Community Care Practice and the Law

also by Michael Mandelstam

Safeguarding Vulnerable Adults and the Law
ISBN 978 1 84310 692 0

Manual Handling in Health and Social Care
An A–Z of Law and Practice
ISBN 978 1 84310 041 6

An A–Z of Community Care Law
ISBN 978 1 85302 560 0

Equipment for Older or Disabled People and the Law
ISBN 978 1 85302 352 1

Community Care Practice and the Law
Fourth Edition

Michael Mandelstam

Jessica Kingsley Publishers
London and Philadelphia

First published in 2009
by Jessica Kingsley Publishers
116 Pentonville Road
London N1 9JB, UK
and
400 Market Street, Suite 400
Philadelphia, PA 19106, USA

www.jkp.com

Library of Congress Cataloging in Publication Data
Mandelstam, Michael, 1956-
    Community care practice and the law / Michael Mandelstam. -- 4th ed.
       p. cm.
    ISBN 978-1-84310-691-3 (pb : alk. paper) 1. Public welfare--Law and legislation--Great Britain. 2. Social service--Great Britain. 3. Community health services--Law and legislation--Great Britain. I. Title.
    KD3299.M26 2009
    344.4103'16--dc22

                                                                    2008020626

British Library Cataloguing in Publication Data
A CIP catalogue record for this book is available from the British Library

ISBN 978 1 84310 691 3

Printed and bound in Great Britain by
Athenaeum Press, Gateshead, Tyne and Wear

CONTENTS

Part II. Social services assessment and provision of services   147

Part III: Housing, home adaptations and the NHS 419

21. Protecting and safeguarding vulnerable adults 582

AUTHOR'S NOTE

I would like to thank in particular Simon Bull and Pauline Thompson for their kindness and patience in pointing me in the right direction; however, any views expressed are those of the author. In a book of this size and complexity, the one certainty is that there will be mistakes. These are down to the author, who would be grateful for any observations or comments by email (michael.mandelstam@btinternet.com).

Otherwise, I owe many thanks to Jessica Kingsley for her support and encouragement, and to her staff who have worked so hard, quickly and efficiently.

Michael Mandelstam, August 2008

PART I

Introduction, overview, underlying themes, remedies

CHAPTER I

Introduction

1.1 OVERVIEW

This book principally covers social care, health and some housing services for various groups of vulnerable people including some elderly people, younger adults with disabilities (physical, sensory or learning), people with mental health needs, people with drug or alcohol problems, and informal carers. It deals mainly with adults only, but services for children in need and their families are touched on.

'Community care services' defined in legislation are provided by local social services authorities. That is, local councils with social services responsibilities, namely county councils, metropolitan councils and other unitary councils. Services are of many sorts, including residential or nursing home accommodation, practical assistance in the home, personal assistance, home help, respite care (breaks for people being cared for, or for their carers), holidays, daily living equipment, home adaptations, Meals on Wheels, day centres, recreational activities and so on.

However, in the sense that community care is about caring for people in their own homes or in institutional accommodation such as care homes, many health care and some local authority housing services are an essential part of the picture as well. For example, NHS policies and practices, including 'care closer to home' are an integral part of, or have a direct impact on, community care in a wider sense. And, in addition to the legislation directly governing the provision of social care, health and housing services, is a range of other relevant legislation. Decision-making by local authorities and the NHS has to be consistent also with the law relating to, for example, mental capacity, information disclosure, human rights, disability discrimination, health and safety at work and the tort of negligence.

On top of all this, some of the work of local authorities in protecting and safeguarding vulnerable adults overlaps with yet more law, including a gamut of criminal justice legislation, civil torts (wrongs) and environmental health legislation.

1.1.1 MENTAL CAPACITY AND SAFEGUARDING ADULTS

This edition has moved on from the past, containing new legislation, legal cases and ombuds-man investigations. The chapter on mental capacity has in particular been expanded to reflect the Mental Capacity Act 2005 and the associated case law. However, the chapter on safe-guarding adults, an increasingly prominent issue, threatened to become outsized. Thus the relevant chapter in this book contains a basic overview only as in the previous edition; the detail has been hived off into a companion book to this one, *Safeguarding vulnerable adults and the law.*

1.2 STRUCTURE

The book is designed for use in different ways and at different levels. For the reader wishing for a brief overview of the legal framework and the underlying mechanisms determining how community care works, Chapters 2 and 3 will serve. The rest of the book comes in more detail:

- **Chapter 4** lists a range of non-judicial legal remedies, that is, remedies which do not generally involve going to court.
- **Chapter 5** outlines a range of judicial remedies available to users of social and health care services. These require going to, or at least the threat of going to, court.
- **Part II** deals with specific elements of community care in relation to local social services authorities, including assessment of people's needs, care planning to meet those needs, providing services and assistive equipment, regulation of organisations providing those services, 'direct payments' (whereby people are given money to buy their own services directly), assessment and provision for family and other informal carers – and finally the rules about charging for services. These lie at the heart of community care.
- **Part III** covers provision of home adaptations, for people classed as disabled, by local housing (and sometime social services) authorities and of health services by the NHS. Although not legally defined as community care services, such services are clearly essential to community care in its wider everyday meaning. They include discharging patients from hospital, NHS continuing health care, and community health services generally.

    The NHS, guided by central government, has sought increasingly over the last few years to restrict its responsibilities and to pass them over to local authorities – thus turning what once was 'health care' into 'social care'. This trend has become more pronounced as policies of health care 'closer to people's homes' are pursued, with some NHS functions being shunted off to local authorities. The legal and financial implications, as well as effect on type and quality of care, are considerable.
- **Part IV** covers two topics that have come to the fore in community care: mental capacity and protecting vulnerable adults from abuse (now frequently referred to as 'safeguarding adults').

1.3. SCOPE AND DETAIL

The detail in the book is not included for the sake of it. It is intended to reflect the type of issues that both users of services, managers and frontline staff come up against on a daily basis. Nonetheless, attempts have been made to limit the size of the book, so that exhaustiveness does not preclude accessibility and usefulness. Boundaries have to be drawn somewhere. Legislation and guidance have been quoted or paraphrased selectively rather than exhaustively; much of this is anyway accessible on the internet through, for example, the Department of Health website (www.dh.gov.uk, for policy and guidance) and the government website for legislation (www.opsi.gov.uk).

The book gives considerable prominence to judicial case law and ombudsman investigations. One reason for this is that the extensive legislation and large volume of Department of Health guidance shed minimum light on how the law works out in practice. Legislation is dry and gives little away; guidance too often brims with wishful and sometimes muddled thinking. By contrast, legal case law and ombudsman investigations illuminate matters much better, providing an insight into what legislation and guidance mean in practice. As well, such case law, about real people, acts as an antidote to what seem to be increasing levels of make believe about health and social care served up by politicians, Whitehall, NHS management and local government. This antidote is particularly required. The great edifice of legislation, guidance, policy, publicity and sheer spin comprising social and health care is at times truly fabulous – in the dictionary sense of exaggerated, incredible and absurd. At times, the author has considered whether he has been writing a work of fiction – so far removed, all too often, is everyday practice from what the law states should be happening, and from what central and local government claim is happening.

For reasons of space and also readability, this book applies in detail essentially to England only. Much of the principle and indeed many of the rules apply across the United Kingdom. Some legislation is identical in effect, if not always the same, applying United Kingdom-wide. However, increasingly, there are divergences, particularly in the case of Scotland (e.g. free personal care, reduced prescription charges, safeguarding adults legislation and an Incapacity Act implemented years ahead of England) and, to some degree, Wales.

1.4 OVERALL AIM

The book attempts to bridge the gap between law and practice. Community care practice is – or at least should be – based on legislation, the decisions of the law courts and Department of Health guidance. It is important for all concerned to be aware of these sources. Neither service providers nor users of services can understand how the system should work without awareness of the legal powers and duties placed on local authorities or the NHS – and of people's legal rights, and the legal or quasi-legal remedies if things go wrong. The value of understanding of this type should not be underestimated; for instance, it might make the difference between receiving vital services or not, or having to sell your house to pay for care – or not.

Few disputes reach the stage of formal legal proceedings, and few even get as far as local authority or NHS complaints procedures, let alone to the local government ombudsmen or the health service ombudsman. Therefore, although the book aims to assist people involved in formal disputes, its predominant aim is to give useful information about legislation and guidance as a way of avoiding disputes, or at least solving them informally. In principle at least, the well-informed statutory service manager is less likely to try to implement a legally doubtful policy. Likewise the front line practitioner will be more confident about decisions he or she makes, whether those decisions are being challenged by a service user or by the practitioner's own manager. More generally, as local authorities and NHS bodies seek ever more routes to minimising their responsibilities and expenditure, an awareness of the legal framework is vital. Otherwise these bodies are liable to overstep the mark, which can result in significant detriment to vulnerable service users and in legal problems.

Conversely, clued up service users (or their representatives) are more likely to be able to challenge successfully, perhaps informally, particular decisions or policies. Local authority or NHS managers, caught red-handed early on in the decision-making process, might simply back down. Not all do so, of course.

CHAPTER 2

Overview of community care

KEY POINTS

The law affecting community care is substantial. This makes an overview all the more essential. Local authorities and NHS bodies are 'creatures of statute', that is, bodies existing by virtue of legislation. Their functions can only be lawfully performed with reference to powers and duties conferred by this legislation. For these local authorities and NHS bodies to apply local policies that are inconsistent with the legislation is illogical and runs the risk of their acting unlawfully.

This chapter provides first of all a summary of the legal framework relevant to community care decision-making as covered in this book. Second, it sets out, in bare form but broken down into categories, a list of the relevant legislation (Acts of Parliament) and other law, in order to give the reader a birds' eye view of this extensive legal landscape.

2.1 SUMMARY OF THE BOOK

The following represents a summary account of the legal framework.

- **Remedies: non-judicial (Chapter 4) and judicial (Chapter 5).** A range of remedies and redress exist, ranging from the informal to the legal. They include local councillors or Members of Parliament, the press, complaints procedures, going to the ombudsmen for redress, and legal cases. Different types of legal case can be brought depending on the nature of the decision or action involved and the remedy sought. Types of legal case include judicial review (challenging the decision-making process of a public body), negligence (seeking compensation for personal injury), health and safety at work (criminal prosecution), human rights (against public authorities), disability discrimination etc. In order to pursue such remedies, the obtaining of information, both public and

private, may be crucial – under the Freedom of Information Act 2000 and Data
Protection Act 1998.

- **Assessment by local social services authorities (Chapter 6)**. The community care
system revolves around assessment under s.47 of the NHS and Community Care Act
1990. Such assessment is to determine people's needs for community care services. These
services are not contained in the 1990 Act but are scattered across five other pieces of
legislation stretching back 60 years to the National Assistance Act 1948. Assessment is
meant to be 'needs' rather than 'service' led. This means in principle that service provision
should be moulded to people's assessed needs, rather than those needs fitted into
whatever services happen to be available.

- **Threshold of eligibility: who is entitled to services (Chapter 6)**. Local authorities
do not necessarily have a duty to meet all the needs that they have identified. This is
because each local authority can, quite lawfully, set a 'threshold of eligibility'. Any needs
that are assessed to come beneath this threshold do not have to be met and are sometimes
labelled 'unmet needs'. In contrast, needs coming above the threshold are sometimes
referred to as 'eligible needs'. They, generally, must be met, irrespective of a lack of
resources within the relevant local authority budget. However, the local authority is
permitted to offer the cheapest option to meet such needs, so long as that option is
consistent with fully meeting the person's assessed needs and with the Human Rights Act
1998.

- **Setting the threshold of eligibility in line with available resources (Chapter 6)**.
This duty on a local authority to meet a person's 'eligible' needs – that is those needs
assessed as coming over the relevant local threshold of eligibility – in principle and law
(though not necessarily in practice) prevents arbitrary refusal or withdrawal of some
services.

    Nevertheless, any absolute duty to make provision is diluted overall by the fact that a
local authority can, from time to time, adjust the threshold of eligibility in the light of its
reduced resources. Raising the threshold allows the authority not only to assess new
applicants for services more restrictively – but also to reassess existing users of services
and accordingly to remove or reduce services even if a person's needs or situation have
not changed. This illustrates how local authorities have considerable legal and practical
leeway in which to tailor services to available resources, by allowing just enough people
to qualify for services within budget. Central government has issued guidance to this
effect, called 'Fair access to care services' (FACS). The direction of the threshold across
local authorities has been upward, thus reducing the overall number of people eligible for
help.

- **Mismatch between threshold of eligibility and resources (Chapter 6)**. A rational
setting of the threshold requires political honesty, which is not easily come by in every
local authority. In other words, there is sometimes a political incentive for an authority to
set a low threshold (and thus demonstrate how generous, caring and deserving of
re-election the ruling body of local councillors is). However, without a correspondingly
generous allocation of resources, a mismatch will arise between the duty to meet people's
assessed, eligible needs and the financial ability to meet those needs.

    Once such a mismatch arises, local authorities are tempted to cut services in an
arbitrary and unlawful manner. For instance, some might unofficially and clandestinely
reset the previously agreed and publicised threshold of eligibility in order to relieve the
pressure on an inadequate budget. Others might – irrespective of a person's assessed,

eligible needs – begin to apply blanket policies in terms of what services they will provide, or impose rigid cost ceilings on care provision for individual service users. Alternatively, they may keep people waiting for services for inordinate periods of time, or meet only a proportion of the eligible need that has been assessed for each person. Such shortcuts risk findings of unlawfulness by the law courts or of maladministration by the local government ombudsmen. They are nonetheless widespread.

- **Review and reassessment (Chapter 7)**. Faced with pressures on resources, local authorities often find themselves reviewing people, with a view not just to checking that a person's needs are being met adequately, but also to changing, reducing or withdrawing services. A reassessment is a prerequisite. Following this, a significant change, reduction or withdrawal of services is only lawful if the person's needs have reduced or changed, they can reasonably be met in another way or the threshold of eligibility has changed. Local authorities can also withhold services in the face of unreasonable behaviour by service users, although there are specific provisos to this.

- **Care plans and provision of services (Chapter 8)**. Following a decision about the services to be provided, various guidance (but not legislation) states that a care plan should be drawn up by the local authority. The plan should contain details about objectives, services, agencies to be involved, costs, needs which cannot be met, date of first review, and so on. The form and complexity of a care plan will vary greatly depending on the level and type of service involved. The law courts have held that either a failure to follow, or at least to have proper regard to, this guidance about care plans can amount to unlawfulness.

  In addition, the courts have accepted that a care plan is likely to be evidence of what a local authority has accepted as its duty to meet a person's assessed needs. Thus significant non-adherence by the local authority to a care plan is likely to indicate breach of its duty to meet a person's assessed, eligible needs.

  Registration and inspection of care providers (both the independent sector and local authorities) come under the Care Standards Act 2000 and have been the responsibility of the Commission for Social Care Inspection and of the Healthcare Commission. From April 2009, under the Health and Social Care Act 2008, a new Care Quality Commission is due to replace both these two Commissions and the Mental Health Act Commission. Local authorities and the NHS are increasingly contracting out services to the independent sector. Whether in-house or contracted out, financial and performance targets can lead to immense pressure on both commissioners and providers, leading to an erosion of standards of care.

  For vulnerable service users, therefore, regulatory legislation is in principle more important than ever. Nonetheless, it is also clear that such regulatory bodies are unable to detect and prevent all poor, and sometimes calamitous, practices. This means that local authorities and NHS bodies, too, have a responsibility to monitor the adequacy of the provision of their own services, as well as those they have contracted out. The local government ombudsman has been highly critical of local authorities that have failed to do this, with detrimental consequences, including the death of service users. And the Healthcare Commission has continued to publish disturbing reports about the erosion of standards of basic care, hygiene and personal dignity within the NHS.

- **Residential and nursing home accommodation (Chapter 9)**. Local authorities have in some circumstances a duty to make arrangements under the National Assistance Act 1948 for the provision of residential accommodation (often in care homes) for people who because of age, illness, disability or other circumstances are in need of care and attention not otherwise available to them. When local authorities have found themselves short of money in relation to this duty, disputes have predictably arisen about when it arises and its extent – involving, for instance, vulnerable older people in the north west of England or destitute asylum seekers in the south east.

- **Charges for residential and nursing home care (Chapters 9 and 10)**. When local authorities place people in care homes, they have a duty to assess them financially and to decide what to charge for the accommodation, if anything. This decision is based on a legally prescribed means test under the National Assistance Act 1948. Depending on what sort of needs people have, and thus what type of home they need to go to, local authorities set a 'usual cost level' which represents the maximum amount they are generally prepared to pay in relation to different levels of need.

    Some, perhaps many, local authorities have attempted to find loopholes in the rules so as to dilute their obligations. For example, there are rules about the 'topping up' of care home fees by a third party, usually a member of the resident's family. If a resident wishes to be placed by the local authority in a more expensive home, then the local authority can agree, subject to this third party making up the difference between the authority's usual cost level and the actual fee charged by the care home. However, such topping up is only lawful if there is a choice involved, and the resident's needs could have been met in a cheaper care home charging fees within the local authority's usual cost level.

    However, in practice, there appears to be widespread flouting of these rules by local authorities, and a concomitant reluctance to explain to families what the rules really are. This results in families being effectively forced by some local authorities to top up care home fees unlawfully.

    People in nursing homes should have the registered nursing care element of the accommodation paid for by the NHS, unless they have what is called 'NHS continuing health care' status – in which case the NHS is responsible for funding all elements of the person's placement (accommodation, board, personal care and nursing care). See below.

- **Non-residential community care services (Chapter 11)**. Community care services are defined by legislation to include a range of non-residential services (such as personal care, recreational activities, travel, day services, equipment and adaptations to people's homes, holidays and meals).

    These services are provided under a range of legislation for groups of people such as those with disabilities (physical, sensory or learning), elderly people, people with a mental disorder, people with drugs or alcohol problems, and people who are ill. Central to non-residential community care services is s.2 of the Chronically Sick and Disabled Persons Act 1970. The 1970 Act has been at the heart of a number of key legal cases which have established that a local authority must meet a person's assessed, eligible need – but that in meeting that need, the authority is only obliged to offer the cheapest option consonant with meeting that assessed, eligible need.

    The other legislation comprises s.29 of the National Assistance Act 1948, s.45 of the Health Services and Public Health Act 1968, s.254 and schedule 20 of the NHS Act 2006, and s.117 of the Mental Health Act 1983.

- **Charges for non-residential community care services (Chapter 12)**. For non-residential services, local authorities have discretion to charge. That is, they can charge if they wish but don't have to. Though only a power rather than a duty, it is the one social services power local authorities generally choose to utilise to the full. Any charge made must be a reasonable one. This is under s.17 of the Health and Social Services and Social Security Adjudications Act 1983.

If the local authority is satisfied, following representations from the person being charged, that it is not 'reasonably practicable' for him or her to pay it, then it must reduce the charge to a level at which it will be reasonably practicable for the person to pay it. Central government has issued guidance, setting out a number of rules, with the purpose of achieving a consistent approach to charging by local authorities. Such consistency has not been achieved.

If people do not pay the assessed charges, the legal position seems to be that local authorities cannot legally withdraw services – at least those that they have a duty (as opposed to a power) to arrange. But authorities do have the power to recover money owed as a debt. One significant and continuing trend has been the shift in definition of certain services to 'social' rather than 'health' in nature. For example, services such as bathing or respite care, previously provided free of charge by the NHS, might now be provided by local social services authorities for a charge.

- **Direct payments, individual budgets (Chapter 13)**. If certain conditions are met, local authorities have a duty under the Health and Social Care Act 2001 to make direct payments to people who have been assessed as having eligible needs. This means that the local authority does not directly arrange the required services, but instead must give people a reasonable sum of money to enable them to purchase services (or assistive equipment) themselves – in order to meet their assessed needs.

  One step beyond direct payments, central government has been attempting to impose on local authorities something called 'individual budgets' as part of what it calls 'self-directed care'. This seems to envisage the allocation, for example per annum, of a certain sum of money based on the person's level of need. The person can then suggest how that money might be spent in order to meet his or her assessed needs. If the local authority concurs with the person's suggestion, either the money can be given as a direct payment, or the local authority can itself – or arrange for somebody else to – organise the services as requested by the person. 'Self-assessment' of need is also encouraged. The nature of such individual budgets is somewhat vague, since to date central government has issued no legislation or policy guidance about them. There remains uncertainty about how they will fit into the existing legal framework; in particular there are questions about whether capping the allocation of money, self-assessment and decisions about services are consistent with the existing legal rules under the NHS and Community Care Act 1990.

  Overall, the policy of direct payments and individual budgets appears to have a threefold purpose: to give people more control over how to meet their needs, to break up local authority provision and commissioning of services, and to put a brake on the amount of money being spent on social care by local authorities.

- **Informal carers (Chapter 13)**. In certain circumstances, local authorities have a duty to assess, or at least to have regard to, the ability of informal carers to provide, or to continue to provide, a substantial amount of care on a regular basis. They must also assess a carer's participation in work, education, training or leisure activities. This is under the Carers (Recognition and Services) Act 1995, the Carers and Disabled Children Act 2000, and the Carers (Equal Opportunities) Act 2004. In addition to this duty to assess, local authorities also have a power, under the 2000 Act, to provide services for carers.

The purpose of the legislation covering carers relates not only to their welfare, but also to a saving of costs. This is because informal caring is widespread and is of similarly high financial value – compared to what it would instead cost local authorities to provide the same amount of care. The argument runs that adequate support of carers, to enable them to continue caring, saves local authorities money. In practice, the extent and thoroughness with which the needs of carers are taken into account by local authorities varies.

Local authorities have, over the past two or three years, increasingly raised their threshold of eligibility for people in need (see above). In addition, the NHS has been shedding many services under the guise of a policy of 'care closer to home' and more care in people's own homes. The consequence of both these trends appears to be that an ever greater burden is being placed on informal, usually family, carers. In the light of this increasing burden, the carers' legislation is arguably inadequate, especially the lack of clear obligation to provide services for carers in their own right.

- **Asylum seekers and immigration control (Chapter 14)**. A prominent part of community care since 1996 has been, at least in some local authorities, the provision of residential accommodation and related services for asylum seekers and other people subject to immigration control. The law and rules concerning such people's eligibility for community care services – or for assistance from the Home Office – have been subject to continual legal challenge, change and confusion. The rules are labyrinthine. The main pieces of legislation affecting social services provision are the National Assistance Act 1948 and other community care statutes as amended, the Immigration and Asylum Act 1999, and the Nationality, Immigration and Asylum Act 2002. Separate rules about 'overseas visitors' apply to the NHS about health care.

- **Ordinary residence (Chapter 15)**. Sometimes the existence of a duty on a local authority to provide community care services depends on whether a person is 'ordinarily resident' within the area of the authority, or indeed on whether he or she is without ordinary residence altogether and is instead of 'no settled residence'. Local authority legal departments are prepared to engage in lengthy disputes if the care package for a person is likely to be an expensive one. Guidance from the Department of Health emphasises that disputes between local authorities should not result in assessment and service provision being delayed.

  As far as the NHS is concerned, the question is one of identifying the 'responsible commissioner', in particular the relevant NHS primary care trust (PCT). Likewise guidance emphasises the principle that any dispute as to ultimate responsibility between PCTs should not result in delay in provision of the service. However, it would appear that this principle is not always adhered to.

- **Housing and home adaptations (Chapter 16)**. The preferred aim of community care is to enable people to remain in their own homes. Housing services, though important therefore, are not for the most part defined legally as community care services.

  It is beyond the scope of this book to examine housing law in detail. However, home adaptations are mentioned in community care policy guidance as one of the key elements in enabling people to remain in their own homes. Such adaptations are available by means of disabled facilities grants provided by local housing authorities under the Housing Grants, Construction and Regeneration Act 1996. Although there are examples of good practice, the local government ombudsmen have consistently found, over many years, maladministration in the provision of adaptations. These findings are indicative of significant disarray in the system, which has been acknowledged by central government. Beyond these mandatory disabled facilities grants, housing authorities have a broad power to assist with adaptations and housing matters under the Regulatory Reform (Housing Assistance (England and Wales) Order 2002.

Local authorities, through their social services functions, also have a duty to assist with home adaptations under the Chronically Sick and Disabled Persons Act 1970. A degree of legal uncertainty attaches to the interplay between the 1996 and 1970 Acts.

- **NHS provision (Chapter 17)**. The NHS has a general duty to provide services under the NHS Act 2006. This includes the provision of medical and nursing services as well as services for the prevention of illness, care of people who are ill, and aftercare for people who have been ill.

  The duty is a general one only (towards the local population, but not towards individuals) and extends only to providing services 'necessary to meet all reasonable requirements'. The effect is that the duty is far from absolute and confers a potentially wide legal discretion on the NHS on whether or how to meet people's needs. Unlike local social services authorities, there is no rule that once an individual person's 'eligible need' has been identified, then it must be met.

  The law courts have generally denied relief to people complaining about the rationing or withholding of health services on grounds of lack of financial resources. They have in the past declined to exercise the much closer scrutiny that they have brought to bear in community care as provided by local social services authorities.

  Nonetheless, the wide discretion enjoyed by the NHS has been checked by the health service ombudsman, in particular over the matter of NHS continuing health care (see below). And, in recent years, the law courts have been called on increasingly to scrutinise NHS decision-making, especially that concerning NHS continuing health care, consultation about changes and closure of services, and the excessive rigidity and rationality of policies designed to ration health services.

- **Discharge from hospital (Chapter 17)**. Of particular importance is whether suitable and effective arrangements for hospital discharge have been made and whether people's needs and wishes have been taken into account.

  When leaving hospital, some people's needs are complicated. The process can be difficult for patients, their families and indeed for the professionals involved. Consideration of many factors is often required including physical ability, mental ability and attitude, social and environmental factors and financial situation. There are sometimes many arrangements to make. This makes the discharge process unpredictable and yet one more uncertainty in community care.

  Keen to continue the reduction in the number of hospital beds across the country, central government has attempted to concentrate minds locally by implementing the Community Care (Delayed Discharges) Act 2003 which imposes financial penalties on local social services authorities if they are in principle responsible for delays in people's discharge from hospital – even if the delay is beyond their practical control.

  The pressure on NHS acute hospitals and their beds is such that – even accepting that acute hospital beds are not a desirable place to be unless absolutely necessary – people continue to be discharged prematurely and with undue haste by acute hospitals. One reason for this is that many slower stream, rehabilitation and recuperation beds have been closed over the last few years – together with such beds in community hospitals as well. This can result in people being discharged inappropriately back to their own home or to care homes, where their rehabilitation and recuperation needs are inadequately met. Another consequence is immediate readmission to hospital; such readmission rates are reported to be increasing.

The overall problem is made significantly worse, because many acute hospitals are reported to operate excessively high bed occupancy levels, leading to reduced care standards, problematic infection control and premature hospital discharge.

- **NHS charges for services (Chapter 17)**. The NHS does not have the same wide powers and duties as local social services authorities to make charges. Some items are charged for if specified in legislation – for example, equipment and drugs prescribed by general practitioners, or wigs, surgical brassieres, and spinal supports provided in hospitals. But everything else, both services and equipment, which is not so specified, must be provided free of charge. Legally, this would seem to be straightforward. However, some NHS bodies have for many years made legally dubious charges, mainly because of confusion or ignorance about what the legislation actually permits.

  Also, the NHS imposes increasing, and controversial though apparently lawful, levels of charges – sometimes exorbitant – for non-clinical services, such as car parking and the use of telephones on hospital wards.

- **NHS continuing health care (Chapter 18)**. If people have a continuing 'primary health need', then they are entitled to what is called NHS continuing health care. This means that the NHS arranges and pays for people's health care, nursing care and personal care in hospital, in care home, in a hospice or in their own home.

  However, people's entitlement to this care has been the subject of consistent and trenchant criticism by the health service ombudsman over a period of at least 14 years. The ombudsman has exposed the fact that the Department of Health's policy about eligibility for such care has been anything but clear and fair; and that many people have consequently been charged large sums of money for care (particularly in nursing homes), which they should not have had to pay. Probably tens of thousands of people have, over this period, wrongly been forced to spend their savings and sell their homes. Instead the NHS should have funded the care, free of charge to the patient.

  As a result of the health service ombudsman's efforts, the Department of Health was forced to authorise significant reimbursement of moneys to individual patients and their families from 2004 onwards. Nonetheless, the evidence has continued to suggest that much NHS decision-making about continuing health care is flawed and potentially unlawful. This is despite a key Court of Appeal legal case in 1999, which set out a relatively low threshold of eligibility for such care, and a more recent 2006 legal case. Perhaps unsurprisingly, given the financial implications, it is a threshold that has not been embraced by the NHS, and in particular by the Department of Health. In both these legal cases, the courts gave short shrift to the coherence of NHS policy and decision-making at both central and local levels.

  Finally, in October 2007, the Department of Health implemented new guidance in the form of a 'national framework', together with three sets of directions, a screening tool and a decision support tool. These were designed, ostensibly, to clarify the rules and lay the problem to rest. However, doubts remain about whether the guidance and associated documents are consistent with the legal position, and whether the political will exists fully to solve the undoubted problem.

  In respect of people placed in nursing homes, a further confusion has arisen in that the NHS has in practice blurred the distinction between NHS continuing health care (attracting full NHS funding for the whole placement) and 'free' registered nursing care (whereby the NHS pays a modest £101.00 per week towards a person's registered nursing care in nursing homes but not for the rest of the placement).

- **Joint working between local authorities and the NHS (Chapter 19)**. Central government has continued to urge greater joint working between local social services authorities and the NHS. The aim of such joint working is generally to reduce duplication of assessment and provision, reduce the chances of patient and clients falling between the two stools of health care and social care, and to save money. In practice, local authorities and the NHS sometimes concentrate on the last aim. This has sometimes resulted in shortcuts being taken with legal obligations to assess and provide services. For example, sometimes NHS bodies – having undertaken to assess and provide services on behalf of the local authority as part of a joint working arrangement – appear to have very little idea about what legally they are meant to be doing. Indeed, the legislation emphasises that underlying legal obligations remain unaffected by the veneer of local joint working arrangements.

  Alternatively, the veneer wears thin when financial pressures arise, and NHS bodies and local authorities continue, much as they have ever done, unilaterally to make decisions about what they will and won't provide, and to pass the buck to each other. This is unremarkable given, for example, the different legislation, legal structures, accountability, priorities, targets and funding sources underpinning the work of local authorities and the NHS.

  Joint working has been explored particularly in relation to mental health services: there are many joint mental health teams in existence. In addition, there has been a particular focus on joint or 'single' assessment of older people, on 'intermediate care' (simple rehabilitation provided for a few weeks after hospital discharge or to prevent hospital admission), and on community equipment services. Of these three policies, it is by no means clear that the single assessment and community equipment policies have made much difference, in law or practice. Community equipment services have long been viewed as poorly organised; as a result central government is now urging local authorities to hive provision off in the main to the independent sector, to create what has been dubbed a 'retail market model'.

  Intermediate care, however, has made an impact, albeit double-edged. On the one hand, it appears to have made available, particularly in people's homes, a basic level of rehabilitation and 'reablement' services for people with relatively simple needs. On the other hand, it seems that instead of enhancing existing rehabilitation services, intermediate care has too often replaced them – leading to a net reduction in specialist rehabilitation services. Arguably, it is the increasing number of people, particularly older people, with more complex physical and cognitive problems associated with multiple pathology, who are losing out as a result.

- **Decision-making capacity (Chapter 20)**. The law relating to the decision-making capacity of adults in relation to health and welfare matters (as well as finance) has become an increasingly prominent issue. Over the past 20 years or so, the law courts have developed common law rules in response to a steady stream of health and social care cases. Finally, the Mental Capacity Act 2005 covering England and Wales was passed in 2005 and brought into force in 2007. The Act seizes upon many of the common law principles and rules already developed by the courts. It also introduces significant changes.

Five key principles apply to decisions and interventions where adults lack capacity to take a decision for themselves. The Act then sets out the rules about a number of matters, including definition of lack of capacity, the legal test for establishing lack of capacity, how to ascertain the 'best interests' of a person lacking capacity, restraint, deprivation of liberty, the law of 'necessaries' (when a contract is enforceable even if a person lacks capacity), lasting powers of attorney, intervention by the Court of Protection, advance decisions (sometimes called living wills), independent mental capacity advocates, and an offence of ill-treatment or wilful neglect of a person lacking capacity.

Particular concern and difficulty have surrounded the circumstances in which people lacking mental capacity are deprived of their liberty in hospitals or care homes. This led to a protracted legal saga, beginning with what became known as the *Bournewood* case, which dragged through the English courts to the House of Lords, then to the European Court of Human Rights – having been subject to an investigation by the health service ombudsman along the way. This culminated in the Mental Capacity Act 2005 having to be amended during 2007, so that certain legal, procedural safeguards would apply to such people. These are due to come into force in 2009.

- **Protecting and safeguarding vulnerable adults (Chapter 21)**. Guidance from central government charges local social services authorities with taking the lead in 'adult protection' or of 'safeguarding adults'. That is, the protection of adults from various forms of abuse including physical, sexual and financial. Legislation relevant to adult protection includes not just community care legislation, but also a range of other law concerning, for example, mental health, mental capacity, environmental health and criminal matters (including theft, assault, manslaughter and sexual offences).

The safeguarding of adults from abuse is now being given increasing priority by local authorities. However, central government in England has not yet passed legislation giving local authorities direct powers to intervene (equivalent to those they already have under the Children Act to protect children). This is in contrast to the Scottish Parliament, which responded to increasing concerns by passing the Adult Support and Protection (Scotland) Act 2007.

2.2 LEGAL FRAMEWORK

The following is a non-exhaustive list of legislation (Acts of Parliament) and other law, providing a bird's eye view of the extensive legal landscape within which community care decision-making lies.

2.2.1 GENERAL (PART I)

Local Authority Social Services Act 1970, s.7: acting under Department of Health guidance. Duty to act under the general guidance of the Secretary of State (see 5.1.6).

Judicial review by the law courts. Decision-making by public bodies such as local authorities and the NHS: reasonableness, rationality, taking account of relevant factors, legitimate expectations, not fettering discretion (not applying blanket policies). These are common law principles (i.e. not to be found in legislation), which are applied by the law courts (see 5.2).

Local Government Act 1974: local ombudsman. Investigations into maladministration by local authorities causing injustice (see 4.9.1).

Health Service Commissioners Act 1993: health service ombudsman. Investigations into maladministration and breach of duties in the NHS (see 4.11).

Health and Social Care (Community Health and Standards) Act 2003. Covers various matters including complaints procedure for local authorities and the NHS.

Health and Social Care Act 2008. Covers various matters, including a new regulatory Care Quality Commission, rules about registration and inspection of health and social care providers, changes to the rules about direct payments and the human rights of care home residents etc.

2.2.2 SOCIAL SERVICES ASSESSMENT AND PROVISION OF SERVICES (PART II)

- **NHS and Community Care Act 1990, s.47: community care assessment**. Duty to assess and to decide about service provision (see 6.1). Directions issued on assessment under s.47. Also plentiful guidance on 'fair access to care' and eligibility criteria, 'single assessment', and on community care generally.
- **Disabled Persons (Services, Consultation and Representation) Act 1986, ss.4, 5: assessment**. Duty to assess disabled person on request (s.4), and to assess in relation to disabled people leaving education (s.5) (see 6.2).
- **National Assistance Act 1948, ss.21–6: residential accommodation**. Care home placements, etc. (see Chapter 9).
- **National Assistance Act 1948, s.22: charges for residential accommodation**. Statutory, detailed test of resources in respect of care home placements (see Chapter 10).
- **National Assistance Act 1948, s.29: range of non-residential welfare services for disabled people**. Social work services, advice and support, etc. (see 11.1).
- **Chronically Sick and Disabled Persons Act 1970, s.2: range of non-residential welfare services for disabled people**. Practical assistance, recreation activities, travel, adaptations and additional facilities, holidays, etc. (see 11.2).
- **Health Services and Public Health Act 1968, s.45: range of non-residential services for older people**. Practical assistance, visiting, support, adaptations and additional facilities, etc. (see 11.3).
- **NHS Act 2006, s.254 and schedule 20: range of non-residential services in respect of illness**. Range of services for preventing illness, caring for people who are ill, or aftercare (see 11.4).
- **NHS Act 2006, s.254 and schedule 20: home help and laundry facilities** (see 11.4).
- **Mental Health Act 1983, s.117: mental health aftercare services** (see 11.5).
- **Health and Social Services and Social Security Adjudications Act 1983, s.17: charges for non-residential services**. Guidance on 'fairer charging' (see Chapter 12).
- **Care Standards Act 2000: registration and inspection of care providers** (see Chapter 8).
- **Health and Social Care Act 2001, s.57: direct payments** (see 13.1).
- **Disabled Persons (Services, Consultation and Representation) Act 1986, s.8: having regard to the carer**. Duty to have regard to the carer's ability to care (see 13.5).
- **Carers (Recognition and Services) Act 1995: carers' assessment** (see 13.5).
- **Carers and Disabled Children Act 2000: carers' assessment and services** (see 13.5).

- **Carers (Equal Opportunities) Act 2004: carers' assessment and services** (see 13.5).
- **Children Act 1989, s.17 and schedule 2: assessment of children in need.** Assessment of children in need, and service provision for those children and their families (see 13.6).
- **National Assistance Act 1948, s.21(1A): prohibition on social services assisting destitute people subject to immigration control** (see Chapter 14).
- **Nationality Immigration and Asylum Act 2002, schedule 3: prohibition on social services assisting some people subject to immigration** (see Chapter 14).
- **Asylum and Immigration (Treatment of Claimants) Act 2004** (see Chapter 14).

2.2.3 HOUSING, HOME ADAPTATIONS AND THE NHS (PART III)

Housing Act 1996. Includes rules for allocating housing and priorities for that housing.

Housing Grants, Construction and Regeneration Act 1996: home adaptations for disabled occupants. System of mandatory disabled facilities grants operated by local housing authorities (see 16.5).

Regulatory Reform (Housing Assistance) (England and Wales) Order 2002. Gives local authorities wide discretion to assist with housing, including (for example) adaptations and helping people move (see 16.8).

Disability Discrimination Act 1995. Specific provisions relating to housing: possession orders (see 16.4), permission for adaptations (see 16.6), making reasonable adaptations including minor adaptations (see 16.10).

NHS Act 2006: provision of health services. General duty on the NHS to provide range of health care services. Guidance on NHS continuing health care, 'free nursing care', the 'care programme approach' in mental health, and 'intermediate care'. Also 'national service frameworks' for older people, mental health and long-term conditions (Chapters 17 and 18).

Community Care (Delayed Discharges) Act 2003. System of local authority reimbursement payments, made to the NHS, in case of local authority failure to enable hospital discharge from acute beds in limited period of time (see 17.11).

NHS Act 2006, s.75: joint working between the NHS and local authorities (see 19.1).

2.2.4 DECISION-MAKING CAPACITY, SAFEGUARDING ADULTS (PART IV)

- **Mental Capacity Act 2005.** Decisions and interventions concerning people lacking the capacity to take those decisions for themselves, including definition of capacity, test of capacity, best interests, limits on restraint, necessary goods and services, lasting powers of attorney, interventions by the Court of Protection including orders and the appointment of deputies, advance decisions about refusing medical treatment, independent mental capacity advocacy (IMCA), offence of ill-treatment or wilful neglect – and legal safeguards concerned with the deprivation of people's liberty in hospitals or care homes (see Chapter 20).
- **No Secrets guidance (DH 2000): adult protection.** Guidance on adult protection policy and practice (see 21.1).
- **Care Standards Act 2000: protection of vulnerable adults (POVA) list** (see 21.4).

- **Safeguarding Vulnerable Groups Act 2006**. (System for monitoring and barring people from working with vulnerable adults, coming fully into force in October 2009, replacing the Protection of Vulnerable Adults (POVA) list (see 21.5).
- **Police Act 1997: criminal record certificate system**. Criminal Records Bureau: standard and enhanced criminal records certificates (see 21.7).
- **National Assistance Act 1948, s.47: removal by local authorities of people from their homes** (see 21.8).
- **National Assistance Act 1948, s.48: protection of people's property by local authority** (see 21.8).
- **Mental Health Act 1983: interventions relevant to adult protection**. Including guardianship (see 21.9).
- **Environmental Protection Act 1990: environmental health interventions** (see 21.10).
- **Public Health Act 1936: environmental health interventions** (see 21.10).
- **Criminal Justice Act 2003: multi-agency public protection arrangements (MAPPA)**. Arrangements for serious offenders (see 21.15).
- **Offences against the person (criminal law), trespass to the person (civil tort)** (see 21.16).
- **Sexual Offences Act 2003: offences relating to people with a mental disorder and to carer workers** (see 21.19).
- **Domestic Crime, Violence and Victims Act 2004**. Includes offence of bringing about, or failing to act to prevent, a vulnerable adult's death (see 21.18).
- **Youth Justice and Criminal Evidence Act 1999: special measures in respect of giving evidence for vulnerable witnesses**. Guidance on 'achieving best evidence' from Home Office (see 21.20).
- **Setting aside transactions (e.g. gifts, wills): lack of capacity** (see 21.23.1).
- **Setting aside transactions (e.g. gifts, wills): undue influence** (see 21.23.2).
- **Theft Act 1968: theft** (see 21.23.3).
- **Care Standards Act 2000: abuse**. Obligations on care providers (under regulations) in relation to safeguarding service users from abuse in connection with the POVA list (due to be replaced in October 2009) (see 21.14).

2.2.5 HUMAN RIGHTS, DISABILITY DISCRIMINATION, HEALTH AND SAFETY AT WORK, NEGLIGENCE, FREEDOM OF INFORMATION, DATA PROTECTION ETC. (CHAPTER 5)

- **Human Rights Act 1998 and European Convention on Human Rights**. Various rights including right to life, not being subject to inhuman or degrading treatment, not being arbitrarily deprived of liberty, right to respect for privacy, home and family life, not being discriminated against (see 5.5).
- **Disability Discrimination Act 1995: goods and services, premises**. Various obligations on local authorities and the NHS in respect of the provision of goods and services, the disposal and management of residential premises (see 5.6).
- **Health and Safety at Work Act 1974, ss.2 and 3: duties of employer toward both employees and any non-employees affected by the undertaking**. Duties subject to reasonable practicability (see 5.4).

- **Management of Health and Safety at Work Regulations 1999: risk assessment, cooperation and coordination etc.** (see 5.4).
- **Manual Handling Operations Regulations 1992: management of risk**. Manual handling risk to be managed by avoidance or reduction, so far as is reasonably practicable (see 5.4).
- **Common law of negligence**. Duty of care, carelessness, causation of harm (see 5.3).
- **Contract law**. Governing contracts held by local authorities or the NHS with the independent sector, in respect of contracted out services (see 5.3 and 8.2).
- **Freedom of Information Act 2000**. Access to non-personal information (see 4.16.1).
- **Data Protection Act 1998: personal data**. Access to personal information, disclosure with or without consent etc. (see 4.17.2).

CHAPTER 3

Underlying themes

KEY POINTS

Community care, in its widest sense, appears to be in substantial disarray. Contributing to this situation are a number of factors, any one of which would be capable of destabilising such a system but which in combination create significant problems. Of these factors, a number stand out.

RESOURCES

First, local authorities and NHS bodies lack adequate resources, relative to demand, to meet the needs of all those people reasonably requiring services. The numbers of people with health and social care needs are increasing, for example, due to an ageing population and more people with learning and physical disabilities surviving at birth and living in the community. One consequence is that, by definition, social and health care policy appears almost always to have a double edge, containing elements of good practice and improvements but coupled with an imperative to minimise expenditure.

WITHDRAWING AND WITHHOLDING OF HELP

Second, the consequence of this mismatch between people's needs and available resources is that services are being increasingly withdrawn from groups of vulnerable people, such as older people with various health and social care needs, people with mental health problems and people with learning disabilities. For instance, the number of people assisted by local social services authorities, but apparently not the money spent, has significantly decreased over the past ten years. Likewise, across the country there has been closure of elderly care, rehabilitation, mental health wards and day hospitals by the NHS. And, for many years, NHS bodies have been refusing to accept their caring and financial responsibilities for people with NHS continuing health care needs – in particular, older people with high levels of chronic illness and disability.

In addition to the actual withdrawal or denial of services, people may find themselves being either charged for services that were previously free, paying very much higher charges than previously – or, although still eligible for social and health care services, nonetheless encouraged to arrange and pay for them privately.

GAP BETWEEN POLICY AND PRACTICE

Third, there has been a signal failure by central government, local authorities and NHS bodies to concede the extent of this situation. This has led to a gap, sometimes gulf, between aspiration and official policy on the one hand, and practice on the other. As this gap and the associated political stakes have grown, so too has a singular lack of transparency and disingenuousness. Such levels of disingenuousness can have a number of undesirable consequences. Some may be serious in that the needs and welfare of patients may as a result not only be glossed over but in some instances positively sacrificed. The Healthcare Commission discovered this when NHS trusts in Buckinghamshire and Kent concealed the extent of infection and resulting mortality in their acute hospitals, thus contributing to the continuing deaths of patients at the time.

PERFORMANCE TARGETS

Fourth, the imposition of performance and financial targets in both health and social care appears to have had some significant adverse consequences. Whilst measurement of performance may have an important place, a balance is clearly required. Yet, too often, it has been reported that targets have resulted in a distortion of priorities, such that users of health and social care services have suffered. Indeed, the Healthcare Commission has attributed serious lapses in standards of patient care partly to the pursuit, by senior NHS management, of government imposed targets. The political parading of targets links to the lack of transparency; behind the facade of the targets, which focus on particular services only, other services – politically invisible – may deteriorate.

UNEVEN AND LABYRINTHINE LEGISLATION

Fifth, the legal framework underpinning social and health care is complex and uneven. On the one hand, social care legislation is labyrinthine and contains a number of duties and rights that potentially pressurise local authorities to spend money they do not have. On the other, health care legislation is so vague that it contains relatively few clear duties to provide services; yet this is out of keeping with the expectations generated by central government for political purposes. Things can become even more confused because the rules are so numerous, that many local authorities struggle to identify them all, let alone stick to them; they then proceed to confuse matters further by making up their own, some of which are not lawful.

Unsurprisingly, this unstable situation – with people's needs not being met and expectations being gravely disappointed – leads to complaints against health and social care bodies as well as sometimes to legal cases.

Notwithstanding this array of legislation in social care, and a monstrous quantity of guidance from the Department of Health aimed at both local authorities and the NHS, central government is quite happy to bypass the law when it suits. For instance, it has for many years happily evaded the legal issues concerning NHS continuing health care, and its introduction of 'individual budgets' into social care – with potentially fundamental implications – is, at the time of writing, being undertaken with no legislation, no definitive guidance and with little reference to how, or even whether, this new system is consistent with the existing legal framework.

In addition, other areas of law are in a state of flux and are forcing their way into social and health care related decisions. These other areas of law include, for example, two relatively recent developments – human rights and disability discrimination – as well as the long established law of negligence. This last is in a state of uncertainty, when it comes to the question of whether or not liability should be imposed on local authorities or the NHS for negligence, if that negligence is connected to statutory functions, policy or resources. And the safeguarding and protecting of adults, an increasingly important part of local authority activity, brings with it a substantial range of legal considerations.

UNCERTAINTIES AND LEGAL ESCAPE ROUTES

Sixth, with such financial, legal and political pressures in play, uncertainties and sometimes chaos flourish and escalate when financial pressures bite. Legal escape routes inevitably beckon, tempting local authorities and NHS bodies to reduce their perceived obligations in relation to the level of resources available. If the courts close off one of these escape routes, another is readily found.

PROTECTING AND SAFEGUARDING ADULTS FROM HARM

Seventh, a growing focus in community care concerns adult protection or the safeguarding of adults – that is, the protection of vulnerable adults from serious harm through abuse or neglect. One question, so far unanswered and almost unasked, is how effective local authorities or NHS bodies are at scrutinising themselves and identifying what is sometimes their own very significant contribution to the harm caused through the abuse (financial or physical) or neglect of vulnerable adults.

PROFESSIONAL GOOD PRACTICE

Eighth, questions arise about the effect on professional good practice of the pressures and uncertainties of the system described above. There is increasing regulation of professionals (and others) working in health and social care, including requirements of competencies and good practice. And yet, some of what is transpiring in social and health care appears to be undermining this aim, forcing staff and managers into policies and practices far removed from these regulatory and professional aspirations. An obvious example of this trend is of the nurses in Kent reportedly telling patients to relieve their bowels and bladder in bed, because of a shortage of staff and over-occupancy of beds, brought about by the NHS trust's pursuit of financial and performance targets (HC 2007a).

3.1 COMMUNITY CARE AND RESOURCES

There are clearly inadequate resources available through statutory services to meet the demand and need for social care (e.g. Caring Choices 2008; Joseph Rowntree Foundation 2006; Wanless 2006; All Party Parliamentary Groups 2006). Likewise, the NHS has been in financial turmoil in the last few years, despite the apparent increase in funding provided by central government.

As a result, it is almost a rule of thumb that government policies in health and social care cut two ways. Partly, they contain many statements and ideas about good practice; at the same time most are aimed at saving money. Too often, apparently good intentions are undermined by the lack of resources.

3.1.1 LACK OF RESOURCES: SOCIAL CARE

When adequate resources are not forthcoming because of the financial policies of the moment in local or central government, the effect on statutory duties laid down by Parliament is corrosive. This has been particularly so in social care, because some of the duties in legislation contain strong duties, non-performance of which cannot be excused by the local authority pleading lack of resources.

Thus, the courts have accepted that resources cannot be conjured up out of thin air (e.g. *R v Islington LBC, ex p Rixon*), but decided also that financial cuts must stop somewhere if specific legal duties (where they exist) are not to become meaningless (*R v East Sussex CC, ex p Tandy*). In this last case, the House of Lords stated that when there is an absolute statutory duty imposed on an authority to do something, it must find the resources, even if it has to raid other budgets. It is not sufficient to claim that one budget in particular has been exhausted and that therefore the statutory duty cannot be performed. This statement confirmed what had been established previously; namely that once an eligible community care need had been assessed, there is an absolute duty to meet it one way or another (*R v Gloucestershire CC, ex p Barry*).

Unremarkably therefore, many of the community care judicial review cases heard to date have focused on an apparent lack of resources to meet people's community care needs. This was predictable. Some 20 years ago, the Griffiths report (1988, pp.iii, ix) on community care emphatically denied that it represented a cost-cutting exercise. It did nevertheless concede that many local authorities felt that 'the Israelites faced with the requirement to make bricks without straw had a comparatively routine and possible task'. It also stated, correctly but naively, that what could not 'be acceptable is to allow ambitious policies to be embarked upon without the appropriate funds'. The ensuing White Paper spoke of better use of taxpayer's money, but arguably did not confront sufficiently forcibly or transparently the inevitable conflict which would follow between people's needs and available resources (Secretaries of State 1989, p.5). Subsequent policy guidance (DH 1990) and practice guidance (SSI/SWSG 1991) tended to camouflage, in verbiage relating to good practice, the issue of resources.

The disparity between the stated policy of central government and practice was highlighted in 1997 by one of the members (Lord Lloyd) of the House of Lords in *R v Gloucestershire CC, ex p Barry*. He confirmed the soundness of the warning about appropriate funding given in the Griffiths report nearly ten years before, pointing out that central government had departed from its 'fine words' in its 1989 White Paper and simply failed to supply the resources required:

Fine words and noble aspiration. The local authority was in an 'impossible position; truly impossible, because even if the Council wished to raise the money themselves to meet the need by increasing council tax, they would be unable to do so by reason of the government-imposed rate capping'. Furthermore, it was the government's departure from its 'fine words' in the community care White Paper that had brought about the situation. The 'passing of the 1970 Act was a noble aspiration. Having willed the end, Parliament must be asked to provide the means' (*R v Gloucestershire CC, ex p Barry*).

3.1.2 LACK OF RESOURCES: THE NHS

In the case of the NHS, the legal, if not the political, problems created by a lack of resources is nowhere near so pronounced as in the case of social services. No legal case has succeeded in arguing that the NHS must find resources to treat patients. The NHS has lost cases on other grounds, such as the rigidity or irrationality of local policies on certain treatments or on lack of adequate consultation before closing down services – but not directly on the issue of resources. However, the political consequences of lack of resources may be uncomfortable when local communities see services closed, or people are denied treatment to prevent them going blind – whether former Labour MPs or war heroes (Mahon 2007; Clout 2008). For this reason, going to the newspapers can be effective in persuading an NHS primary care trust – under pressure in the background from the Department Health which is averse to bad publicity – quietly to authorise a treatment this week, which it was flatly refusing to provide last week.

3.2 WITHDRAWAL OF SERVICES FROM VULNERABLE PEOPLE

Despite apparently increased levels of spending by central and local government, it is arguable that the welfare state is in recession, relative to the needs of the population. Not only is central government breaking up the monopoly of public service provision, but services are being cut back, particularly for older people – who of course represent the largest number of people in need of social and health care services – as well as for other vulnerable groups of people.

3.2.1 WITHDRAWAL OF SOCIAL CARE SERVICES

Local social services authorities have increasingly restricted eligibility for assistance to vulnerable groups of people. They are helping ever fewer people relative to demand and to the needs of an ageing population. For example, in 1997, 479,000 households received home care support from local authorities; this had decreased to 358,000 in 2006 (CSCI 2008, p.6). Given the inevitable rise in numbers of people in need in the community during that period, this actually represents, overall and relative to need, more than the 25 per cent reduction indicated by the figures. This trend of diminishing provision relative to need can presumably only continue; in the next 30 years the number of people aged 85 or over is forecast to rise from just over one million to nearly three million, and the number of people with dementia is expected to double. The number of people aged 50 or over with learning disabilities is projected to rise by 53 per cent between 2001 and 2021 (LAC(DH)(2008)1, para 9).

As a result of the decreasing help being offered, the Commission for Social Care Inspection (CSCI) has found that older people were being denied fundamental services such as gardening, shopping, cleaning and access to the bath in such a way as to undermine seriously their quality of life and dignity (CSCI 2008). Another indication of the apparent unconcern about the basic needs of older people was indicated by an Age Concern England (2008) report, which focused on the social exclusion and isolation of older people and an 'out of sight, out of mind' attitude to them. None of this is new of course; 40 years ago, a foresightful physician at Edgware General Hospital, working in a geriatric department where the 'pips were squeaking', wrote *My brother's keeper*, noting that 'history has never had an equivalent situation; no civilisation has ever had an elderly population of such magnitude, and these older people have to be able to find reasons for living' (Stewart 1968, pp.7–16).

Even in the case of people who were deemed eligible to receive services, the CSCI nonetheless concluded that they, too, may experience a shortfall in what is offered and therefore get too little care to ensure a reasonable quality of life (CSCI 2008, p.120). That this represents a retraction of the welfare state is not hyperbole; especially as it is not just a question of local authorities providing services for fewer people, to the bare minimum, but also charging them ever more money for those inadequate services (Counsel and Care 2006).

Indeed, central government's 2008 vision for social care referred to 'high quality' services available to people who receive social care support 'whether from statutory services, the third and community or private sector or by funding it themselves' – clearly envisaging that many people may indeed be doing the latter. Yet it, too, refers to the inexorable rise in the numbers of people in need, particular of older people (number of over 85 year olds set to almost treble from 2006–2036, from 1.055 to 2.959 million) those with dementia (set to double between 2007 and 2037, from 560,000 to 1.20 million). At the same time, it states that giving more 'choice and control' to people 'must be set in the context of the existing resources and be sustainable in the longer term' (LAC (DH)(2008)1, pp.3–5). Juxtaposing these three points, high quality services, rapidly increasing numbers of people in need, and no more resources, the message and tone would appear absurdly optimistic. Reading between the lines, the message is crystal clear; increasing numbers of people will be left to their own devices.

In financial terms, this is already the case to a significant extent. For instance, in 2007 it was estimated by the CSCI that some half of the total spending on social care in England was funded by people themselves rather than local authorities. Net public spend was calculated at £5.69 billion, slightly less than the £5.9 billion spent privately. Private spend was made up of six categories of people. The first three categories were those people who: (a) chose not to approach public authorities; (b) had assessed needs deemed to be ineligible for support; (c) had assessed, eligible needs but who had savings above the relevant threshold for public support. The remaining three categories comprised people eligible for public support but paying toward that support; who (d) needed residential care but were liable to contribute financially; (e) needed non-residential support but were liable to contribute financially; (f) bought in extra care privately because that provided by the local authority was inadequate (Forder 2007, pp.5–9).

3.2.2 WITHDRAWAL OF HEALTH CARE SERVICES

NHS waiting times may have improved, but apparently at a cost of cuts to many other services, particularly those for older people with more chronic or complex needs, as well as other vulnerable groups (people with learning disabilities and mental health problems). For instance, a 2006 report found that 59 per cent of mental health NHS trusts had reduced staff, and 24 per cent had reduced services, including closure of wards and other units (Sainsbury Centre for Mental Health 2006, pp.5–6).

The British Geriatric Society reports large scale rehabilitation bed closures, largely for older people, without apparent adequate alternatives (British Geriatric Society 2007). Health visiting for the old and the young has likewise been affected; a single health visitor working with 800 families has been reported (Vere-Jones 2007). Local community hospitals or units (in both town and country), maternity units and paediatric services, too, are being affected as local services are increasingly run down or closed, in the name of patient interest and choice but arguably to save money. Specialist services are being centralised into regional centres of excellence, again ostensibly to improve practice, but often it seems to rationalise expenditure. And, the overall policy of making more health services 'local', seems removed from what is happening in practice (see: Mandelstam 2006, pp.112–116). The removal of local services is likely to affect vulnerable groups the most because of difficulties, amongst other things, in travel.

3.2.3 CHARGING FOR SERVICES

Local authorities have a duty to charge for residential accommodation and a power, that is, discretion, to make charges for non-residential services. Increasingly, the latter power is used up to the hilt, in what is sometimes a distinctly flinty and rapacious manner. For example, an older person might receive an hour and 40 minutes essential help in the form of three, barely adequate, short visits a day – and be charged £260 a week for it, until his or her savings run out. Yet, the higher rate of a key disability benefit for older people, attendance allowance, designed to pay for such care is only some £65.00 a week – a huge discrepancy.

In addition to such increased charging, a major change has occurred insofar as health services, by definition free of charge, have increasingly been re-labelled social care – for which a charge can then be made. A range of tasks carried out in people's homes in the past by registered nurses are now undertaken under the umbrella of social care and accordingly are chargeable.

But perhaps the most egregious example of this surreptitious shift comes in the form of NHS continuing health care in care homes or in people's own homes. For the past 14 years at least, the NHS has made strenuous efforts to minimise its responsibilities for people needing such care, and to argue that their needs are primarily social, rather than health-related. This then leaves local authorities free to charge people very large sums of money for such care, and to force people, in some circumstances, to sell their homes to pay for it. Such has been the unseemly rush to effect this change in policy and practice, without full public debate and transparent legislation, that the NHS and local authorities have been acting improperly and unlawfully in a significant number of cases.

Such a diminishing of NHS continuing health care, replaced by means-tested care in care homes and people's own homes, has led to repeated and continuing accusations that central government has abandoned the 'cradle-to-grave' philosophy of the welfare state and broken its promises to people who believed they would be cared for at no cost – with a policy which is unfair and favours the spendthrift over the thrifty (HCHC 1996, p.xxiv). People might feel cheated because they had been led to believe – whilst paying National Insurance contributions, and 'scrimping and saving' all their lives – that the state would care for them in their time of need, that they and their spouses would not be reduced to penury, and that their inheritance would be safeguarded for their children (Salvage 1995, p.3).

A Royal Commission on Long Term Care for the Elderly sat during 1998 with a brief to report on the future funding of long-term care for elderly people, both in their own homes and other settings. In the event, central government failed to implement the Commission's central proposal that personal care be provided free of charge (Royal Commission on Long Term Care 1999). Instead, government in England went only so far as to introduce a limited system of 'free nursing care' for people in certain care homes. (By comparison, free personal care in addition to free nursing care was introduced for older people in Scotland: Community Care and Health (Scotland) Act 2002.)

3.2.3.1 Unfairness of system

More generally, there is widespread agreement that the system of community care and NHS continuing health care is unfair, a situation that has come about precisely because of the lack of hard-nosed public debate about the question of resources and the charges to be paid for services. Some people, increasingly fewer, qualify for totally free care from the NHS. Others have to pay for all their care, assuming they have a certain level of assets (if it is provided by a local authority) or when they are forced to fund it privately.

The system in particular penalises those who have worked hard to build up modest means – and who are rapidly impoverished by disability or illness. Informal carers are inadequately supported, even though they are increasingly relied on to provide sometimes highly demanding – physically and mentally – care for family members. As the King's Fund has put it: 'The evidence…is unequivocal – the current system penalises those who have saved and is particularly hard on those with moderate means. It also fails to meet the needs of thousands of frail older people with serious problems who do not pass the "severe" levels of need test to qualify for help' (Dickson 2007).

3.2.4 BREAKING UP THE MONOPOLY OF WELFARE PROVISION

Apart from withdrawing services from vulnerable groups of people and charging more for service provision, the traditional welfare state is being undermined in another respect. What was a monopoly of public service provision, and public service ethos, appears to be unravelling.

For instance, in social care, local authorities already contract out many care services, both residential and non-residential, to the independent sector. Central government has stated that social care and health care must move toward a 'personalised care system', in order to give people 'maximum choice, control and power over the support services they receive'. It has spoken of the need to 'replace paternalistic, reactive care of variable quality with a mainstream system focused on prevention, early intervention, enablement and high quality personally tailored services' (HMG 2007, p.2). Central government speaks of independence, choice and control – and self-assessment (Secretary of State for Health 2005), which would appear, too, to signal a move away from the traditional notion of the welfare state. The policy appears to be aiming at a 'social care market' containing a wide range of both registered and unregistered care providers, with local authorities receding increasingly into the background. Not only will they be providing fewer and fewer services themselves, but the 'personalisation' policy would appear to mean that they will also be commissioning services less. Instead the idea seems to be that people will be commissioning or purchasing their own services.

In health care, too, the mantra of patient choice appears to herald the breaking up of state provision by the NHS. This includes independent sector treatment providers, general practitioner practices being run by private companies, NHS foundation trusts operating at arm's length from the mainstream NHS – and remaining NHS providers competing with each other for business and advertising their services to that end (DH 2008). And, already, inadequate provision of services such as dentistry, physiotherapy and chiropody has long meant, *de facto*, that many people seek private treatment in the knowledge that timely treatment would not be available on the NHS.

The watch word has become a 'patient-led NHS'. This appears to be a euphemism for 'contestability', competition, new types of provider organisations, and a more diverse range of providers (DH 2005a, pp.13–16). On any view, this is a breaking up of the NHS as we have known it since 1948.

3.3 ASPIRATION, POLICY AND PRACTICE

One consequence of the pressures on the system of social and health care is that rhetoric from central government about how people's needs should be, and are being, met appears ever more detached from reality. Sometimes the extravagance of promises made by central government, local authorities and NHS bodies, are in inverse proportion to the facts. Unsurprisingly, a considerable mismatch appears to exist between public expectation and what local authorities and the NHS are able to deliver with inevitably limited resources.

For instance, government guidance on eligibility for social care services is called 'fair access to care'. It was published following a White Paper which trumpeted the importance of adequate social care for people. Intended in principle and publicity as a guarantor of equity, the Commission for Social Care Inspection reports that in practice it is used to reduce budgetary demands on the council, limit professional discretion, legitimise the diversion of people away from council-funded services, and detrimentally affect the fundamental quality of life and dignity of older people (Henwood and Hudson 2008, p.70).

The discrepancy is seen to full effect in the case of the NHS. Central government policy documents are replete with claims about waiting times, the importance of individual patient choice and also of the involvement of local communities in changes to health services. For instance, the NHS Improvement Plan spoke about 'world class' health service having been partly achieved, and that this ambition would be completed by patient choice. Patients would be choosing from a range of providers by 2008 and have their own personal *Healthspace* on the Internet. Likewise, the NHS would become a 'community based' service; 'the voices of patients and the public, together with greater choice, will play an important role in shaping the health service in future' (Secretary of State for Health 2004, pp.9,78). Yet more guidance spoke of how patients and the public would be heavily involved in decisions about local services by 'strengthening accountability' through public consultation and local council overview and scrutiny committees (DH 2003m).

In reality, however, local health services are reported to be disappearing against the wishes of large numbers of the public. This becomes all the more difficult to reconcile not only with the government policy of more involvement, but also the policy of 'care closer to home', and keeping the NHS local (Secretary of State 2006; DH 2003o). The last few years have seen remarkably widespread local protests about changes and cuts to local NHS services, suggesting not only extensive loss of local NHS provision, but also the failure of another strand of government policy – patient choice and involvement of the local community in local change (Mandelstam 2006). The House of Commons Health Committee was moved to point out that consultations about changes and closures too often appeared to be a sham (HCHS 2007, p.5).

In similar vein, the NHS Plan in 2000 spoke of a consensus for improvement of the NHS in the guise of ten core principles. It spoke of 7000 more beds, of lessening central control, less waiting, the inequity of charging for health services, clean hospitals, better hospital food, bedside televisions and telephones, better rehabilitation services and so on (Secretary of State for Health 2000). Eight years on, waiting times may have been reduced in some respects (although at a high cost to other parts of the service) and telephones introduced at considerable cost to patients, but many crucial elements such as more beds, cleanliness and nutrition of patients remain huge problems. And, in 1997, Tony Blair stated that he didn't want children to be 'brought up in a country where the only way pensioners can get long-term care is by selling their home' (BBC 2006). For the next ten years, his government made every effort to make sure that those pensioners would have to sell their homes (see 18.1).

3.3.1 DISINGENUOUSNESS: COST OF THE GAP BETWEEN ASPIRATION AND PRACTICE

For political reasons, or perhaps self-induced myopia or ignorance, those in power at central, regional and local level employ a pragmatic disingenuousness. It appears, at times, that senior public servants are employed in relation partly in respect of their ability to keep up appearances against the odds, and partly to deceive even themselves about the implications of some of what they are doing.

The loss of transparency in turn makes matters worse, because it then becomes exceptionally difficult for the public at large to understand what is going on. It creates unrealistic expectations. Uncertainty proliferates and meaningful public debate becomes problematic.

Thus, when local authorities reduce services by raising their 'threshold of eligibility', they will typically and publicly speak about fairer services and undertake not to leave a single vulnerable person in need – even when they are in fact removing services precisely from vulnerable people, with the result identified by the Commission for Social Care Inspection (2008). Thus, CSCI found that 'low level needs are often dismissed as trivial by councils and people seeking help with these tasks sometimes [are] seen as trying to dupe the council into giving them help they are not entitled to. This picture did not appear to fit the people seeking help from social services who were interviewed for this study' (Henwood and Hudson 2008, p.9). The CSCI was concerned about the extent to which managers rationalise and justify essentially flawed policy and practice:

Older people trying to trick their way into getting services, or local authority managers not admitting to the harm being caused by their policies? 'Low-level' needs are often dismissed as trivial by councils, yet there is a considerable body of evidence testifying to the importance of support to people with simple tasks… It was not uncommon to find that people seeking such help were viewed by care managers as trying to 'trick' their way into getting help: 'some people like being waited on don't they?' 'I found that those that have got low level needs don't seem to have a need for service – they might have referred themselves. I have lots of people who refer themselves because they want to see what the council can offer (…) they are just testing the water.'

Not one of the people trying to get support from services could have been described in these terms. None of them approached the council without considerable forethought, and none identified frivolous needs or wishes. All were trying (often in some desperation) to get help they viewed as vital to their daily lives; being told they were ineligible was both a surprise and a considerable worry for some people who did not know how they would be able to continue to cope alone' (CSCI 2008, p.143).

In similar vein, when local NHS chief executives are closing beds, without adequate alternatives in place, they maintain that it is all about improving services. Sometimes, the more drastic the reduction in service, so the greater the protestation is that it is all about modernisation and improvement. This is so, even when such closures are not part of any measured, evidenced plan, but simply reflect the need to make short-term finacial savings.

For instance, in 2006, in Southampton, the NHS trust announced the loss of 564 jobs and 160 beds – following the removal of 600 posts and 109 beds the previous year. The chief executive stated that it was all about improving services and that it would even be exciting for staff (Makin 2006). In Ipswich, a debt running into many millions led a senior consultant to talk of the worrying situation and the inability of staff to provide a proper service (Bulstrode 2006). The chief executive put it another way; the cuts were to be about 're-energisation' and efficiency; the people of East Suffolk would have nothing to fear (Dines 2006). Within 18 months, his hospital was waking people up in the middle of the night and sending them home, unplanned – with pressure on the reduced bed numbers being sustained over a period of many weeks of 'black', and even 'blue', alerts (Bond 2008).

Meaningless mantras, such as 'the right care, in the right place, at the right time' become prevalent. Jargon is bandied about, so empty of substance, that it is almost impossible to debate or refute what is being proposed. Thus can it all deteriorate into doublespeak and sophistry. An outstanding example came in East Suffolk. Of 31,302 responses to a consulta-tion to close down all manner of service, some 30,000 expressions of view were opposed to the closures. However, the PCT hired a consultancy to analyse the responses; it advised the PCT that the latter had drafted the consultation questions poorly in the consultation document. This accounted for the overwhelmingly negative response, but also would justify the PCT in not placing undue weight on such overwhelming opposition. (In fact, the PCT had set out its proposals reasonably transparently and bluntly; the consultancy was in effect advising that insufficient gloss or spin had been applied.) The PCT gratefully snatched at this way out of its predicament and went ahead with the closures. It refused to disclose how much it had paid the consultancy for this lifeline, citing commercial confidentiality (Mandelstam 2006, p.120). It was clearly a case of 'no' meaning 'yes'.

3.3.1.1 Consequences of disingenuousness
The consequences of such disingenuousness are serious. For example, if problems are con-cealed or not acknowledged, then meaningful debate and solutions are likely to be elusive. In turn, this may lead to something very much worse than simple lack of transparency, and lead to direct and very serious harm to patients.

For instance, the Healthcare Commission found NHS trusts in Kent and Buckinghamshire either concealing, or providing positively misleading information, about the outbreaks of the bacterium *Clostridium difficile*, in which scores of elderly people died because of poor standards of care and hygiene. Such concealment in turn impeded recogni-tion and remedial action. In addition, the Healthcare Commission pointed out how failings in the commissioning of services by the local PCT – forcing closure of hospital beds before alternative community services were available (a common pattern across England) – had con-tributed to the situation (Healthcare Commission 2007a). That was the reality; but the official line from central government is that PCTs are 'world class commissioners, building trust and legitimacy through local engagement' (DH 2007r). The juxtaposition of the reality of filthy wards and appalling standards of care, with such empty terms as 'world class', is a typical example exposing the rhetoric with which the NHS truly appears to be infected.

Indeed, beneath the much vaunted terms 'modernisation' and 'world class', there are too many examples suggesting that the great escape from history is slower than government would have us believe. Furthermore, the extravagant use of these terms for often political purposes tends to lead to a state of denial about the problems and thus to hinder their solution. For instance, the events in Kent and Buckinghamshire are a reminder of hospitals as 'gateways to death', as Florence Nightingale viewed them in the 19th century. In its biennial report of 2008, the Mental Health Act Commission felt moved to refer to the *Parliamentary Inquiry into Madhouses of 1815/6* and a number of basic evils uncovered. These included (a) 'keepers of the houses' receiving too many patients which hindered recovery; (b) an 'insufficiency in the number of keepers'; (c) the inappropriate 'mixing of patients who are outrageous with those who are quiet'; (d) unnecessary restraint; (e) 'parish paupers in houses for insane persons ... and in parochial workhouses'.

The MHAC drew parallels, from this past of nearly two hundred years ago with 2008, in terms of present (a) overcrowded mental health hospitals, (b) shortage of staff, (c) overcrowding and acute wards which are frightening (e.g. for women locked up with disturbed male patients; (d) undue restraint, taking the form of restraint by 'human hand' with mechanical restraint being more likely to be used on patients with learning disabilities, or who are 'frail or elderly', than on patients formally detained under the Mental Health Act 1983. The parallel with parish paupers was with the current lack of legal protection for patients deprived of their liberty but not formally detained under the 1983 Act. The MHAC also pointed out the uncomfortable parallel of 'asylum dysentery' in the 19th century, caused probably by contaminated water and poor hygiene practices, with the outbreaks of *Clostridium difficile* reported by the Healthcare Commission (MHAC 2008, pp.10-12).

And the apparent separation by some local authorities of elderly couples, who have been married perhaps for fifty years, on financial grounds, carries with it overtones of some aspects of Poor Law and workhouse policy and practice in the 19th century.

3.4 PERFORMANCE TARGETS

A complicating factor in health and social care has been the setting of targets. Designed to improve services, a number of unintended effects have resulted. These include the undermining of clinical priorities and sometimes of the health and welfare of service users, an adverse effect on services not directly related to the targets, and sometimes a reduced concern with adherence to the law. In addition, it has become clear that statistics are in any case subject to manipulation (e.g. Audit Commission 2003; NAO 2001).

Clinical priorities may be undermined. For example, because of targets on new outpatient appointments, follow-up appointments may be set back. This could result in people's urgent treatment being delayed. In one case, an elderly lady who was already deaf, and lived with her completely deaf husband, went blind because her follow-up appointments for glaucoma were delayed several times owing to the need to divert resources to hit targets for first appointments. Near corrupt practices may be uncovered; such as ambulances reaching patients within one minute or even in zero seconds (HCPAC 2003, pp.18–20). More drastically still, the Healthcare Commission has reported on how an obsession with performance and financial targets led to a severe compromising of people's basic care needs by NHS trusts in Kent and Buckinghamshire. This contributed to the death of scores of older people from the bacterium *Clostridium difficile* (Healthcare Commission 2006 and Healthcare Commission 2007a).

Social services assessments, too, may become distorted. For instance, in one case a first level assessment (for which targets had been set) was achieved reasonably quickly. However, the woman then had to wait nearly 18 months for the full assessment; the local ombudsman found maladministration. This length of wait meant that the inadequacies of the first level assessment were not remedied so as to prevent significant harm (*Ealing LBC 1999*). The hitting of the target was a triumph of political form over substance; legally the woman's needs had not been assessed in time, and practically she suffered for it.

It appears that one of the theories behind target-setting is that professionals cannot be trusted to deliver services in the public interest. The theory goes that highly paid managers are more likely single-mindedly to hit targets in the interests of the public. The theory is questionable, supposing as it does (a) the innate selfishness of professionals; (b) that such selfishness is not in the public interest; (c) that optimum and effective targets are set; and (d) that managers are not themselves prone to selfishness and to the manipulation of targets and statistics. Such suppositions are by no means proven; indeed, the ruthless hitting of targets in Kent hospitals was attributed by the departing chairman of the trust as contributing to the deaths of 90 patients (Binmore 2007).

3.5 LEGAL FRAMEWORK

In the light of scarce resources, intense scrutiny has taken place of community care legislation in the search for rights and obligations. Irregular in look even at a distance, it is no surprise that on closer inspection the legislation reveals considerable ambiguity, lack of cohesion and sometimes flaws and contradictions. These all add to the uncertainties.

However, even if the legislation were clearer and more cohesive, it would inevitably still develop cracks if placed under undue pressure and scrutiny. Certainly community care legislation is highly fragmented and extensive; in addition some of the individual pieces of legislation have themselves been significantly amended. Sometimes this not only perplexes local authority staff and managers, but also lawyers. In one case, for instance, the judge concluded by lamenting the fact that during the hearing he had been supplied by the lawyers with defective copies of s.29 of the National Assistance Act 1948 and of s.1 of the Community Care (Direct Payments) Act 1996 (now superseded). He had been shown the originals, yet both had since been amended. Worse, the same had happened to him in a previous case (*R(A and B) v East Sussex CC: no.1*).

Similarly, in a case involving a combination of community care legislation and social security law, the Court of Appeal lamented: 'We cannot conclude this judgment without expressing our dismay at the complexity and labyrinthine nature of the relevant legislation and guidance, as well as (in some respects) its obscurity. Social security law should be clear and accessible. The tortuous analysis in the earlier part of this judgment shows that it is neither' (*Crofton v NHS Litigation Authority*). The disparate nature of the community care statutes has led to calls for new, integrated legislation. The Law Commission announced in 2008 that it would be reviewing adult social care law in England and Wales, since in its view this law was inadequate, often incomprehensible and outdated.

Even once different pieces of social services legislation have been identified and their content understood, their compatibility with one another – or indeed with NHS or housing legislation – is not always evident. For instance, the dividing line between provision of community care services under social services legislation, and of health services under the NHS Act 2006, is ever shifting. The courts have also struggled to explain the distinction between providing housing accommodation under the National Assistance Act 1948 as opposed to the Housing Act 1996.

Nevertheless, as already mentioned, the shortcomings of existing legislation have only been exposed so glaringly because of the close attention it has received in the light of a series of judicial review cases brought over the last 15 years or so. These disputes for the most part arise when local authorities, pleading lack of resources, withdraw or withhold services from people who need them.

In contrast to this legal picture affecting local authority social services authorities, stands the NHS Act 2006. It underpins health care provision in England. It consolidates a range of NHS legislation and replaced the previous NHS Act 1977. It is in some ways a far cry from the legislative fragmentation affecting social services. However, the uncertainties in health care provision under this Act are just as great, for the simple reason that the legislation is drafted in such a way as to confer virtually no individual enforceable rights on patients – whether in respect of assessment, treatment or provision of health care services. This allows NHS bodies to vary, reduce or withdraw provision on both a small scale (e.g. to individual patients) or wholesale (to whole communities) with impunity. In turn, this imports a huge degree of uncertainty into health care provision.

3.5.1 DISPUTES AND LEGAL CASES

Social care legislation and housing legislation (concerning home adaptations) have created a set of potentially strong legal entitlements which neither central government nor local government are either willing, or resourced, to meet.

Such potential entitlements fuel disputes, complaints and legal cases; there have been many of the latter concerning local authorities and their community care duties. Conversely, on the NHS and health care side of the picture, the legislation is so flimsy that people's needs can legally be dismissed and ignored relatively easily in comparison with social services legislation. It confers few enforceable rights on individual patients. Yet such has been the gap between public expectation and service delivery, a surprising number of cases have been taken even against the NHS. This trend has been fuelled by an arguably poor standard of decision-making by the boards of NHS bodies, with evidence, rationality and transparency in short supply. More surprisingly still, given the inhospitable legal landscape afforded by NHS legislation, some of these cases have been successful.

In summary then, over the past 10 to 15 years there has been a relatively large number of community care cases brought against local authorities; and the turmoil affecting the NHS in the last few years has led to an upsurge of legal cases about health care as well. However, these cases have arguably done relatively little overall to clear the smoke and resolve matters satisfactorily, even though some outcomes may have been helpful to individuals or groups of individuals. Legal cases tend to be hit and miss, and the courts anyway are in no position to evolve coherent policy; it is within neither their power nor their remit.

3.6 UNCERTAINTIES AND ESCAPE ROUTES

Community care is thus rife with legal and practical uncertainties. Indeed, these uncertainties are so prevalent as to be an integral and essential part of the system. Perversely, it could even be argued that it is certainty, rather than uncertainty, which is chimerical and anomalous in this context. Central government conceded this some ten years ago:

Nobody knowing what was going on. 'Up to now, neither users, carers, the public, nor social services staff and managers have had a clear idea which services are or should be provided, or what standards can reasonably be expected. There is no definition of what users can expect, nor any yard-stick for judging how effective or successful social services are. Individuals do not know what services are available, in what circumstances they might get them, or whether they will have to pay. This lack of clarity of objectives and standards means that on the one hand social services cannot be easily held to account, and on the other hand they can get blamed for anything that goes wrong.' (Secretary of State for Health 1998, p.6).

There is little evidence that this statement is not equally applicable ten years on. A similar description could be applied to the way in which health services are delivered so unevenly, erratically and, particularly in the case of vulnerable groups of people, inadequately. This is unsurprising. In many ways, the situation described in the White Paper actually suits central government. A lack of clarity veils problems that are difficult to solve and that have large resource implications. The uncertainties identified in 1998 are flourishing in 2008.

It is plain that uncertainties in social and health care multiply in number and degree when resources are short. Their practical function is to give the system some flexibility or 'give', and to allow authorities to regulate it according to their resources and priorities. These uncertainties can be thought of as, for example, safety valves, escape routes, discretionary elements, or variables with unpredictable values. When triggered, they in turn allow a proliferation of problems. In the case of local authorities, they typically include a lack of protection for vulnerable people, poor coordination between services, a lack of clarity about what services are available, and inconsistency in provision both between local authorities and within a single authority (Secretary of State for Health 1998, pp.5–7).

Some escape routes can be adopted lawfully, others cannot. For instance, up to a point it is lawful for a local authority formally to set a relatively high threshold of eligibility on the basis of limited resources. But it is not lawful, having set that threshold formally, for it to be then varied informally, arbitrarily and often covertly – depending on the monthly or quarterly state of local social services team budgets. The more adept amongst local authorities tend to utilise the escape routes that are likely to be lawful or less easily detectable; the less adept err toward routes that are unlawful, sometimes blatantly so.

The NHS generally reacts less subtly, and simply tends to withhold services, or even close them down wholesale, quite brazenly. But this is because the legal impediments to cuts, sometimes severe, to services are less pronounced in the context of the NHS than that of local authorities.

Uncertainties are normally highlighted in proportion to the financial pressures on local authorities and NHS bodies. The latter seek to identify safety valves and escape routes. They try to resolve the tension between people's needs, available resources and political expectations, and to see to what extent people really do have rights to services. In the case of local authorities, the answer has turned out to be that users of their social services have perhaps surprisingly few absolute legal rights or entitlements – although there are a few significant ones. In the case of NHS patients, absolute legal rights or entitlements are even more elusive.

3.7 ADULT PROTECTION AND SAFEGUARDING ADULTS

Protecting and safeguarding vulnerable adults is becoming a very much more prominent topic of concern within health and social care. It is largely about trying to prevent harm to vulnerable adults through abuse or neglect. The scope of such safeguarding work is wide, and to some extent ill-defined, but it covers a range of harm, abuse and neglect including financial, physical, sexual, emotional and institutional – whether occurring in people's own homes, care homes or hospitals.

One key question, unasked and unanswered, is about how far the risks of abuse and neglect are being exacerbated by some strands of government policy. For instance, the reduction of staff and services within the NHS, together with the ruthless hitting of performance and financial targets, has led to an erosion of standards of care amounting in some circumstances to neglect and ill-treatment of NHS patients. Equally, the driving down of costs demanded by central government of local authorities, has led to services being withdrawn from vulnerable people, or services being provided inadequately or to unacceptably low standards – with consequences that give rise to safeguarding concerns.

And current social care policy, which appears to equate service users with consumers – who need to be given independence, choice and control – may not adequately be considering the needs of vulnerable adults to be protected, as well as 'liberated' from what the government considers to be an outmoded welfare state. In practice, giving people control and choice is sometimes equated with abandoning them – because the pressing purpose behind the policy is reduction of expenditure. Yet high levels of support in the community for people living 'independent' lives are not consonant with such a reduction. In Cornwall, this tension was judged relevant to the failure of the local authority to intervene in a particular situation and to prevent a man with learning disabilities, living independently in the community, from being systematically exploited over a significant period, tortured and then murdered (Flynn 2007).

In addition, wholesale and unlawful charging for services, which should be free, calls into question whether local authorities and NHS bodies are themselves perpetrating a form of financial abuse; for instance, in the case of unlawful charges that have been made in respect of

NHS continuing health care, of after care services under the Mental Health Act 1983, and of the 'topping up' of care home fees by the families of residents.

Such practices, stemming from local authorities and the NHS, raise the awkward issue of how effective those bodies are at putting their own house in order, as opposed to investigating abuse and harm perpetrated by others.

3.8 GOOD PRACTICE AND THE LAW

An undercurrent of good professional practice runs through the legislation itself, particularly as it is interpreted and explained by community care guidance issued by the Department of Health. For instance, this is in terms of full and proper assessment, considering people's needs in the round, assessing risks to independence, taking an approach in terms of a social model of disability, considering carefully the role and needs of informal carers (e.g. LAC(2002)13; SSI/SWSG 1991). More recent guidance refers increasingly to choice, control and independence for people (LAC(DH)(2008)1). In addition, the principles applied by the law courts are often supportive of good practice. These include:

Dignity, integrity, etc. When assessing two women with learning and physical disabilities and how they would be physically transferred daily within and without the home, the local authority had to take account of their wishes, feelings, reluctance, fear, refusal, dignity, integrity and quality of life (*R(A and B) v East Sussex County Council: no.2*).

Flexibility. Rigid policies should be avoided and exceptional needs looked out for (*R v Ealing LBC, ex p Leaman; R v North Yorkshire CC, ex p Hargreaves (no.2); British Oxygen v Board of Trade*).

Low threshold for assessment. 'Screening' procedures should not be restrictive (*R v Bristol CC, ex p Penfold*).

Assessment valuable in its own right. Assessment is useful and a potential entitlement in its own right (*R v Bristol CC, ex p Penfold*).

Waiting times. People should not be kept waiting interminably for a decision about services (*R v Sutton LBC, ex p Tucker*).

Preferences. People's preferences should be considered (*R v North Yorkshire CC, ex p Hargreaves*).

Recreational needs. People's needs should be viewed broadly including social, recreational and leisure needs (*R v Haringey LBC, ex p Norton*).

Individual assessment. People's needs should be assessed and reassessed individually and attentively (*R v Gloucestershire CC, ex p Mahfood and R v Gloucestershire CC, ex p RADAR*).

Distinguish need from services. Assessment should distinguish needs from services (*R v Lancashire CC, ex p RADAR*).

Accurate letters. Accurate letters should be written (*R v Bristol CC, ex p Bailey*).

Explanations for decisions. Decisions should be explicable in terms of reasoning rather than unsupported assertions (*R v Ealing LBC, ex p C*).

Value of professional assessment. The courts preferred the comprehensive assessment of a social work team leader, to the decision of a panel – since the latter had given no reasons (*R(Goldsmith) v Wandsworth LBC*).

Human rights. Failing properly to assess vulnerable 95-year-old women could be fatal and a breach of human rights (*R(Goldsmith) v Wandsworth LBC*).

The axioms of good administration applied by the local government and health service ombudsmen also bear a close link to professional good practice (see 4.9.1). The application of such axioms, all consistent with professional good practice, can make a real difference as to whether any one individual service user receives a service – or at least to the fairness of the decision as to whether or not a service is provided. Yet it is surprising how often local authority officers are unaware of the good administration axioms of the ombudsman, of the principles applied in judicial review cases, or of what exactly the relevant guidance states.

The General Social Care Council's Code of Practice for Social Workers states that they must:
- treat each person as an individual
- respect and promote individual views and wishes of users and carers
- support people's rights to control their own lives
- respect and maintain dignity and privacy
- promote equal opportunities, and respect diversity (GSCC 2002).

The Council's Code of Practice for Employers states, amongst other things, that the employer must have written policies and procedures in place to enable social workers to adhere to their code of practice (GSCC 2002a). Healthcare professionals, such as nurses, likewise have professional codes of practice. However, these principles sometimes seem to be treated as rather abstract statements of grand intent but no more; financial and other pressures on local authorities and NHS bodies can make such good practice difficult to adhere to. Yet, often, in both local authorities and the NHS, statements of professionally (and politically) correct principle are made by managers and staff who – most ironically – are at the same time applying inequitable, restrictive and sometimes wholly unlawful policies and practices.

Some professionals may become disenchanted and believe that such codes should be rewritten to reflect a harsher reality. For instance, the Code of Ethics and Professional Practice for Occupational Therapists states that practice should be client-centred and needs led (COT 2005). It has been suggested that the undermining of this, as therapists are forced into drastic gate-keeping roles, means that the Code should be rewritten thus: 'Services could be client-centred and needs-led, if this does not threaten occupational therapists' employment status, career prospects or financial self-interests; or imperil the political and institutional status quo' (Hammell 2007, p.265). This is a fairly extreme and perhaps over-simplified view; but there can be little question that health and social care professionals in the NHS and local authorities routinely feel compelled to compromise on some of their standards.

Perhaps unsurprisingly, the Commission for Social Care Inspection reported a widespread view that social work had become 'de-professionalised'. As one director of services put it, it was all about financial assessments, inputting information on to a computer and hitting targets now (Henwood and Hudson 2008, pp.7, 45). Professionals may be unsure

even as to what constitutes good professional practice; is it to try to follow their gut professional instincts or to follow the organisation's policy to the letter? For instance, up to a third
of social workers may be prepared to bend rules and exaggerate the needs of clients, so the the
latter are not excluded from receiving help (*Community Care* 2007). A CSCI report found the
same trend with staff deliberately placing somebody in a higher band than, strictly, was warranted if their gut feeling told them that the person needed support (Henwood and Hudson
2008, p.48).

3.8.1 GOOD PRACTICE AND LEGAL FAIRNESS IN DECISION-MAKING

Organisational pressures can sometimes cause even experienced and senior social workers
and other care professionals to lose sight of the good practice, which they would as individuals pride themselves upon. The late Sir Douglas Black, president of the Royal College of Physicians and author in 1980 of *Inequalities in health: the Black report*, was reported as making a
telling comment when alluding to organisational aberration: 'People banded together are
capable of follies and excesses beyond what the same people, acting as individuals, would
perpetrate on other individuals. Such activities may be termed corporate tyranny' (quoted in
Richmond 2002).

Such a comment is not to overstate the case. For instance, when a local authority failed to
meet the needs of a disabled child in foster care, apparently concealing or altering the
evidence as to her situation and needs, the judge did not question the good faith of any of the
local authority staff involved. However, he referred to the 'demon' that had entered into and
'infected' the local authority's decision-making for a period of two years (*CD (A Child) v
Anglesey CC*). A comparable situation was reported to the Healthcare Commission in terms of
nurses telling patients regularly to evacuate their bladder and bowels in hospital beds, rather
than assisting them to get to the toilet – and this was against a backdrop of fundamental lapses
in essential patient care and infection control (Healthcare Commission 2007). The nurses
were under intolerable pressure owing to the policy of the NHS trust concerned, but such
practices must inevitably raise questions about the place of professional integrity in the
modern world of health and social care.

3.8.1.1 Fair decision-making: a case study

Sometimes, decision-making can go very badly wrong indeed in social care or health care.
The process can become a mire both for service users and their relatives who struggle to have
their voice heard, and for social and health care staff and managers who are subject to
immense workload, financial and political pressures.

By way of example, the following case illustrates a veritable catalogue of failure: predetermined decision-making, misrepresentations, non-adherence to local good practice guidelines, breach of human rights, apparent suppression or deliberate ignoring of the main
community care assessment, and potential risk to a 95-year-old woman's well-being and
indeed life. In addition to these failings being exposed by the law courts, the local authority
then refused to compensate the woman's daughter for the many thousands of pounds she had
unnecessarily spent – and only finally repaid the money after the daughter took a complaint
(separately from the legal case) to the local government ombudsman. No suggestion of bad

faith was made by the courts or the ombudsman: most of all it was, as the Court of Appeal put it, about a failure in process.

The purpose of setting out this case immediately below is by no means to vilify the local authority concerned. It is a product of the system and could have occurred anywhere:

Manifestly flawed and defective decision-making in the case of a frail 95-year-old woman. A local authority decided that a 95-year-old woman could not continue to live in the care home in which she had lived for many years. Instead she would have to move to a nursing home. Her daughter vigorously opposed the decision. The Court of Appeal ruled that the decision was manifestly flawed. A catalogue of serious criticism of the local authority underlay this judgment.

Misplaced reliance on local continuing care panel. Reliance was placed by the local authority on the recommendations of the local continuing care panel, without ensuring that it had taken account of all relevant factors (which it had not). This meant the local authority was not reaching a lawful community care decision.

Not considering all relevant factors. The local authority had reached a decision without taking account of the most impressive and comprehensive assessment of the woman's needs, carried out by one of its own social work team managers, who knew the woman best. Instead the authority had relied on the panel's recommendations, which in turn rested on the reports of health professionals who assessed the woman in hospital. Furthermore a doctor who had endorsed these reports, had not seen the woman. Thus, the decision was taken without a full and up-to-date community care assessment.

Misrepresenting the daughter's position. A letter written by one of the local authority managers to the doctor involved had misrepresented the dispute. It portrayed the daughter as a lone voice without any professional support; when in fact the team manager's assessment concurred with the daughter that her mother was 'residential care fit'.

Predetermined decision. The court concluded that the decision taken by the local authority was predetermined; those responsible had approached it with 'entirely' closed minds.

Local policy on 'partnership' with service users. The local policy stated that decisions should be made in full partnership with service users and their carers. The team manager's assessment had taken this approach, but was ignored. In addition, the daughter was prevented from attending the panel meeting on the grounds that only clinical matters were being discussed. The court pointed out that this was less than transparent and logical; social work managers were present who could scarcely be called clinicians, and in fact there had been a reference to resources contained in the report submitted to the panel. This was in terms of the additional costs involved if the woman stayed in her present care home. The court pointed out that this was scarcely a clinical issue and so was an irrelevant consideration for the panel.

Furthermore, the panel failed to keep a written record of its meetings; this was unacceptable and extraordinary. In turn therefore the local authority had not put forward a reasoned, balanced and transparent decision.

Human rights. The court also found that article 8 of the European Convention on Human Rights had been breached. This was because the court could not accept that the decision-making process safeguarded the woman's physical and psychological integrity. Interference by the local authority had to be proportionate in terms of weighing up the doctor's and panel's recommendations in the wider context of the woman's needs and rights. The local authority had not done this. And it was not an academic matter since it was not in dispute that a change to a strange environment for such a frail person 'could have serious if not fatal consequences'.

The court ordered the local authority to take the decision again. The court could not determine the outcome; but it hoped that what was left of the woman's life could be lived out with maximum dignity and the minimum of psychological harm (*R(Goldsmith) v Wandsworth LBC*).

Astonishingly, the legal case had a sequel, necessitating a subsequent, also successful, challenge to the local authority through the local government ombudsman. Having been chastised by the Court of Appeal, the local authority doggedly fought on – only to lose the case a second time around:

Seeking compensation for fees paid for nursing care. During the dispute the daughter had taken advice from a variety of professionals about her mother's needs. They had all confirmed that her mother did not need registered nursing care. They included the ward sister, a report commissioned from BUPA nurses, a consultant psychiatrist's report and nursing home managers. So, the daughter agreed that she would pay for the separate, private provision of nursing home in the residential home – this was the only way of getting her mother back into this home. The daughter spent over £27,000 on this nursing care.

But, even after the Court of Appeal case had been won, the local authority refused to pay this money back. The ombudsman found maladministration, since the local authority's assessment had been thoroughly vitiated by the Court of Appeal, and there was plentiful evidence from other sources that the mother did not need registered nursing care. So the ombudsman recommended that the sum of £27,018.84 be reimbursed to the daughter, together with £500 as some recompense for the time and trouble of complaining (*Wandsworth LBC 2006*).

Doubtless, the local authority officers in this legal (and ombudsman) case all acted in good faith in the light of various pressures, but from the point of view of service users and their carers it makes sorry reading. The criticism of the court comes close to a full-scale demolition of the local authority's decision-making process; it referred to 'seriously defective' decision-making throughout. The case appears to serve as something of an object lesson in fairness and in the importance of guarding against 'shortcuts' in decision-making at the expense of extremely vulnerable people.

To conclude on a more optimistic note, the court in the *Goldsmith* case recognised the importance of a good quality professional assessment and documentation. This was the 40-page report by a social work team manager, which had concluded, like the daughter, that the woman was 'residential care fit'. Although it had apparently been largely ignored in the local authority's decision-making process, nevertheless it was ultimately the effort that the team manager had put into the report that served the woman and her daughter so well. Its very quality meant that the court viewed it as 'critical' to the decision-making process. Thus, those social care professionals, who are wont to feel that their efforts are sometimes in vain in the pressured world of community care, should presumably take heart from this aspect of the case.

CHAPTER 4

Non-judicial remedies

KEY POINTS

Remedies are courses of action that people can follow when trying to pursue and resolve disputes. These range from the informal at one extreme to, at the other, judicial review proceedings as well as actions for negligence. These might sometimes be argued up the judicial ladder to the House of Lords and beyond to the European Court of Human Rights. The question of remedy is clearly significant, because apparent obligations in legislation and guidance arguably mean little, if it is unclear when, if at all, they are enforceable. Such remedies are covered in this chapter and the next.

This chapter covers remedies that in principle are not of the 'judicial type'. That is, even if taken to their logical conclusion, they would not normally directly involve the courts – although they could do in some instances. There is a surprisingly wide range of options including going to councillors or the newspapers, complaining, and going to an independent ombudsman. However, it should not be assumed that challenging, informally or more formally, local authorities or NHS bodies, is either an easy process or likely to deliver a just outcome. Courage, stamina, determination and often support are likely to be required, if there is to be any chance of success. Neither should it be assumed of course that those with the most cause to complain or challenge decisions, are the most likely to do so in practice.

Amongst these non-judicial remedies, then, is resort to the local government or health service ombudsmen, who investigate maladministration causing injustice and can also investigate a failure in service. The ombudsmen apply certain axioms or principles of good administration. For local authority and NHS staff, such principles are particularly important because they apply to the process of assessment and provision of services. They also equate closely to professional and administrative good practice. The local government ombudsmen are generally highly regarded; and the health service ombudsman has waged an almost single-handed campaign for over 14 years in order to try to bring about fairness in decisions taken about NHS continuing health care.

Grievances are sometimes collective rather than individual. For instance, cut-backs and changes to NHS services over the past few years have led to a surprising number of local communities across the country to protest. The ingredients of such protest might take various forms including cross political party action committees, public meetings, marches, fundraising events, commissioning independent expert reports, petitioning the prime minister, thousands of letters, extensive use of the local and regional press, Parliamentary questions framed by the local Member for Parliament, judicial review legal cases, referrals to the Secretary of State for Health by the local health overview and scrutiny committee attached to the local council, and the involvement of the Independent Reconfiguration Panel, a notionally independent body appointed by central government to review controversial local changes to the NHS.

This chapter also covers the rules about both obtaining personal information from – and also the rules concerning the disclosure and sharing of personal information by – local authorities and NHS trusts.

4.1 INFORMAL REMEDIES

If something goes wrong, then informal channels for seeking a remedy – for instance, provision or restoration of a service, an apology, undertakings about the future – are various. They might include gently querying actions and decisions without pursuing a formal 'complaint'. Well-informed service users or their advisers may nip in the bud dubious decisions.

Local authority officers or NHS managers are sometimes disconcerted when a service user or a representative refers to legislation or guidance from the Department of Health. Alternatively, well-informed staff and managers might know that they are on firm legal ground and demonstrate this from the outset; in which case a challenge might simply not be worth making. Well-reasoned and well-documented decisions rapidly dismay solicitors and others who may be contemplating a challenge.

Resolving disputes informally is often the preferable option; generally speaking, neither service user nor authority wishes to incur the time, trouble, stress and expense of engaging in a formal dispute. The possible souring of future relations between staff and service user might also be a significant consideration in practice. In addition, many service users, understanding the impossible demands being made all too often on hard-pressed health and social care staff, may be reluctant to complain – for fear of getting those staff into trouble. And, a judicial review legal case, the main type of legal challenge to decision-making by local authorities or NHS bodies, is often too blunt a tool.

4.2 COUNCILLORS, MPS, NEWSPAPERS

MPs and local councillors might take up the cases of constituents not on compelling legal grounds but simply for benevolent, compassionate or local political reasons.

Going to the newspapers can sometimes be effective. For example, in one case a 64-year-old man suffered from Parkinson's disease. Following two major operations and subsequent infections at West Suffolk Hospital, he needed rehabilitation. Because of a shortage of beds at the hospital, the latter stated that he would have to go into a nursing home. However, he would not have proper access to physiotherapy and occupational therapy, both crucial for his rehabilitation. His wife (a retired nurse), to whom he was newly married, understood the implications and urgency and contacted the regional newspaper, the *East Anglian Daily Times*. Within two days of a front page article, the hospital suddenly found a rehabilitation bed (Grahame-Clarke 2005). Making a complaint or even threatening legal action would undoubtedly not have produced the same outcome. In this particular case, speed was everything, if the man was not to miss out on that all important window of rehabilitation.

4.3 LOCAL AUTHORITY MONITORING OFFICERS

Local authority monitoring officers (each authority is obliged to have one) have a duty to report on actual or potential contraventions by the local authority of legislation or codes of practice made under legislation, and on any actual or possible maladministration or injustice caused by the authority. Any proposal, act, omission or actual contravention might be by the authority, any committee, subcommittee or officer of the authority, or by any joint committee, on which the authority is represented (Local Government and Housing Act 1989, s.5).

4.4 DISTRICT AUDITORS

Indirect redress might be had by complaining to the district auditor, who might be concerned at unlawful or wasteful expenditure.

Day services, complaint to district auditor. The mother of an autistic man complained to the local government ombudsman and the district auditor that the council was paying an independent provider for a level of day services which, she claimed, her son was not receiving. The complaint led to the council stating that it would investigate and attempt to recover some money from the provider (*Liverpool CC 1998*).

4.5 LOCAL AUTHORITY SOCIAL SERVICES COMPLAINTS PROCEDURE

A new social services complaints procedure for adults was implemented in September 2006 by means of regulations passed under the Health and Social Care (Community Health and Standards) Act 2003 (ss.114–115, 195). In early 2008, the Department of Health announced legislative reform that would change the system yet again by unifying the social services and NHS complaints procedures (DH 2008a).

4.5.1 GENERAL POINTS ABOUT THE SOCIAL SERVICES COMPLAINTS SYSTEM

The local authority social services complaints procedure is – in principle at least – suitable for most grievances. Furthermore, subject to statutory time limits, it should not be protracted. There is an appeal procedure involving review panels, which have wide powers to examine not only whether an authority has adhered to policy and procedure, but also the factual decisions that it reached. Notwithstanding the potential usefulness of the complaints procedure, there are general provisos:

- The local government ombudsmen have repeatedly found that complaints procedures are in practice too often ineffective and long-winded.
- The law courts have pointed out that the complaints procedure is unsuitable for resolving matters of law.
- If many, maybe over 50 per cent of complaints concern the rationing of resources (Simons 1995, p.40), then arguably the complaints procedure will be impotent in effecting remedies. This will be especially the case if local authorities are utilising lawful loopholes, rather than taking unlawful shortcuts, in order to limit expenditure.

- It is therefore something of an irony that significant political energy and resources are put into complaints procedures, in order to field a potentially large volume of complaints that arguably the complaints procedure is not equipped to resolve. In which case, the complaints procedure runs the risk – up to a point – of being an irrelevant diversion. Clearly, people would rather have good services than a good complaints system.
- Overworked staff can easily become demoralised if they are subject to a continual barrage of complaints; half a day spent recording a complaint made by a relative that morning means they are not seeing other service users. It is not always clear where the balance of the greater public good lies – in terms of how much time should be spent on complaints by scarce professional staff such as social workers and therapists, when they could be assessing and providing services for other people.
- Another potential weakness in the system is that local authorities are not obliged to follow a review panel's recommendations, athough they should have good reasons for not doing so.
- Lastly, and more simply perhaps, a drawback of reliance on complaints procedures to ensure a good quality of decision-making is simply that (a) many service users do not want to be in the spotlight or to upset those providing services; and (b) it is stressful, exhausting and demanding to complain, unless the complainant is a 'persevering, single-handed warrior, who thrives on skirmishes with public authorities'. These are not the characteristics of vulnerable, 'inarticulate and meek' people, in the words of one social services officer (Coombs 1998, p.48).

There is also particular concern that people who are funding their own care directly with independent care providers cannot refer a complaint to the local authority; their only remedy is to complain to that same provider. This is regarded by many as highly unsatisfactory, but central government has given little indication of any imminent change.

4.5.2 SUMMARY OF SOCIAL SERVICES COMPLAINTS PROCEDURE
The following represents a summary of the social services complaints procedure. The rules are drawn from regulations (SI 2006/1681) made under the Health and Social Care (Community Health and Standards) Act 2003, and also Department of Health guidance (DH 2006c). The latter, however, appears not to be 'statutory guidance'; it is described as 'best practice guidance' only, and so lacks the degree of authority it might otherwise have had as statutory guidance (see 5.1.6).

Basically, the complaints procedure consists of three main stages: informal, formal and review. In order that these should operate smoothly, the local authority must appoint a complaints manager (SI 2006/1681, r.16).

4.5.3 IDENTITY OF THE COMPLAINANT
A person can make a complaint if he or she is someone in respect of whom a relevant social services function is being, or has been, discharged. The complaint can be brought by somebody else on behalf of a person. However, the local authority should not consider a complaint brought on behalf of a person lacking capacity, if it is satisfied that it is not in the person's best interests. (However, this bit of the guidance would presumably not apply if the complaint was brought by a person with the requisite power to do so under a lasting power of

attorney or court-appointed deputyship, on behalf of the person lacking capacity to do so himself or herself). Relevant social services functions are defined in s.1A and schedule 1 of the Local Authority Social Services Act 1970 (SI 2006/1681, rr.4–5).

4.5.4 NOT CONSIDERING THE COMPLAINT

A complaint should not be considered by the local authority if it is withdrawn, repeats a complaint already made, has been investigated by the local government ombudsman, is a 'care standards' complaint (see 4.5.5 below), is unclear, is frivolous or vexatious, the complainant intends to take legal proceedings, the local authority is taking disciplinary proceedings against a person complained about and in relation to the substance of the complaint, criminal proceedings have been commenced – or proceedings under s.59 of the Care Standards Act 2000 (that is, General Social Care Council proceedings) have been commenced (SI 2006/1681, r.5).

The guidance adds, a little unclearly perhaps, that a decision made by an approved social worker under the Mental Health Act 1983 would not fall within the complaints procedure, although complaints about the process of assessment would (DH 2006c, p.10).

A complaint, brought over a year from the date of the act or omission complained of, should not be considered. However, the local authority can waive this rule if it believes (a) that it would not be reasonable to have expected the complaint to have been made any earlier; and (b) if it is still possible to consider the complaint effectively and fairly (SI 2006/1681, r.5).

4.5.5 COMPLAINT ABOUT AN INDEPENDENT PROVIDER

A 'care standards' related complaint is defined as relating to services provided by a registered care provider under the Care Standards Act 2000 (in future, the Health and Social Care Act 2008), and which is not about the discharge or failure to discharge social services functions (SI 2006/1681, r.2).

Guidance explains that where 'the local authority is responsible for the original assessment of need that led to a placement and associated funding, then the complainant should, in most instances, have recourse to the local authority's complaints procedure. However, access to the local authority's complaints procedure does not apply to people with private self-funding arrangements'. The latter must use the care provider's own complaints procedure, which the provider is obliged to have under the Care Standards Act 2000 (DH 2006c, p.38).

If part, or all, of the complaint concerns an independent care provider registered under the Care Standards Act 2000, the local authority must within ten days (if part of the complaint) or five days (if all of the complaint) ask the complainant if he or she wishes the relevant details to be sent to the care provider. If so, the local authority must send it as soon as reasonably practicable (SI 2006/1681, r.6).

4.5.6 INFORMAL STAGE OF COMPLAINT

Within 20 days of a complaint being received, the local authority must take all reasonable steps to resolve the complaint informally, inform the complainant about the extent to which it considers the complaint well-founded, give reasons, and inform the person about his or her right to request a formal investigation (SI 2006/1681, r.7). Under the previous social services complaints procedure, the ombudsman took a dim view of stalling tactics by the local authority:

Stalling a complaint at the informal stage. When a response took 219 days, instead of 28 days, the local ombudsman identified the fact that an understandable wish to solve a complaint informally does not mean that the informal stage should go on longer than necessary; otherwise complaints can simply stall altogether (*Sheffield CC 2002*).

4.5.7 FORMAL STAGE OF COMPLAINT

Within 20 working days of receiving notification about the local authority's informal response (or within 20 days of the expiry of the original 20-day period for informal solution – whichever is earlier), the complainant may at any time request that the complaint be investigated formally. On receipt of this request, the local authority must, as soon as reasonably practicable, record the complaint in writing, invite comment from the complainant, investigate the complaint and keep the complainant informed (SI 2006/1681, rr.8–9).

Within a maximum 65 days of the original request (or of a later date on which the record of the complaint was amended following the complainant's comments) the local authority must send a report of the outcome of the investigation. If this is not possible, it should be sent as soon as is reasonably practicable. However, if the report has not been sent within 25 days, the local authority must explain why and when it expects to send a report. If the local authority thinks the complaint is well founded, it must provide an explanation of what action it proposes to take (SI 2006/1681, r.10).

Guidance states that the local authority can choose to appoint a local authority officer or a person independent of the authority to investigate. However, if it chooses to appoint the former, that investigating officer should not be in direct line management of the service being complained of.

Depending on the vulnerability of the complainant and the seriousness of the complaint, the guidance states that the local authority should consider appointing an 'independent person' in addition to the investigating officer. The independent person should not be an employee, or spouse of an employee or of a member of the authority. The guidance sets out the role of this independent person, which essentially seems to be that of shadowing the investigation. The guidance also states more generally that complainants may request assistance from an advocate; in which case, the local authority should facilitate independent and confidential advocacy (DH 2006c, paras 3.4, 3.6, 3.7, Annex 1).

In the past, the local government ombudsman has commented on the need for independence, both in appearance and substance, to attach to formal investigations:

Independence of complaints procedure investigations. The ombudsman had no reason to doubt the 'integrity and professionalism' of the investigating officer; but to the complainants, the officer, who worked within the same directorate of the council involved in the complaint, did not appear to be independent – whilst the ombudsman, too, stated that in fact she may not have been independent (*Manchester CC 1996a*).

In another case (involving a complaint under a non-statutory complaints procedure), the council asked an officer to carry out an initial investigation into the actions of another officer – despite the fact that the two officers were in conflict. As the ombudsman put it, this beggared belief. A highly critical report emerged from the first officer, without the second officer having had the opportunity to put her point of view. Nothing was then done about the complaint until the two officers had left the council; this was 'shocking' to the ombudsman (*Durham CC 1998*).

Furthermore, if an investigation is to be effective, the officer responsible should fully understand her role and have been given guidance and support (*Salford CC 1996*).

4.5.8 REVIEW PANEL STAGE OF COMPLAINT

Following the formal stage (after receipt of the report or on the expiry of the 65-day limit), the complainant can request a review panel within 20 days (SI 2006/1681, r.11).

Within 30 days of this request, the local authority must appoint a review panel and the panel must convene. The panel must consist of three people, at least two of whom must not be members (or their spouses or civil partners) of the local authority. Local authority officers anyway cannot sit on the panel. The chair of the panel must be one of these independent people. Within five days of convening, the panel must decide whether the local authority dealt adequately with the complaint and notify both complainant and authority of its decision. If the decision is that the complaint was not adequately dealt with, the local authority must within 15 days notify the complainant of what action it proposes to take and provide guidance to the complainant about taking the complaint further to the local government ombudsman (SI 2006/1681, rr.12–14).

Guidance states that, amongst other things, the panel should apply the civil standard of proof (balance of probability) rather than the criminal standard (beyond reasonable doubt). The panel should record its findings, which 'should explain simply and clearly any recommendations and the reasons for them' (DH 2006c, paras 3.12, 3.21). The courts have in the past criticised a lack of reasons:

Failure of panel and local authority to give reasons. A failure of either the panel or the local authority to give reasons meant that the applicant was denied what she was entitled to; the court made a declaration that they should have been supplied (in *R v Cornwall CC, ex p Goldsack*).

The guidance also states that the complainant has a right to bring a representative, but that ideally this should not be a lawyer (DH 2006c, para 3.11). Conversely, it might scarcely seem fair to complainants if the authority deploys a member of its legal department in the proceedings:

Involvement of local authority lawyer in panel proceedings. The local ombudsman included in a finding of maladministration the observation that he found it 'hard to see how a solicitor employed by the Council could be seen as an "unbiased observer" and consider[ed] the way in which he joined at the outset in the *in camera* deliberations of the Panel to be unwise at the very least' (*Cleveland CC 1993*).

Whatever the potential shortcomings of the complaints procedure, the courts have ruled that it does not breach article 6 of the European Convention on Human Rights relating to a fair hearing. This is because the fairness of the local authority's reaction to review panel recommendations is subject to judicial review; and, taken together, the complaints procedure coupled with the fallback of a legal case comply with the demands of fairness under article 6 (*R(Beeson) v Dorset CC*, Court of Appeal).

4.5.8.1 Scope of review panel's function and of the complaints procedure generally

In the past, there has sometimes been uncertainty about the legitimate scope of the review panel's deliberations. Some panels have considered the actual merits of decisions, while others have concentrated only on whether procedures have been followed. An example of the broader approach was reported in one legal case, when the complaints review panel found that the social services department had discharged its functions properly in relation to the complainant's application for services – but went on nevertheless to recommend that the department consider providing precisely those services it had hitherto denied (*R v Wigan MBC, ex p Tammadge*).

Arguably a policy that excludes consideration by review panels of the merits of a decision would be an unlawful restriction of the statutory underpinning, which says nothing about not questioning the merits. The courts frequently refer to the suitability of the complaints procedure, rather than of the courts, for investigating disputed facts as opposed to legal issues (e.g. *R v Plymouth CC, ex p Cowl; also R (Ireneschild) v Lambeth LBC*). In turn, the investigation of facts might then lead to a question of the merits of a decision.

Certainly the current guidance says nothing about the scope of the review panel, or of the complaints procedure generally, being limited. For instance, the guidance, non-exhaustively, refers to a complaint being about the following issues, which clearly could include both facts and merits:

- unwelcome or disputed decision
- quality or appropriateness of a service
- delay in decision-making or provision of services
- delivery or non-delivery of services, including complaints procedure
- quantity, frequency, change or cost of a service
- attitude or behaviour of staff
- assessment and eligibility criteria
- a local authority policy and its impact
- assessment, care management, review (DH 2006c, para 2.2).

4.5.8.2 Review panel procedures

The local ombudsman has investigated review panel matters on a number of occasions. Failure to offer the option of a review panel is maladministration (*Manchester CC 1996a*), or even gross maladministration, in the judgement of the local ombudsman:

Gross maladministration and refusal to convene review panel. Two complaints were made by the father concerning assessment and provision for his son on leaving school; his son had mild learning disabilities, a stress-related condition and was later diagnosed as schizophrenic. The first complaint in September 1995 was about the level of care, the second in October about the care provided in a mental health hostel. The father contacted the local ombudsman in January 1996, who in turn wrote to the council. The director of social services then wrote to the father outlining the services being provided but not referring to the second complaint or to the right to a complaints review panel. The local ombudsman asked the council to respond again and to deal with these matters; the council sent a second letter that covered some of the issues concerning the mental health hostel, but still failed to mention the review panel. The ombudsman asked the council to convene a review panel, pointing out that it appeared to be in breach of its duty.

The father received a letter in February asking him to contact the complaints section. He did so by telephone, saying that he would like his solicitor present at the panel hearing; this conversation was never formally recorded. In March he received another letter, asking him for a response to the February letter and saying that if no reply was forthcoming by the end of March, it would be assumed that he did not wish to pursue the complaint. The father never received a letter explaining why his complaints could not be dealt with in 28 days and indicating how long they would take; and a review panel was never convened.

The ombudsman found 'gross maladministration' in the handling of the complaint. The time taken was 'entirely unacceptable' (by July 1996, nothing had been resolved). The council should not have been chasing up letters it had already received a response to. It was only because of the ombudsman's involvement that the father was ever informed about his right to have a review panel convened. Furthermore, although the council pointed out, rightly, that a request for a review panel is required in writing, it was 'disingenuous of the council to imply blame on the complainants when it failed to fulfil undertakings to put matters in writing and failed to respond to correspondence' (*Liverpool CC 1997*).

Basic fairness might be lacking at the panel hearing and mean the local ombudsman will find maladministration:

Procedures at the panel hearing. Not to give advance notice that it would not allow a hearing-impaired complainant to make a tape recording of the panel proceedings was maladministration; as was asking the same complainant to consider at the panel hearing a chronology that he had not been given in advance (*Southwark 2001*).

4.5.8.3 Outcome of review panel recommendations

The regulations do not demand, nor does the guidance suggest, that a local authority must follow the recommendations of a review panel.

However, the courts have with varying force suggested that local authorities should follow the recommendations. In *R v Avon CC, ex p M*, the judge stated that it was unlawful to disregard the review panel's findings without a good reason, given the weight and 'one way' nature of the evidence that had informed the panel's decision. In *R v Islington LBC, ex p Rixon*, the court stated that the greater the departure from the review panel's recommendations, the greater the need for 'cogent articulated reasons'.

Milder was the statement of the court in *R v North Yorkshire CC, ex p Hargreaves* that there was no general rule that local authorities must follow the recommendations of a review panel – but that in some circumstances it might be unlawful not to do so without a good reason.

The local ombudsman has found maladministration where the local authority failed to produce, as requested by the review panel, a detailed report within a year (*Hounslow LBC 1995*). If the complaint is about a decision taken by the director of social services, the ombudsman has stated that the recommendations of the review panel should be referred to someone else, such as the chief executive of the authority or the social services committee (*Carmarthenshire CC 1999*).

There have been many other local ombudsman investigations relating to a review panel's recommendations or to the local authority's response to those recommendations – in terms of compliance, non-compliance or clarity of response. For example:

Inadequate review panel outcomes. A review panel's findings might be flawed on their face and lead to findings of maladministration by the local ombudsman – for instance, because of deficient evidence considered by the panel or apparent misinterpretation of a coroner's report (*Cleveland CC 1993*). Or a panel might fail to evaluate a claim for compensation and to make adequate recommendations back to the council despite being ideally placed to do so (*Warwickshire CC 1997*).

Local authority responses to review panel. It was not maladministration when the local authority refused to follow a panel's recommendation about arranging a residential placement for a man with learning disabilities. This was because no assessment of the man's needs had been carried out, although this failure to assess was itself maladministration in its own right (*Kent CC 1998*).

When a local authority was prepared to follow its review panel's recommendations for compensation after poor advice about state benefits had been given, the local ombudsman nevertheless criticised the panel for taking into account an immaterial factor when coming to its decision about the level of compensation. The panel had been prepared to recommend only £750 instead of the £5000 the woman had lost, on the grounds that it should not reimburse money that it was not responsible for issuing; the ombudsman held that this was an irrelevant consideration (*East Sussex CC 1995*).

When a panel recommended in December 1996 that the local authority carry out an urgent assessment of a woman with learning disabilities, it took seven months for the authority to allocate the task, a further seven months to gather the relevant information, and a further three months to complete the reassessment. It was not sent to the woman's parents for a further two months. Services were not in place until December 1998. This was a year longer than it should have taken. The local ombudsman found maladministration and recommended compensation, including the cost of two hours of day care per week for 50 weeks (*Oxfordshire CC 1999*).

In any event a local authority's response to a complaint and what it proposes to do should be clear. Thus the local ombudsman criticised the fact that the complaints officer first wrote to the complainants stating that the reviewer's conclusions had been accepted; but then a second letter from the chief executive expressed disagreement with some of those conclusions (*Bury MBC 2004*).

4.5.9 REMEDIES

Guidance points out that under s.92 of the Local Government Act 2000, local authorities have the power to remedy injustice arising from a complaint. This can include both financial and non-financial redress. The guidance states that remedies should be appropriate and proportionate, put the complainant in the position he or she would have been except for the fault, consider financial compensation, take into account the complainant's views, and take into account the effect of the complainant's own actions. Financial redress may arise in respect of compensation, quantifiable loss, loss of a non-monetary benefit, loss of value, lost opportunity, distress and time and trouble (DH 2006c, paras 6.3–6.4).

4.5.10 PUBLICITY

Guidance states that local authorities should publicise their complaints procedures (DH 2006c, para 4.1).

4.5.11 SOCIAL SERVICES COMPLAINTS AND LOCAL OMBUDSMAN INVESTIGATIONS

The local government ombudsmen have frequently made adverse findings in relation to the operation of local social services complaints procedures. For instance, the following cases relate to systemic and general failures, the recording of complaints, delay, and failure to focus on the substance of a complaint.

In the following case the local ombudsman identified an aimless approach to complaints and a clear gap between policy and practice:

Worrying attitude to complaints. The ombudsman identified a worrying attitude to complaints. This undermined the assertion by the director of social services that every investigation was approached on the basis that the 28-day timescale would be met. The ombudsman also recommended measures be taken to ensure that adequate staff be available for complaints handling, investigators be promptly appointed who could start their work within the timescales – and that staff required for interview offer interviews within a few days (except in case of holiday or sick leave). The ombudsman was 'appalled' that the council kept no data to inform it about whether it was meeting complaints timescales (*Nottinghamshire CC 1998*).

Confusion, lack of clarity, poor investigation and information, inadequate recording and breached timescales might all lead to findings of maladministration:

General failure to treat complaint properly. Serious concerns (and maladministration) arose as follows. There was confusion about which stage of the complaints procedure was being followed. The complaint was being handled informally but the complainant had wanted it formally dealt with. There was no thorough investigation. 'Presenting problems' were focused on, to the exclusion of underlying issues. Relevant case records were not examined and key people not interviewed. Timescales were not adhered to and the complainant was not informed about progress. A letter sent at the end of investigation neither enclosed the relevant report nor indicated the next step of the procedure (*Newham LBC 1996*).

Failure properly to record complaint. It was maladministration when a local authority could not produce documentary evidence that a complaint had been thoroughly investigated and had failed to send 'a full, written response' following the investigation. The ombudsman made this finding despite the 'enormous staffing problems' (caused by an industrial dispute) in the local authority's neighbourhood office at the time (*Islington LBC 1994*).

A wide gap between aspiration and practice in the complaints procedure may be all too evident and be maladministration:

Delays in handling complaints. One local ombudsman investigation found admirable aims in the local authority's complaints procedure – but serious flaws in practice. The maladministration was based on a number of criticisms. The complaints coordinator apparently made no real attempt to analyse the contents of a letter of complaint. The council did not respond to the complaint within 28 days as the law demanded – nor did it explain in writing to the complainant why it could not respond in that time. No 'substantive reply' to the complaint had been forthcoming from the council after 16 months. Delay is compounded if, despite a special request for the complaint to be handled quickly, the complainant dies before the outcome is known (*Salford CC 1996*).

In another case, the response to a person's complaint took 219 instead of 28 days; and the ombudsman doubted whether it was realistic of the council not to appoint special complaints investigators but instead to use social services managers – who might not be able to take on the complaints task because of pressure of other work (*Sheffield CC 2002*).

The local ombudsman reminds local authorities that they must try to retain a focus on the substance of complaints, even if they are brought by service users regarded by staff as 'difficult' or unreasonable:

Focusing on the substance of the complaint. The local ombudsman has pointed out that the purpose of a complaint is 'first and foremost' to scrutinise a local authority's actions; therefore the focus of an investigation on the complainant's own background and history was maladministration (*Cornwall CC 1996*).

There might be a question of whether the staff involved in investigating a complaint have had sufficient training to 'distance themselves from the personal, and to identify the very real, issues' with which the complainant was concerned (*Haringey LBC 1993*).

The ombudsman sometimes criticises responses to complaints, for instance in terms of gathering facts and evidence, recording meetings, acknowledging fault, conveying decisions, making written responses and taking an objective approach that enables staff to deal with difficult complainants (see e.g. *Islington LBC 1994*).

Similarly, sending responses which do not address what a complainant has written, and inappropriately concluding that the complainant was satisfied, are maladministration; and councils should beware not to filter out complaints informally, thus preventing them from proceeding (*Liverpool CC 1998, Manchester CC 1993*).

A council should not mistake a second complaint about how the original complaint has been handled for an appeal against the outcome of the original complaint (*Sandwell MBC 1995*).

It might be maladministration to refuse to carry out particular home adaptations, simply because the applicant involved is complaining and threatening litigation in relation to other adaptations already installed. But, on the other hand, delay caused by the person's unreasonable demands on the council, the personalising of the dispute, and failure to take up the council's offer of using an independent advocate, were not the fault of the council (*Waltham Forest LBC 1993*).

When information supplied to the ombudsman by the local authority had been 'doctored', the ombudsman reminded the local authority that obstructing the ombudsman could be an offence certifiable to the High Court (under s.29 of the Local Government Act 1974). This had arisen in connection with an email, part of which had been blanked out. The deletion had appeared to describe the complainant as 'awkward' (*Havering LBC 2007*).

4.6 SECRETARY OF STATE'S DEFAULT POWERS (LOCAL AUTHORITIES)

If a local authority fails, unreasonably, to carry out any of its social services duties, the Secretary of State can declare that the local authority is, without reasonable excuse, 'in default' of its duty, and direct it to perform its duty (Local Authority Social Services Act 1970, s.7D).

In some circumstances, the courts use the existence of this power to argue that Parliament did not intend that people should resort to the courts for a remedy to their grievances. However, the usefulness to service users of this judicial approach is in some doubt, given that the default powers have apparently never been used. Even so, the Department of Health does sometimes make preliminary enquiries with a view potentially to using the powers; and these enquiries can be presumed, at least sometimes, to exert pressure on local authorities and to effect informal solutions. Nevertheless, it seems clear that the obligation to use the powers is one that may be extremely difficult to enforce:

Refusal to use the default powers. A challenge was made against a local authority for breach of its duty in providing practical assistance in the home under s.2 of the Chronically Sick and Disabled Persons Act – and against the Secretary of State for failing to exercise his default powers (then contained in s.36 of the National Assistance Act 1948) against the local authority.

The judge dismissed the case, setting out the difficult hurdles to be surmounted. First, the Secretary of State was not to be regarded as a factual review body. Second, his power to intervene would only arise in the same situation in which the court's power to do so arose. For this to occur, the applicant would first have to establish (a) the specific need; (b) the specific arrangements required to meet it; (c) that an express request had been made to the local authority to meet the need; and (d) that the authority had clearly failed to satisfy the request. Third, the applicant would have then to show – 'and no doubt it would be yet more difficult' – that 'the refusal to meet the identified need or contended for need was irrational…that no local authority, properly discharging their duty and having regard to the facts before them, would have declined that request' (*R v Department of Health and Social Security, ex p Bruce*).

Although the new default powers in the 1970 Act differ from the old (in the 1948 Act), the judicial statement in the *Bruce* case is probably still a relevant guide. Nevertheless, in a more recent case involving the present default powers, the courts held that the default powers would be more appropriate where there were disputed facts:

Default powers. In a dispute concerning provision of residential accommodation for asylum seekers under s.21 of the National Assistance Act 1948, the court found that it would be more convenient, expeditious and effective to use the default powers rather than judicial review, especially since in its view the real dispute was apparently about facts (whether or not there was available accommodation in London) rather than law (*R v Westminster CC, ex p P*).

Thus, there appears to be a possible discrepancy in the judicial approach taken in these two cases; the first (*Bruce*) stating that the default powers were not applicable to a factual dispute; the second (*Westminster*) seeming to suggest that they were. Equally, the courts sometimes explain why judicial review is more appropriate than the default powers – for instance, when the issue is one of law in a developing field (*R v Devon CC, ex p Baker*).

4.6.1 SLOW RESPONSE TO REFERRALS FOR USE OF DEFAULT POWERS

Whatever the proper application of the default powers, the Department of Health is unlikely to rush to use them. The Parliamentary ombudsman has in the past been duly critical:

Delay in deciding whether to exercise the default powers (1). The British Deaf Association (BDA) complained of unreasonable delay in the response of the Department of Health and Social Security (DHSS, as it was then) to a claim that a borough council was in breach of its duty to supply a Vistel (deaf communicating terminal) telephone aid under the Chronically Sick and Disabled Persons Act 1970.

The dispute was about whether the council was using blanket criteria precluding the supply of a telephone aid for any disabled person who did not meet the criteria for telephone provision.

Overall, the BDA had to wait over three years before the Department gave its decision. This was 'appalling delay for which they merit the strongest criticism'. The ombudsman felt bound to say that 'the Department's papers in the case suggested prolonged periods not so much of deliberation as of inattention'. The ombudsman accepted the apologies of the Department and assurances about the future handling of such applications as an appropriate response by the Department to his investigation and findings (PCA C.656/87).

Delay in deciding whether to exercise the default powers (2). In another Parliamentary ombudsman investigation, concerning the provision of holidays by a local authority under the Chronically Sick and Disabled Persons Act 1970, the DHSS (as it was then) was again faulted. It took over a year to respond to the Royal Association for Disability and Rehabilitation's application that the default powers be used. In particular, it took over a month even to contact the local authority concerned, and took several months to consider the reply and to prepare a response.

The Department considered that the duties imposed in relation to the default powers were cumbersome and time-consuming; and that local authorities were likely to be helpful in such cases if they were given time to change – rather than if the Department adopted a confrontational approach. However, the ombudsman pointed out that whilst it was not for him to determine the Department's priorities or how it should use its limited staffing resources, nevertheless he was surprised at the delay, in the light of a ministerial assurance in the House of Commons that the investigation would be handled rapidly.

Thus the Department's standard of service fell short of what the complainant was entitled to expect; there was no absolute failure to act, but 'their action was slow'. However, even had progress been quicker, the outcome for the complainant was unlikely to have been markedly different: the local authority had now recognised its potential obligation to assist disabled people with holidays (PCA C.799/81).

4.7 SECRETARY OF STATE'S GENERAL AND SPECIFIC DIRECTIONS (LOCAL AUTHORITIES)

The Secretary of State has the power to make both specific and general directions for local authorities under s.7A of the Local Authority Social Services Act 1970. They can be made in respect of a particular authority, a particular class of authority or authorities generally. The following local ombudsman investigation identified that the Department of Health was somewhat perplexed about how, or whether, to use the power:

Hesitancy to use a specific direction. In a local ombudsman investigation concerning a dispute between two local authorities about where a person was ordinarily resident, the Secretary of State was asked not only to resolve the dispute under s.32(3) of the National Assistance Act 1948, but also to make a specific direction as to which authority should provide a service.

The Department of Health appeared to be somewhat surprised by the request for a specific direction; it had never previously been asked for one and had no established procedure. In the event, it first of all appeared to do nothing; when it did reply after a further request, it stated that it would be improper for the Secretary of State to direct that a council arrange a service that it considered inappropriate. This was because (a) there was no evidence that the judgement of either of the two local authorities involved was unreasonable, and (b) it was natural and proper that professional judgement should differ (*Redbridge LBC 1998*).

4.8 SECRETARY OF STATE'S INQUIRIES

The Secretary of State has the power to institute inquiries in relation to the social services functions of a local authority under s.7C of the Local Authority Social Services Act 1970.

4.9 LOCAL GOVERNMENT OMBUDSMEN

The extraction of legal principle in judicial review cases sometimes entails obscuring untidy realities, in order to identify a point of law. In comparison, the local government ombudsmen consider not only legal principles, but also the everyday, down-to-earth events and facts of a dispute. In this way, on balance, they tend to provide a more detailed and richer, if less boldly delineated, picture of community care than that achieved by the courts.

The local ombudsmen investigate maladministration and injustice perpetrated by local authorities. Recent legislative amendment extends their powers beyond maladministration to investigation of alleged failure in providing, or to provide, a service.

Their findings do not constitute part of 'the law', and their recommendations, though usually followed, are not legally binding. However, they usefully apply axioms of good administration which, if adhered to by local authorities, arguably improve decision-making. They regularly expose both chaotic and sometimes unlawful policies, procedures and practices.

Ombudsman investigations therefore reflect the fact that local authority staff and service users find themselves in the grip of unlike influences: on the one hand, complex legislation and abstract legal principle, on the other humdrum daily administrative activity. Like the courts, within the overall context of an uncertain system, the local ombudsmen attempt to impart a reasonable standard of fairness in decision-making.

Thus, the scope of ombudsman investigations about maladministration covers the legal principles applied by the courts in judicial review cases, but also other practical matters that tend to be administrative rather than legal in nature. This greater scope is significant, because people might in practice suffer just as much detriment through poor administrative practice (e.g. lost letter, poor communication, lack of information) as through an explicit breach of legal duty.

The ombudsmen therefore operate far more freely than the courts and investigate in detail many different types of act and decision, exploring matters both high (legal or quasi-legal) and low (everyday or practical).

4.9.1 LOCAL GOVERNMENT OMBUDSMEN: PRINCIPLES

The local government ombudsmen (there are three in England) investigate maladministration causing injustice. Since April 2008, the ombudsmen can also investigate (a) failure in a service which a local authority had a function to provide, and (b) failure to provide such a service (Local Government Act 1974, s.26).

Findings of maladministration might relate, for instance, to breach of duty, fettering of discretion (rigid policies), poor screening of referrals, failure to prioritise referrals, double-queuing on waiting lists, excessive waiting times for assessment or service provision, unjustified queue jumping, lack of communication and information giving in respect of service users, lack of communication between different departments in the same local authority, lack of communication between different local authorities, withholding information about legal entitlement, absence of policy, and failure of staff to follow a policy (or even to know about it in the first place). And so on.

Maladministration may or may not also potentially constitute unlawfulness (it is not for the ombudsman to state definitively), depending on its particular form and the context. But for service users, administrative failings can be just as detrimental as unlawful actions. So, the following 42 axioms of good administration published by the local government ombudsmen are a useful guide to what decision-making in community care should look like (CLAE 1993):

1 (law) Understand what the law requires the council to do and fulfil those requirements.

2 (law) Ensure that all staff working in any particular area of activity understand and fulfil the legal requirements relevant to that area of activity.

3 (policies) Formulate policies which set out the general approach for each area of activity and the criteria which are used in decision-making.

4 (criteria) Ensure that criteria are clear and relevant, and can be applied objectively so that decisions are not made on an inconsistent, ad hoc or subjective basis.

5 (communication) Communicate relevant policies and rules to customers.

6 (policies) Ensure that all staff understand council policies relevant to their area of work.

7 (policies) Ensure that the council does what its own policy or established practice requires.

8 (exceptions) Consider any special circumstances of each case as well as the council's policy so as to determine whether there are exceptional reasons which justify a decision more favourable to the individual customer than what the policy would normally provide.

9 (consistency) Ensure that decisions are not taken which are inconsistent with established policies of the council or other relevant plans or guidelines unless there are adequate and relevant grounds for doing so.

10 (guidance) Have regard to relevant codes of practice and government circulars; and follow the advice contained within them unless there are justifiable reasons not to do so.

11 (relevance) Ensure that irrelevant considerations are not taken into account in making a decision.

12 (relevance) Ensure that adequate consideration is given to all relevant and material factors in making a decision.

13 (views) Give proper consideration to the views of relevant parties in making a decision.

14 (purpose) Use the powers of the council for their proper purpose and not in order to achieve some other purpose.

15 (hastiness) Ensure that decisions are not made or action taken prematurely.

16 (reasons) Give reasons for an adverse decision and record them in writing for the customer concerned.

17 (time) Ensure that any necessary decisions or actions are taken as circumstances require and within a reasonable time.

18 (delegation) If a decision is being taken under delegated powers, ensure that there is proper and sufficient authority for this to be done and that use of delegated powers is appropriate to the circumstances.

19 (investigation) Carry out a sufficient investigation so as to establish all the relevant and material facts.

20 (advice) Seek appropriate specialist advice as necessary.

21 (consultation) Consult any individuals or organisations who might reasonably consider that they would be adversely and significantly affected by a proposed action.

22 (errors) Detect major errors which materially affect an issue under consideration.

23 (options) Give adequate consideration to the reasonable courses of action which are open to the council in any particular circumstance.

24 (reports) Ensure that a committee is provided with a report when circumstances require and that the report is materially accurate and covers all the relevant points.

25 (correctness) Ensure that the correct action is taken both to implement decisions when they are made and generally in the conduct of the council's business.

26 (systems) Have adequate systems and written procedures for staff to follow in dealing with particular areas of activity.

27 (liaison) Have a system for ensuring proper liaison and cooperation between different departments, different sections of a department or different areas in the authority.

28 (records) Compile and maintain adequate records.

29 (monitoring) Monitor progress and carry out regular appraisals of how an issue or problem is being dealt with.

30 (problems) Seek to resolve difficulties or disagreements by negotiations in the first instance but take formal action when it is clear that informal attempts at resolution are not working.

31 (misleading) Avoid making misleading or inaccurate statements to customers.

32 (responsibility) Formulate undertakings with care and discharge any responsibilities towards customers which arise from them.

33 (enquiries) Reply to letters and enquiries and do so courteously and within a reasonable period; and have a system for ensuring that appropriate action is taken on every occasion.

34 (information) Keep customers regularly informed about the progress of matters which are of concern to them.

35 (information) Provide adequate and accurate information, explanation and advice to customers on issues of concern to them.

36 (fairness) Ensure that the body taking a decision on a formal appeal from a dissatisfied customer does not include any person previously concerned with the case or who has a personal or otherwise significant interest in the outcome.

37 (discrimination) Avoid unfair discrimination against particular individuals, groups or sections of society.

38 (balance) Maintain a proper balance between any adverse effects which a decision may have on the rights or interests of individuals and the purpose which the council is pursuing.

39 (dispute) Where an individual is adversely affected by a decision, or the decision is otherwise one which the individual potentially might wish to challenge, inform him or her of any right of appeal or avenues for pursuing a complaint.

40 (interests) Ensure that members and officers are fully aware of the requirements for declaring an interest where appropriate and the reasons for doing so.

41 (complaints) Have a simple, well-publicised complaints system and operate it effectively.

42 (remedies) Take remedial action when faults are identified, both to provide redress for the individuals concerned and to prevent recurrence of the problem in the future.

4.9.1.1 Local ombudsman investigation and judicial review compared

The ombudsmen have themselves summarised the main differences between judicial review and ombudsman investigations. These include the following points:

- The courts can give a definitive interpretation of the law; the ombudsmen cannot.
- The ombudsmen investigate maladministration causing injustice, neither of which is legally defined.
- The ombudsmen therefore have considerable discretion.
- The rulings of the law courts are enforceable and binding; those of the ombudsmen are not, although most recommendations are in practice adopted by local authorities.
- The courts apply tight deadlines for judicial review applications (promptly and otherwise within 13 weeks), whereas the ombudsmen apply a 12-month deadline.
- The courts can quash decisions and stay actions; the ombudsmen cannot, although local authorities may anyway decide to defer actions during an ombudsman investigation.
- Judicial review decisions are subject to appeal, unlike local ombudsman decisions. The latter can be judicially reviewed, but this would be concerned with procedural matters, rather than interference with the merits of the ombudsman's decision.
- Judicial review proceedings are adversarial, whereas those of the ombudsman are inquisitorial.
- Judicial review may result in the losing side having to pay costs; ombudsman investigations are conducted without charge to either party.
- Financial compensation is a rare occurrence in judicial review, whereas the ombudsmen frequently recommend a financial remedy.
- The courts are bound by precedent; the ombudsmen are not, but attempt nevertheless to be consistent (CLAE 2000).

4.9.2 LOCAL GOVERNENT OMBUDSMEN: PROCEDURES

The local government ombudsmen investigate maladministration in local authorities and can recommend remedies, including financial compensation, when they find that people have suffered injustice (Local Government Act 1974, s.26). There are three local ombudsmen in England.

The ombudsmen can investigate a complaint in respect of an individual person (alive or deceased), and also from an appropriate organisation (s.27). For example, a local advice agency might make representations on behalf of a number of people affected by a common problem. They can also call for and examine information about other service users in a similar situation to that of the complainant (ss.28–29). Complaints can be accepted from a member of the public who claims to have suffered injustice, somebody else authorised by the person – or by a personal representative, or anybody else deemed suitable by the ombudsman, on behalf of a person who has died (s.26A). In addition, the ombudsman is empowered to initiate an investigation if, during an investigation, it appears that a member of the public other than the original complainant has suffered injustice – even if that person has not complained (s.26D).

There is normally a 12-month limit (i.e. from the time the complainant first knew of the matter complained of) on the bringing of the complaint to the ombudsman, but this can be waived if the ombudsman thinks it reasonable (Local Government Act 1974, s.26).

Since August 2007, the health service ombudsman, Parliamentary ombudsman and local government ombudsmen have had the formal power to share information, carry out joint investigations, authorise each other's staff to work on joint investigations and to issue joint reports – when an investigation is relevant to more than just one of these three different ombudsmen (SI 2007/1889: amending the Local Government Act 1974, Parliamentary Commissioner Act 1967 and the Health Service Commissioner's Act 1993). This power is particularly relevant to health and social care, given the increased joint working between the NHS and local authorities, the blurring of boundaries between the two types of care, and a trend of 'passing the buck' from the NHS to local authorities.

This is against a background of people being denied their right to complain where joint working takes place between the NHS and social services. Under joint working arrangements, the statutory social services complaints procedure cannot be delegated to the NHS; yet the local ombudsmen – for instance in mental health trusts delivering 'joined up' services – have found complainants denied access to that complaints procedure. The ombudsmen also consider it unacceptable if the local authority has not established satisfactory arrangements generally with NHS partners for the handling of complaints (CLAE 2007, pp.22–27). The following case was the first investigation to be conducted jointly by the local government ombudsman and the health service ombudsman under the regulatory reform order (SI 2007/1889) making joint investigations and reports possible:

Joint ombudsman report: adult with learning disabilities in care home, joint failure to assess and meet needs. A man with severe learning disabilities was placed in a care home by an NHS mental health partnership trust from 1995 to 2001, and then by the council from 2002. Under s.31 of the Health Act 1999 (now s.75 of the NHS Act 2006), the trust had entered into an agreement for the council to take over the running of the home. A suitable care home placement was eventually found, following a proper assessment.

The man had no speech; could not bathe, shave or dress; needed assistance to go to the toilet; and needed to wear incontinence pads at night or for any lengthy periods spent out of doors. He required one-to-one attention for about 95 per cent of his waking time.

Failure to assess and provide adequate care. The ombudsmen found that during his stay, his care needs were never properly assessed and the level of care was below that which he and his parents were entitled to expect. For example, one matter of particular concern was the locking of doors by staff, who were then unavailable, should residents need them. In addition, his parents had been charged wrongly for items which should have been paid for by the NHS. These included lunches, toiletries, clothes, paint, room furnishings, holidays and incontinence pads.

Joint responsibility. The NHS trust and local authority disagreed about their relative responsibilities for the deterioration of the home's standards. The ombudsman held the trust responsible up to July 2002 when the agreement and transfer to the council took place. The council had to take responsibility once it had assumed managerial control. It was maladministration that the council had failed to apprise itself of the conditions when it agreed to take over responsibility.

Human rights. The ombudsmen were also concerned that the man's human rights had not been considered.

Remedy. Both ombudsmen overall found maladministration. They recommended a payment of £32,000, covering some £10,000 for items paid for by the parents which they should not have had to pay for, acute anxiety and distress as a result of the poor care received, the parents' efforts in physically looking after their son for four months at home unsupported (after he had been afraid of returning to the care home) and the general distress the whole episode had caused the family (*Buckinghamshire County Council and Oxfordshire & Buckinghamshire Mental Health Partnership Trust 2008*).

In addition, the local government ombudsman can investigate local authorities only; but, increasingly, these are contracting out community care services to the independent sector. The question then is how far the local ombudsman can investigate and attempt to hold the local authority responsible. The Local Government and Public Involvement in Health Act 2007 has amended the legislation, making clear that where a local authority exercises a function through another person, then the actions of that person are to be treated as actions of the local authority and so are subject to investigation (Local Government Act 1974, s.25. Also: CLAE 2007, p.45).

4.9.2.1 Exhausting the complaints procedure first

The local ombudsmen will normally investigate only once the local authority complaints procedure has been exhausted (Local Government Act 1974, s.26). However, clearly, where that procedure itself is operating unsatisfactorily, the ombudsmen might take up complaints before such exhaustion. The complaint will then not only focus on the original issue but the failure of the complaints procedure as well. Indeed, not only have the local ombudsmen been critical in a number of investigations of local authority complaints procedures, but they have also published their own guidance on devising complaints systems in local authorities (CLAE 1992).

4.9.2.2 Local ombudsmen precluded if alternative remedy

The local ombudsmen are precluded from investigating where an alternative remedy exists (e.g. a judicial review legal case), unless they are satisfied that it would not be reasonable to expect the complainant to utilise that alternative remedy.

This exclusionary principle was confirmed when judicial review proceedings were brought in a special education case. They were resolved in the applicant's favour by a consent order. A complaint was then made to the ombudsman with a view to obtaining financial compensation, which is not available in judicial review proceedings. The courts held that the ombudsman was justified in refusing to entertain the complaint (*R v Commissioner for Local Administration, ex p PH*).

Another case involved the extension of Liverpool Football Club's ground. The courts held that the ombudsman was justified in taking the case, even though court proceedings would have been possible. The allegations of maladministration could best be investigated by the ombudsman, and it would have been difficult for the complainants to pursue a legal remedy (*R v Commissioner for Local Administration, ex p Liverpool CC*).

The local ombudsmen are also precluded from challenging decisions taken without maladministration (Local Government Act 1974, s.34); for instance, professional judgements.

In many instances in community care, the complaints procedure and possible referral on to the local ombudsman may be the most appropriate route to take. However, if there are clear matters of law involved, and time is pressing, judicial review proceedings may be more appropriate and effective.

4.9.2.3 Local ombudsmen recommendations and enforcement

Local authorities are empowered, though not obliged, to follow local ombudsman recommendations (including payment of compensation). However, they do have a clear obligation at least to consider them (Local Government Act 1974, s.31). Unlike the Commissioner for Complaints in Northern Ireland – acting under the Ombudsman (Northern Ireland) Order 1996 and the Commissioner for Complaints (Northern Ireland) Order 1996 – the local government ombudsmen in England do not have the power to seek enforcement of their recommendations through the law courts.

If a council refuses to follow the ombudsman's recommendations, even after a second report, it can be forced to publish an agreed statement in a local newspaper at its own expense (s.31). Thus, avoidance of bad publicity is an additional incentive for local authorities to comply with ombudsman recommendations. Over a period of ten years from 1994 to 2004, the ombudsmen reported that out of 2145 reports in which maladministration and injustice were found, only 38 cases (less than 2%) resulted in unsatisfactory outcomes in terms of non-compliance (CLAE 2004, p.30).

Nonetheless, occasional non-compliance does arise. This then may result in a second, and usually scathing, report from the ombudsman.

4.9.2.4 Local ombudsmen remedies

When maladministration has caused injustice, the ombudsmen can recommend any lawful remedy, including financial compensation (Local Government Act 1974, s.31).

Recommendations typically include providing the disputed service for the complainant, providing an apology, and rewriting and implementing new policies and procedures to avoid the same thing happening to other service users. If concerned about an issue of wider importance, the ombudsmen sometimes write to the Department of Health or other government department. Financial compensation recommended by the ombudsman, though often involving only smaller amounts, typically ranges from £500 to £5000, but can be considerably larger as the following examples illustrate:

Financial compensation awarded by the local ombudsmen. In two investigations concerning assessment and provision of a residential placement for a person with learning disabilities (*Kent CC 1998*), and rehousing of a family with a severely disabled son (*Bristol CC 1998*), sums respectively of £15,000 and £20,000 were recommended. In another investigation, extreme stress, caused by a rigid ceiling imposed by the council on the cost of home care packages and suffered by the daughter of a woman with severe disabilities and high needs, warranted £10,000 in compensation (*Liverpool CC 1998a*).

When a local authority failed for ten years to make arrangements to enable a person with learning disabilities to leave hospital and live in the community, the ombudsman recommended payment of £20,000 (*Wakefield MDC 2003*). Leaving a man with learning disabilities without an appropriate residential placement for some two years merited £30,000 by way of remedy (*East Sussex CC 2003*). And when a father of a woman with learning disabilities wrongly had to organise and pay for his daughter's care for some two years, an £80,000 remedy was recommended (*Hertfordshire CC 2003*). Considerably more financial redress was recommended when a local authority had wrongly charged one service user £60,000 for aftercare services; this was the amount that the council should repay (*Wiltshire CC 1999*).

When a council badly failed a woman with learning disabilities, the ombudsman recommended that the council recompense the parents £1000 per week, for every week they had been forced to care for their daughter (involving loss of earnings). Since this period was over two years, this worked out at over £100,000. The council refused to accept this recommendation and the ombudsman had to issue a second report (*Trafford MBC 2007; Trafford MBC 2008*).

Typically, the local ombudsmen use their discretion constructively in making recommendations. For instance, in one case involving a catalogue of failure in adapting a seriously ill and disabled woman's home, the ombudsman recommended:

- £5000 compensation for the impact of the delay, as well as an additional £1605 spent by the family themselves on works the council should have carried out
- that an appeals panel be set up for resolving disputes between the social services and housing sectors about adaption works – and that the ombudsmen be informed by the council about how it would work, and subsequently about its implementation and operation
- that all relevant officers be made aware about the council's duty under the Chronically Sick and Disabled Persons Act 1970
- that a report be produced about the lessons learnt by the council, contained guidance for officers (*Leeds CC 2007*).

Legislation makes clear that, in the light of maladministration that has adversely affected a person, the local authority has the power to make a payment to, or provide some other benefit for, the person (Local Government Act 2000, s.92).

4.10 NHS COMPLAINTS PROCEDURE

The NHS complaints procedure is detailed in regulations (SI 2004/1768) made under the Health and Social Care (Community Health and Standards) Act 2003 (s.113). In summary, the procedure provides for:

- designation by each NHS body of a complaints manager
- complaints by patients or their representative
- oral or written complaints
- a six-month time limit for making a complaint, although the complaints manager can choose to disregard this limitation if there is good reason for the delay
- if the complaint relates in part to a local authority, the NHS body must within ten working days ask the complainant if he or she wants the relevant details sent to the local authority. If so, then the NHS body must send them as soon as reasonably practicable
- written acknowledgement of the complaint within two days of receipt
- duty of investigation by the complaints manager

- arranging of conciliation, mediation or other assistance for resolving the complaint if the complainant is agreeable to this
- written response to the complaint, within 25 days of the complaint being made (unless the complainant agrees a longer period)
- onward referral of the complaint to the Healthcare Commission (i.e. the Commission for Healthcare, Audit and Inspection) if the complainant is not satisfied with the result of an investigation
- the Healthcare Commission to, amongst other things, take no further action, make recommendations to the body complained against, investigate the complaint further (and it may appoint a panel made up of three independent lay people), refer the complaint to a health regulatory body or refer the complaint to the health service ombudsman
- a complaints procedure operated by independent providers providing NHS services, run as if the regulations applied to them (SI 2004/1768).

In 2007, the Healthcare Commission identified common themes in complaints made against the NHS. These included safety (22%), care surrounding death (54%), nursing care (quality of, nutrition etc: 7%), discharge from hospital (5%), cleanliness and health care associated infection (5%), record keeping (3%), out of hours GP services (2%). Common problems in terms of responses to complaints included failure to acknowledge the validity of a complaint, failure to apologise, responses containing a lack of explanation as to how a recurrence of the problem will be avoided, responses containing medical or technical terms that may not be understood, failure to involve the staff concerned in the complaint (HC 2007, generally and p.35).

By 2007, too, central government admitted that its reforms to the NHS complaints system had not worked. It had failed to 'deliver the vision' of open and easy access, fairness and independence, responsiveness, and of an opportunity for learning and developing. So, once again, change was in the air, with proposals being put forward for a two-tier system of local resolution followed by resort to the health service ombudsman, thus cutting out the Healthcare Commission stage (DH 2007, pp.18–19).

4.11 HEALTH SERVICE OMBUDSMAN

The health service ombudsman has broad powers of investigation, wider in fact than the local government ombudsmen. His, and more latterly her, investigations have been particularly notable for identifying and continuing to highlight – for a period of some 14 years – the serious problems affecting the provision of NHS continuing health care.

4.11.1 HEALTH SERVICE OMBUDSMAN: PRINCIPLES

The health service ombudsman investigates injustice or hardship caused to a patient through failure in service, failure to provide a service which there is a duty to provide, or maladministration (Health Service Commissioners Act 1993).

Maladministration has been described by the health service ombudsman's office as covering, non-exhaustively (HSC 1996d, p.13):

- bias, neglect, inattention, delay, incompetence, ineptitude, perversity, turpitude, arbitrariness

- rudeness, unwillingness to treat the complainant as a person with rights; refusal to answer reasonable questions; neglecting to inform a complainant on request of his or her rights or entitlement; knowingly giving advice which is misleading or inadequate
- ignoring valid advice or overruling considerations which would produce an uncomfortable result for the overruler
- offering no redress or manifestly disproportionate redress
- showing bias whether because of colour, sex or any other grounds
- omission to notify those who thereby lose a right of appeal
- refusal to inform adequately of the right of appeal
- faulty procedures; failure by management to monitor compliance with adequate procedures; cavalier disregard of guidance which is intended to be followed in the interest of equitable treatment of those who use a service; partiality; and failure to mitigate the effects of rigid adherence to the letter of the law where that produces manifestly inequitable treatment.

Thus, in common with the local government ombudsmen, the health service ombudsman is able to investigate a much wider range of issues than the law courts.

Since April 1996, the health service ombudsman has been able to investigate clinical, as well as administrative, aspects of decisions – and also complaints against GPs, dentists, pharmacists or opticians providing NHS services. Special assessors are used by the ombudsman to investigate clinical matters, who will use the civil law test of the 'balance of probabilities' in reaching conclusions about causation.

4.11.2 HEALTH SERVICE OMBUDSMAN PROCEDURES

Normally, although he or she can decide otherwise, the ombudsman cannot investigate incidents which happened more than a year ago, or complaints for which there are alternative remedies.

Since August 2007, the health service ombudsman, Parliamentary ombudsman and local government ombudsmen have the formal power to share information, carry out joint investigations and issue joint reports – when an investigation is relevant to more than just one of these three different ombudsmen (SI 2007/1889). This power is particularly relevant to health and social care, given the increased joint working between the NHS and local authorities, the blurring of boundaries between the two types of care, and ever more vigorous and sometime dubious 'passing of the buck' from the NHS to local authorities.

4.11.2.1 Health service ombudsman remedies

Legislation does not lay down formal remedies, although the health service ombudsman can make recommendations. The ombudsman will send a report of the findings to the complainant and the NHS. If the complaint, or at least part of it, is upheld the ombudsman seeks a remedy – this could include getting a decision changed, or a repayment of unnecessary costs incurred by patients or their families. Otherwise, the ombudsman does not recommend financial damages. The ombudsman might also recommend that changes be made to procedures so that the same problem does not recur for other people (HSC 1996d, p.7).

4.12 INDEPENDENT COMPLAINTS ADVOCACY SERVICE

Under s.248 of the NHS Act 2006, the Secretary of State has a duty to arrange for the provision of independent advocacy services (ICAS) to assist individuals to make complaints against the NHS. The duty extends as far as is considered necessary to meet all reasonable requirements.

In addition, a non-statutory service exists called Patient Advice and Liaison Services (PALS), to provide confidential advice and support to patients, their families and carers to resolve problems and concerns quickly (Secretary of State for Health 2000, para 10.17). Being a non-statutory service, it is not provided by every NHS trust (DH 2007, p.7).

Under s.130A of the Mental Health Act 2003, when in force (expected April 2009), provision is made for independent mental health advocacy for detained patients, patients subject to guardianship or community patients.

4.13 NHS DEFAULT POWERS (NHS BODIES)

Under s.68 of the NHS Act 2006, the Secretary of State can declare NHS bodies to be in default of their duty. This is on the grounds that 'they have failed to carry out any functions conferred or imposed on them by or under this Act, or have in carrying out those functions failed to comply with any regulations or directions relating to those functions'. The members of the NHS body must leave office; new members must be appointed. It seems unclear whether any such default order has ever been issued.

Likewise under ss.66 ad 67 of the 2006 Act, the Secretary of State may make an intervention order, which allows directions to be made and officers or members of the body to be removed.

4.14 HEALTH OVERVIEW AND SCRUTINY COMMITTEES, PUBLIC AND PATIENT INVOLVEMENT

The government has passed various legislation designed, in principle, to bring a measure of local involvement to health care decisions. It provides for local authorities to set up health overview and scrutiny committees with the power to scrutinise local health services and if necessary refer matters of concern to the Secretary of State for Health. In addition, legislation provides for consultation with the public on some issues, and also local bodies originally called Public and Patient Involvement Forums (PPIFs) but now replaced by Local Involvement Networks (LINKS: see Chapter 17).

4.15 NHS REDRESS ACT 2006

This NHS Redress Act 2006 sets out a scheme whereby personal injury cases in tort (i.e. negligence) against the NHS can be settled without resort to legal action. It involves making an offer of compensation in satisfaction of any right to bring legal proceedings – and giving an explanation, apology and report on action taken or to be taken to prevent similar cases arising (s.3).

4.16 ACCESS TO NON-PERSONAL PUBLIC INFORMATION

In order to explore possible grounds of complaint or challenge to a decision, an individual might need other information beyond the personal – for example, about general council policy, perhaps with a view to finding out how other people have been treated in a similar situation.

The public has a right to attend local authority meetings (with some exceptions) including social services committee meetings. However, access is denied if 'confidential information' is at issue – either information supplied by a government department where disclosure to the public is forbidden, or information, disclosure of which is prevented by legislation or a court order. In addition, councils have the power to deny access in relation to 'exempt information', which includes (amongst various items) information about applicants or recipients of services, legal proceedings – or terms relating to proposed contracts or the acquisition or disposal of property. Access to agendas, reports and background documents must be given three days before a meeting, but items can be excluded if they relate to parts of the meeting which will not be open to the public (Local Government Act 1972, s.100A, schedule 12A).

For instance, when consulting about best value and the transfer of care homes to the independent sector, one local authority attempted to keep secret the best value report it had commissioned from a consultancy firm. It justified this under schedule 12A's reference to disposal of property as an exception to disclosure. In the event, a councillor leaked the report to a local voluntary group opposing the transfers (McFadyean and Rowland 2002, p.9).

The NHS is also subject to a code of practice on openness. Certain categories of information are excluded from disclosure, including personal information, unreasonable or excessively general information about internal discussion and advice, management information that would harm the operation of the NHS organisation, information about legal matters where disclosure would be prejudicial to the administration of justice and law, information given in confidence, and information soon to be published (DH 2003h).

4.16.1 FREEDOM OF INFORMATION

The Freedom of Information Act 2000 applies to public authorities including local authorities and the NHS. Public authorities must have a publication scheme (s.19) and provide information in response to requests (s.1). There are various exempted types of information including the following that are relevant in the context of health and social care:

- information otherwise reasonably accessible to the applicant
- information intended for future publication
- information held in relation to:
  - security matters
  - public authority investigations and proceedings
  - law enforcement that would otherwise be prejudiced
  - audit functions
  - formulation of government policy
  - conduct of public affairs that would otherwise be prejudiced
  - health and safety

- ○ personal information
- ○ information provided in confidence
- ○ legal professional privilege
- ○ commercial interests
- information, disclosure of which is prohibited by other legislation, is incompatible with any European Community obligation or would be a contempt of court (ss.21–43).

4.17 PROCESSING, HOLDING, DISCLOSURE AND ACCESS TO PERSONAL INFORMATION

The law generally affecting the processing, holding and sharing of information consists of the common law of confidentiality, the Data Protection Act 1998 and article 8 of the European Convention on Human Rights, which refers to a right of respect for a person's private life. In addition, there are other specific, relevant legislative provisions that affect the balance to be struck between disclosure and non-disclosure of personal information; for instance, the provision of both conviction and 'soft' non-conviction information by the police in the context of enhanced criminal record certificates (see 21.7).

4.17.1 COMMON LAW OF CONFIDENTIALITY AND HUMAN RIGHTS

A common law of confidentiality has in the past existed and in principle remains to the extent that any particular issue is not determined by other legislation. In summary, confidential information disclosure is – in any particular circumstances – about balancing the private and pubic interests of confidentiality against the private and public interests of disclosure. The following are illustrations of such balancing exercises which the courts have had to perform:

Breaching confidentiality to mental health patient. A consultant psychiatrist prepared a report for a patient prior to a mental review tribunal hearing. The report was unfavourable and the patient withdrew his application. However, the consultant was so concerned about the potential danger that the man represented that he sent the report to both the Home Office and the hospital where the man was detained. The court held that the breach of confidentiality was justified in the public interest (*W v Edgell*).

In another case, the court pointed out that it was not known how, if at all, the relevant information would be recorded and thus whether the Data Protection Act 1998 applied at all. It therefore decided the case with reference to the common law of confidentiality (*R(A) v National Probation Service*; see 17.7). In the following case the Act did apply but did not supply the answer:

Disclosure of files to mother. In a case involving social services, the court noted that the Data Protection Act 1998 did apply but was of limited assistance because of its generality. Instead the judge turned to article 8 of the European Convention on Human Rights (right to respect for privacy) and the common law of confidentiality. Both demanded that a balance be struck in relation to whether a mother should have access to her son's health and social care files. He was subject to guardianship and she was his nearest relative; the balance came down in favour of disclosure to her (*R v Plymouth CC, ex p Stevens*).

Similarly, in a case concerning allegations surrounding the death of a resident in a nursing home, the courts found disclosure by the police to a regulatory body to be justified. Referring to article 8 of the European Convention on Human Rights, the court accepted the disclosure as necessary in a democratic society for the protection of health or morals or for the protection and rights of freedoms of others (*Woolgar v Chief Constable of Sussex Police*).

The courts have generally expected the disclosing organisation to carry out a 'pressing need' test, before any disclosure is made – as it explained in a case about the police informing a caravan site owner about a couple living on the site with convictions for serious child sexual offences (*R v Chief Constable of North Wales, ex p AB*). On this basis, disclosure might be unjustified in the absence of a pressing need test being applied, as the courts held in a case concerning allegations about a man running a bus company with a school bus contract (*R v A local authority in the Midlands, ex p LM*).

In the following case involving a local authority wishing to disclose information about a woman working in a care home in the area of a different local authority, the judge did approve disclosure but was meticulous in weighing up the relevant factors which led to the court's decision:

Disclosure of information, about assault by mother on child, to a care home for older people where the mother was working. A mother had assaulted her eight-year old daughter, who was subsequently removed from the mother after the local authority had applied for and obtained a care order. The mother still worked at a care home for older people in the area of a second local authority. The first local authority wished to inform both the second local authority and the woman's employer about the background to the care proceedings. The judge referred to the *No secrets* guidance and to its exhortation for inter-agency arrangements, as well as to the Protection of Vulnerable Adults list kept by the Secretary of State, and the statutory duty of care providers to refer care workers in case of misconduct causing harm (or risk of harm) to a vulnerable adult).

The first local authority believed that, whatever the Secretary of State decided, nonetheless the employer (and second local authority) needed to be able to discharge their statutory duties under the Care Standards Act 2000. They could only do that if the first local authority disclosed the information to them. The judge then set out the competing considerations

Considerations against disclosure. Potentially militating against disclosure were (a) the impact of disclosure on the child (there would be no benefit for the child in disclosure); (b) the consequences for the family (the woman might lose her job, she might not find easily other employment, the child might be upset if she became aware of the effect on her mother); (c) risk of publicity with potentially serious consequences for the child; (d) importance of encouraging frankness in children's cases (fear of publicity may deter people revealing what is happening to children),

Considerations for disclosure. In favour of disclosure were (a) the gravity of the conduct and risk to public if there were no disclosure (serious assault on child meant that there was a real and potent risk to vulnerable adults); (b) evidence of a pressing need for disclosure (there was both a right and a duty to disclose); (c) interest of other bodies in receiving the information (significant obligations on second local authority and employer to carry out statutory duties); (d) public interest in disclosure (strong and potent – with the need for public safety outweighing the mother's right to respect for her privacy, under article 8 of the European Convention on Human Rights).

Balance in favour of disclosure but with safeguards. The judge was quite clear that disclosure was the proper course, but needed first to be satisfied that confidential discussions between the two local authorities and the employer could adequately address the question of publicity (*Brent LBC v SK*).

On the other hand, the particular legislative context may alter the balance and even create a presumption of disclosure. Certain legislation specifically contemplates disclosure and might affect the nature of any balancing test that the courts bring to bear. For example, the Court of Appeal has held that s.115 of the Police Act 1997 creates a presumption of disclosure by the police in response to information sought in respect of enhanced criminal record certificates (*R(L) V Commissioner Of Police For The Metropolis*).

Similarly, under s.115 of the Crime and Disorder Act 1998, any person who would not otherwise have the power to disclose information to a relevant authority or to a person acting on behalf of that authority (including the police, local authority, probation committee, health authority) shall have the power to do so in any case where the disclosure is necessary or expedient for the purposes of any provision of that Act.

4.17.2 DATA PROTECTION ACT 1998

The Data Protection Act 1998 contains a number of key points that are relevant to the processing – obtaining, holding, sharing, destroying – personal information. In particular, reference needs to be made to the data protection principles which include general rules and safeguards concerning the processing of information.

4.17.2.1 Data Protection Act principles

Data controllers must comply with data protection principles. All processing of personal data must comply with principles in Schedule 1 of the Act and be justified in terms, for example, of fairness and lawfulness, purpose, relevance, length of time held and security.

Following the conviction of Ian Huntley for the murder of two children, Jessica Chapman and Holly Wells, concerns were raised that the Act might have been to blame for some of the police and local authority failings to retain and share information, in which case the principles set out above might have been deficient. However, the subsequent government enquiry concluded that the Act could not be blamed for the failure to retain relevant information (Bichard 2004, para 4.3). Considerable latitude is given by the Act, so that terms such as adequacy, relevance, excessiveness and length of time can be interpreted depending on context and circumstances.

All personal data must also be processed in accordance with at least one of the principles in schedule 2 of the Act. These entail either that the data subject has consented or that various principles are satisfied, including that the data processing is necessary in terms of a legal obligation, vital interests of the data subject, administration of justice, exercise of statutory functions, exercise of Crown functions, or the public interest.

In addition, in the case of sensitive personal data (particularly relevant to social care and health care), at least one of the principles in schedule 3 must be complied with. The person must have consented; otherwise the principles include that the processing is necessary, in terms, for example, of:

- *right or obligation*: for the purpose of exercising or performing a right or obligation conferred by law on the data controller in connection with employment
- *inability to consent, protection of others*: to protect the vital interests of the data subject, where either consent cannot be given by or on behalf of the data subject – or to protect the vital interests of someone else, where consent by or on behalf of the data subject has been unreasonably withheld

- *legal proceedings*: for the purpose of legal proceedings, obtaining legal advice, or otherwise in connection with establishing, exercising or defending legal rights
- *justice*: for the administration of justice
- *legislation*: for the exercise of any functions conferred on any person by or under any enactment
- *Crown functions*: for the exercise of any functions of the Crown, a Minister of the Crown or a government department
- *medical purposes*: for medical purposes and is undertaken by a health professional – or by a person who in the circumstances owes a duty of confidentiality which is equivalent to that which would arise if that person were a health professional.

An order allows sensitive personal data to be processed if, amongst other things, the processing is in the substantial public interest; is necessary for the purposes of the prevention or detection of any unlawful act; and must be necessarily carried out without the explicit consent of the data subject being sought, so as not to prejudice those purposes. The schedule to the order refers to the processing being necessary for the exercise of any functions conferred on a constable by any rule of law (SI 2000/417).

It can be seen that the data protection principles are so broadly drawn that in case of disclosure matters the courts have sometimes held that the Act only gets one so far. It might both justify disclosure and non-disclosure. The balancing act has to be performed with reference to principles established in other areas of law such as human rights and the common law of confidentiality (*R v Plymouth CC, ex p Stevens*). In sum, the important point is that disclosure has to be justified; the Act by no means imports carte blanche for the sharing of information. Equally, it fully supports justified disclosure.

4.17.2.2 Subject access rules under the Data Protection Act

Under the Data Protection Act 1998, people (data subjects) have a general right to find out about and receive copies of personal data of which they are the subject. There are provisos.

One such is where complying with a request for information would also mean disclosing information relating to somebody else. In this case, the data controller is not obliged to disclose, unless the other person has consented, it is nevertheless reasonable in all the circumstances to disclose without that consent – or the other individual referred to is (a) a health professional who has compiled or contributed to the information or has been involved in caring for the data subject; (b) a 'relevant person' (such as a social worker) who has supplied the information in an official capacity or in connection with provision of a service. However, the data controller could anyway communicate so much of the information as could be communicated without disclosing the identity of the individual concerned (s.7 and SI 2000/413 and SI 2000/415).

There are also specific exemptions relating to disclosure of data concerning the prevention or detection of crime, where this would be likely to be prejudiced by disclosure (s.29). Likewise exemptions apply to information about a person's physical or mental health or condition or in relation to social services functions (s.30).

The physical or mental health exemption applies when access by the data subject to the information would be likely to cause serious harm to the physical or mental health or condition of the data subject or any person. If the data controller is not a health professional, then the data controller must consult the appropriate health professional about whether the exemption applies (SI 2000/413).

In the case of information relating to social services functions, the exemption applies if disclosure would be likely to prejudice the carrying out of those functions because serious harm would be caused to the physical or mental health or condition of the data subject or of any other person (SI 2000/415). Department of Health guidance states that there is no general test of what constitutes serious harm, but that restriction on the right of access should be exceptional and restricted to serious harm, such as the risk of harm to a child being such that a child protection plan ins in place (DH 2000, para 5.37).

The Data Protection Act 1998 does not apply to information relating to dead people, since personal data relate only to a living person (s.1). However, issues of confidentiality would still apply. In fact, requests to public bodies would be treated under the Freedom of Information Act 2000 and, in some circumstances, the Access to Health Records Act 1990.

In the case of people lacking capacity, a person with a lasting power of attorney, enduring power of attorney or a court-appointed deputy could ask to see the information under the s.7 subject access provisions, so long as the information related to the decisions that representative had the legal power to make (Lord Chancellor 2007, chapter 16). Arguably, however, disclosure could still be made in a person's best interests in some other circumstances; in fact the Mental Capacity Act 2005 code of practice points out that in consulting about a person's best interests, health and social care staff may need to disclose information about the person lacking capacity in order to make consultation meaningful (Lord Chancellor 2007, chapter 16).

4.17.3 PROCESSING PERSONAL INFORMATION: CALDICOTT GUARDIANS

The Department of Health guidance to local social services authorities expected them to have appointed by April 2002 a 'Caldicott Guardian'. The function of this person is to safeguard and govern the use made of confidential information, particularly in respect of the requirements of the Data Protection Act 1998, including the processing, sharing and security of confidential information (LAC(2002)2). Caldicott Guardians had already been introduced to the NHS at an earlier date.

Sometimes the handling of personal information involves positively prosaic matters, rather than high principle. For instance, the ability to share information at all or to give people the right of access to their own personal information is severely compromised if that information is lost. This would normally constitute maladministration; for example, in one case involving the loss of a person's adoption files, the local ombudsman recommended compensation of £1000 and £200 in addition for the time and trouble expended in complaining (*Birmingham City Council 1993*). In another case, when one file was lost and access to another delayed – with information about a man's time in care and his return home under supervision – the ombudsman recommended £500 compensation (*Tower Hamlets LBC 2004*).

In the following case, the ombudsman found maladministration in relation the council's procedures for disclosing personal information:

Unsubstantiated allegations and information disclosure procedures. A local authority disclosed information to a woman's employer concerning unsubstantiated allegations made by a third party of financial abuse by the woman of a vulnerable adult. The local ombudsman investigated; the council agreed a settlement whereby it would send a letter of apology, make a token payment of £250, seek the woman's permission to send copies of the apology to her employer, review its policy and procedures on disclosure of information and inform her of the outcome. The local authority then delayed in changing its policy and procedures; and its failure to make any contact with the woman about this or with the ombudsman was inexcusable and maladministration (*Kirklees MBC 2002*).

CHAPTER 5

Judicial remedies

KEY POINTS

This chapter outlines considers judicial remedies for when things go wrong. That is, remedies which in principle involve legislation directly related to aspects of service provision and, ultimately, could involve the law courts.

Welfare legislation is the logical starting point, because without it, local social services authorities and NHS bodies would neither exist nor know what their functions were (e.g. Local Government Act 1972; NHS and Community Care Act 1990; NHS Act 2006). Broadly speaking, a public body only acts lawfully if it acts within the relevant legislation. Central government also produces plentiful guidance to back up the legislation; depending on its type, this guidance has greater or lesser legal significance.

Law is not located solely in legislation but in the decisions of the law courts as well. Apart from interpreting the meaning of legislation, the courts bring to bear a number of common law principles when they 'judicially review' the decisions of public bodies such as local authorities and the NHS. These principles broadly translate into what can be termed 'fairness' in decision-making and generally complement professional good practice.

For local authority and NHS staff, such principles are particularly important because they concern the manner in decisions about assessment and services are taken. Whether they are saying 'yes' or 'no' to people, most staff and managers would wish to feel that they were doing so fairly. To some extent, acquaintance with these principles is likely to result in a better quality of decision-making and at the same time reduce the likelihood of successful litigation against the local authority or NHS body.

In addition to welfare legislation, this chapter outlines a range of other law and legislation – including negligence, health and safety at work, human rights and disability discrimination – with which local authorities and NHS bodies must also comply.

5.1 LEGISLATION AND GUIDANCE: FUNCTIONS CONFERRED ON PUBLIC BODIES

Local authorities and NHS bodies are creatures of statute; they exist only by virtue of it. Thus, in a straightforward sense, if their decisions, policies and criteria are inconsistent with legislation, then they will go wrong in law. Beyond their very existence, legislation confers functions on these public bodies. These functions basically comprise duties (what must be done) and powers (what may be done).

5.1.1 GENERAL DUTIES

Duties are generally indicated by words such as 'shall' or 'must'.

Some duties are characterised as general or 'target' in nature, owed to the (local) population at large rather than each individual person. As such they are therefore difficult for individuals to enforce. Typical general duties are to be found in ss.1 and 3 of the NHS Act 2006 (health services: see *R v ILEA, ex p Ali*), s.29 of the National Assistance Act 1948 (welfare services for disabled people: *R v Islington LBC, ex p Rixon*) or s.17 of the, Children Act 1989 (services for children need: *R(G) v Barnet LBC*).

5.1.2 SPECIFIC DUTIES

Other duties are regarded as specific duties towards individual people. These can in principle be enforced by individuals in the law courts. They are sometimes referred to as absolute duties, although the term 'absolute' is to some extent misleading. Such duties are often subject to certain (sometimes stringent) conditions being met. In addition, a failure to perform the duty may be excused if reasonable or best endeavours have been employed (e.g. *R(W) v Doncaster MBC*). Nonetheless, they are very much stronger than target or general duties.

For instance, a strong duty of this type has been identified by the courts in s.2 of the Chronically Sick and Disabled Persons Act 1970 (CSDPA: welfare services for disabled people), s.21 of the National Assistance Act 1948 (residential accommodation) and s.117 of the Mental Health Act 1983 (mental health after-care).

Individual enforceable duty. When a local authority proposed to remove or reduce services from up to 1500 people, the courts examined s.2 of the CSDPA 1970. The House of Lords concluded that in setting criteria of eligibility, the local authority could have regard to its resources. However, once a person was assessed as meeting the criteria, a duty arose to meet need – and lack of resources would be no defence for non-performance of that duty (*R v Gloucestershire CC, ex p Barry*).

The existence of a specific duty is indicated, for example, by the word 'shall', coupled with reference to 'any person'. These words are to be found in s.2 of the 1970 Act. In contrast, s.17 of the Children Act 1989, a target duty only, refers to children in need generally, not to any specific child. Even so, this distinction is not always a reliable indicator; s.21 of the 1948 Act has been held to give rise to just such an individual duty (*R v Sefton MBC, ex p Help the Aged; R v Kensington and Chelsea RBC, ex p Kujtim*), but does not carry such an obvious reference to 'any person', referring instead only to 'persons' generally.

5.1.3 POWERS

Powers constitute what may, but does not have to be, done. An example of a power is contained in s.45 of the Health Services and Public Health Act 1968 concerning the provision of services for older, non-disabled people.

5.1.4 DIRECTIONS

Legislation sometimes gives central government the power to issue directions. Although not strictly legislation and not subject to Parliamentary approval, directions create legal duties; they tell the local authority (or NHS) what it must do. For instance, directions have been issued in relation to residential accommodation (National Assistance Act 1948, s.21), welfare services for disabled people (National Assistance Act 1948, s.29), mental disorder (NHS Act 2006, s.254 and schedule 8), and NHS continuing health care services (see Chapter 18).

Directions normally bear a clear label to that effect. However, in one case concerning the NHS, the courts stated that although the word 'direct' was not necessarily required in order for a direction to be made; nonetheless clarity was desirable (*R v Secretary of State for Health, ex p Manchester Local Committee*).

5.1.5 APPROVALS

Legislation sometimes gives central government the power to issue approvals. Although not strictly legislation, approvals give local authorities legal powers. For instance, approvals have been passed in relation to residential accommodation (National Assistance Act 1948, s.21), welfare services for disabled people (National Assistance Act 1948, s.29), services for illness

(NHS Act 2006, s.254 and schedule 20) and welfare services for older people (Health Services and Public Health Act 1968, s.45).

5.1.6 GUIDANCE FROM CENTRAL GOVERNMENT

Supplementary to legislation is the copious guidance issued by the Department of Health to local authorities and to the NHS. As far as local social services authorities are concerned, there are two types of guidance, stronger and weaker.

Stronger guidance, sometimes referred to as statutory or policy guidance, is identifiable when it states that it is made under s.7 of the Local Authority Social Services Act 1970. This Act places a duty on local authorities, in the exercise of their social services functions, to act under the general guidance of the Secretary of State. Such guidance must normally be followed by local authorities; deviation would be permissible only for good reason, and even then without substantial departure from the guidance (*Robertson v Fife Council*). In which case, a failure to follow it can amount to a breach of statutory duty (*R v North Yorkshire CC, ex p Hargreaves*: local authority failing to take account of the preferences of a service user).

Even the weaker type of guidance, sometimes referred to as practice guidance and not made under s.7 of the 1970 Act, should still be had regard to by local authorities. A failure substantially to adhere to it without good reasons could be unlawful (*R v Islington LBC, ex p Rixon*).

For the NHS, there is no formal distinction between stronger (statutory) and weaker guidance. Nevertheless, a failure to take proper account of guidance could in principle result in unlawfulness. This is so, even if the guidance does not bear a 'badge of mandatory requirement' denoted by words such as 'shall', rather than just 'ask' or 'suggest' (*R v North Derbyshire Health Authority, ex p Fisher*).

In addition to the general run of guidance are codes of practice. Generally, these must be had regard to. A failure to adhere to the code by the relevant decision-making body is likely to be scrutinised closely by the courts. Departure from the code without good reason may lead to a finding of unlawfulness. Examples of such codes include those for the Mental Health Act 1983 (DH 2008c), the Mental Capacity Act 2005 (Lord Chancellor 2007), and the Disability Discrimination Act 1995 (DRC 2006).

5.1.6.1 Judicial approach to community care guidance

The amount of guidance issued by central government to local social services authorities and NHS bodies over the last 20 years is immense. Before the advent of the Internet, there was less guidance but it was difficult to identify and obtain. Now, it is more easily found online, but in such excess that the wood cannot be seen for the trees. The Department itself lost track long ago of what it has issued and has no idea of what is extant and what is not. The result is a morass.

The Department of Health has, over the years, followed incoherent practices concerning the cancellation of guidance. Sometimes it refers to no cancellation date, sometimes to a review date and sometimes to a cancellation date. But even in the case of the last category, the meaning of the cancellation date is not clear; for example, in the case of a policy that is clearly intended to run for years, a 12-month cancellation date has the effect of cancelling the guidance but not the policy – a strange mixture.

The courts have shown themselves willing to scrutinise, sometimes closely, the guidance issued to local authorities and sometimes to the NHS. They have also been prepared to identify its shortcomings, both general and specific, when it is not comprehensible or correct. Even in the case of the NHS, notoriously more difficult to challenge legally than local authorities, the courts have made some inroads over the past nine years – for instance, criticising as inadequate and confusing guidance issued about entitlement to NHS continuing health care (*R(Grogan) v Bexley NHS Care Trust*).

On the one hand, the courts might place considerable weight on adherence to guidance. So, when a local authority failed to follow community care policy guidance and practice guidance in respect of care plans, it was found to have acted unlawfully (*R v Islington LBC, ex p Rixon*). Similarly, when an authority tampered with the wording of policy guidance on eligibility criteria, the court found it had done so unlawfully (*R(Heffernan) v Sheffield CC*). Alternatively, the courts sometimes dismiss government guidance itself with varying degrees of severity.

Critical judicial approach to Department of Health guidance: improper, logically dubious, elusive, unclear. In a case about home care services for disabled people, one of the law lords merely stated of the relevant guidance that he did not regard it as 'proper material for the construction of the critical provision' but still found it satisfactory that his view, arrived at independently of the guidance, nevertheless was consistent with it (*R v Gloucestershire CC, ex p Barry*).

In another case, the judge expressed his respect and sympathy to the authors of practice guidance (SSI/SWSG 1991) – given the complexity of the underlying legislation – but nonetheless questioned its coherence and logic (*R v Gloucestershire CC, ex p RADAR*). In a third, the House of Lords went further, again according its respect to the Department of Health's guidance, but concluding that it was simply wrong (*R v Wandsworth LBC, ex p Beckwith*); the government department had in effect misunderstood its own legislation. In a fourth, the courts referred to aspects of the Department of Health's 1995 guidance on continuing care as 'elusive' and unclear (*R v North and East Devon HA, ex p Coughlan*). Seven years later, new guidance on the same issue was criticised as unclear (*R(Grogan) v Bexley NHS Care Trust*). And guidance on 'fair access to care' and eligibility criteria for social services was not as clear as it might have been (*R(Heffernan) v Sheffield CC*).

5.1.6.2 Guidance: four times cursed?

Thus, guidance issued by the Department of Health and other government departments to supplement legislation may sometimes give helpful pointers to local authorities and NHS bodies – but it tends to introduce substantial uncertainty because of its indeterminate legal status and effect. Quantity, incorrectness, impenetrability, contradiction, jargon, repetitiveness, inconsistency, highly variable quality, incoherence all add to the problems it generates. The Department of Health website is awash with it; local authority staff and managers spend vast amounts of time and money trying to understand and implement the numerous policies contained in it; and community care legal case law is strewn with references to it.

The dichotomy between legislation and guidance is longstanding, and there are various well-rehearsed arguments for and against the greater use of guidance in the implementation of policy (e.g. Baldwin 1995; Ganz 1987). For instance, guidance can be written in ordinary and helpful language, be produced and disseminated more quickly than legislation, and tends to give local authorities and NHS bodies flexibility in how to implement policy.

On the other hand, it is not placed before and considered by Parliament, in contrast to legislation. This means that important policy matters which seriously affect people can bypass Parliamentary scrutiny altogether. Guidance might simply be badly written, and even if the language is clear, the obligations (if any) created might be indistinct.

The general drawbacks and uncertainties of government guidance are nothing new. Some 50 years ago, a court characterised it as 'four times cursed': (a) it did not go through Parliament; (b) it was unpublished and inaccessible by those affected; (c) it was a jumble of legal, administrative or directive provisions; (d) it was not expressed in precise legal language. This was in contrast to legislation which was 'twice blessed' when it passed through both Houses of Parliament (*Patchett v Leathem*). In a more recent case, Department of Health guidance was held to be in effect at least twice cursed by the House of Lords:

Department of Health caught out using a back door unlawfully, to change rules about the employment of doctors. The Department of Health issued guidance about the employment of doctors from overseas. Essentially it was immigration guidance. Such matters fell legally under ss.1 and 3 of the Immigration Act 1971. This meant that they should have been dealt with under the procedure prescribed by that Act – namely changes to the rules must be laid before Parliament, which has the power to annul them.

Instead the Department of Health attempted to introduce the new rules by the back door. Nothing was laid before Parliament. This was legally impermissible. To make matters worse, the House of Lords noted that to speak of any such guidance having been 'issued' at all, suggested a formality that was distinctly lacking. It appeared on the NHS Employers' website, but no official draft, record or statement had been placed before the House of Commons. Instead the House was referred to an email beginning 'Dear All' sent by some official in the Immigration and Nationality Department of the Home Office. The House of Lords observed that it was 'for others to judge whether this is a satisfactory way of publishing important governmental decisions with a direct effect on people's lives' (*R(Bapio Action) v Secretary of State for the Home Department*).

Sometimes, guidance simply does not resolve the issues. For instance, a glance back to the debates in 1989 and 1990 on the NHS and Community Care Bill reveals that some of the proposed amendments, so dismissively rejected by government at the time, were about matters that have continued to be troublesome and have precisely not been solved by guidance. These include hospital discharge procedures, care plans, giving of reasons for decisions, advocacy, incontinence services, assessment of carers, direct payments, and so on. Indeed, some of these issues later triggered legislation: for example, the Carers (Recognition and Services) Act 1995; Carers and Disabled Children Act 2000; Carers (Equal Opportunities) Act 2004; Health and Social Care Act 2001 (covering direct payments); the Community Care (Delayed Discharges) Act 2003.

The very bareness of s.47 of the NHS and Community Care Act 1990 governing community care assessment was deliberate. During the Parliamentary passage of the Bill, the government repeatedly opposed amendments that would have given it rather more substance – on the grounds that such legislative detail would have placed local authorities in a bureaucratic straitjacket. Far better express what was wanted in guidance, and leave local authorities all the

more freedom to get on with it. The following quotes from Parliament, concerning community care legislation, illustrate some of the arguments for and against the use of guidance (the
fourth example being a reminder that it is not just guidance that might be ineffective, but
legislation too):

Forgetting guidance in the hurly-burly and rush. 'We feel that it is important to have such a
provision written into the [NHS and Community Care] Bill. I say that because when a Bill becomes an
Act of Parliament people look upon it as legislation and they forget everything else. They forget about
White Papers and Green Papers and also, with the hurly-burly and the rush which ensue, they forget
about the circulars issued by the department' (*Hansard* 1990).

Ineffectiveness of guidance on incontinence services. 'The Minister referred to government
health notice 88/26… That circular is what the Government recommend. It is from that circular that
the wording of the amendment [duty to provide a district-wide continence service] comes. It is what
the Government want, but the Minister went on to say that district health authorities should be left to
decide on their own priorities. The situation has continued to deteriorate since the health notice
went out. That shows how ineffective notices without legislation can be… There is therefore a need
for an amendment such as this so that provision is guaranteed under legislation' (*Hansard* 1990a).

A couple of 'silly circulars' and inaction. 'Apart from a couple of silly circulars they have sent to
local authorities, the Government's excuse for inaction is that they do not wish to dictate to local authorities. They say that they respect local autonomy' (*Hansard* 1973).

It is 'all in circulars'. Lord Mottistone demanded of Baroness Blatch: 'Is she telling us that effectively
– and until we see it we cannot believe it – regulations and guidance will replace this part of the Bill?
Does she not agree with me that it is very important to have in major legislation underpinning matter
from which circulars can be developed rather than circulars, even if they are already in existence? Circulars can be changed at the drop of a hat because they do not even have to come before Parliament.
The whole burden of my noble friend's remarks, as I saw it, was: "Oh yes, it is all in circulars." Does she
not agree that that is a very inadequate reply? It is terrible that, after seeing my noble friend, this very
important matter is being left to circulars, whether or not they are issued. I just do not like this.'

In reply: 'My Lords…my noble friend has in a sense contradicted himself in his last remarks in that
he has pointed to a matter which is enshrined in legislation and then said that that was not effective –
that is section 117 of the Mental Health Act' (*Hansard* 1990f).

5.2 JUDICIAL REVIEW

Law stems from the decisions of the law courts as well as legislation. In particular, judicial
review cases are of fundamental importance in understanding the meaning and effect of community care legislation.

5.2.1 JUDICIAL REVIEW: PRINCIPLES

The common law principles applied by the courts in judicial review test, overall, the fairness
of decisions, in particular the decision-making process, taken by public bodies. Some of these
principles are summarised, non-exhaustively, below. It should also be noted that these principles tend to run into one another and are used by the courts with a degree of imprecision and
flexibility.

5.2.1.1 Judicial review: 'hands-off' approach

Judicial review is sometimes referred to as a supervisory jurisdiction applying to public bodies. In other words, the courts ensure that public bodies stay within reasonable bounds when they take decisions.

The courts recognise that local authorities and the NHS have a difficult job to do and give them considerable leeway to get on with it. That is, they generally afford public bodies a fairly wide area of discretion, with which the courts will not interfere. However, if public bodies stray outside this area of discretion, the courts will strike down decisions as unlawful.

It is important to remember that judicial review is, in principle at least, about ensuring that local authorities have acted broadly within the law, rather than about the merits of decisions. If a local authority or NHS body has made an unlawful decision, the court usually orders it to go away and retake it – this time in a lawful manner – rather than tell the authority exactly what the outcome of the decision should be.

Indeed, the local authority or NHS body might still reach the same conclusion as it did before, but this time around it will do so on the 'right' grounds. On the other hand, the implications of an adverse ruling might sometimes give little room for manoeuvre; and in some circumstances the court will directly order provision of a service. This occurred, for instance, in three cases concerned with the provision of ordinary residential accommodation (i.e. ordinary housing) by local social services authorities under s.21 of the National Assistance Act 1948 (*R v Wigan MBC, ex p Tammadge, R(Batantu) v Islington LBC and R(Bernard) v Enfield LBC*). Likewise, when there was ongoing delay in providing suitable accommodation for a severely disabled man, the court ordered the local authority to provide weekend respite care within 28 days of the court hearing (*R(Hughes) v Liverpool City Council*).

The courts do not wish generally to step into the shoes of professionals – such as health professionals or social workers – and question the merits of decisions. However, they might do so on occasion (see discussion on proportionality below). There is thus ample room for professionals to make poor decisions without triggering judicial intervention; in other words, a 'bad' decision is not necessarily an unlawful one.

Doubtful decision but not unlawful. A man with multiple sclerosis, receiving a 24-hour-a-day package of care, had his needs reassessed by the local authority. The upshot was that his care package was reduced to five hours. The judge had grave misgivings as to whether the five hours could meet the man's needs, but felt unable to interfere since the decision did not constitute irrationality (*R v Haringey LBC, ex p Norton*; although the reassessment was in fact found to be unlawful on other grounds). Similarly, in another case, the judge could not help but note the care on offer was not 'generous', but then it did not have to be, since adequacy of provision was all that was required (*R (Heffernan) v Sheffield CC*).

5.2.1.2 Fettering of discretion: rigid policies

The courts and ombudsmen generally react against policies applied so inflexibly that exceptions cannot be taken account of. They will look to see whether there was a genuine mechanism for the making of exceptions.

Rigid policies and fettering of discretion. A local authority's policy on holidays meant that it would never, as a matter of policy, render full assistance – whatever the person's needs. The court held that this policy fettered its discretion (*R v North Yorkshire CC, ex p Hargreaves no.2*).

When a local authority set its face, come what may, against paying over a certain amount of money for a residential placement for a young man with learning disabilities, the court found that it had fettered its discretion (*R(Alloway) v Bromley LBC*).

For the local ombudsman, the imposition by a local authority of a ceiling on home care packages for older persons constituted maladministration, because it had fettered its discretion; the mechanism the council had for considering exceptions was ineffective because it never made exceptions (*Liverpool CC 1998a*).

Rigidly imposing a policy preventing council tenants from transferring home, if in rent arrears, resulted in a fettering of discretion and an 'appalling catalogue of neglect' by the local authority which was both welfare authority and landlord. This was because the policy was imposed on a family with a severely disabled son with exceptional needs; the local ombudsman recommended £20,000 compensation (*Bristol CC 1998*).

Notoriously, judicial review cases are more difficult to conduct successfully against the NHS, but increasingly the courts have been prepared to consider whether local NHS policies amount to an unlawful fettering of discretion. For instance, the Court of Appeal found a health authority to be operating unlawfully a blanket prohibition on gender reassignment surgery (*R v North West Lancashire Health Authority, ex p G, A, D*). And, even when the NHS refused a woman cancer treatment but was not fettering its discretion – because its policy allowed exceptions – its inability to demonstrate any rational basis for identifying the exceptions meant the policy was still unlawful (*R(Rogers) v Swindon NHS PCT*). Similarly, a failure to provide a service for a person, who clearly fell within the exceptional circumstances outlined in a primary care trust's policy, was held to be irrational and unlawful (*R(Otley) v Barking & Dagenham PCT*).

Nevertheless, penurious local authorities and NHS bodies can be reassured that the principle of not fettering their discretion does not open floodgates. This is precisely because it is all about making exceptions. On the other hand, because of the prevalence of rigid and crude policies in health and social care, it is a principle that can be employed to challenge local authority decisions and to invalidate them.

The principle of not fettering discretion should therefore not be treated lightly. Furthermore, the courts have held that it applies in the context of not only statutory duties but also powers (*British Oxygen v Board of Trade*). For instance, in one case, a policy never to award discretionary housing grants would have amounted to a fettering of discretion, if this had indeed been the policy (*R v Bristol CC, ex p Bailey*).

5.2.1.3 Taking account of relevant factors and unreasonableness

In the context of community care assessment, the courts have on a number of occasions scrutinised the decision-making process underpinning the assessment in order to ensure that all relevant factors have been taken account of.

Relevant factors identified as part of a lawful assessment have included, for instance, psychological issues (*R v Avon CC, ex p M*), cultural and language issues (*R(Khana) v Southwark LBC*), medical factors (*R v Birmingham CC, ex p Killigrew*), people's preferences, as demanded by Department of Health guidance (*R v North Yorkshire CC, ex p Hargreaves*), a background of domestic violence (*R(Khan) v Oxfordshire CC*), and health and safety of staff (*R v Cornwall CC, ex p Goldsack; R(AandB) v East Sussex CC (no.2)*). It is by no means complicated to achieve this requirement. For example, a purported assessment of the manual handling requirements of a woman with multiple disabilities simply failed to consider the obvious about her needs; namely, the comparative risks of hoisting or transferring her otherwise, and of the specific risks posed by her osteoporosis. This meant that key issues appeared not to have been addressed. The judge therefore gave permission for a judicial review case to be brought against the local authority (*R(Clegg) v Salford CC*).

The principle has also been applied to NHS decision-making. For instance, when considering whether to provide a cancer drug, a primary care trust was held to have failed to take account of the possibility that the drug would prolong the patient's life for more than a few months. It had therefore not taken account of a relevant factor (*R(Otley) v Barking & Dagenham NHS PCT*).

5.2.1.4 Relevant factors: giving them weight

Traditionally, the courts have often looked only to see that all the relevant factors have been taken account of, and not expressed a view about how much weight should have been placed on any particular factor. They would normally interfere only if, despite all relevant factors being taken account of (and irrelevant factors having been disregarded), a decision was so unreasonable that no reasonable authority could possibly have come to it (*Associated Provincial Picture Houses v Wednesbury Corporation*).

Another way of putting such unreasonableness has been to describe it as irrational (*Council of Civil Service Unions v Minister of State for the Civil Service*) or even a taking leave of senses (*R v Secretary of State for the Environment, ex p Nottinghamshire CC*). Thus, when a local authority or NHS body has blatantly overstepped the mark, and none of the other principles used in judicial review spring to mind, the courts may brand a decision irrational. This might typically occur where the lack of logic is blatant. For instance, when a local authority was working out a person's income, in order to make a charge for attendance at a day centre, it took account of the element of a disability benefit that was being received for the purpose of night-time care. This was held simply to be irrational (*R(Carton) v Coventry CC*). Likewise, when a primary care trust blatantly failed to consider the relevant issues in deciding whether exceptionally to provide cancer treatment for a person, the court found irrationality (*R(Otley) v Barking and Dagenham PCT*).

Where human rights are concerned, the courts may employ what they refer to as heightened or even anxious scrutiny (*R(Daly) v Secretary of State for the Home Department*). This means they may feel obliged to interfere to a greater extent with the decision-making of the relevant public body. In such circumstances, the courts may creep closer to considering the merits of a decision, the weighting given to particular factors, and whether a correct balance between has been struck. This was discussed in *R(A&B) v East Sussex CC (no.2)*, a dispute about the tension between manual handling and human rights of two people with profound and physical disabilities. When the courts interfere in this way, they sometimes explain it as the application of a principle known as proportionality. This is used to question whether the decision maker has maintained a sense of proportion and balance when weighing up competing factors.

5.2.1.5 Illegality: breach of duty and blatant contravention of legislation

Sometimes local authorities explicitly breach duties that are clearly set out in legislation. For example, a failure as a matter of policy to consider whether to provide for a person's social, recreational and leisure needs undermined the direct reference to such matters in s.2 of the Chronically Sick and Disabled Persons Act 1970 (*R v North Yorkshire CC, ex p Hargreaves*). Likewise, under the same Act, the failure to consider assistance with holidays, which had not been arranged by the local authority, was unlawful. This was because the 1970 Act explicitly refers to holidays 'otherwise arranged' (*R v Ealing LBC, ex p Leaman*).

In the case of the NHS, simple breach of a statutory duty to provide a service would be difficult to establish, given the vague nature of such duties under the NHS Act 2006. However, establishing a breach of duty to consult according to the obligations imposed by the NHS Act 2006 is more easily achieved (see immediately below).

5.2.1.6 Legitimate expectations and consultation

The courts sometimes consider whether people's legitimate expectations have been properly observed and respected. Such expectations relate sometimes to a right to be consulted before a service is changed or withdrawn; and less often to a right actually to receive, or to continue to receive, a service. The courts might consider that the demands of fairness are higher when an authority intends to remove an existing benefit, rather than in the case of a 'bare application for a future benefit' (*R v Devon CC, ex p Baker*).

Breaking an explicit promise of a home for life. A health authority made an explicit oral promise to a group of severely disabled people that if they moved into a specialist NHS unit it would be a home for life for them. Some years later it proposed to close the unit. The Court of Appeal found that the breach of this explicit promise was not justified by some overriding public interest; that it constituted an abuse of power by a public body; and that it was a breach of article 8 of the European Convention on Human Rights (*R v North and East Devon HA, ex p Coughlan*).

The consultation in issue might sometimes be with a voluntary organisation rather than individual service users. Thus, when a local authority decided to withdraw funding from such an organisation, without informing it about the criteria (based on 'fair access to care guidance': see 6.11) that it was using to take the decision, the court found the decision to be unfair and unlawful (*R(Capenhurst) v Leicester CC*). In any case, and more generally, guidance states that if a local authority is going to tighten up its criteria of eligibility for community care services, it must consult (LAC(2002)13; DH 2003g). It must also consult properly by taking account of all the relevant factors; a failure to consider issues raised by the Disability Discrimination Act 1995 rendered unlawful the consultation to restrict community care services to those in 'critical' need only (*R(Chavda) v Harrow LBC*).

In the case of the NHS, legislation imposes explicit obligations on NHS bodies to consult about changes to services (NHS Act 2006, s.244 and regulations, SI 2002/3048). In addition, the NHS has a duty to involve and consult with the public (directly or through representatives) when it is planning provision, developing and considering proposals, and making decisions about the operation of services (NHS Act 2006. s.242). The last few years has seen a spate of cases reaching the courts, with claimants – to some degree successfully – arguing that the NHS has failed to consult properly (*R(Morris) Trafford Healthcare NHS Trust*).

Even in the context of this statutory duty, the courts still supply on top, from the common law, the key principles of fair consultation. These are that consultation must be undertaken at a time when the proposals are still at a formative stage. Sufficient reasons must be provided for particular proposals so as to permit those consulted to give intelligent consideration and response. Adequate time must be given. The product of consultation must be conscientiously taken into account (*R(Fudge) v South West SHA*).

In addition, both NHS bodies and local authorities should have regard to a code of practice produced by the Cabinet Office, which emphasises the importance of wide consultation, allowing a minimum of 12 weeks for written consultation, clarity of proposals, and provision of feedback regarding responses received and how they influenced the policy (Cabinet Office 2004, p.4).

Nonetheless, even when such legal challenges are successful, the local authority or NHS body may well simply re-consult – this time, cynically going through the correct legal hoops. If it is sufficiently determined, it will push through the same decision, in which case the judicial review may ultimately serve as a delaying tactic only, rather than a complete block on the local closure or reconfiguration of services. Nonetheless delaying tactics may in some circumstances be more permanently effective, because a year or two on, the NHS body or local authority – typically subject to ever shifting policies and priorities – may anyway have changed tack. And, sometimes local authorities and NHS bodies do actually listen and may re-think their plans.

5.2.1.7 Giving reasons

For the most part in community care and NHS legislation, there is no explicit duty to give reasons; and where there is no statutory obligation, a common law duty cannot be assumed in every context (*R v Secretary of State for the Home Department, ex p Doody*). However, the courts may still effectively demand reasons if only as evidence that a local authority has reached a lawful decision concerning a person's needs and how they might be met. If, as already pointed out above, the courts are often exploring not what the final decision has been, but how it has been reached, they will often expect to find an explanation.

Indeed, in judicial review, the courts are generally more interested in how a decision has been reached, rather than in what that decision is. A simple analogy would be with the school teacher of mathematics who points out that most marks will be scored for showing the working out, rather than for the precise answer itself. An absence of reasoning may be taken to equate to an absence of working out. For instance, the Court of Appeal seriously criticised a local authority because 'judicial review is about process; and in my judgment the process here has been manifestly defective'. This was where the decision to place a ninety-five year old woman in a nursing home had been taken without either considering critically important factors or giving reasons (*R(Goldsmith) v Wandsworth LBC*).

5.2.1.8 Judicial review applying only to public bodies

Judicial review applies only to what the courts deem to be public bodies. In the context of care home closures, they have ruled that independent care home providers are not subject to judicial review. It therefore follows that a local authority is not subject to judicial review on account of a care home's actions over which the local authority has no control, nor can the care home itself be subject to a judicial review challenge (*R v Servite Houses, ex p Goldsmith; R (Heather) v Leonard Cheshire Foundation*). However, legislation now states that in some circumstances an independent care home will be amenable to a human rights challenge – but only when a resident has been placed there by a local authority under ss.21 and 26 of the National Assistance Act 1948 (Health and Social Care Act 2008, s.145: when in force).

5.2.2 JUDICIAL REVIEW: PROCEDURES

A number of rules apply to the bringing of judicial review cases.

5.2.2.1 Permission for judicial review

Unlike other types of legal action (such as negligence actions), permission from a High Court judge is first required to bring a judicial review case (SI 1998/3132, r.54.4). Permission will be generally granted if the judge is satisfied that there is an arguable case.

5.2.2.2 Time limits for judicial review

An application for judicial review must be brought promptly and in any event within three months from the date when the grounds of action arose (SI 1998/3132, r.54.5). However, even within the three-month limit, it is open to a court to deny permission on grounds that the application has not been made promptly.

Because of this time limit and the possible requirement that alternative remedies (such as the local authority or NHS complaints procedure) be attempted first, an application for judicial review could be made but then adjourned until the outcome of a complaint brought under the complaints procedure is known. If this were not done, then it might be too late to make the application.

5.2.2.3 Length of judicial review process

Judicial review cases can take a considerable time (months or over a year) to come to court. However, urgency can be pleaded, in which case it might not take more than a few weeks. Similarly, an appeal might be heard quickly in certain circumstances, as occurred in *R v Cambridge HA, ex p B* (about urgent leukaemia treatment for child) when the High Court and Court of Appeal sat on the same day.

If a case is going to take a long time to come to court, an interim injunction (interim relief) is sometimes possible. This might be in a sufficiently serious case where the court could order that services be provided until the dispute is finally heard and resolved (e.g. *R v Staffordshire CC, ex p Farley* involving withdrawal of night sitter services by the local authority). Urgency could justify use of judicial review rather than going through the complaints procedure, which can in practice, despite statutory time limits, be drawn out and ineffective.

5.2.2.4 Standing and status of applicant

The applicant or claimant in a judicial review case must have a 'sufficient interest' in the case (Supreme Court Act 1981, s.31). For example, service users themselves or carers affected by a decision clearly have such an interest. Sometimes established advisory organisations, representing particular groups of people, will also be recognised by the courts (see e.g. *R v Sefton MBC, ex p Help the Aged; R v Gloucestershire CC, ex p RADAR; R v Newham LBC, ex p Medical*

Foundation for the Care of Victims of Torture). In such cases, voluntary organisations may play a useful role in highlighting matters of public interest. Even when the applicant does have sufficient interest, the courts do not welcome intemperate allegations:

Confrontational claimants. A father had, without evidence, alleged unlawful withdrawal of free treatment, wilful aggravation of such breaches of duty by 'illegal public office record fabrication' and 'scurrilous traducing distributed defamation' by the local authority and PCT – in respect of his daughter's treatment. The court understood why the local authority and NHS primary care trust (PCT) had lost patience with this father of a 16-year-old girl. It accepted that 'public servants should not have to put up with such behaviour'. However, the local authority and PCT still had to consider the daughter's needs – it was not her fault her father behaved as he did – but this would require a less confrontational approach from the father (*R(SH) v Camden LBC*).

5.2.3 JUDICIAL REVIEW OR ALTERNATIVE REMEDIES

If the courts believe that there are appropriate 'alternative remedies', then they might insist that those remedies be used first, before judicial review can be applied for. The obvious alternative remedies in the community care field are the social services and NHS complaints procedures, and the powers of the Secretary of State to declare local authorities or NHS bodies in default of their duties. However, there are sometimes reasons why the courts might not insist on such alternative remedies.

5.2.3.1 Judicial review as appropriate remedy

As far as complaints procedures go, service users could argue that a hearing before a panel of non-lawyers without legal representation is inadequate to deal with questions of law. For instance, in a case concerning delay in providing community care services, the court ruled that it would not have been 'convenient, expeditious or effective' for the applicant to argue points of law before a non-qualified body, namely the complaints review panel (*R v Sutton LBC, ex p Tucker*).

Likewise, where the complaints procedure could consider only procedural matters, but not substantially deal with the issue in question – because no investigating officer could substitute his decision for that of the NHS trust involved – the court accepted that judicial review was appropriate. The complaints procedure would not be an effective mechanism (*R(Rodriguez-Bannister) v Somerset Partnership NHS and Social Care Trust*).

Indeed, in a case about the closure of care homes, the court stated that the issue was a question of law in a developing field. It was therefore for the court, not the local authority (through the complaints procedure) or the Secretary of State, to decide it (*R v Devon CC, ex p Baker*).

5.2.3.2 Judicial review not appropriate remedy

If, in the view of the courts, questions of law are absent, then the complaints procedure might be more appropriate (*R v Lambeth LBC, ex p A* about rehousing for child and family; and *R v Birmingham CC, ex p A* about delay in providing a placement for a child). The courts might view the complaints procedure as more effective and quicker than judicial review, and as able to get to the heart of the matter and the facts (*R v Kingston upon Thames, ex p T*: a child care case).

In an asylum seeker case concerning place and choice of accommodation, the default powers of the Secretary of State were regarded as more appropriate than judicial review (*R v Westminster CC, ex p P*). Moreover, some of the community care disputes that have reached the law courts have involved complex problems, which might simply not be amenable to judicial resolution, since they are 'beyond the competence of courts of law' (*R v Islington LBC, ex p Rixon*):

Heavy obligation to avoid litigation. In one case, the Court of Appeal was critical of the fact that a dispute – concerning a care home closure and the adequacy of the assessments of the residents concerned – had resulted in so much litigation. Instead the complaints procedure should have been used; indeed the court declined to decide the matter. The lawyers were under a 'heavy obligation' to resort to litigation only if it was really unavoidable (*R(Cowl) v Plymouth CC*).

Using the courts as a last resort. When a care home was being converted into supported housing, the court stated that the dispute about what was in a care plan was a matter for the complaints procedure; and failure to follow the Secretary of State's guidance should first of all involve reference to the Secretary of State. The courts should be used as a last resort (*R(Lloyd) v Barking and Dagenham LBC, CA*).

Disputed assessment: complaints procedure obvious procedure. When a dispute arose about the assessment of a disabled woman's needs, what was required to meet them, and whether the occupational therapist's assessment had been taken account of, the Court of Appeal emphasised that in judicial review cases, it would not step in lightly to challenge the judgement and discretion of a local authority involved in an assessment. It pointed the local authority complaints procedure as the obvious way to challenge such an assessment (*R(Ireneschild) v Lambeth LBC*).

Failure to consult about an NHS independent sector treatment centre (ISTC): danger of misusing public law. When an NHS primary care trust (PCT) unlawfully failed to consult about a new treatment centre run by the private sector, the court nonetheless seemed to deplore the work and resources that had gone into the case – pointing out that public law could fall into disrepute if it is misused (*R(Fudge) v South West SHA*).

Sometimes the courts might explicitly criticise the lawyers in the case, suggesting that there might have been no need for the case to be brought:

Fallacious ground for bringing litigation. The court stated that the case had been argued eloquently but on the fallacious contention that promises of a home for life had been made to the residents of NHS premises for mentally disordered people; and that this contention had proceeded more on the legal construction of the lawyer involved than on any evidential foundation (*R v Brent, Kensington and Chelsea and Westminster NHS Trust, ex p C*).

5.2.4 JUDICIAL REVIEW REMEDIES AVAILABLE

The court has discretion, not an explicit obligation, to award a remedy in judicial review (Supreme Court Act 1981, s.31). The court can grant a:

- **quashing order**: overturning a decision and ordering the authority to take the decision again (formerly known as certiorari)
- **mandatory order**: obliging an authority to take a positive action (formerly known as mandamus)

- **injunction**: similar to a mandatory order but in an interim form until the full hearing and resolution of the dispute – and obliging an authority to do or not to do something (e.g. not withdrawing services)
- **prohibiting order**: forbidding an authority from doing something inconsistent with its legal powers (formerly known as prohibition)
- **declaration**: that makes a statement about rights, remedies and the general legal position of the parties (formerly known as declaration). It is effective in that public bodies would act in accordance with a declaration (Supreme Court Act 1981, ss.29–33; SI 1998/3132, s.54.2–54.3).

However, the discretion to grant a remedy means that the court does not have to do so, even if the claimant has 'won' the judicial review case in principle. For example, in one case, a judge found himself unable to do more than suggest a declaration that the local authority was 'quite wrong' when it had not acted in accordance with the law (the CSDPA 1970) in refusing nearly two years previously to consider assisting a person with a holiday (*R v Ealing LBC, ex p Leaman*). Likewise, when a primary care trust had failed to consult about an independent sector treatment sector, the court ordered no remedy: what was done could not now be undone (*R(Fudge) v South West SHA*).

5.2.5 PRACTICAL EFFECTS OF JUDICIAL REVIEW

First, when cases go to a full hearing, the decisions of the courts set precedents for the future and have ramifications far beyond the particular applicant or applicants in the case. However, precedents can be sidestepped by, for instance, the courts 'distinguishing' a later from a previously decided case, and so avoiding the precedent set by the earlier case. This seemed to occur in *R v East Sussex CC, ex p Tandy* (about resources in education decisions) in which the House of Lords explained away, without overruling, their earlier decision in *R v Gloucestershire CC, ex p Barry* (about resources in community care). This enabled the court to come to a different conclusion in the later case.

Second, even the threat of judicial review might be effective in resolving a dispute. For instance, if leave (permission) to proceed to a full hearing is given by a judge, then the public body against which the case is being brought will be aware that the case is an arguable one and might be tempted to settle the dispute before it goes further. Authorities might wish to avoid (a) adverse publicity; (b) high legal costs; and (c) the danger of losing the case and the setting of an unwanted, expensive precedent – which might apply to many other service users in a similar position to the applicant. For example, in 2008, Sunderland Primary Care Trust decided to back down, before a full hearing, on the issue of whether it was empowered, as an NHS body, to make direct payments (Booler 2008).

5.2.5.1 Uncertainty of judicial review

The degree to which the courts have brought certainty to community care law is in doubt. Some questions they answer clearly, some not; whilst some are never considered at all if they don't happen to get to court. Even when particular questions are answered, with uncertainty replaced with certainty and perhaps an escape route from potential legal obligations closed off to local authorities, the latter will immediately seek out further uncertainties and alternative escape routes.

Thus, judicial decisions are made on a piecemeal basis, are dependent on which disputes happen to reach them in the first place, and are neither predictable nor consistent. In some cases the courts appear to wish to avoid getting enmired in the detail of community care assessments by local authorities (*R(Ireneschild) v Lambeth LBC*). In others they will go the extra mile and expose shortcuts taken in community care assessments (*R(Goldsmith) v Wandsworth LBC*). Sometimes the cases seem to raise more questions than they answer.

In any case, the tempting belief that law can be learned like multiplication tables and so yield certain answers is false. Such a belief depends on the assumption that there are always right answers that exist in some objective form, waiting only to be uncovered by the correct judicial utterance. This notion was famously dismissed by a leading judge, Lord Reid, as a discredited fairy tale (Lee 1988, p.3). This lack of pre-ordained answers was exposed in the context of community care by the case of *R v Gloucestershire CC, ex p Barry*. It concerned the removal of community care services, and whether disabled people's needs could be measured taking into account the resources of a local authority:

High Court. Two judges in the High Court decided the main issue one way.

Court of Appeal. Three judges in the Court of Appeal reached a 2–1 split decision that which overruled the High Court.

House of Lords. The Court of Appeal was then in turn overruled by the House of Lords, with five law lords arriving at a split 3–2 decision (*R v Gloucestershire CC, ex p Barry*).

Subsequent judicial reflections. The House of Lords seemed to betray, in the later case of *R v East Sussex CC, ex p Tandy* (an education case), some apparent regrets about the *Gloucestershire* decision, though without questioning its basic correctness. The Court of Appeal, in a subsequent community care case about residential care, followed the *Gloucestershire* case only with reluctance and some qualification (*R v Sefton MBC, ex p Help the Aged*).

The *Gloucestershire* case also shows that the uncertainties in community care do not simply affect the odd aggrieved individual. The case was brought originally by four individuals, but in fact stemmed from a reduction in care services to as many as 1500 people. Similarly, the case of *R v Sefton MBC, ex p Help the Aged*, about funding for residential care, concerned a policy applied by the local authority to more than just the two people referred to in that case – and was symptomatic also of what was going on in other authorities. The local government ombudsmen, too, sometimes investigate policies that clearly affect many people within a local authority, for example in respect of long waits for home adaptations or the improper introduction of a system of charges for non-residential services. In other words, the uncertainties affecting community care are far from peripheral.

5.2.5.2 Role of judicial review in community care

The complexity of the legislation, the morass of guidance and the contradictory elements of community care policy were always likely to provoke judicial intervention. Given the instability and uncertainty of community care policy and legislation from the outset, it was eminently foreseeable both to onlookers and to civil servants within the Department of Health that the courts would have to try to work out the legal and practical implications of the new system from 1993 onwards.

Overall, the courts have dealt with a very large number of judicial review cases about the provision of community care services by local authorities – but with a mere handful, relatively speaking, involving the NHS. Nonetheless, there have been significant upheavals and cut backs to services in the NHS from 2005 onwards. This has led to an increase in legal challenges, for example, about the closure of elderly care beds or the contracting out of services to the private sector. At the same time, central government continues to raise our expectations about health care. This has led to cases, for example, about the rationing of drug treatments, such as for cancer or dementia.

Thus, although the NHS remains virtually immune from successful legal challenge if it has made a decision explicitly based on a lack of resources, the courts have begun gingerly and belatedly to explore other ways of holding NHS bodies to account. In these cases, the courts have considered matters such as fettering of discretion (blanket policies), irrationality of decisions and inadequate consultation.

5.3 NEGLIGENCE, BREACH OF STATUTORY DUTY, BREACH OF CONTRACT (PRIVATE LAW)

Civil actions for negligence, breach of statutory duty or breach of contract are known as *private law* actions, compared to judicial review, which is a *public law* remedy.

The common law of negligence is well established in the health care field in relation to clinical decisions, but is perhaps less straightforward in social care. Most private law claims for breach of statutory duty are generally unlikely to succeed in either the health or social care fields.

In addition, a third possible private law remedy, namely an action for breach of contract, appears generally not to be available to individual users of social services or the NHS (except in the case of private patients). The reason for this is that, because the provision of such services is governed by statute, legally enforceable contracts between statutory agencies and service users are generally precluded. Nevertheless, the law of contract is of very considerable importance as between local authorities or the NHS on the one hand, and independent care providers on the other. This is because, increasingly, local authorities and the NHS are making use of the independent sector to deliver services.

5.3.1 NEGLIGENCE: DUTY OF CARE

The law of negligence is largely to be found in the 'common law' and not in legislation. This means that the rules emanate solely from decisions of the law courts. Negligence cases are about physical (or sometimes psychological and in some circumstances financial) harm allegedly suffered.

Broadly, the claimant must show that (a) a duty of care was owed by the person who allegedly caused the harm; (b) the duty was breached by a careless action or omission; (c) this breach directly caused the harm complained of. As in the case of reasonable practicability under health and safety at work legislation, a weighing up of risks, costs and benefits (i.e. to the service user) will often be relevant in judging in whether the alleged tortfeasor (wrong-doer) behaved unreasonably so as breach the duty of care.

5.3.1.1 Judicial protection of local authorities and the NHS from negligence

In many circumstances the duty of care owed by local authority and NHS staff will be straightforward. The large volume of negligence cases brought against the NHS is evidence of this. However, local services authorities and NHS bodies are also afforded protection. The courts have stated that, in some circumstances, there is no duty of care owed by local authorities or their staff to service users. In which case, any carelessness and harm caused are irrelevant, since there can be no breach of a duty of care if that duty does not exist in the first place.

The courts have provided such protection where there are complicated matters of policy, resources or sensitive decision-making involved (such as in the context of child protection). They also tend to avoid identifying a duty of care if its existence would interfere with the carrying out of a statutory duty under legislation (e.g. a duty to assess a person and decide about services). Sometimes the courts contrast this type of decision ('policy'), in connection with which they provide protection from liability, with what they refer to as 'operational' decisions which do not attract this special protection.

The two cases below illustrate the protective approach, the first concerning child protection and the second mental health aftercare services:

No duty of care owed to children. Over a number of years, a local authority failed to protect four children from the severe neglect of their mother. This was despite overwhelming evidence given to the local authority by many different, reliable sources. When a negligence case was brought against the local authority, the courts held there was no duty of care owed (*X v Bedfordshire County Council*). However, a breach of human rights by the local authority in this case was later established in the European Court of Human Rights (*Z v United Kingdom*).

Aftercare services and negligence. A man brought a negligence case, arguing that the health authority had failed to provide him with adequate mental health aftercare services under s.117 of the Mental Health Act 1983 – and that as a result he had stabbed a person to death at a London Underground station. The Court of Appeal held that aftercare services were essentially administrative in nature, rather than clinical. The surrounding legal framework meant that it was not fair and reasonable to impose a duty of care on the health authority (*Clunis v Camden and Islington Health Authority*).

However, the courts have recognised that the law of negligence is in flux in relation to public bodies, when the carelessness becomes entangled with statutory functions, policy and resources. The judges sometimes struggle to decide whether a duty of care should be imposed on local authorities or the NHS. For example, they have at times drawn back from the hard line taken in *X v Bedfordshire CC* (e.g. *Phelps v Hillingdon LBC*: liability for failing to detect dyslexia in a child). Thus, in 2008, the High Court refused to strike out a negligence case in respect of another failure under s.117 of the Mental Health Act 1983, notwithstanding the *Clunis* case. The judge stated that the facts should at least be argued before a court. The case involved a man with paranoid schizophrenia, under s.117, who suffered 'catastrophic injuries' after jumping out of a window whilst in bed and breakfast accommodation. He argued that the failure - to appoint a competent social worker or care coordinator, and to place him in high to medium supported accommodation – was causative of his injuries and negligent (*K v Central and North West London Mental Health Trust*).

The courts continue to blow hot and cold; for example, the Court of Appeal had in two recent cases found the police owed a duty of care to protect witnesses who had been threatened and who were subsequently murdered, but both decisions were overturned by the House of Lords in mid-2008. The law lords held that the police owed no duty of care to protect people from harm from criminals other than in special circumstances (*Chief Constable of Hertfordshire v Van Colle*).

Yet in 2008 also, the High Court made a potentially ground-breaking decision (if it is not overturned on appeal) when it held a local authority liable in negligence for failing to protect a vulnerable couple with learning disabilities (and their children) from harm. This failure was held to have been causative of a culminating weekend of horrific torture perpetrated by a number of youths who had been exploiting the couple. The court held that the local authority should by then have invoked its emergency rehousing procedure, given the information it had about the threat to the couple (*X,Y v Hounslow LBC*).

In the following cases the courts declined to rule that a registration authority could in principle owe no duty of care to a care home:

Duty of care owed to care home proprietors. A care home argued that a local authority owed it a duty of care in respect of excessive requirements relating to the staffing of the care home – even when there was no maximum occupancy. The council argued that in such a situation, connected with statutory functions (at that time, the Registered Home Act 1984), it owed no duty of care – and the case should be struck out. However, the courts were not prepared to state that there could be no duty of care; the case should therefore proceed to a full hearing. This was particularly because the law of negligence in this field was in a state of flux (*Douce v Staffordshire County Council*). The court reached a similar conclusion in a dispute concerning registration of a care home that resulted in its closure (*Strickland v Woodfield Lodge*).

But the Court of Appeal subsequently ruled that such registration bodies should not owe such a duty of care for policy reasons – even if they have acted carelessly and caused a care home to close:

No compensation remedy for negligent emergency application to close down care home. The strategic health authority (SHA), the regulatory body at the time, had made an emergency application without notice for a care home to be closed under s.30 of the old Registered Homes Act 1984. The basis for the application was seriously flawed. For instance, it stated that there had been 12 recent deaths and that seven had been reported to the police. In fact, the police were investigating one death only. The judge found the decision to make the application unreasonable in a public law sense; no reasonable authority could have reached such a decision.

The care home went on to bring a successful negligence case for the loss of the nursing home. It had been forced to close permanently, despite the fact that a registered homes tribunal had subsequently – following the magistrates' order cancelling registration – found cancellation of registration had not been justified.

However, the Court of Appeal overturned the court's finding of negligence. It concluded that the SHA had had powers and duties to protect vulnerable people and that in the course of exercising those powers, loss might be caused to third parties. There was nothing to indicate that the underpinning legislation was in any sense about protecting the economic interests of people registered to run care homes.

The court appreciated that the law was evolving and that human rights had to be taken account of; denial of a duty of care might sometimes infringe those rights. However, first, it stated that the statutory registration scheme generally excluded other remedies. Second, the SHA was a public body, financed out of public funds, and the courts should be cautious in imposing an obligation to pay compensation. Third, in such a situation of an emergency application, there was likely to be a conflict between the proprietor and the interests of residents. If other remedies were potentially available to the proprietor, there would be 'leakage of management time and financial resources from the health authority to the tasks of meeting these challenges, which are not the purposes for which Parliament set up a statutory scheme of regulation' (*Jain v Trent SHA*).

Conversely, the courts declined to strike out as a matter of course two negligence actions against local social services authorities, instead holding that the cases could be pleaded. The first concerned the local authority's role in assisting a girl to find accommodation in hostel premises, where she was subsequently seriously injured when she jumped from a window to escape an attack by three non-residents (*Bluett v Suffolk CC*). The second involved the killing by a father of his daughter after he had returned home in a disturbed and paranoid state of mind from a business trip to India, a trip which had turned out to be a hoax perpetrated by a rival company. He had a past history of mental health problems; it was alleged that, had the local authority acted on the previous concerns, the death of the daughter might have been avoided (*Hall v Monmouthshire CC*).

The NHS, too, will be protected up to a point (although a great deal of the negligence case law brought against the NHS concerns clinical decision-making, which does not attract special protection). In the case immediately below, a duty of care was held to exist and to have been breached, because operationally something had gone wrong. Nevertheless, if lack of resources had been the main cause, therefore rendering it a matter of policy, the outcome of the case would probably have been different:

NHS duty of care and lack of resources. A woman suffered a severe attack of asthma and the ambulance was called. Unaccountably it failed to arrive for 40 minutes, despite several reassurances given by the service over the telephone that its much quicker arrival was imminent. The woman suffered respiratory arrest and substantial memory impairment, personality change and a miscarriage as a result. The Court of Appeal found liability in negligence. However, it held that, had the non-arrival of the ambulance stemmed from a lack of resources (i.e. insufficient ambulances or drivers to respond to demand), the outcome of the case could well have been different (*Kent v Griffiths*).

The courts sometimes distinguish a statutory function (making a decision about services) which will be afforded protection, from a straightforward operational one, such as dropping the service user, which will not:

Dropping a woman or providing a defective bed. A woman with disseminated sclerosis sought damages for negligence against the local authority. This was in relation to the provision of home help, practical assistance in the home and the provision of an invalid bed. She felt the provision had been inadequate. Because the decision whether to provide such services and to what extent was a statutory one – that is, taken under community care legislation – the court dismissed the negligence claim out of hand.

However, the court noted that a claim in negligence might have been possible if, for instance, the home help had dropped the woman and injured her, or if the bed provided by the local authority had been defective, collapsed and caused injury. This was because such matters would not have been connected to statutory decision-making (involving policy, priorities, eligibility criteria, etc.) but would have been straightforward operational matters (*Wyatt v Hillingdon LBC*).

In the following case, the main statutory decision had been made; the failure might have appeared to be merely 'operational', unconnected with statutory functions or policy. On this basis, it was argued by the claimant that the failure to the deliver bed rails in time (to prevent an accident), once a decision had been made to supply them, could give rise to a duty of care. But the court held otherwise:

Failure to deliver bed rails (cot sides) followed by accident. A negligence case was brought against a local authority in respect of injuries suffered by an elderly woman – allegedly from falling out of bed, as a result of not having the cot sides (bed rails) she needed. The local authority had assessed her need for them nearly two months earlier. (There was a causation issue, in that the evidence suggested that she fell after she had got out of bed, which would mean that the absence of the cots sides might have been irrelevant).

But, the causation issue aside, the judge stated that in any case, a duty of care could not arise, and so there could be no negligence. He did not take the view that once the assessment had been made, the delivery of the cot sides was an operational type of issue capable of creating a duty of care. In line with the reasoning in the *Kent v Griffiths* case about resources, he referred to issues such as whether the cot sides were held in stock, where they were held, what resources were available to deliver them, what other calls upon those resources there may have been, delivery times from different suppliers, weighing up of cheaper price against longer delivery time etc.

In other words, the delivery of the cot sides was not capable of giving rise to a duty of care, because it related to statutory functions and resources (as in the *Wyatt* case). Indeed, the court held that the claim had been characterised as a delay in providing the cot sides, but in fact it was really about a failure to deliver the cot sides at all before the accident; and this related to a statutory duty which could not give rise to a duty of care in negligence (*Sandford v Waltham Forest LBC*).

In a child care case, the court felt that a full hearing should proceed, if only to ascertain whether the alleged failures were of the policy or operational type:

Duty of care to child formerly in care. A child formerly in care alleged that, as a result of fragmented and inappropriate arrangements over a period of 22 years, he left care with a psychiatric illness, alcoholic problems and a propensity to harm himself. The local authority attempted to get the negligence case struck out as containing no cause of action. The court refused. It held that although the decision to take a child into care was not 'justiciable' (i.e. it could not found a negligence case), nevertheless a local authority could potentially be negligent thereafter in respect to its employees' actions, if they were of an operational rather than a policy nature (*Barrett v Enfield LBC*).

Nevertheless, the hurdles of policy and resources do not always mean that local authorities or the NHS will not be penalised for a systemic failure (rather than the negligence of an individual employee). For instance, when a woman had twins, far too long a time had elapsed following the birth of the first (and vaginal loss of blood) before a doctor attended. The court found that the health authority was negligent in not operating a system that would have allowed reasonably prompt attendance by a responsible doctor (*Bull v Devon AHA*).

Such problematic cases can be compared with the following examples, in which the courts declined to provide protection for local authorities and stated that a duty of care was owed. They are more straightforwardly operational in nature, unconnected with matters of policy, resources, or sensitive professional judgements:

Duty of care owed to injured foster carer? A woman was the paid foster carer of a disabled teenage boy, who had been placed with her by the council. She claimed that on five occasions between

1991 and 1993 she had suffered back injury when trying to catch, lift, save or restrain him. She now argued she should have been provided with suitable equipment and training in timely fashion and that the local authority had failed to carry out a proper assessment.

The local authority attempted to have the case struck out on grounds of public policy, namely that it was not in the public interest that it should owe a duty of care in such circumstances, even had it acted negligently. The court found that the case should not automatically be struck out. First, it concerned the practical manner in which the local authority was proceeding, not policy; and the judge could not see why the imposition of a duty of care was inconsistent with, or would discourage, the due performance of the authority in carrying out its statutory duties in respect of children. Furthermore, on the public policy question, it would surely be 'poor public policy' to impose a heavy burden on charitable, lowly paid volunteer foster parents, but for those parents to have no recourse if the authority behaved carelessly (*Beasley v Buckinghamshire CC*).

Duty of care to vicar for fire in church. A child with a record of fire raising was in the care of the local authority and set fire to a local church. The court found that in failing to warn his head office, a social worker was not exercising a statutory discretion (e.g. there was no evidence that the decision not to pass on the information had been taken in the interests of the child). Therefore, the scope of the duty of care owed by the local authority was not limited (as it otherwise might have been). The case against the local authority was made out and damages were payable (*Vicar of Writtle v Essex CC*).

Childminder advice. The case concerned the failure of a local authority to deregister a childminder who was under suspicion and investigation. Subsequently, an infant was seriously injured while in the childminder's care. Liability was imposed on grounds of a negligent misstatement made to the mother by the local authority's nursery and childminding adviser. He had said to her that he was quite happy that the child be placed with the childminder, even though there was by then a question mark about an injury suffered by another child in the care of that same childminder (*T (A Minor) v Surrey County Council*).

Duty of care to the public owed by ambulance service. An injured ambulance man brought an unsuccessful personal injury case against an NHS trust in Sussex. The main question was whether the fire brigade should have been called to remove the bedroom window and winch the patient down with a crane – to avoid risk to the ambulance man of using a carry chair down steep and narrow stairs.

As far as negligence was concerned, the Court of Appeal made reference to the weighing up of the risk involved against the social utility of the ambulance service responding to an urgent, if not an emergency, call. It pointed out that whilst the employer had health and safety at work obligations toward its employees, nevertheless it also owed a common law duty of care to the public as well (*King v Sussex Ambulance NHS Trust*).

The extent of any duty of care will vary with the circumstances. For instance, where specific advice is being given, the duty will be all the greater; on the other hand, where general advice is being given, the duty will be less:

Informal advice. A negligence case was brought in respect of informal planning advice given over the telephone. In rejecting the claim, the court pointed out that if it were too ready to impose liability, it would be contrary to the public interest, because local authorities would be likely to cease giving any guidance at all (*Tidman v Reading BC*). On the other hand, where a local authority environmental health officer office gave specific advice, in the form of directing a person as to what should be done (altering a hotel kitchen), gave inaccurate information about his own authority, and omitted reference to the person's statutory rights, the court held that a duty of care did exist (*Welton v North Cornwall DC*).

5.3.1.2 Duty of care to own staff

Local authorities will, as employers, owe a duty of care to their own staff.

Injured social worker. A social worker visited the home of a client who weighed 15 stone. She found him lying half out of bed with a neighbour (who happened to be a nurse) there. Together they moved him; she suffered a serious back injury. She had received neither training nor even information about manual handling. She was awarded over £200,000 compensation (*Colclough v Staffordshire County Council*).

Social worker and stress. A social services team leader working on child abuse cases suffered a nervous breakdown. This was not foreseeable. However, when he resumed work, it was foreseeable that he would suffer further illness unless substantial assistance was provided. This did not happen; he suffered a second breakdown, which led to his retiring at the age of 50. The court found the local authority to be in breach of its duty of care and therefore liable to pay damages in negligence (*Walker v Northumberland CC*).

Social worker and stress. A social worker brought a negligence case in relation to stress she had suffered. The court accepted that she was owed a duty of care by her local authority employer. However, on the facts of the case, the authority had taken reasonable steps so as not to breach the duty. It could not reasonably have foreseen the social worker's reaction, on her return from a three-week holiday, to the fact that a promise had not been kept – namely to implement a 'stacking system' where new cases would not be allocated until existing cases had reduced (*Pratley v Surrey CC*).

In contrast, when a local authority was well aware of a teacher's difficulties in terms of stress, but failed to take action, it was liable. The fact that all the teachers were overworked and stressed did not mean that something could not have been done for this particular teacher (*Barber v Somerset CC*).

5.3.1.3 Weighing up risks and benefits

As already noted above, part of the determination of liability for negligence will concern whether risks and benefits have been correctly weighed up, and any risk proportionately managed. Community care assessment and provision of services may be often not about risk elimination but risk management.

For instance, a certain degree of risk taking will be acceptable rather than, for instance, a compromising of independence and breaking of family or home links (*R(Khana) v Southwark LBC*). Department of Health guidance refers to risks that may be acceptable or viewed as a 'natural and healthy part of independent living' (LAC(2002)13, para 41). In the following case, the fact of the accident did not necessarily mean liability; the court needed to know the background and how risks and benefits had been weighed up:

Road-crossing ability of person with learning disabilities. A person with learning disabilities was knocked down by a car when he was crossing the road to catch a local authority minibus, which would take him to the day centre he attended. He had begun to cross the road, despite being told by an escort to wait. A negligence case was brought on his behalf by the Official Solicitor. Prior to the time of the accident it was not unusual for the man already to be at the pickup point, having crossed the road before the minibus arrived. The evidence indicated that long before the accident he had reached a level of independence and road safety competence so that he was able to cross the road on his own without being exposed to unreasonable risk of foreseeable injury, even in the rush hour. He must have crossed the road in this way, and in safety, many hundreds of times in the five years before the accident. The negligence case failed both in the High Court and Court of Appeal (*Slater v Buckinghamshire CC*).

In another case, the question arose about a local authority's care plan for a highly vulnerable woman with mental health problems and learning disabilities. It was about whether the local authority's care plan should allow continuation of a sexual relationship (to which she could consent) with her longstanding partner. This would be a clear benefit to her, but it would also carry a number of risks in relation to her mental health and to other matters about which she lacked the capacity to decide. The court stated that it was about balancing happiness with manageable risk; there was no point wrapping people in cotton wool if it made them miserable:

Physical health and safety, happiness and manageable risk. The fact is that all life involves risk, and the young, the elderly and the vulnerable are exposed to additional risks and to risks they are less well equipped to cope with. But just as wise parents resist the temptation to keep their children metaphorically wrapped up in cotton wool, so too we must avoid the temptation always to put physical health and safety of the elderly and the vulnerable before everything else. Often it will be appropriate to do so, but not always. Physical health and safety can sometimes be bought at too high a price in happiness and emotional welfare. The emphasis must be on sensible risk appraisal, not striving to avoid all risk, whatever the price, but instead seeking a proper balance and being willing to tolerate manageable or acceptable risks as the price appropriately to be paid in order to achieve some other good – in particular to achieve the vital good of the elderly or vulnerable person's happiness. What good is it making someone safer if it merely makes them miserable? (*Local Authority X v MM*).

The fact that not every accident will entail liability is a point put forcibly in a context wider than community care. In one case the House of Lords stressed the importance of taking account of risk, gravity, cost and social value:

Weighing up risk and social value generally. When a young man dived from a standing position into the shallow water of a council-owned lake, he broke his neck; this was despite warning signs about the dangers of swimming. In rejecting his claim for damages against the council, the House of Lords stated that they had to weigh up risk, gravity, cost and social value. The social value of giving people access to the edge of the lake was very considerable; the risk of such an accident was minimal; and it was not the role of the courts to protect 'the foolhardy or reckless few' who choose to ignore warning notices and put themselves at risk (*Tomlinson v Congleton BC*).

Similarly, the Corporation of London failed in a case which attempted to prevent people swimming in the Parliament Hill ponds at Hampstead Heath, other than in the presence of a lifeguard. Men had been swimming there since 1890, women since 1925. The judge reassured the Corporation that it would not be open to prosecution if something went wrong, because the swimmers swam at their own risk (*Hampstead Health Winter Swimming Club v Corporation of London*).

Continuing the leisure theme, a man had voluntarily undertaken indoor rock climbing activity, fell and was rendered tetraplegic. He claimed that he should have been warned that the matting on to which he fell would not necessarily prevent serious injury. His negligence claim failed; the Court of Appeal held that if training or supervision were required for such an activity, it would be required for a whole range of commonplace leisure activities (*Trustees of the Portsmouth Youth Activities Committee v Poppleton*). This is not to say some cases do not give rise to fears about a culture of litigation; for example, the High Court found negligence on the part of a parent who had not adequately supervised a 'bouncy castle' at a birthday party, during which one of the children suffered a serious head injury. But even this decision was overturned by the Court of Appeal. It held (a) that such a serious injury could not have been anticipated and (b) that the admitted duty of care, to supervise the activity on the bouncy castle, did not amount to a requirement of constant surveillance (*Harris v Perry*).

In another case, a hole had been dug in a village green for the annual fête. Members of the Royal British Legion had filled in the hole with wood, soil and stones. Two years later, the hole had become exposed, and the claimant broke her leg as a result while walking across the green. Her claim for damages failed; the hole had probably been exposed by children, and the Royal British Legion should not be held liable (*Cole v Davis Gilbert*). And when a woman claimed damages from her landlord – after she climbed out of her flat window during a party and fell through the skylight – her case failed. She and her fellow partygoers were sensible, educated, were not sober, and had been dancing on the Perspex roof in poor light (*Siddorn v Patel*).

In cases where there is tension between the risks and benefits to the service user, the solution might not always be easy to find. But the local ombudsman has pointed out that at the very least decisiveness is required, if the service user's needs are not to be neglected. Indeed, while the council argued internally in the following case, the man and his family were perversely at higher risk from manual handling every day. It was not a negligence case, but it illustrates the importance of weighing up risks and benefits of a particular course of action:

Stairlift, health and safety, terminal illness, manual handling. The complainant was the mother of a man with motor neurone disease; she complained that the council had acted unreasonably in providing home adaptations. The man had three children aged between 11 and 15 years; his wife had recently had heart surgery. Part of the complaint related to a stairlift. The council refused to install it because of a lack of clearance at the top of the stairs (demanded by the council's design brief). However, to remedy this would have involved further adaptation work. This was not acceptable to the family because of the fear of dust and draughts during the works – since colds or respiratory illness could be extremely dangerous for people with motor neurone disease. A stairlift with a swivel chair was considered, but the occupational therapy team leader expressed concern because the chair would block the staircase and constitute a risk for other members of the family.

Differences of opinion persisted on the safety ground between the architects' department (which was prepared to proceed) and the building works department, which was not. In the meantime, the man had offered to sign any disclaimer (in case of accident) that the council felt was appropriate. The family felt that the council's preoccupation with safety was somewhat 'hollow', since it appeared to disregard completely the daily risks to the family, when the children and elderly mother carried the man up and down the stairs.

The ombudsman could not 'understand that the importance of the design brief must outweigh' everything else. In the light of the council's policy of enabling people to remain at home, it needed 'to give very careful consideration to those cases where another aspect of their policy contradicts this'. The ombudsman did not believe that the council had thought through adequately the consequences of such a clash; and stated that it should 'put all the facts to Members who will then be in a position to come to a proper reasoned decision' as soon as possible (*Islington LBC 1988*).

Sometimes consideration of risk in negligence cases concerns the risk to staff weighed up against the needs of service users. For instance, an NHS trust was held liable for the injuries suffered by nurses at a high security hospital at the hands of a mental health patient who posed an exceptionally high risk of violence and unpredictable behaviour. The court pointed out that if the trust could 'take precautions so as not to expose their employees to needless risks and still not be in breach of their duty to a patient, then it seems to me that they may well be in breach of duty if they fail to take those precautions' (*Buck v Nottinghamshire Healthcare NHS Trust*).

When a health care assistant was punched hard in the face by a psychiatric patient who was known to be unpredictable, and as a consequence suffered psychiatric injuries, she won her negligence case – because her duties did not require her to be present, and she had not been asked to leave. There was clearly no conflict between her duty of care to the patient and the duty of care of the employer towards the employee (*Cook v Bradford Community NHS Trust*).

5.3.2 BREACH OF STATUTORY DUTY
Seeking financial compensation for breach of statutory duty in private law (as opposed to seeking a judicial review remedy in public law) requires identification of definite, potentially enforceable, individual rights. Such rights are difficult to identify in welfare legislation for a number of reasons – and private law actions in this field do not seem generally to be viable.

At one time, the courts distinguished decisions about whether a duty was owed to a person from the actual carrying out of the duty. Failure to take the first type of decision properly could not result in private law actions for breach of duty; however, failure to discharge the latter 'executive' or operational type of obligation could (*Cocks v Thanet DC*).

However, the courts have since further refined the test for liability and imposed additional obstacles; identification of such executive obligations will not be enough. For instance, the claimant must also show (a) that the legislation was designed to protect a specific class of people and also to confer a right to sue for damages; (b) clear statutory language to this effect; and (c) that there were no alternative remedies such as an appeal to the Secretary of State (e.g. *O'Rourke v Camden LBC*).

The difficulties posed by this test can be seen in cases concerning the neglect of children and the failure of the local authority to act (*X v Bedfordshire CC*), failure to provide housing (*O'Rourke v Camden LBC*), failure to provide adequate home help (*Wyatt v Hillingdon LBC*), and failure to provide aftercare for a mentally disordered patient, followed by his killing of an innocent bystander at Finsbury Park underground station (*Clunis v Camden and Islington HA*). In the light of these cases, the speculation of the judge in *R v Bexley LBC, ex p B* that damages might be possible for breach of the duty to arrange community care services under the Chronically Sick and Disabled Persons Act 1970 appears to signify little.

Even so, there have been some cases in which the courts have entertained the possibility of damages for a breach of statutory duty. For example, the Court of Appeal has ruled that non-payment of a mandatory housing repair grant could give rise to private law rights – which would allow for a private law action to recover, as an ordinary debt, the amount of the unpaid grant (*Dennis Rye Pension Fund v Sheffield City Council*).

5.3.3 NEGLIGENCE/BREACH OF DUTY ACTIONS COMPARED TO JUDICIAL REVIEW

The existence of private law remedies is, or would be, significant (if they were more commonly available in social and health care), because there are a number of differences between private and public law procedures.

First, the claimant does not, at the outset, have to gain the permission of a judge to pursue a private law case. Second, the court in private law normally makes a final decision about the matter in dispute, whereas judicial review often involves authorities themselves retaking a decision about services. Third, when a claimant wins a case, the judge in private law cases must normally grant a remedy of some sort; whereas in public law cases, the judge does not have to do this. Furthermore, a remedy in private law, but not usually in public law, can be in the form of financial compensation (damages).

Lastly, in private law claims for negligence or breach of statutory duty, the claimant must have suffered some sort of harm: physical, psychological (in some circumstances only), property or financial (in limited circumstances only). For instance, if there is no harm, then a negligence case cannot succeed. However, in judicial review, such harm does not have to be shown – although the applicant still has to show that he, she or it (in the case of an organisation) has sufficient interest in the case.

5.4 HEALTH AND SAFETY AT WORK LEGISLATION

A number of duties relevant to community care arise under health and safety at work legislation. Breach of these duties gives rise to criminal offences; in addition, employees can, under some health and safety at work legislation, bring civil law personal injury actions for breach of statutory duty. There are duties toward non-employees as well as employees, on the basis of which health and safety prosecutions may be brought.

5.4.1 REASONABLE PRACTICABILITY IN HEALTH AND SAFETY

The term 'reasonably practicable' recurs frequently in health and safety at work legislation, and is of pivotal importance.

The traditional approach by the courts has been to weigh up the level of risk to employees against the cost of doing something about it in terms of resources, staffing, time and effort. If the cost involved would be clearly disproportionate to the risk, then it might not be reasonably practicable to eliminate or reduce the risk. The courts have stated that the degree of risk should be placed in one scale, and the 'sacrifice' (money, time, trouble) necessary to avert the risk in the other. If there was a gross disproportion, such that the risk was insignificant compared to the sacrifice, then the employer did not have a duty to avert the risk (*Edwards v National Coal Board*). The same principle applied in the following, more recent, case:

Manual handling injury. A local authority carpenter was carrying doors weighing 72 pounds up the stairs of a block of flats. He sustained an injury. The Court of Appeal accepted that the risk of manual handling injury appeared from the evidence to have been relatively low. However, providing him that day with an assistant would not have been a disproportionate drain on the resources of an employer the size of the local authority. The local authority was therefore found to be in breach of the Manual Handling Operations Regulations 1992 (*Hawkes v Southwark LBC*).

5.4.1.1 Risk and public benefit

When an employer is deciding about the reasonable practicability of reducing risk to public service employees, it will sometimes have to take account of the benefit or utility of the activity in question to the relevant member(s) of the public. The courts point out that the test of reasonable practicability can only make sense if one considers the relevant public service context – and the serving of the public by, for example, local authorities and NHS bodies. Public authorities and their staff have both statutory duties to provide services and owe a common law duty of care to the public they serve.

Effectively the courts have stated that, in some circumstances, the provision of certain services may entail a degree of risk to those delivering the service, namely the staff. This risk should not however be at an unacceptable level. The principle entails the striking of a balance between staff safety and the needs of service users. The service provider will have to make proportionate efforts to deliver the service without exposing its staff to unacceptable risk. Proportionality here means that the greater the needs of the service user, so the greater efforts have to made by the service provider to manage the risk at an acceptable level – before concluding that the service cannot be provided. This makes competent risk assessment of the individual situation essential, as pointed out, in the context of manual handling, both by the law courts (*R(A&B) v East Sussex CC no.2*) and the leading professional guidance on the subject (Smith 2005).

Both local authorities and the NHS continue to misunderstand and to misapply this principle. The consequence is that either they put their staff at unacceptable levels of risk, or they pay insufficient attention to the needs and rights of the users of their services. All too often, they fail to find the middle ground, which was the key to solving a dispute about the manual handling of two women with learning disabilities:

Manual handling, health and safety and human rights. A dispute arose about the manual handling of two women with profound physical and learning disabilities. The parents were opposed to the use of hoists within the home and wished their daughters to be manually handled. They also wished their daughters to get out of the house to go swimming, shopping and horseriding. The local authority opposed the parents' wishes because of what it perceived to be the high manual handling risks to staff.

The court held that, when considering reasonable practicability under the Manual Handling Operations Regulations 1992, the local authority had to bring into the equation the assessed community care needs of the women, and most importantly their human rights as well. This would therefore necessitate balanced decision-making by the local authority in weighing up competing considerations.

It would not mean that the rights of disabled people should override those of paid carers; nor would it mean that those of paid carers should override those of disabled people. Nevertheless, it might mean that in certain circumstances paid carers might have to work at higher, but not unacceptable, levels of risk – depending on the needs, and threat to the human rights, of a disabled person.

Thus, in considering reasonable practicability, the local authority would have to consider and weigh up the women's wishes, feelings, reluctance, fear, refusal, dignity, integrity and quality of life, as well as the risk to staff (*R(A&B) v East Sussex CC: no.2*).

The courts may refer explicitly to a degree of risk to health care assistants being justifiable:

NHS care assistant and risk taking. A care assistant in an NHS residential home for disabled children sustained an injury through pulling out and making beds which were low and against the wall. The

Court of Appeal accepted in principle that certain features of the beds, though potentially increasing the risk to staff, might be justifiable in relation to the needs of the children (*Koonjul v Thameslink NHS Health Care Trust*).

In a Scottish case involving the manual handling of a man with dementia in hospital, the judge pointed out that in identifying what would have been reasonable for the safety of staff, it had to be remembered that the load was not a slab of concrete but a person. This meant that hoisting him, though arguably the safest for nurses, was not necessarily the legally reasonable option. From the patient's point of view, another option was to be preferred, albeit one which did not put the nurses at undue risk (*Urquhart v Fife Primary Care Trust*). Similarly, the ambulance service will sometimes be called on to accept at least a certain level of risk, in its role as an essential public service:

Urgent ambulance call and risk-taking. The ambulance service received an urgent call to take a man to hospital. The call required a one-hour response. The man lived in a cottage and was upstairs in bed. There was a steep, narrow staircase with a bend. The two ambulance men began to carry the man down the stairs in a carry chair. One of them momentarily lost his grip on the front of the chair. The other ambulance man briefly had to bear the whole weight. He suffered injuries to his thumb, back and knees.

The injured ambulance man brought a personal injury case. He argued that he should have been trained to give serious consideration to the alternative of using the fire brigade to remove the man through a window with a crane, and that the ambulance service wrongly treated use of the fire brigade as an absolute last resort.

The case failed in the Court of Appeal. This was partly on the basis that public service workers sometimes have to work at higher, although not unacceptable, levels of risk. The court also pointed out that in determining whether to call for the fire brigade, in order to achieve quite a drastic form of removal, various relevant factors had to be taken account of. These included distress to the patient and the reaction of the carers (*King v Sussex Ambulance Service*).

Such judicial decisions are consistent with Health and Safety Executive guidance. This has always pointed out that reasonable practicability does not entail that all risk be removed. Otherwise there would, for instance, be no adequate fire brigade (HSE 1998, p.8). Risk assessment must be performed in context. The Health and Safety Commission also has stated that, within the health service, some situations and activities will call for higher levels of risk taking. One such activity would be rehabilitation (HSC 1998, p.43). This approach is taken in guidance on manual handling issued by the Chartered Society of Physiotherapy (CSP 2002, p.11). Perhaps, above all, it is about individual assessment (*R(A&B) v East Sussex CC no.2*), as emerged in the following case:

Failure to reassess and to take account of osteoporosis in deciding about hoist use. A 23-year old woman with profound disabilities, cared for by her parents, was to be switched from one day centre to another – apparently in order to save the local authority money. She had multiple learning and physical disabilities, compounded by sensory disabilities. She suffered from cerebral palsy, microcephalus and epilepsy, was unable to walk and suffered from a number of spinal problems. A hoist was to be used in the new centre, but the court identified that no reassessment had been carried out. In particular, no consideration had been given to the osteoporosis and the risks it might have posed. Further, it was alleged, with some substance, that the local authority operated a blanket policy that excluded lifting. The woman's parents argued that hoisting was wholly inappropriate. The judge gave permission for a full judicial review case to be brought against the local authority (*R(Clegg) v Salford CC*).

In 2008, a report from Scotland's Commissioner for Children and Young People suggested that striking the right balance between people's needs and human rights on the one hand, and staff safety on the other, too often remains elusive for children as well as adults – resulting in detriment to those children as well as breach of their human rights (Paton 2008).

5.4.1.2 Managing risk

Neither legislation nor decisions of the law courts require the taking of unacceptable risk, contrary to some views that have been expressed (e.g. Griffiths and Stevens 2004).

First, employers will continue to be penalised for obvious failures to protect staff, and it is notable that many reported cases show that staff are put at risk through basic lapses in health and safety, rather than through balanced decision-making involving some degree of carefully managed risk.

For instance, two such cases entailing basic failure involved nurses providing care for highly dependent people in hospital. Serious injury was caused to one nurse because of absent or defective hoists and a system of work that sanctioned routine use of an unsafe lifting technique (*Knott v Newham Healthcare NHS Trust*). In the second case, a lack of adjustable height beds and a flat wheelchair tyre were the main causes of injury (*Commons v Queen's Medical Centre*). The compensation payments in the above two cases, and therefore direct costs to the NHS, were high; over £400,000 in the first case, and over £200,000 in the second (quite aside from the indirect costs of losing highly trained nurses and having to replace them). Yet neither case involved nurses taking planned and managed risk on the basis of people's assessed needs and human rights. Instead they reflected organisational failure to manage risk at the most basic, obvious level.

Second, the Court of Appeal has pointed out that putting staff at unacceptable risk would be a clear breach of health and safety at work legislation – even if the needs of a service user are in issue. This case was about the changing of a boy with faecal incontinence at school. The lack of space and appropriate equipment meant staff were at unreasonably high risk from manual lifting when they changed him. Following a significant injury to the special needs coordinator, the head teacher was more than justified in sending the boy home to be changed, rather than continue to attempt it at school (*K v X Grammar School Governors*).

Third, the courts have emphasised that staff are not expected to be modern day 'Mother Teresas', nor should there be a return to the days of boys being sent up chimneys or women being sent down coal mines (*R(A&B) v East Sussex CC: no.2*).

These legal cases are in principle helpful in assisting organisations to apply health and safety at work legislation in balanced fashion. This is particularly relevant because some local authorities, NHS bodies and other organisations tend in practice to play the health and safety card inappropriately. Some refuse to provide certain services in order to meet service users' needs, not because of unacceptable levels of risk but because management of that risk would require some effort, resources and thought. That is, staff would have to be reasonably trained and be provided with effective systems of work that placed a premium both on staff safety and meeting the needs of service users.

Sometimes both local authorities and NHS bodies artificially or disingenuously use health and safety to circumvent legal duties to consult about the closure of services – instead of admitting that cost savings are the real reason. Sometimes they get caught out; ironically, greater honesty would be a legally better bet, although does not play so well politically of course. For instance, in one case, a local authority tried to close a care home, arguing serious structural faults, on health and safety grounds, even though the report of a structural survey emphasised that the problems were not significant, and the costs to remedy them not great. The judge's reaction to this, which underpinned his decision that the consultation was unlawful, is worth quoting at some length, since such misleading attempts by local authorities or NHS bodies are not uncommon:

True reasons not given for proposed closure of care home. 'Of far greater concern, in my judgment, is the concern of that exercise. In my view, the initial letter of 21 May did not give an adequate summary of the true reasons for the proposed closures. References to the policy considerations that favoured a reduction in the amount of residential service provision were very brief. The specific reasons expressed for the closure, or for the proposals to close the two individual homes, were incorrect or misleading. In the case of Warthfield, the reason was put solely on the basis of health and safety reasons arising out of a structural fault concerning the foundations. Yet the detailed survey report not only fails to support that, but shows that what was said was simply wrong. The survey report goes out of its way to emphasise the very limited nature of the problem with the building, which it is said expressly should not be taken out of context. Yet, in my view, it was taken out of context and was presented misleadingly, whether deliberately or not does not matter. Moreover, the extended timeframe of 12 years envisaged in the survey report for dealing with the problem was not mentioned, and there was no explanation of the costs of remedying the problem on the alternative basis put forward in the report' (R(Madden v Bury MBC).

In another case, the NHS trust argued that rehabilitation wards in a local hospital should be closed on the grounds that the clinical safety of patients could not be guaranteed – but this was only because the trust was inappropriately sending patients with acute needs to those wards which were non-accute in character. Furthermore, the trust had misinformed the professor, whom it commissioned to produce a report, about this issue (R(Morris) v Trafford Healthcare NHS Trust).

Yet some care providers appear to believe that if they can avoid risk altogether (even to the considerable detriment of service users), they can 'get away' with employing staff who are unable to identify, assess or manage risk of any sort. Ironically, even this approach does not save staff from injury, because risk cannot be altogether avoided – and a higher risk well managed by competent staff might anyway pose less risk of injury than a lower risk unmanaged by incompetent staff. Indeed, the House of Commons Work and Pensions Committee (2008) noted that health and safety at work legislation imported a proportionate approach, but that employers were sometimes 'over cautious'. This was partly because of 'over zealous health and safety consultants'. The Committee called for a system of accreditation for such consultants and advisers, in order to rectify this problem (p.3).

5.4.2 DUTIES TO EMPLOYEES

A number of duties are held by employers toward employees.

Under s.2 of the Health and Safety at Work Act 1974, employers have a duty to safeguard the health, safety and welfare of their employees at work, so far as is reasonably practicable. This includes the provision and maintenance of safe systems of work together with instruction, information, training and supervision. It also covers safe use, handling, transport and storage of equipment, as well as a safe working environment. A breach can lead to prosecution. For instance, St George's NHS Mental Health NHS Trust was prosecuted and fined £28,000 for serious breaches of safety procedures which resulted in one of its psychiatric nurses being battered to death (al Yafai 2005).

5.4.2.1 Management of health and safety at work

Under the Management of Health and Safety at Work Regulations 1999 (SI 1999/3242), employers have various duties. These include the duty to assess risks to the health and safety of their employees at work, in order to identify what needs to be done to comply with other, relevant health and safety at work legislation. Employers must also review their risk assessments, and cooperate and coordinate activities in a workplace shared with other employers or self-employed people in order to ensure compliance with relevant health and safety requirements. They are also obliged in a shared workplace to provide health and safety information to other employers or to self-employed people working in the local authority's 'undertaking'.

5.4.2.2 Manual handling

Under the Manual Handling Operations Regulations 1992 (SI 1992/2793), employers must, as far as is reasonably practicable, avoid the need for their employees to undertake manual handling involving a risk of injury. The risk assessment directed to identifying such a risk takes place under the 1999 regulations. If it is not reasonably practicable for an employer to avoid the risk of injury to its employees, then it must carry out a suitable and sufficient assessment of the manual handling operations in issue, and must take appropriate steps to reduce the risk to the lowest level reasonably practicable. If reasonably practicable it must also provide precise information on the weight, and heaviest side, of the 'load'.

The employer must also have regard to the physical suitability of an employee to carry out the tasks together with clothing, footwear and other personal effects being carried out. It must have regard to any relevant risk assessment under r.3 of the Management of Health and Safety at Work Regulations 1999 and whether an employee has been identified by that assessment as coming within a group of employees particularly at risk. It must also have regard to the results of any health surveillance carried out under r.6 of the 1999 Regulations.

Examples of the taking of higher, albeit managed, risks in the manual handling context have already been given (see above). Risk assessment, aimed at identification of manual handling risk in general, is carried out under the 1999 regulations. If the risk cannot reasonably practicably be avoided, then a specific risk assessment concerning reduction of risk must be carried out under the MHOR 1992. Both 1999 and 1992 sets of regulations impose a duty on employers to review these risk assessments if there is reason to believe that they are no longer valid or if there has been significant change in the situation. The employer must then make any changes required.

Maintaining risk assessments and care plans. In one case, the risks posed by a woman who was assisted to walk at a day hospital had increased. This had, correctly, been recorded in her notes. However, the physiotherapist had not taken correspondingly greater precautions, and this had resulted in injury to an occupational therapy assistant. The NHS trust was held liable for the injury (*Stainton v Chorley and South Ribble NHS Trust*: a negligence case).

Thus, the court was not stating that risks should not have been taken, but that they should have been properly managed on an ongoing basis.

5.4.3 DUTIES OF EMPLOYEES

The Health and Safety at Work Act 1974 (s.7) imposes a duty on an employee to take reasonable care of his or her own health and safety and also that of other people who may be affected by the employee's acts or failure to act. Under the MHOR 1992, an employee must make full and proper use of any system of work provided in relation to the reduction of risk. Under the Management of Health and Safety at Work Regulations 1999, employees must use equipment in accordance with any training provided and with instructions provided by the employer.

5.4.4 DUTY OF SELF-EMPLOYED PEOPLE

Under s.3 of the Health and Safety at Work Act 1974, self-employed people have a duty to conduct their undertaking in such a way as to ensure that, as far as reasonably practicable, other people who may be affected are not exposed to risk to their health and safety. In addition, the duties imposed on employers, as outlined above in both the Management of Health and Safety at Work Regulations 1999 and the MHOR 1992, apply also to self-employed people.

5.4.5 DUTY OF EMPLOYERS TO NON-EMPLOYEES

As already explained, employers such as local authorities and the NHS must take account of service users when deciding what is reasonably practicable in order to safeguard their employees under legislation such as s.2 of the Health and Safety at Work Act 1974 or the Manual Handling Operations Regulations 1992.

However, there are in addition more explicit duties owed toward non-employees. Under s.3 of the 1974 Act, there is a duty on the employer to conduct its undertaking in such a way as to ensure, so far as is reasonably practicable, that non-employees who may be affected are not exposed to risks to their health and safety. In addition, under r.3 of the Management of Health and Safety at Work Regulations 1999, there is a duty to carry out a suitable and sufficient assessment of the risks to the health and safety of non-employees arising from, or connected with, the employer's undertaking.

The term non-employee is wide in scope. Non-employees of a local authority include, for example, community care service users, informal carers, NHS staff, employees of independent care providers and self-employed people providing a service to the local authority.

5.4.5.1 Contracting out services: health and safety responsibilities of health or social care commissioner

A local authority could be prosecuted for risks to the health and safety of an independent care provider's employees, as well as to that of service users, if those risks have arisen through failures in the contracting process:

Contracting out services: health and safety at work liability. A local authority contracts out provision of its domiciliary community care services to a local independent care provider. However, the authority is in the throes of what it considers to be a financial crisis. It therefore allocates inadequate funding to the contract. It also fails to check on the safety record of the contractor in question and to monitor the performance of the contract.

Poor practice and unsafe working flourish, leading to two serious accidents to the care provider's staff. The Health and Safety Executive decides to prosecute both the care provider and the local authority under respectively sections 2 and 3 of the Health and Safety at Work Act 1974 (for a comparable case involving a refuse collection service, see *Health and Safety Executive v Barnet LBC*).

However, as illustrated in some negligence cases, if a health or social care commissioner of services takes reasonable care in procuring services from an independent provider, the fact that something then goes awry will not necessarily result in liability (whether in negligence or under health and safety work legislation):

Contracted out services: negligence liability. The Ministry of Defence made arrangements with a London hospital, for the hospital in turn to contract for treatment of army personnel in Germany. The question arose as to whether the hospital should be liable for negligent treatment subsequently given in Germany. The court concluded that the London hospital's duty of care did not extend to ensuring directly that reasonable care and skill were used for hospital treatment in Germany. However, the London hospital might have been liable had it carelessly selected a provider, and mismanaged the contract such that an unsafe regime was permitted and injury to patients caused.

The Court of Appeal upheld this decision, which in effect identified the NHS duty as an 'organisational' duty to use reasonable care that the hospital staff, facilities and organisation provided were appropriate to provide safe and satisfactory medical care. This duty was not breached. Such a duty differed from a duty to ensure that the treatment actually given was administered with reasonable care and skill; however, this latter duty was not applicable (*A Child 'A' v Ministry of Defence*).

In another negligence case, concerning the checking of a contractor's insurance, the NHS was likewise found by the court not to be liable in negligence for the accident that had occurred:

Contracted out 'splat wall' for fair in hospital grounds. An NHS trust organised a fair in its grounds. It contracted with 'Club Entertainments' for a 'splat wall', which allowed people to bounce from a trampoline and stick to a wall by means of Velcro. The equipment was negligently set up and the claimant was injured. The court found that the trust had a duty to satisfy itself about the competence of the contractor. This included factors such as experience, reliability and insurance. The trust was therefore obliged to enquire about insurance, which it did – but not to demand actually to see the policy (which had in fact expired prior to the accident). The trust was held by the court not to be liable (*Gwilliam v West Hertfordshire Hospital NHS Trust*).

However, the routine failure of NHS primary care trusts to carry out full inspections of private mental health providers, as reported in 2008 (Santry 2008), might leave them open to legal action if things were badly to go wrong.

5.4.5.2 Prosecutions for harm to patients: falls, scalding, manual handling, medical treatment

Prosecutions under health and safety at work legislation may be various in respect of non-employees. For instance, the Health and Safety at Work Act 1974 has been used to prosecute the company and manager of a care home, for failure to investigate reports of the abuse and ill-treatment of residents (Mark 2005).

Prosecutions by the Health and Safety Executive (HSE), when hospitals or care homes fail to take sufficient care of older residents, are plentiful. Scalding in baths, or burns on unguarded radiators and pipes, causing serious injury or death, seems prevalent:

Scalded, fully clothed in bath. An 83-year-old resident, suffering from angina, mental health problems and other disabilities, died in 2003, fully clothed in a bath of scalding (50 degrees centigrade) water at 4 am in a care home run by Prime Lift Ltd. The National Care Standards Commission had already warned the home that it needed to fit thermostatic valves. The company was doing so on a rolling programme but not yet in this particular care home. Prosecuted under s.3 of the 1974 Act, the company was fined £100,000 and ordered to pay £49,000 costs (*Health and Safety Executive v Prime Life*).

A range of other mishaps are frequently prosecuted by the Health and Safety Executive, including falls from unguarded windows. Bed rails also feature prominently.

Bed rails. A care home resident fell from her bed, after her bed rail had not been secured properly, face down and died from asphyxiation. This prosecution took place under the Provision and Use of Work Equipment Regulations 1998, because the equipment had not been maintained in an efficient state and working order and in good repair. The fine was £3500 (*Health and Safety Executive v Dukeries Health Care*).

Under the 1974 Act, a prosecution was brought against a care home after a resident died when his head became stuck between dislodged cot sides, on the basis that there was no safe system of work (*Health and Safety Executive v South Church Care*).

A man was left for 15 minutes in a poor posture in a special reclining chair with a lap belt in place. He slipped down the chair, and the belt became trapped around his neck. He subsequently died. The fine was £70,000 (*Health and Safety Executive v Southern Cross Care Homes*). Manual handling and the use of slings and hoists might be implicated:

95-year-old slipping from hoist. A 95-year-old woman slipped from a Sarita hoist, whilst being transferred out of the bath, at a care home run by BUPA Care Homes Ltd. She fractured her shoulder and died four days later. The care assistant involved had not received training in the use of that type of hoists. Assessments and procedures for manual handling and safe bathing were not brought to the attention of care assistants, and supervision of manual handling operations was inadequate. Under s.3 of the 1974 Act, the company was found guilty, fined £90,000 and ordered to pay £19,247 costs (*Health and Safety Executive v BUPA Care Homes*).

Rather than in connection with basic care, the NHS is sometimes prosecuted for lapses in treatment. In one incident, two medical doctors were convicted of manslaughter for failing to make an appropriate diagnosis and seek medical advice for a patient suffering from toxic shock syndrome and who subsequently died. In addition, the NHS trust was prosecuted under s.3 of the 1974 Act, mainly for the absence of adequate supervision, training and appraisal of senior house officers. It was accepted, though, that this failure did not cause the death. The trust was convicted, although the £100,000 fine imposed by the crown court was later reduced to £40,000, with £10,000 costs (*R v Southampton University Hospitals NHS Trust*).

When cardio-angiography treatment was not routinely checked before it was used, air got into the syringe; in turn the air entered the patient's bloodstream causing death. The Crown Court found an absence of a reasonably safe system of work (*Health and Safety Executive v Norfolk and Norwich Healthcare NHS Trust*).

5.4.6 RISK TAKING BY SERVICE USERS

Health and safety at work legislation (and the law of negligence) are sometimes cited as the reasons for a risk-averse approach taken by local authorities and the NHS in relation to service users. Yet risk elimination is not demanded by the law; rather risk management in terms of weighing up risks and benefits is called for. For instance, in a community care case, the Court of Appeal pointed out that a measure of risk taking by users of services may be acceptable, in preference to a compromising of independence and breaking of family or home links (*R(Khana) v Southwark LBC*).

In similar vein, the Health and Safety Executive issued guidance in the past on elective risk taking in the context of community care, basically telling its inspectors not to look for risk elimination, but to consider how risk has been assessed and managed, given that community care packages might quite properly contain certain elements of risk, in connection with independent living (HSE SIM 7/2000/8). And, in pursuit of its policy of giving people more choice and control, the Department of Health points out that 'avoiding risk altogether would constrain the choices people can make' (DH 2007u, p.1).

5.5 HUMAN RIGHTS

In October 2000, the Human Rights Act 1998 embedded the European Convention on Human Rights 1998 into United Kingdom law. The 1998 Act is the vehicle; the main rights themselves lie within the Convention. For the purpose of this book, particularly relevant rights include (but are not confined to):

- article 2 (right to life)
- article 3 (right not to be subjected to torture or to inhuman and degrading treatment)
- article 5 (right not to be arbitrarily deprived of liberty)
- article 8 (right to respect for private and family life, home and correspondence)
- article 14 (right not to be discriminated against).

The Act is, overall, about establishing a balance between individual autonomy and freedom on the one hand, and the incursions of the State on the other. Human rights cases can only be taken against public bodies, or bodies carrying out functions of a public nature. Thus, the decision-making (and actions and sometimes omissions) of local authorities, NHS bodies and other public bodies must be consistent not just with relevant domestic law, but with the Human Rights Act as well.

Human rights cases have arisen in relation to various social and health care issues, including closure of care homes or NHS residential units, provision of suitably adapted accommodation for a disabled woman and her family, disclosure of confidential information, the manual handling of two profoundly disabled women in their own home, renal treatment for a man with learning disabilities, resuscitation in hospital of a man with learning disabilities, assessment of a 95-year-old woman as to her place of residence etc.

5.5.1 HUMAN RIGHTS ACT 1998

The Human Rights Act 1998 (HRA) introduced directly into United Kingdom law the rights contained in the European Convention. Prior to the implementation of the 1998 Act in October 2000, United Kingdom courts could in principle barely apply those human rights, at least directly. Claimants could take their case further to the European Court of Human Rights (e.g. *Z v United Kingdom* concerning child protection) and they can still (e.g. *Pretty v United Kingdom* concerning assisted suicide). In theory, resort to the European Court should be necessary less often in the future.

The United Kingdom courts must, as far as possible, interpret domestic legislation as compatible with the Convention (s.3). This gives the courts wide scope. However, if a court, try as it might, is unable to find such compatibility, it has the power to make a declaration of incompatibility. This does not mean the legislation in question ceases to have effect (s.4). Instead, central government has the power to make a remedial order, in order to change the legislation in question (s.10).

Mental disorder and detention. The courts found that ss.72 and 73 of the Mental Health Act 1983 were incompatible with article 5 of the European Convention, because they effectively placed the burden on the patient – of proving that the criteria justifying detention in hospital no longer existed. The mental health review tribunal had to be satisfied that the person was not suffering from mental disorder in order to direct discharge. This meant that a person could continue to be detained even if the tribunal was not necessarily satisfied that the person was suffering from mental disorder. The courts made a declaration of incompatibility (*R(H) v Mental Health Review Tribunal North and East London Region*); the government subsequently passed the Mental Health Act 1983 (Remedial Order) 2001 (SI 2001/3712) so as to switch the burden of proof to the tribunal. Tribunals now must discharge the patient if they are not satisfied that the person is suffering from mental disorder.

Other Mental Health Act provisions have also been found to be incompatible and had to be amended:

Incompatibility of automatic appointment of nearest relative. A woman was detained under the Mental Health Act 1983. She argued that ss.26 and 29 of the Act were incompatible with article 8. This was because 'nearest relatives' were automatically appointed according to the 'pecking order' in s.26. This would mean her adoptive father, against whom she had previously made allegations of sexual abuse, would be the nearest relative. Under the Act, the woman had no legal means to compel his replacement by somebody else, as the Act does not allow the patient to challenge the status of the nearest relative. This meant the Act was incompatible with a.8 of the Convention. The Secretary of State conceded this incompatibility; the European Court had anyway previously identified it in a 'friendly settlement' case (*JT v United Kingdom*). The Secretary of State nevertheless urged the court not to make a declaration of incompatibility, because the government intended to rectify the situation with new legislation. The judge decided to make such a declaration (under s.4 of the Human Rights Act) because the incompatibility had been identified some time (six years) ago and its anticipated removal had not yet taken place (*R(M) v Secretary of State for Health*).

An amendment to the Mental Health Act 1983, made by the Mental Health Act 2007, is designed to rectify this, and will give the patient a greater say in who the nearest relative should be.

5.5.1.1 Public authorities

It is unlawful for public authorities to act incompatibly with a Convention right, unless an Act of Parliament leaves it with no choice (HRA 1998, s.6). The Human Rights Act applies to public authorities only. A public authority is defined to include, in addition to obvious bodies such as local authorities, any person in respect of whom some functions are of a public nature (s.6).

The courts in the past have ruled (but see 5.5.1.2 below) that independent care providers in the context of community care are not public authorities for the purposes of the Human Rights Act (*YL v Birmingham CC*). However, there is nothing to stop local authorities attempting to place contractual obligations on such providers to observe human rights (*R(Heather) v Leonard Cheshire Foundation*: closure of care home). Central government has made this very point (ODPM 2005).

Consequent on these judicial decisions, the Parliamentary Committee on Human Rights has drawn attention to the problem of numerous, often vulnerable people, being deprived of protection under the Human Rights Act. It recommended legislative amendment, not by way of alteration to the Act directly, but by means of an interpretative statute dealing with the meaning of 'public authority'. It also criticised the notion that contracts, specifying human rights in some way, between public body and independent provider could somehow remedy the problem (JCHR 2007, pp.3–5).

By contrast, in some contexts other than community care, the courts have held that independent providers will be viewed as public bodies for the purposes of the Human Rights Act. For instance, in a case where a large-scale transfer of council housing had taken place from the local authority to a housing association, the courts ruled that the housing association was carrying out public functions in respect of that housing, and so was subject to the Human Rights Act. It has stepped into the local authority's shoes (*Donoghue v Poplar Housing Association*). Likewise, the following example concerning compulsory mental health treatment is in contrast to the community care cases:

Private psychiatric hospital: public functions. A patient was detained under the Mental Health Act 1983 in a private psychiatric hospital where she was funded by the health authority. She was on a ward for therapeutic treatment for women patients with personality disorder. The managers of the hospital changed the treatment focus of the ward to medication treatment for women with a mental illness. She claimed that as a result she was not now receiving appropriate care and treatment. She wished to bring a judicial review case, including human rights points, against the hospital as a public body. The court ruled that the change made to the ward was an act of a public nature, given the context of compulsion, and the public concern and interest concerning the care and treatment for mental health patients (*R v Partnerships in Care Ltd, ex p A*).

The commercial dealings by a local authority with an independent care provider might well be held by the courts to be public in nature and so subject to human rights considerations (*R(Haggerty) v St Helens Council*: closure of care home).

In early 2008, the government undertook to pass legislation to change this state of affairs and ensure that the Human Rights Act applied to residents placed by local authorities or the NHS in independent care homes. However, even with such an amendment, this would leave residents who had placed themselves in a care home without protection.

5.5.1.2 Care homes

The courts had held that independent care home providers were not subject to the Human Rights Act. This meant that a resident of a *local authority care home* could legally argue a human rights case (e.g. in case of impending eviction) against the authority in its role of care home owner. However, the resident of an *independent care home* could not bring a human rights case directly against the care home, even if the resident had been placed there by the local authority. This was because the care home was not deemed to be carrying out functions of a public nature (*YL v Birmingham CC*).

In order to remedy this widely criticised state of affairs, s.145 of the Health and Social Care 2008 (not yet in force) changes the effect of this legal ruling by stating that care homes are, after all, deemed to be carrying out functions of a public nature – and are thus subject to the Human Rights Act 1998 – but only in respect of residents placed by local authorities under ss.21 and 26 of the National Assistance Act 1948. This, however, is a half-hearted legislative amendment, leaving other categories of residents unprotected (see 7.3.4).

5.5.1.3 Victims, time limits, remedies

In order to bring a human rights based case, the claimant must be classifiable as a victim of the allegedly unlawful act and be a person, any non-governmental organisation or group of persons (HRA 1998, s.7, and a.34 of the Convention).

The general rule is that proceedings under the Act must be brought within a year of the act complained of. However, a court or tribunal can waive this requirement if it considers it equitable in all the circumstances. The one-year rule is also subject to any rule imposing a stricter time limit in relation to the procedure in question – such as the time limits applying to judicial review (HRA 1998, s.7).

The courts have discretion to grant a remedy as considered just and appropriate. Damages may be awarded in certain circumstances (s.8). In cases of maladministration, the local government ombudsman's recommendations on compensation for maladministration may be looked to for rough guidance (*R(Anufrijeva) v Southwark LBC*).

Human rights damages for maladministration. The local authority failed for nearly two years to meet the assessed community care needs of a seriously disabled woman. This resulted in her and her family living in conditions that breached article 8 of the Convention. The judge identified maladministration basically as the cause. He awarded damages of £10,000 (*R(Bernard) v Enfield LBC*).

In another case damages were awarded by the court where the article 5 rights of a number of patients detained under the Mental Health Act 1983 had been breached; this had been because of delays in hearing their applications to Mental Health Review Tribunals (*R(KB,MK,GM,PD,TB,B) v Mental Health Review Tribunal*).

5.5.2 EUROPEAN CONVENTION ON HUMAN RIGHTS

The Human Rights Act imports the European Convention on Human Rights into United Kingdom law. The Convention itself contains a number of rights. The following is a selection of rights, illustrated by case law, relevant to health and social care.

5.5.2.1 Right to life (article 2)

Article 2 begins by stating: 'Everyone's right to life shall be protected by law.'

In the context of community care, it has been argued unsuccessfully in a number of cases concerning the closure of care homes. However, in a case about care provided in a person's own home, the judge suggested that leaving disabled people to drown in a bath, because of health and safety concerns about staff, could engage article 2 (*R(A&B) v East Sussex CC: no.2*). In another, it was unsuccessfully argued that the rules on assisted suicide breached article 2 (*Pretty v United Kingdom*). Forcible treatment under the Mental Health Act may raise matters issues under article 2, as well as under articles 3 and 8 (*R v Responsible Medical Officer Broadmoor Hospital, ex p Wilkinson*).

The courts have also held that it is in principle lawful and not a breach of article 2 to withdraw artificial hydration and nutrition, as well as treatment, from a person lacking capacity to decide for himself or herself – if this was in his or her best interests. This arose in the case of a person in a persistent vegetative state (*NHS Trust A v M*).

5.5.2.2 Inhuman or degrading treatment (article 3)

Article 3 states: 'No one shall be subjected to torture or to inhuman or degrading treatment or punishment'.

The courts normally regard article 3 as setting a high threshold; in other words it is not easily breached. The European Court of Human Rights has stated that inhuman or degrading treatment means that the ill-treatment in question must reach a minimum level of severity, and involve actual bodily injury or intense physical or mental suffering. Degrading treatment could occur if it 'humiliates or debases an individual showing a lack of respect for, or diminishing, his or her human dignity or arouses feelings of fear, anguish or inferiority capable of breaking an individual's moral and physical resistance' (*Pretty v United Kingdom*).

In one community care case, involving a failure by the local authority to find suitably adapted accommodation for a disabled woman for two years, the judge seriously considered whether article 3 had been breached. However, in the end he found a breach of article 8 only (*R(Bernard) v Enfield LBC*; see 20.2.4.1). In another, the court held that if manual handling policies or protocols were to mean that care staff would leave disabled people for hours sitting in their own bodily waste or on the lavatory, article 3 might be engaged – that is, the right not to be subjected to inhuman or degrading treatment. On the other hand, the hoisting of disabled people was not to be regarded as inherently degrading; whether or not it was would depend on the particular circumstances (*R(A&B) v East Sussex CC: no.2*).

The European Court of Human Rights found a breach of article 3 in relation to the distress and hardship caused to a heroin addict in prison who subsequently died there. Amongst the key reasons for this finding were the inability accurately to record her weight loss (through dehydration and vomiting), a gap in monitoring by doctors, failure to admit the person to hospital to ensure medication and fluid intake, and failure to obtain more expert assistance to control the vomiting (*McGlinchey v United Kingdom*).

It was a breach also in the case of a severely physically disabled person who had been sent to prison for contempt of court. She had failed to disclose her assets in a debt case. In the police cell she was unable to use the bed and had to sleep in her wheelchair where she became very cold. When she reached the prison hospital, she could not use the toilet herself, the female duty officer could not manage to move her alone, and male prison officers had to assist. The European Court concluded that to detain a severely disabled person – in conditions where she is dangerously cold, risks developing pressure sores because her bed is too hard or unreachable, and is unable to go to the toilet or keep clean without the greatest difficulty – constituted degrading treatment contrary to article 3. Damages of £4500 were awarded (*Price v United Kingdom*).

The unnecessary use of handcuffs on a prisoner receiving chemotherapy treatment in a civilian hospital has been held to be degrading, inhumane and a breach of article 3 – where there was no adequately founded risk of escape or harm to the public (*R(Graham) v Secretary of State for Justice*).

5.5.2.3 Deprivation of liberty (article 5)

Article 5 states that everyone has a right to liberty and security and that nobody should be deprived of it, except in limited circumstances and, even then, only in accordance with procedures prescribed by law. A number of more detailed rules then follow.

Article 5 was held to have been breached by the European Court of Human Rights in the case of informal, compliant but incapacitated mental health patients due to the absence of legal safeguards (*HL v United Kingdom*). In a later case, a local authority was held to have deprived a mentally incapacitated person of his liberty, without proper legal authorisation, when it placed him in a care home and refused to let him return to his own home (*JE v DE and Surrey CC*).

The *HL v United Kingdom* ruling has led to significant amendment to the Mental Capacity Act 2005 and to the introduction, expected in April 2009, of a formal system of authorising the deprivation of liberty of people lacking capacity, not otherwise detained under the Mental Health Act 1983.

Article 5 was also breached in respect of tardiness in mental health review tribunal hearings under the 1983 Act (*R v Mental Health Review Tribunal, ex p KB*. Also: *R(C) v London South and West Region Mental Health Review Tribunal*).

5.5.2.4 Right to respect for private and family life (article 8)

Article 8 states: that everyone has the right to respect for his private and family life, his home and his correspondence. It goes on to say that there should be no interference unless it is in accordance with the law and is necessary in a democratic society. In addition it must be (a) in the interests of national security, public safety or the economic well-being of the country; (b) for the prevention of disorder or crime; (c) for the protection of health or morals; or (d) for the protection of the rights and freedom of others.

In a number of cases, the courts have stated that article 8 embraces a person's physical and psychological integrity (the latter in connection with the development of the personality of each individual in his relations with other human beings (*Botta v Italy*).

A local authority was held to have breached article 8 when it failed to deal with the daily living and accommodation needs of a severely disabled woman (*R(Bernard) v Enfield LBC*). Likewise a health authority when it breached an explicit promise about accommodation for a disabled woman (*R v North and East Devon Health Authority, ex p Coughlan*). The courts have held that article 8 may apply to manual handling issues as they apply to dignity, to hoisting and other transfers, and to the disabled person's participation in the life of the community, including recreational and cultural activities. It was also relevant to paid carers who had rights too (*R(A&B) v East Sussex CC: no.2*).

The courts have accepted also that article 8 is not only about *not* interfering, but that it will sometimes entail *positive* obligations. This would be when there is a direct and immediate link between the provision sought by the applicant and his or her private life. At the same time, it has been held that article 8 does not apply to interpersonal relations of such 'broad and indeterminate scope' that there is no real link between the provision and the individual's private life. Taking this approach, the European Court held that lack of access to beach facilities when a disabled person was on holiday did not constitute a breach of article 8 (*Botta v Italy*).

This means that, generally, article 8 is not simply a broad-brush tool with which to enforce the provision of welfare benefits that a person is aggrieved at not receiving. So, in a case involving the adequacy of accommodation provided by the local authority for asylum seekers, the court held that article 8 could sometimes impose a positive obligation on the state to provide support. However, the court found it hard to conceive of a situation where it would require the provision of welfare support, unless the situation was sufficiently severe to engage article 3 also (*R(Anufrijeva) v Southwark LBC*).

However, article 8 could more easily be engaged in family situations and the welfare of children. For example, the court noted that in *R(Bernard) v Enfield LBC*, family life had been seriously inhibited by the 'hideous conditions' prevailing in the home. Thus, generally, if there is culpable delay in administrative processes (i.e. maladministration) necessary to determine an article 8 right, the courts will not intervene unless substantial prejudice is caused to the person (*(R)Anufrijeva v Southwark LBC*). Similarly, the Court of Appeal has doubted that refusal to fund medical treatment could constitute an interference in terms of article 8 (*R v North West Lancashire HA, ex p G, A and D*).

Despite their caution over article 8, the courts drew a line at the failure of a local authority to assess properly a 95-year-old woman, when deciding that she should not return from hospital to the care home she had been living in. It had failed to weigh up whether it was safeguarding her physical and psychological integrity; it had thus breached article 8 (*R(Goldsmith) v Wandsworth LBC*).

5.5.2.5 Justification of interference with right to respect (article 8): accordance with the law and proportionality

If a local authority is to justify, under article 8.2, the interference with the right to respect under 8.1, the first ground to be satisfied is that the interference be in accordance with the law. This means the relevant domestic law.

In one case involving the decision to close a local authority care home, the judge stated that he could not envisage any circumstances in the present case in which the council could act compatibly with the common law and its other statutory obligations and yet be in breach of human rights, whether under articles 2, 3 or 8 (*R(Cowl) v Plymouth CC*: High Court).

In another case, concerning the lawfulness of offering a care home place instead of accommodation in the community, the court stated that community care legislation was broad, humane and took account of needs including family and private life. Therefore reference to article 8 of the Convention took the case no further (*R(Khana) v Southwark LBC*: High Court).

On the other hand, when a local social services authority breached article 8 by not arranging suitably adapted accommodation for a disabled woman (*R(Bernard) v Enfield LBC*), any justification in terms of the authority's action being in 'accordance with the law' would have failed. This was because the judge had anyway found the local authority to be in breach of the relevant domestic legislation, namely s.21 of the National Assistance Act 1948.

In addition to being in accordance with domestic law, the interference must be 'necessary in a democratic society'. That is, the intervention must be proportionate; a sledgehammer should not be used to crack a nut. For instance, if a supervision order under the Children Act 1989 would suffice to protect a child, a care order should not be granted because it would constitute disproportionate and unjustified interference in family life (*Re O*). However, the European Court held in one case that the decision to close an NHS unit for people with disabilities was both in accordance with the law (consultation etc) and proportionate; the person's welfare and interests had been properly considered before the decision (*Collins v United Kingdom*).

In another case, a decision was made not to allow a man detained under the Mental Health Act to dress as a woman. Amongst the reasons given were security (access to women's clothing might help other patients to escape) and therapeutic need (progress of treatment). The court found that private life was being interfered with under a.8(1) but that it reflected a pressing social need and was proportionate (*R v Ashworth Special Hospital Authority, ex p E*). And the random monitoring of telephone calls in a high security mental health hospital interfered certainly with patients' privacy but was justifiable in relation to security matters (*R v Ashworth Special Hospital Authority, ex p N*).

5.5.2.6 Justification of interference with right to respect (article 8): for a specified purpose

Assuming accordance with the law and proportionality, any interference must also be for a purpose specified under article 8.

For instance, one purpose listed is economic well-being of the country. Inevitably, this has arisen in community care, where most disputes seem ultimately to be about money or resources. Under community care legislation, a duty to meet to people's needs has only to be discharged in the most cost-effective manner, a principle that dovetails with the economic well-being of the country referred to in article 8.

The economic well-being of Walsall justified the local authority's decision to close a care home and place residents elsewhere (e.g. *R(Dudley) v East Sussex CC, R(Rowe) v Walsall MBC*). Closure of a day centre could be justified with reference to the economic well-being of Bromley (*R(Bishop) v Bromley LBC*). Similarly, the European Court has given countries a wide 'margin of appreciation' in how to allocate limited resources for welfare – for instance, when a man could not obtain an essential robotic arm for his wheelchair, to assist him carry out essential daily living tasks (*Sentges v Netherlands*).

Other purposes justifying interference are the protection of health and the protection of the rights and freedoms of others. Thus when the NHS wished to close an accommodation lodge for people with mental health problems, the courts stated that any rights under article 8 were inextricably bound up with the trust's obligation to provide medical care for the benefit of the claimants. Furthermore, the closure would benefit other members of the community to whom the trust owed a duty and who enjoyed the rights and freedoms that the trust had to respect (*R v Brent, Kensington and Chelsea and Westminster Mental Health NHS Trust, ex p C*).

Likewise when a health authority sought to close a purpose-built complex for people with learning disabilities, the European Court of Human Rights held that the decision to move one of the residents into alternative social care gave proper consideration to her interests and was supported by relevant and sufficient reasoning in relation to her welfare. Indeed the court declared the application inadmissible to advance to a full hearing (*Collins v UK*).

5.5.2.7 Discrimination (article 14)

Article 14 states that the Convention rights and freedoms should be enjoyed free from discrimination on any ground such as sex, race, colour, language, religion, political or other opinion, national or social origin, association with a national minority, property, birth or other status.

The list of grounds contained in the article fails to include explicitly age or disability. However, the grounds are illustrative only; therefore age and disability are implicit. However, a.14 cannot be argued in isolation. It must be argued with one of the other articles in the Convention; although breach of that other article is not necessary in order to establish a breach of a.14. The following case related to disability:

Medical treatment for a person lacking capacity to take particular decisions. An 18-year-old man had kidney failure and was receiving haemodialysis. The question arose as to whether in the future he should receive peritoneal dialysis or a kidney transplant. He had severe learning difficulties, was autistic, epileptic and had the mental capacity of a five- or six-year-old child.

The hospital sought a declaration from the courts that neither the transplant nor the peritoneal dialysis would be in the man's best interests. This would be because he would not be able to understand the purpose of the surgery, be prepared for it, be able to cope with it and be managed by hospital staff without undue distress to him and without undue difficulty. However, the parents disagreed with the hospital's view and there was also conflicting evidence given by the professionals involved.

In deciding what declaration to make, the court noted that it was crucial that the man did not get less satisfactory life-saving treatment simply because he did not understand it. Otherwise there would be a breach of both domestic and human rights legislation (*An Hospital Trust v S*).

Although the court did not refer explicitly to article 14 (linked with article 2, right to life), implicitly it was probably referring here to discrimination and to a.14.

In another case concerning the Mental Health Act 1983, the courts considered s.26 of the Mental Health Act 1983, which at the time referred to a person 'living with the patient as the patient's husband or wife' (part of the 'nearest relative' rules). The court held that, to be compliant with a.14 of the Convention, this should be interpreted to include homosexual partners (*R(SSG) v Liverpool City Council*).

5.5.3 HUMAN RIGHTS ACT NOT RESORTED TO

In some cases, the courts find that existing common law principles adequately protect people's rights, without resort to the Human Rights Act 1998. For instance, irrespective of human rights, closure of a care home could not survive such common law principles applied in judicial review, after it became clear that the local authority had not taken account of all relevant factors (including a promise of a home for life) when taking its decision (*R(Bodimeade) v Camden LBC*).

Likewise, when it was proposed that a man be given treatment against his will under the Mental Health Act 1983, the courts ruled that this was such a fundamental issue that the common law demanded that reasons be given by the 'second opinion appointed doctor' under the Act (*R(Wooder) v Feggetter*).

Before the implementation of the Human Rights Act, the courts referred to a common law of humanity when stating that asylum seekers could not be left to starve on the streets. They even referred back to an 1803 case (*R v Inhabitants of Eastbourne*) when the Lord Chief Justice had stated that in relation to maintaining poor foreigners (refugees from France) 'the law of humanity, which is anterior to all positive laws, obliges us to afford them relief, to save them from starving' (*R v Westminster CC, ex p A*: High Court).

5.6 DISABILITY DISCRIMINATION

The Disability Discrimination Act 1995 (DDA) is divided into various sections covering employment, the provision of goods and services, management of premises, education and public transport. The DDA sits alongside the Race Relations Act 1976 and the Sex Discrimination Act 1975. The government intends eventually to repeal all three Acts and subsume discrimination law into a single Equality Act. This will include age discrimination not only in relation to workplace discrimination (at present under the Employment Equality (Age) Regulations 1996), but also – for the first time – in respect of the provision of goods and services. The government has conceded that there is a 'significant amount of evidence that older people are treated in a discriminatory way by those providing goods and services, including health and social care' (Lord Privy Seal 2008, p.16). Given the arguably widespread discrimination against older people, this aspect of the proposed legislation is long overdue (Steel et al; Forder 2008).

5.6.1 DEFINITION OF DISABILITY

Disability is defined under the DDA 1995 as physical or mental impairment which has a substantial and long-term adverse effect on the person's ability to carry out normal day-to-day activities (s.1).

- **Mental impairment** does not have the same meaning as in the Mental Health Act 1983, but a mental impairment under the 1983 Act can be a mental impairment under the DDA (s.68).
- **Long-term** means that the disability must have lasted at least 12 months; is likely to last at least 12 months; or likely to last for the rest of the person's life (schedule 1).
- **Recurrence**. If an impairment ceases to have a substantial adverse effect on a person's ability to carry out normal day-to-day activities, it is to be deemed to continue to have that effect if it is likely to recur (schedule 1).
- **Normal day-to-day activities** are defined as mobility; manual dexterity; physical coordination; continence; ability to lift, carry or otherwise move everyday objects; speech, hearing or eyesight; memory or ability to concentrate, learn or understand; or perception of the risk of physical danger (schedule 1).
- **Substantial**. Guidance states that substantial means more than minor or trivial in effect (Secretary of State 1996).
- **Medical treatment, aids/equipment**. An impairment is still deemed to be such even if measures (including medical treatment, prostheses or other aids) treat or correct the impairment (except in the case of spectacles or contact lenses) (schedule 1).
- **Progressive conditions**. A person who has cancer, multiple sclerosis or HIV infection is deemed to be disabled. A progressive condition, for example cancer, MS, muscular dystrophy and HIV, is taken to be having a substantial effect, even if at present there is only an impairment which has an effect (but not a substantial adverse one) on the person's ability to carry out normal day-to-day activities (schedule 1, paras 6A and 8).
- **Future disabilities** are not covered (except where a progressive condition has begun to manifest itself) (schedule 1).
- **Past disabilities**. People who have had a disability in the past are covered (schedule 2).
- **People deemed disabled (in error)** are not covered (schedule 1).
- **Babies and young children**. If a child under six years old has an impairment which does not have an effect on normal day-to-day activities, the impairment will nevertheless be treated as having a substantial and long-term effect if it would normally have that effect on the ability of a child aged over six years (SI 1996/1455).
- **Severe disfigurement** is included (schedule 1), but not tattoos or non-medical body piercing (SI 1996/1455).
- **Addiction** to alcohol, nicotine or any other substance does not amount to an impairment – unless the addiction was originally the consequence of administration of medically prescribed drugs or treatment (SI 1996/1455).
- **Other exclusions**. Hayfever, tendency to start fires, tendency to steal, tendency to physical or sexual abuse, exhibitionism, voyeurism: however, hayfever can be taken into account if it aggravates the effect of another condition (SI 1996/1455).

5.6.2 PROVISION OF GOODS AND SERVICES TO THE PUBLIC

Providers of goods and services to the public must not discriminate against disabled people by refusing to provide, or not providing, a service that is provided to others, or providing it on worse terms or at a lower standard than it would be provided for others (DDA 1995, s.19).

They must also not discriminate by failing to make reasonable adjustments to practices, policies, procedures to or in respect of physical features – or failing to take reasonable steps to provide auxiliary aids or services. The result of this failure to make reasonable adjustments must be to make it impossible or unreasonably difficult for the disabled person to use the service (ss.20–21).

In one case the Home Office denied that it was providing services to the public in terms of the facilities provided at a detention centre for asylum seekers – namely, reception procedures, access to the toilet and bathroom facilities, access and egress from a room in the centre, suitable bedding and provision of medical services. The claimant was a wheelchair user, paralysed in both legs as a result of spinal injury. The Home Office argued that the case should be struck out, arguing that s.19 simply did not apply. The Court of Appeal held otherwise and remitted the case back to the county court for reconsideration (*Gichura v Home Office*).

5.6.2.1 Less favourable treatment

A provider of services discriminates by treating a person less favourably than others – on grounds relating to his or her disability – where that less favourable treatment cannot be justified. Thus, what would otherwise be discrimination in terms of less favourable treatment or failure to take reasonable steps is capable of being justified on particular grounds (s.20). Less favourable treatment could be in comparison with non-disabled people, or with people with other disabilities.

Wheelchair service at airport. An airline charged for assisting people at the airport to get from the check-in point to the flight at the gate who did not have their own wheelchair, whereas it did not charge people who were more disabled (and who did have their own wheelchair). The judge held that this constituted discrimination on the basis of different classes of disability. The fact that the 'more disabled' were treated more favourably was irrelevant (*Ross v Ryanair*).

When a blind man was turned away from a restaurant because he had a guide dog, he was treated less favourably for a reason (the dog) relating to his disability (*Purves v Joydisc Ltd*).

The alleged discrimination must be disability related. In a case involving local authority charging for non-residential services, the court held that disabled people were having to pay not because they were disabled but because they had the money to pay (*R v Powys CC, ex p Hambidge (no.2)*). In another case, NHS policy on blood product treatment for people with haemophilia rested on people's age or on their history of having had no previous treatment. The more desirable product – recombinant factor rather than plasma-based product – was available on these grounds. But these grounds were held not to relate to disability (*R(Longstaff) v Newcastle Primary Care Trust*).

5.6.2.2 Making reasonable adjustments

The duty to make adjustments applies when a provider has a practice, policy or procedure making it impossible or unreasonably difficult for disabled persons to use a service it provides to other members of the public. The provider has a duty to take steps that are reasonable in all the circumstances to change the policy, practice or procedure.

If a physical feature (e.g. in relation to the design or construction of a building or the approach or access to premises) makes it impossible or unreasonably difficult for disabled people to use the service, the provider has a duty to take steps that are reasonable, in all the circumstances, to (a) remove the feature; (b) alter it so it no longer has that effect; (c) provide a reasonable means of avoiding the feature; or (d) provide a reasonable alternative method of accessing the service.

Thus a failure to provide a wheelchair free of charge, for a person to use between an airport check-in desk and departure gate, constituted a failure to provide a reasonable alternative method of making a service available to the person (*Ross v Ryanair*). In the following case, the train company had failed to provide a reasonable alternative for a wheelchair user to change platforms at Thetford in Norfolk:

Providing a reasonable alternative to accessing a service. It was not possible for a disabled person to change platforms at a railway station, and the half-mile route by road was difficult and attended with risk. The railway company stated that he should travel on to another station, change there, and then return to the original station. This would add an hour to a 36-minute journey. The man argued that the company should instead provide him with a wheelchair-accessible taxi in order to change platforms.

The Court of Appeal agreed with the man, stating that the extra hour required to travel to the other station could not, on any fair view, be considered a reasonable alternative under s.21(2)(c) of the DDA. The court also noted that the policy of the Act was not a minimalist one; it was 'to provide access to a service as close as it is reasonably possible to get to the standard normally offered to the public at large' (*Roads v Central Trains*).

An auxiliary aid or service (e.g. information on audio-tape or a sign language interpreter) might enable disabled people to make use of a service or at least facilitate its use. If so, the provider has a duty to take steps that are in all the circumstances reasonable to provide that auxiliary aid or service (s.21). So, in the *Ryanair* case, the failure to provide the wheelchair free of charge at the airport meant that a disabled passenger was prevented from using the airport facilities and services which were useable by other people (either not disabled or with another type of disability). This was a breach of the duty to provide auxiliary aids (*Ross v Ryanair*).

5.6.2.3 Justifying less favourable treatment or not taking reasonable steps
Less favourable treatment, or the failure to take reasonable steps, can be justified on grounds of (a) health and safety; (b) the incapacity of the person to enter into a contract; (c) the service provider otherwise being unable to provide the service to the public; (d) enabling the service provider to provide the service to the disabled person or other members of the public; (e) a greater cost being applied to the service, because it reflects a greater cost to the provider (but not the costs incurred by making reasonable adjustments) (DDA 1995, s.20).

The justification can only be made out if the service provider believed that one of these defences applied, and that it was reasonable for the provider to believe this. However, if the defence is made out, then there is no discrimination under the Act.

Health and safety justification and inadequate risk assessment. When a school prevented a diabetic pupil from going on a school trip, on purported health and safety grounds relating to his diabetes, the court nevertheless found discrimination. This was because of a totally inadequate process of risk assessment that failed to involve either the pupil or his parents, the provider of the holiday or even to take account of the views of the pupil's consultant paediatrician (*White v Clitheroe Royal Grammar School*).

A health and safety justification failed in the county court, when the supermarket Tesco argued that, for health and safety reasons, its petrol station staff could not help a disabled woman check the air pressure of her tyres (*The Times* 2008). However, in respect of the letting of premises, a successful health and safety argument has been made by a landlord (*Rose v Bouchet*: see 16.4.1 below).

5.6.3 MANAGEMENT, LETTING ETC. OF PREMISES

The DDA contains a number of provisions affecting residential premises and possession orders (see 16.4), permission to carry out adaptations (16.7) and making reasonable adjustments including auxiliary aids and services (see 16.10).

5.6.4 EDUCATION

The Disability Discrimination Act 1995 applies to education at all levels.

In the case of further and higher education, there are duties on the bodies responsible for educational institutions. These must not discriminate by treating disabled students less favourably for a reason relating to their disability, or by failing to make reasonable adjustments so as to avoid putting disabled students at a substantial disadvantage (subject to justification).

Matters to which discrimination could apply include admission of students, terms on which admission offers are made, refusal or deliberate omission to accept application for admission or enrolment, provision of services, and exclusions. Discrimination means less favourable treatment for a reason relating to the disabled person's disability that cannot be justified. It also means failing to comply, without justification, with the duty to take reasonable steps under s.28T of the Act (to ensure that disabled people are not placed at a substantial disadvantage in terms of deciding admissions and of student services).

Justification can be made out if the less favourable treatment (a) is necessary to maintain academic standards or other prescribed standards; (b) is of a prescribed kind. Otherwise less, favourable treatment or a failure to comply with s.28T (reasonable steps) can only be justified if it is for a reason that is both material and substantial (DDA 1995, ss.28R–28T).

5.6.5 DISABILITY EQUALITY DUTY

Under s.49A of the DDA 1995, public bodies have a disability equality duty. They must have due regard to the need:

- to eliminate discrimination that is unlawful under the Act
- to eliminate harassment of disable people related to their disabilities
- to promote equality of opportunity between disabled people and other people

- to take steps to take account of people's disabilities, even if that means treating disabled people more favourably
- to encourage the participation of disabled people in public life.

This duty has come to the fore in both community care and NHS legal cases. When one local authority was making stricter its eligibility criteria for community care services, the s.49A duty was not drawn to the attention of councillors at two crucial meetings. The report under-pinning the changes did not mention what measures could be taken to avoid disadvantaging disabled people. There was nothing in writing. The decision was therefore unlawful and would have to be retaken (*R(Chavda) v Harrow LBC*). And when the National Institute for Clinical Excellence issued guidance about the use of certain drugs for people with Alzheimer's disease, the courts held it had failed to take account of its duties under s.49A of the DDA (*Eisai Ltd v National Institute for Health and Clinical Excellence*).

5.6.6 RELATIONSHIP OF DDA TO OTHER LEGISLATION

Nothing in the DDA makes unlawful any act done in pursuance of another piece of legisla-tion or an instrument made under another piece of legislation (DDA 1995, s.59). This would mean that if the inevitable implication of other legislation were to be discrimination, it would not be unlawful. However, the courts will be slow to find that legislation demands discrimination:

Requirements not prescribed by legislation, so not immune from discrimination chal-lenge. The Department of Education and Science imposed certain requirements in relation to grant-ing a Hong Kong Chinese-trained teacher teaching status in this country. The requirements imposed however were not prescribed by legislation; they were based on administrative practice and discre-tion. They were not therefore automatically protected from being discriminatory under the Race Re-lations Act 1976 (*Hampson v Department of Education and Science*).

PART II

Social services assessment and provision of services

CHAPTER 6

Social services assessment: referral and eligibility

KEY POINTS

This chapter considers the legal underpinning to referral, assessment, and decisions about community care services as made by local social services authorities. It covers access to the assessment process, how referrals are 'screened' by local authorities, the making of priorities in terms of how quickly assessment will be performed, the depth and scope of assessment, and decisions about eligibility for services.

It is at such pivotal points in the assessment process that local authorities are routinely forced to explore and exploit the uncertainties inherent in the community care system and outlined in Chapter 3. They do this in order to limit expenditure and to find escape routes from their potential obligations imposed by law and inflated by the aspiration of central government policy and guidance. The emphasis since 1993 on the process of assessment in both legislation and copious government guidance has been Janus-faced. On the one hand, it has resulted in a focus on good practice in assessment; on the other, it has opened the door to more systematic and formal rationing of services.

ACCESS TO ASSESSMENT

The NHS and Community Care Act 1990 makes assessment a duty and a service in its own right. Assessment is pivotal to the provision of community care services, including both residential and non-residential care services (see Chapters 9 and 11). Access to it is crucial. A number of considerations control who will be assessed, when they will be assessed and what sort of assessment they will get.

The legislation states that a local authority has first to decide whether a person appears to be in possible need of community care services; if the answer is affirmative, there is a duty to assess, if negative, there is none. Having carried out the assessment, the local authority has a duty to decide whether the person's needs call for services.

If, during the assessment, it appears to the authority that the person is disabled then the authority must specifically decide about what services are required under s.2 of the Chronically Sick and Disabled Persons Act 1970.

SCREENING AND ACCESS TO ASSESSMENT

In order to determine who is eligible for an assessment, how quickly they should be assessed and what type of assessment they will get, local authorities operate screening procedures. Such screening is not legally prescribed, but in practice it acts as a potent filter. It can determine what happens to people, and is a tool used by authorities to regulate their responses to the demands made on them. Screening is a shadowy area of activity and occupies a key position amongst the uncertainties identified in Chapter 3 of this book.

The courts have stated that local authorities should set a low threshold for access to assessment, that in any case they should not take account of resources when setting that threshold – and that it is irrelevant that a person is ultimately unlikely to qualify for services, since assessment is a benefit and duty in its own right. The local government ombudsmen, too, emphasise the importance of adequate information-gathering at the screening stage, since otherwise local authorities are simply not in a position to make competent judgements about need and priority for assessment.

In addition, under s.4 of the Disabled Persons (Services, Consultation and Representation) Act 1986, local authorities continue to have a freestanding duty, on the request of a disabled person or carer, to make a decision about services under the Chronically Sick and Disabled Persons Act 1970; in other words, they cannot refuse disabled people some sort of an assessment.

ASSESSMENT OF NEED AND DUTY TO MEET NEED

The concept of need goes to the heart of community care assessment. If a person is not acknowledged by a local authority to have a need that calls for or necessitates provision, then he or she will not get any services. Local authorities in England are obliged to follow central government guidance on 'fair access to care', and to assess people's needs in terms of risks to their independence.

The law courts have confirmed that when local authorities set policy and criteria of eligibility, they can take account of their limited resources when deciding whether it is necessary to meet assessed needs. On this basis authorities can also formally alter their threshold of eligibility from time to time. Consequently, people's assessed needs and the services they receive can fluctuate not just according to their own changing conditions and circumstances, but also as a result of the changing financial situation and policies of local authorities. This can lead over time, in any one local authority, to the application of more stringent tests of eligibility for both existing users and potential new users of services. Removal or reduction of services may or not may be lawful; it all depends on the process underpinning the decision.

The Department of Health guidance on fair access to care states that local authorities should set a threshold of eligibility, the restrictiveness of which will depend on the local resources available. That is, the fewer resources, so the higher the threshold should be set. Over last two years, the trend across local authorities in England has been remorseless; thresholds have been creeping higher and higher, thus restricting community care services to ever fewer people. There is now some unease about the implications of this; the Commission for Social Care Inspection has warned that the dignity, welfare and quality of life older people is being seriously undermined.

If thresholds of eligibility are not set realistically in relation to allocated resources, they might allow too many people to qualify for services and strain budgets to breaking point. Local authorities then attempt to execute shortcuts that run the risk of being unlawful, in order to avoid onerous obligations.

Nonetheless, once a local authority has set its threshold for a period of time, then the local authority has a duty to meet a person's needs insofar as they are assessed to come over the threshold. This is an absolute duty and a lack of resources is no defence. However, if there is more than one option available, then the local authority is obliged only to offer the cheapest – so long as that option will genuinely meet the assessed, eligible needs.

SELF-ASSESSMENT

At the time of writing, central government is introducing a new policy in social care, referred to as self-directed care involving individual or personal budgets (see Chapter 13). Part of this involves local authorities encouraging self-assessment, that is, for people to assess their own needs. What is meant exactly by self-assessment is, at the time of writing, not entirely clear largely because of the absence of any legislation or definitive guidance.

However, there may be some uncertainty as to how self-assessment fits exactly into the existing community care legislation and guidance, especially if service users, rather than the local authority, are in some sense to have the last word about their needs and the services required to meet them. The legislation does not allow this.

6.1 OVERALL DUTY OF ASSESSMENT

Local authority social services departments assess people aged 18 years or over under s.47 of the NHS and Community Care Act 1990. In order to gain services set out in other legislation, people need to 'get through' this assessment process, which therefore serves as a gateway. In summary, section 47 of the 1990 Act is as follows:

- **Main duty of assessment**. If it appears to a local authority that a person, for whom it may provide or arrange for the provision of community care services, may be in need of any such services, then:
  - it must carry out an assessment of his or her needs for those services
  - having regard to the results of that assessment, the authority must decide whether his or her needs call for the provision by the local authority of any such services (s.47(1)).
- **Disabled people**. If, during the assessment, it appears that the person is disabled, then:
  - the local authority must take a decision as to whether he or she requires the services mentioned in s.4 of the Disabled Persons (Services, Consultation and Representation) Act 1986 (in effect services under s.2 of the Chronically Sick and Disabled Persons Act 1970)
  - the authority must inform the person about what it is doing and of his or her rights under the 1986 Act (s.47(2)).
- **Assistance from the NHS or housing authority**. If, during the assessment, it appears to the local authority that the person may need health services under the NHS Act 1977 from a health authority or NHS primary care trust (PCT) or from a housing authority (that is not the social services authority carrying out the assessment), then:
  - the local authority must invite the PCT, health authority or housing authority to assist in the assessment, to such extent as is reasonable in the circumstances
  - in making its decision as to what services the person needs, the local authority must take into account any services likely to be made available by the PCT, health authority or housing authority (s.47(3)).
- **Urgency**. Nothing prevents a local authority from temporarily providing or arranging for the provision of community care services for any person, without carrying out a prior assessment, if the authority is of the opinion that the person requires those services as a

matter of urgency; in which case, the local authority must carry out an assessment as soon as practicable (s.47(5,6)).

6.1.1 TRIGGERING THE OF DUTY OF ASSESSMENT

The duty to assess is triggered if it appears to the local authority that a person for whom it may provide community care services may be in need of such services (NHS and Community Care Act 1990, s.47). The duty is not dependent on a request by the person; it is triggered by the appearance in some way, to the local authority, of possible need. Clearly if a person refused an assessment, the local authority may have difficulty in carrying out an effective assessment. Nonetheless, the authority arguably has to make reasonable efforts.

The duty is not absolute, but has been held by the courts to be a strong one. They have stated that the duty is set at a low threshold; furthermore the state of the local authority's resources is not relevant:

Assessment of person reporting anxiety and depression. A 52-year-old woman suffered from anxiety and depression. She was unintentionally homeless, but had rejected an offer of accommodation under the Housing Act 1996, and sought an assessment and provision of accommodation from social services. Social services refused to assess, partly on the basis that it would be futile and a poor use of resources to do so, where there was no hope of meeting the need.

The court rejected this approach, stating that resources were irrelevant to the duty to assess, that the threshold for entitlement to assessment was very low, and that in any case assessment served a useful purpose even if services did not follow (*R v Bristol CC, ex p Penfold*).

The courts have also held that the duty to assess arises even if a local authority knows that it would only ever have a power rather than a duty to provide services for the person – and even if those services were anyway not physically available within the area of the local authority.

Assessment of a person not ordinarily resident. A seriously disabled man suffering from viral brain damage and epilepsy was resident at the British Home and Hospital for Incurables. His mother, through solicitors, requested that a local authority assess his needs, because she felt he needed different types and levels of care than he was receiving at the hospital. The local authority argued that he was not ordinarily resident in its area, that therefore it had only a power to provide services under s.29 of the National Assistance Act 1948, and that anyway the services in question were not physically available in its area. Thus, it had no duty to assess.

The court rejected the authority's argument, pointing out that the duty of assessment hinged not on a factual capacity to provide services but on a legal capacity (*R v Berkshire CC, ex p Parker*).

Despite legal cases such as the above, local authorities still fail to assess people's potential needs, on the ground that they will probably not be eligible for services. Typically, such a refusal concerns cleaning and shopping needs, as picked up by the local government ombudsman in the following case:

Failure to assess for cleaning and shopping needs. A woman suffered from severe health problems: sarcoidosis, extensive fibrosis of the lungs, chronic obstructive airways disease, atrial fibrillation, epilepsy and a learning disability and a heart problem. The slightest exertion made her breathless. Twice she and her husband requested assistance with cleaning and shopping, but the council did not assess her needs. Instead it had a policy of not providing cleaning and shopping services; it referred her to an independent company. In effect, the woman and her husband had been screened out.

The local ombudsman found maladministration, since the council had failed to carry out an assessment, and it could not lawfully delegate its duty to assess to an independent provider. Furthermore, the ombudsman noted that Department of Health guidance reinforces the legal position that the duty of assessment depends on potential need, and not on the service requested (*Salford CC 2003*).

Sometimes the failure is more haphazard:

Informality with man with mild learning disabilities. A man with mild learning disabilities got 'lost in the system' because of the informal way his long-term social worker had managed his case, without a formal recorded assessment. For a lengthy period he became nobody's responsibility, his mother's efforts gained no response, and he was not even told when the social worker left the council. This was maladministration. His circumstances deteriorated in relation to his drug-taking 'friends' and his ability to clean his flat and prevent damage. He then abandoned his tenancy (previously the social worker had helped prevent him being evicted) (*Derbyshire CC 2001*).

An assessment may not be a full one and so be maladministration:

Lack of full assessment. Over a period of six years, the local authority failed properly to assess the needs of a girl/woman who had multiple and profound mental and physical disabilities. However, it had assessed a need for weekend respite care to be provided at a care home; but when the charity that provided this care was forced to close the home on Sundays, the local authority stated that it could not be held responsible for this effective withdrawal of service. It did not respond with a formal reassessment that would have had to conclude that either there was no longer a need, or that it was in breach of its duty. Instead it simply denied its commitment to the family. The local ombudsman found maladministration (*North Yorkshire CC 2002*).

In another case, the Court of Appeal found a local authority's decision manifestly flawed; it had simply acted on the defective recommendations of a local continuing care panel, the function of which was anyway advisory only. The local authority should have cured the defects by itself taking a fully informed decision (*R(Goldsmith) v Wandsworth LBC*). In some instances, councils appear to go out of their way not to assess people:

Failure to assess person with Asperger's syndrome. A man with Asperger's syndrome was living in a residential hostel and should have been assessed for adult services by the time he was 17 and a half years old. This did not happen. Furthermore, once he was 18 years old and a complaint had been made, still no assessment was carried out. This was despite an assessment having been agreed by a senior manager dealing with the initial stage of the complaint, then recommended by an independent investigating officer, and finally required by the review panel. Still it did not happen.

In the meantime, he had been placed as an adult in supported lodgings. However, the lack of assessment, together with a failure to give the landlady more information about his behaviour and failure to review quarterly his progress, was maladministration. The landlady, who was the complainant, contended that she was not just providing supported lodgings but a care package, such was her input into the man's care, and that she should be paid accordingly. The council refused and stated that she could have ceased to provide lodgings for him at any time.

The ombudsman found this to be an 'extraordinary' argument, given that the man was particularly vulnerable, had already experienced one 'failed' hostel placement, and would have lost the accommodation and a supportive relationship which at least two professionals had assessed was highly beneficial to him. Furthermore, the council would then have had to find a suitable alternative at short notice, using staff and financial resources that appeared to be in short supply. The ombudsman found the delay in making increased payment to the landlady was 'completely unacceptable', and that the system had probably failed others in her position. The ombudsman found serious failings which may have been symptomatic of inherent weaknesses in the system. This was maladministration.

She recommended that the council reimburse the landlady from the man's 18th birthday onward, the difference between the supported lodgings rate and a care package rate – and anyway pay her immediately £5000 on account, of which £1000 was to recognise the time and trouble relating to the complaint. She also recommended that the council consider the action required on various matters: to ensure that assessments for care leavers were completed by the age of 17 and a half years with care packages in place by the time they were 18, to ensure seamless transition from children's to adult services, to ensure that recommendations of independent investigating officers and review panels were recorded, monitored and acted upon, to ensure reviews of individual cases were conducted in appropriate timescales, and to ensure payments to supported lodgings providers were made promptly and reliably (*Birmingham CC 2006*).

A failure adequately to assess can typically lead to a catalogue of woe and maladministration:

Failure to assess leading to catalogue of maladministration. The failure to carry out a detailed risk assessment for an autistic man with fragile X syndrome, on transfer from children's to adult services – together with a lack of respite facilities for autistic young adults – led to a catalogue of maladministration.

This included a lack of precision about how often he needed respite care, a serious assault on a residential social worker who went on long-term sick leave and ultimately left his job, failure to warn the parents that he was about to be excluded from the respite facility he was attending, unreasonable exclusion without making suitable, alternative arrangements, failure to have developed exclusion criteria, failure to refer the exclusion to the Learning Disability Partnership Board, and failure to provide for assessed respite needs for a period of about 15 months (as opposed to a period of three months which might have been acceptable following exclusion) – and failure to arrange the required respite care following the conclusion and recommendations of both the formal and review panel stages of the complaints procedure.

The upshot was that the man did not receive respite care to which he was entitled (a total of 67 days of day care and 30 days of overnight respite). He became bored and withdrawn, which was very damaging to him. His parents had no respite and this caused stress, anxiety and health problems (*Stockton-on-Tees BC 2005*).

6.1.1.1 *Future needs and the triggering of the duty to assess*
The question of whether a local authority is obliged to assess future needs sometimes arises.

In *R v Bristol CC, ex p Penfold*, the court stated that although the National Assistance Act 1948 was couched in the present tense, nevertheless 'imminent events' such as eviction 'must fall for consideration'. Similarly, in *R v Westminster CC, ex p A and in R v Newham LBC, ex p Gorenkin*, the courts referred to the need for local authorities to anticipate reasonably the point at which asylum seekers would come to be in need of care and attention under s.21 of the National Assistance Act 1948. And the local ombudsman has found maladministration when one of the reasons cited by the council for failing to assess a school-leaver was that a full assessment could not be undertaken until the person was in the community. Yet this meant that appropriately supported living was not arranged when he left school (*Knowsley MBC 1997*).

The courts have held that a local authority comes under a duty to assess in case of a deferred conditional discharge under the Mental Health Act 1983, where s.117 services are in clear prospect (*R(B) v Camden LBC*). It has been suggested that the same principle would apply to prisoners before release, but when the release date is known. It has also been argued that, even before release is imminent, a local authority might be obliged to assess a prisoner if he or she has community care needs while in prison (Bowen 2008).

6.1.1.2 Duty to assess and the resources of the person being assessed

The level of a person's resources, and eventual ability to fund their own services, are irrelevant to the local authority's duty to assess their needs. Department of Health guidance has been stating this ever since 1990. For instance, 'the assessment of financial means should...follow the assessment of need and decisions about service provision (DH 1990, para 3.31). More recently, guidance was just as unequivocal: 'an individual's financial circumstances should have no bearing on whether a council carries out a community care assessment. Nor should the individual's finances affect the level or detail of the assessment process' (LAC(2002)13, para 70). Yet still local authorities sometimes either decline to carry out an assessment or carry out a cursory one only, if they believe the person has adequate resources to fund their own care.

6.1.2 DIRECTIONS AND GUIDANCE ON ASSESSMENT

The 1990 Act gives the Secretary of State the power to issue directions about how assessments should be carried out (NHS and Community Care Act 1990, s.47). The Department of Health has issued such directions (DH 2004d):

- When assessing a person under s.47 of the 1990 Act, a local authority must consult the person being assessed, consider whether the person has any carers, and – if the local authority thinks it appropriate – consult those carers.
- The local authority must take all reasonable steps to reach agreement with the person and – if the local authority thinks it appropriate – with any carer, concerning any community care services it is considering providing.
- The local authority must provide information to the person and – if it thinks appropriate – to any carer, about the amount of any charge payable for the services.

These directions link directly to the plentiful guidance issued about involving service users (see 6.8) and informal carers (see 13.5.4) in assessment.

Nevertheless, in the light of this power (finally exercised in 2004) to issue directions on assessment, the courts suggested in one case that guidance on assessment – even statutory guidance made under s.7 of the Local Authority Social Services Act 1970 – is of limited value. It has only to be taken account of; this is because the legislation clearly envisages that it is directions rather than guidance that would carry real weight in determining how assessment is to be carried out (*R(B&H) v Hackney LBC*).

However, in many other cases, the courts have attached importance to policy guidance on assessment. Thus, *Community care in the next decade and beyond* (DH 1990), has been referred to and given weight many times. For example, this guidance underlay findings of breach statutory duty for failing to take account of a person's preferences (*R v North Yorkshire CC, ex p Hargreaves*) and failure in a care plan (*R v Islington LBC, ex p Rixon*). More recently, the court made extensive reference to, and appeared to place considerable weight on, 'fair access to care' guidance (LAC (2002)13), concerning the setting and application of eligibility criteria for the purpose of assessment (*R v Sheffield CC, ex p Heffernan*).

6.1.3 LOCAL AUTHORITY RESPONSIBILITY FOR ASSESSMENT DECISION

The local authority is identified in s.47 of the NHS and Community Care Act 1990 as responsible for assessment and the decision about services. Other than in the case of formally agreed joint working with the NHS (NHS Act 2006, s.75), the local authority must itself take these decisions. This would not preclude the local authority making use of assessment and expertise from another agency; but the final decision about both needs, and whether they call for services, must remain with the local authority.

The importance of this principle is recognised in 'fair access to care' guidance issued by the Department of Health. It stresses the importance of competent local authority staff carrying out reviews, rather than service providers – although the latter would have a useful contribution to make (LAC(2002)13, para 61). Likewise, policy guidance issued about the assessment of informal carers states that the local authorities could contract with another body to carry out part of the assessment process, but that assessment is a statutory function of the local authority, which means that it has to make the final decision. More, this final decision should not simply be a rubber-stamping of another body's view: 'it is not enough for the local authority to simply check on a complete or partial basis the outcomes of another organisation's assessments' (DH 2005, para 45).

Therefore, clarity is required as to who is formally responsible and authorised for carrying out the assessment and taking the final decision about services. In the following case, the court could only conclude that the local authority had not legally taken an assessment decision:

Who is authorised to make the decision about community care needs? A health authority occupational therapist (OT) recommended that an elderly couple should have installed either a vertical lift or a stairlift to give them ingress and egress from their first floor council flat. The recommendation was also backed by an 'advocacy officer' of the council. The recommended home adaptations were eventually refused by the housing department of the council on grounds of cost. The applicants claimed that having assessed the need, the council was obliged to meet it.

The judge decided that, in fact, the council had failed to carry out an assessment under s.47 of the NHS and Community Care Act 1990 and s.2 of the Chronically Sick and Disabled Persons Act. Confusingly for the service users, the statements of the advocacy officer, the care plan she had drawn up and the recommendation of the occupational therapist did not carry sufficient weight, since the provision of services was 'the concern of the council itself or of any committee or officer to whom a specific power is delegated'. The OT and the advocate were not authorised to carry out assessment and to decide about service provision. Thus, the judge found not that the authority was in breach of its statutory duty to provide the stairlift, but that it had been profiting from its failure to carry out the assessment (*R v Kirklees MBC, ex p Daykin*).

It is not wholly clear how self-directed care and self-assessment, in terms of individual budgets (see below and Chapter 13), will sit with the principle of the local authority having the final say and taking the overall decision.

6.1.4 COMMUNITY CARE SERVICES

Community care assessment concerns people's potential need for community care services. Such services are defined in s.46 of the NHS and Community Care Act 1990, by reference to other legislation. This consists of Part 3 of the National Assistance Act 1948, Chronically Sick and Disabled Persons Act 1970 (s.2), Health Services and Public Health Act 1968 (s.45), NHS Act 2006 (s.254 and schedule 20), and Mental Health Act 1983 (s.117). This legislation covers a wide range of non-residential and residential services (see Chapters 9 and 11).

6.2 DUTY TO ASSESS DISABLED PEOPLE

If during the s.47 assessment it appears to the local authority that the person is disabled, the authority has a duty to make a decision as to whether services referred to in s.4 of the Disabled Persons (Services, Consultation and Representation) Act 1986 are required. The services referred to in the 1986 Act are those listed in s.2 of the Chronically Sick and Disabled Persons Act 1970.

This is going round the houses. However, if a local authority is somehow attempting to avoid this duty being triggered during the s.47 assessment, then s.4 of the 1986 Act anyway remains freestanding. In other words, under s.4, a disabled person (or his or carer) would seem able to make a freestanding request that a decision be made as to whether his or her needs call for any of the services contained in s.2 of the 1970 Act. The local authority then has a duty to comply with that request. In one case, a request for assistance by a mother in respect of her disabled child was accepted by the court as a request for a s.4 decision under the 1986 Act. It might not have been a formal request, but the court (and the local authority) had to look at the reality of the situation (*R v Bexley LBC, ex p B*). The 1986 Act was originally passed because some local authorities were reported as arguing, with some sophistry, that the Chronically Sick and Disabled Persons Act 1970 conferred an obligation to meet needs once those had been determined, but no obligation actually to assess or determine those needs in the first place (*Hansard* 1986).

Local authorities will inevitably make priorities in terms of how quickly they assess people (see 7.4). However, this strong duty of assessment does not mean that disabled people with a less urgent, lower priority can simply be ignored – as the local ombudsman has pointed out:

Closing waiting lists for assessment: failure to assess disabled people. A local authority had long waiting lists for occupational therapy assessments. The ombudsman investigated the case of one woman who had had to wait 56 months for assessment. The problems were such that waiting lists were closed.

The ombudsman found serious failures and maladministration. He noted: 'The law makes no distinction between the Council's duty to make an assessment in "urgent" and "non-urgent" cases. Any disabled person is entitled to request an assessment and to expect that the request is met within a reasonable time. In my opinion the Council may be failing to discharge their duties under the Chronically Sick and Disabled Persons Act 1970, and I am concerned that they did not seek legal advice on this matter before the lists were closed… The majority of the service users are elderly people suffering from severe disabilities who may not be able to make repeated enquiries to find out whether the list has been reopened in their area. Many of these people may not approach the Social Services

Department a second time for assistance, and may continue to live in conditions of extreme discomfort and potential danger' (*Hackney LBC 1992*).

The following case illustrates how a local authority failed to assess, under the 1986 Act, a disabled woman's need for shelter for her powered outdoor wheelchair. It had effectively screened her out by means of a letter. For the local ombudsman this was maladministration:

Screening out a disabled person: failure to assess under the 1986 Act. A woman lived in a council house and received income support and mobility allowance. She was in poor health, had difficulty in walking and was entirely reliant on a neighbour to go shopping or to other facilities such as the local library. In order to alleviate these problems, she had bought an electric wheelchair but now required a shelter for it for protection against the weather and vandals. She had identified a prefabricated store costing £1000, and a charity had given her £600 towards the cost. She hoped to enter into an agreement with the supplier to pay the rest by instalment but was concerned that this financial commitment was beyond her means.

No record of assessment. The council had some years ago provided a hard-standing and pavement crossing for the woman when she still had a car (since given up). However, now it claimed that it had 'no budgetary provision' for storage facilities for wheelchairs. It further argued that no legal duty arose under s.2 of the Chronically Sick and Disabled Persons Act 1970 'in the absence of any suggestion of personal danger or serious inconvenience'. The council's files held no record of any assessment of the woman's need. The council wrote to the woman, stating that 'a request had been made for her needs to be assessed, but that from the information received she did not appear to meet the Council's criteria for a service and would not therefore receive a visit'. Enclosed with the letter was a copy of the council's criteria of eligibility; the letter did state that the woman should contact the council if she felt that she had missed out important details from her application.

Failure to make decision under 1986 Act. The ombudsman found maladministration. The council had made no assessment at the outset, and had then on reconsideration decided that she did not merit a visit (an assessment) because she did not meet the criteria it had sent her. Furthermore it had set out its criteria in an 'exhaustive list'. All this meant that the council was in breach of its duty to decide – on a request made under s.4 of the Disabled Persons (Services, Consultation and Representation) Act 1986 – whether services under s.2 of the Chronically Sick and Disabled Persons Act 1970 were needed (*Sheffield CC 1995*).

6.3 REFERRAL, SCREENING AND INITIAL ASSESSMENT

Given the demands made on them, local authorities adopt various types of screening procedures, in order to determine whether a particular person is eligible for assessment – and, if so, what priority should be accorded in terms of how quickly the assessment should be carried out. However this screening is carried out, it needs to be understood in the context of the statutory duty to carry out an assessment under s.47 of the NHS and Community Care 1990. Local authorities must in principle attempt to distinguish between (a) screening a person out from assessment altogether and (b) carrying out a simple assessment of a person and then explaining that he or she does not qualify for services because the need is deemed insufficiently high.

In the first case, people would be screened out because they do not appear to be in need of community care services. In the second, they would be potentially in need of community care services, and would then be assessed as coming beneath the authority's threshold of eligibility and so not be entitled to services. Since the threshold for assessment is low (*R v Bristol CC, ex p Penfold*), it is likely that many more people will fall into the second category than the first; that is, be eligible for some sort of assessment, even if they are probably not going to be eligible for services. The following court case exposed the dilemma for a local authority that wanted both to have its cake and eat it too:

Simple assessment or screening out? A local authority had been unable to make up its mind whether legally it should say that it had refused to carry out an assessment – or that it had carried out an assessment, albeit a simple, informal one. In the event, a letter written by the assessor, that it would have been preferable to maintain that an assessment had been carried out, gave the game away; the judge concluded that it had in fact not been carried out.

The judge added that, if he was wrong in this conclusion, then the authority had still acted unlawfully since any assessment it claimed to have carried out would have been in breach of policy guidance which talks of a comprehensive and flexible procedure able to determine appropriate responses to requests for assessment. The implications of this were that an assessment is directed at a particular person, and should fully explore need in relation to services which the authority has the legal power to supply (*R v Bristol CC, ex p Penfold*).

The local ombudsman, also, has found maladministration associated with an inadequate administrative system for screening out disabled people from obtaining access to home adaptations. The identified inadequacy was made worse by its indiscriminate application to both housing and social services legislation:

Self-completion questionnaires. When people applied for disabled facilities grants under the Housing Grants, Construction and Regeneration Act 1996, they were asked to complete a questionnaire; the application of priority points was based entirely on the replies. If a person was awarded fewer points than the threshold figure, the request was not considered further. Until the person reached that threshold (at a later date), he or she would not be seen by a professionally qualified assessment officer. The questionnaire replies were handled by an administrative assistant. This was maladministration.

However, the council was using the same system also to determine its potential responsibilities to people under the Chronically Sick and Disabled Persons Act 1970. There was no separate assessment in terms of social services responsibilities for adaptations. This too was maladministration (*Neath Port Talbot County BC 1999*).

The courts have not explicitly stated whether or not telephone assessments are unlawful. What they have said is that the simplicity or complexity assessment must be proportionate to the potential needs of the person (*R v Bristol CC, ex p Penfold*). Nevertheless, it is undeniable that the less and the more cursory the contact the local authority has with a person, the more likely it is to make a mistake:

Inadequacy of telephone. In one ombudsman investigation, concerns about the way in which 'first level assessment' operated in determining a person's priority led to a complaints review panel recommending that the referral form completed at this stage should be completed face to face and not just on the telephone (*Ealing LBC 1999*).

So, when councils implement policies and practices to assess ever more people on the telephone, they need to build in safeguards in order to avoid making the type of mistake that would put them in breach of their duty adequately to assess people. The Commission for Social Care Inspection has explicitly referred to this issue, especially since the screening role is now performed so frequently by non-professional staff. Safeguards might include study for national vocational qualifications, managerial supervision, regular meetings of team managers, joint training with professional staff and co-location of both screening and assessment staff (Henwood and Hudson 2007, p.60).

6.4 LEVEL OF ASSESSMENT

Central government guidance issued in 1991 refers to different levels of assessment, which would be applied in proportion to the apparent potential needs of people being referred. Six levels were suggested, ranging from the simple to the comprehensive (SSI/SWSG 1991, para 2.18).

More recent guidance has been issued by central government on what it refers to as 'single assessment' for older people. It too envisages different assessment levels, but this time suggests only four: contact, overview, specialist and comprehensive (HSC 2002/001). This latter guidance does not explicitly supersede the 1991 guidance.

Any such guidance on assessment nevertheless has to be implemented in the context of the legislation. A local authority must decide, in the case of a person clearly entitled to such an assessment, what level of assessment will reasonably satisfy this entitlement. Thus, the local ombudsman has criticised an over simple assessment, for a single service only, of a significantly disabled person:

Single service assessment not a proper assessment. A man who was an amputee, wheelchair user, diabetic and doubly incontinent received what the local authority called a 'single service' assessment for home help. He was not offered an assessment of his potential need for any other service. He subsequently received a further single service assessment for a special chair. The ombudsman concluded that the local authority had failed properly to assess him as it was legally obliged to do under s.4 of the Disabled Persons (Services, Consultation and Representation) Act 1986 and s.2 of the Chronically Sick and Disabled Persons Act 1970 (*Westminster CC 1996*).

6.4.1 SCREENING AND ALLOCATING PRIORITIES FOR ASSESSMENT

The local ombudsman has pointed out that if there is to be screening, then it needs to be of an adequate standard:

Screening and allocating priorities for assessment. In one local ombudsman case a disabled housing association tenant applied for disabled facilities grant. She needed to be assessed by social services in order that the recommendation could be made. She was placed on a waiting list of 549 people, of whom 111 were deemed to be a priority; the average wait was a year. The social services assessment officer conceded that identifying priority assessments was 'hit and miss' because application forms contained inadequate information on which to base the decision. This was maladministration (*Bolton MBC 1992*).

Likewise, failure to remedy poor referral information may result in an excessive wait and maladministration:

Improperly determined priority for a person suddenly blind. A woman suffered a sudden and complete loss of sight. She was referred to the sensory disability team. She was considered not to have a high priority and should have been contacted within six weeks; however, a rigid three-month waiting time was being operated. The local ombudsman investigated and found maladministration; in addition her priority had been improperly determined, since she had been at risk from burning and scalding and suffered injuries, which her doctor had seen. This had occurred because of the inadequacy of the original referral (based on a sparse report) and the failure of the sensory disability team to follow up subsequently with the woman what the issues and risks really were (*Stockport MBC 2003*).

In the following case, too, the ombudsman considered the adequacy of the referral process, in terms of the training and competence of a customer services officer:

Inadequate treatment of referral and competence of customer services officer. The father of a man who had a drinking problem and died subsequently of a heart attack complained that the local authority had not responded adequately to a request that his son be urgently visited. The ombudsman found that the customer services officer had been properly trained and was capable of reaching decisions about people's priority. Furthermore, although it could be argued that a trained social worker would be better placed to make such priorities, the council's wish to free its social workers for more urgent work was understandable. Nevertheless, the ombudsman found that the customer services officer who dealt initially with this referral did not give the request full and proper consideration. This was maladministration (*St Helens MBC 1998*).

Over-simple priorities or categories will also not do for the local ombudsman:

Over-simple system of priorities. A disabled child had to wait 15 months for new seating, including a 12-month wait for assessment. The assessment had been prioritised as complex, which meant that it was on a longer waiting list than existed for cases categorised as emergency or simple. The ombudsman concluded that the system of priorities was 'over-simple', because within the category of complex cases there was 'no provision for relatively simple solutions to tide people over until a full assessment' could be made. Furthermore, there was no provision for treating some cases more urgently within the 'complex' category, even though they were not emergency in nature. This oversimple system meant that the child's needs were not met promptly and was maladministration (*Rochdale MBC 1995*).

6.4.2 FORMALLY COMPLYING WITH DUTY OF ASSESSMENT

The courts will up to a point insist that the local authority complies formally, and is seen to comply, with duties of assessment and decisions about services in the correct logical order. This will be especially so if the shortcuts apparently taken in the assessment process lead to a misunderstanding of the legal questions that need to be asked before a final decision is made.

Asking questions in the right order. When deciding whether an autistic child qualified for a disabled facilities grant (see Chapter 16 in this book), the local authority should have first asked the question whether the proposed adaptation fell, in principle, within the purposes for which such a grant is mandatory (in this case the purpose of safety). Second, it then had to ask whether the adaptation would be 'necessary and appropriate' in respect of meeting need and minimising risk. Instead the local authority had stated that the works were not mandatory because they did not materially meet the child's needs. The court held that this was collapsing two questions into one and was consequently unlawful (*R(B) v Calderdale MBC*).

When a child in need was assessed under s.17 of the Children Act 1989, the care plan concluded that a package of support was required at home, rather than a residential placement. But the package of support was not identified in the care plan; this meant the decision was seriously flawed (*R(LH) v Lambeth LBC*). However, the courts will not always take this exacting approach if they think that in substance the assessment was performed adequately:

Ticking all the boxes: not always required. When a local authority offered care home accommodation to an elderly couple but not ordinary accommodation in the community, the court accepted that the local authority had not filled in every box on the assessment forms relating to unmet needs. However, in the context this did not indicate that it had failed to take account of those needs. In the particular situation, the reasons why only one option was offered was because this was the only reasonable option (*R(Khana) v Southwark LBC*).

Formal assessment: tidy-mindedness not the solution. In a case about housing for a family, the court dismissed the argument that – irrespective of the housing legislation – formal assessments should be carried out under the Chronically Sick and Disabled Persons Act 1970, the Children Act 1989 and the Carers (Recognition and Services) Act 1995. It 'did not accept that at all. There have been numerous assessments in this case... It may be that some are better than others. It may be that some do not explicitly state under what statute or statutes they have been made... The judge exercised his discretion properly...with eminent good sense, when he said that "What this lad needs and what his parents need is a new home"...any correction of a lack of formal assessment in the past would simply be a bit of tidy-minded putting the files in order and would not assist resolution of the real problem' (*R v Lambeth LBC, ex p A*).

Failure to go through the right steps: not fatal to a lawful assessment. A dispute arose about whether a 34-year-old man with severe epilepsy was entitled to have an adaptation for an upstairs lavatory, because of the danger of using the stairs. The local authority occupational therapist's report concluded that he did not qualify, because use of a commode at night would be appropriate, and because his able-bodied partner could empty the commode during the night. The court found that the local authority's assessment had not clearly followed the three-stage process demanded by the legislation, in terms of deciding whether the person might be in need of services, then assessing, then deciding whether needs call for services. The court accepted that there had been no 'formalistic' assessment, but was not minded to intervene since there was no prospect of the decision turning out any differently. This was because the council had in substance, if not in form, asked the right questions (*R v Sheffield CC, ex p Low*).

6.5 HEALTH AND HOUSING NEEDS IDENTIFIED DURING ASSESSMENT

If, during an assessment, it appears that the person may have health or housing needs, the local authority must invite the health authority, NHS primary care trust or housing authority (if different to the assessing social services authority) to participate in the assessment. The local authority must then take account of what the NHS or housing authority is likely to provide, when making its decision about what services the local social services authority should provide (NHS and Community Care Act 1990, s.47).

The courts have pointed out that local authorities should not be wary of this duty to identify housing needs, simply because they fear that they themselves may have ultimately to meet them – if the housing authority is unable or unwilling to. The courts will be slow to impose a duty on social services to provide ordinary housing (*R(Wahid) v Tower Hamlets LBC*), even though a duty may on occasion arise (see 9.2.1). There is in principle no reason why the local authority might not assess that it should provide community care support for a person, whilst also making a priority housing nomination under the Housing Act 1996. In which case, no community care duty will be incurred to arrange, directly, ordinary housing for the person (*R(Mooney) v Southwark LBC*). Indeed, a blatant failure to involve health or housing could be a breach of the s.47 duty. It might also undermine the possibility of a multi-disciplinary assessment and be maladministration (*North Yorkshire CC 2005*).

There is no explicit, specific duty either on the NHS or on the housing authority to respond to this invitation to assist in the assessment. Indeed the courts have pointed out that the implications of s.47 are precisely not that housing authorities are under a statutory obligation to cooperate (*R v Lewisham LBC, ex p Pinzon*). Even so, it is arguable that the social services decision must be reasonable, in terms of what the NHS or housing authority is likely to provide. The following case, though not concerning s.47 of the 1990 Act, exposes a case of unrealistic reliance by social services, on what a housing authority might do, in order to avoid even assessing, let alone providing services:

Unreasonably declining to assess. A seven-year-old autistic boy lived in temporary accommodation with his mother. The need for alternative accommodation had been recognised by the council, but there was no indication as to when it might be forthcoming. However, the social services department refused to assess, on the grounds that the family might move shortly. The court held that, given the uncertainty over any such move, the needs of the child and the burden on his mother, the local authority should carry out an assessment under the Carers and Disabled Children Act 2000 and s.17 of the Children Act 1989 (*R(J) v Newham LBC*).

6.5.1 DECISION ABOUT NURSING HOME CARE

Before a local authority decides to a place a person in a nursing home (ie a care home providing nursing), it must first gain the consent of the primary care trust (National Assistance Act 1948, s.26(1C). However, the converse is not necessarily the case. That is, the local authority does not have to gain consent in order not to place a person in a nursing home. For instance, in one legal case, the Court of Appeal in effect preferred the assessment of a social worker that an elderly woman did not need care in a nursing home – to the assessment of health care staff that she did (*R(Goldsmith) v Wandsworth LBC*).

6.6 URGENCY

If a person's needs are perceived to be urgent, the local authority may provide services on a temporary basis before carrying out an assessment. If it does so, it should then carry out an assessment as soon as practicable (NHS and Community Care Act 1990, s.47). The courts have confirmed the meaning of this reference to urgency:

Urgent provision of temporary accommodation. The claimant was an asylum seeker, destitute and suffering from hepatitis B. The local authority argued that it had no power to provide accommodation under s.21 of the National Assistance Act 1948 until it had carried out a s.47 assessment. The court held that there was a strong case for arguing breach of duty, in the light of the terms of s.47(5). Also, as originally enacted, s.21 of the National Assistance Act 1948 did not require that an assessment take place before temporary accommodation is provided and gave local authorities an unfettered power to provide such. Far from introducing the need for assessment, s.47(5) merely confirmed it was not required (*R(AA) v Lambeth LBC*).

6.7 NEEDS CALLING FOR SERVICE PROVISION

Having carried out an assessment, the local authority must decide whether the assessed needs call for provision of services by it (NHS and Community Care Act 1990, s.47). Logically, this clearly implies that some needs may call for services, whilst others may not. There are three main categories of assessed need that will not call for services.

The first category comprises needs that might readily be met by another statutory body such as the NHS or a housing authority. For instance, some needs may occupy a 'grey area' such that they may legitimately be classed as relating to social care, housing or health care. In such circumstances, if another organisation meets the need, there is clearly no call on the local social services authority to do so. One such example would be where a housing authority will meet a person's needs for a home adaptation by providing a disabled facilities grant under the Housing Grants, Construction and Regeneration Act 1996 (see 16.5). In which case, social services may not be called on directly to assist with the adaptation under the Chronically Sick and Disabled Persons Act 1970.

The second category relates to community care services, which the local authority has a power, but no duty, to provide. In this case, the local authority would not be obliged to provide such services, and therefore could conclude that the assessed needs do not call for services. For instance, certain services for older people falling under s.45 of the Health Services and Public Health Act 1968 (see below) entail only a power but no duty (see 11.3).

Even some of the duties within community care legislation are of the weaker, 'target', rather than the individual or specific, type (see 5.1.6); in which case enforcing provision may be problematic. For instance, duties to provide welfare services for disabled people under s.29 of the National Assistance Act 1948 (see 5.1.1) have been so characterised. The individual duty of assessment under s.47 of the NHS and Community Care Act 1990 – which overlays s.29 of the 1948 Act – has been held not to transmute the generality of the s.29 duty into a more specific, individual, enforceable one (*R v Islington LBC, ex p Rixon*). A little unhelpfully, central government guidance on 'fair access to care' (LAC(2002)13: see below) does not acknowledge these distinctions within community care legislation, let alone consider the implications.

The third category comprises those needs that are assessed as coming beneath the local authority's threshold of eligibility 6.10 and 6.12 below); in which case they will in principle be deemed not to call for services.

6.8 ASSESSMENT OF PREFERENCES AS OPPOSED TO NEEDS

A decision as to whether a person's needs satisfy the threshold of eligibility presupposes that the person has needs. It is the word 'need' that potentially triggers a duty. A mere preference will not do. The courts have identified the important distinction:

Need or preference? A local authority disputed whether a young man with learning disabilities really needed to go to a more expensive care home; it maintained that a cheaper one would be adequate to meet his needs. Thus, it argued, the more expensive home represented a mere preference. However, on the facts of the case, the judge held that the overwhelming evidence (through expert views given to a complaints review panel) was that going to the more expensive home constituted a psychological need, not just a preference. The more expensive cost would therefore 'simply be paying what the law required' (*R v Avon CC, ex p M*).

Likewise, the court found on the assessment evidence that the need of a man with mental health problems – for accommodation in a street house in a residential street, rather than in a flat in a large housing estate – constituted a need, not a preference (*R v Richmond LBC, ex p H*).

A person's preferences may coincide with what the local authority recognises as a need. In principle, this ought to be a not uncommon occurrence, since a whole range of guidance from central government states the importance of placing the individual person and their views at the centre of the assessment. This includes community care policy guidance (DH 1990, para 3.16), guidance on the 'single assessment process' for older people (HSC 2001/001, annex A), and guidance on 'fair access to care' and eligibility criteria (LAC(2002)13, para 35). Furthermore, to enable people to participate in assessments, local authorities should take 'positive steps' in respect of the communication difficulties faced by people with sensory impairments, mental incapacity or other disabilities (DH 1990, para 3.21).

The local authority has only to show that it has taken full account of a person's preferences, not necessarily that it has followed them:

Unlawfully not taking account of preferences. When assessing a woman with learning disabilities for respite care, the social worker had failed to obtain the views of the woman herself but only spoken with her brother. This breached Department of Health policy guidance (DH 1990, paras 3.16, 3.25) to the effect that preferences be taken account of. The court held that the assessment was therefore unlawful (*R v North Yorkshire CC, ex p Hargreaves*).

It is the local authority, rather than service user, that has the final say, since the legislation refers explicitly throughout to decisions being the local authority's responsibility. Department of Health guidance makes this very point when it states that, having weighed the views of the relevant parties, it is the assessing local authority practitioner who is responsible for defining a person's needs (SSI/SWSG 1991, para 3.35). More recent guidance states that, in case of disagreement, the matter should be handled sensitively, safeguarding the best interests of both the service user and carer; and that in many cases it might be appropriate for a solution to be sought through independent or statutory advocacy (LAC(2004)24, para 2.4).

It is not wholly clear how self-directed care and self-assessment, in terms of individual budgets (see 6.15 below and 13.2), will sit with this principle.

6.9 UNMET NEED

There can in principle be no unmet, eligible need. In other words, if a need is assessed by the local authority as coming above its threshold of eligibility, then the need must be met within a reasonable period of time (*R v Gloucestershire CC, ex p Barry*).

First, true unmet need is non-eligible need; that is, need coming beneath the eligibility threshold. Thus those local authorities that instruct their staff not to mention the term 'unmet need' in any circumstances, for fear of the legal consequences, labour under a misapprehension. Indeed, Department of Health practice guidance has always stated that unmet need should be referred to in care plans (SSI/SWSG 1991, para 4.37).

Second, it is nevertheless sometimes the case that the service required to meet an eligible need is simply not available, however much money the local authority is prepared to spend. In which case, unmet eligible need arises. In such circumstances, the courts (and the local ombudsmen) do not demand miracles, but they will expect all reasonable efforts to be made to arrange the service. Therefore, allowing a situation to drift will not do, as the four following examples illustrate:

Lack of recreational facilities. A severely disabled man was assessed as needing to access recreational facilities. Such facilities were unavailable. However, the court found that the local authority had appeared simply to take the existing unavailability of such facilities as an insuperable obstacle to further attempts to provide. The lack of a day centre had been treated, however reluctantly, as a complete answer to the question of provision (R v Islington LBC, ex p Rixon).

Inadequate respite care. A woman with severe mental and physical disabilities received respite care; her parents complained to the local ombudsman about the care she received, including injuries suffered. The local authority had only one respite house available for women in the north of the city. This had no ground floor bathing facilities, and was still being adapted 21 months into use; and reliance was being placed on staff from an agency about which doubts had been expressed by council officers. The facilities were unsatisfactory; this constituted maladministration (Manchester CC 1996a).

Inadequate day services. The complainants to the local ombudsman claimed that the council had failed to assess, and to make adequate day care provision, for the needs of their physically disabled, 25-year-old son. The ombudsman found that the council had 'failed properly to investigate and put in place adequate day provision'. It had not seriously explored the possibility of day services outside the district – indeed it had no policy on the funding of such services, despite recognition that provision for young disabled people was very limited within its own area. Eventually, it was the parents who arranged attendance for their son at a suitable centre. This was maladministration (Trafford MBC 1996).

Lack of respite facilities for autistic young adults. Lack of respite facilities for autistic young adults meant that young adults had to be placed in other areas (away from family) and that 'choice', a key principle of the local disability partnership board did not exist. The local ombudsman found maladministration (Stockton-on-Tees BC 2005).

On the other hand, the courts have held that a local authority may legally be entitled to refuse to provide a service, if that service would be fundamentally unsafe:

Refusal to provide accommodation for released prisoner. A local authority refused to make arrangements for residential accommodation for a person being released from prison. He had been assessed as being at extremely high risk of violent reoffending. His psychopathic disorder was not treatable and so he could not be admitted under s.47 of the Mental Health Act 1983 as a secure patient; he had a need for 'high secure' accommodation.

The local authority attempted to find such accommodation throughout the country but hospitals would not admit him unless he was sectioned under s.47 of the 1983 Act. It argued that it was under no statutory obligation to meet the man's needs by any other means, because less secure accommodation would likely create danger both for the man and other people. The man brought a case arguing breach of s.21 of the National Assistance Act 1948; the court rejected his application, and agreed that no obligation arose under s.21 (R v Swindon BC, ex p Stoddard).

Third, local authority staff sometimes refer to an additional category of unmet need. This occurs when a person is assessed as having eligible needs, the required services are available locally, but the local authority delays provision for financial reasons. In effect this relates to the question of waiting times for services (see section 8.5).

6.10 ABSOLUTE DUTY TO MEET ELIGIBLE NEEDS

The courts have ruled that if a person's need for community care services is assessed as coming above a local authority's eligibility threshold, then the need must be met, irrespective of the local authority's resources. This is therefore an 'absolute' or enforceable duty (*R v Gloucestershire CC, ex p Barry*).

However, such a duty is in principle triggered only if the needs and services relate to certain legislation. This comprises s.2 of the Chronically Sick and Disabled Persons Act 1970 (non-residential services), the duties as opposed to the powers under s.21 of the National Assistance Act 1948 (residential accommodation), and s.117 of the Mental Health Act 1983. The courts have specifically confirmed the existence of such a duty in relation to this legislation (*R v Gloucestershire CC, ex p Barry; R v Sefton MBC, ex p Help the Aged; R v Kensington and Chelsea RB, ex p Kujtim*).

Significance of identifying community care needs in a care plan. A local authority assessed a person (with a family) with significant mental health problems. It stated in his care plan that he required spacious, secure, ground-floor accommodation. The social services department of the authority had hoped that the housing department of the same authority would meet this need under the Housing Act 1996. However, the family had to wait a considerable length of time on the housing register. The court held in effect that if the housing department could not meet such needs, then the social services department would have to. This was because the need for accommodation was an assessed need and had been included in the care plan as a community care need; this gave rise to a duty under s.21 of the National Assistance Act 1948 (*R(Batantu) v Islington LBC*).

For fear of unlawful practices being exposed, some local authority managers instruct their staff to conceal the true reason for not providing services. For instance, in some local authorities it is impressed upon staff that they must not use the terms 'waiting lists' or 'resources', even if these are the real reasons for delay or non-provision. However, despite such instructions, all too often staff still let slip the true explanation – referring not, as should be the case, to a person's assessed need being judged to come below the threshold of eligibility, but instead to resources and financial crisis. Such explanations will sometimes be indicative of unlawful decision-making – for instance, if a person's assessed, eligible need is not going to be met, or if no proper assessment has taken place about whether the person has an eligible need.

Refusing to provide services in the 'financial freeze'. A complaint was made to the local ombudsman that when a man with HIV/AIDS had requested a telephone, his request was refused on the basis that he lived with a carer and that he could use the caretaker's telephone (despite a past breach of confidence by the caretaker). However, the social worker conceded that she had referred to the lack of resources as a significant reason for the refusal and to the 'freeze' until the next financial year. The council also later confirmed that its telephone budget had been spent. In the interim, the man's carer installed a telephone at his own expense. This was maladministration since it confused funding with need (*Salford CC 1996*).

Similarly, in another case, a reduction in service to people with learning disabilities appeared to the local ombudsman to have been taken, in the language of the case notes, purely on grounds of resources – rather than by a proper consideration of individual need. This was maladministration (*Derbyshire CC 2004*).

6.10.1 VARYING THE THRESHOLD OF ELIGIBILITY

The courts have ruled, in the context of s.2 of the Chronically Sick and Disabled Persons Act 1970 that the threshold of eligibility can lawfully vary between local authorities, and that resources are a relevant factor in determining that level. However, resources are not the only factor – the relative cost of providing services should be balanced against the benefit of doing so. It is a question of matching severity of condition or seriousness of people's needs against the resources available to the authority (*R v Gloucestershire CC, ex p Barry*).

In the case, too, of s.21 of the National Assistance Act 1948 (residential accommodation), the Court of Appeal reluctantly accepted this principle, although felt that the scope for taking resources into account when deciding whether a person was in need of care and attention was decidedly limited (*R v Sefton MBC, ex p Help the Aged*).

This principle could mean, as one law lord put it, that the needs of disabled people in Bermondsey may in law differ from those in Belgrave Square (*R v Gloucestershire CC, ex p Barry*). Furthermore, a local authority could lawfully vary the threshold level from time to time. However, such variation would have to be achieved formally at local authority social services committee level (*R v Gloucestershire CC, ex p Barry*). Thus it would not be lawful for individual social services teams informally to vary the threshold from month to month depending on the state of the local team budget.

The need for formality of decision-making in setting criteria is also spelt out in Department of Health guidance. It states that eligibility thresholds should be determined for given periods, and be reviewed in line with local authorities' usual budget cycles – unless major or unexpected changes necessitate the bringing forward of such a review. Furthermore, there should be consultation with users, carers and appropriate local agencies, and criteria should be published in local charters and made readily available and accessible (LAC(2002)13, paras 19–20). Formality, however, will be insufficient if crucial factors are not taken into account:

Setting eligibility for critical needs only under FACS: disability equality duty. A local authority was attempting to restrict eligibility for services to people in critical need only, under its fair access to care (FACS) scheme. There was indeed consultation, and the decision was taken formally at the top of the council at Cabinet level. As one councillor put it, the council's finances were in a desperate state. However, crucially, the attention of councillors was not drawn to the disability equality duty owed to local disabled people under s.49A of the Disability Discrimination Act 1995. This duty included promoting equality of opportunity, and even treating disabled people more favourably.

There was nothing in writing indicating that such consideration of this duty had been given. The court concluded that 'if the relevance of the important duties imposed by the Act had been adequately drawn to the attention of decision-makers there would have been a written record of it'. The decision, to change the FACS banding to critical need only, was therefore unlawful (*R(Chavda) v Harrow LBC*).

Assuming such formalities are complied with, the courts have indicated their reluctance to interfere, on grounds of unreasonableness, with the strictness of eligibility criteria for community care services. They have stated that a local authority's decision would be extremely difficult to review, and that the courts cannot second guess the way in which a local authority spends its limited resources (*R v East Sussex CC, ex p Tandy*). In similar vein, the Department of Health's practice guidance on eligibility criteria states that if resources are scarce locally, then the local authority could decide to assist only those people deemed to be in critical need (DH 2003g, para 3.9).

Thus, the courts have made clear that resources can play a role in setting the threshold for eligibility for services – that is, the point at which assessed needs will call for services. However, they have gone further and stated that in determining what need is itself, local authorities can take account of resources. This was distinctly controversial, a point made by the two law lords in the minority in the *Gloucestershire* case; they noted that needs should be determined by the professional judgement of a social worker, not by the availability of resources. After all, as one put it, a child either needs a new pair of shoes or does not; resources are irrelevant to that judgement.

However, of the majority law lords in the case, one emphasised that resources could affect the setting of eligibility criteria for need; another that resources would come into play when setting criteria for determining the necessity to meet the need (*R v Gloucestershire CC, ex p Barry*). The second approach, that is determining necessity to meet need (but not need itself) with reference to resources, is to be preferred for obvious reasons. This second approach anyway accords with the Department of Health's subsequent guidance on eligibility criteria and 'fair access to care' (LAC(2002)13).

6.10.2 IMPROPERLY MANIPULATING THE THRESHOLD OF ELIGIBILITY

The implication of the rules set out by the courts is that resources are relevant to the setting of eligibility criteria but not to their application in any one case. Once a need has been assessed, either a person is judged to come over the threshold of eligibility for service provision, or not; either way, resources should not come into it. However, as the following local ombudsman investigation demonstrates, knowledge of the law does not always translate into practice:

Assessment of residential placement. A local authority assessed whether to place and pay for a residential placement for a person with learning disabilities. Its policy was legally correct; a decision about eligibility would follow an assessment of need but before a decision about affordability. However, this was not the practice; the chairwoman of the complaints review panel involved had expected to see a detailed assessment report of the young man's needs. Instead it was her view that the council's decision and supporting paperwork had been based solely on the fact that it did not want to pay for residential care. This was maladministration (*Kent CC 1998*).

A second type of improper manipulation occurs when a local authority provides inadequate resources to support the threshold of eligibility that it has set. In other words, if the threshold is 'too generous' in relation to available resources, the local authority will be assessing too many people as having eligible needs. The relevant budgets will then be at risk of being overspent; yet managers are frequently warned that it is more than their job is worth to exceed their financial allocations. In which case, individual team managers sometimes instruct their staff surreptitiously to assess eligibility at a threshold significantly higher than that formally adopted and published by the local authority. This is likely to be unlawful.

For instance, the local ombudsman found an instruction issued to officers stating that they were 'not to spend unless a situation had become critical and inescapable' – irrespective of service users who had been assessed as having eligible needs. Clearly 'inescapability', as a criterion of eligibility for need, lacks coherence and did not represent the local authority's official policy:

Published eligibility and real eligibility threshold. A woman with learning disabilities lived with her elderly parents, aged 77 and 75 years. She needed assistance with most aspects of daily life, including assistance with medication, avoiding certain foods, assistance in getting out of bed, supervision and guidance in meal and preparation, assistance with personal hygiene and bathing, assistance with communication, assistance and support with household tasks, shopping and the use of money, support to go anywhere outside the home. The parents found it increasingly difficult to cope; the GP had written a letter outlining poor hygiene, inappropriate reactions to problems, giving 'considerable cause for alarm'. She was assessed as being in eligible need of a residential placement because she was at major risk of harm – scored against the council's formal, published matrix of need.

Nevertheless, provision was not made until the requirement was eventually recorded as being 'inescapable'. This was significant because staff were under an informal instruction (i.e. not part of the official eligibility framework) not to spend unless a situation was 'critical and inescapable'. Nevertheless, it had taken from August 1998 to November 1999 for funding to be offered.

The local ombudsman found that three months would have been reasonable; therefore the woman had lived in conditions assessed by the council as 'utterly unsuitable' for 11 months longer than she should have done. This was maladministration (*Cambridgeshire CC 2001*).

Indeed, unpublished administrative practices are not uncommon in local authorities, whether in respect of social services or, for example, housing allocation policies (*R(Faarah) v Southwark LBC*).

There may however be more subtle ways of reducing provision without officially or unofficially changing the local authority's eligibility threshold. For instance, the Commission for Social Care Inspection has found that procedural guidelines might often be clarified and tightened to control both staff assessments and expenditure, without changing the eligibility bands (CSCI 2008, p.131).

Third, a significant number of local authorities utilise funding panels or their equivalent (e.g. a supervising manager) to restrict spending. Such panels come in various guises and nomenclature, such as a 'Caring for People Panel' (*Liverpool CC 1998a*), 'Star Chamber' or 'Starlet Chamber' (*Camden LBC 1993*).

The funding panel process is sometimes used, in effect, to manipulate the threshold as it is applied both to individual people and to classes of person. Sometimes panels do not challenge the assessment of eligible need, but simply allocate waiting times. However, on other occasions they query the results of the professional assessment of need and put very considerable pressure on the assessor to alter his or her conclusions; alternatively the panel simply alters the decision itself.

There would be no objection where the panel is genuinely scrutinising whether a competent assessment has been carried out. However, on some occasions, it appears financial anxiety wholly drives the process and this can lead local authorities into unlawful territory, as the court uncovered in the following case:

Unlawfully backtracking on a decision. A complaints review panel recommended that the council find larger accommodation for a family with three teenage boys who were severely mentally handicapped and had behavioural problems. This would be under s.21 of the National Assistance Act 1948 and s.17 of the Children Act 1989. A social services officer visited the family and made it clear that the authority had accepted the recommendation. The local authority subsequently changed its mind when the cost implications became clear. The court ruled that from the point of the social services officer's visit, the local authority had a duty to provide the accommodation. The subsequent change of heart was unlawful. He ordered the property to be identified within three months and made available within six (*R v Wigan MBC, ex p Tammadge*).

Local authorities should not allow such panels to obscure legal responsibilities for decision-making. They should also be aware that the courts are more than capable of detecting improper shortcuts, and sham proceedings where the panel has made up its mind in advance of a case:

Panel usurping local authority's legal duty. It was the function of a local continuing care panel to make recommendations to the local authority about the level (and funding) of care required by service users. The panel's role was advisory only. In one particular case, the panel relied on the views of a doctor, who himself had not seen the woman involved. The panel also failed to consider all the relevant issues (e.g. a detailed social work team manager's report coming to the opposite conclusion to the doctor). The panel's recommendations were therefore flawed. Yet, in turn, the local authority relied on the panel's recommendations.

The court held that the local authority had failed to make a lawful decision as it was required to do, following a full, up-to-date community care assessment and taking account of all the relevant issues. One of the panel members had 'plainly made up her mind' before an (anyway) flawed meeting; the decision as a whole was simply pre-determined.

The court also took particular exception to an improper letter written by that panel member to the doctor, which indicated that it was only the daughter (as a 'lone voice', unsupported by professional opinion) who was opposing her mother's placement in a nursing home – when this was clearly not the case (*R(Goldsmith) v Wandsworth LBC*).

A safeguard for both staff and service users is for assessing staff to put forward well-evidenced and well-reasoned assessments, the conclusions of which are expressed in the relevant terminology – for instance, that of the 'fair access to care' eligibility criteria that local authorities apply. This makes it much more difficult for funding panels or senior managers to set aside assessment on spurious grounds. Indeed, Department of Health practice guidance clearly envisages that staff should be able to argue cases on an individual basis.

The guidance points out that what is 'vital' (a word used in the risk to independence framework: see 6.12) for one person might not be for another. It also states that assessment relies on person-centred conversations; 'frameworks, case examples and the like can only ever support the exercise of person-centred competent judgement' (DH 2003g, paras 3.6, 3.14).

All this is not theoretical; in one case, a comprehensive and well-documented assessment by a social work team leader came to the rescue of an elderly woman, whom the local continuing care panel and local authority were attempting to remove from a care home, on the basis of partial and inadequate information. The court preferred this assessment to the recommendation of the panel and decision of the authority, which lacked documented reasons (*R(Goldsmith) v Wandsworth LBC*).

The Commission for Social Care Inspection refers to the legitimate function of panels in terms of peer review, but also to the view that increasingly their role is associated with budgetary difficulty and that this could lead to an intimidating atmosphere and resentment on the part of practitioners (Henwood and Hudson 2008, pp.51–52).

6.10.3 MEETING ASSESSED NEED: RELEVANCE OF RESOURCES OF SERVICE USERS

Department of Health guidance states that if a person has both the mental and financial (i.e. has resources over the 'capital threshold': see 10.6) capacity to arrange and pay for residential accommodation, then the local authority is not obliged to make the care home placement.

However, for non-residential services, guidance states the opposite, namely that local authorities should arrange services to meet eligible needs – irrespective of a person's financial capacity – if that is what the person wants (DH 2003g, para 8.5). This approach appears to be in line with the original community care policy guidance, which states that the provision of services should not be related to the ability of the people or their families to meet the costs (DH 1990, para 3.31). Nevertheless, one of the law lords has stated that it might not be necessary for the local authority to make arrangements for non-residential services under the Chronically Sick and Disabled Persons Act 1970, s.2, if the person was 'wealthy enough to meet his needs out of his own pocket' (*R v Gloucestershire CC, ex p Barry*).

This approach would seem to be supported by a another judicial decision that in certain circumstances at least, the resources of the parents of two disabled children could be taken into account, when the local authority was deciding whether to provide assistance under the Chronically Sick and Disabled Persons Act 1970. The assistance was alternative to a disabled facilities grant under housing legislation, the means-tested contribution to which the parents claimed they could not afford (*R(Spink) v Wandsworth LBC*). It would seem at least arguable that if the resources of a third party in the form of parents can be taken into account under the 1970 Act, then so too could the resources of an adult himself or herself.

Nonetheless, even were it lawful to take account of a person's resources in deciding whether to provide (as opposed to what to charge the person), the local authority would have to ensure that it was taking a reasonable approach on a case-by-case basis, rather than employing a blanket rule. In terms of good administration at least, this was the view of the local ombudsman:

Taking account of a person's resources in deciding whether to provide a service. A woman applied for help with a hard-standing and shelter for her outdoor, powered wheelchair. The local authority stated that such outdoor mobility needs should be met through her mobility allowance (a social security benefit) and not through the local authority. The local ombudsman accepted that 'an individual's private means may be relevant as to whether or not the Council itself needs to make any provision'. Nevertheless the council had raised this argument only 'very late in the day' – and had in any case apparently made no effort to establish what the mobility allowance was already being spent on in reality (*Sheffield CC 1995*).

6.10.4 FINDING THE MONEY WHEN THERE IS NONE

Hard-pressed local authority managers often ask the legitimate question of how they are meant to perform a legal obligation if their budgets are effectively inadequate. The answer is that when a duty arises, it arises not in respect of a particular social services team but of the local authority as a whole. Thus the courts have considered and answered this very question directly, by stating that the money must be found from somewhere else within the local authority – for example, from other budgets not subject to an absolute duty that demands expenditure.

Finding the money to perform a duty. Referring to education legislation, the court (House of Lords) stated that while the local authority might not want 'to bleed its other functions of resources so as to enable it to perform the statutory duty', nevertheless it could divert money from other discretionary functions. Thus, the 'argument is not one of insufficient resources to discharge the duty but of a preference for using the money for other purposes. To permit a local authority to avoid performing a statutory duty on the grounds that it prefers to spend the money in other ways is to downgrade a statutory duty to a discretionary power.' Indeed, if 'Parliament wishes to reduce public expenditure on meeting the needs of sick children then it is up to Parliament so to provide. It is not for the courts to adjust the order or priorities as between statutory duties and statutory discretions.' At an earlier stage of the same case the Court of Appeal pointed out that a local authority might have to save on non-mandatory items such as a proposed leisure centre or football ground (R v East Sussex CC, ex p Tandy).

Indeed, Department of Health guidance on assessment and eligibility criteria makes just this point when it states that local authorities 'should not adhere so rigidly to budget headings for specific services that resources cannot move from one budget heading to another, if necessary' (LAC(2002)13, para 23).

6.11 MEETING NEED COST-EFFECTIVELY

The courts have consistently ruled that if there are two or more options to meet a person's eligible assessed needs, the local authority can offer the cheapest, so long as that particular option genuinely meets those needs.

Cost-effective options to meet need for residential accommodation. In two Court of Appeal cases, it was lawful for the local authorities concerned to offer care home accommodation, even though the service users wished to be supported in the community. This was essentially because the care home accommodation would meet the assessed needs (R v Lancashire CC, ex p RADAR; R(Khana) v Southwark LBC). The Human Rights Act 1998 has not affected this general principle; the second of these cases (Southwark) was decided after the Act came into force and considered its effect at the High Court stage of the case.

On the other hand, if there were no resource implications in the difference between two options – both of which would meet the person's needs – then it might be unreasonable for the local authority not to offer the option of choice (R(Khana) v Southwark LBC).

Mobility needs of a disabled woman at a day centre. The court stated that a local authority was entitled to take account of resources in deciding how to meet a seriously disabled woman's need for assistance with mobility at a day centre. The choice was between human walking assistance, her walking alone (if the parents agreed to her wearing protective headgear), or use of a wheelchair and rollator (R v Cornwall CC, ex p Goldsack).

Differentiating need from services: stairlift dispute. In a dispute about provision of a vertical lift or stairlift, the court pointed out that need should be differentiated from the means to meet it. The requirement of the stairlift fell into the latter, but not the former, category. Therefore it was 'impossible to regard the provision of a stairlift at home as "the need"'. Instead the need was 'for the applicants to get in and out of the premises' – for which the authority could review various options and take account of cost. Indeed, the authority was 'perfectly entitled to look to see what is the cheapest way for them to meet the needs which are specified' (*R v Kirklees MBC, ex p Daykin*).

Review of services and options for people with learning disabilities. The applicant was a 50-year-old man with learning disabilities, poor eyesight and requiring assistance in looking after himself. In order to save money, the local authority was conducting a review of its care arrangements – and transferring the provision of care for some people to cheaper providers. The social worker was supposed to go down the list, starting with the cheapest, until he or she found a provider who was able to provide the care that was needed. This entailed a change of provider for the applicant – from a male support worker to a female carer – a change he did not want. The authority was accused of fettering its discretion in only making exceptions when the change in provision would be 'significantly detrimental' – and of making resources the prevailing or predominant consideration.

The judge did not find a fettering of discretion, and stated that the authority could take account of resources up to a point. He accepted that the changes were resource led in that they would not have been made unless there was a need to cut costs – but they were not on that account unlawful, so long as the 'correct balancing exercise' had been carried out in reassessing individual needs. The reassessment exercise had in fact resulted in seven out of 13 users remaining with the more expensive care agency. Consequently there was nothing 'to indicate that resources were regarded as paramount or that the Council manifestly got the balance wrong' (*R v Essex CC, ex p Bucke*).

Failure to identify cheaper option for residential placement of person with learning disabilities. When a local authority ruled out a particular residential option for a young man with profound autism and learning disabilities on grounds of cost, it had failed (a) to identify in detail whether another option was available, and (b) to carry out a proper comparison of costs at different establishments. The court therefore held its decision to be unlawful (*R(Alloway) Bromley LBC*).

In the overwhelming desire to save money, however, councils can come unstuck to the substantial detriment of vulnerable users of services. In the following case, the local ombudsman reminded the local authority that it could take account of money and opt for a cheaper placement, only if that placement met the assessed needs – which it did not in this case:

Ending up unnecessarily in psychiatric unit because of breach of duty and failure to make resources available to meet assessed needs. A 22-year-old man had Down's syndrome and exhibited autistic traits, although he had never been diagnosed with an autistic spectrum disorder. He had limited verbal communication and used Makaton sign language. After he left college at 19, the council sought to find a residential placement for him. It prepared a detailed assessment of his needs and identified a placement costing £1400.00 per week.

Cheaper placement in conflict with assessment of need. However, it was determined to place him at a cheaper establishment (£700.00) per week, even though this conflicted with the assessment. Rather than follow the detailed community care assessment, the council accepted the assurance of the manager of the cheaper home that it could meet the man's needs – even though he barely knew the service user. The consequence was that the man's behaviour deteriorated. Staff at the home did the opposite of what should have been done and made a bad situation worse, despite receiving 'excellent' information from the parents and social worker. The council should have anticipated these consequences, since it had been given ample warning by the social worker, the parents, the advocate and the college.

Eight months in psychiatric unit. Ultimately, the man was kept in a psychiatric unit for almost eight months, where he was given medication to keep him calm. He was not formally detained under the Mental Health Act because he had been diagnosed as having no mental health needs. All this had come about because of the council's failure to provide a suitable placement, even though one had been clearly identified by the social worker.

Another, only partially appropriate, placement was then found. It was forced on the family by the council, still did not deal with his behaviour and meant he had little contact with his parents – who themselves had medical and mobility problems. The round trip, by public transport, took seven hours. Finally, a suitable placement was found.

The ombudsman wondered what might have happened to the man without his two devoted parents pursuing the council. It was clear that cost had played a major part in the council's decisions. The ombudsman reminded it that 'only when it has ensured that what is being proposed will actually meet the individual's needs may the Council consider the cost'. The problems with the man's behaviour had been entirely predictable. The council was guilty of maladministration. The ombudsman recommended the council review its procedures for considering placements and their costs, pay the parents £10,000 for the stress and toll on their health, and pay £25,000 to the parents for them to administer on behalf of their son for the failure to meet his needs and the harm caused to him (*Southend on Sea Borough BC 2005*).

The following case reads similarly, the ombudsman finding excessive preoccupation with costs which meant that the needs of a person with learning disabilities were not met by the local authority. Consequently he ended up detained unnecessarily under the Mental Health Act 1983 for 18 months:

Avoidable detention on psychiatric ward. The complainant's son had epilepsy and fragile X syndrome. From an early age he showed characteristics typical of an autistic spectrum disorder. After he left school, the council had to find a suitable residential placement for him. It intended to set up a specialist facility within its area, in the form of two semi-detached houses. This was not yet ready. However, his mother was anyway opposed to this, stating that its location was unsuitable, and that her son and other residents would not be accepted by the local community, that there would be no garden and would be insufficient space for her son to have space for himself.

Managers preoccupied with the effect on the budget. The council persisted however with the idea that he should go there, despite the family's implacable opposition. It did not consider the impracticality of trying to integrate him in a placement which his mother, to whom he was very close, opposed – and despite warnings by the psychiatrist. The ombudsman found a single-minded determination and that, despite the council's protestations to the contrary, the managers concerned were preoccupied with the effect on the budget of any alternative placement. The council also carried out no reassessment of the man's needs. In turn this meant that it could not send a service specification to the National Autistic Society (which had offered a placement favoured by the mother). So this possible placement fell through.

Failure to carry out proper assessment and produce care plan. A record of a meeting between a senior manager and the council's legal department referred to doing a deal with the National Autistic Society to drop the price (£170,000 per year as opposed to £55,000 in the council's preferred placement) – in which case the council would place him at the former. But this meeting had taken place, unknown to the legal department, without an assessment under the NHS and Community Act 1990 and without a care plan (the council subsequently apologised for misleading the legal department). The director of social services expressed his shock and anger at such a discussion and the excessive focus on cost –

even though the more expensive placement would have resulted in an overspend on the social services agency budget of £290,8111. Another, later meeting with the legal department, again referred to there being no objection to the National Autistic Society other than cost.

Detention under Mental Health Act: deterioration foreseeable but which the council failed to anticipate. In consequence of the impasse, the man was placed in a temporary staffed house. His violence and destructiveness then precipitated compulsory detention under the Mental Health Act 1983 in a locked psychiatric ward for a period of 18 months. This was because of a failure of the council to meet his needs. There was no excuse for the council's failure to anticipate the deterioration in his behaviour. It had ample evidence of his behaviour at school, when he was faced with sudden change or social situations which he found difficult or frightening.

Mother gives up work to care for her son. Eventually, his mother gave up work to provide proper care for her son. She suffered stress and loss of income. He suffered untold stress during his detention and 'must have been utterly bewildered by what was happening to him'.

Maladministration: remedy includes £30,000 compensation. The ombudsman identified maladministration causing grave injustice, recommending £10,000 to be paid to his mother for her loss of earnings, stress, worry and inconvenience – and also £20,000 to the mother to administer for her son's benefit. Also the council should review its procedures for considering placements in the independent sector, to ensure that keeping cost to a minimum did not result in unlawful decisions and a failure to meet people's needs (*Bolton MBC 2004a*).

The following case again reveals a local authority's concern with costs at the expense of a person's needs, logical inconsistencies in the council's position, and failure anyway to carry out proper assessments:

Local authority failing to assess adequately a person with learning disabilities, wrongly blaming the parents, not complying with its duties. A woman with learning disabilities was 25 years old, could not speak, had limited communication, difficulty in mobilising and could not look after herself in most ways. Between the age of 19 and 22, she was placed at a college, paid partly by the Learning and Skills Council (LSC) and partly by the local authority. The fees were £65,000 for a 38-week term. She spent the holiday periods with her parents. After the LSC withdrew its funding, the local authority agreed to fund a further year, while preparing the woman for transition to permanent adult residential care. However, her parents and an advocate believed she should remain at the centre. The local authority disagreed, stating that it did not believe the centre could meet her needs (it had never stated this before). It also stated that it was too costly.

Lack of evidence for placement offered by council. The woman's needs had been assessed as 'critical' under fair access to care eligibility criteria. The alternative placement offered by the council was based on no more evidence than a social worker's note that a visit to the centre had been 'positive'. The council argued that this centre's staff had assessed that her needs could be met there. The ombudsman pointed out that there was a risk of the centre having a vested interest. Furthermore, the ombudsman had noted that government guidance stated that assessment should not be carried out by centre managers. This was maladministration.

Inconsistency of council's position. In addition, the council seemed to be inconsistent. It stated that the first centre could not meet her needs. Yet she had attended previously and the council was prepared to place her for interim periods. If it had believed it could not meet her needs, it should not have placed her there at all.

Flawed assessment. Worse, an assessment of need was carried out with no reference to medical records or advice. It was drafted with a residential placement in mind; but in fact in light of the impasse, she had moved back home. So the assessment was not up to date once she had returned home, and was not so for the next ten months. It did not refer to her needs for physiotherapy, hydrotherapy, footwear and speech therapy – all of which she had previously been receiving. Carers' assessments of her parents had not been carried out for the last three years. The local authority argued that the parents had been obstructive, but this contention was supported by no evidence. The parents had only declined one centre – the suitability of which the council had anyway not properly assessed.

Maladministration: significant financial compensation: £1000 per week her parents had had to care for their daughter over a two-year period. All this was maladministration. The ombudsman recommended that the parents be paid £1000 per week for every week they had had to care for their daughter over the past two years (less any weeks where respite care had been provided); that the local authority pay them £3000 for their distress, anxiety, time and trouble; ensure that an 'independent, impartial, credible and comprehensive assessment' of the woman's needs be carried out; and that the local authority should produce a plan with a clear timescale for action to be taken – and report progress to the ombudsman (*Trafford MBC 2007*).

Further report by the ombudsman. In response to the ombudsman's recommendations, the council decided that £10,000 should be paid to compensate the parents for the period since August 2005 they had had to care for their daughter. In doing so, the council did not agree the formula suggested by the ombudsman which, it calculated, would cost £100,000. The council also rejected the ombudsman's recommendation that it report progress to the ombudsman, feeling that this was not appropriate. The council accepted there had been shortcomings and agreed to the independent assessment. The ombudsman published a further report, expressing her disappointment and hoping that the council would now agree to implement her recommendations in full (*Trafford MBC 2008*).

The courts have commented that a certain degree of specificity in how need is assessed and is to be met is clearly required; equally over-specification in every case might mean that even slight changes to services would trigger formal reassessments, and would be excessively cumbersome (*R v Cornwall CC, ex p Goldsack*).

6.11.1 BEST VALUE AND MEETING PEOPLE'S NEEDS

'Best value' authorities must exercise their functions, having regard to a combination of economy, efficiency and effectiveness (Local Government Act 1999, s.3). Thus, best value is not meant to be about always finding the cheapest option. It is essentially about *how* local authorities carry out their duties and not *whether* they should carry them out. In other words, best value cannot negate legal duties, whether performed through the provision of in-house services or contracted services.

The courts have warned local authorities against allowing so-called best value principles to interfere with the basic duty to meet people's assessed community care needs (*R (Bodimeade) v Camden LBC*). In other words, a local authority must ensure that it 'never forgets that the needs of the user are to be regarded as of greater importance than the need to save money' (*R v Essex CC, ex p Bucke*).

Thus, where assessed needs call for a more expensive option, the local authority must find the resources; best value affects how a duty is performed, not whether to perform it. For instance, the refusal to place a person with learning disabilities at a residential home – which the local authority regarded as excessively expensive (and would have provided services in excess of his needs) – was unlawful, because the authority had made the decision before any suitable, cheaper alternatives had been found. The council had fettered its discretion by prematurely ruling out the more expensive option (*R (Alloway) v Bromley LBC*).

Notwithstanding this, local authorities sometimes deprive themselves of the opportunity to decide which option really will meet a person's needs, typically by imposing rigid restrictions or ceilings on what they are prepared to consider – as the two following local ombudsman investigations reveal:

Considering exceptional needs of a woman and the option of remaining at home. A local authority operated a ceiling on home care packages for older people. It argued that this did not represent a fettering of discretion because it had a 'Caring for People Panel' that considered exceptions.

Applying this policy, the council refused to exceed the ceiling in the case of a woman who was blind and deaf, had diabetes, arthritis, hypertension and a heart problem, and was incontinent and depressed. She had become increasingly confused and had a loss of short-term memory. Her mobility was very restricted and she communicated by hand signing. The daughter explained (a) that given that her mother had 'no quality of life' but just existence, her going into a nursing home would mean that she would lose love, affection and understanding and that she could not abandon her mother in that way; and (b) that her mother's needs were exceptional since she required constant one-to-one attention day and night including constant reassurance and stimulation, changing, frequent strip washing (particularly important because of bowel and kidney problems), safety measures (she would crawl around the floor like a baby) – and so on.

The local ombudsman found a fettering of discretion, coming to the conclusion that there was no evidence that the 'Caring for People Panel' ever made exceptions. This was maladministration. The ombudsman also criticised the ceiling as discriminating against older people (*Liverpool CC 1998a*).

Such discrimination, in that younger adults receive much higher cost care packages, is probably not unusual (Henwood and Hudson 2008, p.106). In the next case, the rigid restriction imposed by the local authority would, perversely, probably have resulted in greater expense than if an exception had been made and the service user's need met more appropriately:

Providing services in the last days. A man complained to the local ombudsman about the last days of his parents and the putting to bed service they received. The father was 90 with Parkinson's disease, arthritis and spinal kyphosis; his wife, who was 92, and his main carer, was blind and had angina. The father had been assessed as needing assistance with getting up and going to bed. Evening and weekend cover was provided by an agency.

On 1 February, the agency informed the council it was withdrawing weekend service because it could not recruit staff. On 2 March, the council informed the couple that they might have to attend respite care at a residential home instead; meanwhile district nurses provided the weekend cover on a temporary basis. The agency then informed the council that the evening service would be withdrawn from 26 March. On 24 March, the wife became ill, went into hospital and died on 16 May. The husband went into residential care and died on 21 April. All this had been very stressful; extracts from the woman's journal revealed this.

The council had been unable to find another agency to provide the putting to bed service unless it would pay travel costs of staff, above the flat rate fee for the service, and this was against council policy.

The local ombudsman found maladministration, reminding the council of the importance and sensitivity of its services to vulnerable elderly people. The council should have seized the offer from another home care contractor, even at a higher rate. The man's home care was 'entirely sacrificed to maintain the purity of the council's contractual arrangements'. No one seriously thought of making an exception to the policy, even though the cost of the weekend respite care would probably exceed by far the costs of the agency staff, even with extra travel costs. This was a classic case of the council fettering its discretion and of maladministration (*Essex CC 2001*).

Clearly then, if a local authority holds itself hostage to its rigid policies in the name of best value, this might be at the expense of performing its legal obligations to meet people's assessed community care needs. This will lead to findings of maladministration by the local ombudsman:

Best value policy preventing the meeting of a person's needs. A local authority had a list of approved home care providers; it would not go outside of this list. This was in the name of best value; previously 40 to 50 providers had been used. Now, in the cause of quality control, there were four to five approved providers in each area only. However, a particular approved provider could not provide the two carers that a risk assessment had identified as required to meet the assessed need of a woman to be hoisted in and out of bed. The provider had at first stated that it would not take on situations requiring two carers (because of the logistical difficulty of coordinating their whereabouts during the day); it later corrected this by stating that it would 'double up' its own carers, but would on no account have its carers double up with carers from another agency.

By rigidly refusing to go outside of its approved provider list to enable 'spot purchasing', and by also anyway imposing a £360 weekly limit on how much it would spend, the local authority was found to have 'fettered its discretion' and failed in its duty to meet a person's assessed need. This was maladministration. The ombudsman pointed out that in the final analysis it was the needs of individuals that should have determined the council's response and not its contractual arrangements (*Cambridgeshire CC 2002*).

This sort of harsh approach, which can result in the separation of older couples on financial grounds, continues to be reported. It puts local authorities in the spotlight; proposing such separation on financial grounds is legally permissible, but only if the separation is assessed to be a genuine way of meeting assessed need. This begs the question of whether causing acute psychological distress (together with the concomitant detriment to, and deterioration in, a person's health and well-being) is consonant with meeting assessed community care needs – if there is another practicable, albeit more expensive, way of keeping the couple together. There are also potential human rights arguments, although the courts have barely touched on these; in *R(Khana) v Southwark LBC*, the local authority responded to concerns (including human rights) about separation by offering a place in a care home to both wife and husband, to avoid the wife being placed in the care home alone.

For example, one couple had not spent a night apart since the Second World War and had been married for 69 years. After one of them had suffered a stroke, she was assessed by the council as needing a care home place. Initially, her husband was told he could move in with her and share a double room. Then social services explained that he did not meet the criteria, and he would have to have a care package in his own home instead. For their remaining years, they would thus be separated (*Daily Express* 2006).

These appear not to be isolated cases. In 2002, an elderly couple in Oxfordshire was told it was too expensive for them to live together in the same nursing home. They were placed 20 miles apart. They had been married for more than 60 years. A couple in Portsmouth, married for 61 years were placed in homes five miles apart because of their different needs. The council promised that an adapted taxi would enable them to see each other five days a week.

However, this arrangement broke down when the council needed to save money. When one of them died, the other had not seen his wife for four days.

It appears that one in ten people in care homes is still married, often in marriages of 50 years' duration. Adverse publicity in such cases, especially in the national press, often seems to result in councils backing down. But, as Help the Aged has stated, in other (less trumpeted) cases, financial considerations override the rights of older couples to stay together (Womack 2006). A dentist and his wife were reported as probably having taken their own lives in a suicide pact, to which fears – of the husband being placed in a care home some distance away (rather than close by) – may have contributed (Salkeld 2008).

At the same time, ensuring that a service provider delivers services in accordance with the contract is of course a best value matter and might interest the district auditor:

Treatment day centre, value for money, health and safety. The complainant to the local ombudsman was the mother of an autistic man who attended a day centre run by a voluntary organisation but paid for (including transport) by the council. She became concerned over various incidents, including her son (a) returning from the centre with injuries to the top of his legs (commensurate with a badly fitting climbing harness); (b) drinking river water and being sick; (c) stripping in public; (d) opening the doors of the moving minibus in which he was being transported; (e) going to a park and a carer's home to watch television when he should have been participating in a one-to-one care programme.

The mother had also complained to the district auditor that the council was paying for a service that the centre was not delivering; in response to the auditor's enquiry, the council said it would try to recover money from the centre. Additionally, the Health and Safety Executive had become involved in respect of opening the doors of the minibus; such an incident had occurred more than once and the Executive threatened enforcement in case of recurrence (*Liverpool CC 1998*).

6.12 FAIR ACCESS TO CARE SERVICES (FACS): ELIGIBILITY CRITERIA

The Department of Health has issued guidance to local authorities on what it calls 'fair access to care' in respect of adult social services. This guidance builds upon the rules about eligibility criteria and thresholds set out in legal cases such as *R v Gloucestershire CC, ex p Barry* (see 6.10 above). At the time of writing, it is being reviewed by the Department of Health.

Although it is only guidance, and as such does not amount to law, it is nevertheless stronger rather than weaker and should generally be followed by local authorities unless there are very good reasons for not doing so. This is because it is made under s.7 of the Local Authority Social Services Act 1970, and thus constitutes what is sometimes called 'statutory guidance' (see 5.1.6). Certainly the courts have afforded it considerable attention (*R v Sheffield CC, ex p Heffernan*). The guidance states that when local authorities assess people's needs, evaluation of risks should focus on:

- autonomy and freedom to make choices; health and safety including freedom from harm, abuse and neglect, housing and community safety
- ability to manage personal and other daily routines
- involvement in family and wider community life, including leisure, hobbies, unpaid and paid work, learning and volunteering (LAC(2002)13, para 40).

In order to assist them to do this, the guidance states that local authorities should use a framework in terms of risk to independence. Risks to independence should be categorised as being critical, substantial, moderate or low. Each local authority should then set a threshold of eligibility, above which such risks (when translated into needs) will be eligible for service provision, and below which they will not. Local authorities have not been told where to set the threshold within the framework, but practice guidance states that if a council is short of money, then it should consider moving to a critical threshold (DH 2002a, p.5). Yet, even then, a local authority may engage in wrangling with the NHS, since people in the critical category may have a mix of health and social care needs (Henwood and Hudson 2008, p.21).

It appears that many local authorities have set it either between the substantial and moderate, or between the moderate and low categories. Across the country, year by year, local authorities are pushing up the threshold, some to the critical level. This results in fewer people receiving services from local authorities. However, all things being equal, such restrictions on eligibility are difficult legally to challenge. The principle of the lawfulness of such thresholds was established in *R v Gloucestershire CC, ex p Barry*.

6.12.1 FACS FRAMEWORK

The main guidance on FACS states that the same eligibility threshold should be operated across all services (LAC(2002)13, para 3). The framework is as follows, setting out four different categories of risk to independence (LAC(2002)13, para 16):

- *Critical risk to independence*
  ○ Life is, or will be, threatened; and/or
  ○ significant health problems have developed or will develop; and/or
  ○ there is, or will be, little or no choice and control over vital aspects of the immediate environment; and/or
  ○ serious abuse or neglect has occurred or will occur; and/or
  ○ there is, or will be, an inability to carry out vital personal care or domestic routines; and/or
  ○ vital involvement in work, education or learning cannot or will not be sustained; and/or
  ○ vital social support systems and relationships cannot or will not be sustained; and/or
  ○ vital family and other social roles and responsibilities cannot or will not be undertaken.
- *Substantial risk to independence*
  ○ There is, or will be, only partial choice and control over the immediate environment; and/or
  ○ abuse or neglect has occurred or will occur; and/or
  ○ there is, or will be, an inability to carry out the majority of personal care or domestic routines; and/or
  ○ involvement in many aspects of work, education or learning cannot or will not be sustained; and/or
  ○ the majority of social support systems and relationships cannot or will not be sustained; and/or
  ○ the majority of family and other social roles and responsibilities cannot or will not be undertaken.
- *Moderate risk to independence*
  ○ There is, or will be, an inability to carry out several personal care or domestic routines; and/or

- involvement in several aspects of work, education or learning cannot or will not be sustained; and/or
- several social support systems and relationships cannot or will not be sustained; and/or
- several family and other social roles and responsibilities cannot or will not be undertaken.
- *Low risk to independence*
  - There is, or will be, an inability to carry out one or two personal care or domestic routines; and/or
  - involvement in one or two aspects of work, education or learning cannot or will not be sustained; and/or
  - one or two social support systems and relationships cannot or will not be sustained; and/or
  - one or two family and other social roles and responsibilities cannot or will not be undertaken.

Practice guidance states that local authorities should not vary the wording of this framework (DH 2003g, para 3.1), a point the courts have picked up on:

Unlawfully varying the guidance on eligibility. When a local authority differentiated between 'major health problems' in the critical category, and 'significant health problems' in the substantial category, the court found the authority to be in error. In turn, this had the consequence that any needs related to a health condition should properly have been assessed as falling into the critical category. The local authority had assessed matters such as cleaning, shopping, and attendance at appointments as representing a moderate risk to independence only. However, because they were related to the man's health care condition, they should all have been placed in the critical category and so provided by the local authority (*R(Heffernan) v Sheffield CC*).

Nonetheless, it would appear that local authorities do tamper with the wording in order to make the criteria more restrictive (Lowe 2008). The main guidance states that once eligibility of need is established, a duty arises to meet it (LAC(200213, para 43). However, unhelpfully, the guidance does not distinguish between different pieces of community care legislation and the fact that some of it entails only powers or target duties, neither of which gives rise to enforceable legal obligations; see above, 5.1).

Practice guidance further complicates matters by reminding local authorities that the framework in the guidance refers to 'risk to independence', whereas it is only 'need' that triggers a legal duty to provide services. Therefore, it suggests that needs associated with eligible risk should only themselves be deemed eligible needs if 'through addressing them, risks are ameliorated, contained or reduced' (DH 2003g, para 3.12).

In any case, the setting of a threshold means precisely that not all needs or risks will be met, as in the following case where the risks were not deemed to fall within the substantial category:

Risk of falling on stairs: not substantial. In one case, where assessment under FACS concerned a physically disabled woman at risk of falling on the stairs, the court stated that 'everything is relative' and accepted the view of the local authority decision-maker. This was to the effect that she was at risk, but that it was 'small and acceptable. There are numerous council service users who manage similar or greater risks in their homes and it is neither possible nor desirable for the council to avoid all risks of this nature'. This was further underlined by the point that even though the woman had been allocated the highest number of housing points (25) for the purpose of housing legislation, nonetheless it did not follow necessarily that the risk under FACS should fall within the 'substantial' category (*R(Ireneschild) v Lambeth LBC*).

Similarly, in another case that considered the application of FACS, the court accepted that the local authority's view of what was required was not generous, but that legally it did not have to be (*R(Heffernan) v Sheffield CC*).

6.12.2 FACS: PREVENTATIVE SERVICES

The guidance stipulates that prevention should be built in to the application of this framework (LAC(2002)13, para 22). Nonetheless, in practice a vicious circle of focusing resources on crisis management for those in greatest need has militated against such preventative strategies involving low level services. Councils attempt to justify not meeting needs, by dismissing them as unmet wishes, wants or desires, but not unmet needs. They may even suggest that older people are trying to trick their way into getting help. However, the Commission for Social Care Inspection has taken the view that such services are potentially of fundamental importance (Henwood and Hudson 2008, pp.19, 98; also CSCI 2008, p.148). Older people value so called low level, preventative services (Clark, Dyer and Horwood 1998). Yet local authorities may feel they have little option when faced, for example, with younger adults with very complex needs (including learning disabilities), who might need placements costing thousands of pounds a week. A local authority might point to just six service users costing it a £1 million pounds a year (Henwood and Hudson 2008, p.29).

6.12.3 WIDE RANGING ASSESSMENT REQUIRED UNDER FACS

A glance at the indicators within each category in the guidance makes it clear that assessment should be about far more than physical risk.

Certainly, under the critical category, reference is made to threat to life, significant health problems, little or no choice and control over vital aspects of the immediate environment, serious abuse or neglect, and vital personal care or domestic routines. But beyond such issues, reference is made also to vital involvement in work or education or learning, vital social support systems and relationships, vital family and other social roles and responsibilities. It also states that evaluation of risks should focus on: autonomy and freedom to make choices; health and safety including freedom from harm, abuse and neglect, housing and community safety (LAC(2002)13 para 4).

All this indicates that the scope of assessment under this guidance should be wide, taking an 'independent living' or 'social model of disability' approach. For instance, when disabled parents are assessed, parenting as well as other needs should be covered; something that apparently does not always occur (Morris 2003, p.14).

Overall, the breadth and scope of assessment, as set out in the guidance, is consonant with the implications of the community care legislation, such as the Chronically Sick and Disabled Persons Act 1970 (see 11.2 below), which covers a wide range of needs and services. It is also supported by the approach of the law courts in a number of community care cases, in terms of the potentially wide range of relevant factors that must be taken account of in assessments (see 6.13).

6.12.4 IMPACT OF EVER MORE RESTRICTIVE ELIGIBILITY THRESHOLDS

The Commission for Social Care Inspection delivered unprecedented criticism of this trend in early 2008. It noted that there was evidence that the ever tightening of FACS eligibility criteria was neither appropriate nor effective and failed to save money in the longer term – because the failure to intervene to prevent things deteriorating meant that 'people arrived in the system with more intensive needs than might otherwise have been the case' (CSCI 2008, pp.129–131).

It further pointed out that local authorities, in order to justify cutbacks, often dismissed 'low level' needs as trivial. But in CSCI's view, such support for everyday simple tasks constituted arguably vital help; for instance, housework, cleaning, gardening, companionship, befriending. It noted how a purely functional approach to people's hygiene needs, dismissing them as capable of being met by a strip wash, 'took no account of people's personal dignity or mental well-being'. For people excluded from help, there were 'negative consequences'. Domestic support had fallen foul of local authorities' approach to eligibility, yet was fundamental to people's sense of self-worth and personal identity (CSCI 2008, pp.142–149).

A second CSCI report noted how low level needs might escalate, accidents might occur as people struggled to cope alone, and experiences might be dismal and very poor. The eligibility decisions of local authorities might fail 'utterly to meet people's needs for dignity and self-respect'. With some understatement, it records how a local authority visited a woman at home, assessed her as managing her own personal care and closed the case – having first recorded that she was unkempt, her knickers were around her knees, there was evidence of faeces on the floor and she was not taking her medication (Henwood and Hudson 2008, pp.8–12).

The CSCI report had found also that the signposting, of those excluded from local authority help, to other services, was problematic. There was little evidence of whether it worked (Henwood and Hudson 2008, p.80). It also pointed out that raising the threshold, to critical only, may be 'economically self-defeating'. One council referred to it as involving people stacking up like aeroplanes in the substantial category, waiting to land in the critical by which point they proved more costly (p.37). This observation seems to bear out the contention of one council, bucking the trend of tighter criteria, that providing services across all four bandings, including 'low', was actually cost effective (Hunter 2008). However, even for those people still receiving services, quality of life may be limited because they 'get too little care to have a reasonable quality of life' (CSCI 2008, p.120).

Before these CSCI reports in 2008, the Local Government Association had already spelled out a year earlier that until people's lives were threatened, they had serious physical or mental illness, or were unable to carry out the majority of personal care tasks, they would not receive help (LGA 2006, p.4). The Commission had itself also reported previously that even where people were eligible for services, shortcuts were taken, with shortages of staff, insufficient time allocated to tasks – and assistance only with limited tasks (CSCI 2006, pp.3–5).

6.12.5 BLANKET POLICIES

The FACS guidance expressly states that local authorities should not have blanket policies not to provide particular services (LAC(2002)13, para 23). There are at least four good reasons for the guidance to take this stance.

First, such policies will unlawfully fetter a local authority's discretion, as they would amount to excessive rigidity (see 5.2.1.2 above). Second, such policies might prevent lawful assessment because staff will not bother to carry out a full assessment for a service they believe will not be provided (see 6.1.1). Third, this in turn might signify poor professional practice. Fourth, it is an unfair way of rationing services, because it is then based not on the level of people's needs, but on arbitrary decisions about which services will or will not be provided. The local ombudsman was thus concerned about such a blanket policy involving cleaning services:

Prioritising shopping over cleaning. Local authority staff applied a policy of prioritising shopping over cleaning services, whenever demand for services exceeded the local authority's capacity to deliver services. A man complained about this. He was an amputee, wheelchair user, diabetic and doubly incontinent. He was concerned that his health and indeed his life were placed at risk by this policy, which meant he did not receive a regular and reliable cleaning service.

The ombudsman found maladministration, since there was no evidence that the local authority had considered the man's medical circumstances and whether they justified the maintaining of a cleaning service. Furthermore the policy had not been put to members of the social services committee, nor were there guidelines about how to apply it (*Westminster CC 1996*).

Another simple example, illustrating the importance of an apparently low level service, came in a joint health and local government ombudsman investigation:

Failure to provide a one hour a week shopping service for man with mental health problems unable to do his own shopping. The health and local government ombudsmen investigated together in the context of a joint (health and social care) mental health service . One key issue of the case was that the man required a shopping service in the form of a one hour a week care package. He had particular mental health problems (including suicide attempts), exacerbated by the death of his grandmother. He was unable to cope and suffered from agoraphobia and social phobia and could not manage the shopping. The ombudsmen noted the apparent failure of the health and social care assessment to identify this, which was all the more extraordinary, given that a police constable involved had recognised the problem immediately and had himself actually done some shopping for the man (*Middlesbrough Council 2008*).

Indeed, Department of Health guidance concerned with the provision of assistance for carers states that local authorities that have decided not to provide or commission certain services as community care services – such as gardening, shopping and cleaning – 'should review their positions' (DH 2001b). However, restrictive policies on assistance with bathing are also not uncommon within local authorities; one such was criticised by the local government ombudsman:

Restrictive policy on bathing and showering. An 84-year-old man had suffered a stroke; he suffered greatly reduced mobility, and could walk only in a shuffling gait with a walking frame. He could no longer get into his shower and he requested a level access shower. Initially he was refused because the local authority's policy limited eligibility for such a shower to people with a skin condition, incontinence or arthritis (where the person was under a hospital consultant). The ombudsman commented that it would be unreasonable to set criteria so tightly that people obviously in need do not qualify; yet on the face of it the man had a need but did not meet the criteria (*Castle Morpeth BC 2003*).

Certainly, it is not clear how such restricted eligibility for showering or bathing, as a matter of policy, is consonant with the type of full, 'person-centred' assessment urged by the fair access to care guidance (LAC(2002)13). There might be many other possible reasons why a person's need for access to shower or bath might be categorised, for example, a critical or substantial risk to independence.

As CSCI has pointed out, a mechanistic assessment, focused only on the most basic level of hygiene achievable with a strip wash, may totally fail to meet a person's need for dignity and self-respect. And a housebound person who wants carers to feed the birds might be asking for something of fundamental importance to her, yet have it dismissed as unimportant by the local authority. Likewise, when a person's world is 'reduced to little more than four walls', the state and cleanliness of the house and the garden become all the more important (Henwood and Hudson 2008, pp.9, 76, 95).

Notwithstanding these legal and practical points, busy staff in practice may gratefully snatch at policies that are black and white, and so apply them inflexibly (Henwood and Hudson 2008, p.35). The issue of manual handling, notoriously, is associated with rigid policies; yet the courts will find such policies to be unlawful, largely because they preclude proper individual assessment of need (*R(A&B) v East Sussex CC no.2; also R(Clegg) v Salford CC*).

6.13 TAKING ACCOUNT OF LEGALLY RELEVANT FACTORS IN ASSESSMENTS

The courts' interpretation of what would constitute an adequate assessment is consonant with the breadth and scope of assessment set out in the 'fair access to care guidance'. The following cases, involving matters such as medical or therapy advice, cultural factors, preferences, distress, dignity, etc. are illustrative:

Failing to obtain medical advice. When reassessing a woman with multiple sclerosis, the local authority failed to obtain advice from the woman's general practitioner – advice that the local authority had itself identified as necessary. Nevertheless, it concluded the assessment and reduced the woman's care package. This was unlawful (*R v Birmingham CC, ex p Killigrew*).

Cultural needs. When offering to place an elderly Iraqi-Kurdish couple in a care home, against the husband's and wider family's wishes, the court was concerned to ascertain whether the local authority had taken account of the relevant cultural and language matters. It found that it had, and that the decision was lawful (*R(Khana) v Southwark LBC*).

A person's preferences. A local authority assessed a woman with learning disabilities for respite care. During the assessment, the social worker spoke only to the woman's brother, who was her main carer. Although the brother might have been obstructive, it was still incumbent on the local authority to ascertain what those preferences were, as specified in Department of Health guidance (*R v North Yorkshire CC, ex p Hargreaves*).

Fear, distress, dignity. In a case about the manual handling requirements of two women with profound physical and learning disabilities, the court stated that the local authority would have to take account of the emotional, psychological and social impact on two women with learning and physical disabilities. This would be in terms of their wishes, feelings, reluctance, fear, refusal, dignity, integrity and quality of life. The context was about how to effect physical transfers of the two women, and whether they should be hoisted (*R(A&B) v East Sussex County Council: no.2*).

The local government ombudsmen, too, look to ensure that all relevant factors have been considered:

Failing to seek advice from occupational therapist and physiotherapist. A man had suffered a stroke, substantially paralysing his right arm and leg. He had diabetes, hypertension, ulcerative colitis, coronary disease and deformities to his right hand and foot. When reducing a care package from 31 hours a week to 14 hours, the local authority's reassessment failed to obtain advice from a physiotherapist and occupational therapist as to whether the reduced package would still meet his needs. This was maladministration (*Southwark LBC 2001*).

Reduction of care for woman with severe osteoporosis: missing medical advice. In 1997, the local authority proposed to reduce the weekly package of care for a woman with severe osteoporosis; she suffered constant pain, fear of new fractures, actual new major and micro-fractures, headaches and drug-induced side effects. She had a high risk of developing heart disease and was seriously underweight. She argued for a case review on the grounds that the reduced package would not meet her needs. The review identified the need for specialist advice from an occupational therapist and a consultant physician. The council made no sustained attempt to get the consultant's advice; yet without it, the reassessment could not be completed. There was gross delay. New care plans were issued in 1998 and 1999, altering the level of service but without completed reassessments. All this was maladministration (*Croydon LBC 2000*).

A Court of Appeal decision in 2004 notably illustrates the importance of relevant factors, and their role in achieving fairness in decision-making:

Failing to take account of comprehensive assessment report. The local authority decided that a 95-year-old woman could not continue to live in her previous residential home, but would have to go into a nursing home. Her daughter opposed this decision. The court severely criticised the local authority. Amongst other things, it had failed to take account of a critical piece of information, namely the impressive and comprehensive assessment report of the social work team manager, who knew the woman best. For this and other reasons, the decision was manifestly flawed and failed to consider all the relevant factors (*R(Goldsmith) v Wandsworth LBC*).

On the other hand, the courts will not necessarily make excessively legalistic demands. In the following case, it was not entirely clear how the occupational therapy assessment had been taken account of, but the court gave the local authority the benefit of the doubt:

Judicial leeway given to the assessments of hard pressed social workers. A severely physically disabled woman lived with her two adult sons in a two-bedroomed flat on the first and second floors of a large Victorian house. She could not stand or move unsupported, was more or less in constant pain and used a wheelchair out of doors. She was doubly incontinent. She had to negotiate internal stairs, was concerned about the risk of falling and wanted to be rehoused. It was argued that an occupational therapist's report had not been taken into account in the final decision. It was accepted on both sides that it was not necessary as a matter of law to obtain an occupational therapist's report, nonetheless – having obtained the report – it had to be taken into account.

However, the court held that it had been. Although it was not explicitly dealt with in the final, overall community care assessment and decision, the court accepted that (a) it must have been taken account of, because the assessor and therapist worked in the same building, and (b) the final assessment took account of (and preferred) another and more detailed report from the local authority's principal medical housing adviser – which had in fact referred to the occupational therapist's report.

In addition, the woman had contested some of the information contained in the final assessment and argued that she should have been given the opportunity to comment on it. The court stated that the council was under no legal obligation to do so and, even if it had been, the complaints procedure should be used for such disputes rather than the courts.

The court also went out of its way to state that a community care assessment is 'prepared by a social worker for his or her employers. It is not a final determination of a legal dispute by a lawyer which may be subjected to over zealous textual analysis. Courts must be wary, in my view of expecting so much of hard pressed social workers that we risk taking them away, unnecessarily, from their front line duties'. The court also referred to a twenty-year-old housing case in which the House of Lords had warned that 'great restraint should be exercised in giving leave to proceed by judicial review' (R(Ireneschild) v LBC).

6.13.1 RELEVANT FACTORS: CORRECT WEIGHTING

The courts and the local ombudsmen normally look only so far as to see whether relevant factors have been taken account of. If they have, then unless the decision-maker has taken an irrational or unreasonable decision, the courts or ombudsmen will not interfere. To go further would run the risk of pronouncing on the merits of a particular decision; this would in turn run counter to the notion of the courts' 'supervisory jurisdiction' in judicial review (see 5.2.1 above) and to the statutory prohibition on the local government ombudsman to question matters of professional judgement (Local Government Act 1974, s.34).

Nevertheless, particularly where human rights are in issue, the courts might sometimes go beyond considering only the presence of relevant factors, and look to see whether the decision-maker has struck the correct balance (R(A&B) v East Sussex CC: no.2). This is connected with what is sometimes called the principle of 'proportionality', such that even if the decision is not so outlandish as to be irrational or unreasonable, nevertheless the courts might still decide whether the decision was a balanced one. Such an approach might appear to stray into a questioning of the merits of decisions and of professional judgements.

6.14 GIVING EXPLANATIONS AND REASONS

Community care legislation for the most part does not contain duties to give reasons for decisions; and there is no general common law duty to give them (see 5.2.1.7). However, local authorities would be well advised to have properly recorded reasons for decisions, since their absence may lead the courts to query the lawfulness of a particular decision; and a lack of reasons anyway constitutes maladministration in the eyes of the local ombudsman.

Thus, in measured exasperation, the courts in one case criticised a local authority decision about the needs of a disabled boy, finding a flawed decision-making process: 'Unless the repetition of an assertion is to be regarded as a proper manifestation of a reasoning process, there was none here' (R v Ealing LBC, ex p C). In another, the absence of explanation as to why services were being reduced led the court to conclude that the decision was an unlawful one (R v Birmingham CC, ex p Killigrew).

Withdrawing services without relevant evidence of change of need. When night sitter services were withdrawn from an 86-year-old woman on the basis of her no longer needing them – but without evidence of change of circumstance or need – the court stated that there was a very strong argument that the authority was acting irrationally or unreasonably (*R v Staffordshire CC, ex p Farley*).

In a further case, the Court of Appeal struck down a local authority's purported decision to place a woman in a nursing home. The court pointed out that had the decision taken account of all relevant issues, had it been properly recorded with reasons, and had those reasons been communicated to the woman's daughter – then the local authority's decision would probably not have been susceptible to judicial review (*R(Goldsmith) v Wandsworth LBC*).

6.15 SELF-ASSESSMENT

As already noted, Department of Health guidance stresses the importance of the service user being at the centre of, and fully participating in, the assessment (see 6.8 above). Local authorities sometimes ask people to fill out 'self-assessment' forms in order to help achieve this. As part of a wider assessment, there is nothing objectionable in this. However, sometimes authorities go one step beyond, appearing to rely wholly on such self-assessment. It is difficult to see how this could constitute a lawful assessment under s.47 of the NHS and Community Care Act 1990, since it is the local authority that has to take the final decision; it could not give this duty up and hand it over entirely to the service user. In any event, the following local ombudsman investigation illustrates the confusion that can arise:

Self-assessment system. A council operated a system of providing home adaptations on the basis of what it termed self-assessment. Consequently a disabled woman assessed that she required an extra bedroom. The council then argued that it had no obligation to provide this, since its apparent willingness at one point to provide the extension did not translate into a legal duty to do so. The ombudsman accepted this but found the council's apparent undertaking had been misleading, resulting in acute disappointment and frustration. This was maladministration (*Manchester CC 1994*).

In another context, that of housing allocation based on the 'additional preferences' identified by tenants themselves, the court pointed out that self-assessment would not identify priorities and different degrees of need. This was because the 'individual is inevitably concerned only with his or own situation and may not on any reasonably objective view have greater need' (*Lambeth LBC v A*).

Self-assessment is being advocated ever more by central government, in relation to self-directed care and individual budgets (see 13.2 below), so the question of how it fits into the community care legal framework persists. The Department of Health does, in some but not all of its current, highly fragmented guidelines, dimly recognise that a conflict may arise – and that ultimately it would still be for the local authority to decide, pointing out that people's own assessment of their needs may conflict with those of a professional assessor (Secretary of State for Health 2005, p.31). As the legislation stands, it is difficult to see how the position could be otherwise.

6.16 ASSESSMENT OF CHILDREN WHEN THEY LEAVE SCHOOL

Legislation provides for the assessment by local authorities of children or certain young people who have had statements of special educational needs – when they leave school or further or higher education institutions (Disabled Persons (Services, Consultation and Representation) Act 1986, s.5). In summary:

- Education authorities must obtain an assessment from the local authority social services department – for 15-year-old pupils who already have statements of special educational needs – as to whether or not the pupil is disabled. This is done by notifying the 'appropriate officer' appointed by the local social services authority for this purpose; he or she has to give an opinion as to whether or not the child is disabled. Likewise this duty of notification applies in respect of a child over 14 years old without a statement, but who then has one made for the first time.

- In either case, the education authority must inform the appropriate officer of the date when the child will no longer be of compulsory school age, and whether (and where) he or she intends to remain in full-time education – at least eight but not more than 12 months before that date.

- In addition, further education or higher education institutions, or the Learning and Skills Council, are obliged to notify the local social services authority in writing at least eight, but not longer than 12, months before a pupil with a statement of special educational needs, who has been assessed as disabled, will cease to receive full-time education. This duty applies where the pupil is over compulsory school age, but under the age of 19 years and eight months.

- Once the above has taken place (in respect of school, further or higher education), the local social services authority must then carry out an assessment of the person's needs. This is to determine whether the local authority has a duty to provide services under Part 3 of the National Assistance Act 1948, s.2 of the Chronically Sick and Disabled Persons Act 1970, s.254 and schedule 20 of the NHS Act 2006, or Part 3 of the Children Act 1989.

- The assessment must be carried out within five months of the date of notification. If a disabled student has ceased to receive full-time education or will cease to do so within less than eight months, and no notification has been made to the social services authority but should have been, then the education authority must notify in writing social services – who must then carry out the assessment as soon as reasonably practicable, and in any case within five months.

The intention of notifying the local social services authority is so that a smooth transition can take place and appropriate arrangements be made. However, this does not always work as well as it should, and the local ombudsman has investigated several cases in which the local authority has failed the disabled person involved:

Failure to assess and budget for meeting need. A young man with multiple disabilities was profoundly deaf, partially sighted, and able to communicate only by means of sign language and a computer. From the age of 16 on (statutory school-leaving age), the education authority considered whether he should continue to remain at a specialist residential boarding school. When he was 19 in 1990, it decided that it would cease funding, but that social services might wish to support him for a further period at the school.

Records from 1990 showed that social services had no planned budget for the man, that a newly formed resource centre could not meet his needs and that he should be given priority for assessment. No assessment took place, and some months later in January 1991, the man began attending the resource centre – even though it was recognised from the start that it was not able to meet his needs and that staff could not communicate with him. By 1993, he was still attending the centre, was also attending a local college of further education, and had been assessed by a national deaf association (in February 1993). Social services finally completed its overall assessment by August 1993.

The local ombudsman found various failings including (a) no assessment of need in 1990 as promised; (b) despite the council's knowing about the person since 1986, there had been no planning ahead and budgetary provision made; (c) the placement at the resource centre went ahead despite the unhappiness amongst both its own staff and the mother – and without it being made clear to the mother whether there were any alternatives; (d) a proper assessment had not taken place until 1993 (when the man's own views were finally sought) and this was an unreasonable delay. This was all maladministration which caused distress, anxiety and trouble to both mother and son; the ombuds-man recommended that £1000 and £2000 be paid respectively to them (*East Sussex County Council 1995a*).

Leaving the assessment too late. A 19-year-old man with learning disabilities had attended a resi-dential school outside Knowsley; in August 1993, the school wrote to the social services department inviting an officer to attend in March 1994 the last annual review of the man's statement of special educational needs. It was expected that he would spend the 1994 summer holidays at home with his parents and then move into local accommodation in September.

Despite the council's assurance that an 'appropriately supported living arrangement' would be in place by the time he left school, this did not happen. Apart from one attempt in May 1994 consisting of shared accommodation (the man realised he did not wish to share with the particular man in question), accommodation was not available until November 1995, and there was no evidence that priority had been given to resolving the situation. The council had failed to carry out an adequate assessment of need and to draw up a proper care plan (the council had maintained that a full assess-ment could not be completed until the man was back in the community).

Consequently, the mother had suffered great emotional and physical strain which had affected the relationship with her son. Feeling unable to accept interim provision in the form of domiciliary support or a hostel, she had given up her job and incurred financial loss.

The local ombudsman commended the council for reviewing its arrangements for transition from school to adult services, and recommended it pay £500 in compensation for anxiety, stress and trouble – but not for the mother's financial loss (since it was her decision to reject the temporary solution of hostel accommodation or domiciliary support) (*Knowsley MBC 1997*).

Failure to assess and provide on leaving school and for two years after. This was a complaint about the assessment and arrangements for a young man leaving school, who was initially thought to have mild learning disabilities and a stress-related physical condition, and was later diagnosed as schizophrenic.

First, the local ombudsman found that it was maladministration for the council not to assess him before he left school – as it was required to do under s.5 of the Disabled Persons (Consultation and Representation) Act 1986. However, it was not an injustice, because the ombudsman considered that, at this time, it was most unlikely that the person would have been assessed as disabled – in which case there would have been no automatic involvement of social services.

Second, following a community care assessment (two years after he had left school), nothing was done for nine months. This was 'too long'; the man had 'to wait longer for remedial help in overcom-ing his reclusiveness and…his family had to go longer than was necessary without practical support'. This was maladministration.

Third, it was also maladministration for the council not to have given the parents a copy of the assessment report when requested – even though no injustice flowed from this because the services, which a written report would have recommended, were in fact obtained.

Fourth, a delay in allocating the case to an officer following transfer to another team led to inade-quate provision for seven months; this was maladministration.

Fifth, it was maladministration when a particular officer failed to keep appointments with the father, or to tell him sooner about problems with the appointments; this led to the father taking time off work unnecessarily (*Liverpool CC 1997*).

CHAPTER 7

Reassessing, withdrawing services and waiting

KEY POINTS

REASSESSMENT AND WITHDRAWAL OF SERVICES

Social services legislation does not refer explicitly to review and reassessment but Department of Health guidance has persistently drawn attention to their importance. Apart from ensuring that people's needs are still being met in an appropriate manner, they are also a pre-condition for the withdrawal, reduction or fundamental alteration of service provision for an individual. Following such review and reassessment there is a number of grounds on which a local authority can lawfully withdraw, reduce or alter services substantially. These include a change in the person's needs or circumstances, offer of another way (perhaps cheaper) in which the person's needs can be met, change in the eligibility threshold applied by the local authority, or unreasonable behaviour by the service user.

A particular ground of dispute has been the closure of services, including care homes and day centres. Local authorities must consult adequately before closing down services, and adequately meet people's needs by offering alternative services. Human rights considerations will also be relevant. However, by and large, legal challenges attempting to prevent such closures tend to fail, if the local authority has followed the right procedures of consultation.

WAITING TIMES FOR ASSESSMENT

Alternative to denying people assessment in the first place, local authorities sometimes make them wait a long time. Inevitably the question arises as to the point at which the tardy carrying out of a duty amounts to not carrying it out at all and to unlawfulness. Absent timescales set out in legislation, and both law courts and local ombudsmen state that local authorities must carry out their duties within a reasonable time and without undue delay. What is reasonable will depend on all the circumstances of the case; although the courts might anyway be reluctant to intervene if a dispute about delay involves a consideration of facts only, rather than points of law. The reasonableness approach has both advantages and disadvantages; it sensibly permits flexibility in reacting to individual needs, but denies all concerned an easy, if crude, rule of thumb.

7.1 REVIEW AND REASSESSMENT

From time to time service users will need to be reassessed. The trigger might be, for example, (a) a review date becoming due; (b) needs and circumstances anyway changing (perhaps before a scheduled review date); (c) a change in the local authority's threshold of eligibility.

Failing to reassess on change of need. A complaint was made to the local ombudsman concerning a man with learning disabilities who had in 1991 been placed in a care home jointly by social services and the NHS. In 1998, he was diagnosed as suffering from high functioning autism. However, he was not reassessed by the local authority until February 2003 and not provided with additional services until June of that year. The local ombudsman found maladministration (*Cambridgeshire CC 2004*).

In the legislation, there is no explicit duty of review or reassessment. However, reassessment is in effect covered by s.47 of the NHS and Community Care Act 1990; it is assessment all over again against potential, changed need.

The importance of review is stressed by guidance on 'fair access to care' (FACS) and on the 'single assessment process' for older people. The latter stipulates that reviews should be undertaken on a routine basis, within three months of services first being provided or of major changes to services, and after that annually or more frequently if necessary. It adds that 'one-off pieces' of community equipment do not need review after initial confirmation of suitability and safety, although major items should be reviewed for suitability and safety annually, or more frequently if recommended by manufacturers (LAC(2002)1, annex E). The FACS guidance states that:

- **(reviews)** reviews should consider determine services achieved outcomes, reassess needs, determine continuing eligibility, confirm or amend or close current care plan
- **(three monthly and yearly reviews)** there should be three-monthly reviews where assistance first provided or major change to services, thereafter at least annually

- **(competent professionals)** reviews must be conducted by competent professionals
- **(face to face contact)** reviews may be undertaken without face-to-face contact, but only exceptionally
- **(no delegation to service providers)** reviews must not be delegated to providers
- **(equipment)** one-off pieces of equipment do not need review after initial confirmation of suitability – major items should be reviewed as to their suitability and safety on annual basis
- **(withdrawal and worsening needs)** non-eligibility decision only if the council is satisfied that needs will not significantly worsen or increase in near future for the lack of help, and thereby compromise independence including employment, training, education and parenting responsibilities
- **(withdrawal and exacerbation of need)** non-eligibility: withdrawal of services should not take place if the consequence will be to exacerbate needs and thus make the person eligible again in the foreseeable future
- **(carers)** councils should not make assumptions about the capacity of family members or close friends to offer support
- **(safety of withdrawing services)** it may not be practicable or safe to withdraw services, even though needs and associated risks may initially appear to fall outside criteria – also any commitments given at the outset about longevity of service provision given should be checked before withdrawal
- **(reasons in writing)** refusal or withdrawal of service should be put in writing in terms of the decision and reasons (LAC(2002)13, paras 60–68).

In practice, adequately reviewing people's needs and services would appear to have been a longstanding problem for local authorities. At the outset of community care, central government guidance acknowledged this (SSI/SWSG 1991, para 7.1); the local ombudsmen continue to identify the issue (see Chapter 7 for possible consequences of failure to review):

Failure to reassess. In July 1995, the local authority entered a contract with a voluntary organisation to provide services at a day centre, which two brothers with learning disabilities had been attending for years. The contract expressly stipulated that the services were to be for adults with sensory impairment, physical and invisible disabilities. Reference to learning disabilities was not included. The contract also stated that reassessment of all current service users would be undertaken within six months. However, this did not occur for 18 months, a delay of a year. The local ombudsman found maladministration (*Hackney LBC 1998*).

Failure to review. A woman complained on behalf of her mother, concerned amongst other things about her care in a care home including sitting in urine-soaked clothing, assistance with feeding (she lost over four stone in weight) and inappropriate medication. The mother was 81 years old, had rheumatoid arthritis, angina, was occasionally incontinent and displayed early signs of dementia. Amongst her findings the local ombudsman criticised the failure to carry out a six-monthly review. She pointed out that had a review taken place, the weight loss could have been investigated and dealt with that much earlier (*Wigan MBC 2001*).

In a case involving the failure for many years of a local authority both to assess and review a woman with learning disabilities in a foster placement, the ombudsman stated with some restraint that she was in no doubt that it was inappropriate for a manager to instruct that reviews of someone who is deaf and has learning disabilities should be done by telephone (*Birmingham CC 2008*).

7.2 CONDITIONS FOR LAWFUL WITHDRAWAL OR REDUCTION OF SERVICES

Services can in some circumstances be lawfully changed, reduced or withdrawn by the local authority. First, there must be an individual reassessment (*R v Gloucestershire CC, ex p Mahfood*). Department of Health guidance on fair access to care makes this point, too (LAC(2002)13, para 58). Then one of the following conditions must be met:

- the authority's eligibility criteria have changed such that the person's needs no longer command the same level of service provision
- the assessed needs have changed
- the needs can be met in a different way
- the person no longer wishes to receive the same services
- there is unreasonable behaviour on the part of the service user.

If such conditions are absent, then generally speaking the local authority's decision runs the risk of being unlawful. This follows from the fact that assessed eligible need must generally be met (*R v Gloucestershire CC, ex p Barry*: see 6.9).

7.2.1 REASSESSMENT

The courts have stated that a person's services cannot be reduced, withdrawn or significantly altered unless an individual reassessment has first taken place:

Reassessing on individual basis. When a local authority contemplated withdrawing or reducing home help services from up to 1500 people, the court ruled that it had to reassess each of them on an individual basis. It could not simply take a blanket decision (*R v Gloucestershire CC, ex p Mahfood*).

Changing services. When 13 service users were reassessed, six were allocated a cheaper service provider, seven kept the original, more expensive, one. This balanced outcome reassured the court that individual reassessments had taken place, and that decisions had not been wholly determined by resources. The court accepted that the local authority could take account of resources in respect of the changes, so long as it never forgot that the needs of service users were more important than money (*R v Essex CC, ex p Bucke*).

Furthermore, because of the vulnerable nature of community care service users, a local authority must make reasonable efforts to effect that reassessment:

Making reasonable efforts to reassess. A local authority was reviewing and reassessing people's needs for services they were currently receiving. It wrote to service users offering a reassessment if they replied in the affirmative. If they did not, the implication was that they might anyway have their service reduced or withdrawn. The court found that this approach was not adequate in the context of community care services and vulnerable people, where the duty of assessment did not rely on a request. This contrasted with other contexts, where people might be better able to look after their own interests. Although effective reassessment could not be undertaken without a degree of cooperation from the service user, nevertheless such a letter would not be enough (*R v Gloucestershire CC, ex p RADAR*).

The ombudsman has expressed the view that if a change of service introduces no material difference in terms of meeting assessed needs, then a reassessment is not required; this was in a case involving a change of day centre. However, if the service user then withdrew, as she was entitled to if she was unhappy about the change, the local authority did then have a duty to reassess in order to identify an alternative (*Harrow LBC 2004*). In another ombudsman case, the fact that records showed that a visit was made by local authority staff in order to inform service users about a reduction in service, did not mean that it could be assumed that a reassessment took place (*Derbyshire CC 2004*).

Central government practice guidance originally seemed to suggest that review would be face to face, since it stated that it might be appropriate to conduct the core part of it in the service user's own home (SSI/SWSG 1991, para 7.5). More recent Department of Health policy guidance is more direct, stating that other than in exceptional circumstances, reviews should be face to face, conducted by a competent professional and should not be delegated to the care provider (LAC(2002)13, paras 61–62).

7.2.2 CHANGE IN THRESHOLD OF ELIGIBILITY

If a local authority's threshold of eligibility has changed, it might be the case that certain service users might no longer be entitled to (the same level of) services, even though their own needs remain unchanged. In such circumstances, the courts have held that it is lawful to withdraw or reduce services following individual reassessments (*R v Gloucestershire CC, ex p Barry*).

However, Department of Health guidance points out that caution must nevertheless be exercised, for example, where people may have developed such a dependency on the service that they would not cope without it (LAC(2002)13, para 66). Put another way, such a dependency would, in individual cases, have to be assessed as part of a person's eligible need. This might require a period of adequate notice, as the local ombudsman thought in the following case:

Gradual withdrawal/change. A local authority had been funding psychotherapy sessions for a woman, following the ending of her placement in a therapeutic community home. With no proper assessment or review, the local authority suddenly withdrew the service without adequate notice. The local ombudsman found maladministration; this warranted the local authority paying to the woman the money she owed on some of the sessions she had continued to have, as well as the travel expenses she had occurred and £1250 for distress caused (*Brent LBC 1994*).

The courts have stated their reluctance in principle to interfere with the strictness of eligibility criteria under legislation such as the CSDPA 1970. Thus, on the withdrawal of services following reassessment, they may hesitate to interfere, even if they feel the revised package of care has been pared to the bone.

Reassessment of man with multiple sclerosis. A man with multiple sclerosis was reassessed, with the consequence that a package of care, that had effectively constituted 24-hour-a-day assistance, was reduced to five hours a day.

The judge decided that the reassessment and revised care plan did not constitute legal unreasonableness or irrationality since, on the evidence available, the authority had not 'taken leave of its senses'. Nevertheless, he did say that he had 'grave misgivings as to whether 5 hours per day of care plus Meals on Wheels and domiciliary nursing can meet the applicant's needs consistent with the [authority's] resources'. He went on to give an example of an authority taking leave of its senses and the high threshold necessary to warrant judicial intervention. Under its housing allocation system, an authority had awarded 0 points, on a scale from 0 to 250, to a woman with possibly recurrent cancer and gross breathing difficulty. Two consultants at London teaching hospitals had said in categorical terms that were she to climb stairs this would endanger her life. In such circumstances a court could 'properly but most exceptionally' conclude that the authority must have taken leave of its senses (*R v Haringey LBC, ex p Norton*).

Likewise, in another legal case, the local authority had persistently attempted to reduce and minimise services for a person who had Still's disease (a form of rheumatoid arthritis characterised by high spiking fevers), suffered serious flare-ups and was almost totally blind. The judge remarked that the package was not generous, but then legally it did not have to be. The package was not perverse, but the judge would not have been surprised if a reassessment revealed the need for more hours of care (*R(Heffernan) v Sheffield CC*).

7.2.3 CHANGE IN NEED

If a person's needs have changed then clearly a change in service might be justified, but any such decision should be based on a proper reassessment, as the courts have emphatically stated:

Reassessment and reduction of service. Following a manual handling assessment of a woman with multiple sclerosis, a local authority provided two personal assistants for six hours instead of one for 12 hours. The local authority could not show (a) that this reduction equated to a change in the woman's assessed, eligible needs; or (b) that the needs were to be met in a different way (there was apparently no question of the eligibility threshold having changed).

In particular, the judge found no 'careful assessment' or proper analysis of the whole situation, if the time allotted were to be halved. He noted that it was 'important that the reduction to six hours' care was not driven by the need to have two carers to carry out the task'. The reduction could only be justified if there was no continuing need for 12 hours of care.

The judge held the decision to be unlawful and ordered that the local authority carry out its assessment again. In addition, he found a separate ground of unlawfulness; the assessor knew she ought to discuss matters with the woman's general practitioner, yet failed to do so. This was because the woman had just changed GP and the new GP did not yet feel able to offer any information. This was not good enough; it meant up-to-date medical information was not taken into account, when it should have been (*R v Birmingham CC, ex p Killigrew*).

Alternatively, there might simply be no formal assessment at all, in which case the courts will simply hold the local authority's decision to be unlawful:

Change of residential placement. A 35-year-old woman with autism had been placed by her local authority some years before in a further education placement in Newcastle. Subsequently, she moved out of the hall of residence to a residential address operated by the managers of the college. Seven years from the date of the original placement, the local authority sought to move the woman back to Leicestershire into an alternative residential placement. A letter to this effect was sent to the woman's mother, stating that this move would be for her daughter's long-term health, security and happiness.

However, the judge held that there had been no specific assessment for three and a half years since June 1999, and an assessment had to be carried out with a degree of formality prior to any change of placement. Furthermore he was not prepared to hold that the subsequent greater scrutiny of the woman's needs, which took place through the complaints procedure (when the mother complained), remedied this defect. This was particularly because the independent complaints investigator had first of all taken the approach that because a Leicestershire placement would be more suitable, therefore the Newcastle one was unsuitable. Yet logically this need not follow. Second, there had been an incorrect assumption that the health care services the woman required would not have been available in Newcastle. Thus, the local authority's decision was unlawful and the council would have to start again (*R(S) v Leicester City Council*).

Without a change of need, or of eligibility criteria or some other relevant circumstance, decisions run the risk of being unlawful:

Reassessment and withdrawal of night-sitting service. An 86-year-old woman was reassessed. She suffered from severe arthritis and had poor mobility and a very weak bladder, which meant that she needed assistance from chair or bed to commode or toilet throughout the day and night. This resulted in an altered care plan and the loss of the night-sitting service which had previously been provided. The night-sitting service under the original care plan involved a person in attendance between 10 pm and 7 am to help with undressing, ensure that she was properly provided for and able to visit the toilet frequently during the night. The revised care plan involved only a person in attendance between 10 pm and 10.30 pm, to undress the woman, make her a drink and see that she was comfortable for the night. An interim injunction was sought – and obtained – to prevent this, pending a full judicial hearing.

The judge noted that nothing in the new care plan suggested a change either in the woman's needs or in any other relevant circumstances. This strongly suggested that the apparent decision, that she no longer needed night care, was based on no evidence whatsoever. This would make it irrational or unreasonable. He added that she was indisputably very infirm; and attempts by her to go to the toilet would result in physical problems, danger and possible extreme physical discomfort. To expose her to that sort of indignity and risk would, in the court's judgment, have been inhumane (*R v Staffordshire CC, ex p Farley*).

7.2.4 DIFFERENT WAY OF MEETING NEED

If a local authority can genuinely meet a person's need in another way, then a withdrawal or change of service may be lawful. Nevertheless, local authorities have to be able to demonstrate this; in neither of the two following examples could they do so:

Emergency need. When a local authority reassessed a woman with multiple sclerosis, it substantially reduced the daytime assistance she received. One of the purposes of this assistance had been to ensure that a carer was on hand in case an emergency arose. The new assessment and care plan did not deal with the issue of how an emergency need, in case of epileptic fit, would be met. This was one of the grounds on which the reassessment was held by the judge to be unlawful (*R v Birmingham CC, ex p Killigrew*).

Similarly, the local ombudsman will consider whether a reliable alternative exists:

Unreliable alternative. A local authority reassessed a man and stated that the need for recreational trips could in future be met through a local voluntary organisation rather than the local authority. Yet there was no evidence that the organisation could reliably supply the volunteers that would be required to assist him. The local ombudsman found maladministration (*Southwark LBC 2001*).

Furthermore, the general condition of reassessment – including participation of, and consultation with, the service user – must still be adhered to:

Change in visiting arrangements. A woman with severe learning disabilities had been placed in the care of a foster family. Arrangements for fortnightly Saturday visits home by the sister were agreed. These were subsequently being cancelled at short notice. The local authority proposed a change of day (Wednesday), and informed the mother who disagreed. The council went ahead and confirmed the change. Changing the day without consultation, and confirming the change against the family's wishes, was held by the local ombudsman to be maladministration (*Manchester 1996*).

7.2.5 EXPLICIT REFUSAL BY SERVICE USER

In the case of adults with the capacity to take the relevant decision, community care services cannot be provided without their consent. In other words, such a person is obviously at liberty to refuse a service. If there is such a refusal, the question may arise as to whether or not the service offered was reasonable, and whether the refusal was unreasonable – and thus whether or not the local authority should offer other options. For instance, in the following case, the court did not consider the refusal unreasonable:

Unreasonable refusal of services? A family occupied a two-bedroom flat on the 12th floor of an 18-floor block. The man suffered from severe depression and pain in his knees that prevented him from negotiating stairs. He had psychotic symptoms and some features of post-traumatic stress disorder, and had been preoccupied with suicide and intrusive hallucinations. His wife had become significantly depressed.

Social services assessed and concluded that a ground-floor property was required with enough space for the rest of the family. A care plan was drawn up, stating that he needed a safe, secure, easily accessible and spacious environment in which to live so he had space away from his family, could access the dwelling and reduce the risk of self-harm. The man rejected the idea of short-let private property in principle due to lack of security of tenure and private sector rent rates, and argued that social services still had a duty to meet his needs.

The local authority argued that the refusal was unreasonable and that it had discharged its duty. The court accepted that a local authority does not have a duty 'willy-nilly' to provide accommodation under s.21 regardless of a person's willingness to accept it. However, in this case, the refusal of private, short-let accommodation, and of a three-bedroom flat with a number of unsuitable steps, meant that the man had not begun to stretch the duty 'to the point of willy-nilly'. The refusal was not unreasonable (*R(Batantu) v Islington LBC*).

The following court case provides a clearer example of unreasonableness on the part of the local authority, and indeed of a person's inability to refuse a service, reasonably or unreasonably:

Refusal of hostel accommodation. A woman with physical and mental health problems was evicted from her home on neighbour nuisance grounds. The local authority housing department decided she was homeless but intentionally so. She was told of her right to a review of this decision under the Housing Act 1996. A request for a review was made three days outside of the statutory 21-day time limit (which expired on 21 May), after the Official Solicitor had been appointed to act (9 May) for her because of her mental incapacity. The council's housing department refused to accept the review request. On 28 April, without an assessment, the social services department had offered hostel accommodation to the applicant under s.21 of the National Assistance Act 1948, which she had refused. Social services now stated that it could do nothing more.

The court found that the local authority should have extended the time for review; not least because evidence concerning the woman's mental illness would bear on the question of whether she was intentionally homeless under the Housing Act. The social services department should have assessed the woman; furthermore, the apparent refusal of accommodation by a psychiatrically ill applicant could not put an end to the continuing duty to provide accommodation under s.21 of the 1948 Act (R(Patrick) v Newham LBC).

The local ombudsman has warned that local authorities should not give up too readily when a person apparently refuses services:

Refusal of services: taking this at face value. A man with learning disabilities and autism had rejected offers of service from the local authority; he preferred to rely on his brother (who was however struggling to cope as carer). The local ombudsman accepted that, whilst a local authority cannot 'force services upon an unwilling person', nevertheless it must sometimes be cautious about taking a refusal of service at face value. The ombudsman considered that the local authority should have questioned whether the refusal constituted an informed decision. It should also have found a way to work both with the man and his brother; this was clearly possible because a community nurse, a psychologist and a worker from a voluntary organisation had all successfully interacted with the man; in which case, why could not the local authority do the same (Sheffield CC 2004)?

Even when a local authority is entitled to conclude that it has made a reasonable offer of a service, nevertheless refusal by a person of a particular option under one piece of legislation might not preclude continuing responsibilities under another. For example, an offer to an elderly couple of a care home place, which would have fully met their needs under s.21 of the National Assistance Act 1948, was refused. The court held that that it was a lawful and reasonable offer. However, the question then arose as to whether the local authority should still provide – notwithstanding this refusal of residential accommodation – other non-residential services, such as Meals on Wheels or laundry services, under s.29 of the 1948 Act. The court answered in the affirmative, since the accommodation duty under s.21 was one matter; the duty to provide services under s.29 another (R(Khana) v Southwark LBC).

7.2.6 UNREASONABLE BEHAVIOUR OF SERVICE USERS

Local authorities are often faced with the difficult decision of when to withdraw or withhold a service in the light of difficult or unreasonable behaviour by service users. The duty to meet assessed, eligible need should not be dismissed lightly; and where a person's behaviour stems from the type of need that local authorities are under obligations to meet (e.g. mental health problems), the courts have stated that caution is required in determining what constitutes unreasonable behaviour:

Threats of violence and withdrawal of service. An asylum seeker was being provided with hotel accommodation by the local authority. As a result of violence towards hotel staff, the local authority warned him that they would assist once more. However, if further such problems arose, they would cease to assist. A recurrence took place at different premises and the authority consequently withdrew its assistance.

The court held that the duty of the local authority under s.21 of the National Assistance Act 1948 was not absolute in the sense that it had a duty 'willy-nilly' regardless of the person's behaviour. The duty would be dependent on the cooperation of the person to occupy the accommodation in accordance with reasonable conditions – in terms of health and safety, preventing injury, nuisance or annoyance.

Nevertheless, the court stated that to the extent that s.21 of the 1948 Act was a safety net, the local authority should not lightly refuse to perform its duty; it would have to be satisfied of persistent and unequivocal refusal to comply with reasonable requirements.

Furthermore, such persistent and unequivocal refusal would be unlikely to be identified if the person's behaviour stemmed from a depressive condition associated with the very ill-treatment that had led him to seek asylum. The local authority would be expected to make reasonable efforts to identify a person's needs, although not to conduct a 'CID investigation' (R v Kensington and Chelsea RBC, ex p Kujtim).

The White Paper *Valuing People*, concerned with people with learning disabilities, considered the question of exclusion of people from services. It stated that excluding people with learning disabilities because of challenging behaviour placed great stress on carers who would as a consequence be left unsupported to cope with their son or daughter at home. The 'practice was unacceptable and families must not be left to cope unaided'. Services should not be withdrawn on such grounds without suitable alternative services being put in place where possible. Furthermore, decisions to exclude should always be referred to the Local Disability Partnership Board, which should be responsible for alternative provision (DH 2001d, para 5.7). Department of Health guidance required such local boards to develop policies, procedures and criteria relating to exclusions, as well as procedures for arranging alternative services (HSC 2001/16, paras 37–38). So when an autistic young man was excluded from respite care, an alternative was not found for 15 months, the issue was not reported to the local Board, and there were no exclusion criteria – the local ombudsman found maladministration (*Stockton-on-Tees BC 2005*).

Nonetheless, a point might sometimes be reached where the courts hold that it is reasonable and lawful to withhold a service in the light of threatening behaviour:

Aggressive, abusive and threatening behaviour. District nurses regularly visited a woman at home, who was suffering from disseminated sclerosis, unable to walk or use her arms and hardly able to do anything herself. The nurses were regularly subject to aggressive, abusive and threatening behaviour by the husband. He refused to give an undertaking not to behave in this way. The health authority warned him that it would withdraw the nursing service if this behaviour persisted. The woman challenged this in court, arguing that the authority was obliged to continue to provide nursing, and that husband and wife should be regarded separately. The Court of Appeal rejected this, stating that the authority was doing everything it could, that husband and wife could not be separated for this purpose, and that while the unreasonable behaviour continued, there was no duty to secure the attendance of nurses (R v Hillingdon AHA, ex p Wyatt).

Similarly, a local authority arranged accommodation for an asylum seeker; he failed to take up the offer of the accommodation on the grounds that he could not live in the same house as a Muslim; the council in turn refused to offer alternative accommodation. The court found the local authority's position perfectly reasonable (*R(Panic) v Secretary of State for the Home*

Department). Where exclusion from a service is applied, the local ombudsman has stated that there need to be fair procedures in terms of the exclusion and reinstatement:

Exclusion from a day centre. The case concerned the exclusion of a person with mental health problems from a day centre, following disputes between her and other attendees about the way the centre was run. (At monthly meetings, increasingly more decisions were being taken by users of the centre – one of the complainant's objections concerned this development.)

The local ombudsman stated that if people were excluded from a service on which they rely, then 'natural justice' required that they be told promptly (a) why; (b) the duration of the exclusion; (c) what action was planned to facilitate re-entry; (d) who would decide about re-entry; and (e) how to appeal. Yet none of these requirements was fulfilled.

Managers had not been given clear guidance on how to manage or record difficult events – foreseeable at such centres – and this was maladministration. Also maladministration was the focus on the complainant's background and history in the investigation report produced in response to her complaint, because the 'purpose of a complaint is, first and foremost, to scrutinise the actions of the Council' (*Cornwall County Council 1996*).

If there are such procedures, it is important that they are adhered to and that staff are given appropriate guidance:

Exclusion for smoking marijuana. The case concerned aftercare for a man with schizophrenia under s.117 of the Mental Health Act 1983. He had been discharged from a hostel for people with mental health problems because he had been smoking marijuana. (About a year later he fell to his death from a tower block.) The parents claimed that the council had not dealt properly with the discharge.

The local ombudsman concluded as follows. The council accepted and its procedure stipulated, the events leading to the discharge were grounds for an emergency review, but not an immediate discharge. However, staff had been given no clear written guidance about the procedure, nor about obligations under s.117 of the 1983 Act. The discharge amounted to maladministration (*Hounslow LBC 1995*).

Local authorities also have to bear in mind on the one hand their duty to meet the needs of vulnerable adults, but on the other their duties to their own staff. For example, a failure to protect their staff from racial discrimination, or the detrimental effects of it, could result in proceedings against the employer before an Employment Tribunal:

Racist behaviour toward nurse by child's mother. A very young child with cystic fibrosis had regularly to attend a hospital as an inpatient. The child's mother was known to have difficulties with drink, was dependent on drugs and known to be violent. The mother had approached a consultant, told him that she was racist and did not want a black person to care for her child. The black person in question was a specialist paediatric nurse of Afro-Caribbean origin and of exemplary character.

Thereafter, over an extended period of years, the staff acceded to the mother's wish and the child was moved between wards, or from one end of the ward or the other, to satisfy the mother.

Some years later, another child was admitted and its mother made the same racist request; however, this request was not acceded to by the senior sister. Furthermore, there was no evidence that the first mother had threatened to remove her child if she had not got her way; and if there had been genuine fears that she would and that the child would suffer, the courts or social services could have been involved. The Tribunal therefore had no hesitation in holding that the nurse had been discriminated against and that she had suffered substantial detriment in terms of being hurt, distraught, ashamed to tell her family, and her feelings being injured. An award of £20,000 was made (*Purves v Southampton University Hospitals Trust*).

Similarly, when violence is threatened, local authorities have duties towards their own staff under health and safety at work legislation; under the guise of what measures are 'reasonably practicable', authorities will have to balance the meeting of service users' need with the safety of their employees (see 5.4.1 above).

Thus, it is often about a balanced response, as became clear in the following case, when questions of a client's behaviour to women arose, as well as the buying of whisky by carers. The council did not withdraw services but took a balanced approach which was praised by the ombudsman:

Allegation of sexual deviancy, and whether carers should buy the client whisky as part of a shopping service. A complainant to the ombudsman alleged that the council had branded his uncle a sexual deviant with no evidence. However, the ombudsman found that it was the uncle himself who had informed social workers about his use of prostitutes and a possible investigation against himself for a sexual offence. The warden of the sheltered accommodation where he lived did not want him to return there because of his behaviour. In response to these concerns, the council had responded in a 'proper and appropriate manner', given the duty of care it had both to its service users and its staff. It ruled out a police check, and the man returned home from hospital to sheltered accommodation. Only male home carers were allocated for his care, but were not told the reason for this, thus protecting the man's privacy.

In the same complaint, the nephew complained that the council carers had bought too much whisky for his uncle. Indeed, this was more or less all they were asked to buy. However, the ombudsman found that though the uncle was in poor physical health, his mental faculties were unaffected. If he chose to drink large quantities of alcohol, this was his decision; he enjoyed it and it was a priority for him. The council had assessed that it would provide a shopping service and it continued to do so. This was not maladministration (*North Tyneside MBC 2004*).

The question of smoking cigarettes sometimes arises, and of whether a local authority could insist on a person not smoking in their own home. The Health Act 2006 is not a direct help. It states that a place of work should be smoke-free. However, regulations have been made which means that this rule does not apply to a private dwelling where the work is undertaken solely (a) to provide personal care for a person living in the dwelling; (b) to assist with the domestic work of the household in the dwelling; (c) to maintain the structure or fabric of the dwelling; or (d) to install, maintain or remove any service provided to the dwelling for the benefit of persons living in it (ss.2 and 3. And: SI 2007/76, r.2). So, in case of a refusal by a person not to smoke, a local authority would still have to weigh up on the one hand its duty to meet a person's needs under community care legislation – as against its duty to carers under the Health and Safety at Work Act 1974 (but not under the Health Act 2006).

The courts have held that a ban, under the regulations, on patients at a high security psychiatric hospital - from smoking in the building or leaving the building in order to smoke in the grounds – did not breach the European Convention on Human Rights. Under article 8, the health and safety considerations manifest in the Act and the regulations justified the ban. The court noted, however, that there could be exceptional cases which would demand the availability of facilities for smoking to protect a person's mental health (*R(G) v Nottinghamshire Healthcare NHS Trust*).

7.3 CLOSURE OF SERVICES

Closures of local authority services, including care homes and day centres, are obviously an example of a change in service provision. A considerable number of such closures has been challenged in the law courts. Despite some cases in which the courts notably reached decisions that the proposed closure was unlawful, the majority of such challenges have failed.

A largely similar pattern has emerged in respect of closures of NHS facilities as well (see 17.7).

7.3.1 CLOSURES AND INDIVIDUAL ASSESSMENT

Detailed individual assessment of need and how it will be met will not always have to take place before the decision to close has been taken (*R v North and East Devon HA, ex p Coughlan*). Sometimes it will be enough if it is carried out at a later stage when a decision about individual alternative placements is made (*R(Rowe) v Walsall MBC*). However, individual assessment was required in the following case:

Assessing people with learning disabilities. A health authority wished to close a long-stay hospital for people with profound learning disabilities and physical disabilities such as lack of mobility, incontinence and eating problems. Primary responsibility for the residents would be transferred to the social services authority. In the context of people with learning disabilities and guidance from central government (HSG(92)42) the court stated that individual assessment was required. This meant a detailed assessment had to be undertaken before any decision could be taken to move them out of NHS care (*R v Merton, Sutton and Wandsworth HA, ex p Andrew*).

Likewise, a health authority had to demonstrate, when deciding to close a purpose-built complex for people with learning disabilities, that it was proceeding on the basis of individual need – and not wrongly applying government policy by attempting to discharge all such patients into the community (*R(Collins) v Lincolnshire Health Authority*). Nonetheless, the *Andrew* case involved people with profound learning disabilities, which required detailed individual assessment because of the government guidance (HSG(92)42) for this group of people.

Alternatively, it might be permissible for the process to be in two stages, namely to take a decision in principle to close – to be confirmed only after a full assessment of the impact on the residents (*R(Cowl) v Plymouth CC*). In a case involving closure of a day centre, and transfer to another of people with physical frailty and low to moderate levels of mental health need, the courts held that individual, detailed reassessment was not required before a rational decision to close could be made by the local authority (*R(Bishop) v Bromley LBC*).

There may be more than one way for a local authority to avoid reassessment. For instance, when a local authority proposed to close a day centre for people with learning disabilities, it had no duty to carry out such a reassessment. This was because, those attending had been originally assessed and placed at the day centre by another council (*R(J) v Southend BC*).

7.3.2 CLOSURES AND CONSULTATION

The courts have stipulated that adequate consultation must take place before closure of a care home:

Adequate consultation. Adequate consultation meant that the residents needed to know well in advance of the final decision about the proposed closure; to be given a reasonable amount of time to object; and to have had their objections considered by the local authority. The residents did not necessarily have a right to be consulted individually face to face; meetings held with residents generally could suffice (*R v Devon CC, ex p Baker*).

Consultation containing misleading information. The local authority proposed to close two residential homes. However, the court found the consultation process flawed because the health and safety reasons given for closure were not the true reasons, which in fact related to resources, strategic changes to services and best value (*R(Madden) v Bury MBC*).

Consultation with residents of other homes. The courts held that the duty of consultation extended not only to the residents of the particular home to be closed, but also to those properly interested in the council's other homes (*R v Wandsworth LBC, ex p Beckwith no.2*).

However, a failure to consider a particular option by excluding it from the consultation exercise was not in itself unlawful (*R(Rowe) v Walsall MBC*).

The Cabinet Office (2004) has offered general guidance on consultation by public bodies, stating that a minimum of 12 weeks should be allowed for written consultation at least once during the development of a policy. In any event, it was entirely inadequate when information about the proposed closure of their care home was given to residents only eleven days, and to relatives only six days, before the relevant council committee meeting that voted on closure (*Redcar and Cleveland CBC 1999*). On the other hand, local authorities (or the NHS) may have some latitude in terms of how far the final decision must exactly reflect the options put forward in the consultation:

Exhaustiveness of options. The fact that the consultation put forward four options, and that an NHS trust decided to adopt a fifth, was not necessarily fatal to adequate consultation. In the particular case, involving a reduction of NHS services at a particular site, the court held that the fifth option was not so different from the fourth proposal that had been consulted on. And, in any case, the fifth option emerged from the consultation exercise and so there was no duty to consult again on it (*R v East Kent Hospital NHS Trust, ex p Smith*).

7.3.3 LEGITIMATE EXPECTATION AND PROMISES OF A HOME FOR LIFE

Residents of care homes and of NHS premises have sometimes a 'legitimate expectation', for example if they have been 'promised' that they have a home for life. On occasion, a court may feel that such a promise is so explicit and specific that it carries enough weight to militate against closure, unless there is an overriding public interest (*R v North and East Devon HA, ex p Coughlan*). At the very least, if such a promise has been made, then the courts will demand that the local authority's decision-making process show that it has properly been taken account of:

Failing to take account of the promise of a home for life. Residents of a local authority home were given a booklet, which contained a heading of 'home for life'. When the local authority proposed to close the home, it had not taken this into account. It had therefore not considered all relevant matters, and the decision could not stand on its present basis (*R(Bodimeade) v Camden LBC*).

However, clear evidence of such a promise will be required:

No promise of home for life in interim accommodation. An NHS trust proposed to close an accommodation lodge in which the four claimants with mental health problems were currently living. They argued that they had received a promise of a home for life. The court rejected their claim, not least because the evidence was that the trust had not made such a promise, but had instead made clear that the accommodation had only ever been intended as interim accommodation (*R v Brent, Kensington and Chelsea and Westminster Mental Health NHS Trust, ex p C*).

On the other hand, the assessed needs and interests of residents in moving into the community may outweigh such a promise and the preference of the residents not to move (*R(Collins) v Lincolnshire Health Authority*). Legitimate expectation may arise more generally (not necessarily in respect of a 'home for life' promise). However, even assuming the promise has been made, is specific and it is clear to whom it applied, the courts may still look for 'detrimental reliance' on the promise by the person to whom it was made. In addition, the promise cannot outweigh the fact that the promised service must be able to meet a person's needs:

Promise made but resident did not rely on it: and new care home would not meet his needs anyway. A local authority proposed to close a care home, but promised to move the residents to another particular care home where there needs would be met. For a significant period of time, the claimant resisted being moved on the grounds that the new care home would be unable to meet his needs. When the local authority had further assessed his needs, it agreed. The man now changed his mind and claimed that the authority should be held to its original promise. The court held that he had not relied on the promise to his detriment, so that there was no enforceable, legitimate expectation. Even if there was, it would be outweighed by the local authority's assessment that the new care home would not meet his welfare needs (*R(Lindley v Tameside MBC*).

7.3.4 CLOSURE OR WITHDRAWAL OF SERVICES BY AN INDEPENDENT CARE PROVIDER

Closure or withdrawal of services, with or without previous promises, is increasingly initiated by independent care providers, such as care homes. The legal obstacles for residents to overcome in opposing closure have been formidable.

Independent care home closure. Residents of a care home had received promises of a home for life, so long as their need did not deteriorate to the point where nursing care was required. The owner of the care home, a charitable housing association, maintained that all that had been stated both orally and in its brochure amounted to aims or objectives but not assurances. The judge rejected this interpretation; assurances, amounting to a promise, had been given.

Nevertheless, the judge held that, as an independent provider, the housing association was not open to judicial review, since such a legal remedy can be applied to public bodies only. Judicial review would of course apply to the local authority, but in this case it was not the local authority that had made the promises. The consequence was therefore that judicial review, in respect of the promise, lay against neither the care provider nor the local authority. The latter would meet its obligations by offering to meet the assessed community care needs of the residents elsewhere (*R v Servite Houses, ex p Goldsmith*).

In the *Servite* case, the judge did express his concerns about the outcome, pointing out that it constituted an inadequate response to the residents. However, the response was inevitable because Parliament had permitted public law obligations to be discharged by private law arrangements, thus attenuating the residents' potential rights and remedies.

The *Servite* case was heard before the coming into force of the Human Rights Act 1998; however, subsequent home closure cases confirmed that neither judicial review nor human rights challenges could lie against an independent care home provider, notwithstanding that the residents have been placed in the home by the local authority or the NHS in performance of public law functions (*R (Heather) v Leonard Cheshire Foundation; R (Johnson) v Havering LBC*).

One such case reached the House of Lords on appeal, where the split decision of the five Law Lords revealed the sensitive and controversial nature of the issue. The majority took what might be called a conservative, mechanistic, socially neutral, and strictly 'legalistic' approach (Lords Scott, Mance and Neuberger). The minority duo arguably took a more purposeful, historical and socially aware view of the relevant legislation (Lord Bingham, Lady Hale):

Care of older people deemed to be just another private, rather than public, function: human rights diluted. The case involved an 84-year-old woman with Alzheimer's disease, whom an independent care home wished to evict because of serious conflict with her family when it visited (although not with the woman herself). The question was whether the independent care home was a 'public authority' in respect of residents placed in the home by a local authority, and so subject directly to human rights obligations – which would then have to be taken into account before a decision was taken to evict. Fortunately, a solution had been found, with the council acting as conciliator, resulting in the care home withdrawing its eviction notice. This was fortunate because, as Baroness Hale noted, a consultant psychiatrist's report had stated that she would deteriorate clinically were she to be transferred to an unfamiliar care setting. Furthermore, an alternative care setting would be likely to be located further away from the family home, thus making visits from her 83-year-old husband even more difficult.

Majority view: care home not a public authority. The majority's decision included a number of reasons as to why the care home was not a public authority. For example, it was neither a charity not a philanthropist. It entered into private law contracts both with privately funded residents in its care homes and with local authorities. It received no public funding, enjoyed no special statutory powers, and was at liberty to accept or reject residents as it chose and to charge whatever fee it thought suitable. It operated in a commercial market with commercial competitors. If it were considered to be a public authority, then so too would companies which carried out catering, cleaning or cooking services at a care home. Furthermore, it would be an anomaly if publicly funded residents in a care home had Convention rights, whereas privately funded residents did not.

Majority view: no significant disadvantage to residents in independent care homes. It did not consider that residents placed in an independent care home were significantly disadvantaged compared to those in a local authority care home (who would enjoy rights under the Convention). This was because of the ability of the local authority to impose effective contractual terms on a care home. The contract stated that the home had to observe Convention rights, and a failure to do so would result in a contractual breach. The majority also referred to the regulatory framework covering care homes.

Minority view: need to protect vulnerable people. The minority took a notably different approach. It noted the fact that over the last 60 years, the British state had accepted a social welfare responsibility, in case of last resort, toward the poor, elderly and vulnerable. It pointed out that those in need of residential care under the National Assistance Act were amongst the 'most vulnerable' in the community, along with children, mental patients and prisoners. It recognized also that despite 'the intensive regulation to which care homes are subject, it is not unknown that senile and helpless residents of such homes are subjected to treatment which may threaten their survival, may amount to inhumane treatment, may deprive them unjustifiably of their liberty and may seriously and unnecessarily infringe their personal autonomy and family relationships'. It referred to the 1942 Beveridge report and the fight against want, disease, ignorance, squalor and idleness.

Minority view: risk of violation of human rights. The minority differentiated between public functions and public funding. For instance, the supply of goods and laundry to a care home 'may well not be a public function'. But providing a service to individual members of the public at public expense was different. The home was providing 'health care by arrangement with National Health Service as well as social care by arrangement with the local social services authority. It cannot be doubted that the provision of health care was a public function'. There was a 'close connection between this service and the core values underlying the Convention rights and the undoubted risk that rights will be violated unless adequate steps are taken to protect them' (*YL v Birmingham CC*).

In order to reverse the House of Lords ruling in the *YL* case, s.145 of the Health and Social Care 2008 (not yet in force) states that independent care homes are, after all, deemed to be carrying out functions of a public nature – and thus subject to the Human Rights Act 1998 – but only in respect of residents placed by local authorities under ss.21 and 26 of the National Assistance Act 1948.

However, this amending legislation, at least on its face, does not confer on vulnerable adults human rights where those adults (a) are placed in an independent care home by the NHS; (b) are placed by local authorities and/or the NHS in an independent care home under s.117 of the Mental Health Act 1983; (c) are self-funding residents who have their own contractual arrangements with the independent care home; or (d) who receive services in their own home from independent domiciliary care agencies. Central government has intimated that, in its view, human rights would automatically attach in the case of NHS placements of people in care homes; but it is by no means clear that this is so, given the reasoning of the House of Lords in the *YL* case.

7.3.5 CLOSURES AND HUMAN RIGHTS

For the most part, human rights arguments have failed to prevent care homes, day centres or NHS facilities from closing – even when the care home or facility is run directly by a public body. Even so, in one notable case – when an explicit promise of a home for life had been made to NHS residents (without an overriding public interest justification) – the courts did find a breach of article 8 (right to respect for home and family life) of the European Convention on Human Rights (*R v North and East Devon HA, ex p Coughlan*). But otherwise the courts have tended not to find a breach of article 8; indeed in some cases they have doubted whether it was involved at all, let alone breached:

Article 8 human rights. Breach of an explicit promise of a home for life for a number of severely disabled residents in an NHS unit constituted a breach of article 8 (*R v North and East Devon Health Authority, ex p Coughlan*). In another case, the effect of closure on social ties, familiarity with surroundings, and proximity to friends and relatives did not interfere with article 8 rights (*R(Rowe) v Walsall MBC*). In a third case, the judge suggested that article 8 added little because he could not envisage a breach of article 8, so long as the council was acting compatibly with its relevant common law and statutory obligations (*R(Cowl) v Plymouth CC*: High Court stage).

In some cases, the courts have systematically considered and then rejected arguments based on several human rights together, namely right to life (article 2), right not to be subjected to inhuman and degrading treatment (article 3), and article 8:

Care home closure and human rights generally (1). An independent care home proposed to close. The Human Rights Act did not apply directly to the care provider, and the local authority was not in a position to prevent an independent concern from closing. However, the judge assumed for the purpose of argument that human rights did bear on the matter. In terms of what steps the local authority should take, the court considered articles 2, 3 and 8.

Article 2 (right to life) was not in issue because the council was taking the necessary steps to minimise the impact of the stress on the residents of a move. There was insufficient evidence on the risks to the claimants' lives. Furthermore, the courts give public bodies considerable latitude to decide a fair balance between the interests of the individual and the wider community. For similar reasons, the high threshold required to engage article 3 (inhuman and degrading treatment) had not been reached. The article 8 claim also failed because, first, there was no cogent evidence of disruption of home or family life or interference with physical integrity. Second, the financial resources of the council were an important element, and the council was entitled to consider the care home's fees disproportionately high. Third, the council was entitled to considerable deference in how it allocated its resources.

Throughout, the judge referred to the importance of the precautions taken by the council in order to manage the move, including the preserving of friendship groups (*R(Haggerty) v St Helens MBC*).

Care home closure and human rights generally (2). In another case, the article 2 argument was dismissed because no particularised medical evidence revealed a serious risk to the life of any resident. To bring the case under article 3 would be to strain language and common sense and to trivialise the article and the important values it protects. That article 8 was relevant at all was a generous assumption; if it was, then the court would be slow to interfere with decisions involving the allocation of resources (*R(Dudley) v East Sussex CC*).

Decided on similar lines was *McKellar v Hounslow LBC*, when residents unsuccessfully applied for an injunction preventing their removal from a local authority care home.

And, in a third case, assuming there was an interference under article 8.1, then the closure would be justified on grounds of the 'economic well being' of the council (*R(Rowe) v Walsall MBC*). A like finding was made in relation to the closure of a day centre, given that the financial savings made by the closure was expected to enable the council to deploy resources to domiciliary services and also meet the needs of day services users more cost-effectively at other day centres (*R(Bishop) v Bromley LBC*).

And, even accepting that closure of a day centre for people with learning disabilities could engage article 8 in terms of private life and the existing social relationships at the centre, the courts might still decline to intervene. For instance, it was not for the court to belittle those relationships or underestimate their importance; but nonetheless, other opportunities would come 'from modernisation and from the future', including scope for new relationships and a 'new dimension' in their private life (*R(J) v Southend BC*).

7.3.6 GROUNDS FOR REJECTING CHALLENGES TO CLOSURES

Most challenges against local authorities, about care home and other closures, have failed. The courts – in addition to rejecting human rights arguments – have based their decisions on various grounds, in addition to those already outlined immediately above. In some cases even, the courts have simply not even given permission for a full judicial review hearing to take place:

No permission to challenge closure. In one case, where permission was sought to bring a judicial review case about transfer of local authority homes to an independent trust, it was argued that the local authority had failed (a) to take account of the consequences of the decision; (b) to include a particular option in the consultation exercise; and (c) to analyse the costs of the transfer of the home. The court found that (a) the consultation paper had considered both 'advantages' and 'disadvantages' of the transfer; (b) the additional option was simply not in the consultation paper and so not adopting it was perfectly proper; and (c) an analysis of costs would have been premature at this stage. Permission to bring the case was refused (*R(Hands) v Birmingham CC*; see also *R(Rowe) v Walsall MBC*).

Alternatively, the courts have simply shown a disinclination to become involved:

Using the complaints procedure instead of the courts. A number of residents opposed the closure of a home run by the council. Aged between 77 and 92 they were all frail and in poor health. They claimed that lawful and comprehensive assessments had not been carried out. The Court of Appeal stated that the local authority's complaints procedure should have been used, since the parties did not have a right to judicial review if an alternative procedure existed that would resolve a significant number of the issues (*R(Cowl) v Plymouth CC*).

The local authority subsequently appointed an extraordinary complaints panel that produced a thorough report, including an appendix containing draft guidelines meant to assist other local authorities when they consider whether to close a home (*Plymouth CC 2002*).

In subsequent legal cases, the courts have given these guidelines short shrift. For instance, the panel set up by Plymouth had no authority 'to promulgate guidelines for the world at large' (*R(Dudley) v East Sussex CC*); and the report was simply specific to the particular home closure in Plymouth, and it would be wrong to attach much weight to its views in other contexts (*R(Haggerty) v St Helens MBC*).

In effect, the courts may set the hurdle high, and display apparent unconcern, from a legal point of view, for the effect on vulnerable elderly people of the loss of longstanding social contacts, significant and abrupt changes to environment and routine, longer journeys, more difficult transport arrangements and accompanying stress:

Day centre closure: loss of social contacts, disruption, longer journeys, insensitive decision: still not enough to constitute legal irrationality or illegality. The court might accept that the group of services users affected by closure might be vulnerable elderly and suffering from Alzheimer's disease of varying degrees of severity. Closure of a day centre might mean loss of solid social contacts, a significant and abrupt change to their environment, longer journeys and more difficult transport arrangements – with a significant degree of stress involved in all of this. But this may still not add up to a duty to reassess in detail each individual before closing the centre. Furthermore, even if the local authority takes the decision in an insensitive fashion, leaving people with a strong sense of grievance, nonetheless this is not the same as legal irrationality and illegality (*R(Bishop) v Bromley LBC*).

Sometimes, perhaps often, the local community consulted about closures will believe that the local authority has already made up its mind. In many cases, this may be a correct supposition, but proving it in court is quite another matter:

Hopeless to seek to bring judicial review case before decision to close was taken. The Court of Appeal refused permission for a case to be brought at all in respect of proposals to close a number of day centres and care homes. Although it was argued, on the basis of public documents, that the decision-makers had already made up their minds, and the budget that had already been set was consistent only with the closures going ahead, the court stuck to the substantial point that no final, formal decision had yet been taken. Furthermore the council had given public assurances that it would abide by the law and consult properly. It was therefore a 'hopeless task' to seek to bring a judicial review (*R(Hide) v Staffordshire CC*).

7.4 WAITING TIMES FOR ASSESSMENT

Timescales for assessment are absent from community care legislation with one or two exceptions.

One exception is in the Community Care (Delayed Discharges) Act 2003 in relation to the discharge from hospital of patients from acute hospital beds (see section 17.11). Even in the context of the 2003 Act, failure to assess (and discharge) a person within the relevant time limit is not an actionable breach of duty; it merely entails the payment of money, for the 'blocked' bed, by the local authority to the NHS. There is also a timescale in terms of assessments by local authorities when disabled pupils leave education (see 6.16).

Otherwise, in the absence of timescales set out in legislation or in central government guidance, the legal expectation is for a local authority to perform its duty within a reasonable period of time or without undue delay. In terms of maladministration, the local ombudsmen take a similar approach and have put it as follows in this 2004 example:

Principle of waiting times. The local ombudsman has stated that people must be assessed in a reasonable time; and a reasonable time in any particular case depends on the circumstances and urgency of the client's needs. First, there should be well-defined criteria for assessing priorities. Second, the criteria should be applied after proper consideration and reassessed promptly in the light of any relevant new information. Third, people in need and their advisers should be informed of the criteria, timescales, of their allocated priority, of council services and of reputable alternative suppliers (*Wakefield MDC 2004*).

What constitutes a reasonable period of time will generally depend on all the circumstances of the case. This somewhat vague principle is not as unhelpful as it might appear, since it depends very much on individual need; a one-month wait for assessment may be acceptable for one person, but highly detrimental to another.

Central government in England has set certain targets for assessment in terms of 'performance indicators' which are used to measure and evaluate the performance of local authorities (see 3.4). However, the courts will not necessarily accept that government 'targets' or performance indicators equate to, or are even relevant to, the performance of a statutory duty.

7.4.1 ADEQUATE STAFFING

Staffing levels are not infrequently cited by local authorities as the reason for delay in assessments. Legislation does state that the local authority must provide the director of adult social services with adequate staff (Local Authority Social Services Act 1970, s.6). The minutes of social services committee meetings might provide useful evidence that s.6 of the 1970 Act has been breached, although the duty is usually regarded as rather vague and so difficult to enforce. The case of *R v Hereford and Worcester CC, ex p Chandler* was brought in relation to a breach of s.6(6) of the 1970 Act, given leave to proceed to a full judicial review hearing, but subsequently settled in favour of the applicant (Clements and Thompson 2007, p.4).

The local ombudsmen have investigated the adequacy of staffing on a number of occasions and are generally, but not always, unsympathetic to local authorities that use this excuse.

Waiting times and staff shortages. For instance, if authorities are unable to provide an assessment through their occupational therapists within a reasonable period of time, then they should look at other ways of providing the assessment (*Wirral MBC 1993c*).

Maladministration might be found where problems have long since been reported to, and known by, the social services committee, and yet 'wider failure' in service delivery has continued, including a lack of monitoring and inadequate records of waiting lists (*Redbridge LBC 1993*; *Redbridge LBC 1993a*).

On the other hand, if councils face 'particular resource and staffing difficulties' and have made attempts to remedy the situation, the ombudsmen might not find maladministration. For example, one council responded 'positively and creatively' to staff shortages, offered a recruitment and retention package, set up a special assessment clinic, and seconded health authority staff (*Lewisham LBC 1993*). Likewise, a five-month delay in assessment for a woman allocated a medium priority was not maladministration, given the priorities necessitated by the difficulty of recruiting and deploying occupational therapists (*Islington LBC 1995*).

Even so, in one case, a three-month wait for assessment of a 19-year-old woman seriously disordered with Asperger's syndrome (a form of autism) – for attendance at a day centre – was found to be maladministration. She had been allocated to a particular officer on grounds of the latter's expertise (even though the officer had no experience of the relevant condition: autism). The officer was absent for a considerable period, but the case had not been reallocated. The ombudsman did not 'consider that staff shortages or a departmental reorganisation can ever justify a failure to respond to repeated requests of this seriousness for help' (*Sheffield CC 1994*).

Similarly, a ten-month delay in assessing a woman unable to use her upstairs bathroom was maladministration. Shortage 'of money, communication and administration problems do not absolve the Council from their statutory duty' (*Bolton MBC 1992*).

A related issue is the degree to which a local authority insists on reserving certain tasks for certain types of staff; justified or not in the particular circumstances, this is a form of professional exclusivity. The local ombudsman has considered this matter on a number of occasions:

Waiting times and professional exclusivity. The local ombudsman will not necessarily defer to professional exclusivity.

Locum staff. Following two amputations to a man's foot, it took five months for an occupational therapist to assess him, even though he was deemed to be of 'A' priority and should have been assessed within five days. He subsequently contacted the council again on a further matter, in relation to his bathing needs. This time he was categorised as 'B2' priority and should have been assessed in four months; it took eight. The ombudsman stated that in order to assess people within a reasonable time, the local authority should have taken a pragmatic approach. Its reluctance to employ locum staff, as opposed to permanent staff, was apparently based at least partly on financial considerations. This was unacceptable, given that it contributed to the target time for assessment being exceeded by 100 per cent (*Bridgend CBC 2004*).

Professional occupational therapists. A failure to assess for 21 months was deemed maladministration; in the absence of professional occupational therapists, the council 'should have sought other means to ensure that people did not wait an unacceptable length of time for an assessment'. When 'disabled people ask the Council for assistance in providing adaptations to their homes, they have the right to expect that assistance is provided with reasonable speed' (*Wirral MBC 1992b*; see also *Middlesbrough BC 1996*; *Wirral MBC 1992*; *Wirral MBC 1993c*).

Alternative channels. Similarly, in another case the ombudsman stated that postponement of assessment for a year was not an option, and that an alternative channel for assessment should have been found (as the local authority had now done) if early use of occupational therapists was not possible – even though it would of course be ideal if professional advice were always to hand (*Sheffield CC 1989*).

Recruitment moratorium and industrial action. In one authority, by the end of 1991, disability services were receiving 500 referrals per month and had over 1000 people awaiting assessment. Reorganisation and recruitment recommendations, made in a report to the social services committee, were thwarted shortly afterwards by a moratorium. This was imposed on financial grounds and affected the recruitment of non-qualified staff. Industrial action added to the three-year delay the complainant suffered. The ombudsman still found maladministration in that the local authority should have addressed both the resourcing problems and staffing levels long before (*Newham LBC 1993a*).

Of course, staffing shortages should not be confused with administrative deficiencies, which mean that existing staff are not being utilised properly.

Waiting times and administrative inefficiency. A request by a registered blind person (also at risk of falling and with a rare degenerative disease) for equipment was not passed promptly to the sensory impairment team by an assistant director of social services. A nine-month delay resulted; the local ombudsman found maladministration (*Haringey LBC 1993*).

In another case, the local ombudsman accepted that the failure to carry out a survey for over a year in relation to a disabled facilities grant was due to a huge increase in workload rather than maladministration, but the social services department was still at fault for failing to check matters with the housing department and to refer the case properly (*Barking and Dagenham LBC 1998*).

The local ombudsman has also criticised the phenomenon of 'double queuing'. This sometimes results not just in the service user having to wait longer or negotiate more bureaucratic obstacles, but will also lead to poor use of staffing resources, by virtue of the duplication involved.

Waiting times and double queuing. The local ombudsmen are likely to disapprove of double queuing; that is, where the administrative hoops of a local authority require that a person queues twice on the waiting list.

New start dates. When one man was originally classified as priority but then reclassified as high priority, he did not benefit as quickly as he should have because he was given a new 'start' date and so went to the end of the high priority list. This was maladministration (*Barking and Dagenham LBC 1998*).

Two grants or two assessments. Maladministration also occurred in relation to the double queuing when people applied for both disabled facilities and a renovation grant (*Liverpool CC 1996/1997*) or for two occupational therapy assessments, the first for equipment, the second for adaptations (*Waltham Forest LBC 1994*).

Unnecessary queuing. When a seriously ill and immobile man was referred to the occupational therapy service in August he was put on a waiting list for assessment. However, some of the recorded potential needs (such as cooking) at the referral stage should have triggered the involvement of the physical disability team as well. However, the duty occupational therapist did not refer these matters on to that team at that point; this only occurred later. This meant that there was a delay of five months or so in receiving an assessment and services for these other needs. This was maladministration (*Hackney LBC 1998a*).

Unnecessary wait for repeat assessment. After a man had been assessed as needing a level access shower, conditional on him finding a bungalow to live in, he was visited by an occupational therapist who confirmed the bungalow was suitable for the shower. But he was referred back to the occupational therapy waiting list for assessment. He should then have been assessed within four months instead of the six it actually took; exceeding this target by over two months was maladministration. In addition, the local ombudsman questioned not just the reasonableness but also the lawfulness of this further wait, since the person's need for a shower had already been assessed. The person should have gone straight onto the adaptations waiting list, instead of being subjected to a delay of seven months in joining that list (*Nottinghamshire CC 2000*).

7.4.2 WAITING TIMES FOR ASSESSMENT AND THE COURTS

The courts have barely explored what constitutes a reasonable wait for assessment. They may consider that such questions are best decided through complaints procedures or the local government ombudsman. Indeed, there seem to have been no community care legal cases purely on waiting times for assessment, although there have now been a few concerning waiting times for services (see 8.5.2). Nevertheless, in one case the courts identified a spurious ground for refusal of assessment that had resulted in a vicious circle:

Failure to assess. The local authority refused to carry out an assessment of need for an autistic child aged seven years old under s.17 of the Children Act 1989 and of his mother's ability to care under Carers and Disabled Children Act 2000. The local authority's explanation was that the family might soon be rehoused; and it would be a waste of resources to assess now, when circumstances might soon change.

The court held that, if the change of accommodation was going to occur within one or two months, a postponement might have been justifiable; but on the evidence, there was no indication as to when the accommodation would be found. The local authority was therefore obliged to carry out both assessments, and the s.17 assessment within 35 days (*R(J) v Newham LBC*).

7.4.3 WAITING TIMES FOR ASSESSMENT AND THE LOCAL GOVERNEMNT OMBUDSMEN

In contrast to the courts, the local ombudsmen have investigated delays in assessment many times. The local government ombudsmen have applied a sharper edge to waiting than the health service ombudsman, arguably because of the specific individual duties of assessment that apply to local authorities – under s.47 of the NHS and Community Care Act 1990 and s.4 of the Disabled Persons (Services, Consultation and Representation) Act 1986. There are no equivalent, specific duties applying to the NHS.

The following are but examples covering issues such as the ombudsmen's general approach, setting of priorities for assessment, higher and lower priorities, excessive waiting times.

Waiting times and local ombudsmen's general approach. The local ombudsmen consider the particular circumstances of each case, and so do not necessarily arrive at an easy rule of thumb of what constitutes a reasonable waiting time: it all depends. Nevertheless, faced with sometimes large numbers of complainants in a similar position, they have sometimes considered generally the question of what reasonable waiting times might look like.

For instance, in relation to disabled facilities grants, they suggested in 1997 two months for urgent, four months for serious, and six months for non-urgent cases (*Liverpool CC 1996/1997*; see also *Sheffield CC 1997* and *Sheffield CC 1997a*). Otherwise, the ombudsmen might work out in specific cases what a reasonable waiting time would have been, measure the excess and then assess the resulting injustice, if any (e.g. *Wirral MBC 1992*).

When local authorities have their own policies on waiting times, the local ombudsman has an additional lever to consider whether there has been maladministration over and above what might otherwise have been reasonable (had there been no policy). This is because significant breach by a local authority of its own policy is itself an additional ground of maladministration:

Breach of own policy on waiting times. In one case, even had a wait for assessment of six months been reasonable, the wait was 50 per cent longer than the local policy stipulated; the local ombudsman found maladministration. Likewise, an elderly person – in poor health and a wheelchair, living on the ground floor of her home, using a commode and bathing at a relative's house – should have been assessed within 60 days. It took instead more than seven months (some 215 days). This was maladministration (*Wakefield MDC 2004*).

The ombudsman found maladministration when a joint social services/housing department assessment should, according to policy, have been made within seven days from receipt of referral – but instead took place six weeks later (*Camden LBC 1993*).

Similarly, a council had a policy of a maximum of a two-month wait for assessment. The complainant had already waited much longer than this; the evidence showed that people who did not come into priority categories would normally have to wait in excess of one year. She was not in a priority category because she was not terminally ill, was not being discharged from hospital, and she or a carer was not at risk of injury. She was 30 years old, had spina bifida, was confined to a wheelchair, could not get up the stairs and needed a stairlift fitted at the home she shared with her parents. The delays in assessment to people such as the complainant were 'simply unacceptable'. The efforts of the council to improve matters since previous ombudsman involvement had 'failed lamentably'. This was maladministration (*Northumberland CC 2006*).

Equally, even if the local authority does adhere to its own targets, those targets may be wide of the mark: 'setting time targets which provide the potential for unreasonable delay amounting to maladministration is itself unreasonable'. So, when a man required a stairlift, it took eight months for an occupational therapy assessment to take place and six months for the lift to be installed. The wait for assessment was within the council's target of 52 weeks; but this was unreasonable. The whole process had taken 14 months; it should have taken only six. This was maladministration (*Croydon LBC 2006*).

Since waiting times have been an inescapable part of the community care landscape, and have been accepted up to a point as an unavoidable evil, the local ombudsmen will also look hard at how local authorities can mitigate the effects. One such type of mitigation is for the local authority to inform people about what is happening in terms of the wait. Thus, the local ombudsmen find maladministration when local authorities give people inadequate information about waiting times – whether or not the waiting times themselves are faulted (e.g. *Hackney LBC 1997b*; *Liverpool 1996/1997*; *Rotherham MBC 1995*; *Wirral MBC 1994b*). Even worse is where a local authority knowingly publishes unrealistic waiting times, misleading people almost with intent (*Ealing LBC 1999*).

Another form of mitigation, identified by the local ombudsmen, is that a priority system should mean that the waiting time for any individual person is in some measure proportionate to his or her perceived degree of need.

Waiting times and priorities. When local authorities handle applications for disabled facilities grants by date order, the ombudsmen criticise them on the grounds that such a system cannot take account of differing levels of need or of exceptions; it is 'insufficiently sophisticated' (e.g. *Leicester CC 1998*). Thus, the lack of a priority system, a failure to publicise it when it was adopted and inability to award priority at an early stage are all maladministration (*Liverpool CC 1996/97*). The consequences could be that an adaptation, a stairlift, is not installed before the applicant dies (*Liverpool City CC 1996/1997*).

In another case the housing authority carrying out adaptations stated that it did not prioritise referrals from social services as it did not have the competent staff (i.e. occupational therapists) to do this. However, the social services authority making the referrals stated in its turn that it was not its task to prioritise on behalf of a housing authority. Unsurprisingly (given the unattractiveness of such abnegation of responsibilities), the ombudsman found the absence of a system of priorities to be maladministration on the part of both councils (*Castle Morpeth BC and Northumberland CC 2003*).

A local authority had a waiting list of 392 people waiting for occupational therapy assessments. It operated three priority groups; 360 of those waiting fell into priority group 2. The ombudsman found this to be maladministration because it meant the system of prioritisation was ineffective (*Halton BC 2002*).

Councils sometimes compound the problems. One council failed (in respect of renovation grants) to further prioritise by means of points, within its broad priority bands, and relied on date order only. It then dealt with some applications in priorities 2 and 3, before priority 1, contrary to what its own published information stated. Furthermore, it did not explain the technical distinction between an 'enquiry' and a 'full application'. The failure to provide proper information about what it was doing made the council vulnerable to allegations of bias. All this was maladministration (*Merthyr Tydfil CBC 2005*).

Once there is a reasonable system of making priorities, the further question arises as to how long people should wait, once their priority has been determined. Inevitably, longer waiting times tend to be experienced by people deemed to have needs of a 'lower priority'; but the local ombudsmen have pointed out that this does not mean that they can be kept waiting endlessly.

Waiting times for assessment: lower and medium priority needs. A woman with cerebral palsy lived alone. She had arthritis in her right side, and weakness in both sides. She was unable to cope with shopping and domestic tasks. She worked full time as a teacher. At a first level assessment, a social work assistant stated that she needed a second level assessment, and she was given a priority 2 rating. This should have been completed within three months, the longest waiting time allowed. In fact it took nearly 18 months. This was maladministration (*Ealing LBC 1999*).

In one local authority, the waiting times for the highest priority were some four months, but for people given priorities 2 and 3, they were up to three years. A woman aged 86 applied for adaptations. She suffered from arthritis, asthma and sciatica and had fallen and broken her hip. She had not been able to use the bath for two of the three years she had spent awaiting assessment. The ombudsman's finding was maladministration, the delay being 'totally unacceptable' even though it was a 'relatively low priority' application. The assessment should have started within six months of the first approach to the local authority (*Redbridge LBC 1993*).

The local ombudsman has stated that it is 'not acceptable that a client may wait up to two years for an assessment, whatever the outcome of that assessment'. This was maladministration, though she did commend the council for implementing a system of gathering information at an early stage so as to determine quickly whether it could assist the person (*Wirral MBC 1993b*).

However, gathering preliminary information about a person's disability, but not fully assessing for two years, was maladministration (*Wirral MBC 1993*).

Even allowing for shortage of staff, and the fact that a person is not within the 'at risk' category, the local ombudsman might find that 'it cannot be acceptable for a client in need to face a two-year wait before their needs are even quantified' (*Wirral MBC 1992c*).

Following a stroke, a man was discharged from hospital, awarded 'medium priority' and told that there would be a four-month wait for an assessment; his appalled wife had the bath removed and installed a shower and grab rails. The failure to assess in that time amounted to maladministration (*Barking and Dagenham LBC 1997*).

Even people placed in a higher priority for assessment sometimes wait excessive lengths of time, and this will be maladministration for the local ombudsmen:

Waiting times for people with a higher priority. An elderly woman, placed initially in the second highest and then later in the highest category, had to wait 20 months for an assessment. This was 'totally unacceptable' according to the local ombudsman (*Redbridge LBC 1993a*).

In another case, a woman regarded as high priority had also to wait 20 months; it had taken six months even to get as far as allocating her priority. This was maladministration (*Hackney LBC 1997*).

It was maladministration when the clearing of a backlog of assessments for people with non-urgent needs affected adversely those with more urgent needs (*Wirral MBC 1993d*).

When a roofer became paralysed after a fall and was discharged from hospital, the local authority was at fault in taking ten weeks to produce a draft community care assessment, despite having information from the hospital (*Avon CC 1997*).

Sometimes, the length of wait simply disappears off the scale and turns into not being seen and assessed at all:

Excessively long waits and never seeing people. A wait for assessment of four years and eight months in one case was not even exceptional in that authority; the local ombudsman noted that a number of other people had been similarly affected (*Hackney LBC 1992*). The severe criticism levelled at the local authority did not prevent it some years later from keeping the same woman waiting 20 months, when she requested a reassessment because of worn equipment and of additional needs in relation to looking after her two-year-old son; the local ombudsman found maladministration all over again (*Hackney LBC 1997*).

Long waiting times can turn into never seeing people. In the first of the two cases referred to immediately above, the ombudsman found that the 'non-urgent' waiting lists had been closed indefinitely and believed that this might represent a failure of the council to discharge its statutory duty under s.2 of the Chronically Sick and Disabled Persons Act 1970 (*Hackney LBC 1992*). The ombudsman might recognise the national problem of shortage of occupational therapists to carry out assessments, commend the practice of establishing priorities, but nevertheless find that 'it cannot be acceptable that those with the lowest priority may never be seen by an OT and thus never have their case considered' (*Wirral MBC 1992*).

Even if a potentially acceptable system of priorities exists, the local ombudsmen will also be keen to see that it is applied equitably within a local authority, such that people with similar needs are not treated inconsistently – even if the inconsistency arises, for instance, from the soft-heartedness of local authority staff in individual cases. (Although it should be noted that about variations in waiting times between local authorities the ombudsmen can do nothing.)

Inconsistent application of priority for waiting. It could not be fair that an applicant should wait a few weeks for a renovation grant in one part of the borough, but for years in another (*Newham LBC 1997*).

In another finding of maladministration, one of the 'serious failures' was that a person who had waited four years and eight months for an assessment might have waited only five months had she lived a few hundred yards away in the same authority (*Hackney LBC 1992*). In another case, disabled people's needs for adaptations depended on the competing demands of local area repair budgets from week to week. This meant the ombudsman could not be certain that people with similar needs were dealt with in a similar way; there should have been a borough wide system of prioritisation (*Camden LBC 1993*).

Another investigation found that a council had been misapplying its priority criteria: five people in a sample of 45 cases had been given priority incorrectly ahead of the particular complainant. The case illustrated the difficulties facing local authority staff such as occupational therapists. The reasons for the 'incorrect' decisions included 'soft-heartedness' in the case of a woman with asthma, emphysema and osteoarthritis who could just about manage indoor steps and stairs indoors. A second person 'had great difficulty getting up from a sitting position, and could not bathe without aids, was unable to get in and out of the bath, and lived alone'. Two sisters, aged 82 and 81, with various problems including Crohn's disease, arthritis, osteoarthritis in spine, hips and knees, were both unable to bathe. They should not have been given priority – but were given it, probably because of their joint needs and previous requests. Yet still the misapplication of priority criteria amounted to maladministration (*Lewisham LBC 1993*).

By the same token, if there is consistent and equitable application of priorities, then even significant waiting times will not necessarily constitute maladministration.

Equitable application of priorities for waiting. A six-month delay in assessment for home adaptations was not criticised, since the local authority had applied a system of priorities which took into account relevant factors and had fairly treated the complainant's priority as relatively low (*Ealing LBC 1993*).

Similarly, a 15-month delay was not unreasonable in the circumstances, because the authority had adopted a policy of priority categories as they were entitled to (especially given particular staffing and resource problems) – and the complainant had been properly dealt with under that policy (*Lewisham LBC 1993*).

A two-year wait might not draw the ombudsman's criticism if resources and staff restrictions mean that greater priority is given appropriately to those in greater need (*Wirral MBC 1994b*).

CHAPTER 8

Care plans and provision of services

KEY POINTS

CARE PLANS

Following a community care assessment and decision about what services will be provided, various guidance (but not legislation) states that a care plan should be drawn up containing details about objectives, services, agencies involved, costs, needs which cannot be met, date of first review, and so on. The form and complexity of a care plan will vary greatly depending on the level and types of service involved. The law courts have held that either a failure to follow, or at least to have proper regard to, this guidance can amount to unlawfulness.

At the time of writing, central government is introducing a new policy in social care, referred to as self-directed care involving individual or personal budgets (see Chapter 13). Part of this seemingly involves local authorities encouraging people to decide for themselves how their needs should be met – and to think in terms of overall, general outcomes rather than the specific services required to meet specific needs. It is not entirely clear what the implications are for the traditional notion of a care plan and how this development will fit into the current community care legal framework – especially if service users, rather than the local authority, have the last word about their needs and the services required to meet them. Furthermore, if people's needs and care plans (or their equivalent) are expressed vaguely, it may become difficult to know when, or if, legal duties are being breached.

CONTRACTING OUT OF SERVICES BY LOCAL AUTHORITIES
Care plans are often implemented by independent care providers with whom the local authority contracts, rather than by the local authority directly. The way in which contracts are placed – their content, terms and conditions, and monitoring and review of performance – will therefore bear on how well, and sometimes whether, the needs of service users are met. Unfortunately, the contracting out of services is sometimes seen by local authorities as an escape route from potential obligations; they see it as a further uncertainty in the system (see Chapter 3) which is to be exploited. However, ultimately local authorities remain responsible for the meeting of people's needs in a reasonable and safe manner; therefore an 'out of sight, out of mind' approach is in principle misplaced. The local government ombudsmen have become particularly concerned about local authorities taking this approach, which in some cases has been linked with service users coming to significant harm, including death.

REGULATION OF CARE PROVIDERS
Care providers are themselves subject to regulatory legislation in the form of the Care Standards Act 2000 (to be replaced by Health and Social Care Act 2008). Together with contract specification and monitoring by local authorities, this should in theory protect service users.

WAITING TIMES FOR SERVICES
In practice, waiting times affect the provision of a range of services, for instance residential care placements, day services, domiciliary services, home adaptations and community equipment. Keeping people waiting for services is obviously a major plank in the attempts of local authorities to control expenditure; waiting times therefore represent a potential 'escape route' from obligations, as outlined in Chapter 3. Some waiting times are likely to be lawful and remain within the ambit of good administration; whereas others will err toward the unlawful and constitute maladministration.

In the absence of timescales in either legislation or Department of Health guidance, the legal expectation is that a duty to meet needs will be performed within a reasonable period of time and without undue delay; and that what is reasonable will depend on all the circumstances of the case. The courts have seemed generally reluctant to become involved in such questions, although have done so on some occasions; in contrast, the local government ombudsmen have investigated frequently.

8.1 CARE PLANS

Once a local authority has assessed a person and identified eligible needs, it will generally have a duty to provide services (see 6.10). If services are to be provided, a care plan will be drawn up. Care plans are not referred to in legislation, although community care guidance places considerable emphasis on them (see generally DH 1990, para 3.24 and SSI/SWSG 1991, paras 4.1–4.37). Policy guidance states that care plans should follow assessment and it lists, in order of preference, a number of types of care packages, from support for people in their own homes to institutional long-term care (DH 1990, para 3.24).

Practice guidance states explicitly that users should receive copies of their care plans and goes on to list what their content should be. Guidance issued in 1991 identifies the following as key elements of a care plan. These were:

- overall objectives
- specific objectives of users, carers, care providers
- criteria for measuring these
- services to be provided
- cost to the user
- other options considered
- points of difference
- unmet needs
- named person responsible for implementation
- date of first planned review (SSI/SWSG 1991, para 4.37).

Later policy guidance on fair access to care contains more or less the same list, although explicitly refers also to contingency plans to manage emergency changes (LAC(2002)13, para 47). Yet further guidance, on the 'single assessment process' for older people, states that care plans should refer to:

- 'eligible need' being identified in relation to intensity, instability, unpredictability, complexity, risk to independence, rehabilitation potential
- whether the service user has agreed the plan and has consented to information sharing
- objectives
- of how services will impact on need
- what the service user will do to meet need
- risk management details
- what carers are willing to do
- level and frequency of help, specifying the agency responsible
- details of charges
- nursing plan where appropriate
- level of registered nursing care contribution where relevant
- name of coordinator

- contact number for emergencies and contingency plan
- monitoring arrangements and review date (HSC 2002/001, annex E).

The courts have held in more than one case that failure – without good reason – to draw up a care plan approximating in form to that set out in the 1991 guidance is unlawful.

Inadequate care plan. The case concerned a 25-year-old man with Seckels syndrome. He was blind, microcephalic, virtually immobile, doubly incontinent and mostly unable to communicate. He also suffered from severe deformities of the chest and spine, a hiatus hernia and a permanent digestive disorder. His weight and size were those of a small child, his dependency that of a baby.

The care plan drawn up by the local authority was inadequate to meet his assessed recreational needs; it had not sufficiently attempted to adjust what it was prepared to provide, in order to meet those needs.

The court also held that his care plan breached, without good reason, Department of Health policy guidance (DH 1990, para 3.24) stating that the objective of social services interventions should be recorded. In addition, the plan breached practice guidance (SSI/SWSG 1991, para 4.37) in respect of its contents, specification of objectives, agreement on implementation, leeway for contingencies and the identification and feedback of unmet needs. Practice guidance did not, the judge explained, carry the force of the policy guidance, but even so, the authority should have had regard to it: 'Whilst the occasional lacuna would not furnish evidence of such disregard, the series of lacunae…does, in my view, suggest that the statutory guidance has been overlooked' (R v Islington LBC, ex p Rixon).

Furthermore, the courts have pointed out that a care plan generally provides evidence of a person's eligible needs, of the consequent duty on the local authority, and of the way in which the duty will be performed. On this basis, it follows that a significant failure to provide services in accordance with a care plan could well indicate a breach of statutory duty on the part of the local authority (R v Islington LBC, ex p Rixon). Similarly, a substantial discrepancy between assessed need and the care plan is likely to be unlawful and also to constitute maladministration in the eyes of the local ombudsman.

Significant discrepancy in one-to-one support. A man with dual sensory impairment and ataxia was assessed in 1994 as needing significant one-to-one support because of very high dependency, special needs due to a combination of learning disability, physical disability, blindness, partial hearing, and communication difficulties. However, the care plan did not reflect this assessment and the appropriate level of one-to-one support was not provided. He only received two hours per week over a period of time. In 1999, the council offered an increase to six hours, which his mother found unacceptably low. It was only by 2001 that he was receiving 33 hours per week from a deaf–blind communicator. In addition, Independent Living Fund funding was obtained in 2000 for 27 hours a week care at home; this increased to 41 hours a week in October of that year.

The ombudsman concluded that for a number of years, the local authority had 'failed by a wide margin' to implement the 1994 assessment (Hertfordshire CC 2002).

The failure to produce a care plan, even if an assessment of sorts has been carried out, might lead to costly recommendations by the local ombudsman.

Failure to produce proper care plan for a woman with learning disabilities. A young woman with learning disabilities was in a residential placement. On a visit to her family at Christmas, she decided she wished to live nearby and not return to the placement. The council failed to produce a care plan, relying wrongly on assumptions about what the father wanted. It had now lost the relevant records. However, on the basis of other evidence, it should have been reasonably clear to the council by April that the father was expecting the council either to provide the care or to secure that it be funded with direct payments and Independent Living Fund money if necessary (which eventually happened). It offered only some day centre activity.

The failure to have in place a care plan by April was maladministration. The father had subsequently to look after his daughter for some two years; full local authority funding was not in place for two and a half. As a result, the father had been caused significant financial loss, distress and frustration. The local ombudsman recommended £80,000 by way of remedy to be paid to the father; the council agreed to this (*Hertfordshire CC 2003*).

Not passing a care plan on to the relevant care provider will also be regarded as maladministration:

Care plan not given to care home. When a 101-year-old woman was admitted to a care home, where she subsequently developed a chest infection and pressure sore, the local ombudsman found no evidence that her care plan or any other similar documentation was given to the care home manager. Yet the care plan was an 'important document' and drew attention to significant issues of washing and medication, including treatment for her leg ulcer. This was maladministration (*Kent CC 2001*).

8.1.1 CARE PLANS: INTERRUPTIONS TO SERVICE PROVISION

Interruptions to, or unreliability of, service provision will not always be unlawful or constitute maladministration. It will depend on the degree and the circumstances.

Discontinuity in home care service. Following meetings, conversations and visits from local authority staff, the applicant had been informed that his home care service might suffer from discontinuity in certain circumstances (e.g. when home carers were ill or on leave). The applicant complained about the discontinuity that duly followed.

The judge found that the council had (a) performed a proper balancing exercise 'taking into account resources and the comparative needs of the disabled in their area'; (b) given clear notice about the possible interruptions to the service; (c) provided what they had undertaken to provide and what had been assessed as needed; (d) at no time withdrawn the service; (e) not interrupted a service to a person for whom any interruption of the service would have been intolerable. For instance, missing a day's meal would not have been acceptable, but missing a day's cleaning would have been (*R v Islington LBC, ex p McMillan*).

However, if home help services fail significantly the local ombudsman will find maladministration:

Irregular home help service. Over the course of a year, a man had frequently less than his planned three home help visits a week; no sufficient reason was given for this failure, and the local authority anyway had no system to tell people about cancellation or delay. This was maladministration (*Westminster CC 1996*).

In another case, the care plan stated that a woman with osteoporosis should receive 14.5 hours a week care; yet the council conceded that it had been providing only 12 hours. This was maladministration (*Croydon LBC 2000*). The ombudsman, like the courts in the *McMillan* case (immediately above), has recognised the obvious importance of food:

Meals. The ombudsman criticised the period of two or three months which it took the council to respond to the request from the man's general practitioner to change the type of meal he received – this was important because of his medical condition. He required meals for people controlling diabetes by diet (copper coded), rather than by insulin (red coded). Despite the request, red coded meals continued to be delivered for some time. This was maladministration, caused injustice and warranted a compensation payment of £150.

The man also complained about the irregular visiting times of his home help service; however, the ombudsman accepted that it might take a little time to establish a regular visiting time, and it would be unrealistic to expect visits to be made at exactly the same time each week (*Kensington and Chelsea RB 1992*).

Nevertheless, the court's observation in the particular circumstances of the *McMillan* case, elevating cooking above cleaning, should not be taken as a general dismissal of the importance of cleaning. In one case the local ombudsman found maladministration, because a local authority had prioritised shopping over cleaning without taking account of the individual circumstances of the service user. He was an amputee, diabetic and doubly incontinent with an undoubted and significant need for cleaning (*Westminster CC 1996*).

8.1.2 CARE PLANS: SERIOUS DISCREPANCIES IN PROVISION

Substantial failures in the delivery of services will anyway attract criticism from the local ombudsman, and may relate to the quality of service provision, including the competence of staff, as well as to the amount or quantity of service as set against the care plan.

Serious shortcomings in services in hostel. A woman with epilepsy, severe learning difficulties, behavioural problems and urinary incontinence was placed in a hostel by the local authority under s.21 of the National Assistance Act 1948. The placement failed; the local ombudsman found serious shortcomings. These included the care plan not being fully in place when she moved in, insufficient monitoring of the placement, chronic understaffing, inadequate training, and lack of proper evaluation of the woman's needs (*Hackney LBC 1992a*).

Serious failures in provision of support to a person in a care home. A local authority placed a man with severe learning disabilities in one of its own hostels. The parents complained of poor staffing, their son's sleep disturbance through sharing a room with a man who required attention several times a night, personal belongings being stolen or destroyed, lost laundry, missing lavatory seats, and their son being left with tooth pain. The ombudsman found serious failures and maladministration. Although a support worker was provided, there was a lack of precision in setting, working toward and recording the meeting of targets; this, too, was maladministration – as was a failure on several occasions to administer the medication necessary for his epilepsy (*Manchester CC 1993*).

It is possible that the courts might recognise lack of competence or appropriateness in the provision of care, as they were prepared to do in an education case:

Competence of staff. A dispute arose over the competence of a supply teacher who had been taken on to teach an autistic child. The child's statement of special educational needs required that she be taught by a teacher experienced in teaching children with significant learning difficulties and autism and communication disorders. The court expressed its reluctance to intervene except when a decision appeared legally irrational. However, in this case, the judge found that the local authority could not reasonably have characterised the teacher as 'experienced'. Thus the authority was in breach of its duty to arrange the special educational provision specified in the statement of need (*R v Wandsworth LBC, ex p M*).

Serious failures in care plans might not only mean that people's needs are not met, but be maladministration – and be associated with, if not necessarily proved to have caused, serious consequences including death:

Death of woman with learning disabilities. The case concerned a woman in her thirties who, the coroner found, died accidentally by drowning (perhaps following an epileptic fit or cardiac arrhythmia) in the bath at a six-person residential care unit run by the council.

The woman had an 'Individual Programme Plan', but the ombudsman criticised the fact that it still contained an objective about learning certain skills – despite the fact that the officer with responsibility for the 'Goal Plan', designed to achieve such an objective, said that the woman was not capable of learning those skills. The absence of a formal decision to relax the requirement about these skills was maladministration. More specifically: 'No formal decision was ever taken that Anne had reached a stage where she could safely be left to bath alone. I can understand staff's concern to maximise her privacy and independence. Such concerns needed to be balanced against the needs of safety. It may be that, had a proper assessment been made, a decision could have been properly reached that Anne was able to bath alone but this is not what had happened and no such decision was conveyed to [the parents].'

This, together with a temporarily reduced staffing level, was maladministration, although the ombudsman – in line with the findings of the coroner – did not conclude that it had resulted in the woman's death. However, the staffing level was a factor that delayed discovery of what had happened. The ombudsman concluded that there was maladministration in the way in which the woman was cared for (*Cleveland CC 1993*).

In a similar type of case, considered judicially, the court concluded that the absence of the issue of bathing from the care plan, even if negligent (in civil law), was not sufficient to warrant a charge of manslaughter (in criminal law) on the grounds of gross negligence (*Rowley v DPP*).

If accidents involving bathing seem to be regularly reported, so too do incidents of 'wandering', about which complaints might be made to the local ombudsman:

Death of elderly man with Alzheimer's disease. An 82-year-old man was admitted on 25 April for respite care to one of the council's residential homes. He suffered from Alzheimer's disease but was otherwise fit. He was prone to wandering off and had difficulty finding his way home in an unfamiliar area. Undetected by staff, he left the home on 29 April; he was found dead six weeks later.

The ombudsman found no fault in the local authority's original assessment of the need for respite care. However, it was at fault for not properly checking that the care home could meet his needs. Furthermore, there had already been a 'wandering' incident on 27 April before the final disappearance; the family should have been informed of the incident, invited to think again about the placement and involved in the risk assessment process. In addition, the care home should have reconsidered the suitability of the placement when it finally found and opened his assessment documents on 26 April; ensured that all its staff were aware of his needs and propensity to wander; recorded the 27 April incident; and ensured he was adequately supervised. This was all maladministration (*Hounslow LBC 1999*).

8.2 PROVISION OF COMMUNITY CARE SERVICES: CONTRACTS

Since community care was formally introduced in April 1993, a so-called 'mixed economy of care' has meant that local authorities make extensive use of independent care providers (both voluntary organisations with charitable status and private sector organisations) to deliver community care services. This involves a large scale of contracting, for instance, for residential accommodation (under s.26 of the National Assistance Act 1948) and for non-residential services (under s.30 of the National Assistance Act 1948).

However, overall, it is the local authority that retains statutory responsibility for meeting a person's community assessed care needs and for ensuring that a person's care plan is adhered to – and it is the local authority that is spending public money on the contracts. Therefore, they have to pay serious attention to contracting matters such as the tendering process, allocating sufficient money to contracts, terms and conditions within the contract, penalty clauses, monitoring and review of contract performance, responding to complaints – and so on.

8.2.1 CONTRACTS AND SERVICE USERS

When health or social care is provided by the NHS or by local authorities, the courts have hitherto declined to recognise the existence of a private law contract created between provider and service user. This is despite individual care plans, which bear the language of agreement, being signed by all parties. Users of services and local authority staff sometimes believe wrongly that enforceable contracts are being created. This is not to say that such care plans might not be legally enforceable against local authorities; but this would be by way of judicial review (see 8.1 above) rather than through an action for breach of contract.

The reason for this is that the courts generally hold that the existence of statutory arrangements preclude the free negotiation and bargaining that are meant to be the hallmarks of a genuine contract. This means there will be no contract between the user of a statutory service and a statutory provider. This might be so even when money changes hands – as in a case concerning an NHS prescription charge, when the House of Lords stated that the transaction was governed by statutory obligations and not by contract (*Pfizer Corporation v Ministry of Health*).

A further obstacle to the identification and enforcing of contracts by users of services arises in relation to independent providers. This is the rule in English law called privity of contract. This means that a third party (i.e. the service user) cannot enforce a contract by two other parties (the local authority and the independent provider), even if it has been made for his or her benefit. The Contracts (Rights of Third Parties) Act 1999 was passed in order to enable third parties to enforce, in certain circumstances, a contract made between two other parties. However, whether the courts would interpret the Act as effective in the case of statutory social care and health care services is doubtful.

Of course some people fund themselves privately and enter directly into a contract with independent care providers, in which case contractual obligations exist directly between care provider and service user.

8.2.2 LOCAL AUTHORITY AND CARE PROVIDER CONTRACTS

Under regulations, passed under the Care Standards Act 2000, registered care providers, are obliged to have care plans in respect of each individual service user – for instance in respect of domiciliary care (SI 2002/3214, r.14) and care homes (SI 2001/3965, r.15). This duty is expanded upon further in standards published for the purpose of registration and inspection of such providers – for example standard 7 of both the *Domiciliary care national minimum standards* (DH 2003b), and of the *Care homes for older people national minimum standards* (DH 2003a). In future, such regulation will come under the Health and Social Care Act 2008. Nevertheless, the overall duty of the local authority to draw up a care plan and ensure that it is implemented remains, notwithstanding its contracting out of services to an independent provider.

8.2.3 CONTRACTED OUT SERVICES: OUT OF SIGHT, OUT OF MIND?

Local authorities must beware of improperly shedding their duty to ensure that the needs of service users are met. The local ombudsmen have expressed increasing concern about this issue. For instance, in the following case, a woman died against a background of failures on the part of the care agency involved, and on the part of the local authority to do anything about these known failures:

Woman's death following council's apparent indifference to the fate of elderly people. The complainant's elderly parents were both in their nineties when they began to receive services provided by care agencies on behalf of the council. Even before his father died, he had been complaining to the council that agency staff frequently missed calls, or arrived late – in which case, many elderly people like his mother tried to get up to make their own meals, putting their health in danger. On one occasion, his mother fell in the bedroom at 12.30 pm. She was unable to get up, but expected a lunch time visit so lay on the floor waiting for the carer. After an hour, she realised nobody was coming. She then used her alarm. A few days later there was no breakfast time call; she managed to get herself up, but she went without breakfast or medication.

Carer arriving with no torch: woman startled and falls and dies. The final chapter was when a home help made a tea time call in January. She did not have a torch, which she was meant to have, to illuminate the door entry key pad. So she banged on the living room window. The woman was startled. As she tried to hurry into the kitchen to switch on the light, she fell on to the corner of a table. The home help let herself in, got the woman off the floor, made her a cup of tea and sandwich, wrote up the daily log without mentioning the fall, and left. Two hours later, the woman's son arrived to find his mother slumped in her chair unable to move. A doctor was called. She suffered eight broken ribs as a result of the fall. The doctor made an incorrect diagnosis; appropriate treatment was delayed. She died two weeks later after the onset of pneumonia. The carer was dismissed for failing to report the incident.

Failure of council to respond to reports of missed or late calls: routine contract compliance checks not enough. The ombudsman was scathing. She stated that 'councils must respond to reports of missed or late calls by agency staff and follow up complaints by or on behalf of vulnerable service users as a matter of urgency. It cannot be left to routine contract compliance checks to find out whether planned services are really being delivered. It can never be acceptable for elderly people whose care is the responsibility of the Council to wait long periods of time for the next meal or for their medication to be given.' The council's failure promptly to take up complaints of missed calls was maladministration; likewise its failure to consider whether to make alternative arrangements. When an agency is failing, the council 'must simultaneously look and act in two directions at the same time – to the contractor to improve performance and to the client to assess and respond to the risk posed to them by the contractor's failures.'

Furthermore, the way in which the complaint was then handled – including a failure to coordinate papers for the review panel stage – contributed to the complainant's impression that the council was merely going through the motions and that it 'did not care what was happening to its elderly and vulnerable clients' (*Sheffield CC 2007*).

The report was disturbing. Equally so evidence given to the ombudsman by the woman's social worker in the same investigation, who explained as follows:

Systemic failure in domiciliary care provision, and in reporting and responding to concerns. The council had a traffic light system, with agencies placed on red, amber or green depending on compliance with the terms of their contract with the council. In theory, a move to red or amber triggered a higher level of monitoring. But the system did not work. There was a general problem with care agencies not able to attract staff of a reasonable quality, and not providing basic training. The agency in question had managed to move from red to green, despite missed calls still being reported.

The council had introduced new monitoring arrangements since the woman's death, including financial sanctions for missed calls. But the social worker stated that the care agencies did not inform the responsible social worker when a call was missed. Further, social workers were not completing contract monitoring forms because they had not seen any changes to the system. Home helps were routinely given jobs to complete which were impossible; for example, it was not unusual for carers to be given four one-hour calls within one hour. The social worker also believed that records of visits were often completed fraudulently (*Sheffield CC 2007*).

In another case, the relevant council staff knew that things were going badly wrong with the care agency concerned, but bureaucracy within the council prevented anything being done about it.

Councils wasting money and placing people at serious risk: by paying care agencies for not providing the services they are contracted to provide. The complainant's brother lived alone. He was unable to stand on his own or walk, so he used a wheelchair all day. He had limited use of his arms and hands. He could not get himself in and out of bed or on to and off the toilet. He had some brain damage, diabetes, high blood pressure, hearing impairment and heart problems. Other members of the family could not provide all the care he needed.

The council assessed and drew up a care plan. A care agency was meant to implement it, including personal care needs (with a weekly shower), food preparation, opening/shutting windows and curtains, washing and drying dishes and cutlery, cleaning work surfaces and floors, making the bed daily, changing the bed weekly, attending to laundry weekly. However, the agency did not carry out many of the tasks either at all, properly or regularly (for instance, he had never had a shower from the agency).

The council took no corrective action because there was no mechanism in the council for social workers – who knew about agency shortcomings – to report concerns to the contracts unit. So nothing was done. This meant that the latter was 'paying the agencies without considering the fundamental issue of whether the care plan requirements have been provided'. Thus, in Liverpool, 'agencies can fail to implement care plans yet still get paid because the part of the Council that has the knowledge, on a day to day basis of whether care plans are being met, has no input into the administration of the contract'. This had the potential to put some of the most vulnerable members of the community at serious risk. This was maladministration (*Liverpool CC 2007*).

In yet another case, the complainant's niece brought the complaint, after her aunt lay on the floor all day, after care workers had failed to arrive, and subsequently died. Again the local ombudsman was immensely critical of the council since it had known previously of the systematic failings of the agency involved:

Council fails to do anything about an inadequate care agency: elderly woman lies on the floor all day and dies. The woman, 79 years old, used a wheelchair having had both legs amputated. She had generalised arthritis, diabetes controlled by diet and a hearing impairment. She was highly dependant and required daily contact. On one particular day in March 2003, the care agency contracted to provide care failed to visit in the morning. The carer, who had decided not to work that day, had not informed the agency. The early evening visit did not take place either. Later that evening, she was found on the floor and admitted to hospital. During the period she lay on the floor, she had suffered a stroke, a heart attach and hypothermia. She died eight days later. The time the aunt spent on the floor before she was helped, was some 13 hours after the time set for the morning visit. She was without food or water. The cause of the accident was probably because of the failure of the carers to visit her. 'She was badly let down by the Council and its provider.'

Known inadequacies of care agency. However, the inadequacies of the care agency on that particular day were not uncharacteristic. They were already well known to the council and included inappropriate and untrained staff, a failure to log in and out or report to the office, failure of the back-up telephone system, and failure to ensure all carers had access to a care plan explaining entry and emergency arrangements. In addition, a significant number of complaints had been made in the past about missed or late visits. These problems had existed for nine months, from the start of a block contract the council had with the care agency; yet the council's interventions had failed to protect service users.

Given the background of complaints during 2002 about the care agency involved, the council 'failed to understand that it was dealing with a provider that was acting dangerously towards some service users. It failed to understand the random nature of the problem. The Council failed to monitor the reports of missed visits.'

Previous survey revealing serious shortcomings in agency. By January 2003, an audit of the care agency had revealed that, of a survey of 20 service users, 75 per cent did not have care plans, 60 per cent lacked a written assessment by the provider, and 60 per cent had received no risk assessment. Of 20 staff files reviewed, there was no evidence that the company employed as many people as it claimed to, and staff were averaging considerably more than 48 hours per week of work. There was no evidence of induction training; no training schedule was in place. Complaints made by service users were not recorded on their files. For 25 of 43 visits surveyed, carers provided less than 25 per cent of the time they had been commissioned to spend.

Inadequate investigation of incident. In addition, the council's investigation of the incident involving the death of the woman was inadequate. It lacked a sense of urgency, and the responsible officer was content to leave matters largely with the company and to correspond with it over a number of months. The information the council did obtain showed that, in the week before the incident, the aunt had experienced the same failings experienced by other service users including a lack of continuity in care because of different carers' involvement, truncated visits, possible missed visits, and use of inappropriate staff. The inappropriate staff comprised one who had been banned from working with service users, and another who, in January (so the agency had informed the council), had been sacked for misconduct. All this was maladministration.

Maladministration: and ombudsman's recommendations. Overall, the council failed to consider what measures to take to safeguard service users. It was clearly maladministration. The ombudsman recommended that the council should:

- waive the outstanding home care charge still being asked by the council of the niece (who administering her aunt's estate)
- apologise to the niece and pay her £500 for her time and trouble in complaining
- make a payment of £1000 to the aunt's estate to recognise the failure in service
- offer the niece a form of tribute or memorial to her aunt

- adopt at Member level a policy to ensure risks to individual service users are assessed
- ensure that the contracts unit had adequate resources to monitor contract performance
- review complaints procedures and staff training to ensure a customer care culture which recognises the difficulty and fears that vulnerable service users may have about complaining
- consider, at Member level, annually, information about the performance of care providers
- review all adult service users with critical and substantial needs and ensure that a care plan is available for all service users (*Blackpool BC 2006*).

Of course unreliability and a failure to monitor and investigate complaints are not confined to services that have been contracted out. When a service user's comments about the unreliability of the council's home care services were not treated as a complaint or investigated, it was maladministration (*North Tyneside MBC 2004*). In another case, the failure of a council home carer to report incidents leading up to the client's death also constituted maladministration:

Not reporting falls, followed by death. A home carer employed by the council visited an elderly man and found him lying on the patio floor. She reported the incident to the home care team leader who did not record it in the message book, but orally told a second carer about it. Four days later, the second carer visited and found him lying on the floor inside the house. She told the team leader what had happened. The team leader again failed to record it in the message book and did not tell the first carer about it. The first carer visited again two days later. There was no answer. She looked through the windows but not through the kitchen window (she said it was high and she was short, and it had a net curtain across it). She did not notice the milk bottles on the door step. She went away, thinking he had gone to the shops. Later that morning, his granddaughter went round with her 12-year-old son, looked through the kitchen window (under the curtain) and saw her grandfather leaning over the kitchen unit by the window, with his face close to the window. He was dead.

The ombudsman concluded that the carer appeared to have missed the clue afforded by the milk bottles and did not check the kitchen window. These were faults, but the carer would not have walked away if she had been properly briefed by the team leader, about the latest falling incident. This was serious maladministration, revealing that the passing on of such information was hit and miss (*Leeds CC 2001*).

Local authorities may be all too tempted to take a back seat when it comes to proper monitoring and review, as in the following case involving a failure to review the needs of a man with learning disabilities for five years:

Failing to reassess on change of need. A man with learning disabilities was in 1991 placed in a care home jointly by social services and the NHS. In 1998, he was diagnosed as suffering from high functioning autism. He was not reassessed by the local authority until June 2003. The authority tried to excuse itself by arguing that it did not know of changes in the man's needs during this time, and had no record of recommendations apparently made to it by the care home in 1998.

The local ombudsman pointed out that the local authority was jointly responsible for the placement and for proper reviews of the man's needs and services. No such reviews had been in place; this was maladministration (*Cambridgeshire CC 2004*).

In similar vein, the following case represented many years' worth of failing to assess and review a woman with learning disabilities in an adult placement, with serious detriment to her fundamental welfare.

Woefully inadequate management of woman with learning disabilities in foster placement. The council had failed over a period of many years to assess, review the needs of a woman with learning disabilities in a foster placement, and ensure those needs were met. The woman's welfare suffered, such as ultimately to give rise to an adult protection investigation. She had been obstructed by the foster family from having contact with her previous foster family, was not allowed to use sign language (although this was her preferred means of communication), was deprived of batteries for hearing aids, was treated like a child (being sent to bed at 7 pm), was forced to share a bedroom, was prevented from developing a relationship with a young man at her work placement and was instead encouraged to form an inappropriate relationship with an older man acquainted with the family.

As a baby she had been abandoned on park bench. As a child, she had then been fostered by the council. When she was 18, she remained with her previous foster family who, however, were not registered, as they should have been, for eight years. They were only approved as foster carers for children. She was not reviewed between 1998 and 2004. No assessment of her needs was undertaken until social services launched an adult protection investigation at the end of 2004. The council failed to respond to expressions of concern received from MENCAP and the mother. It did not respond when she lost her placement at a day centre. It delayed in providing funding for advocacy to help find a new centre. Following a complaint, it delayed for seven months in responding to the review panel's recommendations and then took no effective action on a number of points. When she was provided with a new placement, it failed to review it within the 28 days specified in the council's own policy. It failed to involve a signer or the mother in a review in 2006; the review was also unclear and the council failed to maintain a record of it. The learning disabilities team was unable to function as it should have done, with two out of three established posts vacant and a major overspend. The ombudsman was concerned about 'how such a crisis could develop and endure for so long and on how the council, as corporate body and a social services authority, responds in such situations.'

This was all maladministration; it was 'woefully inadequate' management and supervision (*Birmingham CC 2008*).

Either way then, whether services are contracted out or remain provided directly by the local authority, inadequate monitoring might be associated with highly unfortunate outcomes for service users, and be maladministration:

Care home placement and death: lack of monitoring by local authority. A woman was placed in a nursing home by the local authority (before the introduction of free nursing care in 2001 and the implementation in 2002 of the Care Standards Act 2000). She subsequently died as a result of pressure sores. The woman's grandson brought separate complaints against the local authority, the health authority and the private company that ran the home.

The local authority argued that it had no obligation to monitor the standards of nursing care provided in the home; it had to rely on the nursing home staff and the health authority's registration and inspection unit. The ombudsman took a different view, since it was the local authority that had placed her and had a statutory obligation to meet her needs. If the local authority had felt that it was unable to check on her using its own staff, it should have come to an arrangement for the health authority to do it under s.113(1A) of the Local Government Act 1972, under which NHS staff can be made available to a local authority (*Bexley CC 2000*).

Death of young man addicted to alcohol: failure to check, monitor and to contract properly. A local authority placed a young man addicted to alcohol on a residential rehabilitation course in the area of another local authority. The man discharged himself and died shortly afterward from a drug overdose. The ombudsman did not conclude that the local authority was to blame for the death. However, he did find maladministration insofar as the authority failed to make proper checks with the registration and inspection unit of the local authority, within whose area the home was; failed to ensure that a proper contract was in place; and failed to keep in touch with the man (even on the telephone) (*Nottinghamshire CC 1999*).

In another case, the ombudsman identified lack of monitoring and inappropriate placement of a man with learning disabilities:

Council failure to carry out proper assessment, to monitor care home placement, and to ensure person's needs were met. A 25-year-old man with athetoid cerebral palsy was severely physically disabled, had learning disabilities, used a wheelchair, had speech and communication problems, and used an electronic talker. He was placed in a care home, where problems arose. The ombudsman pointed out that although the care home was responsible for his day to day care, the council had a duty to monitor his care and ensure that this needs were being met.

There was a four-month delay in his annual review by the council. But, because of his complex needs, monitoring should anyway have been proactive and frequent, rather than reactive and insufficient. He was not getting the one-to-one support he required, nor gaining access to community facilities. The situation deteriorated. He was then moved to an inappropriate placement, where he spent a lot of time lying on a mattress on his own, very unhappy. He stopped eating. His health deteriorated rapidly. The council had considered how to manage his challenging behaviour, but not the causes (a consultant practitioner identified that his behaviour, caused by physical problems and exacerbated by anxiety or stress, was wrongly thought to be aggressive behaviour).

The lack of monitoring, inappropriate placement, failure to look at the causes of the problem, and a five month delay in dealing with the complaint, were maladministration. The ombudsman recommended £5000 compensation for to the man, and £2000 for his parents (*Essex CC 2006*).

The following example illustrates what can happen when a local authority fails properly to take responsibility for the needs of a person it had contractually placed with a care provider – and to consider properly the health and safety issue raised by the care provider. The upshot was a protracted dispute, the service user's needs not being met and a finding of maladministration by the local ombudsman:

Care home placement and manual handling dispute. A local authority placed a man in a residential home and paid an extra amount to the home, in order to cover additional personal assistance for him. This included manual handling by way of assisted transfers. The care home manager subsequently refused to provide such assistance and insisted instead that the man use a hoist. The manager argued that two carers had been injured while manually handling the man; the man argued that they were in fact injured when assisting other residents. The manager supported his position with a risk assessment, which did not accord with that of the local authority.

The man refused to be hoisted. The manager told him that he would have to stay in bed. His elderly parents began to visit to provide their son with the personal assistance he needed. The man contacted his social worker, who told him that he would have to stay in bed if he refused to use a hoist. This was despite the fact that there was medical evidence that both hoist use and staying in bed would be detrimental.

The subsequent local government ombudsman investigation concluded that there was convincing evidence that the man could safely be given assisted transfers. He also found that the local authority had been in breach of its duty to meet the man's assessed needs (*Redbridge LBC 1998*).

Of course the maintenance of standards applies to NHS in-house providers, as well as to independent providers, as illustrated in the following health service ombudsman investigation:

Respite care. A woman was admitted for respite care to a residential home managed by an NHS trust. She suffered a spiral fracture of her lower right leg. The health service ombudsman found a lack of effective leadership and appropriate supervision, and non-compliance with trust policy on moving handling, safe bathing and personal care (*Surrey Oaklands NHS Trust 2002*).

8.2.4 TAKING REASONABLE STEPS IN RESPECT OF CONTRACTED OUT SERVICES

Conversely, if a local authority does have adequate monitoring and review, it will not necessarily attract criticism from the local ombudsman if things do go wrong.

Monitoring of domiciliary support. Solicitors acting for a severely disabled man's grandmother complained that he had not received adequate care and that she had not been supported properly as a carer. Domiciliary support had been contracted to a care agency. Various complaints were made about the standard of care, financial and security lapses, and violence by a carer. However, the ombudsman found that the local authority initially had no reason to doubt the care agency's ability to provide satisfactory care, and had adequate monitoring procedures in place through regular meetings with the man and his family (*Liverpool CC 1997a*).

8.2.4.1 Reliance on registration and inspection body

Reliance by a local authority on the registration and inspection body (currently the Commission for Social Care Inspection) will not necessarily be enough to discharge its duty to monitor and review in respect of individual service users – as the local ombudsman held in an investigation concerning the standard of nursing care in a care home:

Death in care home. A resident had died as a result of pressure sores. The local authority had sought to rely on the health authority (which had at the time responsibility for registration and inspection of the home) for monitoring the welfare of the residents placed by the local authority. The local ombudsman found that it was maladministration for the local authority not to have taken steps to check the welfare of the resident, in particular her nursing care (*Bexley LBC 2000*).

The health service ombudsman, in a separate investigation of the same case, upheld a complaint against the health authority; its registration team had failed to look adequately into the care home's provision of staff, equipment, or precautions against accidents to residents. The ombudsman also criticised the looseness of the arrangements that the health authority had in dealing with the home (*Bexley and Greenwich Health Authority 1999*).

8.2.4.2 Terms, conditions, standards

The courts have held that there is in principle nothing to stop a local authority imposing contractual terms that exceed what is demanded by national regulatory legislation such as the Care Standards Act 2000 (*R v Cleveland CC, ex p Cleveland Care Homes Association*).

So, a local authority's insistence on high contractual standards, beyond regulatory requirements, coupled with firm and economical means of enforcing them, was held by the courts to be an essential means of balancing statutory requirements to meet needs and the fiduciary duty not to waste taxpayers' money (*R v Newcastle upon Tyne Council, ex p Dixon*). In similar vein, the local ombudsman held that it was within an authority's discretion to run an approved provider scheme and to give a higher council subsidy to such approved providers. To the extent that this might in practice mean higher subsidy being given to council-owned, rather than privately run, care homes, the ombudsman stated that it was not for him to determine; although the district auditor might take an interest (*Isle of Anglesey CC 1999, 1999a; Neath Port Talbot CBC 2000*).

At the same time, the courts have stated that contractual terms should not be so unreasonable as to threaten the ability of care providers to survive, and thus the ability of potential residents to exercise a choice of home as envisaged by the community care legislation (*R v Cleveland CC, ex p Cleveland Care Homes Association*). Such factors must be taken into account when a local authority approves the terms of such contracts (*R v Coventry City Council, ex p Coventry Heads of Independent Care Establishments (CHOICE) and Peggs*).

It is implied – even if not explicitly written – into every contract that a service will be delivered with reasonable care and skill (Supply of Goods and Services Act 1982, s.13). Where a contract does not contain adequate specification within it, this principle may be of assistance if one party is not providing a reasonable level of service.

In terms of trying to ensure standards are adhered to, and that the needs of service users are likely to be met, the courts held in one case that a local authority was not acting beyond its powers or unreasonably when it asked to see the full, rather than the abbreviated, accounts of a home with which it intended to contract. This was to check the financial viability of the home and its ability to provide long-term care and accommodation (*R v Cleveland CC, ex p Ward*).

8.3 REGULATION OF CARE PROVIDERS

The registration and inspection of care providers is currently governed by the Care Standards Act 2000, and by various sets of regulations made under it. In addition, the Department of Health has published national minimum standards that must be taken into account when registration and inspection decisions are taken. The regulatory bodies covering England have comprised the Commission for Social Care Inspection (CSCI), and the Commission for Healthcare Audit and Inspection (known as the Healthcare Commission) set up under the Health and Social Care (Community Health and Standards) Act 2003 (Part 2). CSCI has had a range of functions including the registration and inspection of care providers under the Care Standards Act 2000, including the taking account of standards published under that Act. However, whilst inspection and registration has applied to independent health care providers, the Healthcare Commission had not exercised such functions in respect of the NHS – which has in this respect therefore been subject to a lighter touch.

These two bodies replaced the National Care Standards Commission in April 2004. By 2007, though, central government had published plans to merge both Commissions with the Mental Health Act Commission, with one health and social care regulatory body resulting in the form of a Care Quality Commission (DH 2006c, p.65). These resulted in the Health and Social Care Bill 2007 which became the Health and Social Care Act 2008. The new Commission is due to take over in April 2009, and will operate under new regulations and standards. Under the scheme, registration requirements will be imposed on health and social care providers across the board, including the NHS and probably primary care providers (general practitioners). It is intended that the new scheme of registration be operative from April 2010. It has been suggested by central government that it will focus on safety and quality in terms of outcomes rather than bureaucratic process.

Note. In summary, the Health and Social Care Act 2008 provides for a change to the system of regulation. A Care Quality Commission is created with functions of registration, review, investigation in relation to health and social care, and functions under the Mental Health Act 1983. Health care is defined widely, as is social care (s.2). The new Act will cover both the NHS and local authorities, as well as independent providers of health and social care.

Anybody carrying on a regulated activity, that is the provision of health and social care, must be registered. Such provision includes the supply of staff, the provision of transport or accommodation for people requiring care, and the provision of advice in respect of care (s.8). Health care includes all forms of health care provided for people, whether relating to physical or mental health, and also includes procedures that are similar to forms of medical or surgical care but are not provided in connection with a medical condition. Social care includes all forms of personal care and other practical assistance provided for individuals who by reason of age, illness, disability, pregnancy, childbirth, dependence on alcohol or drugs, or any other similar circumstances, are in need of such care or other assistance (s.9).

It is an offence for a service provider not to be registered for a regulated activity (s.10). Registration can be granted unconditionally or with conditions attached. Registration must be granted if the Commission is satisfied that the requirements have been met of regulations made under s.20 by the Secretary of State (s.12). Managers must also apply for registration as prescribed (s.13).

The Commission can cancel registration on a number of specified grounds; it can also suspend registration (ss.17 and 18). The Act provides for regulations to be made in relation to the quality of services provided, health, safety, welfare, fitness of persons to carry on a regulated activity, management, training, premises, records, financial information and accounts, information about charges for services, requirements for review of the quality of services and for reports, handling of complaints and disputes. Regulations may also be made about preventing health care associated infections (r.20). The Secretary of State may issue a code of practice about compliance with regulations (s.21); and the Commission must issue compliance guidance in respect of the regulations (s.23). The Commission must take account of both the code of practice and the guidance in reaching decisions, and both would be admissible in civil and criminal proceedings; non-compliance would not be decisive in liability (s.25).

The Commission can give statutory warning notices (s.29). It can seek an order from a justice of the peace for urgent cancellation – if there is a serious risk to a person's life, health or well-being (s.30). There is also an urgent procedure for variation or suspension of registration (s.31). Appeals lie to the Care Standards Tribunal (s.32)

It is an offence for providers to fail to comply, without reasonable excuse, with conditions set by the Commission (s.33). It is an offence to carry on regulated activity following suspension or cancellation of registration (s.34). Regulations may specify that it is an offence to contravene them (s.35). It is an offence to give a false description of a concern or of premises, likewise to make false statements in applications for registration (ss.36-37).

The Act gives the Secretary of State power to publish statements of standards relating to health care (s.45). The Commission must carry out periodic reviews of NHS bodies and local authorities. It can conduct special reviews and investigations (s.46). It must recommend special measures to the Secretary of State in the case of failing local authorities (s.50). The Commission has powers of entry and inspection and power to require information, documents and records it considers are necessary or expedient for any of its regulatory functions (ss.60-64).

The Act places restrictions on the disclosure of personal information which the Commission has been obtained, but then provides an extensive list of permitted disclosures (ss.76-80).

8.3.1 REGULATION OF CARE PROVIDERS

Regulation under the Care Standards Act 2000 covers children's homes, independent hospitals, independent clinics, care homes, residential family centres, independent medical centres, domiciliary care agencies, fostering agencies, nurse agencies, voluntary adoption agencies and adult placement schemes. Furthermore, local authorities acting as care providers are covered in the same way as providers in the independent sector. However, the system does not cover the NHS. It is an offence for care providers, who come within the relevant definitions, not to register (Care Standards Act 2000, s.11).

8.3.2 DEFINITIONS OF CARE HOME AND DOMICILIARY CARE AGENCY

A number of definitions are supplied within the Care Standards Act 2000:

- **Care home**. A care home is an establishment (whether or not for profit) that provides accommodation, together with nursing or personal care for people who are or have been ill (including mental disorder), who are disabled or infirm or who are or have been dependent on alcohol or drugs. However, it is not a care home if it is a hospital, independent clinic or a children's home (Care Standards Act 2000, s.3).
- **Assistance with bodily functions**. An establishment is not a care home for the purposes of the Act unless 'the care which it provides includes assistance with bodily functions where such assistance is required' (s.121).
- **Illness**. Illness includes injury.
- **Disability**. A disabled person is defined as having sight, hearing or speech substantially impaired; having a mental disorder; or being physically substantially disabled by any illness, any impairment present since birth, or otherwise.
- **Mental disorder**. Mental disorder means mental illness, arrested or incomplete development of mind, psychopathic disorder, any other disorder or disability of mind (s.121). This will be amended, so as to refer to the new definition in the amended Mental Health Act 1983 of mental disorder meaning 'any disorder or disability of mind' (Mental Health Act 2007, schedule 1).
- **Domiciliary care**. A domiciliary care agency is an undertaking (whether or not for profit) which arranges the provision of personal care for people in their own homes who are unable to provide it for themselves because of illness, infirmity or disability (s.4) – excluding a sole self-employed person (S1 2002/3214, r.3).

8.3.3 PERSONAL CARE AND REGISTRATION REQUIREMENTS

The question of whether personal care is being provided is a crucial one, because the answer determines whether the care provider must go through the registration and inspection regime imposed by the Care Standards Act 2000. The Act does not define what is meant by personal care. However, Department of Health guidance states that its ordinary meaning includes:

- assistance with bodily functions such as feeding, bathing and toileting
- care falling just short of assistance with bodily functions, but still involving physical and intimate touching, including activities such as helping a person get out of a bath and helping them to get dressed
- non-physical care, such as advice, encouragement and supervision relating to the foregoing, such as prompting a person to take a bath and supervising them during this
- emotional and psychological support, including the promotion of social functioning, behaviour management, and assistance with cognitive functions (DH 2002b).

Previous case law under other legislation has given the term 'personal care' a wide meaning so as to include the emotional and psychiatric, not just bodily, functions (*Harrison v Cornwall County Council*). In turn, attention in connection with bodily functions has been interpreted widely. For example, it can include the function of an interpreter for a deaf person, in order that she could communicate during the day with people who were not deaf (*Secretary of State for Social Security v Fairey*).

Under the Care Standards Act 2000, registration as a care home is only required if the care provided includes assistance with bodily functions (s.121). This then is an explicit requirement; however, the *Fairey* case indicates that even assistance with bodily functions has a potentially wide scope.

However, the Department of Health's interpretation of 'personal care' in respect of domiciliary care providers takes a narrow approach. Guidance states that registration is only required in respect of the first two types of care listed above (assistance with bodily functions, and care falling just short of such assistance). It goes on to suggest that the other two types of personal care do not trigger registration requirements, but could be provided, for example, under the Supporting People scheme (see 16.3 below).The guidance supports this approach by arguing that it is s.4 of the Act that restricts registration requirements in this way. Under s.4, a domiciliary care agency is defined as an undertaking that provides personal care that a person is unable to provide for himself or herself without assistance. The guidance maintains that this could not extend to encouragement and emotional support, since it would make no sense to state that a person cannot provide this himself or herself (DH 2002b, para 17). This explanation seems to be not entirely clear.

8.3.4 REGISTRATION AND INSPECTION AUTHORITES

The Commission for Healthcare Audit and Inspection (CHAI, commonly referred to as the Healthcare Commission), and the Commission for Social Care Inspection (CSCI), have been the two main regulatory bodies (Care Standards Act 2000, s.5). They are due to be replaced by the Care Quality Commission in April 2009, under changes in the Health and Social Care Bill 2007.

The Healthcare Commission has registration and inspection responsibilities for independent hospitals, independent clinics and independent medical agencies (s.5A). The CSCI has responsibility for care homes, domiciliary care agencies, children's homes, residential family centres, nurse agencies, fostering agencies, voluntary adoption agencies, adoption support agencies, and adult placement schemes. This has included services of this type provided by local authorities or NHS bodies (s.5).

The CSCI keeps a register of care providers, and has the power to grant, refuse and cancel registration (Care Standards Act 2000, ss.11–16) and to inspect care providers (s.31). It has the power to enter and inspect premises, to inspect and to take copies of documents, and to interview people working there (Health and Social Care (Community Health and Standards) Act 2003, ss.88–89). Its inspections may be unannounced and result in threats to close down homes – for instance, if a culture demeaning to residents is uncovered (*BBC News*, 18 July 2007). Likewise, when suspicions arose concerning the poisoning of one or more residents, the CSCI ordered a care home's emergency closure (*Community Care 2007*).

Appeals against CSCI's decisions go to the Care Standards Tribunal. It can also prosecute for various offences. For instance, it successfully prosecuted a domestic cleaning company, trading as Tender Loving Care, which offered also personal care to people in their own homes without being registered under the 2000 Act (CSCI 2005).

Clearly, any regulatory body cannot always get it right, and registration and inspection is no guarantee that the care provider may not be going badly wrong. For example, physical abuse at a care home in Hull had gone effectively undetected for a period of three years; eventually some care workers were sent to prison and health and safety prosecutions were brought as well (Mark 2005). The local ombudsman in the past found maladministration against a local authority, when it was the regulatory body (before the days of CSCI).

Failure to vary inspection routine. Despite known concerns about a care home, the inspection unit never varied from the routine of one announced and one unannounced inspection per annum. This meant that some of the problems went unresolved and was maladministration. A man with alcohol problems had been placed there; he discharged himself a few months later and was found dead from a heroin overdose. Had the problems been dealt with, he might have received better aftercare, although the ombudsman was not prepared to say that the man would still have been alive (*North Somerset CC 1999*).

8.3.5 CARE STANDARDS: REGULATIONS

Under the Care Standards Act 2000, various regulations have been passed to spell out registration requirements for different types of provider. The following paragraphs outline some of these requirements in relation to care homes and domiciliary care services. Regulations relating to adult placements were reissued in August 2004, so that the regulatory effect and burden would fall on adult placement schemes, rather than individual providers such as families (SI 2004/2070).

8.3.5.1 Regulations for care homes

The Care Homes Regulations 2001 (SI 2001/3965) contain various requirements, including:

- **Information**: home's statement of purpose, a service user's guide, information about fees (r.5).
- **Fitness**: the fitness of the registered provider (including integrity, good character, physical and mental fitness) (r.7).
- **Fitness**: the fitness of the registered manager (including integrity, good character, qualifications, skills, physical and mental fitness) (r.9).
- **Staffing**: registered person must ensure that at all times suitable staff are working at the care home (suitably qualified, competent and experienced), and are appropriately supervised. If the care home provides nursing, medicines or medical treatment, there must be at all times a suitably qualified, registered nurse working at the home (r.18).
- **Employment checks**: for people carrying on, managing or working in a care home, certain information is required including proof of identity, birth certificate, current passport, evidence of qualifications, two written references, evidence of mental and physical fitness, and criminal record certificate issued under the Police Act 1997 (schedule 2).
- **Staffing and training**: there must be suitably qualified, competent and experienced staff working at the care home as are appropriate for the health and welfare of service users; there must be appropriate training (r.18).

- **Health, welfare dignity**: the care home must be conducted so as to promote and make proper provision for the health and welfare of service users. As far as practicable service users should be enabled to make decisions about their care. Arrangements must be made to ensure the privacy and dignity of service users, with due regard to sex, religious persuasion, racial origin, cultural and linguistic background, any disability of service users (r.12).
- **Access to health care**: arrangements must be made for service users to register with a general practitioner of their choice and to receive where necessary services from any health care professional (r.13).
- **Medicines**: arrangements must be made for the recording, handling, safekeeping, safe administration and disposal of medicines (r.13).
- **Health and safety**: arrangements must be made for health and safety matters, including a safe system for moving and handling service users (r.13).
- **Abuse**: arrangements must be made to prevent service users being harmed or suffering abuse or being placed at risk of harm or abuse (r.13).
- **Restraint**: no service user should be subject to physical restraint, unless it is the only practicable means of securing the welfare of that or any other service user and there are exceptional circumstances – or in the case of a person lacking capacity in relation to the matter in question, consistent with s.6 of the Mental Capacity Act 2005. Any such restraint must be recorded (r.13).
- **Assessment of service users**: as far as practicable, service users must have been assessed by a suitably qualified or trained person before accommodation is provided for them, the home must have obtained a copy of the assessment, the service user (or his or her representative) have been consulted, and the home have confirmed in writing to the service user that the home is suitable for his or her needs. The assessment of the service user's needs must be kept under review and revised as necessary. A care plan must be prepared, made available to the service user and kept under review (rr.14,15).
- **Facilities and services**: the care home must have appropriate facilities and services – for example, in respect of telephones, furniture, laundry, kitchen equipment, food, keeping of valuables, arranging social activities, etc (r.16).
- **Premises including adaptations and equipment for disability**: there are many requirements, including suitable adaptations and equipment for old, infirm or physically disabled service users.
- **Informing CSCI**: The care home (registered person) must inform the CSCI of the death of any service users, of any serious injury, of any serious illness at a care home not providing nursing, of any event in the care home adversely affecting the well-being or safety of any service users, any theft, burglary or accident in the care home, and of any allegation of misconduct (SI 2001/3965, r.37).

A number of cases concerning the regulations have come before the courts – or before the Care Standards Tribunal when a home has appealed against a decision of the Commission for Social Care Inspection.

For instance, the following legal case confirmed that the burden lies on the manager of a care home in showing his or her fitness to manage, not on the registration authority:

Fitness to manage. In a case concerning the fitness of a manager of a care home, a care standards tribunal (CST) had in effect given the appellant the benefit of the doubt concerning his background.

The fitness question concerned past misconduct involving physical abuse of residents, in particular hitting a resident on the penis with a pen to stop him masturbating, wheeling a resident into the dining room with a waste-paper bin on her head, forcibly administering medication to a resident, and kicking a resident on her buttocks.

The CST had overturned (what was then) the National Care Standards Commission's decision that he was not fit to be registered. However, in turn the High Court overturned the CST's decision, on the grounds that it had not explicitly addressed the question of whether he was fit to do so in terms of integrity and good character. The Court of Appeal upheld the decision, confirming that the burden lay on the applicant to show his or her fitness, rather than on the registration authority to show unfitness (*Jones v National Care Standards Commission*).

The courts have also held that the requirements under regulations 12 and 13 of the Care Homes Regulations are offences of strict liability which give rise to criminal offences. So mitigating factors put forward by a care home operator might be unavailing, as the courts emphasised:

Strict liability: mitigating factors insufficient. Breaches of the regulations require only to have happened (*actus reus*) to constitute an offence, rather than to have been commissioned deliberately or recklessly (*mens rea*, the guilty mind). For example, the regulations are not qualified by a term such as 'reasonably practicable'. Mitigating factors put forward by the care home operator for non-availability of medicines, such as difficulty in obtaining prescriptions for GPs, would not prevent a breach of the regulations. The protection for the registered person lay rather in r.43 of the regulations, which provided for a notice to be served and for the registered person to make representations to the regulatory body (Commission for Social Care Inspection). Furthermore, it did not follow that every failure would be an offence, since what was 'proper provision' under r.12 would be judged by standards made under s.23 of the Care Standards Act 2000 (*Brooklyn House Ltd v Commission for Social Care Inspection*).

In a Care Standards Tribunal case, the Tribunal confirmed that an enrolled nurse – an owner and manager of a care home – was unfit.

Unfitness of manager: death of resident by scalding. Absence of thermostatic mixing valves contributed to the death of a resident, at 3.30 am, in a bath full of scalding water. There had been no adequate risk assessment. Dangerously hot radiators also posed a risk to residents, whilst there were badly stained and odorous part s of the home. As the Tribunal pointed out, 'when dealing with elderly people who often suffer from incontinence, odour control is a priority to maintain dignity.' Another criticism was that residents had been taken to the bathroom and then led back minus their spectacles. Three sets were lined up in the bathroom; the CSCI inspector noted that this went to the heart of the dignity of residents (*Hillier v Commission for Social Care Inspection*).

Cancellation of registration might be sought on a number of serious grounds relating to the welfare of residents. But evidence is nonetheless required, as the Care Standards Tribunal pointed out in the following case:

Number of CSCI allegations matched only by lack of evidence. In one case, the allegations of failure made by CSCI were legion, but equally so was the lack of evidence.

It was lacking in respect of, for example, manual handling failures, placing chairs against beds because there was a shortage of cot sides, sharing of commodes, shortage of spare mattresses when they needed to be changed because of incontinence, absence of night drainage bags for catheter, absence of disposable gloves and wipes, absence of towels or face cloths in residents' rooms, no sanitary bins, no soap in dispensers, dirt under residents' beds, medication tablets lying on floor, unspecified claims about how many hoists were required, insufficiency of continence aids, manual lifting of residents by staff without the use of appropriate equipment etc.

Despite the list of allegations, the missing evidence meant that the appeal succeeded against the notice to cancel registration (*Bhatnagar v Commission v Social Care Inspection*).

The Care Standards Tribunal has also pointed out that inappropriate interventions by the regulatory body might itself undermine the management continuity in a care home – if the inspector was not merely robust, but apparently overbearing, intimidating, demanding, pedantic and rigorous, such as to himself or herself contribute to the problems of the care home (*Joyce v National Care Standards Commission*).

8.3.5.2 Regulations for domiciliary care agencies

The Domiciliary Care Agencies Regulations 2002 (SI 2002/3214) refer to a number of requirements, including:

- **Fitness**: fitness of registered provider, manager, staff (similar to fitness requirements for Care Homes Regulations above).
- **Safety, independence**: the agency must ensure the safety of service users, safeguard them against abuse or neglect, promote independence, ensure the safety and security of the property of service users.
- **Dignity, etc.**: respect for privacy, dignity, wishes, confidentiality; also have due regard to sex, religious persuasion, racial origin, cultural and linguistic background and any disability.
- **Care plan**: a care plan must specify the service users' needs, how those needs are to be met. It must be made available to the service user, kept under review and revised as appropriate.
- **Meeting need**: as far as practicable the personal care provided must meet the service user's needs.
- **Wishes and feelings**: as far as practicable, service users' wishes and feelings must be taken account of; they must be provided with comprehensive information and suitable choices and be encouraged to make decisions about their personal care.
- **Abuse**: arrangements must be made to prevent service users being harmed or suffering abuse, and a procedure must be specified for dealing with an allegation of abuse, neglect or harm.
- **Medication**: arrangements must be made for the recording, handling, safe keeping and safe administration of medicines; also circumstances must be specified in which a care worker may administer or assist with medication.
- **Mobility**: arrangements to assist a service user with mobility in the home.
- **Agent/money**: there must be a specified procedure where a worker acts as agent for, or receives money from, a service user.
- **Safe system of work**: suitable arrangements must be made, including training, to ensure a safe system of work, to include the lifting and moving of service users.
- **Physical restraint**: (as for care homes).
- **Staffing**: there must at all times be an appropriate number of suitably skilled and experienced staff; suitable assistance, including appropriate equipment, must be provided at their request in respect of the provision of personal care.

8.3.6 CARE STANDARDS

Under the Care Standards Act 2000, national minimum care standards have been published in both England and Wales. The registration authority must take them into account when it takes decisions (s.23); therefore, breach of one or more standards does not automatically mean breach of legislation. Various sets of standards have been published, including one set relating to care homes (DH 2003a), and another to domiciliary care agencies (DH 2003b). In future, equivalent standards will be published under s.45 if the Health and Social Care Act 2008.

8.4 SUPPORTED HOUSING

Since the coming into force of the Care Standards Act 2000, some care homes have decided to 'deregister' themselves as care homes. Apart from avoiding the registration and inspection requirements for care homes, deregistration also results in avoidance of the whole system of local authority placements and charges for residential care. It enables former residents to become tenants and, amongst other things, receive housing benefit. Personal care is then delivered separately by a domiciliary care agency.

Such changes to the status of accommodation have a number of possible legal ramifications. These include their very lawfulness and also the consequent duties of local authorities, who in many instances will have originally placed residents in the care home that is now deregistering. One such instance of deregistration was challenged and the dispute reached the Care Standards Tribunal. It ruled against the deregistration in the circumstances, stressing the absence of choice for service users in choosing a domiciliary care provider. This cast doubt on whether there was a genuine separation between the provision of the accommodation and the provision of the personal care:

Improper deregistration of care home. A company, called Alternative Futures Ltd, provided residential accommodation until January 2002. At that time, having consulted with residents, it purported to deregister itself as a care home. It split itself into two companies. Alternative Housing covered the housing side of things, Alternative Futures the domiciliary care services required. Tenants were given keys and enjoyed exclusive possession of their rooms. The benefits claimed for the tenants were housing benefit, security of tenure, choice of care provider – and extra funding and space that would otherwise have been devoted to registration requirements as a care home.

The Care Standards Tribunal considered various aspects of what had occurred, including whether the residents had the mental capacity to sign the tenancy agreements and whether this would be fatal to the arrangements. Ultimately, however, the tribunal faulted the deregistration, on grounds of choice. This was because in practice the domiciliary care services would have to be delivered by Alternative Futures; there were no arrangements in place to allow tenants to express genuine choice to receive such services from another provider (*Alternative Futures Ltd v National Care Standards Commission*).

The case subsequently ended up in court. It upheld the Tribunal's decision and ruled that even if the service users concerned had valid tenancies, this did not settle the crucial question of whether the establishment was providing accommodation together with nursing or personal care. This was essentially a question of fact. The court stated that the 'establishment of a lessor and lessee relationship can be an indicator of a situation where an establishment does not provide both the accommodation and the care, but cannot be determinative'. It accepted that the residents were assured tenants but did note the Commission's concerns about (a) whether, given their severe learning disabilities, they had the capacity to enter into tenancies; (b) whether grant of the tenancies was nothing more than a sham to enable housing and other financial benefits to be obtained; and (c) that the leases did not appear to be standard leases, because the rent exceeded £700 per week and the tenant received care (*Moore v Care Standards Tribunal*).

The court had noted that the existence of a tenancy is not decisive as to whether or not the establishment is a care home. On similar lines, but conversely, an occupier of a room in a property, run by a person registered to run a care home, could nevertheless be entitled to housing benefit. The residents concerned, in a case before the Social Security Commissioners, were described as 'hostel' residents. They had their own living bed-sitting rooms with cooking equipment but no self-contained washing or toilet facilities. They were not receiving personal care and they did not come within the definition of vulnerable person given in s.3 of the Care Standards Act. They were held not to be living in residential accommodation, not-withstanding the registered nature of the premises (CH/1326/2004).

8.4.1 CARE HOME REGISTRATION: PERSONAL CARE AND ACCOMMODATION

Department of Health guidance states that it would not expect very sheltered housing, extra care housing or group homes (supported housing) to have to register, as a matter of course, as care homes (DH 2002b, para 19). Generally speaking, where personal care is provided, it would be provided by a registered domiciliary care agency. However, it warns that, if the circumstances suggest that an establishment (including personal care) is being run by one (or more than one connected) company, then registration as a care home would be still required (DH 2002b, para 33). Indeed, it was the inability to identify a genuine distinction between the provision of the housing and the provision of personal care which led the Care Standards Tribunal to find that a care home was still being operated in the case of *Alternative Futures Ltd v National Care Standards Commission*.

The Department of Health guidance also lays emphasis on the question as to whether the personal care is being delivered to a person's own home (occupied by the person with, for example, the right to deny entry to people including care workers without this affecting their right to occupy). It states that shared accommodation could be a characteristic of a person's own home; but that the scale of such accommodation is likely to be relevant (para 40). Beyond family or domestic scale, such accommodation might be more realistically regarded as a care home rather than a person's own home. It also suggests that the distinction between a tenancy and a licence to occupy might be relevant, since the latter would not entail the person having exclusive possession of any part of the premises, and so not be consistent with the accommodation representing the person's own home (DH 2002b, para 36). However, the existence of a tenancy does not necessarily mean that an establishment is not functioning as a care home.

On the question of a person's capacity in relation to a tenancy, It has been suggested that if the tenancy were regarded as being a contract for 'necessaries' (under mental capacity law, see 20.9), it would nevertheless be workable and enforceable in that the rent could be recovered – even if the person lacked the capacity to enter into the tenancy. Department of Health guidance summarises the relevant principles as follows. It reiterates the presumption of a person's capacity until proved otherwise, and the importance of taking the functional approach to deciding capacity (see 20.4). It then goes on to state that a contract is binding if the landlord believed the tenant was capable of making it; that the penalty, if any, for a void contract would fall on the landlord; that the 'necessaries' rule could apply; and that the Official Solicitor is of the view that a tenancy can be granted to a person even if he or she has limited mental capacity (DH 2002b, annex B).

The courts have also held that in any case deregistration does not simply happen automatically because there is a change in factual circumstances that appear to take the care home outside of registration requirements; the decision of the registration authority is still required (*Alternative Futures v National Standards Commission*).

8.4.2 CONTINUING LOCAL AUTHORITY RESPONSIBILITIES ON DEREGISTRATION

If a local authority has placed a person in a care home that is now proposing deregistration in order to convert to a supported housing arrangement, it would seem the local authority must review and reassess the needs of the service user. This is to ensure that any new arrangements will continue to meet the needs of the service user and, if so, in order that the care plan is amended. If the new arrangements clearly would not meet the needs of a service user, the local authority would need to make alternative arrangements. This was the inference reached in the following court case:

Change to supported housing and meeting individual needs. A local authority proposed to sell a residential home to a housing association, which would then redevelop the premises and grant tenancies to the residents. The severely disabled claimant argued that she would not as a consequence benefit from communal dining and would lose the social interaction necessary for her well-being. Other concerns related to arrangements for transport, holidays and in relation to her vomiting in the night.

The court held that the care plan for the woman did not have to be worked out fully in advance of the alterations to the premises; and what was important at present was that neither the care plan nor the structure of the new premises obstructed this. So long as this remained the case, then it would be premature to argue that her needs would not be met in the new set-up (*R(Lloyd) v Barking and Dagenham LBC*).

Thus, if a local authority or NHS trust is considering a change for an individual service user from residential care to supported housing, it needs to be able to justify this. Financial considerations can legitimately be part of this justification, as long as the person's needs are properly met under the alternative arrangements:

Supported living rather than residential care. The residential panel of an NHS care trust, providing both NHS and community care services, decided that a man with autistic spectrum disorder no longer required residential care and that his needs could be met in a supported housing context (where he would receive housing benefit). The trust's letter at the time stated that it had to have regard to relative costs; a residential placement would cost £860 per week, whereas supported housing would result in no immediate costs to health or social services, because of access to income support, housing benefit, and other benefits. However, the letter also stated that, such issues aside, supported living would be in the man's best interests. A dispute arose about this.

The court refused to intervene on various grounds. These included the fact that, on the evidence, the trust's belief that the man would benefit from independence in supported housing could not be characterised as legally irrational. The panel had not excluded residential care as a possibility but had preferred the supported housing option, something it was quite entitled to do. Furthermore, article 8 of the European Convention on Human Rights added nothing to the facts of the case (*R(Rodriguez-Bannister) v Somerset Partnership NHS and Social Care Trust*).

8.5 WAITING TIMES FOR SERVICES

Community care legislation contains no time limits on the delivery of services, other than the situation in which people should be discharged from acute hospital beds (Community Care (Delayed Discharges) Act 2003). Even in that case, exceeding the time limit imposed by an NHS discharge notice does not result in a breach of duty; it merely creates a duty on the local authority to pay money to the NHS for the 'blocked' bed. Likewise, government sets targets, by means of performance indicators, for service delivery; but the courts will not necessarily regard such targets as relevant to ascertaining whether undue delay has occurred.

As already noted (see section 7.4), if legislation is silent on the time within which a duty must be performed, then the courts take the approach that it must be performed within a reasonable period of time or without undue delay. The implications of this general rule will depend on the circumstances of the case. The courts and the local government ombudsmen have considered delay on a number of occasions. They are more likely to do so in the context of social services than the NHS, because the duties on local authorities to provide services to individuals are in some circumstances of the specific, 'absolute' and enforceable type – unlike, by and large, NHS duties.

8.5.1 WAITING TIMES AND INTERIM PROVISION

Department of Health guidance points out that interim provision will sometimes be required, for example when the care home place of choice is not yet available (LAC(98)19, para 11). Or, for instance, interim provision might be required in terms of assistive equipment and personal assistance in a person's home, while he or she is waiting for major adaptation works to be carried out or to move house.

Waiting times: interim provision of equipment. The local government ombudsman has referred on a number of occasions to interim provision: for example, a bath aid during a wait for alternative accommodation (*Barnsley MBC 1998*); and provision of a commode by the social services department, while a person waits for a disabled facilities grant from the housing department, which might discharge the authority's duty under s.2 of the Chronically Sick and Disabled Persons Act 1970 (*Barnsley MBC 1998a*; see also *Liverpool CC 1996/1997, Tower Hamlets LBC 1997*).

However, the courts have reminded local authorities that the interim provision should not become an end in itself (*R v Sutton LBC, ex p Tucker*).

8.5.2 WAITING TIMES FOR SERVICES: JUDICIAL APPROACH

In large part, the courts might be reluctant to become involved in the question of waiting times for services.

Judicial reluctance to rule on waiting times. A child had entered a psychiatric unit for assessment. The doctor decided that a special foster placement was required as soon as possible, the accommodation and care to be provided under s.20 of the Children Act 1989. This had proved difficult and the child was still, nearly a year later, in the unit. The judge held that it was not for the court to make a declaration that the authority had not acted with reasonable diligence and speed. This would not be appropriate in the context of judicial review, because the court could not investigate the precise circumstances of the situation. Instead, it was more appropriate that the complaints procedure under s.26 of the Children Act 1989 be used (*R v Birmingham CC, ex p A*).

Nevertheless, in some more recent cases, the courts have in particular circumstances been prepared to refer to timescales.

Delay in care plan. A woman with learning disabilities was assessed as ready for discharge from NHS premises in July 2004. By 1996 she was still there. The judge found the local authority to be in breach of s.47 of the NHS and Community Care Act 1990, since it had still not decided about what services to provide (*R v Sutton LBC, ex p Tucker*).

In a Scottish case, the court also found breach of duty in respect of a considerably shorter timescale than was involved in the *Tucker* case.

Delay funding care home place. A 90-year-old man was admitted to a care home, the need for which the local authority had accepted. He had extremely poor short-term memory, restricted mobility and liability to fall, deafness in both ears, regular confusion, and inability to dress and look after himself. The local authority placed him on a waiting list for funding (in the mean time, his family were in effect being forced to pay the fees). The judge held that placing the man on a waiting list for several months was an abdication of the local authority's responsibility and was unlawful (*MacGregor v South Lanarkshire Council*).

Furthermore, in the *MacGregor* case, the court stated – just as the local ombudsman has on many occasions in respect of waiting times for assessment (see 7.4.3) – that even if waiting lists had some legitimacy, they should not be operated simply in date order. Instead, they should be applied on the basis of priority being allocated according to the degree of individual need.

8.5.3 WAITING TIMES: LOCAL OMBUDSMAN APPROACH

Just as for waits for assessments (see 7.4), the local government ombudsmen have investigated delays in services on a number of occasions. Much might hinge on the individual circumstances:

Undue delay and the individual case. The local ombudsman is likely to consider the circumstances of each case in deciding what a reasonable waiting time should have been. For instance, in one investigation, the local authority claimed, in relation to s.2 of the Chronically Sick and Disabled Persons Act 1970, 'that although they may be under an obligation to provide a facility they do not consider that they have an obligation to provide the facility immediately. Thus, they argue some delay is acceptable.' The ombudsman stated that 'whether or not any particular delay is so excessive as to constitute maladministration will depend on the facts of the individual case' (*Wakefield MDC 1992*).

More recently, the local ombudsmen have stated that, following recommendation of an adaptation, it would be unacceptable for a person to remain on a waiting list for provision for more than six months (*West Lancashire DC 2005*). Waiting times might afflict not just one stage of assessment and provision, but several, turning into a catalogue of delay:

Catalogue of delay. A woman with learning disabilities and autism had completed a university degree in deaf studies and sign language. She now required some form of residential placement as she did not wish to return home to live with her father on a permanent basis. The local authority carried out an assessment of need in July 1997. In February 2000 the need still had not been met, through a catalogue of delay and lack of urgency in obtaining relevant information, holding meetings and making decisions. Even when a decision to provide a tailored assessment had been made, it took seven months from the date of the decision to hold a care planning meeting, and a further five months to request the extra funding that had been identified as needed. This was maladministration (*Wakefield MDC 2000*).

Delay, amounting to maladministration in the judgement of the local ombudsman, might come in terms of days, weeks, months or years.

Long and short waiting times. When a man with paraplegia (following an accident) was discharged home from hospital, it took the local authority 16 months to put a complete care package in place; this was too long (*Avon CC 1997*).

A delay of two or three months in changing the Meals on Wheels for a person with special dietary needs and following a request from the man's general practitioner was maladministration (*Kensington and Chelsea RB 1992*).

It was maladministration also when cleaning and laundry services promised for February did not materialise until late March for a man discharged from hospital after a stroke – and when there was a failure to place straightaway and mark as urgent an order for a gas fire with top controls, given that he was blacking out when bending down to use the existing controls (*Kirklees MBC 1993*).

Delay in providing services of nine months, following the assessment of a young man who had just left school (and was later diagnosed as schizophrenic), was maladministration (*Liverpool CC 1997*); as was a delay of 12 months in making arrangements for an alternative care package, after heavily supported independent living in a bungalow had failed (*Liverpool CC 1997a*). Even a ten-day wait for a visit to be made following the discharge of a man from hospital – when normally a visit would have been made next day – was blameworthy (*Sheffield CC 1996*).

Allowing situations to drift will attract criticism from the local ombudsman:

Avoiding drift. Delay in payment of a housing (renovation) grant could not be justified by the absence of the 'one person' who could make it, even in the absence of an authorised deputy (*Kirklees MBC 1997*). When a stairlift company was slow in responding to the council's request that it assess and estimate the cost of installing a stairlift, the council should have been monitoring the situation and pursuing the company (*Liverpool 1996/1997*).

In order to identify blameworthy, as opposed to justifiable, delay, the local ombudsmen sometimes break down the whole process of referral, assessment and service provision into separate stages. They then give to each a reasonable time that is then measured against the actual sequence of events:

Breaking down waiting times. In establishing a blameworthy period of waiting (18 months), the ombudsman considered the time involved for each of the following: request for assessment, assessment, occupational therapist's report and request for costing, preliminary inspection and completion of grant enquiry form, stairlift estimate, test of resources, sending and return of application package, grant approval (*Liverpool CC 1996/1997*).

In another case, work arranged by the social services department to replace a bath with a shower, which took five months instead of only one, constituted maladministration (*Liverpool CC 1996/1997*).

In the following case, the council failed to act for 18 months in transferring a disruptive service user to alternative accommodation:

Delay in dealing with disruptive service user: severe effects on other residents in group home. When a disruptive service user (with a dual diagnosis in the form of learning disabilities and bipolar mood disorder) was introduced to a group home, she caused considerable problems for other residents – including the complainant's sister (who had a mild learning disability together with visual impairment). The latter found the former's behaviour frightening, to the extent of often not leaving her room.

It took 18 months for the council to resolve the situation, by transferring the disruptive resident to alternative accommodation. Despite the difficulties the council faced, the effect of the disruption on the three other residents of the home was so severe, that the 18-month delay was unreasonable and amounted to maladministration (*Oldham MBC 2006*).

CHAPTER 9

Residential accommodation

KEY POINTS

Local authorities have both duties and powers to arrange residential accommodation of various types under s.21 of the National Assistance Act 1948. Under s.26 of the 1948 Act, such accommodation may be arranged through the independent sector. The fundamental conditions that must be satisfied are:

- a person must be at least 18 years old

- have a need for care and attention
- this need must arise from age, illness, disability or any other circumstances
- the care and attention required must not be available otherwise than by the provision of accommodation under s.21.

Whether in respect of people subject to immigration control, or others in various types of need, s.21 of the 1948 Act continues to be legally scrutinised as to its meaning and scope. Notwithstanding its age, the courts have confirmed that it is a prime example of legislation that is 'always speaking'. Therefore, it should be interpreted in a way that continuously updates the meaning of wording, in order to allow for changes to society since the legislation was originally drafted.

The flexibility of s.21, and this requirement that it be interpreted to keep pace with changing social circumstances, means that uncertainties (as identified in Chapter 3) flourish at times when pressure is put upon the Act because of those changing circumstances. Thus, it has remained a significant battleground as local authorities have sought to limit potentially ruinous expenditure.

For instance, it has continued to be closely scrutinised in the case of asylum seekers and other people subject to immigration control (see Chapter 14). A body of case law has also developed about how far s.21 creates obligations to provide residential accommodation in the form of ordinary housing as opposed to care home placements. These cases have largely arisen as a result of the shortage of social housing, and the inability of local authorities to meet people's housing needs under the Housing Act 1996.

Owing to the costs involved of providing residential accommodation, local authorities predictably tend to exploit ambiguity or uncertainty in order to avoid potential responsibilities. For instance, disputes over where a person was person was 'ordinarily resident' before entering residential accommodation are legion, since this determines which local authority is responsible for making the placement. In the case of some people – particularly perhaps in the case of people with learning disabilities – such placements can run into thousands of pounds each week for one individual.

Likewise, with financial concerns in mind, some local authorities have sought ways to undermine the legal rules about when the 'topping up' of care home fees, typically by the family of a resident, is or isn't lawful. Families may find themselves asked unlawfully by the local authority to add to the fee paid by the authority – when it is in fact the latter that should be covering the whole amount.

Similarly, owing to the failure of central government and NHS bodies to set out and to adhere to clear legal rules about NHS continuing health care (see Chapter 18), local authorities have for many years ended up placing people in care homes (and charging them under the National Assistance Act 1948) – instead of the NHS doing so free of charge under the NHS Act 2006 and its predecessor, the NHS Act 1977). For significant numbers of people, this has meant having to sell their homes and use up their savings unnecessarily and at the unlawful behest of local authorities (see Chapter 18).

Local authorities have also unlawfully or maladministratively sometimes placed people in, and charged them for, residential accommodation under the 1948 Act – when in fact the placement should instead be free under s.117 of the Mental Health Act (following a person's hospital detention and discharge under that Act).

The apparent unconcern with which some local authorities exact legally dubious charges from vulnerable people and their families under s.21 of the National Assistance Act is an irony. It is, after all, local authorities that have been given the lead in protecting vulnerable people from financial harm and abuse.

9.1 NEED FOR CARE AND ATTENTION

Section 21 of the National Assistance Act 1948 refers to the making of arrangements for providing 'residential accommodation for persons aged eighteen or over who by reason of age, illness, disability or any other circumstances are in need of care and attention not otherwise available to them'. The duty has been taken by the courts to be a strong one (*R v Sefton MBC, ex p Help the Aged*). The need specified under s.21 of the National Assistance Act 1948 is for care and attention, but the only service that can be provided is residential accommodation, together with associated amenities and requisites. There would thus appear to be something of a mismatch between the need and the service. The explanation is that the accommodation itself is not the care and attention, but is the only means by which the requisite care and attention, or 'looking after', can be provided (*R(Wahid) Tower Hamlets LBC*). The House of Lords has subsequently confirmed the importance of this term, 'looking after':

The meaning of 'looking after'. Looking after, in the context of s.21 of the National Assistance Act, means more than just 'accommodation'. It means 'doing something for the person being cared for which he cannot or should not be expected to do for himself; it might be household tasks which an old person can on longer perform or can only perform with great difficulty; it might be protection from risks which a mentally disabled person cannot perceive; it might be personal care, such as feeding, washing or toileting. This is not an exhaustive list. The provision of medical care is expressly excluded'. This meant that a person subject to immigration control, and HIV positive, was not in need of care and attention. This was because he was under the care of the National Health Service, took medication which had to be kept in refrigerated conditions, and needed to see a doctor every three months; but otherwise his illness did not affect him and he was able to look after himself (*R(M) v Slough BC*).

The courts have also considered whether the phrase 'not otherwise available' refers back to 'care and attention' or to 'residential accommodation'. They have concluded that it means care and attention not otherwise available (not residential accommodation not otherwise available: *R(M) v Slough BC*). The courts have held a local authority should look ahead to some extent, if the circumstances are such that a person is not in immediate need of care and attention but is likely soon to be so (*R v Newham LBC, ex p Gorenkin*). However, the legislation refers to people who 'are' in need of care and attention, and the House of Lords has stated that therefore (a) the primary focus must be on present rather than future needs, (b) there needs to be sensible flexibility, and (c) intervention should be premised on a need for care already existing, but (d) if there is a present need for some sort of care, then the local authority is empowered to intervene before the need becomes a great deal worse (*R(M) v Slough BC*).

In formulating eligibility criteria about when a person is to be deemed to be in need of care and attention, local authorities may up to a point (in terms of a 'limited subjective element') consider their resources (*R v Sefton LBC, ex p Help the Aged*). It is thus permissible for local authorities to apply a threshold of eligibility to determine whether a person is eligible for a care home placement, or for some other form of residential accommodation. Since 2002, the threshold used by local authorities derives from guidance issued by the Department of Health on 'fair access to care' (see section 6.12).

9.1.1 AGE, ILLNESS, DISABILITY OR ANY OTHER CIRCUMSTANCES

The care and attention required must be due to age, illness, disability or any other circumstances. Age, illness and disability are not defined. The term, 'any other circumstances', means precisely what it says. The following two court cases illustrate this in terms of destitution and domestic violence; both were held to be relevant circumstances, although the law was subsequently altered in respect of the destitution of asylum seekers or other people subject to immigration control (see Chapter 14).

Any other circumstances: asylum seekers. The Court of Appeal ruled, upholding a decision of the High Court in relation to asylum seekers, that the term 'any other circumstances' did not necessarily have to be of a kind with age, illness or disability (the other conditions for assistance under s.21 of the 1948 Act).

However, the court also stated that, even if it were wrong and it did have to be of a kind with these other terms, it was clear that the circumstances of the asylum seekers – without food and accommodation, inability to speak the language, ignorance of Britain, and stress – could result in illness or disability, thus establishing potential eligibility under these terms of s.21 rather than 'any other circumstances'. Nevertheless, this did not mean that s.21 was a safety net for just anyone who happened to be short of accommodation and money (*R v Westminster CC, ex p A*: decided before the 1999 and 2002 Acts relating to immigration and asylum).

Similarly, domestic violence could be a relevant 'other circumstance' when a local authority considers whether the needs of an asylum seeker stem from destitution alone or something more (*R(Khan) v Oxfordshire CC*).

The open-ended, though not limitless, nature of 'any other circumstances', and the subsequent history of how the term has been applied, was indeed foreseen in 1948 at the time the Bill was passed in Parliament. It was described as not concerning age or infirmity (the original criteria in the section) but was to cover the difficult or marginal case, such that its absence might 'run us into trouble'. At the same time, it was not intended to place 'indefinite responsibility' on local authorities (*Hansard* 1948). Such limitation was illustrated in 2004, when the High Court held that a local authority did not simply have to accommodate en masse a group of Chagossian islanders who had arrived in England claiming to be destitute. However, it would have to accommodate some of the islanders, if relevant need were demonstrated in individual cases (*R(Selmour) v West Sussex CC*).

9.1.2 TAKING ACCOUNT OF PEOPLE'S ABILITY TO MAKE THEIR OWN ARRANGEMENTS

In deciding whether care and attention is otherwise available, the local authority must disregard the person's capital resources beneath the relevant capital upper threshold applying to care home fees (National Assistance Act 1948, s.21(2A) (see 10.6 below).

Even before the National Assistance Act 1948 was amended to put this beyond doubt, the Court of Appeal had held that to treat a person as able to make her own arrangements for residential accommodation – once her capital had fallen below the relevant threshold – was not lawful. The local authority had in fact been pursuing a policy that allowed a person's resources to fall to the £1500 required for funeral expenses – far below the capital threshold – before it would assist (*R v Sefton MBC, ex p Help the Aged*). In similar vein, the local ombudsman has stated that, when people are already in residential care and their capital dips below the relevant financial threshold, a policy of delaying council funding and not back dating it would be likely to be unlawful and was in any case maladministration (*Cumbria CC 2000*).

Undue delay in funding decision for person already in a care home. A local authority told the wife of a self-funding resident of a care home to contact the local authority when his resources fell below the capital threshold. She did so, assuming that as soon as this point was reached, the council would contribute to the funding. In fact, from the point of the wife contacting the council, it took the local authority a total of 17 weeks to decide on the funding. The local ombudsman felt that seven weeks would have been reasonable; this meant that there were ten weeks of undue delay. This was maladministration (*Staffordshire CC 2000*).

However, the local ombudsman in one case suggested that the effect of the *Sefton* judgment was limited to those already in residential care (and currently paying for themselves). She suggested that this still left open the question of whether waiting lists for those people in hospital or in their own homes were lawful – even where savings are below the capital threshold (*Liverpool CC 1999*). In fact, the effect of the *Sefton* judgment seems not to be limited to those already in residential care; the court's conclusions appear to apply to any person assessed to be in need of care and attention, not just a person already in a care home. Furthermore, central government subsequently amended the relevant regulations to make it quite clear that the rules concerning the test of resources applied not just to residents but also to prospective residents (SI 1992/2977, r.2).

The Department of Health guidance points out that the effect of this rule does not mean that people who do have capital over the threshold will necessarily have to make their own arrangements. This is because, in some circumstances, the person might be unable to make their own arrangements (for example, because of physical or mental inability to do so); in which case, the local authority would still have a duty to do so (albeit then charging the person). Likewise if a person were to become 'self-funding' through sale of his or her property, the local authority should only sever its contract with the care home if the person is able to manage their own affairs or has assistance in doing so (LAC(98)19, paras 10–11).

This same principle applies in relation to the '12-week disregard' rules (see section 10.6.3.2), whereby for the first three months of a permanent stay in a care home arranged by the local authority, the value of a person's home is disregarded. Guidance points out that, at the end of the period, the local authority will have to consider whether the value of the resident's assets mean that council support is no longer needed and that the authority's contract with the care home should be terminated (LAC(2001)10, para 12). But the proviso concerning the inability of a potential self-funder to manage his or her affairs is equally applicable in these circumstances.

For a person who can afford to pay the full amount of the fee, the question of whether a person makes the arrangements, that is contracts, with the care home – or whether the local authority does so – remains important. This is because many care homes tend to charge private individuals more for a placement, than they would charge a local authority. In effect, because local authorities continually attempt to keep down the amount of fee they are prepared to pay, care homes charge private individuals that much more – in order to cross-subsidise those residents placed by local authorities (CCC 2007, p.4). It could therefore be highly advantageous financially to a resident to be placed by the local authority, rather than to place himself or herself in the home.

In any event, irrespective of the financial means of a person, a local authority still has a duty to assess a person's needs under the umbrella of s.47 of the NHS and Community Care Act 1990. This is not just a legal technicality. For prospective residents it may be useful because they will receive assessment, information and advice. The local authority can point out that if they choose a more expensive home, but their money then runs out, the local authority might try to move them to a cheaper home – subject of course to a reassessment and decision that their needs could reasonably be met by moving them. Equally, for the local authority it is useful, because if too many people are, unknown to it, paying for themselves in care homes, its budget may then get unexpectedly hit by these residents – whom they some-times term 'depleters' – when their money reduces to the threshold at which the local author-ity is obliged to step in (Spiers 2007). Nonetheless, evidence suggests that local authorities continue to avoid (a) assessing people about to go into a care home who will be self-funding, and (b) reviewing those self-funders already in care homes (Dalley 2008, p.8).

9.1.3 PROVISION DIRECTLY BY THE LOCAL AUTHORITY

Local authorities may directly provide residential accommodation themselves under s.21 of the National Assistance Act 1948, rather than contract with the independent sector.

9.1.4 MAKING ARRANGEMENTS THROUGH THE INDEPENDENT SECTOR

Under s.26 of the 1948 Act, the local authority may arrange for provision of residential accommodation by entering into arrangements with independent sector providers. The courts have held that a s.26 arrangement is only in place when the local authority is paying (i.e. has a contract with) the independent provider (see e.g. *Chief Adjudication Officer v Quinn; Steane v Chief Adjudication Officer*). For instance, providing somebody with advice on entering a care home (where the person would pay his or her own fees), and even providing transport to it, would not constitute 'making arrangements' under s.26. This principle has since been reiterated:

No community care services being provided in the absence of a s.26 agreement. Responsibility for certain residents of a care home, with 'preserved rights' and funded by social security benefits, was transferred to the local authority. The residents remained in the home, and the authority made payments based on the previous (social security) rate with some adjustments. However, no agreement under s.26 of the 1948 Act was in place. The care home subsequently sought more money for the care provided; the local authority argued that it was providing community care services and was obliged to pay only up to its usual cost level for such care. The court found that community care services were not being provided, given the absence of a s.26 agreement; and therefore the care home proprietor might have an arguable case to claim a 'reasonable sum' for the care provided (*Yorkshire Care Developments v North Yorkshire CC*).

9.1.5 EDUCATIONAL PLACEMENTS

Sometimes the question arises about responsibility for funding what are sometimes called specialist college placements for people aged 18 years or over. The local social services authority, the local education authority department or the Learning and Skills Council may all be involved. In summary the position appears to be broadly as follows and by no means straightforward.

First, the Learning and Skills Council (LSC) has general duties to secure the provision of proper facilities for people aged 16 to 18 years, and of reasonable facilities for those aged 19 years or over (Learning and Skills Act 2000, ss.2–3). In carrying out those general duties, the Learning and Skills Council must have regard to people with learning difficulties (s.13). However, there are two further particular duties and one power in respect of residential placements for people with learning difficulties:

- **Duty to under 19-year-olds.** For a person with learning difficulties and under 19 years old, if the LSC cannot secure sufficient (in quantity) and adequate (in quality) education or training without securing also boarding accommodation, then it must secure provision of boarding accommodation as well.

- **Duty to those aged 19 to 24.** For a person with learning difficulties who is 19 years old or over but under 25, if the LSC is satisfied it cannot secure the provision of reasonable facilities for education or training unless it also secures provision of boarding accommodation, then it must secure the provision of boarding accommodation for him.

- **Power in respect of those aged 25 years or over.** For a person who is 25 years old or over, if the LSC is satisfied that it cannot secure the provision of reasonable facilities for education or training for a person with a learning difficulty who is 25 or over unless it also secures the provision of boarding accommodation for him, it may secure the provision of boarding accommodation for him.

In respect of all placements, the Learning and Skills Council imposes a number of conditions, and applies additional criteria to determine whether a residential placement is appropriate (LSC 2006).

Second, education authorities have a power to secure the provision of further education for people who are 19 years or over. In exercising this power, authorities must have regard to the needs of people with learning difficulties (Education Act 1996, s.15B).

Third, as to social services responsibilities, the courts have from time to time grappled with the issue. In one such case, the judge did make a general comment on the dividing line between what should be regarded as education or as community care:

Community care or educational need. A 20-year-old man with learning disabilities was due to take up a residential college placement. However, neither the local authority nor the Further Education Funding Council (FEFC: since superseded by the Learning and Skills Council) would agree to fund the placement.

In the event, the court dismissed the case against both local authority and the FEFC. For some reason that is not entirely clear, the court referred only to social services legislation covering non-residential services (National Assistance Act 1948, s.29; Chronically Sick and Disabled Persons Act 1970, s.2) – and not to s.21 of the 1948 Act covering residential accommodation. Nevertheless, the judge considered whether educational and community care needs were mutually exclusive.

He concluded that formal instruction in an academic sense would obviously not correspond to a community care need. For a person with a learning difficulty, teaching him or her to read or the basic principles of mathematics (addition, subtraction, multiplication and division) would obviously be purely educational. However, instruction on how to deal with money or to read or how to recognise certain signs (e.g. on food labels or on male and female facilities) could amount to community care needs, notwithstanding an educational element. There would sometimes be overlap; but the correct approach – where the real purpose was to meet a community care need – was to regard it as welfare provision, notwithstanding its educational content.

However, this approach might not necessarily apply to a 'quite additional educational content for which statute provides a duty or power to provide' (R v Further Education Funding Council and Bradford Metropolitan District Council, ex p Parkinson).

The following local ombudsman case also illustrates the confusion and maladministration – and significant financial recompense to be paid by the local authority – that can arise when responsibilities are not clarified and funded:

Funding specialist college placements. In 1999, at the age of 21, a young man with learning disabilities started his final year at an out of county residential college specialising in providing services to people with a variety of learning disabilities, for developing life skills and work skills. His first year was funded fully by the Further Education Funding Council (FEFC, since superseded by the Learning and Skills Council). This funding was progressively reduced and by the final year the local authority paid the fee with contributions from state benefits.

Another charity-run further education college was identified, to which a number of his friends were moving on as well. He was offered a place there; but the council delayed for some months in approving funding; by which time he had lost his place. The consequence was that he was without appropriate care for two years, before his parents themselves funded a residential placement, located such that their son could still benefit from the day services of the charity-run further education college.

The ombudsman found maladministration; had the council made the funding available at the appropriate time, he would have been placed at the second college. Having accepted the need and the duty to meet it, the council should have made specific budgetary provision more quickly. The ombudsman recommended that the council pay £30,000 to the man or to his parents on his behalf (East Sussex CC 2003).

9.2 DIFFERENT TYPES OF RESIDENTIAL ACCOMMODATION

The 1948 Act refers to the need to provide for different types of accommodation and to have regard to the welfare of residents (s.21). However, the courts have held that this does not mean that local authorities are obliged themselves to provide or manage care homes; they can contract with other care providers instead (R v Wandsworth LBC, ex p Beckwith).

The duty as to different types of accommodation has been construed widely, both legally and in practice. For instance, local authorities typically place people in care homes and sometimes hostels, bed and breakfast and hotels where necessary (often in cases of urgency and temporarily); and the courts have held that s.21 is capable of extending also to ordinary housing.

Different types of accommodation. In certain circumstances, the courts have ordered local authorities to arrange (and pay for) ground floor flats or four- or five-bedroom houses for people with mental health problems or physical disabilities (e.g. *R(Batantu) v Islington LBC; R(Bernard) v Enfield LBC*). In other circumstances, small flats and bed and breakfast accommodation for asylum seekers were accepted as coming within s.21, since board and any other services required did not necessarily have to be part of provision under s.21 (*R v Newham LBC, ex p Medical Foundation for the Care of Victims of Torture*).

These cases clearly indicate that accommodation without board or personal care can be arranged under s.21 of the National Assistance Act 1948. Conversely, the provision of food without accommodation would not be lawful (*R v Newham LBC, ex p Gorenkin*).

Where care home accommodation is provided with nursing or personal care, as referred to in s.3(2) of the Care Standards Act 2000, then it must be registered under the 2000 Act (National Assistance Act 1948, s.26(1A)).

9.2.1 PROVIDING ORDINARY HOUSING ACCOMMODATION

Some local social services authorities have been surprised by the courts' insistence that in some circumstances they must provide ordinary accommodation – and thereby made anxious that they are being asked to take on the role of housing providers. In summary, the legal position appears to be as follows.

The courts recognise the importance of the distinction between provision of accommodation under the Housing Act 1996 (a housing function) and under s.21 of the National Assistance Act 1948 (a social services function). They are astute to the danger of people attempting to jump the queue and obtain ordinary accommodation more quickly through the social services authority than through waiting on the register of a housing authority (*R(Wahid) v Tower Hamlets LBC*).

However, it appears that if ordinary accommodation has been assessed as a community care need, and that need cannot be met in any other way, then the social services authority may nevertheless incur a duty to arrange the accommodation under the 1948 Act – in the absence of anybody else doing so. In particular, for example, the housing authority might not meet the need either at all or sufficiently speedily. One reason for this might be that the person has been lawfully judged to be intentionally homeless, and therefore ineligible for accommodation under the Housing Act 1996. Another might be that the person will have a long but lawful wait on a housing register for the type of accommodation required.

Nonetheless, if the wait is, in the circumstances of the case, unduly long – and if there is no other way for assessed community care needs to be met – a duty might arise for the social services authority itself to arrange the accommodation under s.21 of the National Assistance Act 1948.

Provision of ordinary housing as a community care service. A local social service authority assessed a man with mental health problems and stated, as part of his care plan, that he required spacious, secure, ground-floor accommodation. After many months he was still waiting on a housing register with no real indication about when the housing department of the same local authority would be able to offer suitable accommodation under the Housing Act 1996. The court held that the responsibility now fell on the local authority social services department under s.21 of the National Assistance Act 1948, because of its assessment and care plan (*R v Islington LBC, ex p Batantu*).

In a second case, a local authority occupational therapist had assessed a woman (who had suffered a stroke) as requiring suitably adapted accommodation. The present accommodation could not be made suitable by adapting it. The housing department of the same local authority would not assist under the Housing Act 1996, because it had made a finding of intentional homelessness on grounds of rent arrears; this decision had been upheld by the courts. Thus, it was for the local authority to find a suitable house under s.21 of the 1948 Act (*R(Bernard) v Enfield LBC*).

In a further case, the court held that the failure on the part of the local authority to find suitable accommodation represented a breach of duty under s.21 of the 1948 Act. The person concerned had cerebral palsy, severe learning difficulties, poorly controlled epilepsy, extremely erratic sleep pattern, ataxia, decreasing mobility, double incontinence and no speech. Early in 2003, the need for ground floor accommodation had been identified. Two years later, the need had still not been met. This constituted a breach of s.21 (*R(Hughes) v Liverpool CC*). Nevertheless, in the following example, the local authority successfully argued that the person's community care needs could be met through means other than a change of accommodation. Effectively, it had succeeded in separating the community care, from the housing, need:

Social services not obliged to provide ordinary accommodation. A 53-year-old man suffering from schizophrenia lived with his wife and eight children in a two-bedroom flat on the ground floor of a council block of flats. He had refused alternative accommodation on grounds of unsuitability offered by the housing department under the Housing Act 1996. A psychiatric nurse wrote to a social services team leader, arguing that the man's mental stability could only be maintained in a more congenial and relaxed environment.

Social services refused to arrange alternative accommodation. The team leader conceded that better accommodation was required; but social services had to consider whether he needed care and attention under s.21 of the National Assistance Act. It concluded that he did not, since he was currently in good mental health, better in fact than for many years. He also argued that the man (and two of his adult sons) had unreasonably rejected offers of alternative accommodation by the council. He also concluded that the chances of mental breakdown from the overcrowding were small.

The court accepted this reasoning; it also referred to the effect of s.21(8) of the 1948 Act which precluded provision that could or must be made under another Act. Thus, ordinary housing needs that fall under the Housing Act 1996 could not come under s.21 of the 1948 Act. Lastly, it pointed out that social workers, traditionally strong advocates for clients, should not be deterred from identifying needs that properly come under other services – for fear that social services will have to meet them (*R(Wahid) v Tower Hamlets LBC*).

The 'anti-duplication' provision (in s.21(8) of the National Assistance Act 1948), referred to in the *Wahid* case, is potentially a significant obstacle to social services authorities being forced to provide ordinary housing. There are increasing signs that the courts are less likely to entertain arguments that ordinary housing should be provided under the 1948 Act, no doubt concerned about the floodgates which they prised ajar in the *Islington* and *Enfield* cases. For instance, the approach in Wahid was adopted in the following case, with the court raising formidable obstacles to the provision of housing under the 1948 Act:

Adequacy of local authority's assessment not to provide ordinary accommodation. A 52-year-old single parent was severely physically disabled with arthritis of the spine, neck and feet – and experienced pain and breathlessness on walking short distances. She had three children; the twins had learning disabilities and little sense of danger. She lived on the ground floor; she could not get up the stairs to the children's bedrooms. The oldest child (17 years old) had for years taken on child care. There were difficulties finding alternative accommodation. Other people had the same priority needs as the woman. Not every four-bedroom dwelling could be fitted with a lift. She would not accept just any offer, because she wished to remain close to extended family who provided support. In addition, she had previously suffered domestic violence and did not want to be in proximity to her former partner or his family. She had been overly selective in what property she would accept. She argued the local authority was in breach of 21 of the 1948 Act.

The court found the local authority's approach lawful, giving six reasons. First, there was a substantial gap between establishing a need for housing and triggering a duty under s.21 of the 1948 Act. Second, the 1948 Act was not relevant to the children's needs. Third, the social services assessments were detailed and thorough; the need for accommodation was 'substantial' (under fair access to care eligibility criteria). Fourth, there was no suggestion in the assessments that the woman was in need of care and attention not otherwise available to her other than by providing s.21 accommodation. Fifth, the local authority had assessed that it would provide additional support to the family in the current accommodation and nominate the family for priority housing under the Housing Act. This was in line with s.47(3) of the NHS and Community Care Act 1990 (involving housing in a community care assessment). Lastly, since suitable accommodation could be provided under the Housing Act 1996, s.21(8) of the 1948 Act – the anti-duplication provision – was brought into play. This prevented s.21 from imposing an obligation on the council (*R(Mooney) v Southwark BC*).

Sometimes the need for ordinary accommodation arises for a family with members both 18 years old or over and under 18 years old – that is, both adults and children. The National Assistance Act 1948 s.21 applies on its face only to those over 18 years old. The courts have stated that, normally at least, s.21 should not be taken to apply to people under 18 years old (*R(O) v Haringey LBC; (R(Mooney) v Southwark LBC*).

Thus in some cases, where provision is both for a disabled adult and a child in need, both s.21 of the 1948 Act and s.17 of the Children Act 1989 (general duty to safeguard and promote the welfare of children in need) apply. Where the provision is primarily related to a child in need, s.17 of the 1989 Act would in principle suffice because of the provision it contains for providing for other family members and not just the child (e.g. *R v Birmingham CC, ex p Mohammed*). Nevertheless it would be as well for s.21 of the 1948 Act to be argued, at least in respect of adults, since the courts have read into s.21 a significantly stronger duty (*R v Sefton MBC, ex p Help the Aged*) than they have into s.17 of the 1989 Act (*R(G) v Barnet LBC*).

9.2.2 PROVIDING ACCOMMODATION WITH NURSING

Arrangements for accommodation together with nursing can only be made with the consent of a primary care trust or health authority (National Assistance Act 1948, s.26(1C)). In the following case, the High Court also held the converse; that a local authority could not place a woman in a residential home, if NHS staff judged that she needed to be a nursing home. However, the Court of Appeal reversed this decision; it was for the local authority ultimately to decide:

Return to care home with or without nursing? A 94-year-old woman wished to be discharged from hospital, following a fall and fracture of femur, back to a flat in a registered residential care home. Differing professional views emerged about whether her needs could continue to be met at the home – or whether she would require a place in a care home that provided nursing care. The High Court ruled that, quite apart from being entitled to rely on a particular medical doctor's expertise, the local authority had no choice but to accept the decision he had made on behalf of the NHS. This was because of s.26(1C) of the National Assistance Act 1948 (*R(Goldsmith) v Wandsworth LBC*: High Court).

Strictly speaking, the logic of this last judicial point appeared open to some doubt, since s.26(1C) applies only where it is proposed to place a person in a care home with nursing. Where the proposal is simply a care home without nursing (in this case, the woman's current care home), then s.26(1C) does not, on its face at least, apply.

The High Court's decision was duly overturned, when the Court of Appeal found that the decision about whether or not the woman should return to her original care home was for the local authority to take. The doctor's advice was given to the local continuing care panel. It was for the panel in turn to advise the local authority, but not to usurp the latter's duty to take the final decision. In fact the doctor's advice was anyway based on only limited information, and the panel's reasoning also left out of account a detailed report by a social worker which was at variance with the doctor's view (*R(Goldsmith) v Wandsworth LBC*: Court of Appeal).

9.2.3 AMENITIES ASSOCIATED WITH RESIDENTIAL ACCOMMODATION

The provision of residential accommodation under s.21 of the 1948 Act does not refer only to the provision of bare accommodation. Accommodation is defined to include reference to board and to other services, amenities and requisites provided in connection with the accommodation – except where in the opinion of the authority managing the premises their provision is unnecessary (National Assistance Act 1948, s.21(5)).

Likewise, a local authority has a power to provide, where it considers appropriate, transport to and from the accommodation, and also to make available on the premises any services that appear to it to be required (s.21(7), and LAC(93)10, Appendix 1). Directions made under s.21 of the 1948 Act state that local authorities must make arrangements, in respect of residents for whom accommodation has been provided under s.21:

- for their welfare
- for the supervision of hygiene
- to enable residents to obtain medical attention, nursing attention or the benefit of other NHS services (but the local authority is not required to provide anything that is authorised or required to be provided under NHS Act 1977)
- for provision of board and other services, amenities and requisites provided in connection with the accommodation, except where in the opinion of the authority managing the premises their provision is unnecessary
- to review regularly the provision made and to make necessary improvements (LAC(93)10, appendix 1).

In one case, the council claimed that, in arranging accommodation for asylum seekers under ss.21 and 26 of the 1948 Act, it could offer accommodation only if it included also a package of services such as food, laundry and personal hygiene facilities. Because, it argued, there was no such accommodation in Newham, it would therefore have to offer accommodation to asylum seekers in Eastbourne. The court ruled that the effect of ss.21(5) and 26(1A) was that residential accommodation without board and personal care could in some circumstances be offered (*R v Newham LBC, ex p Medical Foundation for the Care of Victims of Torture*).

However, the reverse situation, of providing food without accommodation under s.21, has been held to be unlawful. In a case, also concerning asylum seekers, the High Court ruled that because the need for care and attention was a condition for arranging residential accommodation, a local authority was not empowered under s.21 to provide food (vouchers) alone without accommodation (*R v Newham LBC, ex p Gorenkin*). On the other hand, although the courts have held that food is an amenity provided in connection with accommodation, they have also held that clothes or toiletries, for instance, are not, since they are have nothing directly to do with the accommodation (*R(Khan) v Oxfordshire CC*). In any event, failure to provide for basic welfare and hygiene has been held to be maladministration:

Welfare, hygiene, medical attention. The local ombudsman has investigated arrangements for welfare, hygiene and medical attention provided in a council hostel, finding serious failures relating to, for example, sleep interruption, theft, missing lavatory seats, lost laundry, failure to observe a resident's pain and need for dental treatment – and a failure to provide the required medication for epilepsy on several occasions (*Manchester CC 1993*).

9.3 DUTIES AND POWERS TO PROVIDE RESIDENTIAL ACCOMMODATION

If the need for care and attention is evident, consonant with the application of a local authority's eligibility criteria, then the local authority has to consider whether it has a power or a duty to arrange the accommodation. The Act gives central government the power to issue directions and approvals under s.21; from these flow duties and powers respectively.

It should be noted, however, that there is a prohibition in the making of arrangements for people subject to s.115 of the Immigration and Asylum Act 1999 – applying to people subject to immigration control excluded from welfare benefits – if their need arises through destitution, or the physical effects, actual or anticipated, of destitution (s.21(1A)). See Chapter 14.

9.3.1 DIRECTIONS AND DUTIES

Directions have been issued so as to create a duty in the case of people who are ordinarily resident within the area of the local authority, and in need of care and attention not otherwise available to them, by reason of age, illness disability or any other circumstances. Without prejudice this overarching duty, a duty is also imposed as follows:

- provision of temporary accommodation for those in urgent need of it, in circumstances where the need for that accommodation could not reasonably have been foreseen
- provision for people who are or have been suffering from mental disorder, for preventing mental disorder, for people who are ordinarily resident within the authority (LAC(93)10, appendix 1).

9.3.2 APPROVALS AND POWERS

A power arises where a mere approval, rather than a direction, has been issued by central government. The approvals issued apply – without prejudice to the duty to provide for people who are ordinarily resident and in need of care and attention – to the making of arrangements:

- for a person who is of no settled residence
- for a person who is ordinarily resident in the area of another local authority (but such provision subject to the consent of the other authority
- for a person who is or has been suffering from mental disorder, or for the prevention of mental disorder, and who is ordinarily resident in the area of another authority but has become resident in the authority's area following discharge from hospital
- for the prevention of illness, the care of those who are ill, or their aftercare
- specifically for people who are dependent on drugs or alcohol
- for expectant and nursing mothers of any age, in particular the provision of mother and baby homes (LAC(93)10, appendix 1).

9.3.3 SPECIFIC, ENFORCEABLE DUTY

Where a duty is established against an assessed eligible need, the courts have accepted that the duty is absolute in the sense that it must be met irrespective of resources (see e.g. *R v Sefton MBC, ex p Help the Aged; R v Kensington and Chelsea RBC, ex p Kujtim*). This is notwithstanding that the actual language of both the Act and the directions is more suggestive of a general target duty than an individual enforceable duty (see 5.1.1 above). Nevertheless, the courts seem to have taken the view that s.21 is such a fundamental provision that a specific duty is to be read into it.

9.4 ORDINARY RESIDENCE

The ordinary residence and no settled residence conditions, referred to within the directions and approvals, are further defined in s.24 of the National Assistance Act 1948 (see Chapter 15).

9.5 CHOICE OF RESIDENTIAL ACCOMMODATION

Directions issued by the Department of Health state that a local authority should make arrangements for the residential accommodation of a person's choice – if certain conditions are satisfied. These are as follows. The person must have an assessed, eligible need. The preferred accommodation must be suitable for the person's assessed needs and be available. The cost of the placement must be within the usual cost level for the degree of need. The accommodation must also be provided subject to the authority's usual terms and conditions, having regard to the nature of the accommodation (LAC(92)27, direction 3).

Department of Health guidance makes clear the importance of local authorities' giving people information in order to allow them to exercise choice; of encouraging the presence, wherever possible, of a relative, carer or advocate; and of keeping a written record of the conversation and in particular of decisions taken and preferences expressed (LAC(2004)20, para

7.2). Thus, a failure to consult and indicate choice will be maladministration for the local ombudsman:

No consultation and no choice. The grandson and main carer of a 101-year-old woman received a telephone call from the local authority stating that a placement had been arranged in a particular nursing home; while the grandson was being told this on the telephone, a van arrived to collect his grandmother. The local ombudsman found that the failure to consult and indicate any sort of choice was maladministration (*Kent CC 2001*).

Department of Health guidance gives examples of reasons why a local authority might have to incur higher than usual costs, in order to meet a person's assessed needs. These include specialist care for specific user groups with high levels of need, special diets or additional facilities required for medical or cultural reasons (LAC(2004)20, para 2.5.8). Likewise if a person's assessed needs mean that it is necessary to place him or her in a care home in another area (e.g. to be near relatives), where the costs of placement exceeded the authority's usual cost level, the authority should nevertheless meet the additional cost (para 2.5). This last point is illustrative of the difference between an assessed need, which will trigger an obligation to pay a higher cost, and a 'mere' preference, which will not – as the courts have confirmed:

Preference, psychological need and more expensive accommodation. The case involved a 22-year-old man with Down's syndrome, for whom the local authority was under a duty to make arrangements for residential accommodation under s.21 of the National Assistance Act 1948. The man had an 'entrenched' wish to go to a particular home, whilst the council had decided to place him in a cheaper one which would still, it claimed, meet his needs. The dispute went to the complaints procedure review panel, which recommended that the council make arrangements for provision at the man's home of choice. The panel found, having consulted expert opinion, that the assessment should be based on current need including psychological, educational, social and medical needs. The entrenched position of the man formed part of his psychological need. The social services committee of the council, worried about setting costly precedents, rejected the panel's findings.

The judge stated that needs 'may properly include psychological needs' – and that the authority was not therefore being forced to pay more than it otherwise would have normally (something it was not required to do under the Choice of Accommodation Directions in LAC(92)27: it would 'simply be paying what the law required'. He also referred to guidance (LAC(92)15) on adults with learning disabilities, which stated that services should be arranged on an individual basis, 'taking account of age, needs, degree of disability, the personal preferences of the individual and his or her parents or carers, culture, race and gender' (*R v Avon CC, ex p M*).

Similarly when a local authority refused to place a person with learning disabilities at a residential home – which the local authority regarded as excessively expensive for his needs – the court found the decision to be unlawful, because it was made before any suitable alternatives had been found (*R(Alloway) v Bromley LBC*). In some other circumstances, however, the courts have simply evaded the question:

Choice of accommodation for asylum seekers: not for the courts. The case concerned whether asylum seekers had a right to exercise their entitlement to choice of accommodation (i.e. so that they could remain in London instead of being sent to the south coast). The court stated that the dispute (a) was suitable for referral to the Secretary of State with a view to exercise of the default powers (see 4.6 above); and (b) was primarily factual (as to whether or not there was alternative accommodation in London) and was a matter which could not be resolved one way or another by legally deciding about the existence and nature of the duty imposed by the directions on the local authority (*R v Westminster CC, ex p P*).

9.5.1 TOPPING UP CARE HOME FEES

The principle of topping allows a resident, over and beyond exercising a reasonable choice of which care home to enter, to live in a more expensive one. That is, more expensive than the local authority believes is necessary to meet assessed needs. However, for this to happen, a third party must be willing to pay the difference. Regulations allow for this; likewise they allow for self topping up (by the resident himself or herself), but only in the case of the 12-week disregard of a person's property or in a deferred payment agreement (SI 1992/2977, r.16A).

In the late 1990s, 14 per cent of residents funded by local authorities received third-party top-ups; by 2004, this had risen to 33 per cent. In addition, 40 per cent of local authorities believe that more top-ups are being paid than they know about, because they are being negotiated directly between the home and the relatives. This is a practice which appears to be consistent neither with the legal rules nor with the Department of Health's guidance. In short, this pattern seems to indicate 'widespread illegal conduct' (CCC 2007, pp.4, 17).

9.5.1.1 Third party topping up

The regulations concerning third party top-ups state that a local authority may place a person in more expensive accommodation if (a) a third party other than a liable relative (see 10.5.1) agrees to make up the difference between the usual cost level and the actual fee; (b) the third party can reasonably be expected to make the additional payment (SI 2001/3441, made under s.54 of the Health and Social Care Act 2001). This does not therefore amount to a duty on the local authority to allow such third party contributions. For instance, in the following example, the local authority, quite lawfully, had serious doubts about the ability of the third party to do top up and accordingly refused to allow it:

Refusing to allow a third party top-up. An 81-year-old woman applied for permission to apply for judicial review. In October 1999 she had indicated her preferred care home accommodation; her daughter had agreed to pay the difference between the local authority's usual cost level and the actual fees charged by the care home. Two years later, the daughter ceased to pay the top-up; the council then had to pay the full cost. The daughter then issued proceedings against the council for repayment of the top-up amounts she had paid for the two years. The grounds were that she had been induced into the agreement by unlawful duress and misrepresentation on the part of council officers. The county court proceedings had not yet been decided.

In January 2004, the woman was assessed as now needing nursing home care; her preferred accommodation cost £520 a week, which contrasted with the local authority's usual cost level of about £450. The daughter offered to pay the top-up; the local authority refused on the grounds that it was entitled to take into account what had happened previously – at least until the county court proceedings had been resolved.

The court refused to hold that the local authority was – at least pending the outcome of the county court proceedings – acting unlawfully by refusing to enter into the top-up agreement (*R(Daniel) v Leeds CC*).

Thus, guidance points out that in order to safeguard both residents and councils from entering into top-up arrangements that are likely to fail, local authorities should make sure that third parties will have the resources to continue to make top-up payments.

Directions state that the third-party top-up must be an amount which is at least equal to the difference between what the local authority would usually pay and what the standard charge for the accommodation is. The Directions also remind local authorities that nothing in the Directions prevents a local authority from making or continuing to make arrangements for a person to be accommodated in preferred accommodation – even at a higher cost than the local authority would usually pay – 'having regard to the person's assessed need' (LAC(92)27, direction 4).

However, the principle of topping up appears to have been seriously undermined in those local authorities that offer such a low usual cost level that there is little choice (if any) of a care home at that cost. In which case, it seems that families are pressured into topping up, in order to meet not additional preferences but those basic needs that should properly be met by the local authority. Such practices are likely to be unlawful.

9.5.1.2 Choice of topping up

Ascertaining the lawfulness of a topping up arrangement is surprisingly simple in principle. The question to be asked is whether the resident has been placed in a more expensive home out of choice, and therefore whether a cheaper home could have met his or her needs fully (including, for example, an assessed need to be near relatives).

If there has been a genuine choice, and if a cheaper home (with the local authority's usual cost) was available, then the top-up would be lawful. If, however, no cheaper home was available that would meet the assessed needs, then, clearly, entering the more expensive home would not be through choice. In which case, the local authority should cover the more expensive cost, and a top-up should not be paid. Even where there is no choice involved, some local authorities do not request a top-up themselves, but leave it up to the care home to try to exact such a contribution from the family. This, too, is unlawful, since in such circumstances, the local authority remains responsible for the whole fee. The Department of Health guidance stresses that councils 'must never encourage or otherwise imply that care home providers can or should seek further contributions from individuals in order to meet assessed needs' (LAC(2004)20, paras 4.4–4.5).

Department of Health guidance points out that residents should not be asked to pay more because of market inadequacies or failures in local authority commissioning. Thus, where a resident has not expressed a preference for more expensive accommodation but, for whatever reason, there is no place available at the authority's usual cost level – then the local authority must pay the more expensive cost (LAC(2004)20, para 2.5.5).

9.5.1.3 Local authorities paying low usual cost levels

Local authorities should not set 'arbitrary ceilings on the amount they expect pay for an individual's residential care. Residents and third parties should not routinely be required to make up the difference between what the council will pay and the actual fees of a home' (LAC(2004)20, para 2.5.7).

Thus, when setting its usual cost level, the local authority should be able to demonstrate that it is sufficient for meeting the assessed need of residents and providing residents 'with the level of care services that they could reasonably expect to receive if the possibility of resident and third party contributions did not exist' (para 3.3). Where there are no placements available at the council's usual rate, local authorities should not just leave individuals to make their own arrangements – but instead make alternative, suitable arrangements and seek no additional contributions from the person (other than under the means test).

Low usual cost levels paid by local authorities might mean in practice that a care home may have to limit the number of local authority-funded residents they take, unless third party top-ups are demanded as a matter of course – or otherwise take privately-funded residents who are then charged more for the same facilities. For instance, in one local ombudsman investigation the owner of the care home explained that for a council-funded resident the fee was £215 per week; for privately-funded residents it was between £260 and £320 (*Kent CC 2001d*).

Excessively low usual cost levels have not in general been successfully challenged either in the courts or through the local ombudsmen, but this does not mean that local authorities cannot be challenged in individual cases. For instance, the following local ombudsman case exposed the practice of some local authorities of not providing clear information for people and their carers, relatives or friends; of paying a usual cost level that meant that the choice of home was in reality restricted; and of failing to exercise their discretion (or arguably perform an obligation) to exceed the cost level in individual circumstances:

Failure to exceed usual cost level. A 98-year-old woman lived on her own. She was finding it increasingly difficult to cope. A friend, whom she had looked after when she was a child, had remained in close touch. In September 1994, the friend identified a care home that would be suitable for the woman. In March 1995, the council assessed the woman as eligible for a care home placement. The social worker's assessment recommended the placement at that same care home; however, it was some £33 more expensive per week than the council's usual cost level. The friend would have to top up; she was prepared to do this. However, when the woman found this out, she refused to take up the placement; she wouldn't hear of her friend making up the difference. Her health deteriorated; she was admitted to hospital in September 1995.

In October, the friend searched for suitable homes charging at the council's usual cost level. She found none; the council then decided it was willing after all to pay up to £285, that is above its usual cost level. The ombudsman found, amongst other things, that the council had failed to explain the choice of accommodation rules properly; and had fettered its discretion by not considering at the outset whether the circumstances meant that it should exceed its usual cost level in the particular circumstances (*Merton LBC 1999*).

9.5.1.4 Third party topping up and usual cost levels generally

It is not clear to what extent, if at all, the courts are prepared generally to interfere with the levels of payment offered by local authorities to independent care home providers. Nevertheless, they have stated that the various factors – including payment levels – that affect the availability of care home places must be taken account of by the local authority (see variously *R v Cleveland CC, ex p Cleveland Care Homes Association; R v Coventry City Council, ex p Coventry Heads of Independent Care Establishments (CHOICE) and Peggs).* However, the courts may display a distinct reluctance to get involved in such matters:

Local authority cost levels. A consortium of care homes in Birmingham challenged the rate at which the council would pay for placements of residents in those homes. It was principally contended that this rate would result in home closures and therefore undermine the council's ability to meet needs under s.21 of the National Assistance Act 1948 and to afford people some choice of care home. The council had partially accepted the results of a Laing and Buisson report that it had commissioned – but not wholly. In particular it had not accepted the recommended rate of return/profit for care homes.

The court found that the case was not made out; that, except in case of a statutory duty specifically compelling expenditure, decisions about affordability and allocation of resources were for the local authority. Furthermore the courts should be slow to intervene where there had been a long process of consultation and there was in effect contractual negotiation in train between local authority and care providers (*R v Birmingham CC, ex p Birmingham Care Consortium*).

An alternative avenue of approach to challenging local authority 'usual cost' levels appeared to beckon in the form of the Office of Fair Trading (OFT). Nonetheless, as the following case demonstrates, this did not bear fruit:

Complaint about usual cost levels to the Office of Fair Trading. In connection with arguments that local authorities were abusing their dominant position in the market under the Competition Act 1998, by setting unfairly low cost levels for placements in independent care homes, a complaint was made to the Office of Fair Trading (OFT). The complaint concerned the fees paid for care home accommodation by the North and West Belfast Health and Social Services Trust. The OFT rejected the complaint on the basis that the trust was not an undertaking for the purposes of the Act.

On appeal, the Competition Commission Appeal Tribunal then ruled that such contracting did constitute 'economic activity', and that the trust was therefore a relevant undertaking. The complaint was remitted to the OFT (*BetterCare Group v Director General of Fair Trading*).

Nevertheless, the OFT subsequently rejected the complaint (identifying in effect a vicious circle that precluded it from interfering). It held that the Eastern Health and Social Services Board, which commissions services through health and social services trusts, was not itself an undertaking for the purpose of the Act. It then held that the trust, which was of course a relevant undertaking, could not be committing an abuse even if it was paying excessively low prices. This was because it did not set the prices; the prices were set by the Eastern Health and Social Services Board. In any case, the OFT concluded that: (a) there was insufficient evidence that the prices were excessively low; (b) excessively low prices were likely to amount to an abuse only in exceptional circumstances; (c) there was no reason to believe that there were exceptional circumstances (*BetterCare Group v North and West Belfast Health and Social Services Trust*).

The Office of Fair Trading launched in 2004 a market study of care homes, to focus on how and in what circumstances people choose homes, and the transparency of pricing and contracts. Its published findings in 2005 concluded that there was a lack of clarity about third party (top-up payments), a lack of transparency about prices, a large number of contracts containing unfair or unclear terms, and particular difficulty for people in making complaints arising from general lack of awareness and of support for people wishing to complain (OFT 2005, pp.2–3). It also published a report on unfair terms in contracts between care homes and residents and families. Typical examples included contracts that allowed care homes:

- to make frequent and arbitrary increases in residents' fees
- to impose unfair penalties, restrictions or obligations on residents
- to exclude liability for loss or damage to residents' property even where the fault lay with the care home
- to impose unclear charges (including for how long fees were payable after death) (OFT (2005a).

Similarly, its guide on unfair contracts set out a long list of things to look out for including:

- lack of clarity about charges
- exclusion of liability for causing death of personal injury
- changing a resident's room without consultation
- right to keep or dispose of the resident's possessions
- charge unreasonable penalties for overdue fees
- lack of clarity about the notice to be given (by either the home or the resident) about leaving the care home
- lack of clarity about access to the room after death (OFT 2005b, p.6).

9.5.1.5 Transparency about care home fees

In recognition of the muddle and confusion about how care home fees are set, explained and charged, the Care Homes Regulations 2001 were amended in 2006, in order to force care homes to provide more transparent information about fees. (In future, regulations to be made under the Health and Social Care Act 2008 will cover this issue). They stipulate that the service user's guide provided by the home must include various information, including the following:

- statement of purpose
- description of standard services offered
- terms and conditions (other than relating to fees) in respect of the provision of accommodation (including food), personal care and nursing care
- details of the total fee payable for the standard services, accommodation (including food), personal care and nursing care
- arrangements in place for charging and paying for additional services
- a statement as to whether the above charges differ if the person is not funding themselves [e.g. the local authority is paying]
- a standard form of contract
- the most recent inspection report
- summary of the complaints procedure.

In addition, specific information must be given to each service user, on the day they become a service user, setting out:

- fees payable for the accommodation (including food), nursing and personal care (and, except where a single fee is payable, the services to which each fee relates)
- the method of payment.

Further, the registered person must inform the service user of any increase in fees, together with reasons for the increase, or of variation in the method of payment. Such notification must be, where practicable, at least one month in advance, or otherwise as soon as practicable.

Where relevant, the registered person must inform the service user about whether a nursing contribution from the NHS is payable. If it is paid, the registered person has to give the service user a statement specifying the date of the payment and the amount of the nursing contribution and either (a) the date on which the registered person will pay the amount of the nursing contribution to the service user or deduct the amount from the fees; or (b) if the nursing contribution is not to be so paid or deducted, whether and how it is taken into account in calculating the fees. These rules do not apply where the NHS primary care trust – as opposed to the local authority – has actually arranged for the provision of accommodation itself (SI 2001/3965, rr.5–5A).

Thus, lack of adequate information given by the local authority to a man, when he was considering a nursing home placement for his wife (with Alzheimer's disease) and using an insurance policy to pay some of those fees, meant that he ended up topping up far in excess of what he had anticipated. In the circumstances, the local authority should have spelt out matters to him in writing, especially since its leaflet was written in very general terms (*Wiltshire CC 2007*).

9.5.1.6 Self topping up of care home fees

In addition to third party top-ups, it is possible for residents themselves to make top-up payments – either during the 12-week property disregard (see 10.6.3 below), or where a deferred payment agreement is in place (see 10.9.4) (SI 2001/3441). For self-funders generally, whose assets reduce so that they now need local authority financial support, guidance points out that they should be assessed. If they are already in a home that is more expensive than the local authority would usually pay for, they may have to move or find a third party to top up. However, if the assessment reveals that their needs can be met only in the current accommodation, then the local authority would have to cover the whole cost, and no top-up payment could be requested (LAC(2004)20, para 4.1).

9.5.1.7 Topping up and rises in fees

Department of Health guidance further explains that a home's fees and the local authority's usual amount of contribution might change. But they might not change at the same rate. Thus a rise in fees will not automatically be shared between the local authority and the third party, since the fees might rise more quickly than the authority's usual cost level (LAC 2004(20), para 3.5.7).

Nevertheless, the following case illustrates this principle taken too far, resulting in what the local ombudsman deemed an absurdity. It involved a local authority operating different usual cost levels, depending on how long residents had been in a care home. This resulted in unjustifiable, variable 'top-up' contributions from the relatives of residents:

Unacceptable variable usual cost levels. A local authority's policy meant that the relatives of a resident who had lived longest in a care home contributed more to charges (by way of topping up) than the relatives of more recently placed residents. This was because up-ratings to the authority's usual cost level, its standard rate of payment, did not necessarily apply to existing residents. This had come about because the local authority was not contractually bound to the care home to increase the rate to such residents; and so long as the care home was receiving fees from somebody, it would not object.

The ombudsman found maladministration. First, she pointed out that Department of Health guidance (LAC(92)27) stated that such usual cost levels can only vary in response to assessed, individual need. Second, an absurd situation was created whereby had the resident moved to a different home (or even been discharged and readmitted to the same home), she would have been entitled to a higher standard rate, with a lower third party contribution involved (*Bolton MBC 2004*).

9.5.1.8 Topping up: local authority with overall responsibility for payment

Department of Health guidance makes quite clear that when a local authority places a person in an independent care home under s.26(3A) of the National Assistance Act 1948, the local authority is responsible for the full cost of the accommodation. Even if an agreement had been reached, by which the resident and the third party paid their contributions direct to the care home, nevertheless in case of default the local authority would remain liable (LAC(2004)20, para 3.5.2).

This rule has apparently not stopped widespread direct pressure from care homes, for families to top up local authority contributions – with local authorities turning a blind eye (CCC 2007, p.4).

9.5.2 CROSS-BORDER PLACEMENTS WITHIN THE UNITED KINGDOM
See Chapter 15.

9.6 CARE HOME PLACEMENTS: OTHER ARRANGEMENTS

First, if local authorities place people in care homes registered to provide nursing, the NHS is responsible for funding the registered nursing care element that the person requires (see section 17.9). The local authority remains responsible for the accommodation, board and personal care.

Second, in some circumstances, the NHS places in care homes people who are deemed to have NHS continuing health care status. In this case, the NHS is responsible, under the NHS Act 2006, for funding the entire placement in terms of accommodation, board, personal care, registered nursing care and any other health care required (see Chapter 18).

Third, under s.117 of the Mental Health Act 1983, certain patients must be provided with aftercare services when they are discharged from hospital. The duty of provision is a joint one, placed on both local authority social services departments and the NHS. Aftercare services can include both residential accommodation and non-residential services and either way must be provided free of charge to the resident (see 11.5.8).

The question of whether the NHS and local authorities may allow choice and topping up under s.117 has arisen. The courts have pointed out that there is no 'statutory basis' for it, possibly casting some doubt on it, but coming to no conclusion (*Tinsley v Sarkar*). However, some local authorities take the view that there is a discretion to allow it, as in the following local ombudsman case where the authority accepted a top up in principle, but was not entitled in fact to ask for it in the particular circumstances:

Topping up under s.117 of the Mental Health Act 1983. A council backed down from asking for such a top-up, because it accepted that it was only the more expensive care home that could meet the woman's assessed needs. The cheaper home would have made family contact difficult, and the care plan had referred to the need for frequent family contact. The council's delay in sorting this out, and its attempt to place the woman in a cheaper care home contrary to her assessed needs, was therefore maladministration (*North Yorkshire CC 2007*. See also: *York CC 2006*).

Fourth, the provision of NHS community health services in care homes has long been a vexed question; it is highly variable in type and quantity (see 17.10).

Fifth, is the question of whether a person subject to guardianship can be charged for care home accommodation. Neither the 1983 Act, nor the main Department of Health guidance on charging for residential accommodation (CRAG 2004), refers to residential accommodation provided for a person under a guardianship order (under ss.7–8 of the Mental Health Act 1983). It is unclear as to whether a person, subject to guardianship and required to live in a care home under s.8, should be exempt from charges or not. If the accommodation were regarded as provided under the National Assistance Act 1948 (rather than under s.8 of the 1983 Act itself), then charges would potentially apply. However, in a case about s.117 of the Mental Health Act 1983, the House of Lords expressed the view that to make charges under s.117, for accommodation that is not freely chosen by patients recently subject to compulsion, would be surprising and morally objectionable (*R v Manchester City Council, ex p Stennett*). Similar arguments might be raised in respect of charging under s.8.

CHAPTER 10

Charging for residential accommodation

KEY POINTS

When local authorities arrange to place people in care homes under Part 3 of the National Assistance Act 1948, they are obliged to apply a statutory test of resources, or means test. This is to determine what contribution, if any, the resident must pay toward the cost of the accommodation. This is in contrast to charging for non-residential services, which is discretionary only and not governed by detailed legislative rules. Broadly, the charging rules for residential accommodation are as follows:

- **Test of resources**. If a local authority places a person in residential accommodation under s.21 of the National Assistance Act 1948, it has a duty to apply a test of resources in order to ascertain what, if anything, the resident should have to pay toward the accommodation, board and personal care.
- **Registered nursing care**. However, the registered nursing care element of the care provided, in a care home providing nursing, is the responsibility of the NHS and is thus free of charge to the resident (see section 17.9 below). This is payable in respect of privately funded residents as well, who have not been placed by the local authority.
- **NHS continuing health care**. If a resident has been deemed by the NHS to have continuing health care status, then the NHS should fund the accommodation, board, personal care and nursing care – all of which will then be free of charge to the resident (see Chapter 18).
- **Mental health aftercare services**. If a person is placed in residential accommodation by way of aftercare provision under s.117 of the Mental Health Act 1983, then provision is free of charge to the resident (see 11.5.8).
- **Self-funding**. In some circumstances, if a person is assessed as having resources over the relevant threshold, and as having the mental and physical ability (albeit with assistance) to make his or her own arrangements, then the local authority may decline to place the person in a care home. If the person then makes his or her own arrangements, he or she is known as 'self-funding'. However, when his or her resources are reduced to the relevant financial threshold, the local authority should then become responsible for making the placement.

The rules are detailed and complicated; the following represents an outline only. Reference should be made to the full, original sources of legislation and guidance, to expert advice or to specialist publications. The application of these rules sometimes proves controversial when people's savings or homes have to be used to pay for residential or nursing home accommodation – or when assets, which have previously been gifted to somebody else (e.g. another family member), are nevertheless taken account of by the local authority in the means test.

Note. The extracts in the following chapter are drawn in the main from the National Assistance Act 1948, the National Assistance (Assessment of Resources) Regulations 1992 (SI 1992/2977), and the Charging for Residential Accommodation Guide (CRAG 2008), a loose-leaf, regularly updated manual of guidance available from the Department of Health. The Regulations frequently cross-refer to, and rely on, the Income Support (General) Regulations 1987 (SI 1987/1967).

10.1 OVERALL DUTY TO CHARGE

Generally speaking, local authorities have a duty to apply a test of resources to each person for whom they make arrangements for the provision of residential accommodation (National Assistance Act 1948, s.22). The test of resources is set out in regulations. In deciding whether a person needs residential accommodation – that is, whether the person needs care and attention not otherwise available – the local authority must disregard so much of the person's resources as is specified in regulations.

If the authority is providing the accommodation directly, then the charge should be at a standard rate and represent the full cost to the local authority of provision. However, if the authority is satisfied, according to the statutory test of resources, that a person cannot afford to pay at the standard rate, then it must assess the person's ability to pay, and charge a lower rate accordingly (National Assistance Act 1948, s.22).

In the case of independent care providers, the charging procedure is more or less the same: the local authority pays to the provider the cost of the place, and the resident repays the authority the amount he or she has been assessed to pay (National Assistance Act 1948, s.26).

10.2 PERSONAL EXPENSES ALLOWANCE

In calculating the weekly amount payable by a resident, the authority must assume that he or she will require a certain amount of money for personal requirements. This is called the personal expenses allowance (PEA; National Assistance Act 1948, s.22). The amount of this is determined by regulations and is currently (2008–9) set at £21.15 per week (SI 2003/628). Department of Health guidance states that its purpose is to allow residents to have money to spend as they wish, and that it should not be spent on services that have been contracted for, or that have been assessed by the local authority or the NHS as necessary to meet a person's needs (CRAG 2008, para 5.001).

The amount of the PEA can be varied (National Assistance Act 1948, s.22) in the case of less dependent residents; when the person in the residential accommodation has a dependent child; when the resident is in receipt of an occupational pension and is paying it to his or her partner, but is not married (so that the statutory disregard of half of the pension has not been triggered); or when the person is responsible for a property (and associated costs) that is disregarded in the test of resources (CRAG 2008, para 5.005).

Guidance also states that residents must be left with the full PEA, following the test of resources (CRAG 2008, para 5.002); in other words it should not be used toward paying care home fees.

10.2.1 ADEQUACY AND MISUSE OF PERSONAL EXPENSES ALLOWANCE

Blatant misuse of personal expenses allowance is sometimes reported in practice. For instance, owners or managers of care homes sometimes pool people's allowances, and spend them collectively. This means that individual residents not only lose control of their money, but that there might not even be an itemised account of how it has been spent (OFT 1998, p.26).

Pooled 'extras account' in care home: paying for newspapers she couldn't read. A man complained to the local ombudsman about his mother's placement in a council care home. Part of the complaint related to a pooled general 'extras account' operated by the home to cover personal items not included in the care home fees. This resulted in his mother effectively being charged for newspapers that she was unable to read, as well as for piano tuning, aquarium maintenance and plants for the garden. The ombudsman found this to be maladministration, insofar as items to be charged for were not clearly identified to residents in advance and some, such as piano tuning, were arguably not the responsibility of residents anyway (*Hampshire CC 2001*).

Likewise, if people do not have their needs for incontinence pads (see 17.13.2) met by the NHS in care homes, they might end up spending their personal expenses allowance on the pads (*Hansard* 2001).

Quite apart from improper erosion of the allowance, a thorough study – providing a salutary reminder of the 'modest-but-adequate' living standard that residents reasonably require – concluded that the allowance should anyway, even in 1997, have been nearer £40 than the £14 it was at that time. It considered the recurrent cost of items such as personal food (fruit, biscuits, tea/coffee, sugar, milk, soft drinks), alcohol (e.g. a glass of sherry to give a visitor), clothing, personal care (e.g. plasters, cough mixture, aspirin, hairbrush, shampoo, bath oil, sponge bag, walking stick, watch, small mirror), household goods (e.g. furniture, linen, electrical appliances, crockery, batteries, shoe brushes), household services (e.g. postage, telephone call, footwear repair, dry cleaning), leisure goods (e.g. television, radio, newspapers, magazines, books, games, knitting, embroidery), leisure services (e.g. cinema, keep-fit classes, dancing, social club), transport (e.g. to dentist, optician, hairdresser, shopping, cinema, dancing, keep fit classes) (Parker 1997).

Department of Health guidance stresses that local authorities should ensure that an individual resident's need for continence supplies or chiropody is 'fully reflected' in their care plan; and that neither local authorities nor care homes have the right to require residents to spend their PEA in particular ways. It states that pressure of any kind is extremely poor practice (LAC (DH) (2007)4, annex).

10.3 TEMPORARY RESIDENTS

A temporary resident is a person whose stay is unlikely to exceed 52 weeks or, in exceptional circumstances, is unlikely substantially to exceed 52 weeks (SI 1992/2977, r.2).

For the first eight weeks of a temporary stay, the local authority has discretion, subject to reasonableness, to limit what it charges (National Assistance Act 1948, s.22). In other words, it is not obliged to follow the statutory test of resources in these circumstances although it can do so (SI 1992/2977, r.22(5A). This gives local authorities considerable discretion in deciding what to charge for respite care or short-term breaks. Beyond a stay of eight weeks the local authority is obliged to apply the statutory charging procedure, subject to special rules applying to 'temporary residents'.

Guidance explains that if a stay, which was thought to be permanent, turns out to be temporary only, then it would be 'unreasonable' for the authority to continue to apply the permanent residence rules to the resident. Conversely, if what was expected originally to be a temporary stay turns out to be permanent, the permanent residence rules should only be applied from the date of this realisation, not from the outset (CRAG 2008, paras 3.004–4A). A failure on the part of the local authority to be clear about when such a change of status occurs and to inform the resident and relevant family, may lead to a finding of maladministration by the local ombudsman:

Informing relative of change status of mother. A complaint was made to the local ombudsman about a woman with senile dementia who had been placed in a care home on a temporary basis. Following a meeting, the local authority decided that her status had changed to that of permanent resident. However, the son was not informed until nine months later, when he was also notified that there were accumulated arrears (representing the difference between temporary and permanent resident charges).

This was maladministration. Furthermore, because the son would have sold his mother's house that much earlier, it meant that interest had been lost on the sum that would have been realised. The ombudsman recommended that the council pay £3300 in lost interest and that it issue clear guidance to its staff (*Humberside CC 1992*).

10.3.1 DISREGARDING CERTAIN ASSETS OF TEMPORARY RESIDENTS

When applying the test of resources for temporary residents, a local authority must disregard certain assets.

These include, for example: (a) the person's own home (when he or she is intending to return there, or is taking steps to dispose of it with a view to acquiring another more suitable); (b) the housing costs element of income support/pension credit; (c) housing benefit; (d) housing support charges under 'Supporting People' arrangements (including charges for a warden in sheltered housing, emergency alarms, cleaning of rooms and windows, general support and counselling; (e) reasonable home commitments not covered fully by income support/pension credit, housing benefit or Supporting People payments (e.g. fixed heating charge, water rates, mortgage payment not covered by those payments, insurance premiums, housing support charges not met by the local authority); (f) reasonable home commitments where income support/pension credit, housing benefit or Supporting People payments are not in payment; (g) cash payment made in lieu of concessionary coal; and (h) attendance allowance and disability living allowance, care component (SI 1992/2977, schedule 3).

10.3.2 INTERMEDIATE CARE

A care home placement, made as part of intermediate care, must be free of charge for up to six weeks (see 19.6).

10.4 LESS-DEPENDENT RESIDENTS

For people classed as less-dependent residents, authorities are explicitly given the option of not applying the normal charging rules. A less-dependent resident is defined as a person for whom accommodation is provided in premises not registered under the Care Standards Act 2000 (SI 1992/2977, rr.2, 5). The courts have accepted that residential accommodation arranged under s.21 of the National Assistance Act 1948 can embrace a wide range of accommodation including, at one extreme, ordinary housing (see 9.2.1).

Factors the local authority should take account of include the resident's commitments (in relation to necessities such as food, fuel, clothing), independence, and incentive to become more independent (CRAG 2008, para 2.010).

10.5 ASSESSMENT OF COUPLES

Legislation does not authorise the financial assessment of the joint resources of a couple; local authorities are not empowered to apply the statutory means test under regulations (SI 1992/2977) to ascertain the potential liability of the spouse of a resident (CRAG 2008, para 4.001).

Each person entering residential care should be assessed individually, whether or not the other member of the couple is also a resident or remains at home. Before being excluded from assistance on grounds of capital, the resident must have in excess of £22,250 in his or her own right, whether separately or a share of jointly owned capital (CRAG 2008, para 4.003).

10.5.1 LIABLE SPOUSE

The liability of a married person to maintain his or her spouse should in principle be taken into account when the statutory means test is applied (CRAG 2008, para 4.001). This refers to s.42 of the National Assistance Act 1948, under which spouses have an obligation to maintain each other. Such liability applies only to husband and wife, and not to unmarried couples. The Department of Health has told local authorities that they 'should exercise their right to NOT apply the liable relatives rule' (LAC(DH)(2007)4, para 11).

The Health and Social Care Act 2008 contains provisions which will abolish the liable relative rules. Nonetheless, pending that abolition, the position is as follows. Guidance states that under ss.42 and 43 of the National Assistance Act 1948, local authorities may ask a spouse to refund all or part of the authority's expenditure on residential accommodation for his or her husband or wife (as well as on other non-residential services under the Act). However, it states that this does not mean that an authority can demand that a spouse provide details of his or her resources. It should not use assessment forms which require information about the means of the spouse.

According to the guidance, the authority should instead use tact in explaining to residents and spouses the legal liability to maintain and point out that the extent of the liability is best considered in the light of the spouse's resources. In each case the authority should decide if it is worth pursuing the spouse for maintenance, and what sum would be appropriate. This will involve discussion and negotiation with the spouse, and will be determined to a large extent by his or her financial circumstances in relation to his or her expenditure and normal standard of living. It suggests that following such negotiation, the local authority should, if appropriate, secure a retrospective contribution from the spouse.

The guidance also states that, in the Department of Health's view, it would not be appropriate, for example, necessarily to expect spouses to reduce their resources to Income Support/Pension Credit levels. In any case, it concludes by saying that, ultimately, only the courts can decide what is an 'appropriate' amount (CRAG 2008, paras 11.001–6).

An Age Concern England study pointed out the defects of the liable spouse provision. These included:

- lack of operational policies in many local authorities
- arbitrary nature of whether a spouse is pursued for payment
- England-wide, only a small number of spouses are anyway being pursued
- where pursuit did take place, Department of Health guidance was breached and spouses were asked for financial details on the same form used for the financial assessment of the spouse entering the care home
- huge variations in the approach to establishing a 'reasonable' spouse contribution
- finance officers struggling to apply the rules, which most felt were unclear
- some spouses, unaware of the local authority policy, had felt intimidated into agreeing a level of payment, unaware that they could negotiate a reasonable level of payment
- the rules apply only to spouses, not to unmarried couples, and so are inequitable (Thompson and Wright 2001).

10.6 ASSESSMENT OF CAPITAL

Resources are assessed in terms of both capital and income. If a resident individually has more than a prescribed upper capital figure, then he or she will automatically pay the whole amount due and receive no financial support from the local authority. This means that there is then no call to assess income. However, beneath that upper figure, but above a lower prescribed figure, any capital over the lower figure is deemed to produce a weekly tariff income of £1 for every £250.

At the time of writing the upper and lower figures are £21,250 and £13,500 respectively (SI 1992/2977, rr.20, 28).

10.6.1 WHAT IS COUNTED AS CAPITAL

Capital is not defined in legislation. Guidance states that capital, distinguished from income, is generally (a) not in respect of a specified period; and (b) not intended to form part of a series of payments.

Guidance gives a non-exhaustive list of examples of capital. Included are buildings, land, national savings certificates, premium bonds, stocks and shares, capital held by the Court of Protection or a receiver it has appointed, building society accounts, bank accounts, SAYE schemes, unit trusts, trust funds, cash and Cooperative share accounts. The guidance states that the position concerning investment bonds is complex and that local authorities should seek legal advice (CRAG 2008, para 6.002). Income from capital is generally treated as capital (not income), except in the case of certain disregarded capital (SI 1992/2977, r.22).

10.6.1.1 Valuation of capital

Capital (other than National Savings Certificates) is valued at the current market or surrender value, less 10 per cent if there would be actual expenses arising directly from the sale of the asset, and less any outstanding debts secured on the asset (e.g. a mortgage) (SI 1992/2977, r.23).

10.6.2 JOINT BENEFICIAL OWNERSHIP OF CAPITAL ASSET

A capital asset normally belongs to the person in whose name it is held, that is, the legal owner. However, sometimes, somebody else will be the beneficial owner, in part or in whole. However, evidence would be required. For instance, a resident may have £10,000 savings and £6500 in shares, but be able to show that the shares were bought on behalf of his son (who is abroad) and will be transferred to him on his return. In which case, the son is the beneficial, though not yet legal, owner of the shares. The resident's capital therefore is confined to the £10,000 savings only (CRAG 2008, para 6.008).

For joint beneficial ownership of a capital asset, except for an interest in land, the total value should be divided equally between the owners (SI 1992/2977, r.27).

10.6.3 DISREGARDED CAPITAL

Certain capital is disregarded either indefinitely or for a period of time.

10.6.3.1 Capital disregarded indefinitely

Capital disregarded indefinitely includes, for example, property in specified circumstances, surrender value of life insurance policies and annuities, payment of training bonus up to £200, age-related payments to pensioners (under the Age Related Payments Act 2004), payments in kind from charities, personal possessions such as paintings or antiques (unless bought to reduce the accommodation charge payable), capital treated as income or student loans, payments from various trust (the MacFarlane Trusts, Skipton Fund payments, the Fund (payments for non-haemophiliacs infected with HIV) or Independent Living Funds, Social Fund payments, value of funds held in trust or administered by a court (e.g. Court of Protection) following payment for personal injury, value of a right to receive income (under an annuity, outstanding instalments under an agreement to repay a capital sum, personal injury trust, life interest or liferent, income payable abroad which cannot be transferred to the UK, occupational pension, rent), ex gratia payments paid to former Japanese prisoners. And so on (it is a long list) (SI 1992/2977, schedule 4; CRAG 2008, 6.028).

10.6.3.2 Personal injury settlements: capital rules

From April 2008, the rules were amended so as to make clear that any payments actually made in consequence of personal injury to the person or his her partner should be disregarded, in the calculation of capital, for 52 weeks – unless the payment was made specifically (and identified by a court as such) for the purpose of covering the cost of care. In addition, the disregard, in the calculation of capital, of awards of personal injury damages relates not just to court-held damages, but also where the damages are held subject to the order or direction of the court (SI 1992/2977, schedule 4, as amended by SI 2008/593).

Where the capital is to be disregarded, the disregard applies to the whole of the capital (and also the value of the right to receive payments from the trust) – as the courts have confirmed:

Disregarding all the capital of personal injury payments held in trust by a court. It was argued in one court case that the capital disregard for personal injury payment held in trust by a court should apply only to the part of the compensation payment awarded for pain, suffering and loss of amenity – not, for example, to the part covering future care costs or loss of earnings. If this were so, the local authority could take account of at least some of the personal injury payment capital, for the purpose of charging for the residential care being provided to the person involved. (He had sustained a severe head injury at a textile mill, when retrieving a cricket ball from the roof of a shed.)

The case focused on a reference to 1987 Income Support Regulations, which referred to disregard of a payment 'for' personal injury, as opposed to the term 'in consequence of' personal injury. It was argued that the 'for' implied damages only for the pain, suffering and loss of amenity; and not damages for the cost of care and loss of earnings. The court rejected this argument, and found that whole of the capital fell to be disregarded (*Firth v Ackroyd*; see also *Bell v Todd*, and subsequent confirmation of this approach by the Court of Appeal in *Sowden v Lodge*; also *Peters v East Midlands SHA*).

The frustration this rule causes local authorities can be seen from the following court case in which the local authority attempted to hold an NHS trust liable for the costs of residential accommodation:

Circumventing rule about personal injury trusts. A local authority incurred costs of some £81,000 for the residential accommodation of a person who had suffered a stroke due to the negligence of an NHS trust. The damages award resulted in a structured settlement, with £40,000 payable annually into the Court of Protection. This sum had to be disregarded by the local authority under the charging rules. Instead, it sought to reclaim the costs from the NHS trust, on the basis that the latter could reasonably have foreseen that the consequences of its negligence would be a personal injury settlement paid into trust (and therefore to be disregarded); and also that the situation was unjust.

The case failed; the court held that the NHS trust could not reasonably have foreseen that the damages would be paid to the Court of Protection or a trust fund. It also held that the relevant charging rules were a necessary consequence of the interface between central government and local authority; and it was an abuse of language to call the consequence a gross injustice. The Court of Appeal, in substance, upheld this ruling, whilst having sympathy for the council which was having to pay for the NHS Trust's negligence (*Islington LBC v University College London Hospital NHS Trust*).

The rules means also that damages awarded, to the claimant and against the defendant, in personal injury cases, will be reduced to the extent that it is clear that the local authority will in future be meeting the person's needs for residential accommodation and care. However, the situation is complicated, because the principle of the reasonable meeting of a person's needs in the law of negligence may not equate to a local authority's view of meeting a person's needs reasonably.

Therefore, in some cases, the damages payable by the defendant may be reduced, but the claimant receive a 'top-up' award – to reflect what he or she may reasonably need over and above what the local authority is likely to provide in future (*Sowden v Lodge*). So, the defendant may fail to show either that a privately funded, as opposed to a publicly funded care home, for the clamant is unreasonable – or to show that the local authority will make reasonable provision for the claimant. In which case, the court may award compensation to reflect the cost of such private provision (*Godbold v Mahmood*. Also: *Walton v Calderdale Healthcare NHS Trust*). Equally, the damages payable may reflect the whole cost of private privately funded care, even if the person would be eligible for local authority assistance. In the following case, the judge was in no doubt that this was the case, since relying on the local authority in the future would be fraught with uncertainty. Such a situation gives rise to the danger that the claimant will benefit from "double recovery"; that is, receive compensation and then claim free care from the local authority. However, the court did not regard this as likely:

Full compensation for privately funded care, despite eligibility for local authority care. A woman had been born with congenital rubella syndrome and was severely disabled – as a result of the negligence of the NHS. The health authority argued it should not have to pay damages to cover all her care, because the local authority would be under an obligation to fund residential accommodation under s.21 of the National Assistance Act 1948. The local authority in turn argued that if it was required to pay for such care, then it should be able to make a charge against the personal injury compensation payable by the health authority.

The court ruled, first, that the local authority was not entitled under the rules to make a charge, against the personal injury compensation held in a trust or administered by the High Court of Court of Protection. Second, that if full compensation were not paid for her care, in reliance on what the local authority would have a statutory obligation to provide, then she would be exposed to considerable uncertainty. This was because the rules might change in future, allowing the local authority to make a charge against the personal injury award. In which case, she would then lose other elements of the award intended for different purposes. Furthermore, the constraints on the local authority budget would 'inevitably' mean a reduction in the future level of care and facilities provided for the woman. The care that would be provided by the local authority would be 'unlikely to provide her with the quality of care she presently enjoys for the rest of her life'. The only way to ensure that she would receive such care in the future was for her to be self-funding and for the compensation payment to reflect this.

On the issue of double recovery, the court noted that 'it would be folly' for her to make herself dependent on local authority resources, because she would receive a lower standard of care. However, the court stated that there was no legal basis for the woman's deputy (appointed by the Court of Protection) to undertake not to rely on the local authority in the future, and that in any case such an undertaking would be undesirable. Nevertheless, the court noted that the deputy was of the view that future care should be privately funded, and that the local authority would not be called on, barring 'some wholly unexpected development' (*Peters v East Midlands SHA*).

The courts have applied similar reasoning to the provision of accommodation under s.117 of the Mental Health Act 1983 (*Tinsley v Sarkar*). Likewise, the religious beliefs of an individual were relevant in determining whether compensation payable in a specialist care home or (at greater expense) in their own home (*Ahsan v University Hospitals Leicester NHS Trust*).

10.6.3.3 Capital disregarded for 12 weeks or 26 weeks

During the first 12 weeks of a permanent resident's stay, the value of the dwelling normally occupied as his or her only or main dwelling should be disregarded (SI 1992/2977, schedule 4, para 1A. CRAG 2008, para 6.028A). If the resident is temporary to begin with, the relevant rules for temporary residents apply (including disregard of the person's home). If the resident then becomes permanent, the 12-week disregard then runs for a further 12 weeks (LAC(2001)10, annex).

Some other capital is disregarded for up to 26 weeks or more, including the assets of a business owned or part-owned by the resident in which he or she intends to work again; money acquired for replacement of the home or repairs to it – or premises which the resident intends to occupy but to which essential repairs or alterations are needed; premises for which the resident has commenced legal proceedings to obtain possession; the capital proceeds of the sale of a former home which are to be used to buy another home; money deposited with a housing association and to be used to buy another home; or a grant obtained under housing legislation to buy a home or to repair it, so as to make it habitable (SI 1992/ 2977, schedule 4).

10.6.3.4 Capital disregarded for 52 weeks
Yet other capital is disregarded for 52 weeks, for example arrears or compensation in relation to non-payment of a range of state benefits, payments or refunds in relation to the NHS (dental treatment, spectacles and travelling expenses), free milk, vitamins or prison visits (SI 1992/2977, schedule 4, para 17).

10.6.3.5 Other disregarded capital
The assets of a business – owned or part-owned by the resident who is no longer a self-employed worker in it – must be disregarded for a reasonable period, so that the resident can dispose of the business assets (SI 1992/2977, schedule 4; CRAG 2008, para 6.031).

Payments made, in respect of variant Creutzfeldt–Jacob disease, to a victim's parent should be disregarded for two years from date of death of the victim. If made to a dependent child or young person, the payments should be disregarded until the person is no longer a member of a family (i.e. until they leave school between 16 and 17) but in any case for at least two years (SI 1992/2977, schedule 4; CRAG 2008, para 6.030A).

10.7 INCOME TREATED AS CAPITAL
Some income is treated as capital, including tax refunds, holiday pay, income from a capital asset, bounty payments, advance of earnings or loan from employer, irregular charitable and voluntary payments, including any payments made by a third party to the resident to help clear arrears of charges for residential accommodation (SI 1992/2977, r.22).

10.8 NOTIONAL CAPITAL
In certain circumstances, a resident may be assessed as possessing capital – even though not actually in possession of it. This is called notional capital and might be capital (a) of which the resident has deprived himself or herself in order to decrease the amount payable for the accommodation; (b) which would be payable if he or she applied for it; or (c) which is paid to a third party in respect of the resident.

However, the rule that capital, which would be available on application by the resident, should be treated as belonging to him or her does not apply where that capital is held in a discretionary trust, a trust derived from a personal injury compensation payment (or a court administered sum arising from personal injury compensation), or a loan that could be raised against a capital asset (e.g. the person's home) which is being disregarded (SI 1992/2977, r.25; CRAG 2008, para 6.052–3).

10.8.1 SHOWING DEPRIVATION OF CAPITAL·

A local authority can treat a resident as still possessing a capital asset, and thus possessing notional capital, if it believes that the resident has deprived himself or herself of it, in order to reduce accommodation fees (SI 1992/2977, r.25 and CRAG 2008, para 6.057). The local authority can only consider deprivation of capital, if it is capital which could otherwise have been taken into account.

For example, the giving by a woman of a diamond ring to her daughter a week before entering residential accommodation could not be deprivation because such personal possessions cannot be taken into account as capital anyway. However, had the resident bought the ring for her daughter, for example from money in a building society account, this could be deprivation (CRAG 2008, para 6.058). The capital in question might, for instance, involve a car. In one case the question was whether or not it was deprivation to stop spending the mobility component of disability living allowance on the leasing of a car through the Motability scheme – and instead to buy a new Vauxhall Zafira for just over £12,000 (an income support social security commissioner case on deprivation: CIS/2208/2003).

Guidance states that avoiding the charge 'need not be the resident's main motive but it must be a significant one'. Furthermore, it would not be reasonable for the authority to identify such deprivation of income if the resident was, at the time of the disposal, 'fit and healthy and could not have foreseen the need for a move to residential accommodation' (CRAG 2008, para 6.064).

The courts in England and Scotland (where the deprivation rules are roughly the same as in England) appear to have taken a different approach to what is required to show a significant motive. Effectively the Scottish courts have tended toward an objective (and arguably harsher) approach; the English toward a more subjective one.

Inference of motive for giving the house away. An elderly woman, aged 78 years, transferred her house in early 1995 to her granddaughter for love, favour and affection, though retaining a right to live there. She also executed a power of attorney in favour of her son. A year or so later, she fell, breaking her arm; by June 1996 her physical and mental condition had deteriorated such that she entered a nursing home. The son indicated, before admission to the home, that his mother had deteriorated over the past few years and had harboured paranoid ideas regarding a neighbour. The local authority could not show directly that the woman's motive for the transfer had been avoidance of future care home costs. However, it received no explanation as to why the woman had not left her house in her will, as opposed to transferring it in life.

The court held that the local authority was entitled to draw inferences on the basis of all the material available to it; furthermore, it did not have to make a specific finding as to the exact state of knowledge or intention of the woman (*Yule v South Lanarkshire Council (no.2)*).

In another Scottish case, the courts took a similar, arguably even harsher, line, because there was no evidence that at the time of the transfer anybody either knew or suspected that the person had begun to suffer from senile dementia:

Transfer of home. An elderly woman transferred to her children, for love, favour and affection, her home, but continued to live there. It was argued that this was in part to discourage the pestering of her brother who wished to come to live with her. The head of the local authority's social work department stated that he was not satisfied that this was a satisfactory explanation; and that it appeared to him that the property was transferred at least in part for the purpose of reducing residential accommodation charges. The local authority succeeded on this point in both the Outer and then, on appeal, the Inner House of the Court of Session (*Robertson v Fife Council*).

The above Scottish cases seemed to place considerable burden on the resident to provide an explanation, and gave considerable latitude to the local authority to draw inferences. They appear to contrast markedly with the approach taken by the English High Court, which emphasised the importance of the subjective state of knowledge of the person transferring the asset:

Giving the house away. A man had a stroke in March 1997 at the age of 90. Discharged from hospital a month later, he went home 'on a wing and a prayer' (as a social worker put it), receiving intensive home care three times a day including personal care, meal preparation, shopping, cleaning and laundry. For some eight years previously, he had been in receipt of home care comprising assistance with domestic tasks for three hours a week. In April 1997, a week after hospital discharge, he transferred his house to his son by deed of gift. This was later explained with reference to the fact that his son's 24-year marriage had broken down, and that he was concerned that his son would become homeless. The father had no thought of dying anywhere else than in his own home.

In April 1999, the man was admitted to hospital in a state of collapse and exhaustion. He returned home in May, was readmitted to hospital in August – and in September assessed by social services as requiring residential care. Social services decided that he had deprived himself of an asset which would have funded his residential care. The son complained, and the complaint reached the final complaints review panel stage. The panel rejected the son's complaint, and the director of social services accepted the panel's findings. One of the panel members at one stage pointed out that ignorance of the law was no defence.

The court found the local authority's decision to be unlawful. The test to be applied was meant to be a subjective one in terms of the father's state of mind. If the son's evidence was rejected on this point, the panel had to explain why with adequate reasons. The absence of such reasons suggested the panel was not applying the right test. The 'ignorance of the law' comment betrayed a misunderstanding of that test (*R(Beeson) v Dorset CC*, High Court).

10.8.2 DEPRIVATION OF CAPITAL AND CONSEQUENCES

If deprivation of capital is shown, the local authority can attempt to recover the assessed charge owing from either the resident as normal – or, if the resident cannot pay, then in some circumstances from the third party to whom the asset was transferred – but only if the deprivation took place less than six months before the person was placed by the local authority in the care home (SI 1992/2977, r.25; CRAG 2008, para 6.067, Annex D).

If notional capital is taken into account, it must be regarded by the local authority as reduced each week by the difference between the (greater) amount the resident has been assessed to pay because of the notional capital, and the (lesser) amount he or she would have paid but for the notional capital (SI 1992/2977, r.26). There is no rule about how long ago the deprivation must have occurred, although the greater the period between the 'deprivation' and the entry into the care home, the more difficult it is likely to be for the local authority to argue relevant motive.

Notional capital and timescales. In one Scottish court case, where the rules are the same in England, the petitioner claimed that the power to take account of notional capital conferred by r.25 of SI 1992/2977 was limited to disposals of assets only up to six months before entry into residential accommodation – a limit deriving from s.21 of the Health and Social Services and Social Security Adjudications Act 1983. However, the court confirmed what had been widely supposed to be the case, that there was no such time limit (the limit of six months applying only when an authority wishes to make liable a third party, to whom the asset in question had been transferred) (*Yule v South Lanarkshire Council*).

Of course, demanding payment, notwithstanding deprivation, will not be greatly to the authority's benefit if the resident does not have sufficient actual, as opposed to notional, capital. If the asset was transferred to a third party more than six months before the resident entered the care home, the rules are that the authority cannot legally hold the third party liable) Health and Social Services and Social Security Adjudications Act 1983, s.21) – unless insolvency proceedings are contemplated (see section 10.12).

An incentive for identifying notional capital would be for the local authority then to argue that it has no duty to contract for the care home placement at all. This would be on the basis that notionally, if not actually, the person had sufficient resources to make his or own arrangements. In practice the local authority might seek to rely on the third party (e.g. a family member), who now had the actual property or other asset, to pay the fees.

However, there would be no legal (as opposed to moral) obligation on that third party to do so, always assuming the six-month rule were not relevant. In which case, so the argument runs, the person would have to remain in the care home until his or her resources (actual rather than notional) ran out. Then, he or she could in principle be evicted for non-payment. The Scottish courts were prepared to countenance this happening. However, the House of Lords overturned the decision and ruled that in Scotland at least this would not be lawful; and that local authorities are obliged to continue to fund the care home placement, notwithstanding the existence of notional capital (*Robertson v Fife Council*).

There is a degree of uncertainty about the extent to which the Scottish case of *Robertson* case applies in England. This is because some of the court's reasoning referred to elements of the Scottish legislation that differ from the English. Possibly there is material in the *Robertson* case to argue the position either way. The Court of Appeal, in a subsequent English case, came to no conclusive view on this but perhaps seemed unconvinced that the outcome of such a case in England would be so very different (*R(Beeson) v Dorset County Council*). Thus, it is doubtful whether the English courts would allow a vulnerable, disabled person (particularly without, but may be even with, the mental capacity to decide or arrange welfare matters for himself or herself) to be abandoned by both care home and local authority and put out on the streets.

10.8.3 INSOLVENCY PROCEEDINGS FOR DEPRIVATION OF CAPITAL

Alternatively, the local authority may consider insolvency proceedings in respect of what it considers to be a deprivation of capital (see 10.12).

10.9 ASSESSMENT OF REAL PROPERTY (HOUSE OR LAND)

In some circumstances, a resident's property might be disregarded in the assessment of assets, but otherwise it is fully taken account of.

10.9.1 TEMPORARY RESIDENTS: DISREGARD OF PERSON'S HOME

The value of the dwelling, normally occupied by a temporary resident as his or her home, will be disregarded if he or she intends to return to the dwelling or is taking reasonable steps to dispose of the property in order to acquire another more suitable one to return to (SI 1992/2977, schedule 4).

Guidance states that if a person's stay was thought to be permanent, but turns out to be temporary, he or she should be treated as if the stay were temporary from the outset. In which the case the dwelling should disregarded (CRAG 2008, para 7.002).

10.9.2 PROPERTY OCCUPIED BY OTHER PEOPLE AND JOINT OWNERSHIP

10.9.2.1 Property occupied by other people: mandatory disregard

The value of the resident's home must be disregarded if it is occupied, whether wholly or partly, (a) by the resident's partner or former partner (except in case of divorce or estrangement); (b) by a lone parent who is the claimant's estranged or divorced partner; (c) by a relative or member of the family who is at least 60 years old, or is under 16 years old and is liable to be maintained by the resident, or is incapacitated (SI 1992/2977, schedule 4; CRAG 2008, para 7.003).

Guidance points out that 'incapacitated' is not defined in the regulations, but that a reasonable test might be whether the person receives, or could receive, a disability-related social security benefit (CRAG 2008, para 7.005). The regulations set out a long of list relevant relatives. Family includes married or unmarried couple or civil partnership and any person who is a member of the same household and is the responsibility of either or both members of the couple. It also includes a person who is not a member of a married or unmarried couple or civil partnership and who is a member of the same household and the responsibility of the resident (CRAG 2008, paras 7.004,7004A).

The dwelling must in any case be disregarded for the first 12 weeks of a permanent resident's stay (SI 1992/2977, schedule 4, par 2). If the resident leaves residential care before the end of the 12 weeks and then re-enters on a permanent basis within 52 weeks, he or she is entitled to the balance of the 12-week disregard. If he or she re-enters more than 52 weeks later, the 12-week disregard applies afresh (CRAG 2008, para 7.003B).

10.9.2.2 Property occupied by other people and discretionary disregard

Outside the mandatory disregard, if anybody else is living in the home, local authorities have discretion to disregard the property, if they 'consider it would be reasonable' (SI 1992/2977, schedule 4). Guidance suggests that it might be reasonable where, for example, 'it is the sole residence of someone who has given up their own home in order to care for the resident, or someone who is an elderly companion of the resident particularly if they have given up their own home'.

However, it would be for the authority to decide when and whether to review the exercise of any such discretion – for example, when the carer has died or moved out (CRAG 2008, paras 7.007–8). It should be noted that the example given in the guidance is just that; the discretion is a wide one – although in the following court case, the local authority had lawfully decided not to exercise it:

Discretion to disregard value of house. In 1991, a man gave up his job in Australia (as a welfare officer working with Aboriginal Australians) to return to England to look after his mother; she was suffering from Parkinson's disease and had been forced to go into residential care. On his arrival, she returned to her own home, and he looked after her with constant assistance and support. However, she suffered a series of strokes and was admitted to hospital in July 1993. In March 1994, the son returned to Australia to resume his job; but this did not work out and he had returned by July.

In May 1994, his mother had been discharged from hospital to a nursing home. In April 1997 she died. There was a shortfall in the payments she had made to the local authority for this nursing home care; the local authority decided to take account of her home in the test of resources. During this period, it did not force the son to sell the house, but created a charge of £500 a month on it. The mother died with a bill of £25,000 outstanding – and interest began to accrue from date of death. The authority would not enforce the charge (i.e. force a sale) until the son ceased to occupy the property.

The judge decided that 'in all the circumstances of the case it was not unreasonable to take account of the house'. One factor – though not the only one – in the overall decision was that the son had returned to Australia after his mother had gone into residential care for the second time, in order to attempt (unsuccessfully) to resume his career. This meant that on his second return to England, occupation of the house had become attributable not to the need to look after his mother, but to the decision to give up the job and accommodation in Australia. Overall, the judge was satisfied that the decision had been taken by the local authority's officer within the ambit of the regulations, was 'properly based on conclusions of fact to which he was entitled to come on the material which he had to consider', and 'was based on full and proper assessment of all the facts and circumstances of the case' (*R v Somerset CC, ex p Harcombe*).

Nevertheless, even if the local authority is entitled to take account of the house, it needs to provide clear information; a failure to do so may mean a finding of maladministration by the local ombudsman:

Misleading advice about taking account of the value of the house. A son lived with his elderly mother. The council wrongly advised him that if she moved into a care home, the value of her house would not be taken into account when calculating her contribution to the care home fees. Four and a half months after she had entered the care home, the local authority told the son that the house would after all be taken into account and that there was now a legal charge on the property. The son stated that had he received proper advice at the outset, he would have given up his job to care for his mother at home – something he had done for relatively long periods in the past.

The ombudsman found maladministration in that the local authority failed to give clear written advice and took far too long in carrying out its financial assessment. The council agreed to waive £2000 from the charge and not insist on a sale of the property (although the mother had now died). Nevertheless, the ombudsman did not recommend that the charge on the property be lifted, since the mother had received the residential care, the cost of which was property recoverable (*Cumbria CC 2001*).

Wrong information. The local authority assessed, wrongly, an elderly woman's liability for residential care fees in December 1995. In April 1997, when it had obtained the information to correct the error it did not do so; it only did so in September 1999, the delay being because of insufficient debt recovery procedures. By now there was £13,500 owing. All this was maladministration. The son claimed he would have taken more urgent action regarding the house, either selling it earlier or renting it out (*Kent CC 2001a*).

10.9.2.3 Legal and beneficial ownership of property

There will be some circumstances in which the local authority might have difficulty practically taking account of the value of a property where somebody else is living, if the person has a beneficial interest in that property.

Guidance points out that legal owner means the person in whose name a property is held; beneficial owner means the person entitled to receive the proceeds or profits of the property. Normally the two will be one and the same. However, this is not always so. Where the care home resident is a legal owner of a property but has no beneficial interest in it, the property should not be taken into account for charging purposes. However, if the resident has a beneficial interest in the property, then the property should be taken into account, even though he or she is not the legal owner (CRAG 2008, paras 7.009–11).

The guidance goes on to suggest that the law of equity might resolve doubts about beneficial ownership, by considering the original intentions involved between the parties (CRAG 2008, para 7.014A). The following court case was about a beneficial type of interest or ownership:

Beneficial interest of lodger as against local authority's interest. A relatively fit and healthy couple had a lodger. Their physical and mental capabilities declined into frailty, helplessness and incontinence; the lodger in effect became an unpaid live-in carer, until they went into a care home. Although he stopped paying rent at a certain point, the lodger had been providing substantial personal care and incurred out-of-pocket expenses of £1700. The lodger claimed that the couple had repeatedly assured him that he would have a home for life.

After the couple had both died, the lodger resisted sale of the property by the executors of the will, on the grounds that he had a right to live there. The court found that he had a claim in equity under the principle of proprietary estoppel. The couple had, through assurances, induced the lodger to act as he did, and he then acted to his detriment (the level of care he provided was greater than could be accounted for by friendship and a sense of responsibility). The claim amounted not to a right to live there for life but instead to a sum of £35,000; and this claim ranked ahead of the local authority's charge (£64,000) that it had placed on the home for the couple's residential care (*Campbell v Griffin*).

Purchase of council houses has sometimes given rise to legal dispute in respect of a local authority attempting to take account of a person's house for the purpose of care home fees:

Purchase of council house: legal or beneficial interest and liability for care home fees. A secure tenancy of a council property passed from a woman's father to her mother when he died. The mother then exercised her right to buy; the property was worth £120,000 but it attracted a discount of £50,000. The daughter funded the whole purchase by means of a mortgage; she and her mother became joint legal owners. Just before the transfer the mother went into hospital and was subsequently discharged to a care home; she then died. The local authority subsequently registered a caution against the property by way of seeking a contribution to the care home fees. The daughter argued that the property had only ever been intended for her use and not her mother; she had paid the entire purchase price; and her mother had only joint legal title, but no beneficial interest.

The court held that on the evidence it was not clear that the mother had no beneficial interest. There was no express declaration by the mother and daughter concerning the beneficial interest at the time of purchase. In the absence of such declaration, the court would normally decide that the joint purchasers held the property on a resulting trust for themselves in proportion to their original contributions (as in *Springette v Defoe*). In this case, this would mean the mother holding a beneficial interest of 5/12 of the property (representing the £50,000 discount value attributable to her being the tenant), compared to the £70,000 contributed by the daughter.

The court ruled that it was not unlawful for the local authority to have registered the caution; but that further proceedings could be brought by the daughter to try to show specific evidence of common intention by herself and her mother – to displace the presumption of the existence of the resulting trust (*R(Kelly) v Hammersmith and Fulham LBC*).

10.9.2.4 Joint ownership and willing buyer

In the case of land, the resident's share should be valued at an amount equal to the price which his or her interest in possession would realise. However, this would be on the basis of it being sold to a willing buyer, and taking into account the likely effect on that price of any incumbrance secured on the whole beneficial interest (e.g. somebody in occupation with a beneficial interest). The price would also be less 10 per cent, representing the costs involved in selling (SI 1992/2977, r.27).

This rule means that the value of a property might therefore have only a nominal value if a co-owner is still living in it, since in reality there may be no willing buyer to purchase the resident's interest. In some circumstances the value could therefore be nil. For example, no other relative (or anybody else) might be willing to buy the resident's interest, if the financial advantages did not significantly outweigh the risks and limitations involved of somebody else having part ownership (CRAG 2008, para 7.014).

In one case concerning income support, the Court of Appeal held that in the case of father and daughter who had a beneficial interest in the family home, the value of the father's interest was to be taken by reference to the current market value (minimal), not to his share of the beneficial interest taken as a whole, given that a sale of the property could not be forced (*Chief Adjudication Officer v Palfrey*). In another, the local authority attempted to circumvent this rule. It approached the question on the basis of a hypothetical 'open market value' that effectively assumed the existence of a willing buyer, whilst ignoring the 'real circumstances'. The property in question was jointly owned by the care home resident and his son; the latter had intended to move in when he retired. The local ombudsman found that the council's approach was inconsistent with both Department of Health guidance and legal case law. Without significant evidence or opinion to support such a contrary position, this was maladministration (*Lincolnshire CC 2004*).

Nevertheless, in the context of income support, a 2004 decision by the Social Security Commissioner suggested, without deciding, that it should not be assumed that in every such case the resident's share of the value is little or nothing. For example, it might have value for inheritance tax purposes (the resident was now deceased). In the particular case, however, the

Commissioner accepted that the resident's share (one-third) of the house (the other two-thirds owned by her daughter) was minimal (CIS/3197/2003).

The whole matter was considered in yet another case, in which the court found, in the particular circumstances, that there was no impediment to the forcing of a sale of jointly owned property (in which case the value of the each share would be realisable, and so should be taken into account in the income support means test):

Share in the house realisable if no impediment to sale of house. A parent had left her house, half to her daughter, half to her son. Her daughter was claiming income support; her share of the house would take her above the capital threshold and thereby remove her entitlement. She argued that she could not sell the house, because her mother had intended that her brother should live there with his son, when he returned from Australia (he did in fact return and take up occupation). She maintained that this purpose had not been stated expressly in the will, because of the uncertainty about her brother's return. She maintained that this meant her share in the house was effectively nil, because nobody else would be interested in buying her share, with her brother in occupation.

The court ruled that there was nothing stopping the daughter selling the house, because the house was an absolute gift, with no restriction or superadded purpose. (Under the Trusts of Land and Apportionment of Trustees Act 1996, the court – before ordering a sale – would have to consider the intentions of the person who created a trust, the purpose for which a property subject to trust is held, the welfare of any minor occupying the property, and the interests of any secured creditor or any other beneficiary.) If the brother wished to remain in occupation, he would have to pay his sister the value of her share or a market rent. If he was unable or unwilling, a sale with vacant possession would be inevitable. The case could be distinguished from one such as the *Palfrey* case, where property was acquired for joint owners for a collateral purpose, such as accommodation for both joint owners, and that purpose would be defeated if one were to insist on a sale.

However, one of the three judges dissented, stating that even on the limited evidence available, the 'collateral purpose' of the gift (i.e. occupation by the brother) could be established – and did not have to 'an express or implied term of the trust'. He held that an order for sale would probably have failed (*Wilkinson v Chief Adjudication Officer*).

10.9.3 INTENTION TO OCCUPY PROPERTY

If the resident has acquired a home that he intends to occupy, then it should be disregarded for up to 26 weeks or for a longer period if reasonable (SI 1992/2977, schedule 4, para 18; CRAG 2008, para 7.006).

10.9.4 PROPERTY AND DEFERRED PAYMENTS

Local authorities have the power to make deferred payments (Health and Social Care Act 2001; SI 2001/3069). This means that, where a local authority would be otherwise entitled to take account of a resident's home and force a sale, it will not do so (SI 2001/3067). Instead, it can agree not to force the sale, but instead place a progressively increasing land charge for an agreed period (i.e. until the person dies or until the elapse of some other agreed period of time). The purpose is so that people do not have to sell their homes during the period of the agreement. Guidance stresses a number of points.

- Local authorities have only a discretion, not a duty, to enter a deferred payment agreement.

- Authorities should ensure that the resident will have sufficient assets eventually to repay the money owing and meet other commitments (e.g. mortgage payments).
- If an authority enters into a high value agreement with one person, it might affect its ability to enter agreements with others.
- A deferred payment agreement would only take effect after the 12-week mandatory property disregard (see 10.6.3.2 above).
- Such agreements should not supplant the use of the discretion not to take account of the property at all, where there is somebody (such as a former carer) still living in it (see 10.9.2.2).
- An agreement lasts until the end of the exempt period, that is, 56 days after the resident dies or when it is otherwise terminated by the resident. The authority cannot terminate the agreement of its own accord. The debt is only payable, and interest only chargeable, from the day after the exempt period ends.
- Authorities should distinguish the placing of a charge on the property under a deferred payment agreement (Health and Social Care Act 2001, s.54) from placing a charge on a property when the resident is simply failing to pay an assessed charge (under the Health and Social Services and Social Security Adjudications Act 1983, s.22) (LAC(2001)25, annex).

The setting up of a deferred payment agreement in any one case is a discretion only. But, clearly, in order to exercise that discretion, the council needs to set up a deferred payment scheme, so that the possibility of an agreement with a particular resident is possible. Legal powers and funding for such a scheme were given to local authorities in October 2001. So, for example, a failure to set up such a scheme until October 2004 was maladministration. Arguing that there were other priorities was not good enough; if more resources were required to set up the scheme, the council should have provided them (*Manchester CC 2005*).

10.10 ASSESSMENT OF INCOME

A payment of income (other than earnings: see below) is generally distinguished from capital on the basis that it is made in relation to a period and is part of a series (regular or irregular) of payments (CRAG 2008, paras 8.001–2). As with capital, income might be wholly or partly disregarded, or be taken fully into account. Residents may also be assessed as having notional income if, for example, they have deprived themselves of income in order to reduce the charge payable.

10.10.1 NOTIONAL INCOME

A resident may be treated by the local authority as having notional income, even though he or she does not actually receive it, if it is income: (a) paid by a third party as a contribution towards the cost of the accommodation (unless paid directly to the local authority); (b) which would be available on application; (c) due but not yet paid; (d) which the resident has disposed of (SI 1992/2977, r.17; CRAG 2008, paras 8.059–70A).

However, the rule that income, which would be available on application by the resident, should be treated as belonging to him or her does not apply in a number of circumstances – including where that income is payable under a discretionary trust, or a trust derived from a personal injury compensation payment (SI 1992/2977, r.17; CRAG 2008, para 8.070).

A resident will be treated as possessing income, of which he or she has deprived himself or herself 'for the purpose of paying a reduced charge'. Deprivation occurs if the person ceases to possess the resource. There 'may have been more than one purpose of the disposal of income, only one of which is to avoid a charge, or a lower charge. This may not be the resident's main motive but it must be a significant one.' The local authority should make a judgement about this 'only after balancing all the person's motives, explicit and implicit, and the timing behind the action (CRAG 2008, paras 8.071–8.079).

The authority can then attempt to recover the assessed charge owing from either the resident as normal – or, if the resident cannot pay, from the third party to whom the asset was transferred (subject to its having been transferred less than six months before the person was placed in the accommodation by the local authority: Health and Social Services and Social Security Adjudications Act 1983, s.21).

10.10.2 INCOME FULLY TAKEN ACCOUNT OF

Income fully taken account of includes most social security benefits, annuity income, cash in lieu of concessionary coal (permanent residents only), child support maintenance payments (if the child is accommodated with the resident under Part 3 of the 1948 Act – i.e. mother and baby unit), ex gratia incapacity allowances from the Home Office, income from certain disregarded capital (e.g. from property or business assets which have been disregarded), insurance policy income, income from certain sublets, occupational pensions, income tax refunds, payments made by third parties to meet higher fees of a care home, trust income, and war orphan pension (SI 1992/2977, r.15).

Income actually received in consequence of a personal injury is disregarded for up to 52 weeks, unless the payment was made (and identified by a court as such) specifically for the purpose of covering care (SI 1992/2977, schedule 4, as amended by SI 2008/593).

10.10.2.1 Top up payments as income of resident

If a local authority places a person in a higher cost home, on the basis of a third party topping up the excess, any lump sum payment made by the third party should be divided by the number of weeks for which the payment is made and then taken into account fully as the resident's income.

During the 12-week property disregard or during a deferred payments agreement, the resident may himself or herself be paying toward a higher price home. In the case of the 12-week property disregard, the payment made by the resident should be treated as part of his or her income. If made as a lump sum, it should be divided by the number of weeks for which the payment is made and then taken into account fully as the resident's income (SI 1992/2977, r.16A).

In the case of deferred payments, the capital value of the person's home (once realised in the future) will be used to repay the council (SI 2001/3441, r.4).

10.10.3 INCOME PARTLY DISREGARDED

Income partly disregarded includes a £10 disregard for payments made under German or Austrian law to victims of National Socialist persecution, war disablement pension, war widow's pension and civilian war-injury pension. There is also a savings disregard.

In addition, various amounts are disregarded including occupational pensions, personal pensions and retirement annuity contract payments; some charitable payments; annuity income from a home income plan; subletting income; income from boarders; insurance policies for mortgage protection; income from certain disregarded capital, for example disregarded might be the element of the income representing mortgage repayments, council tax or water rates (CRAG 2008, paras 8.021–37; SI 1992/2977, schedule 3).

10.10.4 INCOME FULLY DISREGARDED

Income fully disregarded includes disability living allowance/attendance allowance (while still in receipt) for temporary residents, income support/pension credit, home commitments of temporary residents (see above); Supporting People housing support payments; certain charitable and voluntary payments; child support maintenance and child benefit payments (unless the child is living with the resident in accommodation: i.e. mother and baby unit); child tax credits; Guardian's Allowance; Christmas bonus associated with certain benefits; age-related payments under the Age Related Payments 2005; payments from the Macfarlane Trusts, Independent Living Funds, Eileen Trust and the Fund, council tax benefit, disability living allowance (mobility component), mobility supplement for war pensioners; dependency increases associated with some benefits; gallantry awards; income in kind or frozen abroad; income in kind; social fund payments; certain payments made to trainees; special payments to war widows and widowers; work expenses paid by employer and expenses payments for voluntary workers; adoption related payments under the Adoption and Children Act 2002; childcare cost payments under s.63 of the Health and Social Services and Public Health Act 1968; payments under s.14F of the Children Act 1989 (CRAG 2008, paras 8.038–56; SI 1992/2977, schedule 3).

10.11 RESPONSIBILITY FOR PAYMENT OF FEES

The ultimate responsibility for paying an independent provider of accommodation is the local authority as a party to the contract. However, the resident can make payment direct to the provider if this is agreed by the authority, the provider and the resident. Where this is agreed, but the resident fails at some point to make the required payment, the local authority is obliged to pay the shortfall to the provider (National Assistance Act 1948, s.26(3A); CRAG 2008, para 1.023).

10.12 PURSUIT OF DEBT

Local authorities are empowered under the National Assistance Act 1948, without prejudice to any other method of recovery, to recover money owing for care home fees, as a civil debt. However, proceedings must be brought within three years of the sum becoming due (National Assistance Act 1948, s.56).

10.12.1 PURSUING THIRD PARTIES FOR FEES: SIX MONTH RULE

Local authorities are empowered to pursue money owing to them from a third party, to whom the resident transferred assets not more than six months before entry into residential accommodation. This must have been done knowingly and with the intention of avoiding charges for the accommodation. The transfer needs to have been at an undervalue or for no consideration at all (Health and Social Services and Social Security Adjudications Act 1983, s.21).

This six-month rule is only triggered when the local authority has assessed the person as needing residential accommodation under Part III of the 1948 Act, and has arranged a placement. The rule does not apply if the resident is self-funding in an independent sector home, has not been assessed, or has not had his or her placement arranged by the local authority. Even if the requisite conditions are met, the rule applies only to assets that would have been taken into account when assessing the charge (CRAG 2008, annex D). This would mean valuation at time of transfer, namely the amount that would have been realised on the open market by a willing seller. However, debts secured on the asset would have to be taken into account together with a reasonable amount (10%) in respect of the expenses of a sale (CRAG 2008, annex D).

10.12.2 PLACING A CHARGE ON LAND OR PROPERTY

If a resident fails to pay assessed charges for accommodation, the local authority is empowered to place a charge on any land or property in which the resident has a beneficial interest. The legislation states that such a charge will only bear interest from the day after the resident dies. The rate of interest should be a reasonable one as directed by the Secretary of State; otherwise, as the local authority determines (Health and Social Services and Social Security Adjudications Act 1983, s.24). Guidance states that the local authority should advise or assist the resident to consult a solicitor (CRAG 2008, annex D).

The Department of Health believes that because a specific power to create a charge is contained in the 1983 Act, local authorities cannot decide instead to use other general powers contained in s.111 of the Local Government Act 1972 in order to be able to charge interest during the person's lifetime (CRAG 2008, annex D).

The placing of a charge on property when a resident fails to pay should be distinguished from the situation of deferred payments. The placing of the charge occurs in different circumstances and under different legislation. It is by mutual agreement under s.54 of the Health and Social Care Act 2001 in respect of deferred payments. Where there is a lack of agreement and the resident fails to pay, it is under s.22 of the Health and Social Services and Social Security Adjudications Act 1983.

10.12.3 INSOLVENCY PROCEEDINGS

If local authorities attempt to enforce charges, but the person being pursued has no or little money left (e.g. following a deliberate deprivation of resources), they clearly have a problem. However, authorities might consider utilising provisions under the Insolvency Act 1986 to enable them to pursue debts that are owing from other parties.

First, steps might be taken (under ss.339–341 of the 1986 Act) to have the resident declared bankrupt, in which case any of the resident's transactions made at an undervalue in the past two years can be set aside (or in the last five years, in the unlikely event that the resident was already insolvent at the time of the transaction).

Second (under ss.423–425), a gift, no matter how long ago it was made, can be set aside if the court is convinced that the purpose (not necessarily sole or even dominant, but at least substantial) of the gift was to place the assets beyond the reach of a possible creditor or otherwise prejudice a creditor's interests (i.e. to avoid paying residential care charges). However, this test does not necessarily mean that a transaction designed primarily to minimise tax liabilities would fall foul of s.423, as the following legal case illustrates:

Tax planning not to be equated with avoiding potential creditors. A successful businessman and solicitor had for many years put his assets, as he accrued them, into his wife's name. He was subsequently investigated by the Law Society for breaches of accounting rules. The man died. The Law Society sought to recoup £283,000 in costs incurred by its intervention, relying on s.423 of the Insolvency Act 1986 to do so. The court rejected the Law Society's arguments; stated that the evidence clearly showed that the transfer of assets to the wife was based on the advice of his accountant for the purpose of minimising tax liability; and that the Society should not have engaged in speculative litigation against an elderly lady (*Law Society v Southall*).

However, the outcome was different in the following case concerning s.423:

Insolvency proceedings: based on real and substantial purpose of avoiding care home fees. A man suffered a heart attack and stroke and was admitted to a nursing home, following discharge from hospital. A month before entering the nursing home, he made a gift of his house. In reaching the conclusion that the purpose was to put assets beyond the reach of a person (the local authority) who was, or would, make a claim against him, the judge had concluded as follows. First, he was ill and had to go into a care home. Second, there was knowledge in the family generally that his resources would be called on to pay care home fees. Third, he had never before made legal documents, but now did so in contemplation of going into a care home. Fourth, there was no explanation (other than avoiding care home fees) as to why, at the same time as he made a will, that he should make a gift of the house to his children. Fifth, he was not a sophisticated man used to legal dealings, but had a number of meetings with his solicitor in the relevant few weeks before entering the care home.

Overall, the judge found that a 'real and substantial purpose' of making the gift was to put the house beyond the reach of people who in future might require payment for the provision of residential care. The judge also pointed out that it was a 'very common, understandable and in no way morally reprehensible reason, but a clear purpose nonetheless' (*Derbyshire County Council v Akrill*).

10.13 CARE HOMES: PERSONAL FINANCIAL ISSUES

Possible or actual need for residential or nursing home accommodation raises various financial issues for people and their families, including how to raise capital on their own home, the making of gifts and the transferring of assets to avoid possible charges.

For instance, fearful that they will in effect be forced by local authorities to sell their home in order to pay residential or nursing home fees, some people contemplate making a gift of their home – typically to close family – so as to put the property out of the reach of the local authority.

However, there exists a range of possible complications and pitfalls, and it is clear that expert advice should be sought by those considering gifts of property or other assets, or other forms of alienating them (such as trusts). The following two legal cases are cautionary reminders of how things can go wrong in the case of lifetime transactions within families:

Undue influence of great nephew on elderly man. An elderly man contributed (£43,000) towards the purchase (for £83,000) of a house by his great-nephew (and in the latter's sole name) in return for living in it for the rest of his life. The nephew defaulted on the mortgage repayments, and the man tried to retrieve his money ahead of the mortgage lender. The Court of Appeal ruled there had been undue influence exercised, and that he could recover a proportion, but not the whole, of the original amount. This was because the house was sold for only £55,000. The man could not recover his original £43,000, but only an amount (£28,700) corresponding to the proportion (i.e. 43:40) he had contributed to the original purchase price (*Cheese v Thomas*).

Sharing of house, breakdown of arrangements. A man provided the money (£33,950) towards purchase of a house for his son and daughter-in-law. The agreement was that he would then live there rent free for the rest of his life. The arrangement broke down when the son accused the father of sexually molesting the latter's young granddaughter; it was subsequently clear that the accusation was unfounded and made without reasonable grounds. The High Court ruled that the full sum was recoverable on the basis of a doctrine known as proprietary estoppel (basically about a person's expectation, which has arisen because he or she has acted to his or her detriment in reliance on a promise or assurance).

However, the Court of Appeal ruled that the expectation lost was not the full sum, but the value of the father's expectation to live in the house rent free for the rest of his life. This would be a smaller amount than the original sum he had contributed (*Baker v Baker*).

CHAPTER 11

Non-residential services

KEY POINTS

A substantial range of non-residential community care services is covered by various community care legislation applying to local social services authorities. Access to these services is governed by assessment conducted under s.47 of the NHS and Community Care Act 1990 (see Chapter 6). However, these services are not contained within the 1990 Act itself, but instead are scattered within five other pieces of legislation. These are the National Assistance Act 1948 (s.29), Chronically Sick and Disabled Persons Act 1970 (s.2), Health Services and Public Health Act 1968 (s.45), NHS Act 2006 (schedule 20), and the Mental Health Act 1983 (s.117).

On the positive side, the services are wide ranging. They include social work services, advice, support, holidays, practical assistance in the home, assistance to take advantage of educational facilities, recreational activities, additional facilities (equipment), home adaptations, holidays, night sitter services, home help, laundry service, visiting services, assistance in finding accommodation etc.

Less helpfully, the very extent, overlap and fragmentation of the legislation governing non-residential services feeds the type of uncertainty outlined in Chapter 3. Not only are service users unaware of what services could or must be provided, but so too sometimes are local authority officers. Furthermore, it is particularly in the case of non-residential services that local authorities have so effectively deployed the government policy of 'fair access to care' – by imposing ever stricter thresholds of eligibility for services, thereby denying services to increasing numbers of older people. This minimising of assistance given to older people in their own homes, with local authorities treating eligibility as highly a moveable feast, is a typical escape route from potential legal and financial obligations, also explained in Chapter 3.

The legislation contains individual duties which are more easily enforceable such as under the Chronically Sick and Disabled Persons Act 1970; general duties less easily enforceable such as those under s.29 of the National Assistance Act 1948; and powers, not enforceable, such as those under schedule 20 of the NHS Act 2006. The 1970 Act probably remains the epitome of welfare legislation creating a strong, legally enforceable duty (with the associated resource implications), which sits increasingly uneasily with the broad brush, resource-limited approach which both central and local government are striving for.

11.1 NON-RESIDENTIAL SERVICES FOR DISABLED PEOPLE: NATIONAL ASSISTANCE ACT 1948, S.29

A number of non-residential services for disabled people are listed under s.29 of the National Assistance Act 1948. However, s.29 states that the provision of such services is subject to either approval or direction by the Secretary of State. An approval confers a power, whilst a direction created a duty, to provide services.

11.1.1 NON-RESIDENTIAL WELFARE SERVICES (1948 ACT): DUTIES

By means of directions issued under s.29, there is a general duty to arrange services for disabled people who are ordinarily resident within the area of the local authority. For disabled people who are not ordinarily resident, arranging these services is a power only (LAC(93)10, appendix 2). Ordinary residence is discussed in Chapter 14. The duty consists of:

- compiling and maintaining a register of disabled people
- providing a social work service and such advice and support as is needed for people at home or elsewhere
- providing, whether at centres or elsewhere, facilities for social rehabilitation and adjustment to disability including assistance in overcoming limitations of mobility or communication
- providing, either at centres or elsewhere, facilities for occupational, social, cultural and recreational activities – and, where appropriate, payments to persons for work they have done.

Although the directions do create a duty, the courts have held that it is of a target, general nature only. This means that in the event of non-provision of a service, it is likely to be difficult legally to enforce provision for any one individual. For instance, in one case the court stated that it would be impermissible to adjudicate on the s.29 target duty with reference to an individual case (*R v Islington LBC, ex p Rixon*; see also *R v Cornwall CC, ex p Goldsack*).

Walking assistance at a day centre. The court concluded that the walking assistance being given to a young disabled woman at a day centre was being provided under s.29 of the 1948 Act rather than under s.2 of the CSDPA 1970. It might have been provided under s.2 if it had been closely associated with meeting her recreational needs, but this was not so in the particular case (*R v Cornwall CC, ex p Goldsack*).

Even so, a number of local ombudsman investigations have concerned s.29 services and identified maladministration in relation to them, irrespective of the strength of duty:

Failure to provide social work services. In one investigation relating to support and advice given to people entering or resident in nursing homes before April 1993 (when social services departments assumed responsibility for nursing home funding), the local ombudsman stated that a social work service should in principle be available to 'all those living in their area', i.e. residents of private nursing homes should not be excluded (*Buckinghamshire CC 1992*).

In another, the ombudsman found maladministration because, in considering whether to provide social work support, the authority had not balanced the views of relevant professionals against the resources it had available (*Tower Hamlets LBC 1993*).

Failure to provide adequate advice. On more than one occasion the local ombudsman has found maladministration because of a failure on the part of local authority staff to provide directly – or at least to ensure provision of (e.g. by pointing people to other sources) – adequate advice about welfare benefits (e.g. *Stockton-on-Tees BC 1997; Wakefield MDC 1993*).

In one case, the ombudsman pointed out that either the council should offer adequate training to social workers to enable them to give proper advice, or it should instruct them to advise clients to obtain advice elsewhere (*Devon CC 1996*).

Social rehabilitation and adjustment to disability. A person with learning disabilities was placed in a residential home by the local authority. The authority provided, in addition, a support worker for 30 hours a week, in order to meet his developmental needs (under s.29 of the National Assistance Act 1948) by way of social rehabilitation and adjustment to disability. The amount of time allocated seemed reasonable to the ombudsman; however, the lack of precision in setting, working towards and recording the meeting of targets was maladministration (*Manchester CC 1993*).

11.1.1.1 Registration of disabled people

The duty to keep a register of disabled people under s.29 of the 1948 Act is one that has by and large not been rigorously carried out by local authorities. Nevertheless, in the case of partially sighted people, local authorities are sent a form known as the Certificate of Vision Impairment (CVI) 2003, signed by a consultant ophthalmologist (DH 2003f). This notification should then trigger registration of the person by the local authority; in turn the person is then eligible for certain benefits, for example a television licence. Also, such certification and registration means that the person is deemed to be disabled under the Disability Discrimination Act 1995 (SI 2003/712).

For hearing impairment, Department of Health guidance states that there is no formal examination procedure for determination, under s.29, as to whether a person is deaf or hard of hearing (LAC(93)10, appendix 4).

Department of Health guidance asks local authorities to keep registration data under three main headings: very severe handicap, severe or appreciable handicap and other persons (for example, people with a less severe heart or chest condition or with epilepsy). The first two of these categories are themselves further explained (LAC(93)10, appendix 4):

- **Very severe handicap** includes those who:
  ○ need help going to or using the WC practically every night. In addition, most of those in this group need to be fed or dressed or, if they can feed and/or dress themselves, they need a lot of help during the day with washing and WC, or are incontinent
  ○ need help with the WC during the night but not quite so much help with feeding, washing, dressing, or, while not needing night-time help with the WC, need a great deal of day-time help with feeding and/or washing and the WC
  ○ are permanently bedfast or confined to a chair and need help to get in and out, or are senile or mentally impaired, or are not able to care for themselves as far as normal everyday functions are concerned, but who do not need as much help as the above two categories.
- **Severe or appreciable handicap** includes those who:

- either have difficulty doing everything, or find most things difficult and some impossible
- find most things difficult, or three or four items difficult and some impossible
- can do a fair amount for themselves but have difficulty with some items, or have to have help with or two minor items.

11.1.2 NON-RESIDENTIAL WELFARE SERVICES (1948 ACT): POWERS

By means of approvals (as opposed to directions) issued by the Secretary of State under s.29, there is a power to arrange a further range of services for disabled people irrespective of whether they are ordinarily resident in the area or not (LAC(93)10, appendix 2). The services are:

- providing holiday homes
- providing free or subsidised travel for people who do not otherwise qualify for other travel concessions
- assisting a person to find accommodation which will enable him or her to take advantage of arrangements made under section 29
- contributing to the cost of employing a warden in warden-assisted housing, and to provide warden services in private housing
- informing people to whom s.29 relates about services available under that section
- giving instruction to people at home or elsewhere in methods of overcoming effects of their disabilities
- providing workshops where such people may engage in suitable work and for providing associated hostels
- providing suitable work in people's own homes or otherwise, and to help people dispose of the produce of their work.

The power to give instruction to people at home or elsewhere in relation to overcoming their disability is clearly a wide one. However, instruction is not the same as education. In *R v Further Education Funding Council, ex p Parkinson*, the court held, in its attempt to separate out the education and social services functions of the local authority, that instruction could not include a service that was 'purely educational'.

The House of Lords has in the past confirmed (in a rating valuation case) that s.29 could not authorise the arranging of residential accommodation (*Vandyk v Oliver (Valuation Officer)*).

11.1.3 DEFINITION OF DISABILITY

A basic condition of eligibility for the provision of non-residential welfare services under s.29 of the National Assistance Act 1948 (and under the Chronically Sick and Disabled Persons Act 1970, s.2) is that the person be disabled. Avoiding use of the words disabled or disability, the blunt language – which now seems anachronistic – states instead that a person must, in order to be eligible, be (a) blind, deaf, dumb; (b) have a permanent and substantial handicap through illness, injury or congenital deformity; or (c) have a mental disorder of any description.

The definition is elaborated upon in longstanding guidance. The approach advocated by the guidance, and by the government during the passing through Parliament of the NHS and Community Care Act 1990, appears to be a generally inclusive one. This should discourage local authorities from setting narrow definitions of disability in order to exclude people from eligibility for services. The definition applies also to the Disabled Persons (Services, Consultation and Representation) Act 1986, s.4, the Housing Grants, Construction and Regeneration Act 1996, and s.17 of the Children Act 1989.

First, Department of Health guidance points out that registration of disability is not a condition for provision of service. It is instead a question of whether or not the person is to be regarded as having a hearing, vision or speech impairment or is substantially and permanently handicapped by illness, injury or congenital deformity (LAC(93)10, appendix 4, para 5). It is about registerability not actual registration.

Second, for people with blindness or partial sight, the guidance refers to the established procedure of medical certification and local authority registration. For people with hearing impairment, it states that the 'deaf' category should include people who are deaf with speech, deaf without speech, or hard of hearing (that is, those who, with or without a hearing aid, have some useful hearing and whose normal method of communication is by speech, listening and lip-reading (LAC(93)10, appendix 4).

Third, the guidance states that it is not possible to give precise guidance on the interpretation of the phrase 'substantially and permanently handicapped'. However, it asks local authorities to give a wide interpretation to the term 'substantial', which should always 'take full account of individual circumstances'. With regard to the term 'permanent', it states that authorities would wish to interpret this 'sufficiently flexibly to ensure that they do not feel inhibited from giving help under s.29 in cases where they are uncertain of the likely duration of the condition'. However, the guidance does suggest registration categories and gives examples of 'very severe' and 'severe' handicap (LAC(93)10, appendix 4).

11.1.3.1 Categorising disabled people in practice

Despite the inclusive approach urged by the guidance, it appears that in practice some local authorities, faced with what they perceive to be excessive demand for services under the Chronically Sick and Disabled Persons Act 1970, are sometimes tempted to restrict what they mean by 'substantial handicap'. These authorities might, for instance, attempt to exclude certain groups of older people on the grounds that they might be frail, but that they are not disabled. It is then argued that those people are not eligible for services under s.29 of the National Assistance Act 1948 and s.2 of the Chronically Sick and Disabled Persons Act 1970. In which case, they might at best qualify for services for 'aged' or 'old' people under either the weaker duty contained in schedule 20 of the NHS Act 2006, or for services under the Health Services and Public Health Act 1968, which an authority has a power but no duty to provide.

However, such an approach carries the risk of discriminating against older people and being potentially unlawful, by implying that the effects of frailty and age do not 'count' as disability, even if the consequence is that those persons are in fact significantly disabled in daily life. Indeed, Department of Health guidance (LAC(93)10), providing examples of 'substantial handicap', refers to handicap in terms of function, not of condition or of age. And frailty would often be associated with an 'illness' such as arthritis (so as to bring it within the overall s.29 definition which refers to illness, injury or congenital deformity).

Alternatively, some local authorities may take 'permanent' to mean, strictly, for the rest of a person's life. Others, more generously, tend to draw on the definition of 'long term' in the Disability Discrimination Act 1995, and take disability likely to last longer than 12 months to be a 'permanent' disability. The interpretation of 'substantial and permanent handicap' appears never to have arisen directly in a legal case.

Local authorities also increasingly have to consider the question of obesity and whether it constitutes substantial and permanent handicap. It would appear that if obesity has arisen from illness or impairment resulting in disability – or alternatively has itself caused illness or impairment (which has then in turn resulted in disability) – then the person would come under the definition contained in s.29. However, if the obesity has not arisen from, or resulted in, illness or impairment, then it is unclear whether obese people would fall under s.29 and be eligible for assistance – for instance, if they were to approach the local authority asking for assistance simply because they have outgrown their living room chairs or their bath. Likewise there is some doubt about how obesity fits into the definition of disability in the Disability Discrimination Act 1995 (Doyle 2005, p.16).

11.1.3.2 Other definitions of disability
In addition to the term 'substantial and permanent handicap' under s.29 of the 1948 Act, related terms also apply under other legislation:

- The term 'handicapped' is one of the conditions governing community care services arranged under schedule 20 of the NHS Act 2006. There is a question as to whether this term (a condition for receipt of home help services or laundry facilities) is to be construed as including the whole class of so-called handicap (i.e. both mild and substantial) or only the mild. The correct construction is probably the former, inclusive of both mild and substantial disability.
- 'Disability' is one of the qualifying conditions for provision of residential or nursing home care under s.21 of the National Assistance Act 1948, where, however, it is not defined.
- The term 'illness' is used in s.3 of the NHS Act 2006 in respect of health care and in schedule 20 in respect of certain community care services. As defined in s.275 of the 2006 Act, it includes mental disorder (as defined in the Mental Health Act 1983), and 'disability' requiring medical or dental treatment or nursing.
- The definition applied by the 1948 Act should be distinguished from the definition in the Disability Discrimination Act 1995, although there are some similarities. The 1995 Act definition does not directly supplant the s.29 definition in the 1948 Act. Arguably though, to the extent that a local authority is using its discretion to interpret the s.29 definition, it could, or perhaps should, seek to utilise the 1995 Act definition.

11.1.4 PAYMENTS AND PROHIBITIONS
There are two particular prohibitions contained in s.29 of the 1948 Act.

11.1.4.1 Prohibition on payments
The payment of money to disabled people is prohibited (except in relation to workshops and provision of suitable work). However, the effect of this prohibition is now reduced in the light

of the existence of direct payments made under the Health and Social Care Act 2001 (see 13.1 below).

11.1.4.2 Anti-duplication provisions

Also prohibited is the provision under s.29 of any accommodation or services required to be provided under the NHS Act 2006. This latter provision has caused some confusion. For example, in one case it was argued that because home help could be provided by a local authority under schedule 8 of the NHS Act 1977 (predecessor to schedule 20 of the 2006 Act), it could therefore not be provided under the Chronically Sick and Disabled Persons Act 1970 (in the guise of practical assistance in the home). This would be because the 1970 Act was in effect an extension of s.29 of the 1948 Act. The judge rejected this, stating that what authorised services under s.2 of the 1970 Act was precisely s.2 of the 1970 Act – and not s.29 of the 1948 Act.

This decision may appear straightforward and pragmatic, but does not sit easily with the Court of Appeal's decision, in another context, that s.2 of the 1970 Act is not freestanding and is firmly hitched to s.29 (*R v Powys CC, ex p Hambidge*).

The term 'required to be provided' is suggestive of a duty. However, as far as NHS provision goes under the NHS Act 2006 as a whole, not many services are listed in the Act (medical, nursing, ambulance and services in relation to illness are explicitly referred to in s.3 of the Act). So it becomes difficult to discern what exactly is 'required' to be provided by the NHS under the 2006 Act.

It is clear that social services legislation is not capable of being used to provide registered nursing care, because this is legally prohibited. However, registered nursing care is limited to those services provided by a registered nurse and involving the provision, planning, supervision, or delegation of care – so long as the nature of the services and the circumstances of their provision are such that they need to be provided by a registered nurse (Health and Social Care Act 2001, s.49).

Other than registered nursing care, one way of pinpointing NHS, as opposed to social services, responsibilities might be to scrutinise relevant Department of Health directions and guidance. For instance, Department of Health guidance – on NHS continuing health care (see 18.3) and on NHS services in nursing homes (see 17.9), and in residential homes and people's own homes (see 17.10) – lists various services.

Sometimes it is unclear when a service should be regarded as health or social care, sometimes it is more straightforward. In a case concerning tracheostomy care for a child, the court concluded that such medically related care was inherently health care provision and beyond the power of a local social services authority to provide. It noted that 'the gravity of the consequences of a failure in care, the duration of the care need, which required her carer always to be present lest something had to be dealt with rapidly, underscores the medical rather than social service nature of the provision'. Otherwise, the obligations placed on social services would be far too broad (*R(T) v Haringey LBC*).

However, in another case about an anti-duplication provision (albeit in a different context), the court held an item could be regarded as either medical or non-medical, depending on the way in which it was being used:

Incontinence pads as non-medical items. The Social Fund (a social security agency) was prohibited, legally, from providing assistance with medical items. On the basis that incontinence pads were medical items provided by the NHS, a Social Fund officer had denied a 26-week supply of pads to a woman who was incontinent, arthritic and had asthma. The relevant health authority did provide free incontinence pads in principle, but in practice its criteria were so stringent – regular double incontinence or terminal illness – that the woman did not qualify. Hence her application to the Fund.

The judge found that the decision of the Social Fund officer, that the pads were medical items and thus excluded by the Social Fund rules, was wrong. She had asked whether the pads were needed for a medical problem and were thus necessarily a medical item. However, it was 'quite clear that a handkerchief might not be needed, but for a severe attack of a runny nose in a heavy cold. It is quite clear that a bowl might not be needed unless there was a medical problem of a severe bout of vomiting but nobody would think of those articles, the handkerchief or the bowl, as medical items' (*R v Social Fund Inspector, ex p Connick*).

On the same basis, the Social Fund has in the past assisted on occasion with powered wheelchairs, which would normally be regarded as the statutory responsibility of the NHS.

Whatever the answer, it is clear that local authorities argue all the more about divisions of responsibility when they are short of resources; and then tend to take decisions improperly, expediently and in a hurry, as the local ombudsman found:

Provision of psychotherapy services. The local authority had, from 1987, been making up the difference between the charges of a residential therapeutic community home and the DHSS (as it was then) funding available for a woman with mental health needs. When the placement came to an end, the authority agreed to fund psychotherapy sessions for the woman. The dispute arose around the authority's subsequent attempt to stop such funding, and its rather belated attempt to suggest that such provision was health, rather than social, care – and so was properly an NHS responsibility.

The local ombudsman concluded that whatever view the authority took in hindsight, it had obligations to the woman. Although it was entitled to reduce or stop the funding, it had to take into account the woman's needs as well, not focus solely on an overspent budget, and to make the 'promised assessment' of the benefit and value of the therapy. Had a proper review been carried out, the authority might have decided to stop the payments earlier than it did. However, the failure to carry out proper review and assessment meant that the authority made a sudden decision to withdraw without giving adequate notice.

Once the director of social services had decided that these were health rather than social care needs, no approach was made to the health authority about alternative sources of funding.

All of this was maladministration; the ombudsman recommended that the council pay the woman (a) the amount she owed to the psychotherapist for the sessions in 1993 that had not yet been paid for; (b) travel expenses; and (c) £1250 for distress caused and for the time and trouble in pursuing the complaint with both ombudsman and council (*Brent LBC 1994*).

Also suggestive of fluid statutory boundaries was the local ombudsman's doubt in one investigation, about whether the local authority social services department simply had no responsibility at all for the provision of powered wheelchairs under s.2 of the Chronically Sick and Disabled Persons Act 1970 (*North Yorkshire CC 1993*).

11.1.5 EMPLOYMENT OF AGENTS
For the purpose of arrangements for welfare services under s.29 of the 1948 Act, local authorities are empowered to employ, as agents, voluntary organisations or any other person carrying on, professionally or by way of trade or business, activities that consist of or include

the provision of such services. This is so long as the organisation or person in question appears to the local authority to be capable of providing the relevant services (National Assistance Act 1948, s.30).

The courts have held this provision to cover a local authority's agreement with, and payment of money to, a user independent trust – which would then apply the money to set up and implement a care package to meet a person's assessed needs (*R(A&B) v East Sussex CC*).

11.2 NON-RESIDENTIAL SERVICES FOR DISABLED PEOPLE: CHRONICALLY SICK AND DISABLED PERSONS ACT 1970, S.2

Under s.2 of the Chronically Sick and Disabled Persons Act 1970 (CSDPA), a local authority has a duty, if certain conditions are met, to arrange non-residential services for disabled people. The conditions are:

- that the local authority has functions under s.29 of the 1948 Act (see above)
- that the person is ordinarily resident in the authority's area
- that the person has a need
- that it is necessary, in order to meet that need, for the local authority to arrange services.

The section also states that, in carrying out its functions under s.2, a local authority must act under the general guidance of the Secretary of State issued under s.7(1) of the Local Authority Social Services Act 1970. The services are listed as follows:

- **practical assistance**: provision of practical assistance for the person in his or her home
- **recreation**: provision for the person of, or assistance to that person in obtaining, wireless, television, library or similar recreational facilities
- **recreation/education**: provision for the person of lectures, games, outings or other recreational facilities outside his home or assistance to that person in taking advantage of educational facilities available to him or her
- **travel**: provision for the person of facilities for, or assistance in, travelling to and from his home for the purpose of participating in any services provided under arrangements made by the authority under the said section 29 or, with the approval of the authority, in any services provided otherwise than as aforesaid which are similar to services which could be provided under such arrangements
- **adaptations and additional facilities**: provision of assistance for the person in arranging for the carrying out of any works of adaptation in his or her home or the provision of any additional facilities designed to secure his greater safety, comfort or convenience
- **holidays**: facilitating the taking of holidays by the person, whether at holiday homes or otherwise and whether provided under arrangements made by the authority or otherwise
- **meals**: provision of meals for that person whether in his home or elsewhere
- **telephone**: provision for that person of, or assistance to that person in obtaining, a telephone and any special equipment necessary to enable him to use a telephone.

11.2.1 STRONG DUTY TO MEET ASSESSED NEED UNDER THE CSDPA 1970

The duty to arrange services, in contrast to the duty in s.29 of the National Assistance Act 1948, has been held judicially to be strong and amenable to legal enforcement by an individual service user. The courts have held under s.2 of the CSDPA 1970 that, once a person is deemed to have an eligible need (see 6.10), then non-performance of the duty to meet that need will not be excused by a lack of resources (*R v Gloucestershire CC, ex p Barry*).

The reason for this strength of duty lies in the fact that s.2 of the 1970 Act refers to 'any person' and states that, once the local authority is satisfied that it is necessary to meet the need of that person, it must do so by providing any or all of the services listed.

11.2.2 NEED, NECESSITY AND THE LOCAL AUTHORITY'S RESOURCES

A number of matters concerning the assessment of a person's needs have already been covered in Chapter 6. In *R v Gloucestershire, ex p Barry*, one of the law lords held that a local authority could set a threshold of eligibility as to what is meant by *need*, in relation to the resources it had available. Another law lord took a different view, emphasising the relevance of resources to setting criteria in respect of the *necessity* to meet need (but not in respect of need itself). The latter approach is more in keeping with central government guidance on 'fair access to care' (LAC(2002)13: see 6.12). However, guidance issued in 1970 in association with the CSDPA 1970 stated that criteria of need were matters for authorities to determine in the light of resources (DHSS 12/70, para 7).

The courts have subsequently added that they would be slow to interfere with the level of strictness of an authority's threshold of eligibility under s.2 of the 1970 Act. This is because once the reasonableness of an authority's actions depends on a decision about the allocation of scarce resources, it becomes extremely difficult for the courts to review that decision by second-guessing the local authority about how it spends those resources (*R v East Sussex CC, ex p Tandy*). Nevertheless, the effect of this judgment, delivered before the implementation of the Human Rights Act 1998, would be tempered by human rights considerations – albeit in individual cases. For instance, if the severity of the criteria were such as to breach a person's article 3 right not to be subjected to inhuman or degrading treatment – or person's right to respect private life (including physical and psychological integrity) under article 8 – then the courts might feel obliged to interfere after all in an eligibility decision.

11.2.3 NECESSITY: RELEVANCE OF A PERSON'S OWN RESOURCES

This is discussed above (see 6.10.3).

11.2.4 NECESSITY: AVAILABILITY FROM OTHER SOURCES

If a person's needs could readily be met from other sources, then there would clearly not be a necessity for the local authority to meet the need. For instance, a need for home adaptations might be met by the local housing authority under the Housing Grants, Construction and Regeneration Act 1996, by means of a disabled facilities grant. However, failure of another statutory body to meet a person's assessed community care needs would not necessarily be an excuse for a local authority to do nothing. For instance, failure of the housing department to meet a disabled woman's essential needs for alternative accommodation under the Housing Act 1996 did not mean that the social services department could avoid meeting her assessed needs under the National Assistance Act 1948 (*R(Bernard) v Enfield LBC*).

11.2.5 CSDPA 1970: SERVICES

The range of services listed in s.2 of the CSDPA 1970 is extensive.

11.2.5.1 Practical assistance in the home

Practical assistance in the home is a broad term that could range from a small amount of home help each week, to full-scale personal assistance 24 hours a day. The major community care case of *R v Gloucestershire CC, ex p Barry* concerned the provision and withdrawal of such practical assistance. The need for local authorities to avoid acting unlawfully, for instance by ruling out, as a matter of policy, cleaning or shopping services, has been considered by the local ombudsman (see 6.12.5). In *R(Heffernan) v Sheffield CC*, the court held that, in the circumstances of the particular case, the local authority was obliged to provide such services. The Commission for Social Care Inspection has criticised heavily the exclusion of such services by local authorities (CSCI 2008).

11.2.5.2 Wireless, television, library or similar recreational facilities

In 1971, an example of a local authority deciding that it was not necessary to provide a radio was given in Parliament. A severely disabled man, using an environmental control system with an interface for a radio, wished to take an educational degree and required a radio. The local authority refused because he already had one; so he had, but he could not operate it because he was completely paralysed (*Hansard* 1971). The Department of Health has issued no guidance on the provision of radio or television.

Note. In Northern Ireland, following the passing of the Chronically Sick and Disabled Persons (Northern Ireland) Act 1978, the Department of Health and Social Services (DHSS) gave guidance on the provision of televisions by health and social services boards (HSSBs). The person had to be housebound and living alone, or confined to a room that meant that a television was needed in that particular room. As well as providing the sets, the licence fees of eligible applicants could also be paid (HSS(PH) 5/79). The Northern Ireland DHSS also issued guidance stating that HSSBs should provide batteries free of charge for people who had radio sets provided by the British Wireless Fund for the Blind (HSS(OS5A) 4/76).

11.2.5.3 Lectures, games, outings or similar recreational facilities

When a local authority ruled out, as a matter of policy, providing for a person's social, recreational and leisure needs, stating that he could arrange these for himself by approaching a local resource centre, the court found that it had acted unlawfully.

Not providing for social, recreational and leisure activities as a matter of policy. Following a reassessment, a man with multiple sclerosis received a letter from the local authority. It outlined the care plan, which would only cater for the man's personal needs; the letter explained that in relation to the man's social, recreational and leisure needs, he could approach a local resource centre himself. The authority was unable to meet these needs because it was not in a position 'to meet or address all the demands made [and so was] forced to make decisions upon prioritising need and working within existing resources'.

The judge held that it was 'impermissible to carry out the reassessment by putting social, recreation and leisure needs on one side and saying, "I would be happy to provide you with details of the Winkfield Road Resource Centre." The care package that should have been assessed...had to be a multi-faceted package. This Applicant has been able to overcome or at least live with some of the most awful characteristics of his illness by the social intercourse achieved in recreational facilities such as the playing of bridge, swimming, etc. A reassessed care package should have comprehended such matters and should not have discriminated in the manner that it did' (*R v Haringey LBC, ex p Norton*).

In another court case, a local authority had similarly failed to meet a person's recreational needs:

Failure to meet recreational needs of person. The case concerned a 25-year-old man who suffered from Seckels syndrome and who was blind, microcephalic, virtually immobile, doubly incontinent and mostly unable to communicate. He also suffered from severe deformities of the chest and spine, a hiatus hernia and a permanent digestive disorder. His weight and size were those of a small child, his dependency that of a baby. The dispute concerned the provision for his social, recreational and educational needs; having left a special needs school, the applicant had requirements which the local authority could not meet because, it pleaded, it was short of resources.

The judge found that the local authority had failed to provide for the person's recreational needs under s.2 of the Chronically Sick and Disabled Persons Act. The duty under the Act was 'owed to the applicant personally' to provide 'recreational facilities outside the home to an extent which Islington accepts is greater than the care plan provides for. But the authority has, it appears, simply taken the existing unavailability of further facilities as an insuperable obstacle to any further attempt to make provision. The lack of a day centre has been treated, however reluctantly, as a complete answer to the question of provision' (*R v Islington LBC, ex p Rixon*).

The local ombudsman, too, has found local authorities improperly excluding consideration of a person's recreational needs (*Southwark LBC 2001*).

11.2.5.4 Taking advantage of educational facilities

Taking advantage of educational facilities, under s.2 of the CSDPA 1970, has been held by the courts not to include actually making arrangements for the provision of education – but merely the taking advantage of what is already potentially available (*R v Further Education Funding Council, ex p Parkinson*). This very point was made in guidance issued in 1970 (DHSS 12/70, para 7). Likewise, in the *Parkinson* case, the court stated that the power under s.29 of the National Assistance Act 1948 to give instruction to disabled people in their own homes could not be read into the duty regarding educational facilities in s.2(1)(b) of the 1970 Act.

Department of Health guidance has stated that such assistance could cover, for instance, personal care that might be required to assist a person study. This might be in addition to any educational disabled student allowance that a person might already be receiving (LAC(93)12, paras 9–10). The following local ombudsman investigation illustrates the potential difficulty surrounding the meeting of a person's education-related needs – in this case a communication aid:

Loss of college placement for want of a communication aid. A young person with moderate learning difficulties, poor fine and gross coordination and some mobility problems had the use of a communication aid at school from the age of six years onward. He subsequently had a 'light-writer', with a lightweight keyboard, a voice synthesizer and two-sided visual display. The cost of such an item was £2000 plus VAT. On leaving school, he was accepted on a course at a post-16 further education college. The education authority allowed him to keep the communication aid for a few months, but then stated that it must be returned. Funding was sought to no avail from the general practitioner, the health authority and the Further Education Funding Council (since superseded by the Learning and

Skills Council). The local authority stated that its duty extended only to giving advice on sources of funding, and that the CSDPA 1970 was never intended to be used for such aids.

However, without the aid, the young person would lose his place on the college course; he felt he had 'lost his voice'. Eventually, the local authority agreed to loan a communication aid under the Children Act 1989. The ombudsman concluded that communication aids fell within a 'grey area', and that central and local government needed to produce a clear, unambiguous statement of responsibilities (*Kingston upon Hull C 2000*).

In the above case, the ombudsman appears to have accepted that the local authority social services had no potential duty to provide such equipment. Nevertheless, this conclusion is questionable, given the reference in s.2 to assistance in relation to education, the absolute duty to meet eligible need – and more recently the reference in Department of Health guidance on eligibility criteria to 'vital involvement in education' (LAC(2002)13). If the assistance under s.2 might include personal assistance (as stated in guidance: LAC(93)12, paras 9–10), why not equipment?

11.2.5.5 Assistance in arranging for the carrying out of any works of adaptation

The duty to make arrangements in relation to home adaptations is qualified by a lengthy and tortuous chain of wording: '…making arrangements for the provision of assistance for that person in arranging the carrying out of adaptations'. This suggests to some local authorities that direct provision is not contemplated.

The correct view would seem to be that in some circumstances an arm's-length approach might legitimately be taken, but if the need cannot be met in any other way then the local authority is probably committed to some form of direct arrangement – always assuming that the applicant has surmounted both the need and necessity tests: see above. This view would also be consonant with the judicial approach taken to the word 'facilitate' in the context of holidays (see immediately below).

For a full discussion of this social services obligation, see section 16.9.

11.2.5.6 Additional facilities for greater safety, comfort or convenience

The term 'additional facilities' is a broad one and covers, amongst other things, the wide range of daily living equipment that local authorities provide. The purpose for which such facilities might be provided is also broad, since not just safety, but also comfort and convenience are referred to. Local authorities might be tempted to focus only on safety and regard comfort and convenience as surplus – but they should beware not to cut words out of the legislation. They may nonetheless attempt to construe a term such as convenience narrowly:

Safety, comfort or convenience. In one case, the local ombudsman referred not only to the potential danger, but also to the 'extreme discomfort' and the 'inconvenient' accommodation, in which a disabled woman had to live – whilst waiting four years and eight months for the simple aids that eventually made such a difference to her life (*Hackney LBC 1992*).

On the other hand, an authority might maintain that its priorities or criteria conform, albeit strictly, to the statutory wording by referring to safety in terms of 'personal danger' and to convenience as the absence of 'serious inconvenience' (*Sheffield CC 1995*).

11.2.5.7 Facilitating the taking of holidays

The provision of holidays has been examined in several court and local ombudsman cases:

Unlawful refusal to assist with privately arranged holidays. The local authority had – in order to save money – adopted a blanket policy of only providing assistance with holidays which it had arranged itself. The judge found this blanket policy to be 'quite wrong', since the legislation expressly contemplated that authorities might assist with holidays 'otherwise arranged'. The local authority's policy had prevented it asking the question of whether the person's needs were such that they required to be met through a privately arranged holiday (*R v Ealing LBC, ex p Leaman*).

Unlawful refusal to assist fully with a holiday. The local authority argued in court that its role under s.2 of the CSDPA 1970 was not to relieve poverty, and that it would only assist with the extra costs (such as special accommodation or transport expenses) of a disabled person's holiday arising because of disability – in other words, not with the ordinary travel and hotel expenses which everybody has to pay when they go on holiday. It also argued that the term 'facilitate' precluded it from paying for the full cost. The judge found that the policy fettered the local authority's discretion and was not consistent with the wording of the legislation (*R v North Yorkshire CC, ex p Hargreaves (no.2)*).

Inadequate arrangements for holiday: maladministration. A complaint was made to the local ombudsman; a local authority had been assisting an older woman with learning disabilities to take a holiday. She arrived at the hotel, but such serious problems arose in relation to her behaviour that the hotel owners drove her home again that same evening (a distance of 115 miles). The council complained to the local tourist information centre and the English Tourist Board, and wanted the money for the holiday refunded by the hotel both to itself and to the woman. However, the hotel owners consulted a solicitor and themselves demanded an apology and compensation.

The local ombudsman concluded – from the 'total absence' of records about how the hotel was identified and about the taking up of references – that the 'proper degree of care' in arranging the holiday had not been exercised. The hotel owners had not been given the 'full and accurate information', about the needs of the woman, to which they had been entitled. This was all maladministration, as was the precipitate complaint to the tourist organisations before the hotel owners had had the opportunity to put their case (*Buckinghamshire CC 1998*).

11.2.5.8 Telephones and related equipment

The Department of Health has issued no guidance on the provision of telephones and related equipment. Their provision has sometimes been subject to inappropriate application of policies and criteria, as in the following local ombudsman case:

Minicom telephone equipment: unduly restrictive policy. A local authority was restricting provision of Minicoms (telephone equipment for deaf or hearing impaired people) to people who already had a telephone; the local ombudsman agreed with the British Deaf Association that this criterion was a legally irrelevant consideration (*Wakefield MDC 1992*).

Withdrawal of telephone line rental payments from 1000 people: maladministration. The local authority decided in 1994 to pay telephone rental charges for the complainant. In 1996, it decided not to pay them for new applicants. In 1999, as part of the 'budget making process', it ceased to pay the charges even for the existing 1000 or so recipients. Although minuted, no written report was presented to the social services committee, which took the decision. The council argued that it had received legal advice that such payments were unlawful; however, it refused to provide the ombudsman with a copy of the advice and to identify who gave the advice. It referred to s.29(6) of the National Assistance Act 1948, which prohibits cash payments. Subsequent legal advice from leading counsel stated that the original advice was wrong.

The ombudsman declined to express a view on the correctness of either set of legal advice. However, he found maladministration of a fairly serious nature because (a) the decision to withdraw the payments implied that many other councils, and Haringey up to that time, had been acting unlawfully; (b) therefore, a clear written report backed up by considered opinion was required; (c) in reality the decision seemed to have been taken without any proper consideration by the committee (*Haringey LBC 2000*).

Note. In 1971, the Association of County Councils (ACC) and Association of Metropolitan Authorities (AMA) – now both part of the Local Government Association (LGA) – issued a joint Circular (note: not a government Circular). In summary, people would qualify if, in the view of an authority, they lived alone, or were frequently alone – or lived with a person who was unable, or could not be relied on, to deal with an emergency or maintain necessary outside contacts. In addition to this, the person either (a) would have a need to get in touch with a doctor, other health worker or helper and would be in danger or at risk without a telephone; or (b) be unable to leave the dwelling in normal weather without assistance or have seriously restricted mobility – and need a telephone to avoid isolation. Also, there should be no friend or neighbours willing and able to help (ACC, AMA 1971). Guidance on telephones was issued in Scotland and Northern Ireland and contained similar criteria to the AMA/ACC guidance (SW7/1972; HSS(OS5A)5/78).

11.2.6 CSDPA 1970 LINK TO S.29 OF NATIONAL ASSISTANCE ACT 1948

The reference in s.2 of the 1970 Act, to the exercising of functions under s.29 of the National Assistance Act 1948, has given rise to dispute in the law courts. This is not just a theoretical matter, since it has focused on, for instance, (a) whether CSDPA services are legally 'community care services' at all under s.46 of the NHS and Community Care Act 1990; and (b) whether local authorities are empowered to charge for CSDPA services under s.17 of the Health and Services and Social Security Adjudications Act 1983.

The problem is that s.2 of the CSDPA 1970 is not listed in the 1990 and 1983 Acts at the relevant place; and if s.2 were to be regarded as freestanding and not embraced by s.29 of the National Assistance Act 1948, then services under s.2 could be neither community care services nor capable of being charged for.

In fact, the Court of Appeal ruled in 1998 that s.2 of the CSDPA 1970 is not freestanding (*R v Powys CC, ex p Hambidge* about charges). This confirmed the High Court ruling in the same case, another Court of Appeal judgment of nearly 20 years before (*Wyatt v Hillingdon LBC*), and the House of Lords finding that s.2 of the 1970 Act was clearly embodied in the whole of the community care regime (*R v Gloucestershire CC, ex p Barry*).

11.2.7 MAKING ARRANGEMENTS FOR SERVICES

The term, 'make arrangements', does not mean that a local authority must itself make direct provision under s.2. The National Assistance Act 1948, s.30 authorises the employment by local authorities of agents to deliver services, in the form of voluntary organisations or any other person carrying on, professionally or by way of trade or business.

11.2.8 INFORMATION FOR INDIVIDUAL DISABLED PEOPLE: CSDPA 1970, S.1

Local authorities have a specific duty under s.1 of the CSDPA 1970 to inform existing service users about other services which the authority thinks relevant and which it knows about. This is a strong duty that a local authority has towards individual people, not just a general duty. Failure to provide this information might give clear grounds for challenge, although even this duty is qualified since it depends on the authority's opinion about other relevant services and on its having particulars of those other services.

Nevertheless, the local ombudsman does sometimes find maladministration in relation to the giving of information by local authorities in specific instances – for example, poor advice about social security benefits, or unclear information about disabled facilities grants.

Provision of information. The local ombudsman has on occasion considered provision of information under s.1 of the CSDPA 1970, finding maladministration when inaccurate advice is given, for example about entitlement to state benefits (*East Sussex CC 1995*), or when a social services authority fails to discuss the possibility of home adaptations available through a housing authority with a disabled person (*Leicester CC 1992a*). However, in another case, there was no maladministration in respect of information provision. First the complainant had been given a range of leaflets in response to his request for information. Then, following a complaint the man had made, a council officer visited him to go through the relevant legislation and to leave copies with him (*North Yorkshire CC 1993*).

11.3 NON-RESIDENTIAL SERVICES FOR OLDER PEOPLE: HEALTH SERVICES AND PUBLIC HEALTH ACT 1968, S.45

Under s.45 of the Health Services and Public Health Act 1968, local authorities may (if approved by the Secretary of State) and must (if directed by the Secretary of State) make arrangements for promoting the welfare of old people. The Secretary of State has only ever approved, and never directed, the making of arrangements by local authorities for the following services (DHSS 19/71: approvals):

- **meals and recreation**: to provide meals and recreation in the home and elsewhere
- **information**: to inform the elderly of services available to them and to identify elderly people in need of services
- **travel**: to provide facilities or assistance in travelling to and from the home for the purpose of participating in services provided by the authority or similar services
- **finding accommodation**: to assist in finding suitable households for boarding elderly persons
- **visiting and advice**: to provide visiting and advisory services and social work support
- **practical assistance, adaptations, additional facilities**: to provide practical assistance in the home including assistance in the carrying out of works of adaptation or the provision of any additional facilities designed to secure greater safety, comfort or convenience
- **wardens**: to contribute to the cost of employing a warden on welfare functions in warden assisted housing schemes and to provide warden services for occupiers of private housing.

This list represents a wide range of services and assistance that local authorities may, but are not obliged to, provide for older people. Department of Health guidance states that the purpose of s.45 is to enable authorities to make other approved arrangements for services to the elderly who are not substantially and permanently handicapped. This would promote the welfare of the elderly generally and so far as possible prevent or postpone personal or social deterioration or breakdown (DHSS 19/71, para 2). It refers to home help, including laundry services and other aids to independent living, social visiting organised and coordinated by the local authority but largely undertaken by voluntary workers and Meals on Wheels (para 10).

11.3.1 SERVICES FOR OLDER PEOPLE: POWER ONLY

Section 45 of the 1968 Act gives central government the ability to issue directions and thereby turn these services into a duty, or to issue approvals that would confer a power rather than duty. No government, over the past 40 years, has issued directions and thereby created a duty. Instead the approvals issued in 1971 have made the provision of these services a mere power.

It is possible that if, in developing its community care policies and services, a local authority could be shown not even to have taken account of the approvals and guidance in respect of s.45, then a case might be arguable in the law courts. Even in respect of a power, local authorities should not fetter their discretion by failing to consider how and when that power should be exercised (*British Oxygen v Board of Trade*).

Exercise of the power is not restricted to those elderly people ordinarily resident in the area of a local authority; and the power is capable of being used creatively. For instance, it might be relevant where local authorities extend adult protection activity to vulnerable older people generally. In 1993, the Social Services Inspectorate suggested in its report, *No longer afraid*, that the 1968 Act would be a key statute for preventative strategies in respect of the abuse of older people (SSI 1993, p.5).

11.3.2 EMPLOYMENT OF AGENTS

For the purpose of arrangements for welfare services under s.45 of the 1968 Act, local authorities are empowered to employ, as agents, voluntary organisations or any other person carrying on, professionally or by way of trade or business, activities that consist of or include the provision of services for old people. This is so long as the organisation or person in question appears capable of providing the service to which the arrangements apply (s.45).

11.3.3 PROHIBITIONS

There is an anti-duplication provision in s.45 of the 1968 Act that precludes the making available of any accommodation or services required to be provided under the NHS Act 2006 (see 11.1.4 above) for discussion of such a provision. Likewise there is a prohibition on the making of cash payments: but this prohibition is tempered by the provisions for making direct payments under the Health and Social Care Act 2001 (see 13.1).

11.4 NON-RESIDENTIAL SERVICES: NHS ACT 2006, S.254, SCHEDULE 20

Local authorities may (if the Secretary of State approves) or must (if the Secretary of State directs) make arrangements for various non-residential services (NHS Act 2006, s.254 and schedule 20). These services relate to expectant and nursing mothers; and to the prevention of illness, the care of people who are suffering from illness and the aftercare of people who have been so suffering. In addition there is a general duty to provide home help services and a corresponding power to provide laundry facilities.

Provision is subject to s.3 of the NHS Act 2006, under which the NHS has functions in relation to such services; in other words, this would appear to be an anti-duplication provision, such that schedule 20 social care provision should not duplicate health care provision by the NHS under s.3. There is no ordinary residence condition stipulated. Illness is defined as including 'mental disorder within the meaning of the Mental Health Act 1983 and any injury or disability requiring medical or dental treatment or nursing' (NHS Act 2006, s.275).

11.4.1 NON-RESIDENTIAL SERVICES FOR ILLNESS AND MENTAL DISORDER

A major part of schedule 20 of the NHS Act 2006 deals with non-residential services for the prevention of illness, the care of people who are ill, the aftercare of people who have been ill – including specific duties towards people with a mental disorder. Both directions and approvals have been made in respect of these services; the directions relate only to illness in the form of mental disorder; the approvals refer simply to illness and so are not confined to mental disorder.

11.4.1.1 Directions: illness, mental disorder

By means of directions issued in respect of schedule 20, there is a general duty to arrange various non-residential services for people with a mental disorder (LAC(93)10, appendix 3). The duty includes:

- the provision of centres (including training centres and day centres) for the training or occupation of such people
- the exercise of their functions towards people received into guardianship under Part 2 or 3 of the Mental Health Act 1983
- the provision of social work and related services to help in the identification, diagnosis, assessment and social treatment of mental disorder and provide social work support and other domiciliary and care services to people living in their homes or elsewhere.

However, because these services appear to be covered only by a general, target, rather than a specific, duty, it is likely that legally enforcing provision for any one individual would be difficult.

11.4.1.2 Approvals: illness generally

By means of approvals issued under schedule 20, there is a power to arrange a further range of services in respect of illness. The services comprise arrangements for the provision of:

- centres or other facilities for training or keeping people suitably occupied, to equip and maintain such centres, and for the provision for those people of ancillary or supplemental services
- meals at centres and at other facilities, and Meals on Wheels for housebound people (not already provided for under s.45 of the Health Services and Public Health Act 1968, or schedule 9 of the Health and Social Security Adjudications Act 1983)
- the remuneration of people engaged in suitable work at centres or at other facilities
- social services (including advice and support) in order to prevent the impairment of physical or mental health of adults in families where such impairment is likely, or to prevent the break-up of such families, or for assisting in their rehabilitation
- night sitter services
- recuperative holidays

- facilities for social and recreational activities
- services specifically for alcoholic or drug-dependent people.

11.4.2 HOME HELP AND LAUNDRY FACILITIES

Local authorities have a general duty to arrange, on a scale adequate for their area, home help
– and a power to provide or arrange laundry facilities – for households where it is required
because there is somebody who is ill, lying in, an expectant mother, or is aged or handicapped
as a result of having suffered from illness or congenital deformity. The power to arrange the
laundry facilities is dependent on the household either receiving, or being eligible to receive,
the home help (NHS Act 2006, s.254, schedule 20).

Assistance is for the household, suggesting that it could be made for other members of
the household, not just the disabled, aged or ill person. The duty is probably to be regarded as
a general, target one and therefore difficult to enforce in individual cases (see section 5.1).

11.4.3 SERVICES FOR EXPECTANT OR NURSING MOTHERS

Through approvals made under schedule 20 of the 2006 Act, local authorities have the power
to make arrangements for the care of expectant and nursing mothers, other than for residential accommodation.

11.5 MENTAL HEALTH AFTERCARE SERVICES: S.117 MENTAL HEALTH ACT 1983

NHS primary care trusts or health authorities, and local social services authorities – in cooperation with voluntary organisations – have a duty to provide aftercare services, when certain
categories of patient detained in hospital under the Mental Health Act 1983 are discharged
from hospital. The duty also applies to those patients on leaving hospital, even if they had
previously ceased to be detained, but who had remained in hospital for a while as informal
patients.

This duty persists until the primary care trust or health authority and the local authority
are satisfied that such services are no longer required (Mental Health Act 1983, s.117).

11.5.1 ENTITLEMENT TO AFTERCARE SERVICES

The people covered by s.117 are those who have been detained under the 1983 Act, under s.3
(treatment), s.37 (convicted offenders with hospital or guardianship orders), or s.47 and s.48
(prisoners – serving a sentence, on remand, civil prisoners, people detained under the Immigration Act 1971 – for whom a transfer direction has been made). Aftercare services under
s.117 do not apply to informal mental health patients. However, they have been held to apply
to a person granted leave of absence under s.17 of the 1983 Act – and to a person who has
been transferred into guardianship (via s.19 of the 1983 Act), having originally been
detained under s.3 (*R v Manchester CC, ex p Stennett*: High Court).

11.5.2 RESPONSIBLE AUTHORITIES FOR AFTERCARE SERVICES

The responsible primary care trust, health authority and local authority are those for the area
in which the person is resident or for the area to which he or she is sent on discharge (s.117).

This has been taken by the courts to mean that the responsible bodies are those where the person was resident at the time of detention. However, if there was no (ascertainable) place of residence at the time of detention, then the responsibility would lie with those relevant bodies in the area to which he or she is discharged under s.117 (*R v Mental Health Review Tribunal, ex p Hall*; High Court stage). Thus in the following local ombudsman case, involving three different local authorities, it was the original local authority which retained responsibility – despite the fact that the man and his advisers had at one point determined the aftercare with the original local authority uninvolved:

Three local authorities involved: original retaining responsibility; chain not broken by service user's choice of aftercare facility. A man was detained in hospital under s.3 of the Mental Health Act 1983. He was discharged to a specialist rehabilitation unit outside of his area (local authority A) in the area of a second local authority (B). He was then placed by the rehabilitation unit in accommodation in local authority C. The ombudsman held that as he had been resident in local authority A prior to his detention, it was local authority A that retained responsibility for funding aftercare services.

Local authority A had argued that because the man and his advisers had chosen the rehabilitation unit, and the authority had not done so, its duties were discharged at that point – meaning that he had in effect voluntarily taken up residence in local authority C which should therefore be responsible. The ombudsman was not convinced. First, local authority A had failed to involve itself at the time of the discharge; it did not attend the relevant meeting and its contribution was therefore both 'limited and ill-informed'. Furthermore, even had it attended, the ombudsman saw no reason to suppose the outcome would have been any different; there was no specialist facility in local authority's A's area and the facility chosen in local authority B was an appropriate placement. Worse, local authority A's social worker had, at the time of discharge, doubted that the authority could help him, because of his financial resources. The ombudsman pointed out that this was 'irrelevant' to the question of eligibility for s.117 services (*Wigan MBC* 2008).

11.5.3 AFTERCARE UNDER SUPERVISION

`Aftercare under supervision' orders, made under ss.25A-25J of the Mental Health Act 1983, are due to cease to exist from November 2008; the repeal of these sections of the 1983 Act is through the amending Mental Health Act 2007.

11.5.4 SETTING UP AFTERCARE SERVICES

The Mental Health Act Code of Practice states that in establishing a care plan for aftercare, a number of people should be involved. These may include the responsible clinician, nurses and other professionals involved in caring for the patient in hospital, a clinical psychologist, community mental health nurse and other members of the community team, the patient's GP and primary care team, (subject to the patient's views) any carer who will be involved in looking after them outside hospital, the patient's nearest relative or other family members, a representative of any relevant voluntary organisation, the Probation Service, a housing authority representative, an employment expert, an independent mental health advocate, an independent mental capacity advocate, the patient's attorney or deputy, any other representative nominated by the patient (DH 2008c, para 27.12).

The Code states that a thorough assessment is likely to involve consideration of continuing mental healthcare, the psychological needs of the patient (and of family and carers), physical healthcare, daytime activities or employment, appropriate accommodation, risks and safety issues, specific needs arising (from e.g. co-existing physical disability, sensory impairment, learning disability or autistic spectrum disorder, drugs, alcohol or substance misuse), any parenting or caring needs, social and cultural and spiritual needs, counselling and personal support , assistance with welfare rights and managing finances, involvement of authorities and agencies in a different area (if the patient is not going to live locally), involvement of other agencies including the Probation Service or voluntary organisations, the conditions (for a restricted patient) which the Secretary of State for Justice or the Tribunal has imposed or is likely to impose on a conditional discharge, contingency plans (should the patient's mental health deteriorate), and crisis contact details (DH 2008c, para 27.13).

11.5.4.1 Setting up services before discharge

In one case, the courts found that the local authority and health authority were obliged to complete a multi-disciplinary assessment before a mental health review tribunal hearing (*R v Mental Health Review Tribunal, ex p Hall*). Subsequently, this has been held not to be a legal requirement, although there would be nothing to stop those authorities making plans before a tribunal sat if they wished (*R(W) v Doncaster MBC*).

Thus, no express duty arises under s.117 until discharge takes place. There is a power for the local authority and health authority to take preparatory steps, but this does not extend to an obligation to monitor the condition of the patient before the discharge decision. The local authority, under s.47 of the NHS and Community Care Act 1990, would come under a duty to assess in the case of a deferred conditional discharge. Nevertheless, it cannot appear to the authority that the person in is in need, which is the trigger for assessment under s.47, until it knows of that need (*R(B) v Camden LBC*).

11.5.5 RANGE OF AFTERCARE SERVICES

Services under s.117 are effectively undefined and comprise both residential and non-residential provision. The Mental Health Act Code of Practice lists the following non-exhaustively: daytime activities or employment, appropriate accommodation, outpatient treatment, counselling and personal support, assistance with welfare rights and managing finances (DH 2008c, para 27.13). The courts have confirmed that such services are provided under s.117 itself, and that s.117 is not merely a gateway to the services contained in other community care legislation (*R v Manchester CC, ex p Stennett*).

11.5.6 STRENGTH OF DUTY TO PROVIDE AFTERCARE SERVICES

In 1993, the courts interpreted s.117 of the Mental Health Act as placing a strong duty on health authorities and local authorities – contrasting it with the less specific duty in relation to aftercare owed by the health authority under s.3 of the NHS Act 1977 (*R v Ealing DHA, ex p Fox*). By the same token, the duty placed by s.117 on local authority social services departments is likewise a stronger duty (towards individuals) than the general duty to provide aftercare for mentally disordered people under schedule 254 of the NHS Act 2006.

Even so, it should be noted that although the court in the *Fox* case emphasised the strength of the s.117 duty, it also seemed deliberately to exclude from the ambit of its judgment the situation where authorities plead lack of resources for non-performance of duty. The strength of the duty was subsequently referred to in a later case, when the courts stated that s.117 did not constitute an absolute duty, but merely a duty to exercise best endeavours (*R(IH) v Secretary of State*). In an earlier case, the courts had referred to reasonable endeavours (*R(K) v Camden and Islington Health Authority*).

Local authority failing to find hostel under s.117. The patient suffered from schizophrenia and had a long history of mental illness. In 1994 he had stabbed at a woman with a knife. He was hospitalised under ss.37 and 41 of the Mental Health Act 1983. By 2000, he had improved dramatically. A mental health review tribunal recommended his discharge on condition that he receive psychiatric treatment and supervision from a social worker, and that he live at appropriate accommodation approved by both doctor and social worker. The local authority faced 'perfectly genuine difficulties'. These related to professional concerns about a proposed placement, lack of necessary staff at the placement, lack of support for the placement by the treating psychiatrist, other suitable placements not being identified. The man was therefore not discharged over a certain period. He argued that the local authority had breached s.117 of the 1983 Act, as well as breaching article 5 of the European Convention by committing the tort of false imprisonment amounting to a deprivation of liberty.

The court rejected the claim, pointing out that the s.117 duty was to use best or reasonable endeavours only. It pointed out that there was neither a bottomless pit of funds nor an adequate supply of suitable accommodation and support in relation to difficult cases. Local authorities and health authorities had to do the best they could; the former faced particular difficulties in finding out-of-area placements (*R(W) v Doncaster MBC*).

The Court of Appeal has also pointed out that s.117 imposes a duty to provide aftercare facilities, but that the nature and extent of those facilities would to a degree fall within the discretion of the health authority, which must have regard to other demands on its budget (*R(K) v Camden and Islington Health Authority*). Thus, 'it is unrealistic and wrong to require section 117 authorities to act without exploring funding issues. Resources are limited, and any authority is entitled to consider whether a suggested placement would involve an efficient use of resources and therefore whether there is a possibility of that placement being funded by central government [in this case, through Supporting People money rather than the social services budget] or by another authority' (*R(B) v Camden LBC*).

In summary, these cases probably bring the s.117 duty roughly into line with the other strong community care duties – s.2 of the CSDPA 1970 and s.21 of the National Assistance Act 1948 (see sections 6.10 and 9.1). That is, finance alone would not be a defence for non-performance of the duty, but financial resources can lawfully be a factor as to how (but not whether) to provide aftercare services. Genuine practical difficulties, as is the case with the other community care duties, will also be a defence for non-performance of the duty.

11.5.7 ENDING PROVISION OF AFTERCARE SERVICES

The legal requirement not to charge for s.117 services (see below) means that there is sometimes an incentive for a local authority to discharge the person from his or her s.117 status, but nevertheless to continue to provide services for the person through other legislation under which charges can be made. Nevertheless, it is clear from local government ombudsman investigations and judicial comments in a legal case that caution is required.

First, the decision to discharge s.117 is a joint one. It arguably cannot be made unilaterally. Therefore a local authority would be acting erroneously if it were to base its decision solely on what the NHS stated, since it must make its own decision as a social services authority. This was the reasoning of the local ombudsman:

Social services decision-making. A local authority decided to discharge s.117 services in the case of a woman in a residential care home, even though she was to continue to live in a specialist care home for elderly, mentally infirm people. The council had argued that the decision was a medical one, and it had followed the NHS decision to withdraw. This was maladministration because the local authority had a responsibility to come to its own decision (*Clwyd CC 1997*).

Second, local authorities have in the past sometimes taken the view that s.117 could be discharged if the service user has become stable in the community and is unlikely to require readmission to hospital. Taken alone and as a decisive indicator, this would appear to be a suspect ground, because the fact that the aftercare services are meeting the need does not mean they are no longer required. If anything, the opposite conclusion beckons. Furthermore, the courts have stated that so long as a person's mental disorder persists, then so too must the s.117 services.

Discharging s.117 provision of services. The court explained in one case that, on the person leaving hospital, following s.3 detention under the Mental Health Act 1983, the local authority would owe a duty under s.117. It considered that there might be cases where accommodation would no longer be required for a person's mental health condition (under s.117), but still be needed for physical disabilities (under s.21 of the National Assistance Act 1948). In this situation the person could then be charged for services under the 1948 Act. However, the court stated that in the case of a person with dementia, it was difficult to see how such a situation could arise in practice (*R v Manchester CC, ex p Stennett*, High Court).

The local ombudsman has come to a similar conclusion:

Discharge of s.117, despite worsening dementia. A local authority decided to discharge s.117 services in the case of a woman in a residential care home, even though she was to continue to live in a specialist care home for elderly, mentally infirm people. This would enable the local authority to charge her under the National Assistance Act 1948. Nevertheless, at the time of the discharge she was assessed; her dementia was getting worse, she was extremely paranoid and suffered from hallucinations. The discharge therefore was maladministration (*Clwyd CC 1997*).

More recently, the local ombudsman referred directly to the *Stennett* case in an investigation concerning a woman whose care home placement was initially funded under s.117. However, following a review, the s.117 basis was withdrawn and it was decided she would have instead to pay for her placement under the 1948 Act. The ombudsman roundly rejected the stability or 'settled' argument:

Local authority trying to avoid its public responsibilities by removing care homes from the definition of aftercare services. The ombudsman considered that 'to remove those costs [of the care home] from aftercare would only be appropriate where the services of the residential home were no longer needed. It is my understanding that those services are still required and that if they were withdrawn then Mrs. Fletcher would be at risk of admission to hospital… Whether or not a person is 'settled in a nursing or residential home' is an irrelevant consideration. They key question must be, would removal of this person (settled or not) from this nursing or residential home mean that she is at risk of readmission to hospital. If the answer is yes then the person cannot be discharged from aftercare.'

The ombudsman went on to indicate the logical conclusion of the council's approach: 'the practical effect of the council's criteria is to remove long term nursing or residential home accommodation from the definition of aftercare services. If that were to remain the position, the council's criteria would allow it to avoid its public responsibilities under section 117' (Bath and North East Somerset Council 2007).

The local ombudsmen have thus underlined that local authorities cannot casually re-categorise services being provided under s. 117 as suddenly coming under other community care legislation, with a view to imposing financial charges (which are barred under s.117). They have therefore criticised local authorities for attempting to discharge s.117 in retrospect, in order to justify charging, and at the same time failing to perform a proper review and to consult the person and his or her carer in accordance with Department of Health guidance (HSC 2000/3) and with the Mental Health Act Code of Practice.

Retrospective discharge of s.117. A woman was detained under s.3 of the Mental Health Act 1983; she was discharged to a care home under s.117 of the 1983 Act. The council charged her, from May 1995, for the next few years' care a sum of £60,000. By March 1996, the local authority had received legal advice that such charging was likely to be unlawful; however, the policy was not changed for over two years. This was maladministration.

On reviewing matters in 1998, the council argued that since July 1996 the woman had been self-funding and had effectively been discharged from s.117 at that point. The ombudsman found no scope for retrospective judgments, since discharge had to be based on proper review at the time and (under the old Mental Health Act Code of Practice: DH 1999, section 27) involve consultation with others who were involved with the person. The failure to adhere these requirements was maladministration; her care costs should be reimbursed to her (Wiltshire CC 1999).

In another case, the local authority decided only after a person's death that she had in fact been previously discharged from s.117, and that part of her estate should be paid to meet the charges. Yet the ombudsman quoted Department of Health guidance (HSC 2000/3) that the patient and his or her carer should always be consulted. As the ombudsman pointed out, the woman (who was dead) could not be consulted about the retrospective decision. She had therefore been in receipt of s.117 aftercare to the day of her death (Leicestershire CC 2001).

In another case, a local authority tried to withdraw aftercare services on the spurious ground that circumstances had changed because of the illness of the person's main carer – and without convening a meeting with relevant professionals, the patient, family and carers. A care plan had only been belatedly drawn up, and there appeared to have been no multi-disciplinary assessment:

Multiple flaws in withdrawal of s.117 status. A woman was discharged home with a care package under s.117 of the Act. Her husband was nevertheless her main carer. He then had a stroke was taken into hospital. The council subsequently then placed the couple in a care home in a different part of the country so they could be near family. The council, without convening a meeting with the relevant professionals, patient, carer or nearest relative to review the care plan, simply withdrew the s.117

aftercare – on the ground of the change of circumstance brought about by the illness of her main carer, the husband.

The ombudsman found that this was not a valid reason to withdraw s.117. The failure to convene the meeting was maladministration. The ombudsman also noted that the care plan review document was produced only after she had moved into the care home, and that moving to another area is not adequate justification for ending s.117 aftercare. It had been manually altered to show that s.117 was no longer required, and had been signed by a community psychiatric nurse only (suggesting that no multi-disciplinary approach had been taken). And the file note written by the care home stated clearly that she was subject to s.117 aftercare.

All this was maladministration. The ombudsman recommended that the council compensate the woman's son the cost of nursing home fees he had paid for some 17 months: over £33,000 (*Poole BC 2007*).

Decisions to cease aftercare services are likely to become all the more problematic when staff are anyway uninformed about what s.117 entails. This is maladministration for the local ombudsman:

Absence of guidance for staff on s.117. A man with schizophrenia had been discharged from a hostel with mental health problems for smoking marijuana. A year later he fell to his death from a tower block. The parents complained about how the local authority had dealt with the discharge. The local ombudsman found maladministration, since staff were given no written procedural guidance about the requirements of s.117 of the Mental Health Act 1983 (*Hounslow LBC 1995*).

Lastly, some local authorities have in the past set a rigid time limit for discharging s.117 – for instance, after six or 12 months in all cases. As can be seen from the above points, such a policy would be legally indefensible.

11.5.8 CHARGING FOR AFTERCARE SERVICES

The courts have held that it is unlawful to make charges for services, residential or non-residential, provided under s.117 of the 1983 Act. They have rejected the argument that s.117 contains no services itself, and is instead merely a gateway duty to other community care legislation, under which services can be provided (and charged for).

However, it was also argued before the courts that this conclusion created an inequitable anomaly. It would mean that a mentally disordered person who had been sectioned under the Mental Health Act would receive free aftercare services; whereas an informal but compliant patient, with a similar disorder, would be charged for services on discharge from hospital. The courts rejected this argument, pointing out that s.117 arises from the use of compulsory powers under the 1983 Act. Thus, in some cases patients would not be voluntarily availing themselves of aftercare services; this would be a good policy reason for not charging them (*R v Manchester CC, ex p Stennett*).

During the judicial review proceedings, it became clear that many local authorities had been charging for such services over a long period of time. As a consequence of the courts' decision, they potentially owed substantial sums of money to relevant service users, whom they had unlawfully charged for s.117 services. For instance, in one local government ombudsman investigation, the ombudsman recommended that the local authority reimburse £60,000 to one person whom it had wrongly charged (*Wiltshire CC 1999*). In another instance, the ombudsmen reported the sum owing to an individual service user as £294,000 (CLAE 2004, p.7).

The local ombudsmen were aware that local authorities were in some cases attempting to avoid making retrospective payments either by retrospectively discharging people from s.117, or employing restrictive cut-off dates for money owing. As a consequence, the ombudsmen issued their own guidance on how local authorities should go about things (CLAE 2003):

- Local authorities should in general not carry out retrospective assessments to remove aftercare services from an earlier date.
- Any such retrospective assessments that have taken place should be reviewed.
- Out-of-time complaints should not be rejected (for 12 months from July 2003).
- Where aftercare was improperly ended, financial restitution with interest was appropriate.
- No generally applicable date should be applied when repayments were being calculated.
- Local authorities should put in place mechanisms to identify those people who had been improperly charged.

Notwithstanding the controversy surrounding s.117, local authorities continue to try to find a way around it. For instance, in one case a local authority attempted to place a woman in a cheaper care home that would not meet her assessed needs and the requirements of a care plan. If she wished to go into the more expensive home, she would have to top up. The ombudsman found maladministration; it was obliged to cover the cost of a care home that would meet her needs (*North Yorkshire CC 2007*).

In a second, seemingly extraordinary, case, the local authority persuaded the patient to sign away her statutory right to free placement in a care home. Having done so, she was then forced to pay full cost for the placement.

Persuading service users to waive their legal right to free aftercare services. The local authority told a woman being discharged from hospital, who had previously been detained under s.3 of the Mental Health Act, that she would have to wait for up to 12 months for s.117 funding for a care home placement. The family proposed a residential placement that was more expensive than the council would usually pay. The council's legal advice was that the council could pay its usual cost and then allow the family to top up. The council disregarded its own legal advice. The woman then signed a form, stating that she was 'no longer in need of the services for which she was assessed within the provisions of Section 117 of the MHA'. The woman then moved into the residential home in question and paid the full costs.

The ombudsman was in no doubt that this was maladministration. First, the delay in funding a placement of up to 12 months was 'wholly unacceptable'. Understandably, the family was not prepared to risk such a long wait. Second, there was no reason why the council should not have followed its own legal advice and allowed the top up; it certainly should not have discarded this advice without careful and considered debate. Third, the council gave the impression that in order for her to move to that home, she had to waive her rights to s.117 aftercare. Fourth, the only assessment of the woman's needs, a month before discharge, identified an extensive care plan of aftercare. Short of a 'miraculous improvement', the ombudsman could not see how aftercare could no longer be considered necessary. The ombudsman recommended that the council calculate the financial loss suffered by the woman and repay the sum with interest, agree to fund her aftercare, pay £250 to her husband for his time and trouble, and review relevant policies and procedures (*York CC 2006*).

CHAPTER 12

Charging for non-residential services

KEY POINTS

Unlike in the case of residential accommodation (see Chapter 10), local authorities do not have a duty to charge for non-residential services. Instead, they have only a power to do so under s.17 of the Health and Social Services and Social Security Adjudications Act 1983 (HASSASSA). Although authorities generally exercise powers (as opposed to duties) sparingly, the power to charge is the one power that is employed increasingly extensively.

Local authorities can charge for non-residential services if they wish but only (a) if the charge is a reasonable one; (b) to the extent that they are satisfied that it is 'reasonably practicable' for the individual person to pay it. In addition to these two conditions contained in the legislation, the Department of Health has issued 'statutory' guidance that effectively sets out elements of what it considers to be a reasonable charging system.

Significant points in the guidance include not reducing people's weekly income to income support levels, not taking account of earnings, and – where a person's disability related benefits are being taken into account as income – carrying out an assessment of that person's disability-related expenditure. If people do not pay the charges for the services they have been assessed as needing, the guidance states that local authorities should not legally withdraw services but do have the power to pursue the ensuing debt.

The local government ombudsmen have investigated charging systems on a number of occasions, setting out what they consider a reasonable system to be, especially in terms of formulating, consulting on and providing information about the system and about how decisions can be challenged.

As the boundaries between health and social care blur, the redefining of certain services as 'social' rather than 'health' care can result in services such as bathing or respite care, previously provided free of charge by the NHS, now being charged for by local authorities. It makes it all the more important therefore that – despite central government's insistence on joint working and 'seamless' services – there should be clarity as to which part of a care package is health care and which social care. This will avoid unlawful charging for those health care services that should be free.

Overall, inconsistencies in charging continue to flourish, with local authorities displaying varying degrees of adeptness and financial rapaciousness. Charging for non-residential services remains one of those significant uncertainties inherent in the community care system referred to in Chapter 3. Likewise, as pointed out in the same chapter, the increasingly prevalent and high charges made by local authorities for providing services in the community arguably represents another aspect of the receding of what was known as the welfare state.

12.1 LEGAL POWER TO CHARGE FOR SERVICES

Under s.17 of the HASSASSA 1983, local authorities have the power to make a charge for non-residential services. The charge must be a reasonable one. In addition, if a person satisfies the local authority that it is not reasonably practicable for him or her to pay it, then the local authority must reduce the charge to a level at which it is reasonably practicable for the service user to pay. Non-residential services that can be charged for under s.17 of the 1983 Act are defined with reference to specific social services functions:

- National Assistance Act 1948 (s.29: welfare arrangements for 'blind, deaf, dumb and crippled persons, etc.')
- Health Services and Public Health Act 1968 (s.45: welfare of old people)
- NHS Act 2006 (schedule 20: prevention of illness and care and aftercare and home help and laundry facilities)
- Carers and Disabled Children Act 2000 (services for carers).

Though a power only, it is one which local authorities are understandably eager to use. Some older people in some councils may be paying up to £315 weekly for local authority services. Nonetheless, the picture is highly variable (Counsel and Care 2006, p.5). In fact the maximum weekly a charge a local authority might make varies between authorities from £23.50 to £400.00 (Coalition on Charging 2008, p.11). A third of local authorities do not have a maximum charge, and at a top rate of £17.30 an hour, care charges can mount up to a very high level (Counsel and Care 2007, p.8).

12.2 SERVICES EXCLUDED FROM CHARGING

Some non-residential services simply cannot be charged for.

Central government guidance states that community care assessment should not be charged for. In any case, s.47 of the NHS and Community Care Act 1990 is not listed as a relevant, chargeable function in s.17 of the HASSASSA 1983. The guidance also states that advice about assessment or services should not be charged for (DH 2003i, para 8). And the courts have made clear that aftercare services under s.117 of the Mental Health Act 1983 cannot be charged for (*R v Manchester CC, ex p Stennett*).

In addition, other legislation in the form of regulations prohibits charges being made for social services' provision of any community equipment (whatever it costs the local authority to provide), or of any minor adaptation to property that costs £1000 or less (SI 2003/1196). Guidance states that the cost of minor adaptations can be calculated to include buying and fitting, and that councils retain the discretion to charge in relation to minor adaptations that exceed £1000 in cost (LAC(2003)14). It should be noted that additional guidance issued in 2004 states the law ambiguously, appearing at one point to imply (wrongly) that equipment costing over £1000 can be charged for (ODPM 2004, para 2.26).

The same legislation also states that intermediate care cannot be charged for. Intermediate care is defined as consisting of a structured programme of care provided for a limited period of time to assist a person to maintain or regain the ability to live in his or her home. The charging exemption for intermediate care lasts up to a maximum of six weeks (SI 2003/1196).

These exemptions concerning equipment, adaptations and intermediate care are not limited to the context of the discharge by hospitals of patients. The legislation – the Community Care (Delayed Discharges) Act 2003 – under which the relevant regulations (SI 2003/1196) have been made, is concerned largely, but not only, with hospital discharge.

12.2.1 CHRONICALLY SICK AND DISABLED PERSONS ACT 1970: CHARGES

Section 17 of the HASSASSA 1983 refers to the legislation under which charges are made. It omits s.2 of the Chronically Sick and Disabled Persons Act 1970. Nevertheless, it has been confirmed by the courts that s.2 of the 1970 Act is to be regarded as an extension of s.29 of the National Assistance Act 1948 and therefore subject to charging (*R v Powys CC, ex p Hambidge*). This decision, although it confirmed earlier judicial findings about the relationship between the two Acts (*Wyatt v Hillingdon LBC*), appears to sit uneasily with a previous High Court decision which stated that what authorised services under s.2 of the 1970 Act was indeed s.2 of that Act – and not s.29 of the 1948 Act (*R v Islington LBC, ex p McMillan*).

12.3 REASONABLENESS OF CHARGES

Under s.17 of the HASSASSA 1983, any charge imposed must be reasonable. The courts have held that this is a very broad test.

Reasonableness and retrospective charging: attempt to recoup £232,000. The courts in one case emphasised that the flexibility of the 'overriding criterion of reasonableness' enabled the local authority to make charges retrospectively (i.e. when the resources of the service user had increased long after services had been provided). The reasonableness of such conduct on the part of the authority had to be assessed at the time of the conduct and with regard to all the relevant circumstances. For example, in the case of retrospective charging, the local authority would have to justify its reasonableness, notwithstanding the delay involved.

This was in the context of a seriously brain-damaged man who had been provided with residential accommodation by the local authority (s.17 of the 1983 Act applied in respect of the charging because the accommodation had been provided under schedule 8 of the old NHS Act 1977 – before it was amended so as to exclude residential accommodation). The man had subsequently been awarded damages for negligence on the part of the NHS. The local authority attempted to recover the cost (£232,000) of the care it had provided; it hoped to do this ultimately from the health authority (not the person's estate: the man was now dead), since part of the negligence settlement had involved the health authority indemnifying the person against any liability for care prior to the date of settlement.

The court found in favour of the local authority (*Avon CC v Hooper*).

In another case, the court considered what 'disability-related expenditure' (see 12.5 below) was reasonable and should thus be disregarded by the local authority, when assessing a person's means and how much she should pay for services. The case revolved around payment by the disabled person to a family member for care, and also to the annual and monthly costs attributed to the costs of disability equipment and associated repairs. The Court of Appeal held that the local authority's policy – of only taking into account (as disability-related expenditure) payments made to family members on grounds of ethnicity, religion or race – was too narrow. It also questioned the local authority's approach to assessing the person's expenditure, including repairs, on disability equipment which she had bought privately:

Charging policy and reasonableness: payments to family members. A local authority assessed the outgoings of service users in order to identify 'disability-related expenditure' (which would then be disregarded from the calculation of a person's income available for paying charges). In doing so, it applied a 'family member' rule that meant that allowance would not be made for any payments made to family members – unless there were cultural issues, or other (so the council claimed, though did not state in its policy document) exceptional circumstances. This policy was on the basis that provision of care by a family member was generally by choice, except in a particular cultural situation where it might be due to necessity, because it would not be acceptable to have a non-family member undertaking the caring role. In which case, an exception might be made in respect of making allowances for any payment made.

Payment to daughter. The claimant paid her daughter, an experienced nurse, £45.00 a week for a range of assistance (laundry, ironing, correspondence, finances, some housework, toenail cutting, outings) – over and above that which the council carers provided. Her daughter had reduced her working week as a nurse, in order to spend more time with her mother. To compensate her for loss of earnings, her mother paid her.

Choice as opposed to necessity. The High Court held that this distinction between choice and necessity in relation to paying family carers was not an irrational policy – and that, other than in cases of necessity, support offered by a family member could reasonably be expected to be provided without charge (indeed it was only the mother who insisted on making the payments). Furthermore there were other legitimate justifications for the policy: prevention of fraudulent claims, the impracticality of investigating claims of payments to family members, and the otherwise possible effect that family members would be increasingly tempted to charge for the care they provided.

Unlawfully rigid application of policy. However, the Court of Appeal overruled the judge. It stated that the policy had to be applied so as to take account of exceptions, where care provided by a family member was not in reality voluntary – and that the exceptions could not be limited to cultural issues based on race, religion or ethnicity. The concept of cultural issues could include those issues arising within the relationship between mother and daughter. There was no doubt that the woman's insistence on paying her daughter was genuine. Furthermore, 'nobody challenged the cost to [the daughter] of the 80 mile round trip to visit her mother. Nobody appears to have evaluated what must have been the enormous psychological benefit to the [woman] of a weekly trip out shopping and visiting her elderly brother…'. In this case, the proposition on which the policy rested – that the family member would perform the tasks without payment – did not apply. The council had not exercised the discretion which it claimed to have exercised. It had instead applied the rule rigidly and unlawfully.

Human rights. The High Court had also rejected an argument that article 8.1 of the European Convention on Human Rights was breached in terms of interference with family life. This was because the policy did not prevent a person being cared for by a family member, but merely prevented any payment being treated as disability-related expenditure. Furthermore, the local authority could anyway treat any case as exceptional and thus make an exception to the rule. Thus article 8 was not engaged; the Court of Appeal agreed with this. In any case, the High Court held, even if family life were being interfered with under 8.1, it was an interference that could be justified under 8.2 in terms of prevention of crime or the economic well-being of the State. However, if article 8 had been engaged, the Court of Appeal was unclear that the defence to a breach of 8.1 would be so straightforward.

Discrimination. The High Court also rejected the argument that the woman was being discriminated against under the Race Relations Act 1976, since s.35 of the Act states that it is not unlawful to afford facilities or services in order to meet the special needs of people belonging to a particular racial group.

Equipment. The woman had bought disability equipment costing some £1800 (reclining bed and chair, and bath lift). The local authority treated it as having a lifespan of ten years and so assessed (i.e. made allowance for) her expenditure on it at £3.46 per week over that period. The woman argued that the lifespan of the equipment should have been regarded as only five years, thus her weekly expenditure should have been assessed at over £6.00. The court held there was no evidence put forward (e.g. from manufacturers) that the ten-year estimate was irrational.

However, it did not appear to the High Court altogether rational for the local authority to regard repair costs in the same way by 'amortising' the costs over the estimated lifetime of the equipment. Likewise, it was not rational to defer treating repair costs as disability-related expenditure until the next accounting period, instead of considering them as they arose (*R(Stephenson) v Stockton-on-Tees BC*).

The local ombudsman has criticised arbitrariness in rules on charging:

Unreasonableness: arbitrariness in charging. The local ombudsman has questioned the reasonableness of a charging policy when the council (a) failed to give careful thought as to how much a person receiving income support could be expected to pay; and (b) adopted a threshold above which charges would be automatically exempted, but only if weekly expenses exceeded income by £10 – a criterion which was 'quite arbitrary' and not well thought out (*Essex CC 1991*).

The courts have in one case identified irrationality:

Unreasonably charging for daytime services by taking account of night-time income. It was unlawful, unfair and irrational for a local authority to take account of that part of disability living allowance (higher rate) paid in respect of night care – in order to assess the amount to be charged for day care (*R(Carton) v Coventry CC*).

If staff are not made aware of the local authority's local charging policy, that too is maladministration: for example when invalid carer's allowance and carer's premium were taken account of contrary to the local policy (*Durham CC 2000*).

12.4 REASONABLE PRACTICABILITY OF PAYING THE CHARGE

If a person satisfies the local authority that it is not reasonably practicable for him or her to pay a charge, the authority should charge no more than appears, to it, to be reasonably practicable for the person to pay (HASSASSA 1983, s.17).

The courts have stated that it is for the service user to 'discharge his burden of persuasion' by showing that he or she had insufficient means to pay (*Avon CC v Hooper*). In the same case, which concerned a charge being imposed retrospectively, the court also gave a wide interpretation of 'means':

Reasonable practicability of paying a charge. Under the legislation, the courts stated that the person had to show that he had insufficient means. The time at which he had to do this was when the local authority was seeking to make a charge. If his means were now reduced – for example, if the business was in difficulty following a personal injury – the person could rely on this reduction in arguing he could not pay, even though at an earlier date he might have been better off.

The court also stated that the word 'means' in s.17 of the 1983 Act referred to more than just cash, since as a 'matter of the ordinary use of English, the word 'means' refers to the financial resources of a person: his assets, his sources of income, his liabilities and expenses. If he has a realisable asset, that is part of his means; he has the means to pay... If he has an asset which he can reasonably be expected to realise and which will (after taking into account any other relevant factor) enable him to pay, his means make it practicable for him to pay' (*Avon CC v Hooper*).

The local ombudsman considers that the word 'hardship' is not a simple substitute for 'reasonable practicability', suggesting that the latter is of wider scope (*Gateshead MBC 2001*). In determining reasonable practicability, the local ombudsman will look for reasoned decision-making:

Arbitrary decision-making. A failure to explain how a decision is reached on reasonable practicability – beyond expressing scepticism of the parents' breakdown of expenditure in relation to their adult children with learning disabilities – suggested arbitrary decision-making by officers not familiar with the specific care needs of those individuals concerned. This was maladministration (*Gateshead MBC 2001*).

One way in which the service user can discharge this burden of persuasion is to take advantage of appeal procedures, about which the local ombudsman has commented on a number of occasions. Even if the burden is on the service user to convince the local authority about reasonable practicability, a local authority should provide adequate information and procedures in order to give the person a decent chance of discharging that burden. The local ombudsman has considered this issue in several cases:

Information and appeals procedure. The local ombudsman has pointed out that for people to be able to exercise their statutory right to satisfy the authority that they cannot afford charges: (a) they must be informed that the local authority has the discretion to waive charges; (b) a proper appeals procedure must exist in order to assess people's cases (*Greenwich LBC 1993*).

Decision letters omitting reference to appeals procedure. The fact that an appeals procedure existed in principle, but that the decision letters made no clear reference to it, was maladministration (*Derbyshire CC 2004*).

Appeals procedure: clear criteria, information and reasons for decisions. The ombudsman stated that essential to the appeals procedure was (a) the application of clear, thought-out criteria; (b) accurate and sufficient information on which decisions were based; (c) information about how to challenge the outcome of the appeal; (d) clear reasons explaining decisions. In particular, criteria applied by the local authority should have been relevant – for example, they should have related to ability to pay (as demanded by s.17 of the 1983 Act) and not to a reassessment of degree of need – and been applied consistently. The information on which appeal decisions were based should have been of good and consistent quality (*Essex CC 1991*).

In another case, the ombudsman likewise referred to the need for simple and transparent procedures, information about them, and clear reasons for decisions. All this was very difficult if a new charging system was implemented before the appeal criteria were formally adopted; in which case service users had 'no idea' of the factors that would support their case or be taken into account (*Gateshead MBC 2001*).

In sum, the local ombudsman is likely to place great emphasis on a local authority having a clear policy and information about its charging system generally:

Having a clear policy on charging. The local ombudsman has found maladministration when a local authority has failed to have (a) 'a properly recorded policy on financial assessment'; (b) 'a statement of the criteria for the basis of assessing financial resources and need'; (c) 'advice and explanation of this together with information on what information must be submitted for the assessment'.

In this particular case, part of the problem had arisen because the local authority refused to disregard charitable pledges obtained by the applicants for adaptations for their daughter. The applicants claimed that this was inconsistent with the purpose of the pledges, which were designed to bridge the shortfall between the authority's contribution and the actual cost of the works. The ombudsman did not fault the authority for wanting to practise 'prudent' budget management, but for the lack of policy and criteria for such practice, and of advice and explanation (*Hertfordshire CC 1992*).

12.4.1 TAKING ACCOUNT OF THE SERVICE USER'S RESOURCES IN DECIDING WHETHER TO PROVIDE THE SERVICE

Charging for providing a non-residential service should be distinguished from taking account of a person's resources in order to decide not what to charge, but whether to provide a service in the first place (see section 6.10.3).

12.5 DEPARTMENT OF HEALTH GUIDANCE ON CHARGING

The Audit Commission issued a critical report in 2000 about home care charges, identifying significant inconsistencies and also disadvantages suffered by those service users on the lowest incomes and with the highest costs related to their disability (Audit Commission 2000). In response, the Department of Health issued guidance in 2001 with a view to achieving greater consistency across local authorities.

The guidance was to be implemented partly by October 2002 and fully by April 2003 (LAC(2001)32; with attached guidance that was slightly amended in 2003: DH 2003i). It was issued under s.7 of the Local Authority Social Services Act 1970, which makes it of the stronger, policy variety (see 5.1.6 above). The main points include the following:

- **No presumption that local authorities should charge**. The guidance makes no presumption that local authorities will charge for non-residential social services, since the 1983 Act creates only a power, not a duty (para 4).
- **Discretion on local policies**. The guidance notwithstanding, local authorities retain substantial discretion as to how to implement local charging policies, so long as they are consistent with the clear objectives set out in the guidance (para 5).
- **Income Support levels**. Local authorities should not charge people on levels of income equal to basic levels of income support plus 25 per cent. For service users with higher income levels, charges should not be imposed that have the effect of reducing the person's income below those income support levels plus 25 per cent (para 20).
- **Taking account of disability benefits**. Some disability benefits may be taken into account as income, namely the income support severe disability premium, attendance allowance, disability living allowance (DLA), constant attendance allowance, and exceptionally severe disablement allowance. War pensioners' mobility supplement and the mobility component of disability living allowance may not be taken into account (paras 30–31) and likewise age-related payments to pensioners under the Age Related Payments Act 2004 (LAC (2004) 25).
- **Assessment of disability-related expenditure**. If disability benefits are taken into account, the service user must not be left without the means to pay for other necessary care and support or for other costs arising from their disability. In order to ensure this happens, local authorities should specifically assess the disability-related expenditure of any service user, whose disability benefits are being taken into account (para 33).
- **Disability-related costs**. The guidance gives a non-exhaustive list of disability-related expenditure, needed for independent living. The list includes payment for community alarm system, costs of privately arranged care services, specialist washing powders or laundry, special dietary needs, special clothing or footwear, additional bedding costs (e.g. because of incontinence), additional heating costs, reasonable costs of domestic tasks (maintenance, cleaning, domestic help) where the assistance is required because of the disability, disability-related equipment costs (e.g. purchase, maintenance, repair, hire), and other transport costs over and above the mobility component of DLA (para 46).
- **Day and night care services**. When assessing a charge for daytime services, local authorities should avoid taking account of, as income, the element of benefits that are payable for night care. This reflects the case of *R(Carton) v Coventry CC*). The guidance suggests that normally it would be reasonable to treat the difference between, DLA care component high rate and middle rate as representing the element paid for night care (although this might not always be so) (paras 35–43).
- **Taking account of savings**. Service users with savings over the upper capital threshold used for the residential accommodation test of resources may be asked to pay the full cost of the service. The guidance suggests that the same approach to capital should be taken as for residential accommodation (para 58).

- **Taking account of capital**. Various types of capital can be taken account of in line with the test of resources for residential accommodation; however, the person's home should be disregarded (para 59).
- **Parents and other members of the family**. Under s.17 of the 1983 Act, only the service user's means may be assessed, not those of other members of the family. However, the guidance then goes on to suggest that in some circumstances the service user may have a legal right to share in the value of an asset, even if the asset is not in his or her name. This may be through statutory or equitable rights (para 64).
- **Earnings**. All earnings should be disregarded as income. This is so that a disincentive to work is not created (para 72).
- **CJD**. No charges should be made for people suffering from any form of Creutzfeldt-Jakob disease (para 75).
- **Full cost of the service**. The maximum charge must not exceed the full cost of providing the service, which cannot include costs associated with the purchasing function or costs of operating the charging system (para 77).
- **Notional costs**. If the costs of services vary within a local authority's area (e.g. because of diverse provider charges), it is for the local authority to decide whether to set a notional average (e.g. to avoid people in rural areas being disadvantaged, para 79).
- **Carers**. If informal carers are being charged for carers' services under the Carers and Disabled Children Act 2000, then the local authority should take account of costs that the carers may be bearing, before deciding what to charge. For example, private purchase of care (to allow short breaks), adaptations to the carer's home (e.g. where the disabled person has moved in), additional transport costs (e.g. taxis because there is not time to use public transport), and additional costs relating to the person's disability (see above) that the carer meets (para 83).
- **Direct payments**. Direct payment recipients are to be charged in the same way as if they had received the equivalent services from the local authority (para 86).
- **NHS payments**. If a person's community care services are being in effect paid for by NHS money, transferred to the local authority via the NHS Act 2006, service users could still be charged up to the full cost of the service. However, s.17 of the 1983 Act is not a revenue-raising power. In joint working generally, charging arrangements must be clear, because there is no power to charge for NHS services (para 88).
- **Refusal to pay charge**. A service should not be withdrawn because a person refuses to pay a charge; however, the debt could be pursued through the civil courts (para 97).
- **Refusal to disclose resources**. If a person refuses to disclose their resources, it may be reasonable to charge them the full cost of the service (para 97).
- **Consultation**. Changes to charging policies, including increases, should be consulted on with users and carers (para 98).
- **Scope of review in considering reasonable practicability of person paying the assessed charge**. The fairness of the charge should be considered in the light of individual circumstances. The review may need to go beyond consideration of the terms of the council's policy, since the policy is unlikely to make provision for all conceivable personal circumstances (para 101).
- **Information about a review**. Users must be provided with information making it clear that they can seek a review of the charge or can make a formal complaint (para 102).

Various issues arise from the guidance.

12.5.1 DISABILITY-RELATED EXPENDITURE

Local authorities may set notional averages for certain types of disability-related expenditure. However, such averages may not be an accurate way of assessing an individual's necessary expenditure.

For instance, setting such a notional weekly amount for single or double incontinence would run the risk of (a) generally being set anyway too low; and (b) even if it was not set unduly low, and represented a reasonable average, it would still not obviously equate to each individual's actual expenditure. This is because one person's incontinence needs might necessitate considerably greater expenditure (in terms of both quality and quantity) than another's. In fact further Department of Health guidance alludes to this very pitfall, stating that to a limited degree it might be possible to set standard allowances for costs such as laundry, but that the main emphasis should be on each individual's verifiable expenditure (DH 2002a, para 48).

More generally, an Age Concern England report (Thompson and Mathew 2004, p.57) revealed the rough, ready and arbitrary nature of how some local authorities assess disability-related expenditure. For instance, disallowed were vitamin drinks (because not prescribed by the doctor), heating costs (not great enough to qualify), plastic bags to put incontinence bags in, chiropody (simply not 'allowable'), hairdresser who visits (because this was not in the care plan), incontinence pads bought from the chemist because the woman found those provided by the district nurse too bulky, transport to day centre and physiotherapy sessions, and special transport to take a spouse (who had suffered a stroke) on holiday.

A more recent report suggests that a range of expenditure continues still not to be fully considered by local authorities when they assess people's essential living costs. Further examples of expenditure which might not be taken into account include heating (need for set temperatures), laundry (additional washing or drying required because of incontinence, spilled food or drinks), specialist clothing (e.g. custom made shoes), wear and tear on clothing, essential dietary requirement relating to an impairment, daily living equipment (including maintenance, repair, replacement), internet costs (e.g. ordering shopping), respite care, high costs of accessible transport (Coalition on Charging 2008, p.20).

12.5.2 CHARGING IN THE LIGHT OF NHS CONTRIBUTIONS TO SERVICES

The Department of Health guidance claims that even if services are being provided through money given by the NHS to the local authority (under s.256 of the NHS Act 2006), so that the services are not costing the local authority anything, nevertheless the local authority could still charge the person up to the full cost of the service (para 88). This may seem controversial; but although s.17 of the HASSASSA 1983 is not a general revenue-raising power, nevertheless all it says is that the authority may recover such a charge as it considers reasonable. It says nothing about recovering only the actual overall cost to it of providing the service to any particular service user.

12.5.3 DISABILITY BENEFITS

As far as taking account of disability benefits as income is concerned, the courts have held that charging a person receiving disability benefits more than a person who does not receive them is not contrary to the Disability Discrimination Act 1995 (*R v Powys CC, ex p Hambidge (no.2)*).

However, the fact that a person is receiving income from benefits does not necessarily mean that this income is disposable and can be taken account of by local authorities in assessing charges. This is because there may be a significant discrepancy between maximum state benefits payable and the actual expenditure faced by disabled people. For example, a 2004 report concluded that, for 'high to medium' needs, the weekly benefits payable amounted to £235, but that budgetary requirements (excluding personal assistance) were £467, resulting in a weekly shortfall of £232 (Smith *et al.* 2004, p.77).

12.5.4 TAKING ACCOUNT OF THE RESOURCES OF ANOTHER PERSON

The guidance states that only the resources of the service users may be taken into account, not those of other family members. However, it does state that sometimes a person may have a share in resources, even if they are not in the service user's name.

The answer to the question, whether in some circumstances the resources of other members of the family (partner, parents etc.) can be taken into account in deciding what to charge, is unclear. For instance, in two cases concerning the provision of home adaptations under s.2 of the Chronically Sick and Disabled Persons Act 1970, the courts declined to answer the question. One case concerned the resources of the partner of the disabled person (*R (Fay) v Essex CC*), the other the resources of the parents of a disabled child (*R (Spink) v Wandsworth LBC*).

Although it has not been commonly realised, the 'liable spouse' rules (see section 10.5.1), under ss.42 and 43 of the National Assistance Act 1948, have applied to non-residential services provided under the 1948 Act, as well as to residential accommodation. The rules have involved the liability of a husband or wife to support the other – and the power of the local authority to ask one spouse for payment in respect of services provided for the other spouse. The liable relative rules are due to be revoked, imminently, under s.147 of the Health and Social Care Act 2008.

12.5.5 CAPITAL

The Department of Health guidance states that local authorities should use the capital threshold as set out in the rules for charging for residential accommodation (see 10.6) – in order to determine what capital to taken into account (other than the person's home). It states that users with savings of more than this upper limit of capital may be asked to pay the full amount – and that while councils could set more generous limits, they should not set lower ones (DH 2003i, para 58).

12.5.6 CONTINUING INCONSISTENCIES IN CHARGING

In April 2004, an Age Concern England report concluded that the Department of Health guidance had resulted in greater consistency for poorer service users, but otherwise there remained large inconsistencies between authorities – in how they set their maximum charges, what they charged per hour and what they allowed in terms of disability-related expenses (Thompson and Mathew 2004).

12.6 CONSULTATION WITH SERVICE USERS ABOUT CHARGING

The courts have confirmed that when a local authority is making fundamental changes to its charging system, fairness requires that proper consultation should take place. Up-rating and adjustment of charges is one thing, but quite another are changes to the policy and rules that result in significant differences for service users. The latter requires consultation (*R(Carton) v Coventry CC*).

Six weeks of consultation, and only then with too small a group of local representatives, meant the local authority was inadequately informed about the concerns of local voluntary bodies. It was not legally fair and was unlawful. However, the local authority subsequently went on to cure this defect with a second round of consultation which, although it stretched over the summer holidays, was held by the court to be adequate (*R(Berry) v Cumbria CC*).

On any view, introducing a charging system from scratch marks a significant change, making consultation all the more imperative; a failure to ensure this was maladministration (*Derbyshire CC 2004*). Moreover, the Department of Health guidance states that consultation must take place about increases in charging (DH 2003i, para 98). This does not stop local authorities attempting sometimes to take blatant shortcuts, involving gross deficiencies in the consultation, as well as attempts to backdate increased charges unlawfully:

Consulting without explaining what was being proposed. The local authority consulted on extremely large increases in charges, but did not explain this. Even the report to the council's Cabinet at no point made clear that some people would now have to pay £46 per day for attendance at a day centre instead of £1. The council argued that to have provided this sort of detail would have led to accusations that it had already made up its mind.

The ombudsman was highly critical: 'There is little point in a consultation exercise unless you tell the consultees what you are consulting them on. To say that it might prejudice the decision, if consultees were told the proposals, is as absurd as informing neighbours that a planning application has been received but that they cannot know what the application is for as it might prejudice the decision of the Planning Committee.'

Things got worse. Apart from this fundamental flaw, the consultation letter was 'extremely difficult to understand, complex and unfocused. It does not make responding easy, even if people could work out what they were being asked. This is poor practice in general but, given that this letter was going to some very vulnerable people, it is exceptionally ill considered.' The complainant's wife suffered from dementia.

Nor was this the end of the matter. The council was itself unsure about the changes it had implemented. In February, it wrote to the complainant saying her new charge was £6.50 a day from 6 March. In April it invoiced for £46 per day from 6 March. In May, she was told this was the cost for full payers. Ten days later, an explanation of the rise was sent, but only explaining a cost of £6.50, not the £46 charge now being made.

In any case, the council had no power to back date the charge. When it remedied this, describing the forfeiture of the backdated amount as a goodwill gesture, the ombudsman remained critical. Far from this being a good will gesture, the ombudsman pointed out that the local authority had no choice – since such a backdated charge was anyway unlawful (*Oldham MBC 2007*).

12.7 CHARGING AND PERSONAL INJURY COMPENSATION PAYMENTS

The HASSASSA 1983 is silent on the matter of whether a local authority can take account of a personal injury compensation payment (not just actual income received, but also the capital and right to income), even where it is held in trust. The Department of Health guidance on non-residential charging does not deal clearly with the issue. This situation contrasts with the rules for charging for residential accommodation, which prohibit the capital and income from it, where it is held in trust, being taken into account. New rules from April 2008 concerning residential accommodation mean that actual income received from such a compensation payment will be disregarded for 52 weeks, unless it is a payment made specifically to cover the cost of care (see 10.6.3.2).

Nonetheless, the Department of Health guidance (DH 2003i, para 59) states that the same approach to capital should be taken for non-residential charges as for residential accommodation charges. Searching for something concrete, the courts have seized upon this and stated that therefore trust-held personal injury compensation capital sums cannot be taken into account. However, because the guidance does not state that the income from such capital sums should be treated in the same way as for residential accommodation, the courts have also held that the local authority would retain a discretion to take account of such income for non-residential services (*Crofton v NHS Litigation Authority*).

If it is clear that a local authority will thus meet a person's needs in the future, without making a charge (because it will be ignoring the capital), the amount of damages assessed as payable by the defendant in a personal injury compensation case may be reduced. This is because otherwise the claimant would be receiving a windfall, by receiving compensation, which he or she then does not need to spend on the care for which it was awarded.

However, the damages payable in negligence cases are to meet the person's reasonable needs; and these may not always coincide with what the local authority considers to be reasonable. In which case, a 'top-up' award may be made to the claimant, to reflect the difference between the two (*Crofton v NHS Litigation Authority*).

Indeed, the courts sometimes display little confidence in the stability and extent of local authority funding to meet all the needs of a personal injury claimant. This is particularly so, given that a personal injury claimant's needs may stretch over decades to come. The courts have pointed out that the statutory scheme for the provision of domiciliary care services is flexible, leaving significant discretion with local authorities. For instance, under the government-imposed scheme of 'fair access to care' (FACS), local authorities can change the threshold for eligibility for services from year to year, in response to budgetary demands. The courts may anyway recognise that reasonable needs (in a negligence case) may encompass a claimant's wish not to rely on local authority support; such a wish might contribute to the claimant's sense of well-being. The courts may sympathise, taking the view that the claimant should not be exposed to risk and uncertainty (*Freeman v Lockett*). For instance, there could in the future be a change in government policy about how charging will work in relation to ring-fencing personal injury compensation payments (*Crofton v NHS Litigation Authority*).

In a case involving compensation to a child, who had suffered severe brain injury from a road traffic accident, the questions arose as to (a) whether his accommodation needs reasonably included a secure private garden, and (b) if so, whether there was a reasonable prospect, within a reasonable time, of the local authority offering such accommodation. The answer to the first question was yes, and to the second, no. Thus, the compensation payable should reflect the need for such accommodation (*Williams v Williams*).

In trying to work out the legal rules, the Court of Appeal has expressed its dismay at the complexity, labyrinthine nature and obscurity of the relevant legislation and guidance. Clarity and accessibility were lacking, and tortuous analysis was required (*Crofton v NHS Litigation Authority*).

12.8 PLACING A CHARGE ON A PERSON'S HOUSE

Some local authorities, when assisting people with home adaptations under s.2 of the Chronically Sick and Disabled Persons Act 1970, place a charge on the person's house, with the consent of the person. The value of the charge is then payable if and when the house is sold. The courts have confirmed the lawfulness of placing such a legal charge in the home in a case involving adaptations under the 1970 Act for a disabled child (*R(BG) v Medway Council*). Presumably, the same principle would hold in the case of an adult, under the same Act.

12.9 PEOPLE WHO FAIL TO PAY

There seems to be nothing in legislation to suggest that authorities can withdraw, or refuse to provide, services solely on the grounds that a person will not pay. However, the legislation empowers authorities to recover charges as a civil debt (in a magistrates' court), without prejudice to any other method of recovery (HASSASSA 1983, s.17).

The generally accepted legal view seems to be that if an authority has a duty to provide a community care service, then non-payment of a charge cannot justify withdrawal of the service. Certainly this is the stance taken by statutory guidance from the Department of Health (DH 2003i, para 97). This is on the assumption that a duty to provide a service cannot be overridden by a mere power to make a charge. Nevertheless, this approach would appear to leave open the possibility that a service provided under a mere power (e.g. for an older person under the Health Services and Public Health Act 1968) could in principle be withheld lawfully if the person refused to pay.

There is evidence that significant numbers of people are declining services because they feel unable to afford to pay. Equally, if they continue to pay for services, people are cutting back on their personal lives because they can no longer afford to undertake various activities. For instance, they go out less and experience social exclusion, stop education, stop activities beneficial to health and well-being (swimming, physiotherapy), and cut back on food and heating (Coalition on Charging 2008, pp.16, 22).

The local ombudsman has questioned the dividing line between a service user declining services (in reaction to charges being imposed), and the local authority withdrawing them – particularly where both staff and service user were ignorant of the legal position on withdrawal of services.

Suspending or withdrawing services for non-payment? Faced with difficulty in meeting the charges being demanded, a man suspended the local authority care being provided to his wife. Local authority staff had not explained to him that the authority had a duty to continue to provide the services even if he did not pay. However, staff were unaware of the authority's guidance that explained this point. This was maladministration. In such circumstances the ombudsman also questioned whether the man's decision to suspend care was in fact the equivalent of withdrawal of care by the local authority (*Durham CC 2000*).

The problem for local authorities lies in deciding in what circumstances to pursue debt for unpaid charges, especially given the sensitivity and potentially adverse publicity surrounding the legal pursuit of disabled, elderly or vulnerable people. At the same time authorities may come under pressure from the district auditor to chase up what might in some cases be a substantial sum of money owing by individual, or groups of, service users. In deciding whether to recommend pursuit of a debt, some local authority staff might be faced with difficult decisions and react in ways little related to the law – as the following study revealed:

Moral judgements about whether to pursue a debt. Social care practitioners might react in various ways, for example, when faced with a man with learning disabilities who owes money to the local authority, who has recently won several thousand pounds through a lottery, but who refuses to reduce the debt. Some practitioners might inform the finance department and urge that the debt be pursued for the sake of equity (i.e. having regard to other users of services).

Also in the name of equity, practitioners might even suggest that, since services cannot legally be withdrawn on non-payment, they should instead be withdrawn by means of a reassessment and a downward adjustment of assessed need and service provision. Others might wish to preserve confidentiality and not pass on the information; yet others still might decide to keep quiet because to do otherwise would be 'snitching' and taking away the luck that had come the client's way (Bradley and Manthorpe 1997, pp.70–73).

12.10 GENERAL LOCAL GOVERNMENT LEGISLATION ON CHARGING

Some local authorities have considered making use of another statutory route for making charges, namely s.111 of the Local Government Act 1972. This enables authorities to do things to facilitate, or which are conducive or incidental to, the discharge of any of their functions. However, the courts have sounded a clear warning against use of this section by local authorities to make charges for services (*McCarthy v Richmond LBC*).

Likewise, any attempt to circumvent restrictions on charging by utilising s.93 of the Local Government Act 2003 – which gives local authorities a broad power to charge for certain services – would almost certainly be unlawful. First, this would be because it only applies to discretionary services as opposed to services that a local authority has a duty to provide. Second, even if discretionary services could be identified (e.g. provided for older people under s.45 of the Health Services and Public Health Act 1968), s.93 of the 2003 Act cannot be used if there is a power outside of s.93 to charge for those discretionary services (see ODPM 2003, paras 11–13). There is of course just such a power: in s.17 of the HASSASSA 1983.

CHAPTER 13

Direct payments, individual budgets, carers, children in need etc.

KEY POINTS

DIRECT PAYMENTS AND INDIVIDUAL BUDGETS

If certain conditions are met, local authorities have a duty to make direct payments to people, so that the latter can purchase their own non-residential community care services – rather than have the local authority provide or arrange them. The conditions are, in summary, that the person has an assessed eligible need, that the service to be purchased will reasonably meet that need, that he or she consents to the payment, and that he or she is able to manage the payment with or without assistance. The overall stated purpose of direct payments is to give service users greater independence and control over their daily lives.

Since they were introduced about ten years, the number of direct payments has remained relatively small. This has disappointed central government. Because of this, it is now introducing a system known as individual or personal budgets. This is expected to be applied to all those people eligible for community care services. It provides an option whereby a person is allocated a particular sum of money, according to their community care needs. The person can then choose how they would like their needs met. They can opt to manage the money directly by means of a direct payment, or choose instead what could be called a virtual budget and request the local authority that a broker (such as a social worker or independent organisation) should arrange the services. With this latter arrangement, the person does not have to control the money directly.

However, the introduction of individual budgets is, at the time of writing, being implemented with no new legislation or even definitive, statutory guidance from the Department of Health. This means that to describe individual budgets precisely is not straightforward.

Furthermore, it is not entirely clear how certain key elements of individual budgets – in particular self-assessment of need, service users themselves determining how their (self-assessed) needs should be met – are consistent with existing community care legislation and guidance.

In addition, at the time of writing, the legal rules about direct payments are due to change, allowing somebody else to be the recipient of a direct payment when the disabled person is unable to consent to it.

INFORMAL CARERS

Various pieces of social services legislation now make provision for informal carers. In summary, informal carers providing substantial and regular care, and who request an assessment, have a right to have their ability to care assessed. Carers' involvement in (or wish to do) work, training, education or a leisure activity must also be taken into account in the assessment. The local authority also has a duty, having carried out an assessment, to decide whether such an informal carer requires services. However, the legislation does not contain a duty to provide any such services, but only a power.

The lack of duty actually to provide services means the legislation is arguably flawed, since informal carers appear to be taking on ever more of a caring burden. This seems particularly to be so, as local authorities apply stricter eligibility criteria under their 'fair access to care' policies, and are assisting ever fewer people. At the same time, the NHS has closed significant numbers of rehabilitation and recuperation beds for older people and is pursuing a policy of 'care closer to home', including in people's own homes. Inevitably greater burdens fall on informal carers, especially since there is little evidence that the NHS is adequately resourcing its community health care teams. On the matter of carers, legislation applying to the NHS is all but silent.

CHILDREN IN NEED AND THEIR FAMILIES

Under the Children Act 1989, local authorities owe a general duty toward children in need (including disabled children) and may provide services also for any member of the child's family. Therefore, in considering the legal basis for meeting the needs of disabled children and their families, or disabled adults with children, local authority staff will sometimes have to carry out assessments under both adult community care legislation and under the Children Act.

OTHER GROUPS OF PEOPLE

The Department of Health has issued specific guidance in relation to specific groups of people; these include, for example, deaf-blind people, people with learning disabilities, people with HIV and people with drug or alcohol problems.

13.1 DIRECT PAYMENTS: OVERVIEW

Legislation obliges local authorities to give service users money, by way of 'direct payments' to purchase their own services, rather than have the local authority arrange the services. This obligation is triggered if certain conditions are met in any individual case. Department of

Health guidance states that the overall purpose of direct payments 'is to give recipients control over their own life by providing an alternative to social services provided by a local council' (DH 2003c, p.3).

The duty to make direct payments extends to older people as well as other groups of service users; however, a study published in 2004 questioned the extent to which such payments were making possible greater independence when compared with payments made to other groups of service users. This was because older people's social and leisure needs were not deemed by local authorities as essential or 'eligible' as they would be for other adult groups; despite the fact that this was contrary to Department of Health guidance (LAC(2002)13, para 12) on 'fair access to care' that cautioned against such discrimination (Clark *et al.* 2004, p.56).

More widely, it has continued to be reported that uptake of direct payments in general has been slow. This has been attributed to a number of factors, including a lack of clear information, unawareness on the part of local authority staff, restrictive or patronising professional attitudes, inadequate advocacy and support services, inconsistency between the legislation and local practice, excessive paperwork. In addition, there have been difficulties in the recruitment, employment and retention of personal assistants, and in assuring quality (CSCI 2004, p.5).

There have been consistently reported problems with banks, which are reluctant to allow direct payment recipients to open separate accounts, owing to queries about people's capacity, their credit rating, ability to sign cheques and so on (see e.g. CO, DH 2005). In principle these difficulties are not insuperable; for instance, banks should accept a letter from social services confirming that the person is capable of managing the account (BBA). And instead of signatures, rubber stamps can be used or, for example, electronic banking or standing orders (Mullen 2006).

Despite these reported difficulties, central government has consistently encouraged local authorities to increase the numbers of people receiving direct payments (DH 2004f). It has also included direct payments amongst the performance indicators, the targets, which local authorities are told to hit. This has brought about greater numbers of direct payments. It appears to have resulted in some local authorities making direct payments unlawfully to some people who lack the ability to consent or to manage the payment (even with assistance). Nonetheless, after a decade, uptake has remained relatively limited. Disappointed at the relatively limited impact of the direct payments policy, central government has introduced a new system of individual budgets. These are intended to encompass direct payments, as well as give service users greater control of meeting their needs in other ways. In addition, the legal rules about who is permitted to receive direct payment are being broadened.

13.1.1 ELIGIBLE GROUPS OF PEOPLE FOR DIRECT PAYMENTS

Eligible for direct payments are community care service users aged 18 or over with an assessed eligible need and informal carers aged 16 or over for whom the local authority has decided services are called for (Health and Social Care Act 2001; SI 2003/762). Also eligible are the parents of disabled children, disabled parents of children, and children aged 16 or 17 years old. In the last three categories, the child in each case has to be a child in need under s.17 of the Children Act 1989, for whose needs the local authority has decided services are called for (Children Act 1989, s.17A; SI 2003/762).

There is a number of exclusions relating to mental health and criminal justice legislation. In summary, the exclusions are: (a) patients detained under mental health legislation on leave of absence; (b) conditionally discharged detained patients subject to Home Office restrictions, status; (c) patients subject to guardianship under mental health legislation; (d) people receiving aftercare or community care that is part of a care programme initiated under a compulsory court order; (e) offenders serving a probation or combination order, or offenders released on licence, subject to an additional requirement to undergo treatment for a mental health condition, or drug or alcohol dependency; (f) people subject to equivalent restrictions in Scottish mental health or criminal justice legislation (DH 2003c, annex C; see SI 2003/762 for details). However, draft regulations issued in August 2008, propose that local authorities – rather than be prohibited as at present - should instead have a power (but not a duty) to make direct payments to individuals subject to this mental health legislation (DH 2008e).

13.1.2 CONDITIONS TO BE MET FOR DIRECT PAYMENTS

The conditions that have to be met for a direct payment to be given are as follows:

- The person has to have an assessed, eligible need (Health and Social Care Act 2001, s.57; Children Act 1989, s.17A).
- The local authority must be satisfied that the service can meet the relevant need or, in the case of child-related services, the welfare of the child concerned will be safeguarded and promoted (SI 2003/762).
- The person must consent (Health and Social Care Act 2001, s.57; Children Act 1989, s.17A). This implies both ability or capacity to do so and willingness.
- The person must be able to manage the payment with or without assistance (SI 2003/762).

If all these conditions are met, a duty arises. The prior requirement that the local authority must first have decided that services are called for in the individual case – that there must be an assessed, eligible need – indicates that direct payments are not a 'back door' route to services, which the person would not otherwise be eligible for. In other words the normal rules of assessment and eligibility apply (see Chapter 6).

Nonetheless, with this hurdle surmounted, there is a duty. Thus, when a woman was already receiving direct payments, she nonetheless required additional care. The local authority determined to provide this through an agency, but did not explain to her that she was entitled to receive all her care via direct payments. This failure was found by the local government ombudsman to be maladministration (*Ealing LBC 2008*). Another common way in which local authorities have sometimes sought to evade the duty to make a direct payment is simply to drag their feet. In the same case, a request for an increase in a direct payment was made in March 2005, not presented to the local authority's resource allocation panel until October, and then referred for further investigation and reconsidered in December. The required package of care was not implemented until May 2006. This was too long and was held to be maladministration.

13.1.2.1 Consent of direct payment recipient

Department of Health guidance points out that blanket assumptions should not be made about whether certain categories of person will or will not be able to manage direct payments. The guidance goes on to state that assistance might include, for instance, keeping records, management of day-to-day relationships with staff or using a payroll service; the assistance itself might be bought in (DH 2003c, paras 47, 52). Therefore the question would be whether, overall, the recipient could control what was happening, even if he or she could not necessarily handle the day-to-day administration.

Managing a direct payment with assistance. A complaint was made to the local ombudsman. A woman with learning disabilities visited the family home at Christmas and decided not to return to her residential placement. The father wanted the council to pursue the possibility of a direct payment in combination with Independent Living Fund money so that she could live nearby. The council initially refused direct payments on the ground that she lacked the capacity to manage such payments without assistance. This was maladministration (*Hertfordshire CC 2003*).

The organisation, Values into Action, provides pointers to thinking through the question of consent and control in the case of people with learning disabilities; although it also makes the point that direct payments are not the only way of enabling people to achieve greater independence (Bewley 2002, p.5).

If a person does not agree with the local authority about his or her capacity to manage, the guidance states that the person should have access to an advocate and that arbitration should be available (DH 2003c, para 54). In addition, it might be that a person could manage some services and not others, or simply wish to manage some but not others. This would not prevent the making of a direct payment, since a person's needs could be met in part by the making of a direct payment, and in part by directly provided services arranged by the local authority (DH 2003c, para 50).

Local authorities should pay attention to these rules; a failure to do so could result in the local authority being deemed to have employer responsibilities. The following employment tribunal case, albeit drawn from a slightly different context, is illustrative:

Local authority as employer. Two people with learning disabilities ostensibly had a contract with a personal assistant, who was paid with money from the Independent Living Fund (a grant-giving body) and from a local authority social work department.

The assistant was bringing a case against her employer, based on allegations of sex discrimination and breach of contract, but was unsure who her employer really was. An employment tribunal held that because the local authority retained overall control of the situation in a number of respects, and that conversely the two people with learning disabilities appeared to take little responsibility, the local authority was in reality the employer. In other words, with or without assistance, the disabled people were not managing the payment. The tribunal's decision was upheld on appeal (*Smith v South Lanarkshire Council*).

13.1.2.2 Consent of somebody else: change to the law

At the time of writing, consent to receiving a direct payment cannot be given by anybody else other than the service user (Health and Social Care Act 2001, s.57). For instance, in one case involving two adult sisters with profound learning disabilities, it was clear to the judge that a direct payment could made to neither the women themselves nor their parents (R(A&B) v East Sussex CC (no.1)).

Department of Health guidance also states that, in its view, a person operating an enduring power of attorney could continue to receive direct payments on behalf of a person who had already consented (before loss of the requisite capacity). However, such an attorney could neither provide the original consent nor continue to receive the direct payments if, on review, services change (DH 2003c, para 59). This is because enduring powers of attorney relate only to property and financial affairs, not to welfare decisions.

However, the law is due to change. The Health and Social Care Act 2008 provides for another person, the recipient, to give consent to a direct payment on behalf of a person who lacks capacity under the Mental Capacity Act 2005.

There are two key conditions to be met. The first is that the requisite consent be given; the second, is that the recipient be suitable.

As to consent, the recipient must in any event give consent. If there is a surrogate for the person lacking capacity, then that surrogate has to consent as well. Draft regulations state that a surrogate must be a donee of a lasting power of attorney or a Court of Protection appointed deputy – either of whose powers, under the Mental Capacity Act 2005, must have been set up so as to include the power to secure a community care service. The recipient and the surrogate may, but not necessarily, end up being one and the same person (i.e. the surrogate may act as representative and so receive the direct payment). As to suitability, the other person (the recipient) giving consent is suitable as follows (Health and Social Care Act 2008, s.57 as amended):

- if the recipient is a representative of the person, then he or she is by definition suitable
- a representative is defined in draft regulations as a being either a donee of a lasting power of attorney or a deputy appointed by the Court of Protection (but not necessarily having welfare powers relating to community care services: DH 2008e)
- if the proposed recipient is not a representative of the person, he or she might still be suitable, but only if both the local authority and any surrogate consider the representative to be so
- if the recipient is not a representative of the person, and there is no surrogate, then the local authority alone has to consider whether the proposed recipient is suitable

In establishing whether a person, who is not a representative, is nonetheless suitable, draft regulations prescribe a number of conditions, which involve the local authority (DH 2008e):

- as far as is reasonably practicable, consulting with family members and friends involved in the provision of care for the person lacking capacity – as to whether they believe direct payments are the best option
- obtaining a criminal record certificate, if the proposed suitable person is not a family member or friend involved in providing care, from the Criminal Records Bureau (in future, this will be a check from the Independent Safeguarding Authority)

- being satisfied that the suitable person will act in the best interests of the person lacking capacity
- being satisfied that that suitable person has the ability to manage the direct payment
- being satisfied that the needs of the person lacking capacity can be met by a direct payment.
- being satisfied that in all the circumstances it is appropriate to make the direct payment to the suitable person.

The Act also provides for regulations to be made specifying the steps – such as consulting family members – to be taken by a local authority in deciding about who is suitable to receive a direct payment on behalf of a person lacking capacity. It also provides for regulations covering the case of a person's fluctuating capacity (e.g. in the early stages of dementia), such that if a suitable recipient were receiving the direct payment, he or she could continue to do so even if the person regained capacity. However, the person would decide how the payment was used while he or she enjoyed the capacity to do so.

Regulations may also provide for repayment of the money if, for example, the recipient were to misuse it.

13.1.2.3 Willingness to receive a direct payment

The condition of consent implies not only capacity to decide to receive direct payments, but also willingness: people should not be 'forced' into them, as the local ombudsman noted:

Only offering direct payments for domiciliary care. The local ombudsman criticised a local authority, when it would only offer assistance for an elderly woman in her own home by way of direct payments; otherwise only permanent residential care or temporary (institutional) respite care was offered. The woman rejected both these options; she was on file as having threatened suicide rather than enter a care home and had previously had a bad experience in respite care. She reluctantly accepted the direct payments option in order to be able to stay at home; but, as the local ombudsman pointed out, direct payments 'are not something that everyone can reasonably be expected to take on' (*Cambridgeshire CC 2002*).

Nonetheless, a not uncommon question is whether a local authority can, having run down certain of its own directly provided services, effectively force a person to accept a direct payment by claiming that there is no practical alternative. This has not been answered head on, but the following case went some way to dealing with it. It concerned a direct payment to a parent for the welfare of a 12-year-old child. The court considered further the issue of consent and its implications. In summary, consent is required. In its absence, the local authority must make a reasonable response, but the speed with which the local authority must provide an alternative may depend on the reasonableness of the person's refusal:

Refusal of a direct payment. First, it was clear that the use of direct payments was dependent on the consent of the person concerned. Second, the consent condition did not apply to the offer of a direct payment, but only to the obligation of having to make a direct payment. Third, the court considered but did not decide 'whether the person concerned has an unqualified right to refuse to consent to direct payments'. It stated that 'if the prospective recipient does have a reason to believe that the needs cannot be met in this way or (in the case of a child) that his or her needs will not be safeguarded or promoted by the use of direct payments or that the proposed amount is an unreasonable estimate of the cost of providing the services, the expectation of the statute and regulations is no doubt that these concerns will be articulated and a dialogue take place between the authority and the carer.'

Where a direct payment is refused, a local authority may claim that it will take longer to arrange the required services because appropriate carers may be hard to find. In deciding whether in such circumstances the local authority exceeds a reasonable time in arranging services, the court 'may have to take into account whether the objections which [the recipient] raises to the direct payment alternative have been reasonable or arbitrary and, if reasonable, whether they have met a reasonable response' (R(P) v Hackney LBC).

13.1.2.4 Direct payments and tax

One hurdle sometimes to be overcome, if direct payments are to be made more attractive, is the question of tax. Issues identified by the Low Incomes Tax Reform Group include direct payments users being categorised as 'non-business micro employers', but support services and information are not tailored to direct payment circumstances. Complex technical questions may arise over national minimum wage payments and sleep-in carers, as well as the tax position where living accommodation is provided for the sleep-in carer. A 'simplified' deduction offered to non-business domestic employers is not designed specifically for direct payments and is viewed as far from simple.

Status issues, such as whether a personal assistant is an employee or self-employed, are far from straightforward. Her Majesty's Revenue and Customs (HMRC) have on occasion conducted a status enquiry in the context of direct payments, with 'harrowing' results for the older person concerned and her daughters. HMRC advice on this issue is far from clear or easy to apply. Questions may also arise about the proper tax analysis for user-controlled or independent living trusts used to administer direct payments; and whether the money-laundering regulations apply to payroll agencies in the voluntary sector in the context of direct payments (LITRG 2008, p.2).

13.1.3 RELEVANT SERVICES FOR DIRECT PAYMENTS

Direct payments are available for non-residential services including community equipment. They may also be used for residential accommodation but only on a limited basis. This is that the accommodation be provided for no more than four continuous weeks in any period of 12 months. Stays of shorter duration are to be added together, unless they are separated by a period of four weeks or more. However, they must anyway not exceed 120 days a year (SI 2003/762). Thus substantial, regular respite care throughout the year is possible under these rules, so long as there are four-week gaps and the 120-day limit is not exceeded.

However, in a case involving a child, the court accepted that the placement of a child in a residential educational placement involved the provision of a significant amount of social care and practical assistance, which did not amount to residential accommodation. Therefore, direct payments could be available for this element of the child's needs, even to a child in residential accommodation (R(M) v Suffolk CC). In the case of adults, this case would appear to open the door to direct payments being made to a person in residential accommodation, for needs and services unconnected to the provision of the accommodation but nonetheless provided in the context of that accommodation.

13.1.3.1 Direct payments and health care

The direct payments legislation covers social services, but not NHS or housing services (Health and Social Care Act 2001, s.57; Children Act 1989, s.17A). This means that under the direct payments legislation at least, the NHS cannot make direct payments in respect of health care services.

Nevertheless, the NHS could, under s.256 of the NHS Act 2006, make money available to social services to bolster a direct payment. Section 256 allows the NHS to make payments to local authorities to help the latter carry out their social services functions. However, any such money made available by the NHS could not be for health care services.

Even given such apparent restrictions, there remains a significant grey area of uncertainty as to what constitutes health or social care. Clearly to the extent that a service (e.g. bathing) could be regarded as either, then for the purpose of direct payments it could be labelled as social care (i.e. a social services function) and be eligible. For recipients of direct payments, it may seem advantageous to have all, or at least the greater part of, their needs met through the flexibility of direct payments. However, two further issues arise.

First, the more services are categorised as coming within social services functions, the more they are subject to charging (the NHS is not empowered to charge for most services). Second, the extent to which local authorities have a legal power to provide 'health care' type services is governed in part by a prohibition in s.29 of the National Assistance Act 1948 (see 11.1.4 above). One study considered the very question of the dividing line between social care and health care in the context of direct payments. It found that in practice:

- Health professionals considered that tasks such as simple surgical dressings, giving suppositories and regular physiotherapy exercises could be performed by non-professionals; they lay in the grey area between health and social care (and so could arguably be included in direct payments).
- Health professionals considered the following type of task as not suitable for non-professionals (and so, arguably, should not be included within direct payments): care of leg ulcers or deep tissue wounds, assessing effectiveness of treatment, giving bladder washouts, tube feeding, enemas, manual bowel evacuation, colostomy care, tracheal suction, other aspects of tracheostomy care, changing urinary catheters (Glendinning *et al.* 2000).

In addition, local authorities are prohibited, under s.49 of the Health and Social Care Act 2001, from providing registered nursing care.

13.1.3.2 NHS ability to make direct payments under the NHS Act 2006

The courts have held that an NHS primary care trust (PCT) can pay money into a user independent trust, a voluntary organisation or private care agency. This would be under the wide powers a PCT has under s.12 (and schedule 3, para 15) of the NHS Act 2006:

Legality of NHS payments to user independent trust to allow disabled woman to live in the community. A woman who was blind, suffered from diabetes and had suffered several strokes. She required 24-hour nursing care, which had been provided by her parents in a home setting with private 24-hour nursing support. The parents now wished to withdraw hands-on care.

The PCT decided on a residential package, the main factor involved being cost and specialist attention being to hand in case of a crisis. A case was brought on the woman's behalf, arguing that the

PCT should provide support in her own home. This would be a cost-effective solution, it was argued. There was doubt as to whether it was lawful to make such a payment. The court held that it was lawful under the wide NHS powers. Furthermore, a reconsideration of the case was required, with a view to utilising and IUT.

However, the court would not order the PCT to enter into such an agreement, and there were various problems that had to be overcome. For instance, the IUT would need to be registered, some past track record would be needed, financial accountability would be required and the PCT would have to remain ultimate decision-makers. Nonetheless, the reconsideration was required because the interference with family life under article 8 of the Convention was clear. Whilst cost was relevant under article 8, so too was the evidence of the improvement in the woman's condition at home, the quality of life in the family environment and the her expressed views that she wished to remain at home (*R(Gunter) v South Western Staffordshire PCT*).

Section 12 of the Act states that the Secretary of State 'may arrange with any person or body to provide, or assist in providing, any service under this Act'. In addition this power may be exercised on 'such terms as may be agreed, including terms as to the making of payments by or to the Secretary of State'. Under schedule 3, a primary care trust 'may do anything which appears to it to be necessary or expedient for the purposes of or in connection with its functions' (NHS Act 2006). Nonetheless, it is also clear that whilst such a power exists to make payments to a user independent trust, it is just that; it is a discretion not a duty (*R(Whapples)* v *Birmingham East PCT*).

It is arguable that these powers are so wide that they go beyond the ambit considered in the *Gunter* case and enable PCTs to make payments direct to patients. Thus, in 2008, a PCT settled an imminent judicial review case by agreeing to make a direct payment to the parents of a severely disabled girl of more than £35,000 per annum – and to meet their legal costs. The parents claimed that this would save the NHS money because she could be treated at home instead of in a high dependency unit. They argued that their daughter, with learning disabilities and severe heart problems, would accept care only from her parents. The PCT had argued at the preliminary legal hearing, that it would be unlawful to make such a payment, that to do so would be contrary to policy and that if such payments had been intended, then Parliament would have said so explicitly (*R(Patnaik)* v *Sunderland Teaching PCT*; also Booler 2008).

13.1.4 USING DIRECT PAYMENTS TO PURCHASE SERVICES FROM CLOSE RELATIVES OR LOCAL AUTHORITIES

A direct payment recipient may not use the money to pay close relatives living in the same household, unless this is necessary in order for the recipient's needs to be met satisfactorily – or, in respect of a child-related direct payment, it is necessary for promoting the welfare of the child. The list of relatives comprises parent or parent-in-law, son or daughter, son-in-law or daughter-in-law, stepson or stepdaughter, brother or sister, aunt or uncle, grandparent, spouse, or any person living as spouse with anybody on this list (SI 2003/762).

The local authority may also make a direct payment subject to whatever other conditions it thinks fit, including that the payment should not be used to purchase services from a particular person (SI 2003/762). Such conditions might also relate to financial procedures, including methods of payment, monitoring procedures and accounting procedures; guidance on such matters is published by the Chartered Institute of Public Finance and Accountancy on such matters (CIPFA 2007).

The Social Security Commissioners have held that, where a husband was paid by his wife to provide care for her, using her direct payment, that money counted as income for the purpose of his claiming income support (thus reducing his entitlement (CIS/1068/2006). This decision was upheld by the Court of Appeal (*Casewell v Secretary of State for Work and Pensions*).

13.1.5 AMOUNT OF DIRECT PAYMENT

The local authority must make the payment at a rate that it estimates 'to be equivalent to the reasonable cost of securing the provision of the service concerned' (Health and Social Care Act 2001, s.57).

Department of Health guidance emphasises that the payment should be sufficient to enable the recipient 'lawfully to secure the service of a standard that the council considers is reasonable to fulfil the relevant needs'. There should be 'no limit on the maximum or minimum amount' of the amount of care to be purchased, or of the value of the direct payment (DH 2003c, para 82). Thus, when a local authority announced a freeze on its direct payment rates, it was argued that it would amount to a cut in service. Threatened with judicial review proceedings, the local authority backed down, deciding instead on a two per cent inflationary increase, in line with its own annual budget increase for other social services provision (NCIL 2007). The guidance also states that a local authority can pay a higher amount, if the benefits of doing so outweigh the costs and 'best value' is still adhered to (para 85).

Therefore, financial ceilings imposed irrespective of individual circumstances and as a matter of policy – for example, on the total weekly amount, or on the hourly rate that the direct payment will cover – are likely to be unlawful in the light of both the legislation and the guidance. They would also risk unlawfully fettering the local authority's discretion if applied in blanket fashion (see 5.2.1 above). Certainly the local ombudsman criticised a ceiling of £360 per week offered by way of direct payment, to pay for two evening carers for a woman; that amount was insufficient for the purpose of meeting her assessed needs (*Cambridgeshire CC 2002*). In 2008, the organisation SENSE reported on people who are deaf and blind receiving direct payments, and how restrictive hourly rates could be inadequate for the hiring of staff with the required specialist skills (SENSE 2008, p.10).

The direct payment might also include, for instance, an amount to cover recruitment costs, national insurance, statutory holiday pay, sick pay, maternity pay, employers' liability insurance, public liability insurance and VAT (DH 2003c, paras 82–83). In one legal case, the court accepted that the direct payment had to be 'at such a rate as the authority estimates to be equivalent to the reasonable cost of securing the provision of the service concerned'. In the context of the particular case, this reasonable cost would have seemed to include the provision of insurance to cover liability for injury caused to the service provider by the service user, or possibly an indemnity against any such liability. It also needed to include provision for income tax and national insurance payments (*R(P) v Hackney LBC*).

Flat rates of payment are likely to offend against the principle that the payment be reasonable. For instance, people living in rural areas may find costs of employing assistants or contracting with care agencies higher than those living in more urban areas. Alternatively, a person with more specialist needs may need to purchase a higher standard of care at a higher hourly rate. Furthermore, and more generally, if direct payment amounts, flat or otherwise, are too low, direct payment recipients will be unable to gain a 'fair stake' in the market and will experience difficulty in obtain the assistance and services they require (Davey *et al.* 2007, pp.2–3).

Questions sometimes arise about the degree of flexibility which a local authority affords to direct payment recipients. Guidance from the Chartered Institute of Public Finance and Accountancy gives an example of a person being allocated £750 to purchase a riser recliner chair. Instead they purchase a second-hand one for £250 and spend the remaining money on satellite television and some air flights for relatives abroad to come and visit and give the house a spring clean. It is suggested that local authorities should embrace this sort of thing. More generally, the guidance states that people may wish to put some of their money aside, for instance, for a holiday – and that this is perfectly appropriate so long as it helps to achieve outcomes agreed in the person's support plan (CIPFA 2007, paras 2.24, 2.42).

Another example of the direction in which central government would appear to wish social care to move came in the form of the 88-year-old man, who was reported in the newspapers as seeking a companion, at a rate of £7.00 per hour, to be his drinking partner in the local public house. Teenagers, women and anybody who was just going to 'get wrecked' were excluded (Pavia 2008). If such a person were eligible for social services assistance under fair access to care rules, then he would be able to determine what was most important to him, in terms of his recreational and social needs.

13.1.5.1 Direct payments: best value and cost-effectiveness

In some circumstances, the reasonable cost of making a direct payment might appear to the local authority to be more expensive than directly provided services. For instance, in the case of personal assistance or equipment, the local authority might benefit from bulk contracts. If so, the personal assistance hourly rate or the equipment per item might be cheaper for the local authority to purchase than the individual with the direct payment.

Some local authorities are tempted to argue 'best value' or cost-effectiveness as a reason for not making the payment, or at least not making it up to the reasonable amount required for the person to purchase the service. However, this would seem legally dubious. First, if the relevant conditions are met, a duty arises to make a direct payment. And, in turn, if this duty arises, the legislation states that it must pay a reasonable amount to allow the person to purchase the service required. So, a failure to make the payment at all or up to the reasonable amount would breach this duty and run the risk of reducing it to a mere power. Second, best value would normally be relevant to *how* a duty is performed, not to *whether* it is performed.

Nevertheless, there remains uncertainty about how the courts might respond if a particular direct payments package was markedly and demonstrably more expensive than direct provision by the local authority. On this issue, guidance from the Chartered Institute of Public Finance and Accountancy has in the past suggested that if the cost of a direct payment is greater than the cost to the local authority of providing the service itself, then a direct payment does not have to (although could still) be given (CIPFA 2004, para 5.1).

13.1.5.2 *Charging for direct payments*

The reasonable amount of a direct payment that the local authority must estimate is a gross payment. However, it can make a 'net' payment. That is, it can reduce the payment if it is satisfied that it is reasonably practicable for the recipient to make a contribution toward the cost of the service. Alternatively, even where it is reasonably practicable for the recipient to make a contribution, the local authority can still make the gross payment, but then seek reimbursement of that assessed contribution (Health and Social Care Act 2001, s.57; SI 2003/762).

13.1.6 COMMUNITY EQUIPMENT

Department of Health guidance makes clear that direct payments apply to equipment, as well as to other community care services. It states that the recipient should be supported by adequate expertise, especially where major items of equipment are concerned. The local authority should also clarify responsibilities for ongoing care and maintenance, as well as what should happen when the person no longer needs the equipment (DH 2003c, paras 78–81).

13.1.7 TOPPING UP DIRECT PAYMENTS

If a direct payment recipient wishes to purchase a service or equipment to a standard over and beyond that which the local authority judges necessary for the meeting of the need, there would seem no legal impediment to a recipient 'topping up' with their own, or a third party's, resources – so long as other relevant conditions are met and the local authority agrees.

However, as with the case of topping up in respect of residential accommodation (see section 9.5), local authorities, or rather service users, should beware. Local authorities are likely to be tempted not just to allow a person to top up to obtain a service over and beyond their assessed need – but also to award too low an amount of direct payment in the first place even to cover the cost of the basic service required. This would then effectively force the person, assuming he or she could afford to do so, to top up in order to meet even the basic assessed need. Alternatively, those who could not afford it might be unable to meet all their assessed needs. Either way, the local authority would risk acting unlawfully.

13.1.8 DIRECT PAYMENTS, AND HEALTH AND SAFETY

Some local authorities tend to express concerns over health and safety issues in the context of direct payments. For example, a disabled person might on occasion use the payment in such a way as to give rise to serious health and safety concerns on the part of the local authority. If, in response, the local authority takes a 'hands-off' approach it is likely to be anxious about negligence litigation in respect of any accident that occurs – even if the recipient has, as a condition of the direct payment, taken out insurance.

In addition to a claim against the disabled person, a local authority would still represent an additional and tempting target for litigation because of its relatively deep financial pocket. In some circumstances, the disabled person might anyway attempt to argue that the accident was the local authority's fault (e.g. because of lack of information or poor initial risk assessment) and so to try to deflect the litigation away from himself or herself on to the local authority.

In such circumstances, the local authority might be legally vulnerable because, overall, it remains statutorily responsible for assessing need and making a direct payment in order that the need be met. Yet, an excessively 'hands-on' or interventionist approach would risk undermining the whole purpose of direct payments – which is to give people greater choice and control over their own lives. With this purpose in mind, Department of Health guidance states that recipients should be given information about health and safety and also the results of any risk assessment carried out. In addition, recipients should be encouraged to develop strategies on manual handling. However, the guidance clearly states: 'As a general principle, local councils should avoid laying down health and safety policies for individual direct payment recipients' (DH 2003c, para 96).

This guidance would appear therefore to represent a hands-off approach, and one taken perhaps by most local authorities. It is an approach consistent with the underlying purpose of direct payments, namely to give disabled people more control, including responsibilities. It is also an approach which some local authorities believe may protect them from liability in case of accident, because it would indicate that the statutory framework inevitably reduced the extent, if not the existence, of the local authority's duty of care. Even so, in case of things going very badly wrong, it is at least conceivable that local authorities could in some circumstances be legally vulnerable not only to negligence litigation, but also to prosecution under s.3 of the Health and Safety at Work Act 1974, which contains a duty toward non-employees (see 5.4 above).

In any event, local authorities have the power to set reasonable conditions when they make direct payments (SI 2003/762). Guidance states that local authorities 'may set reasonable conditions on the direct payment, but need to bear in mind when doing so that the aim of a direct payment is to give people more choice and control over the services they are assessed as needing... Conditions should be proportionate' (DH 2003c, para 63). They also have the power ultimately to withhold a direct payment (and instead arrange services themselves for the person) if it is not being used in a reasonable manner (SI 2003/762).

13.1.8.1 Health and safety at work legislation
It is probable that, because of the effect of s.51 of the Health and Safety Work Act 1974, health and safety at work legislation does not apply as between a direct payment recipient as employer and his or her employees. However, the employee could still bring negligence litigation if necessary; in other words the recipient has a common law duty of care to his or her employees. The local authority would still *potentially* have health and safety at work responsibilities toward both the recipient and any employee employed by the recipient – since both would be 'non-employees' of the local authority for the purpose of s.3 of the Health and Safety at Work Act 1974. However, the arm's length nature of direct payments would call into question the extent of local authority responsibility.

If the recipient contracts with an agency, then the agency has duties toward its employees under s.2 of the Health and Safety at Work Act 1974 and various regulations, for example, manual handling (SI 1992/2793) – and toward the direct payment recipient under s.3 of the 1974 Act. Employees of the agency have duties towards themselves and others under s.7 of the 1974 Act.

If the personal assistants supplied through an agency are not employees of the agency but are genuinely self-employed, then the agency has a s.3 duty toward them as non-employees and likewise to the direct payment recipient. Self-employed persons, too, have duties towards themselves and others under s.3 of the 1974 Act.

13.1.9 WITHDRAWING OR WITHHOLDING A DIRECT PAYMENT

The effect of the legislation is to allow a local authority to withdraw a direct payment if any of the relevant conditions are no longer being satisfied – for example, in relation to need not being met or the person's ability to manage the payment (SI 2003/762).

Department of Health guidance states that councils should encourage people to plan for the unexpected and be prepared to step in to provide services, or to help a person continue to manage his or her own care, particularly if the problem is temporary or unforeseen (DH 2003c, para 154). Indeed, the legislation itself states that if a person is unable, temporarily, to manage the payment, the local authority can continue to make the payment if somebody else is prepared to accept and manage it, and the service provider agrees to accept payment from that other person (SI 2003/762).

The legislation allows the local authority to seek repayment if the money involved has not been used to secure a relevant service or if a condition of the direct payment agreement has been breached (SI 2003/762). However, Department of Health guidance states that this power to recover money should not be used to penalise honest mistakes, or to seek repayment where the recipient has been the victim of fraud (DH 2003c, para 161).

13.1.10 THIRD PARTY OR INDIRECT PAYMENTS

Hitherto, when a person has clearly lacked capacity to consent or to manage the payment with or without assistance, a direct payment has not been permitted lawfully to be made by a local authority to the person himself or herself or to anybody else. (The law is due to change: see 13.1.2 above.)

However, there are ways around this involving what are variously referred to as third party or indirect payments. These may involve what is sometimes called a user independent trust. This became clear during the course of a manual handling dispute that ended up in court:

Manual handling dispute and user independent trust. One legal case concerned two women with profound physical and learning disabilities cared for by their parents at home. The local authority and parents engaged in an extended dispute about manual handling for the two women. It was accepted by all involved that direct payments would not be possible because of the two women's inability to consent or to manage the payment with or without assistance.

However, the judge stated that it would be possible for a 'user independent trust', in the form of a registered company, to be formed. The local authority could make payments (sometimes referred to as 'indirect' or third party payments) to the trust, which in turn would purchase personal assistance including manual handling assistance. The arrangements would lie not under direct payments legislation but under s.30 of the National Assistance Act 1948. If the judge was wrong about this possibility under s.30, then he suggested such an arrangement could come under s.111 of the Local Government Act 1972, that allows a local authority to do things to facilitate, or which are conducive or incidental to, the discharge of any of its functions. Alternative to either of these two, s.2 of the Local Government Act 2000 would also serve, under the power to promote or improve social well-being in the local authority's area (*R(A&B) v East Sussex CC: no.2*).

Section 30 of the National Assistance Act permits local authorities to employ, as agents, voluntary organisations or any other person carrying on, professionally or by way of trade or business, activities that consist of or include the provision of such services. This is so long as the organisation or person in question appears to the local authority to be capable of providing the relevant services (National Assistance Act 1948, s.30).

It should be noted that the judge was astute to the above arrangement not simply being a covert or sham means of giving the parents the money, and so undermining the rules about direct payments. In this particular case, the trust would be in the form of a registered company, with five members on the trust board; this would mean the parents had neither a veto nor majority voting rights. The daughters could not have received direct payments in their own right because of their lack of relevant mental capacity. Had it been raised as a possibility, the parents (in their role of informal carers) could not have received carers' direct payments because these cannot involve anything of an intimate nature (see 13.5.6). It should be noted however, that the local authority has no duty to make payments to such a user independent trust – unlike the case of direct payments.

As already indicated above, the courts have stated that the NHS, too, has a power to make payments into a user independent trust (*R(Gunter) v South Western Staffordshire PCT*).

13.2 INDIVIDUAL BUDGETS

At the time of writing, local authorities have been implementing a new way of allocating funding and arranging services for people, called 'individual budgets'. Introduced with no legislation and no formal guidance, it is not entirely clear exactly how they should be accurately described. However, several key elements are apparent (see e.g. CIPFA 2007).

First, they may involve the lumping together of a number of funding streams for meeting people's needs, including community care services, community equipment (see 19.7), independent living fund (see 13.4), access to work, supporting people (see 16.3) and disabled facilities grants for home adaptations (see 16.5).

Second, at least as far as community care services go, the level or extent of a person's assessed need is to be equated with a certain amount of money (e.g. weekly or annually). The person concerned can then indicate how and on what the money should be spent. If the local authority believes that what is suggested is a reasonable way of meeting a person's needs, then it will agree.

Third, the money might be given to the person in the form of a direct payment, that is, an actual budget. Alternatively, an agent or broker might arrange the services and allocate the money on the person's behalf – so that the person does not have to handle and take direct responsibility for the money. This could be referred to as 'virtual budget'. As a government

White Paper put it: 'Individuals who are eligible for these funds will then have a single transparent sum allocated to them in their name and held on their behalf, rather like a bank account. They can choose to take this money out either in the form of a direct payment in cash, as provision of services, or as a mixture of both cash and services, up to the value of their total budget. This will offer the individual much more flexibility to choose services which are more tailored to their specific needs' (Secretary of State for Health 2006, p.83). Fourth, it appears that the money should be spent with a view to achieving specified general outcomes for the service user, rather than achieving a particular type of service provision.

Fifth, 'self-assessment' is actively encouraged so that a person's own view of their needs increasingly determines what their statutory needs are accepted to be by the local authority (under the NHS and Community Care Act 1990).

Sixth, there is meant to be an integrated charging system applied to individual budgets, somehow taking account of the different charging rules underpinning some of the funding streams.

13.2.1 INDIVIDUAL BUDGETS: RAMIFICATIONS

Central government has made clear that individual budgets are intended to bring about a major change to the way in which social care is provided. This is part of moving toward a 'personalised care system', giving people 'maximum choice, control and power over the support services they receive'. It is about replacing what has been labelled paternalistic, reactive care with enablement and high quality personally tailored services (HMG 2007). Independence, choice and control are the watchwords (Secretary of State for Health 2005).

Nonetheless, individual budgets appear to be Janus-faced. On one view, they are likely to be welcomed insofar as they give people more control and say in how their needs are perceived and how they are met. Given the rigidity, bureaucracy and restrictions that have sometimes characterised local authority support and assistance for people, there is an arguable case that such change is needed. On the other hand, and at another extreme, they could appear to be directed primarily at (a) saving money, (b) leaving vulnerable people to their own devices to sink or swim with decreasing support and help from the State, and (c) dismantling local authority adult social services and indeed a significant part of the welfare state as it has been understood since 1948. There is, therefore, some unease that such a potentially major change to social care is so far being introduced with no legislation, definitive guidance or Parliamentary debate. From a legal point of view, it is almost as though individual budgets are being implemented by the back door. One consequence of this is that it is by no means clear how they fit into the existing framework of community care legislation and statutory guidance.

First, the legislation states that it is for the local authorities to carry out assessments and to take final decisions about needs and services. This seems to sit uneasily with the individual budget emphasis on service users both assessing their own needs, and then determining how those needs should be met.

Second, if the meeting of people's needs is expressed in terms of very general outcomes only, rather than specific services, it may be difficult to establish whether a local authority is actually meeting a person's needs. Whereas at the moment, more detailed care plans represent a measure against which the authority's performance of its duty can be legally gauged (see 8.1).

Third, the allocation of fixed amounts of money corresponding to certain levels of need is likely to lead to tight caps being placed on the amounts of money available to relative need. This is inevitable because of the financial straits in which local authorities find themselves. It has already been pointed out that, where the individual budget is less than the value of existing support arrangements, a greater burden may fall on family and friends to support the person (Ibsen 2007). Topping up – of money or care – of what the local authority is providing, in terms of finance or informal care, is likely to become widespread. As the community care rules stand, allocation of insufficient money to meet a person's assessed need would run the risk of being unlawful – always assuming, under the new way of doing things, it were possible to identify what those assessed needs were.

Fourth, individual budgets will only be available to those deemed eligible under the fair access to care policies of local authorities (LAC(DH)(2008)1, para 19). Yet the current trend is for fewer people to be treated as eligible.

Fifth, central government wishes a unified system of charging for services to cover the different funding streams making up individual budgets. Given that the charging rules currently differ – for example, disabled facilities grants are financially assessed very differently than community care services, and community equipment cannot be charged for at all – this would appear not straightforward.

13.3 VOUCHERS

Local authorities have a power to issue vouchers (Carers and Disabled Children Act 2000; SI 2003/1216). These can be issued in respect of the informal carer (16 years old or more) of an adult aged 18 years, or of the parent of a disabled child.

Department of Health guidance describes vouchers as offering flexibility in timing and choice of short breaks, and as giving service users and carers an alternative to direct payments or to direct provision of services. A key difference between direct payments and vouchers is that, in the case of the former, the recipient of the payment takes on contractual responsibility; whereas with vouchers, the local authority retains that responsibility. Thus, for service users and carers, vouchers will be simpler to operate (DH 2003d, paras 4–5). They are something of a halfway house.

A voucher enables a person to obtain services which he or she would have otherwise obtained through the local authority. A voucher is issued where a local authority agrees with an informal carer (including a parent) that a temporary break from caring would help him or her to care for the person being cared for (Carers and Disabled Children Act 2000, s.3; Children Act 1989, s.17B). Such breaks must not last longer than 28 days at any one time and cumulatively not exceed 120 days in any 12-month period (SI 2003/1216).

Vouchers may be expressed in terms of money or of time. A time voucher must specify the service for which it is valid; and it may, but does not have to, specify the supplier of services (Carers and Disabled Children Act 2000, s.3; Children Act 1989, s.17B; SI 2003/1216).

In the case of community care services for adults, time vouchers may be issued either to the person cared for, or to the carer – if the cared for person consents or lacks capacity to give that consent. In respect of children in need, they may be issued to the parent. However, money vouchers can be issued only to the person cared for or the parent of a child in need.

If the voucher holder wishes the care provider to provide additional or more expensive services over and above those covered by the voucher, a third party may pay the extra (i.e. 'top up'). However, vouchers must not be issued either to a cared for person or a carer who comes into any of the categories of people subject to certain criminal justice and mental health legislation and who are prohibited from receiving direct payments (SI 2003/1216).

Department of Health guidance states that a local authority's normal charging system for non-residential services should be applied to the provision of vouchers (DH 2003d, para 25).

13.4 INDEPENDENT LIVING FUND

Grants are available to disabled people through a trust fund, funded by central government, known as the Independent Living Fund. It is beyond the scope of this book to enter into detail. The following is a summary only.

Up to September 2007, there were two funds. The first had been closed to new applicants since April 2003 and was known as the Independent Living (Extension) Fund. Eligibility was basically in terms of the person being in receipt (other than exceptionally) of the higher rate of care component of disability living allowance (or of attendance allowance) or constant attendant allowance, and having capital of under a certain threshold (£18,500). The maximum weekly payment available through the Extension Fund was £785 per week.

The second fund, known as the Independent Living (1993) Fund, was for new applicants since April 1993. Eligibility was established by the person being aged over 16 years old, and under 66 years (at the time of first application); receipt of, or entitlement to, higher rate care component of disability living allowance or (attendance allowance) or constant attendant allowance; receipt of local social services authority support of at least £200 per week; capital under a certain threshold (£18,500); and an expectation of living independently at home for at least the next 12 months.

In calculating the cost of care a local authority contributed, the Fund considered the cost to the local authority, less any charge it imposed on the service user (i.e. the £200 had to be net of any charges made to the service user). The maximum weekly amount payable by the Fund was £455 per week, which would be set against £330 contribution by the local authority, making a total of £785.

13.4.1 INDEPENDENT LIVING FUND (2006)

From October 2007, the two previous funds ceased, and a new fund, the Independent Living Fund (2006) took their place under s.1 of the Disability (Grants) Act 1993. In summary the trust deed for the new fund gives powers to the trustees of the fund 'to make payments to assist certain severely disabled people to live independently'. The following picks out a few key points from the trust deed (DWP 2006).

People who were eligible under the Independent Living (Extension) Fund remain eligible if they meet the 'common eligibility criteria' (see below) and remain entitled (other than exceptionally) to the higher rate of the care component of disability living allowance, attendance allowance or constant attendance allowance.

People who were eligible under the 1993 Fund, and new applicants (who must be under 65 years old on application), remain eligible if they meet the common eligibility criteria, are receiving at least the rate highest rate of the care component of disability living allowance (or attendance allowance) or constant attendance allowance – and are receiving from a local authority ongoing 'qualifying support and services' or direct payments at least to the value of a 'threshold sum' (currently £16,640 per annum, or its equivalent worked out weekly, £320).

This threshold sum was introduced in April 2008 and represented a steep increase in the threshold from £10,400 per annum, that is, £200 per week. The reason for this change was that the annual fixed budget of the ILF was no longer adequate to make awards to all qualifying applicants. The maximum amount payable from the ILF remains at £455, dependent on the amount of local authority contribution.

For the same reason, the ILF introduced also a new rule about allocating a priority system to applications. The first priority is afforded to applicants who are in work – that is remunerative employment or self-employment of at least 16 hours a week. The next level of priority is awarded to the poorest applicants – those receiving Income Support, Income Based Job Seekers' Allowance and Pension Credit Guarantee Credit or people whose other income is at an equivalent level. In addition, people who have received substantial compensation for personal injury will normally be excluded from applying.

The common criteria include the conditions that the person:

- be severely disabled (physically, mentally, sensorily) so as to require extensive help in terms of qualifying support and services, to enable the person to live independently
- be at least 16 years old
- be receiving income support, or the guarantee credit part of the state pension credit (and have capital under a certain threshold), or must have weekly resources less than their weekly needs (as defined) and capital under a certain threshold.

The qualifying support and services are defined as:

- cleaning and other domestic duties
- cooking and preparing food and drink
- laundering and ironing
- shopping
- personal hygiene and grooming
- dressing
- eating
- drinking
- physical movement such as turning, walking
- supervision in order to avoid substantial danger to him or herself or others.

The Fund can pay the money to a third party to administer it, usually where the disabled person is unable to manage his or her own money. The 2006 Fund is primarily intended to pay for the cost of employing personal assistants to provide personal and domestic care. The money cannot be used to employ or pay close relatives living in the same household. There is also a range of services on which the money cannot be spent, including holidays, care homes, wheelchairs, equipment, home adaptations, furniture, physiotherapy, etc.

It will be seen that there is a close link with social services support (the £320 rule), which local authority staff therefore need to be aware of. For instance, when a local authority reduced a person's weekly care package, and told her that it would not affect her entitlement to ILF, this was incorrect and the local ombudsman found maladministration (*Croydon LBC 2000*).

13.5 INFORMAL CARERS

At least six pieces of legislation are directly relevant to informal carers in the community care context. These are the Carers (Equal Opportunities) Act 2004, Carers and Disabled Children Act 2000, Carers (Recognition and Services) Act 1995, Children Act 1989 (s.17), Disabled Persons (Services, Consultation and Representation) Act 1986 (s.8) and the NHS Act 2006 (s.254 and schedule 20).

This legislation relevant to carers is important because, increasingly it seems, informal carers (largely families but others as well) are shouldering ever more substantial caring burdens, as statutory services in the form of both the NHS and local authorities seem to be withdrawing services and leaving people to fend more for themselves. As has been pointed out, breaking point, physically and emotionally, can be reached with the endless pressure of intensive care, including sleep deprivation, moving and handling and being only the person who can provide what is needed (MENCAP 2006, p.5).

13.5.1 RIGHT OF INFORMAL CARER TO AN ASSESSMENT

Under the Carers (Recognition and Services) Act 1995 and the Carers and Disabled Children Act 2000, informal carers are entitled, if certain conditions are met, to have their ability to care assessed by local authorities. Under the 1995 Act, for an informal carer to be entitled to an assessment, the local authority must be carrying out an assessment of the person cared for under s.47 of the NHS and Community Care Act 1990. In the case of a disabled child, there must be an assessment of that child under Part 3 of the Children Act 1989 or s.2 of the Chronically Sick and Disabled Persons Act 1970.

By contrast, under the 2000 Act, an assessment of the person being cared for is not a pre-requisite. The condition for a carer's assessment is simply that he or she must be caring for a person for whom the local authority is satisfied that it has the power to provide or arrange community care services. In principle, it would be possible to for a carer to be an entitled to an assessment, even if the cared for person has been assessed as not being eligible for services under 'fair access to care' (FACS) eligibility criteria – because his or her needs do not come above the eligibility threshold. The carer might still be entitled, because even a cared for person with 'low' needs under FACS is still a person for whom the local authority may provide community services. It is just that, by means of FACS, the local authority has chosen not to exercise that power.

In the case of a parent of a disabled child, the local authority must be satisfied that it has the power to provide or arrange services for the child and family under s.17 of the Children Act 1989. In other words, a carer's assessment under the 2000 Act is an entitlement irrespective of whether an assessment of the person cared for has taken place. Whereas, under the 1995 Act, a carer's assessment could not proceed unless associated with a community care assessment of the cared for person.

The Carers (Equal Opportunities) Act 2004 amended the 2000 Act, so as to extend the scope of assessment. It must now consider not just the person's ability to care but also whether the carer is engaging in, or wishes to engage, in work, training, education, leisure.

13.5.1.1 Request for carer's assessment

The carer must request the assessment for the assessment duty to be triggered. What legally constitutes a request is not always clear; the following two court cases are arguably inconsistent:

Requesting a carer's assessment. A local authority maintained that it had not carried out an assessment of the mother of a disabled child under the Carers (Recognition and Services) Act 1995, because it had not received a request to do so. The court held that a letter sent by the woman's solicitors, requesting a full enquiry into both mother and child's 'total needs', was not specific enough. So no request had been made, and there was no duty to assess (R(AB and SB) v Nottingham CC).

This apparently restrictive judicial approach in the *Nottingham* case seems inconsistent with the approach taken in another case concerning the need for a request (by a disabled person or carer) to trigger an assessment of the disabled person under s.4 of the Disabled Persons (Services, Consultation and Representation) Act 1986. A mother had requested assistance for herself and her disabled ten-year-old son. The judge accepted that she had made no formal request for assessment, but held that the courts should look at the 'reality of the situation'; her request for assistance was in effect a request for assessment under the 1986 Act (R v Bexley LBC, ex p B).

Unsurprisingly, as the local ombudsman has found, it is easier if informal carers are informed about this right to request an assessment:

Complete failure to inform carers about their right to an assessment. A profoundly disabled girl was cared for by her parents; the local authority provided weekend respite care in a care home. The local ombudsman found that, over a period of several years, the authority had done absolutely nothing to inform the parents of the statutory provisions for the assessment of carers. Its efforts at publicising the 1995 carers' legislation fell far short of what government guidance stated should happen. Yet there could not have been another family whose need was more pressing. This was maladministration (*North Yorkshire CC 2002*).

In the light of such failings, the Carers (Equal Opportunities) Act 2004 confers a duty on the local authority to inform carers about their right to request an assessment.

Any informal carer aged 16 years or over would potentially be entitled to an assessment under either the 1995 or 2000 Act. Less than 16 years old, as a young carer, he or she would be entitled to an assessment under the 1995 Act only. However, arguably such a child would also have a right to be assessed as a child in need under s.17 of the Children Act 1989.

Some local authorities continue to attempt to avoid carers' assessments; in one case, when an authority argued that it had fully assessed the family circumstances when assessing the disabled person, the local ombudsman found maladministration, since a clear assessment of the carer's needs had in fact not been undertaken (*South Tyneside MBC 1999*). Likewise:

Failure to assess the father of a woman with learning disabilities. A woman with learning disabilities visited home at Christmas and decided not to return to her residential placement. She wanted to live close to her family. The father suggested direct payments and Independent Living Fund money. The council failed properly to assess and to draw up a care plan; as a result the father had to take responsibility for the care of his daughter for over two years. During this time, his needs as a carer were not assessed. The local ombudsman found maladministration (*Hertfordshire CC 2003*).

So, when a social worker failed to visit an elderly couple – requiring help with cleaning and shopping needs – in order to carry out a community care assessment, the council was not in a position to consider properly whether a carer's assessment was required; this was maladministration (*Salford CC 2003*). And, in another local ombudsman investigation, the local authority failed to respond to a carer's request for assessment for over two years. It was then unacceptably critical, by implication of the carer's wishing to discuss his own mental health problems, which he felt were exacerbated by caring for his highly dependent brother who had learning disabilities and autism (*Sheffield CC 2004*).

13.5.2 INFORMAL CARERS: DEFINITION

Under both the 1995 and 2000 Acts, the definition of carer excludes both paid carers and volunteers from a voluntary organisation. Under the Disabled Persons (Services, Consultation and Representation) Act 1986 (see below) only paid carers, but not such volunteers, are excluded. It also appears that, under the 1986 Act, paid carers working for a voluntary organisation would also not be excluded, since s.8 of the 1986 Act excludes only paid carers working for an organisation exercising functions under legislation – which a voluntary organisation would presumably not be doing.

13.5.3 SUBSTANTIAL CARE ON A REGULAR BASIS

The duty of a local authority to assess a carer arises only if substantial care on a regular basis is involved. Department of Health policy guidance states that local authorities should judge substantial and regular care in relation to the overall impact of the whole caring situation and that it is not just about the amount of time spent. For instance, caring might not necessarily be based on physical tasks, and the caring may be periodic, sporadic or preventative in nature. It might involve the carer not physically or practically caring at all times, but nonetheless being subject to anxiety or stress waiting for or trying to prevent the next crisis. Caring responsibilities may conflict with either family or work responsibilities (DH 2005, p.22). This would mean that an over-simple criterion, such as the number of hours spent each week on the caring role, should not in itself be decisive.

13.5.3.1 Ability to care

The assessment under both 1995 and 2000 Acts must be of a carer's ability to care. The Carers (Equal Opportunities) Act 2004 amended both Acts so as to oblige the local authority to consider, in addition, whether the carer works or wishes to work – or is undertaking, or wishes to undertake, education, training or any leisure activity. Notwithstanding this, a local authority continued to state, six months after the 2004 Act came into force, that direct payments for a carer were not available for childcare purposes, so that the carer could attend a university course. This was maladministration (*City and County of Swansea 2007*).

In addition, the 2004 Act enables local authorities to call on other local social services, housing authorities, as well as NHS bodies, to assist in supporting carers. These other authorities and NHS bodies must give due consideration to any request made by the assessing local social services authority (see below).

13.5.4 RIGHT OF INFORMAL CARER TO BE HAD REGARD TO

If an informal carer of a disabled person does not wish for an assessment, or does not request it, the local authority is still obliged to take account of that carer's ability to care when deciding what welfare services to provide for the disabled person (Disabled Persons (Services, Consultation and Representation) Act 1986, s.8). However, this duty under the 1986 Act does not apply where a carer's assessment is carried out under the 1995 or 2000 Acts. The proviso that the carer be providing substantial and regular care applies under the 1986 Act, just as it does under the 1995 and 2000 Acts.

13.5.5 SERVICES FOR CARERS: CARERS AND DISABLED CHIILDREN ACT 2000

Under the Carers and Disabled Children Act 2000, where the cared for person is 18 years or over (i.e. excluding disabled children), a local authority has a duty to consider:

- whether the carer has needs in relation to the care being or intended to be provided
- whether those needs could be satisfied wholly or in part by services that the local authority has the power to provide
- if so, whether or not to provide these services (Carers and Disabled Children Act 2000).

This threefold duty is expressed in a tortuous manner and in any case only seems to create obligations in terms of considering the question of whether to provide services. It is expressed in such a way that the final stage simply falls off the edge of the cliff, as it were. There is a duty to assess, to decide whether needs exist, to decide whether those needs could be met by the local authority, and then to decide whether or not to provide the services – but there then appears to be no duty actually to provide any services. It would seem that provision of services appears to amount only to a power and not a duty.

However, a local authority cannot simply choose never to exercise the power. It is a power, a discretion, arising in the case of each individual assessed carer. The local authority has to decide in each case whether to exercise that power. Never to do so would fetter its discretion (*British Oxygen v Board of Trade*).

In addition, it has been suggested that if a carer had 'critical needs' (as set out in the Department of Health's 'fair access to care guidance', LAC(2002)13), the local authority would be under an obligation to provide services (Clements and Thompson 2007). Leaving human rights aside, potential breach of which could oblige an authority to exercise the power, this would on the face of it turn what is only a power into a duty. It is unclear whether this can be the case.

Practice guidance sets out a framework of risk, similar to the 'fair access to care' framework (see 6.12) and consisting of critical, substantial, moderate and low categories; within this framework, authorities should set a local threshold of eligibility. It states that local authorities 'should consider the level at which they fix eligibility in relation to sustainability of the caring role' (DH 2001b, paras 67–70). Once a local authority has adopted such a policy, it may be arguable that public law principles mean that it has largely to stick to it; but there still remains the question as to whether the adoption of a policy in respect of a power could bind the local authority in every case – otherwise the distinction between a power and a duty is lost. Nonetheless, a local authority would unlawfully fetter its discretion (see 5.2.1), were it to adopt a blanket policy not to provide carers' services either at all, or if it were inflexibly to provide for certain classes of person only or provide certain services only.

Perhaps in recognition of the essential weakness in the legislation, central government has continued to award special grant to local authorities for carers. In addition to this annual grant, it made available in 2007 an additional £25 million under s.31 of the Local Government Act 2003, in order to support the development of emergency respite services for informal carers – that is where carers are unable to provide care for a short period because of an emergency or personal crisis (DH 2007j).

The power to provide services in the 2000 Act applies only in the case of carers aged at least 16 years old, who are caring for a person 18 years old or over. For parents (as carers) of disabled children, services would fall to be provided under s.17 of the Children Act 1989 (see 13.6.3).

13.5.5.1 Range of carers' services

Assuming that the provision of carers' services is merely a power, then this is clearly a weakness in the Act. Nevertheless, a potential strength is that services are not defined, and therefore a local authority would have very wide scope indeed. This is clear from examples of services given in Department of Health practice guidance. They include shopping, cleaning, a washing machine in the informal carer's own home (to deal with incontinence laundry), a travel warrant for the brother of a person with a psychotic illness to come and stay for a week (thus giving the mother a break), and trips to art galleries (for a 17-year-old carer to get a break while caring for his dying father) (DH 2001b, paras 80–102). The policy guidance states that services 'may take any form', for example, a gardening service; and that practitioners are encouraged to be flexible and innovative (DH 2005 combine policy, para 52).

Providing instruction and training for informal carers could be another form of service. For instance, it has been pointed out in the *Selfish pig's guide to caring* that, in respect of the manual handling of disabled people, paid staff might receive training, specialist equipment and have assistants. In contrast, unpaid carers all too often receive no information, little equipment and have to lift alone (Marriott 2003, p.123).

The potential availability of services under the 2000 Act contrasts with the position previously, when there was no explicit legal power to provide services at all for carers. For example, in a 1996 case, informal carers living in upstairs premises wished to apply for assistance with modification of their dwelling. This would help them to care better for the elderly family members they were caring for in downstairs premises. The judge pointed out that the assessment under the Carers (Recognition and Services) Act 1995 did not get anyone anywhere in terms of services, and that the Chronically Sick and Disabled Persons Act 1970 anyway did not explicitly cover provision for carers (*R v Kirklees MBC, ex p Good*). Since the advent of the 2000 Act, this example contrasts with that given by Department of Health guidance of a washing machine provided not in the cared for person's home, but in the (separate) home of the informal carer.

13.5.6 SERVICES FOR THE CARER OR FOR THE CARED FOR PERSON
Some services will be capable of being characterised as either being for the disabled person or for the cared for person – for instance, a laundry service. However, there is an important proviso to this flexibility. Regulations made under the 2000 Act state that carers' services may not involve anything of an intimate nature in respect of the person being cared for (SI 2001/441). A service of an intimate nature is indicated in policy guidance as involving:

- lifting, washing, grooming, feeding, dressing, bathing, toileting, medicine administration, or other forms of physical contact
- assistance in connection with washing, grooming, feeding, dressing, bathing, administering medicines or using the toilet
- supervision of the person while he or she is dressing, bathing or using the toilet (DH 2005 Policy, para 56).

Nevertheless, the regulations also contain an exception to the rule. During the delivery of what was meant to be a non-intimate service, the carer may deliver an intimate service:

- if the person providing the service is asked by the cared for person to provide a service of an intimate nature
- if the person lacks capacity to consent to such a service but it is provided in accordance with the principles of the Mental Capacity Act 2005; or
- (except where the person lack such capacity to consent) if the person cared for is likely to suffer serious personal harm if the intimate service is not provided and (a) the person cared for is unable to consent to the service; or (b) the person providing the service reasonably believes it is necessary to provide the service because the likelihood of serious personal harm is imminent.

The overall purpose of the rule is to 'prevent any services being delivered to unwilling disabled or frail people' (DH 2005, para 57).

13.5.7 DIRECT PAYMENTS FOR CARERS
Where the local authority has decided to provide a carer's service, the service could be provided or arranged by the local authority or by means of direct payments (see 13.1).

13.5.8 OTHER LEGISLATION FOR CARERS
Services for informal carers are also potentially available under at least three pieces of legislation other than the 1986, 1995 and 2000 Acts.

The first is the Children Act 1989, s.17, which contains a 'general duty' to safeguard and promote the welfare of children in need by provision of services not only for the children but also for other family members.

The second is s.254 and schedule 20 of the NHS Act 2006, which places a general duty on local authorities to provide home help for households (and a power to provide laundry facilities) where it is required owing to the presence in the household of a person who is ill, disabled, aged etc. (see 11.4.2). The way in which the duty is couched would appear not to exclude provision in respect of informal carers, since providing for a household could presumably mean providing for any person in that household.

Third, the Carers (Equal Opportunities) Act 2004 imposes a twofold duty of cooperation on other authorities, including the NHS. These other authorities are any other local social services authority, housing authority, education authority or NHS body (listed as special health authority, local health board, primary care trust, NHS trust or NHS foundation trust):

- If a local authority requests these other authorities to assist it in planning the provision of services – for carers entitled to assessment under the 1995 or 2000 Acts, and for those receiving substantial and regular care from those carers – the authority must give due consideration to the request (s.3).
- If a local authority is carrying out, or has completed, a carer's assessment, and believes that the carer's ability to care might be enhanced by services from another authority (as defined above), it can ask the other authority to provide the services. The other authority must give the request due consideration (s.3).

The term 'due consideration' is a relatively weak term; although the NHS could not simply operate a blanket policy of refusing local authority requests for assistance, nevertheless the duty is a far cry from imposing a strong duty to assist in the planning of, or to provide, services for carers. This absence of concrete obligation upon the NHS is all the more glaring, since the present NHS policy of health 'care closer to home' – and, where possible, in people's own homes – carries wide implications for informal carers.

Policy guidance explains that giving due consideration means giving 'appropriate thought' to an individual request. For instance, the authority or NHS body could not 'fail to consider it, dismiss it arbitrarily, or have a blanket ban on considering certain types of request'. Thus an NHS body could not 'refuse to to consider any request made to them in relation to the provision of lifting and handling support for carers'. However, the guidance confirms that there is no duty to comply with the request, just so long as it is not ignored (DH 2005, para 36).

Lastly, the NHS Act 2006, in terms of NHS provision, does not explicitly refer to carers at all. On the other hand, it is couched in such broad terms that there would appear to be nothing to stop the NHS making plentiful provision for carers. For instance, under schedule 3 of the NHS Act 2006, a PCT can do anything appearing to it to be necessary or expedient in relation to its functions.

13.5.9 COST-EFFECTIVENESS OF CARERS' SERVICES

Cost-effectiveness, applied to an absolute duty, relates to how that duty is performed, not to whether it is performed. In the case of a power, it may apply in terms of whether that power will be exercised at all. Carers' services are seemingly governed by a power only. Therefore, in practice, local authority staff are likely to have to support their recommendations about such services with strong arguments about cost-effectiveness.

Cleaning assistance: example from Department of Health guidance. An older woman is caring for her husband. She carries out all the care, but would like help with cleaning. The local authority assessor understands the stress she feels at not being able to clean, and that this is undermining the sustainability of the whole caring situation. Her husband would be eligible for home care provided by the local authority but neither he nor his wife want this. The authority instead assists with the cleaning. This solution meets the couple's wishes and is more cost-effective (DH 2001b, para 81).

This example illustrates how useful a relatively small-scale service can be in a caring situation. It might even save the local authority money, since if the situation breaks down because the cleaning service is not provided, then the ensuing care package would be very much more expensive to provide. Department of Health practice guidance makes this very point, stating that carers sometimes approach local authorities, only to be told that they are entitled to expensive personal care (which they do not want) but not the cheaper cleaning service (which they do want). The guidance states that authorities who do not provide shopping-only, cleaning-only or other low level services should rethink their position – in the cause of genuinely assisting people and of cost-effectiveness (DH 2001b, para 80).

13.6 CHILDREN IN NEED AND THEIR FAMILIES

Local authorities have a general duty to safeguard and promote the welfare of children in need within their area. So far as it is consistent with that duty, they must promote the upbringing of such children by their families by providing a range and level of services appropriate to those children's needs (Children Act 1989, s.17). Section 17 of the 1989 Act contains notable strength and weakness. The strength essentially lies in the breadth and scope of provision that can be made; the weakness is that such provision is barely enforceable in any individual case.

Under s.11 of the Children Act 2004, there is a very broad duty on local authorities and NHS bodies (as well as other bodies such as the police) to ensure that they discharge their functions having regard to the need to safeguard and promote the welfare of children.

13.6.1 DEFINITION OF CHILDREN IN NEED

A child in need is defined as:
- unlikely to (or have the opportunity to) achieve or maintain a reasonable standard of health or development without the provision of services
- one whose health or development is likely to be significantly impaired, or further impaired, without the provision of services
- disabled.

A disabled child in turn means a child who is 'blind, deaf or dumb or suffers from mental disorder of any kind or is substantially and permanently handicapped by illness, injury or congenital deformity'.

Development means 'physical, intellectual, emotional, social or behavioural development'. Health means 'physical or mental health' (Children Act 1989, s.17). A child is defined as being under 18 years old (s.105).

13.6.2 RANGE OF SERVICES FOR CHILDREN IN NEED

The duty under s.17 of the Children Act 1989 is couched in such general terms – accommodation, assistance in kind and, in exceptional cases, cash – that a wide range of services could in principle be provided. For the purpose 'principally of facilitating' the discharge of this general duty, a local authority has a duty to provide, as it considers appropriate, the following services (s.17):

- advice, guidance and counselling
- occupational, social, cultural or recreational activities
- home help (which may include laundry facilities)
- facilities for, or assistance with, travelling to and from the home, in order to take advantage of any other service provided under the 1989 Act or any similar service
- assistance to enable the child and family to have a holiday (schedule 2).

The local authority also has a duty to minimise the effect on disabled children within their area of their disabilities and to give such children the opportunity to lead lives that are as normal as possible (schedule 2).

Services may be arranged in the form of direct payments in respect of the parents of disabled children, disabled children aged 16 or 17 years old, or disabled parents of children – where the child concerned is deemed to be in need of s.17 services (see 13.1). In addition, the parent of a disabled child may obtain services designed to give a short break to him or her, by means of time or money vouchers (s.17B: see 13.3).

13.6.3 PROVISION FOR THE FAMILY

Any service provided under s.17 of the 1989 Act may be provided for the child's family or any member of the family, so long as it is with a view to safeguarding and promoting the welfare of the child (s.17).

13.6.4 DUTY OF ASSESSMENT

There is no explicit duty on the local authority to assess a child in need under s.17 of the Children Act 1989; although the Act (schedule 2) does state that an assessment under s.17 may take place at the same time as an assessment under other legislation such as s.2 of the Chronically Sick and Disabled Persons Act 1970 (CSDPA).

However, policy guidance, *Framework for the Assessment of Children in Need*, assumes such a duty and sets out timescales of responding to referrals within one day, conducting an initial assessment within seven, and completing an in-depth, core assessment within 35 days (DH 2000a, paras 3.8–3.11). The courts have ruled that such guidance should be followed:

Assessment of child in need. The court stated that in terms of carrying out a core assessment of a child in need, the local authority had either to follow the guidance, or at least adopt a similarly systematic approach to achieve the same objectives. In the case of a core assessment this was to assess the child's developmental needs, parenting capacity, and family and environmental circumstances. It was then to identify the needs, produce a care plan and provide services. Failure to take this approach 'without good cause would constitute an impermissible departure from the guidance' (R(AB and SB) v Nottingham CC).

In another case, the court specifically ordered the local authority to carry out the s.17 assessment that it had been attempting to avoid, within 35 days (R(J) v Newham LBC).

Second, the courts have anyway confirmed that s.17 implies a duty of assessment of each child in need, whenever it appears necessary to assess (R(G) v Barnet LBC). It should be noted that unlike much of the community care legislation, s.2 of the CSDPA 1970 applies to children as well as adults. There is a condition contained in s.2 of the CSDPA that, for s.2 to apply, a local authority must have functions under s.29 of the National Assistance Act 1948 (welfare services for disabled adults). In the case of disabled children, this condition is substituted and replaced by a reference to Part 3 of the Children Act 1989 (CSDPA 1970, s.28A).

There is a duty, on request by the disabled child or a parent, to decide whether a disabled child's needs call for services under s.2 of the CSDPA 1970 (Disabled Persons (Services, Consultation and Representation) Act 1986, s.4).

13.6.5 DISABLED CHILDREN

The courts have pointed out that in contrast to s.17 of the Children Act 1989, an enforceable duty to provide for assessed, eligible need does arise in the case of a disabled child under s.2 of the Chronically Sick and Disabled Persons Act 1970. Therefore, artificial attempts to avoid providing for a disabled child, by arguing that provision of a respite service) concerned s.17 of the 1989 Act rather than s.2 of the CSDPA 1970, was treated with scepticism and as unlawful by the courts (R v Bexley LBC, ex p B).

13.6.6 LEAVING CARE: CHILDREN PREVIOUSLY LOOKED AFTER

In some circumstances, local authorities retain specific responsibilities (both duties and powers) into adulthood for certain people who, as children, were in the care of the local authority ('former relevant' children: Children Act 1989, s.23C).

There are also other wider responsibilities toward not just people previously looked after as children by a local authority, but also those who as children were (a) accommodated by a voluntary organisation or in a private children's home; (b) for a period of at least three consecutive months accommodated by an education authority, by the NHS, or in a care home or independent hospital; (c) privately fostered (Children Act 1989, s.24). The legislative provisions are complicated and the following is a rough summary only.

Where a child is a former relevant child or was otherwise looked after by a local authority, the responsible authority is the authority that last looked after him or her. Otherwise, it is the local authority in whose area the person now is (Children Act 1989, ss.23–24). Such responsibilities are known as 'leaving care' provisions; the duties are expressed toward each individual child. They normally cease when a child has reached 21 years but can in some circumstances continue beyond that age (Children Act 1989, ss.23C, 24B).

For former relevant children, the duties include keeping in touch with the former relevant child (now an adult); continuing the appointment of an adviser to the person; keeping a 'pathway plan' under regular review; and giving assistance in terms of living or other expenses incurred in relation to employment, education or training. Other assistance, in kind or exceptionally cash, must be given to the extent that the person's welfare requires it (Children Act 1989, ss.23C, 24B).

The courts have held that these duties, under the Act and relevant regulations (SI 2001/2874), apply as much to disabled children as to able-bodied children (*R(P) v Newham LBC*). A pathway plan has clearly to identify a child's needs, and also what is to be done about them and when; aspiration is not enough. Even if the child is uncooperative, the local authority still has to carry out its obligations under the regulations by doing its best. A child's lack of engagement, by way of hindrance, should be fully documented in the assessment and pathway plan (*R(J) v Caerphilly CBC*). Likewise, merely recording a person's self aspirations is not enough to constitute a pathway plan (*R(C) v Lambeth LBC*).

For the other categories of children mentioned above, duties and powers include advising and befriending, providing assistance in kind (exceptionally accommodation or cash), living or other expenses in connection with education or training (Children Act 1989, ss.24A–24B).

The definition of 'looked after' excludes children who have received services under s.17 of the Children Act 1989 (see s.22 of the Act); however, Department of Health guidance warns that local authorities should not on that account artificially label the provision of accommodation as s.17 (rather than s.20) provision merely to avoid 'leaving care' obligations at a later date (LAC(2003)13). Identification of the responsible local authority, for the purpose of leaving care functions, is covered below (see 15.2.4).

The courts have held that social services cannot sidestep s.20 responsibilities by arguing that it has provided under s.17 of the 1989 Act instead, if s.20 was clearly the relevant duty. Yet not every 16- or 17-year-old homeless child will necessarily be eligible for s.20 assistance, and thus excluded from provision under the Housing Act 1996. However, bed and breakfast accommodation is unlikely to be a suitable solution for a 16- or 17-year-old in need of support. Thus, if the criteria for s.20 involvement are met, then social services rather than housing is responsible – giving rise subsequently to leaving care duties (*R(G) v Southwark LBC*). However, in one particular case, when a housing authority should have, but failed to, refer a child to social services for s.20 provision, a legal claim that the social services leaving care duties were owed did not succeed (*R(M) v Hammersmith and Fulham LBC*).

In determining a ward of court's age – with an implication for leaving care duties arising – the courts have held that they have jurisdiction themselves to determine a child's age, notwithstanding that the local authority had conducted an earlier age assessment (*E By her litigation friend PW) v X LBC*).

13.6.7 DUTY OF COOPERATION IN RESPECT OF CHILDREN

Under the Children Act 2004, a duty is imposed on local authorities to promote cooperation with 'partners', including district councils (if the local authority is a county council), the police authority, local probation board, youth offending team, strategic health authority and primary care trust, and Learning and Skills Council. Arrangements made can include the provision of staff, goods, services, accommodation and other resources. The arrangements may, in addition to children, be made for people aged 18 and 19, people over the age of 19 receiving leaving care services under the Children Act 1989, and people over age of 19 but under the age of 25 who have a learning difficulty (s.10).

Under s.11 of the 2004 Act, these partners and other specified bodies must make arrangements to ensure that they discharge their functions 'having regard to the need to safeguard and promote the welfare of children in need'. This duty applies also where somebody else is providing services on their behalf (s.11) – for example, a contracted out service.

13.7 OTHER SPECIFIC GROUPS OF PEOPLE

The Department of Health has issued various guidance relating to specific groups of people, including people with HIV/AIDS, people with dual sensory impairment, people with learning disabilities, and people who misuse alcohol and drugs.

13.7.1 HIV SOCIAL CARE SERVICES

Guidance has been issued in respect of support grant for people with HIV/AIDS, which is provided by central government under the Local Government Grants (Social Need) Act 1969. The grant overall is to 'enable social Services Departments to finance the provision of social care for people with HIV/AIDS, and where appropriate, their partners, carers and families'. Guidance lists matters that local authorities should consider, including:

- effective joint planning arrangements
- comprehensive population needs assessments to ensure that minority groups are not overlooked (including women, children, people from newly arrived minority ethnic communities, and men who have sex with men)
- flexible care management arrangements including direct payments
- eligibility being determined on basis of assessed need, not just HIV status
- assessment and support for informal carers
- carers' rights
- integration of HIV services with those services for other service users, particularly children, families and people with drug-related problems
- review of continuing health care eligibility to ensure that people with HIV/AIDS have access to such services (LAC(2008)3).

13.7.2 DEAF–BLIND ADULTS

The Department of Health guidance (under s.7 of the local Authority Social Services Act 1970) in respect of deaf-blind adults recognises the particular impact of dual sensory loss; and of the fact that such dual loss does not necessarily mean profound deafness coupled with profound blindness. Even separately milder sensory loss can cause difficulty in combination (LAC(2001)8). The guidance states that local authorities should:

- make contact with and keep a record of deaf-blind people in their catchment area
- ensure that assessment is carried out by a specifically trained person or team in respect particularly of the need for one-to-one contact, assistive technology and rehabilitation

- ensure that services for deaf-blind people are appropriate, since mainstream services or those aimed at people who are either blind or deaf (but not both) may not be of benefit to deaf-blind people
- ensure that deaf-blind people are able to access one-to-one support workers where this is an assessed need
- ensure that a senior manager includes amongst his or her responsibilities responsibility for deaf-blind services.

13.7.3 PEOPLE WITH LEARNING DISABILITIES

Department of Health guidance issued in 1992 set out three basic service principles for people with learning disabilities (LAC(92)15, paras 9–15):

- People with learning disabilities should be treated as individuals and thus services should be provided on an increasingly individual basis, taking account of age, needs, degree of disability, personal preference of the person or his or her parents or carers, culture, race gender.
- Parents and carers should be fully involved in decisions about services; conciliation and counselling should be offered in case of conflicts between parents/carers and people with learning disabilities – but generally the views of the person with learning disability should be respected.
- Local authorities should give assurance that people's essential needs would be met on a lifelong basis, for instance to reassure ageing parents about continuity of service in the future for their sons or daughters with learning disabilities.

In 2001, central government published a White Paper, entitled *Valuing People*. It set out what it called four key principles: rights, independence, choice and inclusion. It referred to improving 'life chances', enabling more choice and control (e.g. through use of direct payments), improving health, more options for housing and education and employment, better quality of services, and partnership working by agencies (DH 2001d).

Subsequent policy guidance instructed the chief executives of local social services authorities to set up Learning Disability Partnership Boards. Representation on the boards should include social services, NHS bodies, housing, education, Employment Service, Jobcentre Plus, independent providers and voluntary organisations. The boards should promote effective arrangements for enabling young people with learning disabilities to move smoothly from children's to adult services in respect of all relevant agencies. Directors of social services should ensure the existence of good links between children's and adult's services in local authorities (LAC(2001)23).

The guidance stated that boards should also collate information about advocacy services to inform decisions on the funding of advocacy; foster the development of support services and schemes so that more people with learning disabilities benefit from direct payments; recommend procedures for dealing with the exclusion from services of people with learning disabilities. Boards should, amongst other things, also ensure that arrangements were in place to enable people currently in NHS long-stay hospitals to move to more appropriate accommodation by April 2004; introduce a 'person-centred' approach to planning services by spring 2003; begin to modernise day services; and have a local housing strategy for people with learning disabilities etc. (LAC(2001)23).

Person-centred planning was described in subsequent guidance as an approach based on what is important to a person from his or her own perspective, with a view to the person's fuller inclusion in society. It was to be distinguished from community care assessment and care plans under s.47 of the NHS and Community Care Act 1990 (DH 2001b). In other words, there might be no duty actually to provide what was important to the person and was necessary for his or her fuller inclusion in society.

13.7.3.1 Further consultation about valuing people

In 2007, the Department of Health consulted on the next steps in *Valuing People*. The gist of the proposals was that people with learning disabilities should (a) have 'real choice and control over their lives and services' by means of direct payment and individual budgets; (b) not go to traditional day centres, rather should get a 'job and education and a life'; (c) have better health care from the NHS; (d) have more control and choice over where and how they live; and (e) access to advocacy and protection of their human rights (DH 2007s, executive summary).

13.7.4 DRUGS AND ALCOHOL

The Department of Health issued guidance in 1993 in respect of misuses of drugs and alcohol (LAC(93)2). Some of the main points include:

- **Priority**. Local authorities are expected to attach a high priority to alcohol and drug misusers in community care (para 1).
- **Special circumstances**. Misusers of alcohol and drugs present a particular challenge. Assessment procedures must be capable of identifying alcohol or drug misuse. People might have complex needs, move between areas frequently, and have no settled residence. They might self-refer to agencies in areas in which they are not resident, avoid contact with statutory services, and require services several times before they bring the misuse under control. Their behaviour might be unpredictable, and they might require rapid responses to avoid deterioration (paras 12–13).
- **Eligibility criteria**. Local authorities should ensure that eligibility criteria are sensitive to the circumstances of alcohol and drug misusers (para 14).
- **Assessment by the independent sector**. Local authorities should consider involving the expertise of the independent sector in the assessment process, although ultimate responsibility for the decision to provide services remains with the local authority (paras 16–17).
- **Out of area placements**. Generally, local authorities, within certain financial bounds, must attempt to give people a choice of residential accommodation. There might be 'therapeutic benefit in referring people to a residential area away from the area in which they are experiencing their alcohol and drug problems… LAs should ensure that resources can be identified for out of area placements' (para 23).
- **Probation service**. For people who misuse drugs or alcohol and who might require residential or non-residential care, local authorities should liaise with probation services (para 25).

Despite the firm tone of the guidance, it should be noted that the provision of non-residential services (NHS Act 2006, schedule 20 and LAC(93)10) or residential accommodation (National Assistance Act 1948, s.21 and LAC(93)10) 'specifically for persons who are alcoholic or drug dependent' is a power only. Nevertheless, if the need, or the service required by, the user of alcohol or drugs can be equated with more than just the substance misuse, then a duty could be identified – for instance, if the person has in addition, or as a consequence of the substance misuse, a mental disorder, an illness or a disability etc. – so as to bring him or her under a duty elsewhere in the legislation.

CHAPTER 14

Asylum seekers and other people subject to immigration control

KEY POINTS

The law as a whole relating to asylum seekers and other people subject to immigration control is beyond the scope of this book. The following is a summary only, designed to give a few pointers on matters relating to community care specifically. Much of the legal case law involving community care revolves around s.21 of the National Assistance Act 1948; therefore this chapter should be taken in conjunction with Chapter 9 in particular.

Since about 1996, a significant part of community care for some local authorities has concerned the provision of services for asylum seekers and others who are subject to immigration control. The relevant law continues to be in a continual state of flux and uncertainty; a situation reflected in the large amount of legal case law on immigration matters generally, a significant part of which has involved local social services authority responsibilities. This represents an additional and unexpected layer of complexity in the community care system, which even in its basic form contains uncertainty enough. Local social services authorities have continued fully to explore legal loopholes and escape routes, referred to in Chapter 3 of this book, in order to extricate themselves from unwanted financial legal obligations.

In summary, there are perhaps three key questions for local authorities. First, in respect of asylum seekers is the all important decision about whether the asylum seeker is in need merely because of destitution or the effects of destitution – or whether there are needs beyond those which are destitution related. This is often referred to as the 'destitution plus' test. In the former case, the Home Office is responsible for relieving that destitution, whereas local authorities are responsible in the latter circumstance. Likewise, if a person is here lawfully but on condition of not accessing public funds, then the same destitution plus test has to be applied.

Second, asylum seekers apart, local authorities have to establish whether they are prohibited from assisting other people who may be subject to certain immigration-related rules. For instance, they are prohibited from assisting people with refugee status abroad, European Economic Area (EEA) citizens, unsuccessful asylum seekers who have failed to cooperate with removal directions, and other people unlawfully present under immigration legislation.

Third, however, these prohibitions do not prevent the local authority assisting a child; they are also disapplied if they would mean a breach of human rights or contravention of an EEA treaty.

The NHS is subject to separate rules about providing treatment and services for overseas visitors in the context of hospital treatment. Depending basically on degree of urgency, some treatment is provided free of charge, other treatment must be provided but is chargeable (albeit retrospectively) and still other treatment should not be given until payment is made.

Overall, provision of welfare support (including community care) for asylum seekers and others subject to immigration control is an especially complex and specialist area. This chapter attempts to give a number of pointers only. Other specialist sources of information should be consulted for greater detail.

14.1 IMMIGRATION CONTROL: BACKGROUND

Asylum seekers and people subject to immigration control have featured prominently in community care since at least 1996. In attempts to deal with this unexpected development, something of a 'cat-and-mouse' game has emerged, played out between central government, local government and the courts. Parliament has passed a great deal of legislation. Because of the fundamental issues involved, the courts have closely scrutinised this legislation for loopholes. And, owing to the financial implications, local authorities have made sustained attempts to avoid responsibilities that they have felt to be unfair.

In 1996 regulations were introduced to deny certain classes of asylum seeker access to income-related benefits including income support and housing benefit. The courts struck down these regulations as unlawful in the light of the rights implicit in the Asylum and Immigration Appeals Act 1993 (*R v Secretary of State for the Home Department, ex p Joint Council for the Welfare of Immigrants*).

Central government then reacted via the Asylum and Immigration Act 1996, so as to restore the effect of the regulations that the courts had just held to be unlawful. Consequently, certain asylum seekers were deprived of accommodation, funds, benefits and permission to work (for at least six months). A possible last resort was then identified; namely s.21 of the National Assistance Act 1948. This placed a duty on local social services authorities to arrange residential accommodation in certain circumstances for those in urgent need of it. The 1948 Act had not been on the list of exclusions contained within the 1996 Act.

Faced with potential unexpected and significant expenditure, the affected local authorities resisted and fought out several issues in the courts, including whether (a) s.21 was relevant at all to asylum seekers (*R v Westminster CC, ex p A*: it was); (b) cash payments could be made to those being provided with residential accommodation (*R v Secretary of State for Health, ex p Hammersmith and Fulham LBC*: they could not); (c) food vouchers could be given under s.21 even if residential accommodation was not being provided (*R v Newham LBC, ex p Gorenkin*: they could not); (d) accommodation alone – without food, laundry and other facilities for personal hygiene – could be provided (*R v Newham LBC, ex p Medical Foundation for the Care of Victims of Torture*: it could); and (e) choice could be exercised in relation to where the accommodation was arranged (*R v Westminster CC, ex p P*: the question was not answered).

One case was particularly significant. The Court of Appeal emphasised that the plight of the asylum seekers was horrendous and that the National Assistance Act 1948 was a prime example of legislation that was 'always speaking' in response to changing social circumstances (*R v Westminster CC, ex p A*). Up to October 2000, this type of case was being decided without recourse to the Human Rights Act 1998, which had not yet come into force. The courts instead referred on several occasions to an 1803 case (*R v Inhabitants of Eastbourne*), in which the 'law of humanity, which is anterior to all positive laws', had been invoked and which obliged that relief be given to prevent poor foreigners (Napoleonic refugees) from starving (see e.g. reference in *R v Westminster CC, ex p A*: High Court).

By 1998, it was clear that the pressure on some local social services authorities had become considerable. In 1999 and 2002 further major legislation was passed to give the basis of the present position. This was elaborated upon by further legislation in 2004. The

1999 legislation was designed to shift the burden of asylum seekers away from local authorities; the subsequent case law and judicial interpretation suggests that the Act did not achieve this to the extent intended. The 2002 legislation aimed at reducing further the assistance given by local social services authorities to people subject to immigration control (other than asylum seekers).

The approach of central government, which effectively reduces to destitution asylum seekers and others – including those who may be particularly vulnerable for a variety of reasons – is seen by some as controversial and as using destitution as a public policy tool (e.g. Amnesty International 2006; Refugee Council 2004; Refugee Council 2006).

14.2 IMMIGRATION CONTROL: SOCIAL SERVICES

The following paragraphs outline the position concerning responsibilities owed by local social services authorities, in the community care context, to asylum seekers or other people subject to immigration control.

14.2.1 'DESTITUTION PLUS' TEST

People to whom s.115 of the Immigration and Asylum Act 1999 applies (those subject to immigration control including asylum seekers) may not be provided with community care services by local authorities, if the need for care and attention arises solely (a) because the person is destitute; or (b) because of the physical effects, or anticipated physical effects, of destitution.

Basically, s.115 applies to people who are denied a wide range of social security benefits because they are subject to immigration control. A person is subject to immigration control if he or she is not an EEA national and (a) requires leave to enter or remain in the United Kingdom but does not have that leave; (b) has leave to enter or remain on condition of not having recourse to public funds; (c) has leave to enter or remain as a result of a maintenance undertaking by another person; (d) during an appeal concerning leave.

The prohibitions on community care services are contained in the National Assistance Act 1948 (s.21(1A) NAA), the Health Services and Public Health Act 1968 (s.45(4A)) and the NHS Act 2006 (schedule 20, para 6). However, s.117 of the Mental Health Act 1983 is not listed. Nor is s.29 of the 1948 Act, or s.2 of the Chronically Sick and Disabled Persons Act 1970; this is presumably because it is assumed that the various disabilities required to trigger this legislation (see 11.1.3) would not normally be regarded as solely destitution related.

The prohibitions refer to destitution or to the physical effects, or anticipated physical effects of, destitution. The courts have held that mental illness can come within physical effects. So in one case a local authority failed to ask the question, whether depression arose solely from destitution, or whether there was another cause as well. In the former, but not the latter, circumstance, it would be prohibited from assisting (*R(PB) v Haringey LBC*).

A person is defined as destitute if he or she does not have adequate accommodation or any means of obtaining it (whether or not other essential living needs are being met); or if he or she does have adequate accommodation or has the means of obtaining it, but cannot meet other essential living needs (Immigration and Asylum Act 1999, s.95).

Ineligible for assistance through destitution. The applicant was a 51-year-old British citizen, holder of a British passport with right of abode in the United Kingdom. He was ineligible for social security benefits because he was not classed as habitually resident in the UK and did not speak English. The manager of a night shelter – where the man had been staying, but which was now closing – wrote on his behalf, seeking for residential accommodation to be provided by the local authority under s.21 of the National Assistance Act 1948.

An assessment was carried out by the local authority, with the conclusion that, though without benefits and homeless, the man was able-bodied and had worked previously as a ship's captain and cook, was not physically disabled except for dental problems for which he could receive NHS treatment, and was aware of his situation. On this basis his application was refused.

The judge held that it was not 'perverse' of the local authority to have refused assistance. For instance, the present applicant was not ineligible from seeking accommodation under homelessness legislation, was not 'under any physical or mental disability', was able-bodied and of working age. He also referred to the Court of Appeal's judgment in *R v Westminster CC, ex p A*, which emphasised that s.21 of the 1948 Act was not a safety net for anybody short of money or accommodation. Nor could the judge fault the local authority's assessment, finding that it was 'not arguable that they left out of that consideration any material matter' (*R v Newham LBC, ex p Plastin*).

However, the courts have held that a disabled asylum seeker might be eligible for provision of accommodation under s.21 of the National Assistance Act 1948, but nevertheless have other essential living needs (e.g. for clothing) unrelated to the accommodation or to the amenities and requisites that go with it (see 9.2.3). In which case, the Home Office might have potential responsibility under s.95 of the 1999 Act for meeting those additional needs (*R(O) v Haringey LBC*).

The courts have also held that an asylum seeker, who was a nursing or expectant mother and in need of accommodation, did not have needs other than destitution, and should be a Home Office responsibility (*R(Gnezele v Leeds City Council*).

In the case of various categories of people subject to immigration control other than asylum seekers, there are further prohibitions in respect of community care services – even if their needs are not solely related to destitution.

14.2.2 ADULT ASYLUM SEEKERS

The effect of the Immigration and Asylum Act 1999, the amended community care legislation and associated legal cases, is that if an adult asylum seeker has a community care need going beyond destitution, then he or she will be eligible for community care services. This will be so, even if the level of need falls below the normal threshold of eligibility applied by the local authority (see 6.10 and 6.12).

Where the local authority has such an obligation, the Home Office is precluded from assisting under its own scheme to assist asylum seekers. This is because of the effect of s.95 of the 1999 Act, allowing Home Office provision only if the person is destitute – which the person will not be if he or she is eligible for assistance with accommodation and essential living needs from a local authority under its social services functions.

Thus, in relation to the provision of residential accommodation under s.21 of the National Assistance Act 1948, an asylum seeker is eligible for assistance from the local authority if his or her need for care and attention (arising from destitution) is to a material extent made more acute by age, illness, disability or any other circumstances (i.e. the reasons why care and attention must be required under s.21). This test was set out in the following legal case involving not asylum seekers but others subject to immigration control – but nevertheless applicable to asylum seekers also:

Differentiating need solely caused by destitution from need otherwise caused. In a case involving two people subject to immigration control, the court considered two possible approaches. The first was to ask whether the applicant would still need assistance under the 1948 Act, even were he or she not destitute. The second was to ask whether the applicant's need for care and attention was to any material extent made more acute by some circumstance other than the mere lack of accommodation and funds. The court was in no doubt that the second, more inclusive, approach was to be preferred. This was because the 1948 Act had been the last refuge for the destitute; and if there were to be immigrant beggars on the streets, 'then let them at least not be old, ill or disabled' (*R v Wandsworth LBC, ex p O*).

Although concerning non-asylum seekers, the test as formulated in the above case is applied also to asylum seekers to determine whether or not they are in need of care and attention (e.g. *Westminster CC v NASS*). The consequence is that the normal test of eligibility for community care services (see 6.12) is not straightforwardly applicable to asylum seekers.

Furthermore, the courts have to date maintained that entitlement to s.21 assistance by way of accommodation does not depend on a need for care and attention of a kind only available through the provision of residential accommodation. In other words, assistance is not confined just to those asylum seekers who would otherwise be eligible for s.21 accommodation (even if they did not have a need related to immigration status). So, asylum seekers have a substantially better chance of qualifying for s.21 accommodation than their 'indigenous counterparts' (*R(Mani) v Lambeth LBC*).

It has been argued that it is absurd that local authorities, rather than the Home Office, should have to support people who are eligible only because they are asylum seekers, rather than because they have an 'eligible' need, as normally understood, for s.21 accommodation. The courts, whilst acknowledging the substance of such concerns, have declined to say more (*Westminster CC v NASS*). The following court cases illustrate the test as to whether a person's need is to a material extent made more acute for some reason other than lack of accommodation or funds:

Eligibility for accommodation of wheelchair user with spinal cancer. An infirm, destitute asylum seeker had spinal cancer; she required accommodation that was wheelchair accessible. The local authority argued that, had she been an ordinary resident rather than an asylum seeker, she would not have required, or been eligible for, accommodation under s.21 of the 1948 Act. She would have had her own accommodation, at which other services could have been provided if required. The court disagreed and stated that she was eligible under s.21 (*Westminster CC v NASS*). Likewise, a destitute asylum seeker who had a leg abnormality needed help with bed-making, hoovering and heavy shopping; he too was eligible for s.21 accommodation (*R(Mani) v Lambeth LBC*).

HIV status and destitution. A local authority took a decision without medical evidence to decide that a person with HIV was not in need over and beyond destitution – and so was ineligible for assistance under s.21 of the 1948 Act. In other words, it was not the case that all people with HIV would automatically be eligible. However, the court stated that in the light of subsequent medical evidence, there would be at least a strong case for the local authority to reassess and find that the woman would be in need of care and attention (*R(J) v Enfield LBC*).

Asylum seekers with a status of HIV have long been a bone of legal contention. For instance, in one case:

Eligibility, AIDS and refrigeration. A woman with AIDS had been seriously ill-treated in Uganda by the Lord's Resistance Army, and ill-treated and raped by the National Resistance Movement (part of the Ugandan security forces). She was a failed asylum seeker, although was pursuing her case to the European Court of Human Rights. This followed a rejection by the House of Lords of her appeal not to be deported (*N v Secretary of State for the Home Department*). In fact, subsequently, the woman lost her case against removal in the European Court as well. The court held that the fact that life expectancy would be reduced significantly, because the standard of treatment in another country would be considerably lower, did not of itself mean that article 3 (inhuman and degrading treatment) would be breached by removal. Exceptionally, it might do so, but not in this case (*N v United Kingdom*).

     The local authority involved attempted to invoke the Department of Health guidance on 'fair access to care services', arguing that the guidance spoke of risk as a relative concept, thus allowing the local authority to argue that it need not provide accommodation. The judge rejected this attempt, especially as it appeared that the local authority was trying to supplant the important statutory questions under s.21 of the 1948 Act, with reference instead to guidance. The local authority also attempted to argue that care and attention in the form of accommodation was not required because the medication did not have to be refrigerated. The judge found this surprising (*R(N) v Lambeth LBC*).

However, the House of Lords subsequently considered another case of a person with HIV and subject to immigration control. The court emphasised that for care and attention to be needed, a person needed 'looking after' (see 9.1). This person was therefore not in need of care and attention from the local authority. This was because he was under the care of the National Health Service, took medication which had to be kept in refrigerated conditions, and needed to see a doctor every three months. But otherwise his illness did not affect him and he was able to look after himself (*R(M) v Slough BC*). The decision in this last case still left open the issue as to whether the local authority would be responsible if and when the man deteriorated in the future and so needed care. At that point, the question would be whether he needed care and attention solely because of destitution (or the anticipated effects of destitution) (see 14.2.1), in which case the s.21 duty under the National Assistance Act 1948 would not arise for the local authority – or because of some additional reason, in which case the duty would arise. One of the law lords stated that:

Need arising solely from destitution. The question would arise only once it was established that 'the person has a need to be looked after – a need beyond merely the provision of a home and the means of survival. If a person reaches that state purely as a result of sleeping rough and going without food…then clearly the need for care and attention will have arisen solely from destitution. If, however, that state of need has been accelerated by some pre-existing disability or infirmity – not of itself sufficient to give rise to a need for care and attention but such as to cause a faster deterioration to that state and perhaps to make the need once it arises that much more acute – then, for my part … I would not regard such a person as excluded' from the National Assistance Act (R(M) v Slough BC).

Nonetheless, the threshold, at which a person becomes eligible for assistance under the National Assistance Act 1948, remains a low one. Furthermore, the conditions in s.21, that might take an asylum seeker out of the 'destitution only' category, include not only age, illness and disability, but also 'any other circumstances', the ambit of which is potentially wide, as the following case shows:

Domestic violence. A woman had been granted leave to enter the United Kingdom from Pakistan to join her husband. She was subjected to violence; he tried to strangle her and threatened her with a knife; she was kidnapped and locked up in a house. She escaped. The local authority now considered whether it had a duty to accommodate her. Under s.115 of the Immigration and Asylum Act 1999 she was subject to immigration control, because her condition of entry was that she did not have recourse to public funds. This meant that unless she could show her needs stemmed from more than just destitution, she would not be eligible for local authority assistance under s.21 of the 1948 Act.

The court accepted that a background of domestic violence could be a relevant 'any other circumstance' for the purpose of showing this. Thus the local authority had to show that it had genuinely considered, when rejecting her application for assistance, whether the woman's needs stemmed solely from destitution or whether she was more vulnerable because of such a background. In fact, the local authority could show this and the court would not interfere with its reasoning (R(Khan) v Oxfordshire CC).

14.2.2.1 Care and attention not otherwise available

Nevertheless, even with this low threshold, a need for care and attention not otherwise available still needs to be demonstrated in order for the legal duty to provide residential accommodation to be triggered:

Care and attention otherwise available from wife or family overseas. The court found that the local authority was acting lawfully in the following circumstances. A United States citizen with mental health problems was not currently living with his wife (a British citizen, who was disabled and suffering from epilepsy) because, following his discharge from hospital, she did not feel she could cope living with him. However, they were on good terms. He also had family in the United States. He was in the country lawfully but subject to immigration control insofar as he had leave to remain so long as he did not have recourse to public funds. He therefore came under s.115 of the Immigration and Asylum Act 1999. This in turn meant that the local authority would be prohibited from assisting him under s.21 of the 1948 Act, if his need for care and attention arose solely from destitution or the physical effects of destitution.

However, apart from contesting the question of destitution, the local authority also argued that care and attention was otherwise available to him either from his wife or from his family in the United States. The court held that the local authority was entitled to take this stance, both in principle and on the facts of the case (R(P) v Camden LBC).

Local authorities have tried to argue that not all medical needs will automatically and necessarily be sufficient, in addition to destitution, to show that the need for care and attention is materially more acute as a result of those needs. In one case, such an argument succeeded in the High Court but was overturned in the Court of Appeal:

Medical needs being met by the NHS. The two claimants suffered severe depressive episodes, which were not simply caused by their destitution but by traumatic periods of detention undergone in their country of origin and which had a serious effect on them. The local authority maintained the needs arising from this depression could be met by the NHS and that therefore there was no need for social services to do anything.

However, the court pointed out that they still had a 'separate and additional need for the care and attention that is required by all who are condemned to a life on the streets, being care and attention in the shape of shelter and warmth capable of being provided by the type of residential accommodation (including ordinary housing) available under section 21.' The question for the local authority to ask was whether 'their need for this separate head of care and attention is made the more acute by the depressive disorder from which they are both suffering and the fact that, absent any section 21 assistance, they have to cope with that disorder on the streets, albeit with the benefit of NHS counselling.' The local authority had not asked that question; so its decision was materially flawed. It would now need to reconsider (R(Pajaziti) v Lewisham LBC).

In sum, it can be seen therefore that there has been considerable incentive for dispute between local authorities, the Home Office and asylum seekers.

14.2.2.2 Home Office responsibilities

The Home Office has a power to support destitute asylum seekers under s.95 of the Immigration and Asylum Act 1999. However, as explained above, this power does not arise in the case of any asylum seeker who is eligible for social services assistance because his or her needs amount to more than just destitution or destitution-related need. If such a person is eligible for social services assistance, he or she is not then destitute for the purpose of s.95.

Likewise under s.4 of the 1999 Act, the Home Office has discretion to provide accommodation for failed asylum seekers, who are unable to return to their country of origin. This is known as 'hard cases' support. However, the courts have held that in the case of a failed asylum seeker, with more than just destitution-related needs, then social services is obliged to take responsibility under s.21 of the National Assistance Act 1948 – in order to avoid a breach of the person's human rights (R(AW) v Croydon LBC).

Regulations set out the conditions on which the Home Office may offer hard cases support. These are (a) the person has taken all reasonable steps to leave the United Kingdom; (b) inability to leave because of physical impediment or some other medical reason; (c) inability to leave because in the view of the Secretary of State there is no viable route of return; (d) an application for judicial review has been made; (e) provision of accommodation is necessary to avoid breach of human rights (SI 2005/930).

For instance, in one case, the courts held that the needs of two expectant/nursing mothers needs arose, for the purposes of s.21 of the National Assistance Act 1948, from destitution alone. The local authority therefore did not have the legal power to provide accommodation for them. But, as failed asylum seekers, they came within the Home Office responsibility under s.4, because of physical impediment in travel – either because of late stages of pregnancy or because of having very young children. In neither case would airlines carry them (R(Gnezele) v Leeds City Council).

14.2.3 ASYLUM SEEKERS WITH CHILDREN

If an asylum seeker eligible for social services assistance (under s.21 of the National Assistance Act 1948 because of a need relating to more than destitution) has a child, then the Home

Office is normally responsible for supporting the child under s.95 of the Immigration and Asylum Act 1999. To avoid fragmented practical arrangements, with the local authority providing for the adult and the Home Office for the child, the courts have suggested that the Home Office could come to an agreement with the local authority, whereby the local authority would make arrangements for the child on the Home Office's behalf (*R(O) v Haringey LBC*).

This issue was considered in the case of a woman, who was an asylum seeker and was HIV positive, with two children aged three and five years old. The following points were made (*R(O) v Haringey LBC*):

- Local social services authorities cannot provide assistance under s.17 of the Children Act 1989 for children of asylum seekers or their families, if they are eligible for assistance under s.95 of the 1999 Act (Immigration and Asylum Act 1999, s.122).
- The family would be eligible under s.95, only if its accommodation and essential living needs could not be met elsewhere (Immigration and Asylum Act 1999, s.95).
- The court held that s.17 of the Children Act 1989 contained such a vague duty (because it was not enforceable) that it could not be relied upon as evidence of accommodation being otherwise available for the family (nor were ss.20 or 23 of the Children Act 1989 relevant to deciding the issue).
- The National Assistance Act 1948, s.21, placed an obligation on the local authority to provide for the adult (whose needs were more than just destitution related); but there would be no entitlement or enforceable expectation under s.21 of the 1948 Act that children would be accommodated with their parents.
- Thus the family as a whole was destitute under s.95 of the 1999 Act, essentially because the children had no other reliable means of support. The family was therefore eligible for Home Office support; however, the mother's eligibility under s.21 of the 1948 Act had to be taken into account.
- Therefore the Home Office would have to provide support for the children under s.95 of the 1999 Act, whilst the local authority would provide the accommodation for the mother under s.21 of the 1948 Act. However, to avoid fragmented arrangements, the Home Office would request the local authority to make arrangements for the child on the Home Office's behalf and at the Home Office's expense.

If the child is disabled, but the adult asylum seeker parent is not, then the effect of the legislation is that the Home Office has responsibility for the whole family under s.95 of the Immigration and Asylum Act 1999.

The courts have also held that 'adequate accommodation' for a disabled child, under s.95 of the Immigration and Asylum Act 1999, should be suited to the disabled child. The National Asylum Support Service had argued that, even in the case of a disabled child, adequacy should be tested with reference only to able-bodied children (*R(A) v National Asylum Support Service*).

14.2.4 UNACCOMPANIED CHILDREN

Local social services authorities have potential responsibilities toward all unaccompanied children in need who are subject to immigration control (including asylum seekers). Such support is prohibited neither in s.122 of the Immigration and Asylum Act 1999 nor in schedule 3 of the Nationality, Immigration and Asylum Act 2002.

An unaccompanied child will be the potential responsibility of the local authority under the Children Act 1989. Faced with the possible choice of different sections in the Children Act under which assistance could be given, local authorities have received guidance from the Department of Health. This states that there will be a presumption that accommodation provided for unaccompanied asylum seeking children will be under s.20 of the 1989 Act (thus attracting the 'leaving care' provisions: see 13.6.6) rather than s.17 (which does not bring a child into the leaving care provisions). A local authority that took the opposite position (that s.17 was the norm) would be potentially in breach of the guidance and acting unlawfully (*R(Berhe) Hillingdon LBC*).

Thus, if on the facts of a case, a duty arises under s.20 of the Act to provide accommodation, a local authority cannot purport instead to be acting under s.17 of the 1989 Act. To do so would be to 'finesse away their specific or particular duty by claiming merely to act under a general one'. The judge criticised, though did not find unlawful, Department of Health guidance (LAC(2003)13) on the s.17 and s.20 issue. The guidance drew the distinction between a requirement of accommodation (which triggers s.20) and a need for 'help with accommodation' which might properly come under s.17. The judge stated that it came very close to being wrong. What a local authority should do is to decide whether the child requires the provision of accommodation, or merely help with accommodation, 'without regard to the implications of his being or not being a looked after child' (*R(H) v Wandsworth LBC*).

Local authorities should also take care when making a decision about an unaccompanied asylum seeking child's age. For instance, they should not simply follow the Home Office's view but come to their own conclusions, should explain the purpose of the interview to the person, and give him or her the opportunity to address the issues. If a view is taken that the person is lying about his or her age, he or she must be given an opportunity to address the issues (*R(B) v Merton LBC*). They should also be able to demonstrate that all relevant factors have been taken into account:

Age of asylum seeker: not taking account of material considerations. An immigration and asylum adjudicator had concluded that an asylum seeker was only 17 years old, and the Secretary of State for the Home Office had accepted this, giving her leave to remain in the United Kingdom until her 18th birthday.

The local authority now reached a different decision to the adjudicator. It might have been entitled to this, but it was unable to show that it had taken account of the relevant considerations. It failed actually to ask the asylum seeker from Angola, who had suffered horrific experiences there, why it was that she was maintaining that she was under 18 years old. It failed also to take account of the report of a consultant paediatrician, or of the views of the Child Guidance team and of the person's mental health worker. In addition, the questioning of the person was unduly hostile; this led her to 'clam up' and to the local authority assessors wrongly disbelieving her evidence (*R(T) v Enfield LBC*).

So, when a local authority rejected expert evidence about a person's age being under 18, its decision letter needed to explain why. Although it might have carried out a fair and lawful assessment, taken adequate account of the person's birth certificate – it had failed properly to consider and refute expert medical opinion (*R(C) v Merton LBC*). The irony in this case was that had it done so, the judge accepted that the local authority might well have had sufficient grounds for its view. Similarly, in the following case, the local authority failed to apply commonsense analysis to an expert dental report:

Common-sense approach. When a local authority obtained a dental report stating that the asylum seeker in question was an adult, at variance with a paediatrician's report that stated the opposite, the authority failed to subject to the dental report to a reasonable analysis. In any group of individuals showing the same dental characteristics as the claimant, some would be under, and some over, 18. The local authority should therefore have considered other matters, in order to judge better what the claimant's age really was. Those 'who are making age assessments on behalf of local authorities are not expected to be experts in statistics, but they can be expected to consider assertions which are made in reliance on statistics and to apply common sense to those assertions' (*R(A) v Liverpool CC*).

As with asylum seekers generally, the costs of supporting unaccompanied children has been considerable for some local authorities. This led one, unsuccessfully, to challenge a reduction in discretionary grant paid by central government for such children. The court held that central government had created no legitimate expectation that the grant would be held at the rate it had been paid in the first year of the programme (*R(Hillingdon LBC) v Secretary of State for Education and Skills*).

14.2.5 OTHER ACCOMPANIED CHILDREN

In respect of asylum seekers, the position is as set out above (14.2.3). If the parent with a child is not an asylum seeker, but nevertheless subject to immigration control, support or assistance can be given by a local social services authority to the child but not to the family (Nationality, Immigration and Asylum Act 2002, schedule 3, paras 1–2). However, regulations have been made to allow the provision of temporary accommodation for such a parent and dependent child (see 14.2.7 below).

14.2.6 PEOPLE SUBJECT TO IMMIGRATION CONTROL (OTHER THAN ASYLUM SEEKERS): ADULTS

For certain classes of adult who are subject to immigration control, social services are barred from providing support or assistance under nearly all the community care legislation (Nationality, Immigration and Asylum Act 2002, schedule 3).

This prohibition covers the National Assistance Act 1948 (ss.21 and 29 and by implication s.2 of the Chronically Sick and Disabled Persons Act 1970), Health and Services and Public Health Act 1968, s.45, section 21, and schedule 8 of the NHS Act 1977. Also listed is the Children Act 1989, insofar as provision can be made for adults under ss.17, 23C, 24A and 24B. The prohibition does not extend to s.117 of the Mental Health Act 1983; and children in their own right are likewise not excluded from assistance. Furthermore, assistance is not prohibited, if there would otherwise be a breach of human rights or of European Community treaties.

The prohibition in the 2002 Act applies to (a) people who have refugee status abroad; (b) certain people who are members of a European Economic Area state other than the United Kingdom (but see 14.2.9 below); (c) failed asylum seekers who are not cooperating with removal directions; (d) any other person, not an asylum seeker, who is in breach of the immigration laws (defined in s.11 of the Act).

This prohibition further means that, whereas previously the courts had stated that a local social services authority should concern itself with meeting people's community care needs and leave it to the Home Office to determine immigration status (*R v Wandsworth LBC, ex p O*), now local authorities have an obligation to make efforts to comply with this prohibition. Nonetheless, they have to proceed with caution and not make unwarranted assumptions about the merits of people's human-rights based immigration related applications:

Local authority's unwarranted refusal of assistance and anticipation immigration decisions. As an unaccompanied asylum seeker from Uganda, a child had been assisted by a local authority under s.20 of the Children Act 1989. When he was 19, the Home Office refused a further application for leave to remain, a previous application having been made and rejected. Yet another application was then made to the Home Office, arguing that it would be a breach of article 8 of the Convention for the person to be removed. At which point, the local authority decided to cease supporting him, on the basis that he was present in breach of the immigration laws and was not an asylum seeker.

The court held that the local authority asked itself the wrong question, by considering (and concluding) that the person's article 8 rights would not be breached by removal. Whereas, what it should have asked was whether the claimant's article 8 application to the Home Office was 'manifestly unfounded'. Furthermore, it was 'only in the clearest cases that local authorities should make decisions on the predicate that the application in question would be dismissed by the immigration authorities' (*R(Binomugisha) v Southwark LBC*).

Thus, except in case of manifest inadequacy, a further claim for asylum on human rights grounds means that a local authority will have to provide support for a failed asylum seeker (on those human rights grounds) pending the Home Office's decision (*R(AW) v Croydon LBC*).

Further complication has arisen, because the courts have held that following the rejection of an asylum claim, there are two classes of failed asylum seeker for the purpose of prohibitions under the 2002 Act. A failed asylum seeker who lodged the original asylum claim on entry to the United Kingdom, and who has not yet failed to cooperate with removal directions, continues to be eligible for social services support. However, a failed asylum seeker who did not apply for asylum on entry, but only later and 'in-country', falls into the category of being present in breach of the immigration laws – and so is straightaway denied social services support (unless human rights would be breached: (*R(AW) v Croydon LBC*). It may of course not be possible to cooperate with removal directions. For instance:

Failure to comply with removal order. In one legal case (heard prior to the 2002 Act), a man who had originally been granted political asylum in the United Kingdom was subsequently convicted of drug offences and imprisoned. A deportation and removal order was made, but Sweden would not permit his re-entry. The court pointed out that the applicant had served a lawful prison sentence and was unable to leave through factors entirely beyond his control. He was therefore not exercising a choice not to comply with the deportation order (*R v Lambeth LBC, ex p Sarhangi*).

14.2.6.1 Prohibitions: asylum seekers with children

A failed asylum seeker with a dependent child remains eligible for Home Office support (Immigration and Asylum Act 1999, s.94).

However, a prohibition applies to failed asylum seekers with dependent children who, according to a certificate issued by the Secretary of State, have failed without reasonable excuse to take reasonable steps to leave the United Kingdom voluntarily (Nationality, Immigration and Asylum Act 2002, schedule 3, para 7A). This system of certificates has barely been used by the Secretary of State, although there have been pilot schemes. Though not a success, the provision remains on the statute book.

The Refugee Council reported that the Home Office failed in its objective to persuade families to return to their country with assistance – for example, a third of the families involved were reported to have responded by disappearing, a number of families had been inappropriately categorised, and many of the families had serious health and mental health problems made worse by the application of the rule (Refugee Council 2006a).

14.2.7 PEOPLE SUBJECT TO IMMIGRATION CONTROL: ADULTS WITH CHILDREN

The prohibitions placed on a local authority's ability to provide support for an adult subject to immigration control (other than an asylum seeker) does contain an exception – if he or she is accompanied by a dependent child. This is possible through regulations issued under schedule 3 of the 2002 Act – the Withholding and Withdrawal of Support (Travel Assistance and Temporary Accommodation) Regulations 2002 (SI 2002/3078). These regulations give local authorities the power to accommodate a person who is unlawfully in the United Kingdom, with a dependent child, so long as he or she has not failed to comply with directions for removal.

Although it is only a power that is conferred, a failure to exercise it could result in separation of the parent from the child, with the child alone then being cared for under s.20 of the Children Act 1989. But this could, depending on the circumstances, infringe the right to respect for family life under article 8 of the European Convention on Human Rights (*R(Grant) v Lambeth LBC; see also R(M) v Islington LBC*).

The same regulations confer on local authorities a power to make travel arrangements for an adult and child to return to their country of origin only in the case of nationals of European Economic Area (EEA) Member States and those with refugee status in such an EEA state. Otherwise, paradoxically, a local authority could not make such travel arrangements, but instead have to consider providing accommodation under the regulations. However, the courts have held that a local authority could offer instead to make travel arrangements under s.2 of the Local Government Act 2000, in order to avoid breach of human rights – for a family for whom it could not make travel arrangements under the regulations themselves (*R(Grant) v Lambeth LBC*).

14.2.8 HUMAN RIGHTS

The prohibitions placed on local social services authorities in schedule 3 of the 2002 Act do not apply if a person's human rights (or rights under European Community law) would otherwise be breached. Likewise the prohibitions placed on Home Office assistance under s.55 of the Act:

Human rights and assistance for an illegal overstayer. In a case heard prior to the Nationality, Immigration and Asylum Act 2002, the courts considered whether a local authority should assist a Brazilian man with advanced HIV/AIDS who had illegally overstayed on his six-month visa. In making its decision, it had to decide whether or not he was fit to travel back to Brazil to receive care and treatment. If not, the local authority had to consider the effect of the absence of shelter and accommodation. This could in turn give rise to considerations under articles 2 and 3 of the European Convention on Human Rights (*R v Brent LBC, ex p D*).

There has been a number of court cases argued concerning whether human rights would be breached if no assistance were given. Many of these have hinged on article 3 of the European Convention and the question of inhuman or degrading treatment – in relation to denial of support by the Home Office under s.55 of the 2002 Act. These culminated in a House of Lords judgment, outlining the circumstances liable to give rise to a breach of article 3:

Human rights generally. 'When does the Secretary of State's duty under section 55(5)(a) arise? The answer must in my opinion be: when it appears on a fair and objective assessment of all relevant facts and circumstances that an individual applicant faces an imminent prospect of serious suffering caused or materially aggravated by denial of shelter, food or the most basic necessities of life. Many factors may affect that judgment, including age, gender, mental and physical health and condition, any facilities or sources of support available to the applicant, the weather and time of year and the period for which the applicant has already suffered or is likely to continue to suffer privation.

It is not in my opinion possible to formulate any simple test applicable in all cases. But if there were persuasive evidence that a late applicant was obliged to sleep in the street, save perhaps for a short and foreseeably finite period, or was seriously hungry, or unable to satisfy the most basic requirements of hygiene, the threshold would, in the ordinary way, be crossed' (*R(Limbuela) v Secretary of State for the Home Department*).

In a case involving a woman with AIDS, who had been hospitalised suffering from serious and life-threatening related illnesses – but whose health had now improved – human rights issues were considered. The judge pointed out that it was difficult to understand how the local authority 'could have properly arrived at a conclusion that sleeping on the streets in the case of this claimant, a person who is acknowledged to be suffering from a chronic illness, which if not medicated in the appropriate way will lead to terrible consequences, could be regarded as a person who can be refused support without any breach of her convention rights'. He also rejected the dubious argument that any breach of human rights would not have been deliberately inflicted by the local authority, and so would not constitute a breach of article 3, because schedule 3 of the 2002 Act explicitly imposes prohibitions (and the human rights exception) on the local authority which it had no choice but to obey (*R(N) v Lambeth LBC*). (But see p.383 above: *N v UnitedKingdon*).

14.2.8.1 Human rights and a person's ability to return home

Of key importance in ascertaining a local authority's potential obligations – to avoid a breach of human rights arising from the prohibitions contained in schedule 3 of the 2002 Act – is the question of whether the person is able to return to his or her own country, freely and without impediment (*R(K) v Lambeth LBC*).

Offering to make travel arrangements back to the country of origin might be enough to prevent a breach of human rights, all other things being equal (*R(Grant) v Lambeth LBC*). That is, if there is no impediment to such travel – for instance, there is no ostensible reason why the children's needs for accommodation would not be met, or that they would be destitute when getting off the plane in Jamaica. Likewise if there is no issue under article 8 of the European Convention on Human Rights – for example, in a case where the relationship between the children and their father in the UK was almost non-existent, and bearing in mind that article 8 does not anyway confer an absolute right on family members to live together (*R(Blackburn-Smith) v Lambeth LBC*).

However, the position would be different if the local authority had inadequately considered breach of article 8, if a return to Jamaica would mean that the mother was unable effectively to take part in care proceedings in relation to her children. In turn, if she were to remain here and be street homeless, then issues under article 3 of the Convention would arise (*R(PB) v Haringey LBC*).

14.2.9 EUROPEAN ECONOMIC AREA NATIONALS

People from the European Economic Area are excluded from support under schedule 3 of the 2002 Act, unless such an exclusion would breach European Community treaty and, by extension, the Immigration (European Economic Area) Regulations 2006 (SI 2006/1003).

A note of clarification from the Department of Health in 2003 explained that, generally speaking, European Economic Area nationals who have worked or work in the United Kingdom, their families, self-employed and former self-employed people and students are eligible for assistance from social services. This was because of European Community law on freedom of movement and the enjoyment of social advantages in other EEA states (DH 2003e). However, the rules are slightly modified for the eight so-called accession countries.

Other EEA nationals who have entered the United Kingdom, on the understanding that they had sufficient resources so as not to become a burden in terms of social welfare, should not be provided with support – beyond temporary support. The guidance goes on to suggest that local authorities could seek to determine such matters by examining documents such as P60 forms in the case of employed (or formerly employed) people. Establishing self-employment status might, the guidance concedes, be difficult (DH 2003e).

In one case, the court backed the local authority's refusal to provide accommodation under s.17 of the Children Act 1989 to an EEA national:

Denial of assistance to Spanish woman. A Spanish national had applied for housing assistance for herself and her two children under s.17 of the Children Act 1989. She had been subjected to domestic violence in Spain, for which her husband had been convicted and sentenced, but not yet incarcerated because of prison overcrowding in Spain. She was seeking work in England. The council refused, stating that there was no reason she could not return to Spain where, it argued, she would be protected by the police or courts if necessary from further violence. Furthermore it argued that schedule 3 of the 2002 Act prevented it helping her as she was an EEA national.

The court held that, although she was a work seeker, nonetheless this did not, under European Community law, entitle her to housing – thus the refusal by the council did not breach any European Community treaty (any such breach would create an exception the prohibition on assisting EEA nationals). Furthermore, the local authority denied that it was discriminating in any way on grounds of her nationality, since if the woman had come from the north of England, it would have said to her equally: 'You can go back up to the north of England' (*R(Conde) v Lambeth LBC*).

14.2.10 LOCAL GOVERNMENT ACT 2000

Apart from utilisation of the Human Rights Act 1998 to test the various prohibitions placed on local authorities from assisting asylum seekers and others subject to immigration control, some attempt has been made also to use the Local Government Act 2000. In particular s.2 of this Act allows a local authority to do anything it thinks will achieve the promotion or improvement of the social well-being of the area. However, this power does not enable a local authority to do anything that other legislation prohibits, restricts or limits (s.3).

In a case where a person subject to immigration control under s.115 of the Immigration and Asylum Act 1999 was not eligible for residential accommodation under s.21 of the National Assistance Act 1948 (because her need was essentially destitution related), the courts took a fairly restrictive approach to use of the 2000 Act. They held that the rules under s.21(1A) of the Act (see 14.2.1) constituted a prohibition on the provision of accommodation for such a person – and on the provision of the amenities and requisites provided in connection with the accommodation (such as food). However, clothes or toiletries, for instance, had nothing to with the accommodation; so s.2 would give the local authority a power to provide such items (*R(Khan) v Oxfordshire CC*).

However, in another case, it was accepted that under schedule 3 of the Nationality, Immigration and Asylum Act 2002, the local authority was precluded from assisting a Jamaican woman and her children, unless to avoid a breach of human rights. It could avoid such a breach by exercising a power to provide temporary accommodation under the Withholding and Withdrawal of Support (Travel Assistance and Temporary Accommodation) Regulations 2002 (SI 2002/3078). Alternatively, the court accepted that the local authority could make travel arrangements back to Jamaica under s.2 of the Local Government Act 2002, use of which was not prohibited in order to avoid a breach of human rights, even though such travel arrangements could not lawfully be made under the 2002 regulations themselves (*R(Grant) v Lambeth LBC*).

14.2.11 EXCEPTIONAL LEAVE TO REMAIN

Outside of the normal rules on immigration, the Secretary of State had, under the Immigration Act 1971, discretion to grant 'exceptional leave to remain'. In April 2003, this type of leave was replaced for asylum seekers by policies (under the same general provisions of the 1971 Act) labelled 'humanitarian protection' and 'discretionary leave' (exercisable in a number of listed circumstances, and also other 'compelling circumstances').

In addition, in cases other than asylum seekers, a residual discretion still remains to grant leave to remain in the form of 'leave outside the rules'. In one such case, the courts found that the discretion should be properly exercised in relation to the general policy of 'care in the community':

Leave to remain. A Polish couple in their sixties came to the United Kingdom to care for their ageing mother. Their leave to remain was extended so that they could care for the wife's brother, a British citizen who suffered from epilepsy, had learning difficulties and spoke no English. They again applied for leave to remain, with the support of Hackney Council, which pointed out that the alternative of residential care was very costly, not acceptable to the brother and in its view not an appropriate solution. The Secretary of State refused the application.

The judge stated that the critical issue was that the brother was a British citizen who was entitled to remain in the United Kingdom and to be cared for in accordance with the policies and duties (i.e. in relation to community care) applying to citizens in general. First, he drew a parallel with another immigration case in which the Secretary of State had not performed the appropriate balancing exercise in comparing immigration issues with the rights of British citizens. Second, there was no evidence supporting the Secretary of State's assertion that he was satisfied that alternative arrangements could be made for the brother. In fact, the government's community care policy, to enable people to remain in their own homes, was consistent in this case with domiciliary care provided by the family rather than residential care. He concluded that the Secretary of State's decision was unreasonable and should be overturned (*R v Secretary of State for the Home Department*, ex p *Zakrocki*).

In a further case, also relevant to community care concerning more permanent, indefinite leave to remain, the courts also queried the approach taken by the Home Office, though refrained from a finding of irrationality:

Moroccan hairdresser and care in the community. The claimant was Moroccan. His sister had married an Englishman serving in the Grenadier Guards, who was blown up and severely injured, needing constant 24-hour care. He was now 75 years old. His sister was herself ill with lupus. She died in 2002. The claimant devoted his life from 1996 to looking after the family and his two nieces.

He sought leave to remain in the country, but had no right to do so. Under the instructions relating to carers, he was given leave only 12 months at a time. On each application he had to show he was financially independent. He achieved this by returning to Morocco for a period each year where he worked as a hairdresser to earn sufficient money.

The continual need to produce evidence, every 12 months, with uncertainty about the success of the application, put a continual strain upon the family. He therefore applied for indefinite leave to remain. He was supported by both his brother-in-law's GP and by Devon County Council social services. They pointed out that if he were not allowed to remain, social services would incur the cost not only of looking after the brother-in-law, but also taking the daughters (15 and 12 years old) into care. The application for indefinite leave to remain was refused; another 12 months stay was granted, up to 31 March 2007, shortly before the daughters would be taking exams.

Overall the claim failed. However, the judge stated that the Secretary of State had not been obliged to grant such leave, but was required to consider on merit the compassionate circumstances in accordance with the policy. Normally indefinite leave cannot be applied for until a person has been in the country for ten years, lawfully. The Home Office letter stated that, even when the ten years had been reached, any such application would be unlikely to succeed. The judge stated that this was an improper statement to have made in advance, especially since article 8 (European Convention) rights would appear to have been very strong in this case – which the judge pointed out was a 'wholly exceptional case'. This was a matter for the future (*R(Belcaid) v Secretary of State for the Home Department*).

Likewise, in a case about the Home Office's family reunion policy, the court found that the Asylum and Immigration Tribunal had not taken account of the compelling compassionate circumstances clearly present:

Human rights require proportionate approach to compelling compassionate circumstances. A man and wife had arrived as asylum seekers from China, because of their father's membership of the Falun Gong movement. His father was already in the United Kingdom and had refugee status; he had been imprisoned and tortured in China. The father needed very considerable help and medical opinion was that without the help of his son and daughter-in-law, he would present a high suicide risk. Compliance with human rights meant a proportionate approach was required; this did not necessarily preclude removal but proportionality had at least to be considered. The Tribunal had not done this. It was to be noted that had the son been applying from abroad, he would have come within the Home Office's family reunion policy; the only reason he did not was that he was applying from within the UK. The case was remitted to the Tribunal for reconsideration (*Miao v Secretary of State for the Home Department*).

14.3 NHS SERVICES AND OVERSEAS VISITORS

In April 2004, the government amended the relevant regulations (SI 1989/306) and issued new guidance concerning the provision in England of hospital services to overseas visitors (DH 2004a). The main rules, as set out in the guidance, are outlined below. They place a duty on NHS trusts to charge overseas visitors for health services, unless specified exemptions apply.

The overall purpose of the changes was to deal with alleged 'health tourism'. The Joint Committee on Human Rights, and the House of Commons Health Committee have drawn attention to the lack of cost–benefit analysis in relation to the regulations – and to the lack of monitoring of their operation (JCHR 2007a, para 165). It is also doubtful about how far the term health tourism is applicable to people, such as asylum seekers, who are now chargeable under the regulations. It has been pointed out that health tourism implies not only deliberate fraud, but also the possibility of returning to one's country of origin for treatment – yet this may be a practical option (Kelley and Stevenson 2006, p.6).

14.3.1 NORMAL RESIDENCE

The NHS, in respect of hospital services, has a duty to establish whether a person is normally resident in the United Kingdom, to assess liability for charges and to charge those liable to pay – that is, those who are not ordinarily resident (SI 1989/306, r.2, made under what is now s.175 of the NHS Act 2006).

Ordinary residence is not defined in the regulations and therefore the test formulated in *R v Barnet London Borough Council, ex p Shah* must be used. Ordinary residence is about a person being in a 'particular place or country which he has adopted voluntarily and for settled purposes as part of the regular order of his life for the time being, whether of long or short duration'. The guidance suggests that a person should be resident for at least six months, but this is not a hard and fast rule and is not a legal minimum (DH 2004a, p.51).

This test could mean, for instance, a British citizen, resident in South Africa visiting the United Kingdom for a holiday, and being charged for treatment. Whereas an Indian national, just arrived with a 12-month visa to join a British citizen spouse, could be regarded as ordinarily resident (Hundt and Willman 2007). Thus, if people are ordinarily resident, then they are entitled to NHS services as normal and are not categorised as an overseas visitor. If, however, they are not deemed to be ordinarily resident, then they will be subject, as overseas visitors, to the rules below about payment for services. However, this is subject to another overarching rule that if an overseas visitor has been resident lawfully in the United Kingdom for at least 12 months then they, too, are eligible for NHS services as normal, whether or not they are deemed to be an ordinary resident (SI 1989/306, rr.2, 4).

14.3.2 FREE SERVICES AND EXEMPTIONS

Some services must be provided free to everyone, regardless of their status, including treatment at an accident and emergency or casualty department or walk-in-centre providing the same services (SI 1989/306, r.2).

Treatment is also free for family planning services, certain diseases to protect the wider public health (a list of exempt diseases is included in the Regulations), initial diagnostic test and associated counselling for HIV/AIDS (but not for treatment), people detained under the Mental Health Act 1983 (ST 1989/306, r.3).

14.3.2.1 Asylum seekers

Department of Health guidance states that refugees and asylum seekers are exempt from charges if they have made a formal application to the Home Office, which has not yet been determined. It goes on to state that the fact that: 'exemption for asylum seekers only lasts until their claim is determined means that trusts should be prepared to check that the application is still ongoing at intervals if treatment is being provided over a long period. If the claim is finally rejected (including appeals) before the patient has been in the United Kingdom for 12 months, they cannot be charged for a course of treatment they were receiving at the time their status was determined. That remains free of charge until completed. They must, however, be charged for any new course of treatment. If that is routine elective treatment, then payment should be handled in the same way as for anyone else seeking non-urgent treatment, i.e. payment should be obtained before payment begins. Once they have completed 12 months' residence they do not become exempt from charges' (DH 2004a, para 6.24).

These rules, as interpreted by the guidance, mean that, for example, once an asylum claim has been refused, 'no patient is too vulnerable to escape charging'. For example, the victim of a near fatal care accident would receive free accident and emergency care but, once in the intensive care unit, would incur charges of up to tens of thousands pounds. Children, people with acute mental problems or learning disabilities and elderly patients with dementia would all be charged (Kelley and Stevenson, p.8). The Parliamentary Joint Committee on Human Rights has recommended that HIV/AIDS treatment (and not just diagnosis and counselling) should be free for failed asylum seekers – on the basis not just of humanity but also the wider public health (JCHR 2007a, para 152).

However, in early 2008, the courts held that at least one aspect of the guidance was unlawful in relation to failed asylum seekers:

Failed asylum seeker regarded as ordinarily resident rather than overseas visitor. The court held that an asylum seeker who claimed asylum at port of entry (as opposed to a later in-country application: see 14.2.6 above) could argue – with reference to the case of R v Barnet LBC, ex p Shah – that he or she was in the country lawfully and therefore ordinarily resident. This would be by dint of his or her wish to settle, coupled with residence for a significant period, and at least before he or she had failed to cooperate with removal directions. The court went on to hold that although under *Shah*, the in-country applicant could not be ordinarily resident because he or she would be here unlawfully, nonetheless making such a complex distinction between these two classes of failed asylum seeker would be unworkable for the NHS. Thus, in short, the guidance on charging failed asylum seekers was unlawful (*R(A) West Middlesex University Hospital NHS Trust*).

The effect of this judgment – at least until the appeal is heard - is that asylum seekers granted temporary admission to the United Kingdom, with an intention to remain, will be treated as ordinarily resident – whether at-port or in-country applicants. Likewise, people who have applied for leave to remain under article 3 of the European Convention on Human Rights – and also, for example, someone who lawfully entered with a visa, then applied for an extension (before it ran out), and with an intention to remain for a reasonable period of time (Hundt 2008).

Department of Health guidance makes the following points in the wake of the case, namely that (a) not all failed asylum seekers will be ordinarily resident, (b) NHS trusts must consider each case to decide whether the person is ordinarily resident, (c) they must take account of the relevant factors signalled by the judge, (d) there is no specific time frame but the judge referred to a `significant period', (e) however, even if a person has been in the United Kingdom for less than the six months' guideline (contained in the guidance), he or she could still be ordinarily resident (DH 2008d).

14.3.2.2 Other exemptions

There is a long list of other exemptions from charging in the guidance. These include students pursuing a course of study longer than six months (or less than six months but substantially funded by the United Kingdom government), refugees, a number of exceptions related to employment arrangements, United Kingdom pensioners who reside in the United Kingdom for at least six months each year and in another member State for less than six months a year and who are not registered as resident of another member State – and British nationals or others with a right of abode who return to the UK to resume permanent residence (DH 2004b, pp.25-30).

14.3.3 IMMEDIATELY NECESSARY TREATMENT

The guidance states that immediately necessary or emergency treatment – given other than in an accident and emergency or casualty department where it would anyway be free – should not be delayed in order to establish the chargeable status of patient (delay could breach the Human Rights Act 1998).

Such treatment will not exempt a person from charges. If a person is admitted to a ward, or given an outpatient appointment following treatment in an accident and emergency department, the exemption from charging ceases. A distinction should be made between what treatment is necessary and what is clinically appropriate. Some of the treatment might be appropriate, but not necessary, and so be deferred – allowing the person to return to his or her own country to receive it there. If immediately necessary treatment is being given, and the NHS trust knows that payment is unlikely, then the treatment should be limited to what is clinically necessary to enable the person to return to their own country. Thus the treatment given in these circumstances should not normally include routine treatment, unless this is necessary to prevent a life-threatening situation (DH 2004a, pp.9, p.22, 49).

The practical implications of these rules are as follows. A man from Romania with stomach cancer was operated on but then billed for over £1000 and denied the follow-up radiotherapy unless he could pay in advance. An Arab with disputed nationality, suffered from bowel cancer and was admitted as an emergency with uncontrolled bleeding. He was scheduled for an operation, but the hospital then discovered that he was a failed asylum seeker. The operation was cancelled, he was given a bill for thousands of pounds, and told to come back when his condition had deteriorated. A Rwandan with bowel cancer and a colostomy bag had been refused care from the local NHS trust, and the local GP would not register him (Kelley and Stevenson 2006, p.12).

In respect of degrees of urgency of treatment, the above guidance would seem in general principle to be in accord with what the law courts have found, albeit under the previous version of the regulations and guidance (and before the implementation of the Human Rights Act 1998):

Dialysis treatment for overseas visitor. A Nigerian overseas visitor suffered renal failure and required dialysis three times a week. This had been paid for in advance by a company, of which the man's father was an employee. The company would not now make further payments to the London hospital concerned; however, treatment was available in Nigeria. The hospital would continue to treat him, so that he was fit to return to Nigeria for continuing treatment. Furthermore, the court noted that if non-treatment were to lead to an emergency, then on humanitarian grounds the hospital could exercise its discretion to treat without insistence on a deposit or advance payment (*R v Hammersmith Hospitals NHS Trust, ex p Reffell*).

14.3.4 URGENT TREATMENT
The guidance refers to this as treatment which is not immediately necessary but cannot wait for the person to return to their home country. The patient should be booked in for treatment, and the intervening period used to establish chargeable status. Whenever possible, deposits should be sought (DH 2004a, p.9).

14.3.5 NON-URGENT TREATMENT
Where the treatment could wait until the person returns to their own country, the guidance states that the patient should be placed on a waiting list, but not until a deposit equivalent to the cost of the treatment has been obtained. The guidance maintains that this is not a refusal to provide treatment, merely a requirement that the payment condition be met before treatment can be commenced (DH 2004a, p.9).

14.3.6 MATERNITY SERVICES
Maternity services are not exempt from charges. However, because of the severe health risks associated with conditions such as eclampsia and pre-eclampsia, maternity services should not be withheld if the woman is unable to pay in advance. The patient remains liable and the debt should be pursued in the normal way (DH 2004a, p.49).

Even the Department of Health has conceded that the regulations and guidance are not being adhered to. It wrote to NHS trusts warning them against charging women who are exempt (e.g. asylum seekers), refusing proper care because they cannot pay, pursuing women for payment to the extent of intimidating them and deterring them from receiving necessary maternity services (Hundt and Willman 2007).

For instance, a completely destitute 15-year-old Vietnamese girl received a letter from an NHS trust demanding payment within five days of £2300 for maternity services; otherwise a debt collection agency would be notified. Another destitute woman gave birth in hospital and her baby was admitted to the special care unit. She received an invoice for over £3000, which she was wholly unable to pay. She then refused to attend follow up checks, for fear of debt collectors. And a woman from China was turned away by the local NHS trust unless she could pay several thousand pounds in advance. She gave birth at home with no medical care. Serious problems arose, and she had to be admitted to hospital. She then received bills which so frightened her that she fled her home (Kelley and Stevenson 2006, pp.11–12).

14.3.7 PRIMARY MEDICAL CARE SERVICES

At the time of writing these are free (e.g. services from a GP). From a district nurse employed by a GP services would be free, but chargeable if the nurse was employed by an NHS trust. At the time of writing the Department of Health has proposed to remove this exemption (DH 2004b).

Other Department of Health guidance states that for treatment that is not immediately necessary and non-emergency, GPs are not obliged to accept overseas visitors onto their list – but are encouraged to treat on a private, paying basis (HSC 1999/018, paras 13–14).

In practice, it appears there is sometimes misinterpretation of the rules, with the rules applying to hospitals being wrongly applied to primary care (Kelley and Stevenson 2006, p.17).

14.3.8 BILATERAL HEALTH CARE ARRANGEMENTS

Bilateral health care arrangements exist between all member states of the European Economic Area (EEA) and Switzerland. Residents of the relevant countries are entitled to treatment if they have a form E112 from their home country that covers them for treatment – or if the treatment is immediately necessary. There are also bilateral agreements between the United Kingdom and some other countries (DH 2004a, p.29).

Further guidance deals with people from the eight recent 'accession countries', that is countries that have recently joined the European Union (EU). These are the Czech Republic, Estonia, Hungary, Latvia, Lithuania, Poland, Slovakia and Slovenia – and also Malta and Cyprus (but not the Turkish part of Cyprus). These have the same residence rights in the United Kingdom as people from the original 15 EEA countries – as long as they are exercising EU treaty rights.

The exception to this is if they are seeking to live in the UK for the purpose of employment. If so, they can only reside legally if, within 30 days, they register on the Worker Registration Scheme. Following 12 months of continuous employment, they will be eligible for state benefits, including income support and local authority accommodation. They will be exempt from charges. If they cease work before the end of the 12 months, they are not entitled to state benefits and lose the right of residence.

In contrast, short-term visitors from these countries such as tourists or visiting relative are eligible to receive all necessary treatment, if they are insured under health care arrangements in their own country. People staying in the longer term and exercising EU treaty rights (self-employed people, students, those who are self-sufficient) are eligible for exemption from charges if they meet one of the exemption criteria.

The guidance gives an example of a pregnant Polish woman who comes to the UK to live with her boyfriend, by whom she is supported and maintained. She would be self-sufficient and exercising a treaty right, be here legally and might be deemed an ordinary resident. In which case, she would be entitled to health care as any other ordinary UK resident – likewise, an Estonian student on a qualifying college course. However, a Lithuanian woman, claiming to be employed as a cook in an office canteen, would only be exempt from charges if she could show that an application to the Worker Registration Scheme was made within 30 days of her starting work – or that she has completed 12 months employment whiles being registered on the scheme (DH 2007h).

14.3.9 DEBT RECOVERY

The regulations place a duty on NHS trusts to make charges, where overseas visitors are not exempt (SI 1989/306, r.2). The Department of Health guidance points out that overseas visitors' bad debt cannot be waived. It recommends employing the services of a debt recovery agency specialising in overseas debt. Bad debt, which proves irrecoverable, should be written off and properly recorded. Invoices should still be raised even if it is believed that the person cannot pay. The NHS trust can decide to write off debt if all reasonable steps for recovery have been taken, or the patient has died (DH 2004a, p.44).

CHAPTER 15

Residence and eligibility for services

KEY POINTS

This chapter considers the issue of how a person's residence can affect the obligations of both local social services authorities and the NHS.

The question of a person's ordinary residence is a recurring one in community care – in both social and health care. The reason for this is that various duties are conditional on a person being an ordinary resident within the area of a local authority or NHS primary care trust; and the resource implications might be considerable. Ordinary residence is yet one more escape route, referred to in Chapter 3, away from unwanted obligations and expenditure. Department of Health guidance makes clear that any such disputes should not be to the detriment of the service user caught in the cross fire.

Local authorities have long since engaged with one another in frequent and sometimes lengthy disputes, particularly about the ordinary residence of people being placed in residential accommodation under s.21 of the National Assistance Act 1948. And, as the NHS becomes more fragmented, with NHS providers urged to compete with each other, it would appear that disputes about residence and the 'responsible commissioner' are becoming more prevalent.

15.1 RESIDENCE IN COMMUNITY CARE: OVERVIEW

Some local authority obligations to provide community care services (both residential and non-residential) depend on whether a person is 'ordinarily resident' in the authority's area. In some cases, a duty is converted to a mere power, if the person in question is not ordinarily resident; in others, absent the duty, and there is not even a power.

Should a dispute arise between local authorities about where a person really lives, Department of Health guidance makes it clear that assessment and service provision should anyway not be delayed or prevented. The decision, about which authority is responsible for arranging and paying for services, should be made subsequently.

If a person has housing and health care needs as well, there is scope for uncertainty because social services, housing and NHS rules for residence and responsibility differ.

15.2 ORDINARY RESIDENCE: SOCIAL SERVICES

A number of rules, both legislative and at common law, bear upon where a person is deemed to be legally ordinarily resident, for social services purposes.

15.2.1 COMMUNITY CARE LEGISLATION AFFECTED BY ORDINARY RESIDENCE

Community care legislation affected by the ordinary residence condition comprises the National Assistance Act 1948 (s.21: provision of residential accommodation and s.29: welfare services) and the Chronically Sick and Disabled Persons Act 1970 (s.2: welfare services).

For instance, what might be a duty towards an 'ordinary resident' to arrange a care home placement might be a power only towards a non-resident of the area, under s.21 of the National Assistance Act 1948 and directions made under it (see 9.3.1). Under s.29 of the 1948 Act, a general duty to provide certain services for disabled people is rendered a power only in the case of those not ordinarily resident (see 11.1). And s.2 of the Chronically Sick and Disabled Persons Act 1970 anyway extends to ordinary residents only, there not being even a power to provide those services to disabled people who are not ordinarily resident (see 11.2).

15.2.2 MEANING OF 'ORDINARILY RESIDENT'

There is no statutory definition of 'ordinarily resident' and it is ultimately for the courts to decide what it means. Department of Health guidance states that the term should be given its ordinary and natural meaning subject to any interpretation by the courts. It states that the concept of ordinary residence involves questions of fact and degree, and factors such as time, intention and continuity in the particular context (LAC(93)7, para 2). A number of court cases that have considered 'ordinary residence' are cited in the guidance (paras 12, 13):

- *R v Barnet LBC, ex p Shah* defined a person's ordinary residence as 'abode in a particular place or country which he had adopted voluntarily and for settled purposes as part of the regular order of his life for the time being, whether of short or long duration'.
- *R v Waltham Forest LBC, ex p Vale* and *R v Redbridge LBC ex p East Sussex CC 1992*.

Of these two latter cases, one involved provision for autistic twins who had apparently been abandoned by their parents:

Ordinary residence: parents returned abroad. A dispute arose between two local authorities about which authority had a statutory responsibility for making arrangements for two autistic twins with learning disabilities. Their parental home had been in Redbridge but they had attended a residential Rudolf Steiner school in East Sussex. The parents then sold the house in Redbridge and returned to Nigeria. The imminent closure of the school subsequently sparked the dispute between the two councils about which would be responsible for making arrangements for the provision of residential accommodation under s.21 of the National Assistance Act 1948.

The judge, referring to the case of *R v Barnet LBC, ex p Shah*, found that the parents' departure and sale of the family home meant that the twins had ceased to be ordinarily resident in Redbridge, and that the duty to make provision fell to East Sussex (*R v Redbridge LBC, ex p East Sussex CC*).

The other case concerned the ordinary residence of a woman with learning disabilities:

Ordinary residence: parental home. The person concerned was 28 years old and mentally handicapped from birth. In 1961 she had moved to Ireland with her parents where she lived in residential homes. Her parents returned to England in 1978 to live in Waltham Forest; she returned in 1984 and lived for one month with her parents before being placed in a home in Buckinghamshire. Waltham Forest now denied financial responsibility for the placement on the grounds that she had been ordinarily resident in Ireland and that the stay with her parents had been merely temporary.

The judge disagreed. First, the woman concerned was so mentally handicapped that she was totally dependent on her parents and was in the same position as a small child. Concepts such as 'voluntarily adopted residence' or 'settled purpose' – used in *R v Barnet LBC, ex p Shah* – were irrelevant to the case. Therefore, the woman's ordinary residence was that of her parents, which was not her 'real home' (a concept rejected in the *Shah v Barnet LBC* case) but her 'base'.

Should he have been mistaken in this view, and she did have capacity, the judge went on to state that in any case the one-month stay with her parents was sufficient to constitute ordinary residence – since the *Shah* case made clear that ordinary residence could be of short duration. Alternatively she might have been of no settled residence; but she could not be resident in the area in which she had been accommodated before moving back to the parents' home.

Thus, responsibility lay with Waltham Forest and not Buckinghamshire (*R v Waltham Forest, ex p Vale*).

15.2.3 COMMUNITY CARE RESIDENTIAL ACCOMMODATION AND ORDINARY RESIDENCE

The rules concerning ordinary residence and the provision of residential accommodation – when, due to age, illness, disability or any other circumstances, care and attention is not otherwise available for a person – are contained in s.24 of the National Assistance Act 1948 and in directions issued by the Secretary of State. The Department of Health has also issued guidance on the matter. In substance, the position is as follows:

- **Ordinarily resident**. A local authority has a power to provide residential accommodation to a person ordinarily resident in the area (this is turned into a duty by directions: see 9.3.1).
- **No settled residence**. A local authority has a power to provide residential accommodation for people with no settled residence and for people ordinarily resident elsewhere but who are in urgent need of accommodation.
- **Provision on behalf of another local authority**. A local authority has a power to provide residential accommodation for a person ordinarily resident in the area of another authority with the consent of that other authority.
- **Placement in another area**. If a person is provided with residential accommodation, he or she is deemed to be ordinarily resident in the area in which he or she was ordinarily resident immediately before the residential accommodation was provided.
- **NHS patient**. An NHS patient is deemed to be ordinarily resident, for local authority purposes, in the area (if any) he or she was living in immediately before entering hospital (National Assistance Act 1948, s.24).

    (The Health and Social Care Act 2008 amends this, substituting the term NHS accommodation for the term hospital, and making clear that the rule applies both to accommodation provided under the NHS Act 2006 and also provided by a Primary Care Trust under s.117 of the Mental Health Act 1983.)

Department of Health guidance advises that when a person states that he has no settled residence or describes himself as having no fixed abode, the social services authority where he presents himself should normally accept responsibility (LAC(93)7, para 16). Nonetheless, if a person is deemed to have no settled residence, he or she is less well protected (Secretary of State for Health 2007, determination no.1). Thus:

No settled residence and urgency. 'The point that was made, having regard to the combination of the primary statutory provisions and that direction, is that in respect of persons ordinarily resident in their area local authorities owe a duty. However, they only have a power in respect of persons who are not ordinarily resident in their area. That can occur in circumstances when the person is ordinarily resident in the area of another local authority, or it could occur in circumstances when the person is not ordinarily resident in any authority. When the person is ordinarily resident in another authority, then the power is exercisable with the consent of the authority that owes the duty, that is, the authority where the person is ordinarily resides. Where there is no settled residence there is a power, save that that power is converted into a duty in circumstances of urgency.

I accept the submission made on behalf of Greenwich that a message derived from the statutory provisions (which expressly envisage the Secretary of State making directions against the backdrop of the subject matter of provisions which are the last safety net) is that the preservation of a duty is a relevant feature. Thus it seems to me that that is a factor to be taken into account in considering whether or not a person has ceased to become ordinarily resident in a local authority which owed him a duty. It is, however, naturally, no more than a factor' (*R(Greenwich LBC) v Secretary of State for Health*).

So, the power of a local authority to provide for somebody of no settled residence is converted to a duty in case of urgency; and physical presence in the area of a local authority is enough to trigger this. For instance, in one legal case a person had lived for some three years in Lambeth before being imprisoned for drugs offences. On release, she went to stay with a friend in Hackney for about two weeks; one day she travelled by public transport to

Lewisham (where her half-sister and son lived), where she presented herself at the social services office. The court held that Lewisham was the responsible authority (*R(S) v Lewisham LBC*).

The guidance states also that if a person is placed in a care home by one local authority in the area of another local authority, then it is the former that retains responsibility. However, if by 'private arrangement' the person then moves, he or she 'may' become ordinarily resident in the area of the second authority, 'depending on the specific circumstances'. If the person makes his or her own arrangements to enter a care home in a different local authority's area, and subsequently requires social services assistance, he or she will normally be ordinarily resident in the second authority's area (LAC(93)7, paras 7,10).

15.2.3.1 Entering a care home: ordinary residence

Thus, a key issue inviting dispute is the legal rule in s.24 of the 1948 Act sometimes referred to as a 'deeming' provision. That is, a person is deemed to be ordinarily resident in the local authority where he or she was resident, immediately before residential accommodation or services were provided.

Furthermore, in determining whether such accommodation was provided under the 1948 Act, it is essential that the contractual arrangements with the care home be made by a local authority (*Chief Adjudication Officer v Quinn*). When a person has adequate funds to pay for his or her own care, this has sometimes led to a local authority carrying out an assessment and even making travel arrangements for a person to enter a care home in the area of another local authority. But it is the person himself or herself who makes contractual arrangements with the care home. However, when that person's funds run down and he or she needs local authority assistance, it the second rather than the first local authority that is normally responsible. This is because the person had voluntarily taken up residence in the area of the second local authority, where he or she was resident immediately before requiring provision of residential accommodation under the 1948 Act.

This rule was tested in the following case, referred initially to the Secretary of State for resolution and then to the courts. It included the all too common allegation of 'dumping' made by one local authority against another:

Dumping a care home resident over the border? A woman was in a care home in Bexley – apparently placed there by the local authority. Complaints were made about her behaviour and the conclusion was reached it was no longer appropriate for her to remain there. Two other placements in the local authority were considered but rejected on grounds of suitability or lack of an available place. A third option was identified 100 yards over the border with Greenwich. She moved to that home.

Bexley Council knew that within five weeks her capital would have reduced such that a local authority would have to step in and start to contribute to some (and progressively more) of the cost. Bexley left it up to the family to fund the placement for those five weeks – before claiming that, once the five weeks were up, she would be Greenwich Council's responsibility. Greenwich argued that the woman had not voluntarily adopted residence in Greenwich (since the placement was arranged in all but contract by Bexley) – and that moreover it was intended to be a temporary placement only.

Muddle rather than deliberate dumping. The dispute was referred to the Secretary of State who applied the deeming provision and held that Greenwich was now the responsible local authority. The case subsequently went to court. The judge did not accept that Bexley had acted in bad faith by deliberately 'dumping' the woman in Greenwich. In fact, it appeared to be a muddle rather than anything else. Bexley had not informed Greenwich; furthermore the contractual arrangements for the relevant period had been entirely unclear. The family made no contractual arrangements with the home, nor did Bexley Council – Greenwich Council knew nothing of what was going on. The judge had sympathy with the woman and her family, because Bexley had effectively withdrawn and Greenwich was in ignorance.

Severing of residence in first council. The Secretary of State had relied on the fact that, at the end of the five weeks, the woman had severed ties with Bexley whether or not her move was voluntary. Her house had been sold anyway, and she was no longer living in the area. She was either of no settled residence or ordinarily resident in Greenwich; either way she was no longer ordinarily resident in Bexley. And she could not be deemed to be so, because Bexley had not contracted with the Greenwich care home for those five weeks.

Residence in second council. The judge pointed out that this lack of contracting by Bexley could not be determinative, even though it was significant – because in principle she could have remained ordinarily resident in Bexley if the placement had been regarded as an emergency one with a view to her being found another home in Bexley. Nonetheless, he pointed out that she might have remained in the Greenwich home for days, weeks, months and that it was difficult to say she had not acquired ordinary residence there. The judge was not prepared to hold the Secretary of State's decision unlawful. So Greenwich ended up responsible (*R(Greenwich LBC) v Secretary of State for Health*).

Likewise in the next case:

Moving into a care home in another council. An elderly woman, suffering from vascular dementia, required placing in a care home. She lived in Council B. Her husband died. The family became concerned. She moved to live temporarily with her son in Council A. He could not cope. He placed her in a nursing home for two days on 10 June; during this time Council A did an assessment. He then moved her to another nursing home, this time for seven days, on 12 June. On 19 June, Council A took over the funding in the interim, pending resolution of its dispute with Council B.

The Secretary of State held that the woman's stay with her son and then at the first nursing home did not have sufficient settled purpose under the *Shah* test. However, when she went into the second nursing home, the position changed. There was a settled purpose of meeting her care needs there for the foreseeable future; and it was chosen by the son on behalf of the mother. Council A had some involvement, but had not made the placement; so it was in effect a voluntary move by the woman. This meant that immediately before a local authority provided residential accommodation, she had been ordinarily resident in Council A, which now had responsibility for the placement (Secretary of State for Health 2006, determination no.5).

The frustration of, and disputes between, councils can be understood when it is a matter of mere days or weeks, prior to placement under s.21of the 1948 Act, that determines many thousands' of pounds worth of commitment by the local authority in future.

Private placement in second local authority area: money running down in four weeks. An elderly woman was displaying aggressive behaviour in a care home, in which she had been placed by Council B where she had previously lived. She moved into a nursing home, identified by Council B, in the area of Council A. Council B emphasised to the family that it would not be involved in contractual negotiations with the nursing home; the family would have to do this. Four weeks after moving, her capital of £21,308 had diminished to £19,000, the threshold for local authority involvement. Thus her move had been facilitated by Council B, but up to that point there had been no provision of accommodation under the 1948 Act. Applying the *Vale* test, the position was as follows. If she lacked capacity, the arrangement had been made in her best interests by Council B (and effectively she had taken up residence in Council A). If she had capacity, she had given up residence in Council B, whether or not the move was voluntary. This was because her house had been sold and she was no longer living in the area. However, if the move had not been voluntary, she would have been of no settled residence (in which case Council A had to assume responsibility anyway). Either way Council A was responsible (Secretary of State for Health 2007, determination no.4).

In the following case, the Secretary of State, in a determination of a dispute between authorities, applied the test outlined by the courts in the *Vale* case. The woman was judged to lack capacity to choose where to live, to be dependent on her parents, and so to be ordinarily resident where they lived:

Entering care home: ordinarily resident where parents living. A woman with severe learning disabilities, together with challenging and abusive behaviour, had been placed by Council B in residential accommodation in Council A. Meanwhile her parents had moved from Council B to Council A. The care home then said that she had to leave the placement because of her behaviour. She did so and stayed with her parents for some three months, before she began a placement in residential accommodation in Council B.

The Secretary of State judged that she lacked the capacity to choose her residence, The *Vale* case therefore applied, and she was in the same position as a small child, dependent on and ordinarily resident with her parents. She was therefore resident in Council A. If, on the other hand, she had capacity, the outcome would be the same – she would have been voluntarily resident (albeit for a short period of some three months) with her parents in Council A, immediately before entering residential accommodation (Secretary of State for Health 2005, determination no.8).

15.2.3.2 Moving from residential accommodation into the community

If a person placed by Council A in a care home in Council B leaves the care home voluntarily and lives in the community in Council B, the latter would normally be responsible for any non-residential community care services required. These would be provided, for instance, under the Chronically Sick and Disabled Persons Act 1970, on the basis that the person is now voluntarily, ordinarily resident in the area of Council B. The common law test for ordinary residence set out in the *Shah* case refers to voluntary adoption of a place of residence for a settled purpose of longer or shorter duration.

However, if the person lacks the capacity to decide to move out of a care home into the community, the position may become more complicated. The two key questions would be as follows. First, whether the person really did lack capacity. Second, if not, and following the judge's approach in the *Vale* case, then it should be assumed that the person did have capacity, and residence decided on the facts of the case. This would have the outcome of ordinary residence being determined in Council A or Council B. Alternatively, the person might be deemed to be of no settled residence – in which case, the council of the moment would have responsibility. This approach was taken in the following case decided by the Secretary of State:

Moving from a care home to supported housing. A care home was to close and the relevant resident would instead live in supported housing in Council B. She had originally been resident in Council A, which had taken responsibility for the care home placement. The evidence suggested that the person, with mild to moderate learning disabilities, had the capacity to form a settled purpose for residing in a particular area. In which case, Council B would be responsible. However, if she lacked capacity, the outcome would be the same.

First, the *Vale* case in the main did not apply (i.e. person to be treated as small child in terms of dependence on parents), because the woman had not had contact with her family in the present case. Nor was she totally dependent for her everyday needs on either the local authority or other care provider. However, in the *Vale* case, the judge had stated that if the small child analogy (totally dependence on parents) was wrong, the decision would have to based on treating the person as being mentally capable on the facts of the situation. In the *Vale* case this would have meant either that the woman was residing with parents for the settled purpose of being looked after and having her affairs managed – or that she was of no settled residence. In the present case, the woman had rented accommodation, had unpaid work and a social network of friends – all in Council B. Therefore, on the facts, she was ordinarily resident in Council B (Secretary of State for Health 2005, determination no.5).

The same question arose in another disputed case:

Care home deregistering and turning into supported housing. A care home in Council B deregistered as a care home, and turned itself into a supported living environment on the same site. The person concerned, who had been placed by Council A, now signed a tenancy agreement for private residential accommodation, but required personal care support. The dispute was about which local authority was responsible for providing this.

The Secretary of State judged that he had the mental capacity to choose and that his residence had a settled purpose. He had a tenancy, attended adult education courses, worked in a coffee shop, attended a craft group and religious worship, and had formed friendships in the area. So Council B was responsible. Even had he lacked capacity, the outcome would have been the same. The *Vale* analogy with a small child was not appropriate in this case because he had had a residence independent of his parents for a considerable period of time.

So the alternative *Vale* test had to be applied – that is to assume he had capacity and to decide factually whether he was 'voluntarily' resident with his parents (or other base) or of no settled residence. On the facts, his ordinary residence could not be Council A (where he was no longer present), so either he was ordinarily resident in Council B or of no settled residence. Council B was the answer (Secretary of State for Health 2006, determination no. 3).

15.2.4 ORDINARY RESIDENCE: ADULTS WHO WERE PREVIOUSLY LOOKED AFTER CHILDREN

The 'leaving care' provisions under the Children Act 1989 place certain responsibilities (duties and powers) on local authorities in respect of people formerly looked after as children by the local authority, or otherwise accommodated as a child. The responsibilities are usually up to the age of 21 years of the person, but may extend beyond (for details of the leaving care provisions, see 13.6.6).

In the case of a disabled person requiring, for example, non-residential community care services under s.2 of the Chronically Sick and Disabled Persons Act 1970 (CSDPA), uncertainties could arise concerning responsibility – if that person were subject as well to the leaving care provisions.

Where the person (as a child) was looked after by a local authority (as opposed to another body), but is now in the area of another authority, the original authority retains certain responsibilities and duties, including the provision of assistance in kind.

Therefore any uncertainties about responsibilities (between the former authority and the present authority) might centre on the individual case, and on the interpretation placed by the courts on the word 'assistance' in the leaving care provisions. It is possibly unclear whether the courts would hold that the assistance referred to in the leaving care provisions extends to the services contained in s.2 of the CSDPA 1970. Section 23B(4) of the Children Act 1989 might suggest not, since it refers to a leaving care assessment as being separate from a CSDPA assessment. The implication would seem to be that the present authority would retain its responsibilities under s.2 of the CSDPA to the person, who is now ordinarily resident within its area; whilst the former authority would retain the leaving care responsibilities. Guidance issued by the Department of Health on inter-authority arrangements for care leavers does not explicitly clarify this issue in respect of disabled persons (LASSL(2004)20).

Unsurprisingly, residence questions arise when a local authority has taken responsibility under the Children Act 1989 and placed the child in another local authority area. When the person becomes 18 years old, a dispute then arises as to ordinary residence under the National Assistance Act 1948. The question becomes complicated because s.105(6) of the 1989 Act states that in determining ordinary residence for any purpose under the 1989 Act, the period in which a child lives in accommodation arranged by the local authority should be disregarded. Thus up to a person's 18th birthday the child remains ordinarily resident in the original area; but at that age, ordinary residence has instead to be ascertained under the 1948 Act. The Secretary of State takes the approach that although ordinary residence under the Children Act will be an important factor in determining ordinary residence under the 1948 Act when the child reaches 18; nonetheless it is not decisive (Secretary of State 2006, determination no.4). This is in line with the Department of Health guidance which states that local authorities could 'reasonably have regard' to the definition in the 1989 Act, for the purposes of the 1948 Act (LAC (93)7, para 21).

In the *Vale* legal case (see above), the judge held that in the case of a person lacking capacity, her total dependence on her parents meant she should be treated as ordinarily resident at her parents' address. The Secretary of State followed this approach in the following disputed case:

Adult previously in foster care, ties with parents maintained ordinary residence in original council. A young man (lacking capacity to state where he wished to live) had not lived with his natural parents (in Council A) since he was 21 months old. However, he had not formally been taken into care, since he was accommodated with foster carers under a voluntary arrangement in Council B. Furthermore, his natural parents had retained parental responsibility, a role in making decisions about his future and had had regular contact with him. Aged 18, he had now entered residential accommodation. In these circumstances, he was deemed by the Secretary of State to have been ordinarily resident (immediately before entering the accommodation under the 1948 Act) in Council A, the council of origin (Secretary of State for Health 2005, determination no.3).

However, the outcome may be different even in apparently similar circumstances, if contact with the parents has lapsed – as the Secretary of State decided in the following determination:

Adult, previously in foster care, ties severed with parents: ordinary residence in new council. A person with severe disabilities and generally lacking mental capacity to say where he wanted to live, had been placed by Council A (where his parents lived) with foster carers in Council B under the Children Act 1989. When he reached 18 years and legally became an adult he remained with the foster carers, under s.29 of the National Assistance Act 1948. The Secretary of State held that he had not had any contact with his natural parents for many years, and that he had now resided with his foster carers for nearly 17 years. Thus his ordinary residence was now in Council B (Secretary of State for Health 2005, determination no.1).

Likewise in a further case along similar lines:

Adult, previously in foster care: ties with father severed: ordinary residence in new council. A person with severe learning disabilities had been placed by Council B with foster carers at the age of 16 (in Council A). He remained with them for four years, until they could no longer have him. The Secretary of State held that if he had capacity to decide where to live, then he was ordinarily resident in Council A, since he had been happy there for four years – and so had been resident there voluntarily for settled purposes as part of the regular order of his life (the *Shah* legal test). Even if he lacked the capacity, he would still be ordinarily resident in Council A, because he had not had any contact with his father for many years, and the father wished for no contact. Under the *Vale* test therefore, his dependence would be not on his natural parent but on his foster carers (Secretary of State for Health 2004, determination no.1).

Similarly in the following case, although contact with the mother had been retained:

Adult, previously in foster care, ties with mother but not otherwise with original council of residence: ordinary residence in new council. A woman with profound mental, physical and visual disabilities, together with epilepsy, had been placed with foster carers as a child by (what was now) Council A. As an adult she had been placed in residential accommodation. Although she maintained contact with her mother in Council B, it was not her 'base' in any meaningful sense. She had never lived there, and it was not a place from where she set out and to where she returned. It was the place she visited for short periods to maintain contact with the family. So Council A was the area of ordinary residence (Secretary of State for Health 2005, determination no.4).

And again, in another similar case:

Looked-after child. A girl at the age of 15 had been looked after in Council A, the council in which she had lived with her mother up to that point. At age 18 she was continuing to be provided with accommodation but it was now under the National Assistance Act and ordinary residence had to be determined. She retained contact with her mother who lived in Council B, but the Secretary of State considered that her real base was still in Council A, where she lived and had ongoing contact with relatives. Thus, under the Children Act she was ordinarily resident in Council A immediately before turning 18 and being provided with accommodation under the 1948 Act. Council A was her place of ordinary residence, too, under the 1948 Act (Secretary of State for Health 2006, determination no.4).

In yet another similar case, the man with Asperger's syndrome involved did retain ties with his mother in Council A, but that council area could not be called his base. Before he turned 18 he had been living for two years in Council B with a foster carer. He had put down roots there, had friends, participated in outside activities, had a part-time job and indicated he wished to remain in Council B. He was judged to have the mental capacity to decide. He was ordinarily resident in Council B and fell to be provided by that council with residential accommodation under the 1948 Act (Secretary of State for Health 2007, determination 3).

15.2.5 HOMELESSNESS AND HOUSING ISSUES

Social services and housing authorities apply different tests to establish the 'ordinary residence' of homeless people. Therefore the responsible housing authority will not necessarily be the same as the responsible social services authority. The test for 'local connection' in the context of homelessness legislation is to be found in s.199 of the Housing Act 1996 and covers normal residence (past or present), employment, family associations or special circumstances.

Department of Health guidance explains that when a person states that he or she has no settled residence or fixed abode, the social services authority where he presents himself should normally accept responsibility. This is because, for a person in urgent need, that social services authority cannot argue that the possible existence of a 'local connection' elsewhere excuses it from its duty to assess and provide necessary services. In particular, the guidance warns against using the housing rules to identify ordinary residence for social services purposes (LAC(93)7, para 16).

15.2.6 ORDINARY RESIDENCE OF PEOPLE IN HOSPITAL, NURSING HOMES, PRISON AND SIMILAR ESTABLISHMENTS

The legislation states that people in hospital/NHS accommodation are to be regarded by local authorities as ordinarily resident in the area (if any) they were ordinarily resident in before entering hospital (National Assistance Act 1948, s.24).

Department of Health guidance suggests that local authorities could reasonably apply this approach to people in comparable situations, such as prisons, resettlement units and other similar establishments. These people might be without a permanent place to live and might require social services involvement at the time of their discharge (LAC(93)7, para 14). In the following case, a prolonged stay in a hospital-like establishment, which the person concerned wanted and had the capacity to decide, broke the link with the original council (where he had been originally ordinarily resident before entering the establishment). He was now ordinarily resident in the area of the new council, where the establishment was situated and from which he would be discharged into the community:

Stay in specialist establishment for epilepsy: breaking of link with original council. A man with cognitive disabilities and epilepsy living in Council B, was placed by the NHS in the area of Council A, in a residential centre for assessment and rehabilitation of people with epilepsy run by the National Society for Epilepsy (NSE). He remained there for two years, at which point the NHS ceased to fund the placement. There was no compulsion that he remain there. However, he stayed on for a year until June 2004, funded by Council B, until he could be discharged into the local community. He wished to continue living in the area of Council A. However, there was a hitch in the discharge, and he remained living, and wished to remain living (he had the capacity to choose), at the NSE establishment.

The Secretary of State held that the NSE centre was not a hospital for the purposes of s.24. He took it nonetheless to come under the guidance and that there was a rebuttable presumption that he remained ordinarily resident in Council B (the original council). However, in this case, the presumption was rebutted, because he was capable of forming his own intention of where he should continue living – and he had done so (Secretary of State for Health 2005, determination no.7).

The Secretary of State also resolved the following, complicated case, which involved a number of councils and hospitals:

Hospital care required after accident to a person in transit and of uncertain residence. A woman left Council A in a transit van for an unknown period of time. There was a traffic accident. Her boyfriend was killed, and she received multiple, severe injuries to brain, neck and spine, resulting in a coma of several months. She was admitted initially to a hospital in Council, then a hospital in Council C, another in Council F, a rehabilitation hospital in Council B and finally a rehabilitation centre in Council D – all fully funded by the NHS. Another placement now had to be identified and arranged by a local authority.

The rule in s.24 of 1948 Act is that a person be deemed ordinarily resident in the area of ordinarily residence immediately before hospital admission. However, the Secretary of State held that she had left Council A, probably intended to return to Council A in the longer term, but had no intention of doing so until after the expiry of her tenancy in Council A (which would mean she would not then have had a base to which she would have had a right of return). This meant that she was of no settled residence and, in any event, Council A was therefore not responsible for funding.

The Secretary of State decided that she had become ordinarily in Council D, where she had lived at the rehabilitation centre for over four years. The original intention had been a stay of only 12 weeks, but she stayed for much longer and it seemed likely that there had been some element of choice as to which rehabilitation centre to reside in. If not at the outset, then by the end, of her stay, she had acquired ordinary residence in that area (Secretary of State for Health 2006, determination no. 1).

In the following case, provision of residential, rehabilitation accommodation by an NHS primary care trust broke the link with the local authority area in which the woman had lived:

Placement in rehabilitation facility by PCT, then by local authority. A 31-year-old woman lived in Council B. She suffered a brain haemorrhage, and was admitted to hospital in Council B. Then she was placed in a privately run rehabilitation facility in Council A (near her family) by the NHS primary care trust, on the basis that she had NHS continuing health care status. It subsequently reviewed her needs and decided that she no longer met continuing health care criteria. So it would fall to a local authority to fund the placement.

Immediately before she fell to be provided by a local authority with this accommodation under the National Assistance Act 1948, she was held to be ordinarily resident in Council A. While she was in hospital she remained ordinarily resident because of the effect of the rule about this in the 1948 Act. As for the placement in the rehabilitation facility, it was true that a person's ordinary residence is not lost because of temporary absence, but this had been more than temporary. She did not retain a property in Council A and had no intention of returning. It was also likely that she would eventually be placed in supported living near her family, which was in Council A. In the *Shah* case, the court had distinguished voluntary adoption of a place or residence from enforced (such as kidnapping or imprisonment). But in this case, her wishes and proximity to family played a part in the choice of this particular facility. Furthermore, though the rehabilitation facility was never meant to be permanent, under the *Shah* test it did not have to be; 'settled purpose' could be of long or short duration.

The Secretary of State also considered whether she might have been of no settled residence but decided against this, stating that such a conclusion should not be hastily drawn. This was because it conferred a lesser degree of protection on the person (Secretary of State for Health 2007, determination no. 1).

15.2.7 ORDINARY RESIDENCE DISPUTES AFFECTING SERVICES

Uncertainty and disputes about ordinary residence sometimes arise between local authorities. Circular guidance states that delay in assessment and service provision should not occur: 'If there is a dispute about the ordinary residence of a person in need of services it should be debated after the care assessment and any provision of service' (LAC(93)7, summary and para 3). A failure to follow this guidance will attract judicial censure:

Washing hands of responsibility all round. A 28-year-old woman with learning disabilities lived in Camden. Her relationship with her husband broke down. She went to live with a boyfriend in Hackney. She had been receiving community care services in Camden from the local authority, including a vocational training placement. Camden proposed to withdraw the services in the context of a dispute with Hackney about her ordinary residence. Neither council was prepared to accept responsibility for her. Pending resolution of the dispute, the courts granted an injunction obliging both authorities to provide her with accommodation for people with learning disabilities – at accommodation where she had previously lived. Eventually the woman anyway moved back to Camden, which resumed its community care responsibilities toward her.

In a subsequent court case about disputed legal costs, the court criticised both authorities for 'plain breach of the guidance'; the wrangling between the authorities over a period of months meant the woman was left in limbo (the training placement was interrupted for eight months). Both authorities 'washed their hands' of the woman. Since there was no good reason for the departure from the guidance, this meant that the authorities had acted unlawfully (*R v Hackney LBC, ex p J*).

Similarly the local government ombudsman will find maladministration if the guidance is not followed and undue delay occurs:

Dispute concerning responsibility. Two questions arose about responsibility and ordinary residence in the case of a man in a care home, in a different local authority area to his previous residence. The first complication was that he had moved to the care home on his own initiative and only sought funding from his original authority after the event. The original authority therefore questioned its responsibility, since it had not placed him there. The second question concerned responsibility for a community care package, were he to leave the care home to live in the community in the second local authority's area. Whatever the correct answer, the maladministration lay in the delay of a year, before a determination from the Secretary of State was sought (*Redbridge LBC 1998*).

15.2.8 RESOLUTION OF DISPUTES ABOUT ORDINARY RESIDENCE

Guidance refers to the fact that disputes about ordinary residence under Part III of the National Assistance Act 1948 are ultimately to be determined by the Secretary of State under s.32 of the same Act.

Disputes about ordinary residence could therefore relate to non-residential services under s.29 of the 1948 Act, as well as to residential services under s.21. The guidance states that each case has to be considered on its own facts; that the Secretary of State's decision is final subject only to judicial review; that the question of establishing ordinary residence is essentially a legal one; and that authorities must have agreed provisional liability for service provision before the dispute is referred to the Secretary of State. The guidance describes the procedure to be followed by local authorities (LAC(93)7, paras 24–28).

The Secretary of State's powers of dispute resolution under s.32 of the National Assistance Act 1948 do not apply to s.117 of the Mental Health Act 1983 (aftercare for discharged patients) (LAC(93)7, para 24). There is however reference to residence within s.117, and the courts have interpreted how the rules should be applied (see 11.5.2 above).

The courts have also held that in the past that the s.32 resolution procedure does not apply to disputes concerning ordinary residence under s.2 of the Chronically Sick and Disabled Persons Act 1970 (*R v Kent County Council, ex p Salisbury*). This is another example of the strained relationship between s.29 of the 1948 Act and s.2 of the 1970 Act; sometimes the courts hold that they function separately as in this instance, and in the case of *R v Islington LBC, ex p McMillan.* Yet in other respects, for example for the purpose of charging, the courts have held that they are firmly hitched together (*R v Powys CC, ex p Hambidge (no.2)*).

The Health and Social Care Act 2008 provides for an amendment to s.2 of the 1970 Act, which will make quite clear that the s.32 dispute resolution procedure applies to s.2, just as it does to Part 3 of the National Assistance Act 1948.

An arrangement exists between England and Wales, such that in case of dispute, the place where the person is living at the time of referral determines whether that referral is made to Welsh Ministers or the Secretary of State for Health (DH 2007k).

15.3 NHS: RESPONSIBLE COMMISSIONER

The legal framework regarding NHS commissioning responsibilities is set out in regulations (SI 2002/2375) concerning Primary Care Trusts (PCTs). Such trusts are in England now responsible for commissioning most health services for the population in each of their areas. Guidance issued by the Department of Health includes the following points (DH 2007t):

- **Delay or refusal of treatment**. Treatment should not be delayed or refused because of uncertainty or ambiguity in funding responsibility relating to a person's place of residence (para 2).
- **Basic test/usual rules: registration with GP or usual address**. A PCT is responsible for commissioning services for people registered with a general practitioner (GP) associated with the PCT; and also for people usually resident in the area or non-UK residents present in their area who are not registered with a GP. In summary, the responsible PCT is identified by the GP with whom a patient is registered or, where not applicable, by the person's usual residence (para 6). If a person is of no fixed abode, then the address the person gives as their "usual residence" should determine responsibility; for example, this may be a hostel. If no address of usual residence can be established, then the area in which the person is present establishes responsibility (paras 17-18).
- **Changing place of residence**. If a person moves residence during a course of treatment, the same basic test applies as above (i.e. depending on GP registration). However, the guidance suggests the original PCT may wish to continue to provide the treatment on behalf of the new PCT for a certain length of time (para 19).
- **Overseas visitors**. See 14.3.
- **Asylum seekers.** During any stage of the application, an asylum seeker is regarded as a member of the resident population, so the usual rules apply (para 16).
- **Prisoners**. The PCT within whose area a prison is located is responsible for commissioning services for the prisoners (para 79).

- **NHS walk-in centres**. Responsibility lies either with the patient's PCT under the usual rules or, for unregistered patients, with the PCT within the area of which the centre is.
- **Emergency ambulance services**. These are the responsibility of the PCT within the boundary of which the emergency has occurred. Non-emergency transport responsibility lies with the PCT identified under the usual rules (para 44).
- **Mental Health Act 1983**. For people detained for treatment under the Mental Health Act 1983, the basic test applies. If GP registration or residential address cannot be established, the responsible PCT is determined by the location of the mental health unit (para 64). A separate rule governs responsibility for aftercare under s.117 of the Mental Health Act 1983; the responsible PCT is that where the person was resident before he or she was detained; if such previous residence is not ascertainable, then responsibility for s.117 services falls on the PCT for the area to which the person is discharged (see 11.5.2).
- **NHS Continuing health care**. The original, placing PCT remains responsible for a placement in residential accommodation (care home or independent hospital), even if the placement is in another area. If continuing health care is provided in a person's own home, then responsibility is ascertained under the usual rules; likewise if the person is transferred to an NHS hospital for inpatient care (Annex C).
- **Registered nursing care**. If a person is placed in a care home outside the original PCT, it is the receiving PCT that becomes responsible – albeit after being informed by the original PCT (Annex C).
- **Disputes**. Ultimately, if disputes cannot be resolved locally, the relevant strategic health authority should be consulted (para 9).
- **Children**. The guidance explains the effect of the regulations on children. In the case of four groups of children, the originating PCT retains responsibility, even if a child is placed in the area of another PCT and has changed his or her GP. The four groups are as follows: (a) looked after children and children leaving care; (b) pupils with statements of special educational needs attending residential special schools; (c) children with continuing health care needs requiring residential care who are not looked after children; (d) young adults (18 years or over) with continuing health care needs. However, in respect of the latter, the guidance states that the person will need to be reviewed as he or she approaches 18 years of age, because the 'threshold for PCTs and local authorities providing continuing care needs may be higher for adults than it is for children' (para 30).

15.4 RESIDENCE: CROSS-BORDER RESPONSIBILITIES

Uncertainty commonly arises concerning cross-border issues, that is, between England, Wales, Scotland and Northern Ireland, in respect of both health and social care responsibilities.

15.4.1 CROSS-BORDER SOCIAL SERVICES PLACEMENTS IN CARE HOMES

The position as to the placement of people in care homes across the borders of the four United Kingdom countries is a confused one. The following is a broad summary of the apparent position.

The Choice of Accommodation Directions (in LAC(92)27) reflect s.26 of the National Assistance Act 1948, which restricts placement to homes in England and Wales, because residential accommodation providing personal and nursing care must be registered under the Care Standards Act 2000 (which applies to England and Wales only).

In the case of Scottish local authorities wishing to place people in English or Welsh care homes, the position is not as clear. First of all s.13A of the Social Work (Scotland) Act 1968 apparently prohibits such placements in respect of care homes that provide nursing, although the wording is not without possible ambiguity. However, under s.59 of the 1968 Act which covers placements in care homes not providing nursing, there is apparently no prohibition on such placements (see e.g. Scottish Executive 2001, paras 31–35).

The Health and Social Care Act 2001 provides for regulations to be made to rectify this situation and to allow English (and Welsh) local authorities to place people in residential homes in Scotland, Northern Ireland, the Channel Islands and the Isle of Man (s.56). There is a similar Scottish provision in the Community Care and Health (Scotland) Act 2002 (s.5); when passed, the position of Scottish local authorities placing people in England and Wales will in any event be clarified. However, at the time of writing, neither English nor Scottish regulations have been made.

In the absence of such regulations, the Department of Health's 1993 guidance appears still to hold good. It states that Scottish authorities have a discretion to arrange residential accommodation for people resident in England and that where prospective residents wish it, English authorities are expected to approach Scottish authorities to exercise this discretion (LAC(93)18). In which case, although the contract for care would be between the Scottish local authority and the care home, an arrangement between the two authorities concerned should allow for the Scottish authority to be reimbursed by the English one.

In the case of Scottish local authorities wishing to place people in English care homes, the position would be the same in reverse (LAC(93)18; and see also equivalent Scottish guidance: SWSG 6/94).

The statutory provisions allowing such reimbursement in both directions lie in the National Assistance Act 1948, ss.32–33; and s.86 of the Social Work (Scotland) Act 1968. However, in the light of the uncertainty in Scotland referred to immediately above, it appears that in practice some Scottish local authorities simply place people directly in English care homes anyway, believing that they have the legal power to do so.

The Department of Health guidance states that such reimbursement arrangements would not be possible in respect of Northern Ireland – that is, for English authorities to arrange to pay for residential care in Northern Ireland or for health and social services boards in Northern Ireland to pay for residential accommodation arranged by English authorities (LAC(93)18, para 11).

15.4.2 CROSS-BORDER NHS RESPONSIBLE COMMISSIONER
Department of Health guidance, based on regulations, states (DH 2007, replacing DH 2006, and SI 2002/2375).

- **Moving to England**. If a patient moves from Scotland, Wales or Northern Ireland to England, there is an expectation that he or she will register with a general practitioner (GP). This would then determine the responsible PCT (para 69).
- **Living in Scotland, Wales or Northern Ireland with English general practitioner**. In Wales, Scotland and Northern Ireland, the responsible authority for health care is determined by where the person is usually resident, and not by general practitioner registration. Therefore, if a person is registered with an English GP but lives in Scotland, the responsible commissioner will be Scottish. If a person is resident in Wales or Northern Ireland but registered with a GP in England, both Wales/Northern Ireland or England could be held responsible as commissioner; it would be up to local organisations to come to an agreement about this (paras 58–60).
- **Living in England, but registered with a GP elsewhere**. If a person is resident in England, but registered with a general practitioner in Wales, Scotland or Northern Ireland, the responsible commissioner is the English PCT (para 69).

15.4.3 CROSS-BORDER REGISTERED NURSING CARE IN ENGLAND AND WALES

A protocol developed by the National Assembly for Wales and the Department of Health concerning registered nursing care in care homes includes the following principles: first, that the level of funding provided will be that of the destination (i.e. receiving) PCT (in England) or Local Health Board (LHB in Wales); second, that the PCT or LHB, within which the home is located, will arrange the funding for the registered nursing care (Department of Health 2003l).

PART III

Housing, home adaptations and the NHS

CHAPTER 16

Housing and home adaptations

KEY POINTS

It is beyond the scope of this book to cover housing legislation in general. This chapter therefore makes only passing reference to the interface between housing and social services legislation in terms of provision of accommodation and also a scheme of assistance called Supporting People. In addition, it touches on three particular aspects of the Disability Discrimination Act 1995 relating to (a) landlords and premises, (b) eviction, permission to adapt a dwelling, and (c) the making of reasonable adjustments including provision of auxiliary aids and services.

It does however set out in more detail the law concerning home adaptations, provision of which overlaps in several significant respects with social services legislation. Adapting people's homes was recognised in the original community care policy guidance as a key method of enabling people to remain in their own homes (DH 1990, para 3.24).

The system of home adaptations is subject to considerable complexity, relying as it does on a high degree of cooperation between local social services authorities and local housing authorities, and on more than one set of legislation. Local housing authorities operate a system of disabled facilities grants (DFGs) under the Housing Grants, Construction and Regeneration Act 1996. If certain conditions are met, a strong duty arises to approve the grant, subject to a statutory means test to determine how much the applicant should contribute financially. In addition, housing authorities have a broad discretion to assist in other ways, apart from these mandatory grants, under the Regulatory Reform (Housing Assistance) (England and Wales) Order 2002. Local social services authorities, too, retain responsibility for assisting with adaptations under s.2 of the Chronically Sick and Disabled Persons Act 1970.

The system of adaptations has been beset by funding problems in relation to demand, and consequently by long waiting times. Local housing authorities in some areas attempt to dilute the duty to approve disabled facilities grants by deploying a range of restrictive policies, some of which are legally dubious. This is because the strong duty to award such grants does not allow as many lawful, as opposed to unlawful, 'escape routes' as other, weaker legislation might do (see Chapter 3). In addition, both local housing and social services authorities sometimes attempt to exploit their divided responsibilities for home adaptations, by engaging in disputes and passing the buck from one to another. Practice in local social services authorities seems to vary considerably, some providing substantial assistance for major adaptations under s.2 of 1970 Act, others being most reluctant to do so.

Strangely, given the extent to which the relevant legislation is stretched to its limits by local authorities when it is not being disregarded altogether, few cases have reached the courts about on home adaptations. However, this dearth of legal cases is balanced by the large number of investigations conducted by the local government ombudsmen into the provision of home adaptations.

16.1 PROVISION OF HOUSING ACCOMMODATION

Principal duties in terms of allocating public sector housing and providing accommodation for homeless people lie under the Housing Act 1996. Nevertheless, in a number of cases local social services authorities have been found unprepared for the courts' findings that, in certain circumstances, they too have a duty to provide 'ordinary' accommodation under s.21 of the National Assistance Act 1948. In other words, some local social services authorities have in the past assumed that any duties in respect of ordinary accommodation might extend to making referrals to housing authorities (e.g. under s.47 of the NHS and Community Care Act 1990), but not to social services authorities themselves arranging the accommodation. The courts have not always shared this view (see 9.2.1 above).

16.2 COOPERATION BETWEEN HOUSING AND SOCIAL SERVICES AUTHORITIES

Various legislative provisions entail cooperation between social services and housing authorities. For instance, s.47 of the NHS and Community Care Act 1990 places a duty on the local social services authority to invite a housing authority to assist in a community care assessment (see 6.5). The Housing Grants, Construction and Regeneration Act 1996 places a duty on local housing authorities to consult with local social services authorities about whether a disabled facilities grant is necessary and appropriate.

In addition, social services authorities have a duty of cooperation with housing authorities generally in respect of housing allocation and homelessness, and specifically in respect of children (Housing Act 1996, ss.213–213A). Likewise housing authorities have a duty of cooperation with social services authorities under s.27 of the Children Act 1989; and social services authorities have a duty to assist housing authorities with the formulation of a local homelessness strategy and to take it into account when exercising their functions

(Homelessness Act 2002). Nevertheless, such duties of cooperation only go so far, as the courts may feel unable to enforce them:

Duty of cooperation: limited enforceability. A housing authority decided that it had no duty to secure permanent accommodation for a homeless family (because it judged that the homelessness was intentional). The social services authority then declined to exercise its power to give assistance in cash to the family – as part of its duty to safeguard and promote the welfare of the children – under s.17(6) of the Children Act 1989. Instead it tried to rely on s.27 of the 1989 Act which stated that it had the power to request the assistance of other authorities, who 'shall comply with the request if it is compatible with their own statutory or other duties and obligations and does not unduly prejudice the discharge of any of their functions'. The housing authority, unsurprisingly, having already assessed the application in the negative, now refused to offer long-term accommodation.

On the issue of cooperation between authorities, the House of Lords stated that the 'two authorities must cooperate. Judicial review is not the way to obtain cooperation. The court cannot decide what form cooperation should take. Both forms of authority have difficult tasks, which are of great importance and for which they may feel their resources are not wholly adequate. The authorities must together do the best they can... In this case the housing authority were entitled to respond to the social services authority as they did' (*R v Northavon DC, ex p Smith*).

16.3 SUPPORTING PEOPLE

During the 1990s, a number of challenges were made about the type of service that could legitimately be covered by housing benefit (e.g. *R v North Cornwall DC, ex p Singer; R v St Edmundsbury Housing Benefit Review Board, ex p Sandys*: concerning counselling and support services).

As a consequence, changes were made to the housing benefit system, and funding for a number of housing support services, formerly paid through housing benefit, is now available instead through a central government funded scheme, administered by local authorities. Under the umbrella of a policy called Supporting People, such services are to be distinguished from community care services, since it is not part of a local authority's social services functions.

The basic legal framework consists of the *Supporting People (England) Directions 2007*, the *Supporting People Programme Grant and Grant Conditions 2007*, the *Supporting People Programme Grant and Grant Conditions for Excellent Authorities 2007*, the *Supporting People Guidance 2007*. These all emanate from the Department for Communities and Local Government. For people receiving housing benefit on 31 March 2003, charges may be made under the *Local Authorities (Charges for Specified Welfare Services) (England) Regulations 2003* (SI 2003/907 – otherwise charging is through the powers contained in s.93 of the Local Government Act 2003. Funding and provision decisions are the responsibility of the 'administering authority' (the local authority, other than an 'excellent authority') and of the commissioning body within the local authority's area which must implement the Supporting People strategy and arrangements.

Guidance, aimed at all local authorities except those deemed to be excellent authorities (which are not subject to detailed rules), explains that eligible welfare services are defined as being housing-related support services, with a view to developing or sustaining an individual's capacity to live independently in accommodation. They should be distinguished from general health, social services or statutory personal care services. Any service provided as part of a statutory duty is not eligible for supporting people funding (DCLG 2007, p.8).

For instance, an eligible service might help with life skills such as cooking or budgeting – or the general support of a visiting support worker to give the person confidence to sustain his or her own home. The guidance states that Supporting People services should focus on developing or sustaining more independent living skills. 'Occasional welfare services' can also be included – for instance, arrangements for tidying the garden of an elderly person (perhaps to allow support workers to access the property to deliver support), and services provided for the carrying out of maintenance and minor repairs to a vulnerable person's home through a handyperson scheme. Otherwise, welfare services must be part of an agreed package of support services, not ad hoc (DCLG 2007, pp.8–9).

Supporting People services are not aimed at the general public but at people at risk of losing their own home due to an inability to cope, for reasons such as homelessness, rough sleeping, previous imprisonment, mental health problems, learning difficulties, domestic violence, teenage pregnancy, vulnerability due to age, drug and alcohol problems, physical or sensory disability, HIV or AIDS, and being a refugee etc. (DCLG 2007, p.11).

Specifically excluded from Supporting People are residential care, the type of service provided by a registered care provider, personal or nursing care, services that local authorities have a statutory duty to provide, building works (other than advice and personal support services), equipment (e.g. stairlifts or specialist adaptations), psychological therapy or therapeutic counselling, services to enforce court of law requirements, and general housing management services (*Supporting People Programme Grant and Conditions 2007*, schedule 1).

The need to draw a dividing line, between Supporting People welfare services and other services provided under statute, became clear in the following case, in which the court held that a number of services being provided should have come under community care legislation and not Supporting People:

Relationship between Supporting People and community care services. A local authority assessed a person with significant health problems related to Still's disease (a form of rheumatoid arthritis) involving frequent, painful and highly debilitating flare-ups; he was also nearly blind. It had categorised some of his needs as moderate only, in particular cleaning, shopping, and attendance at appointments. This meant that under the authority's 'fair access to care' eligibility criteria, those needs would not attract social services support. Instead these needs were met through the Supporting People scheme. However, because they were related to the man's health care condition, the court held that these needs should all have been assessed as coming within the critical category of the eligibility framework, and so been provided as community care services, and not through Supporting People (*R(Heffernan) v Sheffield CC*).

16.4 DISCRIMINATION IN MANAGEMENT AND LETTING OF RESIDENTIAL PREMISES

Under the Disability Discrimination Act 1995 (DDA), it is unlawful to discriminate against disabled people in the selling, letting or management of residential premises.

Discrimination could occur in relation to the terms of disposal of premises, to refusal to dispose, or to the way in which a disabled person is treated in respect of a list (e.g. waiting list or register for allocation of housing) of people in need of the premises (DDA 1995, s.22).

In terms of management, discrimination against a disabled person occupying the premises could occur in relation to (a) the way in which the disabled person is permitted to make use of any benefits or facilities; (b) refusing or omitting to allow the disabled person to use such benefits of facilities; (c) evicting the person or subjecting him or her to any other detriment.

Discrimination means less favourable treatment of the disabled person for a reason relating to the person's disability – and which the other person cannot show to be justified.

16.4.1 JUSTIFYING LESS FAVOURABLE TREATMENT

Less favourable treatment is justifiable if, in the other person's opinion, certain conditions are satisfied. However, it must also be reasonable in all the circumstances of the case for him or her to hold that opinion.

The conditions relate to (a) health and safety; (b) incapacity to make an enforceable agreement; (c) that the less favourable treatment is necessary in order for the disabled person or the occupiers of other premises, forming part of the building, to make use of a benefit or facility; (d) that the refusal to allow the disabled person to make use of a benefit or facility is necessary in order for the occupiers of other premises forming part of the building to make use of the benefit or facility (s.24). There is a small dwellings exemption (DDA 1995, s.23). The following case illustrates a health and safety justification which was successfully argued in the Scottish courts:

Refusing to let a flat. A blind person with a guide dog was refused by a landlord the let of a flat for a week during the Edinburgh Festival. This was on the grounds of the absence of a suitable handrail on the steps leading up to the flat. The man brought a case in the Scottish courts under the DDA. The landlord argued a health and safety justification for the less favourable treatment; he succeeded because he brought forward genuine evidence including his attempts to get a suitable rail installed, and also his past letting of premises to disabled people. In particular, the court held that the opinion of the landlord was a reasonable one for him to have reached. He knew that the man was blind and used a guide dog, that the steps without a handrail posed a threat to safety because of the unguarded drop on both sides. This threat to safety was subsequently confirmed by an environmental health officer (*Rose v Bouchet*).

In respect of the eviction of tenants, several cases have reached the courts in which possession orders by landlords were disputed with reference to the DDA. These cases centred on whether, in the case of assured or secure tenancies, it was reasonable under the Housing Act 1985 for the court to grant the possession order sought.

Even before the advent of the DDA, the courts sometimes found that such an order would be unreasonable: for example, if the tenant suffered from a mental disorder that might be amenable to treatment (*Croydon LBC v Moody*). However, the judgment of what is reasonable now has to be made in the light of the DDA.

The questions to be asked in such cases are whether: (a) the tenant disabled within the meaning of the DDA; (b) if so, is the reason (e.g. aggressive or antisocial behaviour) why the landlord is seeking possession related to the tenant's disability; (c) if so, is there a health and safety justification for the less favourable treatment (which treatment would otherwise inevitably constitute discrimination). In the first of these cases, the possession order was denied:

Possession order denied on grounds of discrimination. A tenant of a housing association was in a chronic state of conflict with her neighbours. She had been diagnosed as suffering a form of paranoid schizophrenia. Following police and social services involvement she was transferred to another property. She continued to be disagreeable and aggressive. She kept the neighbours awake at night by banging and shouting, and used abusive language and rude gestures. The landlord brought possession proceedings. The High Court concluded that there was no doubt that she suffered from a psychotic disorder and that her behaviour stemmed from her illness. Thus the only justification for the eviction would be on grounds of health and safety; but the court found no evidence that the landlord had considered the eviction necessary on such grounds. Nor did the court find that the physical health and safety of neighbours had actually been at risk (*North Devon Homes v Brazier*).

However, in two subsequent Court of Appeal cases, the tenants failed in their objections:

Possession orders not discriminatory. A tenant had a depressive mental illness, which meant that she was regarded as disabled under the DDA. The courts held that the conduct complained of – loud hammering and music during the night – could reasonably be held to be endangering the health of a neighbour who was a driving examiner and suffering sleep deprivation as a consequence of the nightly disturbance. In addition, the court anyway doubted whether the music and hammering could be linked to the mental impairment – in which case no issue would arise under the DDA.

A second tenant suffered from a personality disorder, producing violent behaviour, depression and anxiety. The court concluded that by reason of her illness she was unable to learn how to cope with stressful situations and to react appropriately. This resulted in abusive language toward a neighbour and her children; the neighbour was on anti-depressants, felt suicidal and could not leave her house without being called names. The evidence from the neighbour to this effect was sufficient to constitute reasonable justification on health and safety grounds.

The court said that it was enough if a person's health or safety was endangered, not necessarily seriously; it did not have actually to be damaged (*Manchester CC v Romano*).

Nevertheless, in the *Manchester* judgment, the Court of Appeal heavily criticised the way in which the DDA had been drafted and predicted a possible deluge of such cases with possible unfair and absurd consequences. In the meantime it suggested that local authority landlords would need to liaise more closely with social services at an earlier stage, in order to try to deal with problems that could lead to attempted eviction. The court was further concerned that a landlord might perform a discriminatory act, contrary to the DDA, even when it did not know that the tenant was disabled.

In a later case, the Court of Appeal (which was subsequently overruled) held that a notice to quit did constitute discrimination, on the basis that there was a link between the person's schizophrenia and his subletting of his flat – which was a breach of the tenancy agreement and the reason why the possession order was sought:

Link between schizophrenia and the breach of the tenancy agreement: possession order sought was discriminatory. A man suffering from schizophrenia sublet his council flat in breach of the tenancy agreement. The local authority sought a possession order. The court held that he was protected under the DDA.

First, he should have been regarded as disabled under the Act. In terms of whether his disability had a substantial adverse effect on his ability to carry out normal everyday activities, the right question was to ask was whether the effect was more than minor or trivial.

Second, it had to be shown that the local authority was seeking to evict him for a reason relating to his disability. However, whilst his disability had to be related to the action in question, the subletting, it did not have to the sole cause of the action, nor did it have to be a matter without which the action would not have occurred. At the time of the subletting he had not been taking his medication, and there was no evidence that he had approved the subletting in a lucid phase when he was able to understand the consequences of it. However, there was evidence that the nature of his condition led to distortions in thinking; this was sufficient to establish the link, the relationship, between his disability and the action, the subletting.

Lastly was the question of whether the local authority had to be aware of the disability for discrimination to be shown. The court held that less favourable treatment can occur even if the local authority did not know of it. In any case, the court pointed out that the local authority could have asked why he sublet the flat, and could have spoken to the social worker about the man's unmedicated schizophrenia. On this basis the possession proceedings were dismissed, and the notice to quit was held to constitute unlawful disability discrimination (*Malcolm v Lewisham London Borough Council*).

The Court of Appeal had found discrimination on the basis that the claimant had been treated less favourably (for a reason relating to his disability) than another person (to whom that reason did not apply) would have been treated. Following previous case law, the Court of Appeal had taken this 'reason relating to his disability' to mean that the comparison should be with a person who had not sublet a flat, as opposed to the more obvious comparison with a non-disabled person who had sublet a flat. The Court of Appeal's approach was on the basis that (a) the subletting of the flat was the 'reason', and (b) it related to the disability, because without the latter, the subletting would arguably not have taken place. The Court of Appeal had also confirmed that it made no difference that the local authority didn't know about the disability.

The House of Lords, on further appeal, was in no doubt that the Court of Appeal had got it wrong. First, the House was clear that the comparison should be with another statutory tenant, with no mental illness, who had sublet (although one of the five law lords strongly dissented on this point). Second, there was no evidence that the local authority was aware that the tenant was mentally ill. For there to be discrimination, it had to be shown not only that there was a causal connection between the disability and the subletting, but that the mental condition played a motivating part in the council's possession proceedings. The local authority won its appeal (*Malcolm v Lewisham LBC*).

On the other hand, when a person had got into rent arrears because the landlord had increased the rent, but did not suggest that his disability was the reason for non-payment of rent of 132 weeks, no question of unlawful discrimination could anyway arise (*S v Floyd*).

16.5 HOME ADAPTATIONS: DISABLED FACILITIES GRANTS

Home adaptations have, since 1990, been identified as a key part of community care. Continually, too, it is argued that they represent an effective, and cost-effective way, of meeting people's needs (ODPM 2005a, p.5; Heywood and Turner 2007).

In October 2005, the government published a review of the system of disabled facilities grants which, though identifying certain strengths, highlighted a long list of problems, at the heart of which were an absence of strategy and of adequate funding. This led to, amongst other things, older people being screened out inappropriately from the process, delays with serious consequences, inequalities, grant amounts falling short of building costs, an unfair test of resources (means-test), lack of suitable staff to carry out assessments, and insufficient capital resources in local authorities to provide adaptations to which people were entitled by statute (ODPM 2005a, pp.4–10).

Following this review, the government then consulted on possible changes to the system. These included:

- increasing the maximum grant payable to £30,000 and maybe up to £50,000
- placing a charge (applicable up to ten years) on an adapted property in owner occupation (enabling the grant to be recouped when the property is sold
- changing the test of resources (e.g. 'passporting', on the basis of other social security benefits received, easier – or taking into account outgoings in term of housing costs)
- clarifying the question of adaptation of gardens to enable access
- simplifying the funding system for housing associations
- increasing the use of home improvement agencies in the delivery of home adaptations
- define stairlifts as equipment which would be provided through social services, rather than as major adaptations (DCLG 2007).

In February 2008, a number of changes were duly announced. From April 2008, these were to be:

- maximum grant to be raised to £30,000
- changes to the means test meaning applicants claiming council tax benefit, housing benefit and tax credits won't have to provide any further financial information, and working tax credit and child credit will no longer count as income
- enabling a local authority, where it deems it to be appropriate on a case by case basis, to place a charge on the property. This is where the cost of the DFG exceeds £5000. The maximum charge will be £10,000
- change to the legislation to make it clear that access to gardens is potentially mandatory
- transfer of Social Housing Grant from the Housing Corporation to local authorities as part of the 'DFG baseline'
- cessation of the arrangement whereby 60 per cent of funding for DFGs came from central government, matching the other 40 per cent provided by the local authority
- the removal, ultimately in 2010–11, of the 'ring-fencing' of DFG funding provided by central government (DCLG 2008).

16.5.1 HOME ADAPTATIONS: DISABLED FACILITIES GRANTS (DFGS)

Under the Housing Grants, Construction and Regeneration Act 1996 (HGCRA), housing authorities have a duty, if certain conditions are met, to approve applications for disabled facilities grants for the carrying out of home adaptations.

The conditions are basically that (a) the adaptation in question falls into one of the purposes in the Act that attract mandatory grant; (b) if so, that it is necessary and appropriate;

(c) if so, that it is also reasonable and practicable. The three questions should be asked and answered logically and discretely; not to do so has been held by the courts to be unlawful:

Collapsing two questions/answers into one. In one case involving a loft conversion to provide an extra bedroom for a boy with autism, the local authority's reasoning in effect stated that the works were not necessary and appropriate because there was no clear case for a mandatory grant. The court held that this was impermissibly to collapse the first question about the mandatory nature of the grant with the second question as to whether it was necessary and appropriate (*R(B) v Calderdale MBC*).

16.5.2 PURPOSES FOR MANDATORY DISABLED FACILITIES GRANT

The 1996 Act lists a number of purposes that will in principle attract mandatory grant. These are to facilitate access by the disabled occupant:

- **dwelling**: to and from the dwelling (including the garden: SI 2008/1189)
- **family room**: to a room used as the principal family room
- **sleeping room**: to, or providing for the disabled occupant, a room used or usable for sleeping
- **lavatory**: to, or providing for the disabled occupant, a room in which there is a lavatory – or facilitating its use by the disabled occupant
- **bath, shower**: to, or providing for the disabled occupant, a room in which there is a bath or a shower (or both) – or facilitating its use by the disabled occupant
- **washhand basin**: to, or providing for the disabled occupant, a room in which there is a washhand basin – or facilitating its use by the disabled occupant (s.23).

Other purposes are:

- **safety**: making the dwelling or building safe for the disabled occupant and other persons residing with him
- **cooking**: facilitating the preparation and cooking of food by the disabled occupant
- **heating**: improving any heating system in the dwelling to meet the needs of the disabled occupant or – if there is no existing heating system or an existing system is unsuitable for use by the disabled occupant – providing a heating system suitable to meet his needs
- **use of power, light, heat**: facilitating the use by the disabled occupant of a source of power, light or heat by altering the position of one or more means of access to, or control of, that source – or by providing additional means of control
- **disabled occupant as carer**: facilitating access and movement by the disabled occupant around the dwelling in order to enable him to care for a person who normally resides in the dwelling and needs such care (s.23).

As detailed immediately above, the legislation, together with the guidance (see below), provides a firm base from which to answer the question as to whether the proposed works will in principle attract mandatory grant.

16.5.3 SAFETY IN THE DWELLING

Guidance from central government gives examples of adaptations relating to safety. These include provision of specialised lighting, adaptations to minimise the danger if a disabled person has behavioural problems, enhanced alarm system in connection with cooking facilities, fire escapes, toughened or shatterproof glass, fire or radiator guards, reinforcement of floors, walls or ceilings, and cladding of exposed surfaces and corners to prevent injury (ODPM 2006, annex B, para 18–20). The examples indicate just how wide the safety purpose goes. The Court of Appeal has considered the implications of the safety purpose in the circumstances of the following case:

Additional bedroom for safety. The parents of a boy with autism applied for a loft conversion. The boy had for the last few years subjected his younger brother, with whom he shared a bedroom, to dangerously inappropriate horseplay and to violent interference with his sleep, day after day, night after night. The local authority declined to approve the application on the ground that the danger to the younger brother was confined to the shared bedroom; therefore an extra bedroom would still not make the dwelling safe for him. The High Court upheld the local authority's argument; the case went to appeal (R(B) v Calderdale MBC).

This judgment was overturned by the Court of Appeal, which ordered that the local authority re-take its decision. This was on the basis that the works could not necessarily be expected to make the premises completely safe for the disabled person and other people he lived with. The question was whether it was enough if the works simply made the premises (a bit) safer, or whether there was some threshold of safety that the works would have to get over, in order for them to be deemed necessary and appropriate:

Reducing risk. The Court of Appeal found that there was a threshold, namely that the proposed works must minimise the material risk – in other words reduce it as far as is reasonably practicable, if it could not be eliminated. In turn, this would mean that it would be immaterial even if there were other areas of risk that the works did not ameliorate (R(B) v Calderdale MBC).

The Act refers to the safety of the disabled occupant and other people living with him or her:

Safety of other people. The court held that so long as the safety of the disabled occupant is involved in some way, a grant would not be precluded; there was not a requirement that the principal purpose of the works be the safety of the disabled person. For example, a fire escape or cooking alarm might benefit several other occupants of a dwelling, and not just the disabled occupant. Thus, the fact that the disabled occupant (who might injure himself) was not the immediate and direct source of danger did not preclude a grant. By the same token the danger could arise from a person's behaviour, and not just the condition or lack of facilities in the dwelling (R(B) v Calderdale MBC, High Court stage).

Some local authorities effectively stated in the past that they would never approve applications for works to the garden, either to allow access or to make the garden safe. However, logically, such policies were unlikely to be lawful if applied in every case. This is because dwelling is defined in s.101 of the 1996 Act to include garden; and the mandatory purpose relating to safety is stated to apply to the dwelling. It would seem to follow that the barring of all such works was to prevent the housing authority coming to a proper decision on the individual facts of the case, and to be a fettering of its discretion (see 5.2.1).

In any case, from May 2008, amending regulations make clear that gardens fall legally within mandatory grant in terms both of 'making access to a garden safe for a disabled occupant', and also of 'facilitating access to and from a garden by a disabled occupant' (SI 2008/1189).

16.5.4 SLEEPING ROOM

Central government guidance states that provision of a room usable for sleeping should only be undertaken if the adaptation of an existing room in the dwelling (upstairs or downstairs) or the access to that room would be unsuitable in the particular circumstances. Where the disabled occupant shares a bedroom, grant could be given to provide a room of sufficient size, in order that normal sleeping arrangements be maintained (ODPM 2006, annex B, para 21).

16.5.5 FAMILY ROOM

The legislation refers to facilitating access to a room used or usable as the principal family room. Guidance states that in considering applications for grant toward such works, the presumption should be that the occupant have reasonable access to the main habitable rooms, including the living room.

Thus, when a local authority approved a shower and toilet adaptation downstairs for a seriously ill and disabled woman, but did not accept that a family room should be retained, the ombudsman found maladministration. The room to be sacrificed was the only one where the family could sit together; the hoist, hospital-type bed and other medical treatment she needed meant that there was no space to use the front room (*Leeds CC 2007*).

16.5.6 BATHROOM

Guidance points out that, compared to the previous legislation containing DFGs (Local Government and Housing Act 1989), the 1996 Act separated the provisions relating to lavatory and washing, bathing and showering facilities. This was to make clear that 'a disabled person should have access to a wash-hand basin, a WC and a shower or bath (or if more appropriate, both a shower and a bath)'. Therefore DFG should be given 'to provide a disabled person with each of these facilities' and to facilitate their use (ODPM 2006, annex B, para 22).

16.5.7 FOOD, PREPARATION AND COOKING

Guidance states that eligible works include the rearrangement or enlargement of a kitchen to ease manoeuvrability of a wheelchair and specially modified or designed storage units, gas, electricity and plumbing installations.

However, it also states that, if most of the cooking and preparation of meals is carried out by somebody else, it would not normally be appropriate to carry out full adaptations to the kitchen. Nevertheless, certain adaptations might still be appropriate, to enable the disabled person to do some things, such as prepare light meals or hot drinks (ODPM 2006, annex B, paras 23–24). Similarly, it was maladministration when a local authority proposed adaptations – for a quadriplegic man in his early twenties with leukaemia – which meant that the only family room, the dining room, be given up. This would mean that the family would have to eat in the kitchen. This was despite the fact that a foster child had special needs and behaviour problems which meant he had to sit at a table and was not safe near kitchen appliances (*Kirklees MBC 2008*).

16.5.8 HEATING, LIGHTING, POWER

Guidance states that people with limited mobility who remain in one room for long periods usually need more warmth than able-bodied people. If there is no heating system or where the existing heating arrangements are unsuitable to meet his needs, a heating system may be provided. However, the works should not involve adaptation or installation of heating in rooms that are not normally in use by the disabled person. Installation of central heating should only be considered where the disabled person's well-being and mobility would otherwise be adversely affected. As far as operating heating, lighting and power, power points could be relocated, and suitably adapted controls provided (ODPM 2006, annex B, paras 25–26).

Local authorities should beware of adopting restrictive approaches, as highlighted in a court case:

Policy on central heating too narrow. In a dispute about a person's needs for central heating, the local authority conceded that its existing policy was unlawfully rigid. It had stipulated that the applicant must (a) be receiving home kidney dialysis and the treatment room be inadequately heated; (b) have a medical condition that made a constant temperature, 24 hours a day, necessary; or (c) have been assessed by social services as requiring extended bedroom/bathroom facilities that required heating (*R v Birmingham CC, ex p Taj Mohammed*).

The local ombudsman has criticised too limited an approach:

DFGs and assessment for central heating: restrictive approach. The social services occupational therapy service considered that it could only provide assessments for heating if a disabled occupant's need arose from a severe functional loss or if there was a risk of injury: that is, risk of burning because of the dysfunction, or inability to control the existing heating where the person lived alone (or was frequently left alone for four hours or more). The occupational therapy service did not consider that it should assess when poor housing conditions (e.g. damp and cold) affected people with a medical condition. The local ombudsman concluded that the council did 'have a duty to consider a request from one of its tenants for installation of central heating on medical grounds and to reach a decision'.

After consulting with the Department of Environment, Transport and the Regions, he concluded that the criteria used by the occupational therapy service for assessing heating requests amounted to maladministration because they 'placed a narrow construction on legislation and guidance about the circumstances in which grants might be awarded for heating improvements... I can understand the difficulty for the occupational therapy service; its concern is with functional loss. But if that service is not able to advise on applicants with medical need, the Council should have some other mechanism which can' (*Hackney LBC 1997a*).

16.5.9 DISABLED OCCUPANT

For the purpose of DFG, a person is disabled if (a) his sight, hearing or speech is substantially impaired; (b) he has a mental disorder or impairment of any kind; or (c) he is physically substantially disabled by illness, injury impairment since birth or otherwise. A person is also to be taken to be disabled if he or she is registered under s.29 of the National Assistance Act 1948 (see 11.1.3 above), or is a person for whom welfare arrangements have been made under that Act or in the opinion of the social services authority might be made under it (HGCRA 1996, s.100).

16.5.10 DFG FOR ONLY OR MAIN DWELLING

Unlike for social services or the NHS (see Chapter 15), the residence qualification for DFGs is given in terms of dwelling rather than area of residence. The dwelling must be the person's only or main residence, either as owner (s.21) or occupier of a houseboat or caravan (HGCRA 1996, s.22A). It is improbable, but not impossible, that the courts would hold that a person could have more than one only or main residence. This would normally rule out the provision of disabled facilities grants for two dwellings (e.g. in the case of shared care).

This residence condition is to be contrasted with that in s.2 of the Chronically Sick and Disabled Persons Act 1970, which also covers home adaptations. The 1970 Act refers to ordinary residence in the area of the authority, and not to the only or main dwelling. Thus, duties under the 1970 Act could in principle apply to more than one dwelling, if the need for this was made out. Therefore, in the case of shared care, home adaptations might be possible (where the needs call for it) in two dwellings via both a disabled facilities grant under the 1996 Act and assistance under s.2 of the 1970 Act. This assumes that a duty on social services to fund such a second adaptation could be made out in terms of assessed, eligible needs (see 16.9 and 11.2.5.5).

16.5.10.1 Owner's application for DFG

A certificate is required that the applicant has or proposes to acquire a qualifying owner's interest, and that the disabled occupant will live in the dwelling or flat as his only or main residence throughout the grant condition period, or for such shorter period as his or her health and other relevant circumstances permit (s.21). The grant condition period is ten years. In the case of an applicant who proposes to acquire a qualifying owner's interest, the application must not be approved until he or she has done so (HGCRA 1996, s.24). Repayment is not required in case of breach of the time condition.

16.5.10.2 Tenant's application for DFG

A certificate is required that the applicant intends that he or she (if the disabled occupant) or the disabled occupant will live in the dwelling or flat as his or her only or main residence throughout the grant condition period, or for such shorter period as his or her health and other relevant circumstances permit. The grant condition period is five years. Unless it is unreasonable in the circumstances, a tenant's certificate must be accompanied by an owner's certificate (HGCRA 1996, s.22). Repayment is not required in case of breach of the time condition.

One drawback identified by the local ombudsman involved the case of a man who had to accept the offer of a council tenancy before he was eligible for a disabled facilities grant. However, the house would not be habitable until the works were complete. This meant that he had to pay for two dwellings for an indeterminate period (*Birmingham CC 2002*). This situation arose because although a prospective (rather than actual) owner can apply for a DFG, it appeared that only an actual tenant, as opposed to a prospective tenant, could apply (HGCRA 1996, s.19). However, guidance issued subsequently by central government states that the offer and acceptance of a tenancy in principle, subject to the completion of adaptations, should be treated as a residence qualification for the purpose of DFG (ODPM 2006, para 6.6).

16.5.10.3 Caravan and houseboat applications for DFG

An 'occupier's certificate' must certify that the applicant intends that he or she (if he or she is the disabled occupant) or the disabled occupant will live in the qualifying houseboat or caravan as his or her only or main residence throughout the grant condition period (five years) or such shorter period as his or her health or other relevant circumstances permit. Repayment is not required in case of breach of the time condition.

Unless it is unreasonable in the circumstances to require such a certificate, the local authority cannot consider an application unless a consent certificate is received from a person who is entitled to possession of the premises at which the houseboat is moored or the land on which the caravan is stationed – or who is entitled to dispose of (sell) the houseboat or park home (s.22A).

Qualifying park home was restrictively defined in the HGCRA 1996 (s.58) so as to exclude, for example, disabled people living on gypsy sites, as well as various others. An amendment contained in the Housing Act 2004 changed the reference from qualifying park home simply to caravan, as defined in Part 1 of the Caravan Sites and Control of Development Act 1960 – and thus widened its application.

16.5.11 DFG MUST BE NECESSARY AND APPROPRIATE

The works must be necessary and appropriate. This is a decision for the housing authority to take, but if the housing authority is not itself also a social services authority, then it is under an obligation to consult the latter about this issue (s.24). Social services and housing functions might come under one (e.g. in a unitary or metropolitan local authority) or more than one (e.g. county council and district council) roof.

Where the authority is unitary, covering both housing and social services functions, it would nevertheless be assumed that housing would call on social services expertise. The reason, why the Act states that the authorities must be separate for consultation to take place, is because when the legislation was drafted and under discussion, it was thought that logically an authority could not consult itself. Thus, previous guidance (now superseded) made clear that, in the case of unitary authorities, the housing department should still consult the social services department (DoE 17/96, annex I, para 37).

The dangers of losing control over recommendations about necessity and appropriateness were illustrated in the following local ombudsman investigation:

Loss of control of assessment and recommendation for a DFG. Following treatment for cancer, a woman living alone had difficulties in managing at home. Supported by Macmillan nurses to some extent, she needed more help and wished to have an additional room in which a carer could stay overnight.

The county council social services department purportedly assessed her and made a recommendation to the district council that such an adaptation/extension was necessary and appropriate, and so qualified for a disabled facilities grant. The district council refused to provide one, explaining that the proposed adaptation did not come under the mandatory category of grant, but only under the discretionary; and the council had a policy of not awarding discretionary grants.

Relying on guidance from central government, which stated that in such circumstances (i.e. rejection by the district council of a social services recommendation) the social services authority had a continuing duty to meet the person's needs, the woman asked the social services authority for help. In the course of refusing, the authority disowned its previous recommendation to the district council.

It transpired that, at the relevant time, the occupational therapy assistant originally involved had no substantial support or supervision from a qualified occupational therapist; and the possibility of using NHS therapists had been rejected on grounds of cost. As a consequence, and unknown at the time to the director of social services, the original assessment had been delegated to another organisation altogether (a home improvement agency) – and the recommendation, made without the use of qualified staff (e.g. therapists), had been forwarded as the council's own and without question by the social services department to the district council.

Amongst other findings, the ombudsman found maladministration insofar as social services had throughout failed to assess the woman's needs properly (*Dyfed CC 1996*).

Some councils might avoid even getting to the stage of properly considering an application for a DFG and whether works might be necessary and appropriate. This will be maladministration for the local ombudsman:

Self-completion questionnaires. When people applied for disabled facilities grants, they were asked to complete a questionnaire; the application of priority points was based entirely on the replies. If a person was awarded fewer points than the threshold figure, the request was not considered further. Until the person reached that threshold (at a later date), he or she would not be seen by a professionally qualified assessment officer. The questionnaire replies were handled by an administrative assistant. This was maladministration (*Neath Port Talbot County BC 1999*).

Previous guidance also stated that if 'both the social services and housing authorities collaborate effectively it should be a rare occurrence where a housing authority determines not to approve particular adaptations recommended by a social services authority' (DoE 17/96, annex I, para 4).

The replacement guidance states that local housing authorities, having consulted social authorities about what is necessary and appropriate, must then decide what action to take on the basis of the advice provided by social services. The decision must be taken in respect of the statutory provisions for mandatory DFG under s.23 of the HGCRA 1996 (ODPM 2006, annex B, para 34). The guidance goes on to make a number of points about assessing the need for adaptations including (ODPM 2006, Chapter 5):

- Occupational therapists will generally assess for adaptations, but others who may be involved include occupational therapy assistants – and specialist staff working with people with sensory impairments, learning disabilities or mental health problems.
- Disabled people must be involved in the assessment of needs and carefully listened to, since they are the experts on their own needs (this includes children, young persons and their parents).
- 'Self-assessment' may be part of the consultation with the disabled person.
- Particular materials may have to be used or avoided in the adaptation for the protection of a person with learning disabilities or of other people living in the dwelling.
- Adaptations might be required for the protection (from harm or from intrusions provoking their problems) of people with mental health problems.
- People with autism may require additional quiet space, without which serious adverse consequences may occur.

The guidance refers to three other pieces of guidance containing the 'general principles' of social care assessment, namely 'fair access to care' (LAC(2002)13), the single assessment for older people (HSC 2002/001), and the assessment framework for children in need (DH 2000a). However, elsewhere the guidance reminds local authorities that they cannot straight-forwardly apply to DFG decisions the social care eligibility rules under the social services 'fair access to care' guidance (ODPM 2006, para 4.7).

Some councils in practice apply dubious policies. For example, they might insist that the adaptations must make the whole dwelling 'barrier free', in order for adaptations to be necessary and appropriate. Applying such a policy, they then refuse to carry out adaptations to the bathroom, for example, on the grounds that access to the dwelling will remain difficult for the disabled occupant. However, the pointers given in the guidance do not necessarily equate to a completely barrier free dwelling. Given the variety of needs, circumstances, reasons (and care plans), in respect of which people might need adaptations, such policies are excessively restrictive. They arguably run the risk of being held to be unlawful or to be maladministration if applied in blanket fashion.

Similarly councils which state that they will 'never' build extensions or extra space run the risk of acting unlawfully or with maladministration. This is because if an adaptation is deemed to be necessary and appropriate, and there is no reasonable way of achieving it through use of existing space, then an extension might be the only option for meeting the need. Indeed, the guidance states that sometimes an extension will be necessary where existing space cannot be reasonably used (ODPM 2006, annex B, para 21).

Nonetheless, since most extensions will cost in excess of £30,000 (the current mandatory maximum disabled facilities grant in England), and local authorities are not obliged to exceed this amount, it is not too difficult for councils to avoid approving extensions. Even so, they may exercise discretion to add in extra grant, over and above the £30,000, under the *Regulatory Reform (Housing Assistance) (England and Wales) Order* (see 16.8 below).

16.5.12 RELEVANCE OF RESOURCES TO NECESSITY AND APPROPRIATENESS

The courts have stated that the decision about whether works are necessary and appropriate is 'directed to a consideration of a technical question'. Local housing authorities were therefore not entitled to take resources into account (*R v Birmingham CC, ex p Taj Mohammed*).

The courts distinguished the rules under the 1996 Act from those under s.2 of the Chronically Sick and Disabled Persons Act 1970. The latter allows local authorities to set a threshold of eligibility, at least partly based on the local authority's resources, to determine the sort of circumstances in which it is necessary to meet them (*R v Gloucestershire CC, ex p Barry*). The *Birmingham* case appears to state that such an approach is not legally permissible under the 1996 Act.

In the light of this judicial decision, both social services and housing authorities must guard against applying the rules for one set of legislation to another. For instance, there is a danger that social services authorities will apply the eligibility threshold for community care services (including 'fair access to care': see 6.10 and 6.12) to the recommendation about whether a DFG is necessary and appropriate under housing legislation. Legally this would appear to be impermissible, since it would in effect be collapsing two quite distinct sets of leg-islation into one. Guidance points out that a person might be eligible for DFG assistance but not for social services assistance (ODPM 2006, para 4.7).

Collapsing two Acts into one. The local ombudsman found maladministration because a local authority had collapsed into one procedure its dealing with applications for adaptations under the HGCRA 1996 and the Chronically Sick and Disabled Persons Act 1970. The situation was exacerbated by the inadequacy of the self-assessment questionnaire that was used to make a judgement about a person's priority under both Acts (*Neath Port Talbot CBC 1999*).

The distinction is by no means academic. Not only might a person be eligible for a DFG but not for social services assistance, but the reverse might also be the case and the person be eligible for social services assistance but not for DFG. For instance, the adaptation in question might be one that does not come under one of the DFG mandatory purposes; in which case it might fall to social services to consider whether to assist under the CSDPA 1970.

Where people have deteriorating conditions, housing authorities often hesitate to approve adaptations. Some tend to impose blanket-type conditions that the adaptation must be likely to be of use for a certain length of time, if the works are to be deemed necessary and appropriate. Guidance states, however, that the fact that an adaptation might be appropriate for only a limited period of time, should not of itself be regarded as 'sufficient reason' for delaying or withholding provision (ODPM 2006, para 5.22).

16.5.13 DFG MUST BE REASONABLE AND PRACTICABLE

In addition to deciding whether a proposed adaptation is necessary and appropriate, housing authorities must also decide whether it is reasonable and practicable in relation to the age and condition of the dwelling. Central government guidance gives examples of issues that relate to this condition. These include:

- architectural and structural characteristics of the dwelling
- practicalities of carrying out adaptations to smaller properties with narrow doorways, halls and passages which might make wheelchair use difficult or, for example, steep flights of steps making access for wheelchair use difficult and continued occupation of the dwelling open to question
- conservation considerations and planning constraints
- the impact on other occupants of proposed works which would affect existing facilities in the dwelling (ODPM 2006, annex B, para 37).

The courts have indicated that resources might in some circumstances legitimately inform the decision; for example, it might not be 'sensible use of resources to make a DFG to improve an old dilapidated building, or a dwelling which was not fit for human habitation' (*R v Birming-ham CC, ex p Taj Mohammed*).

Therefore it would seem legally suspect for housing authorities simply to argue that a DFG is not reasonable and practicable because the budget cannot cope. Instead, the rejection of an application must relate (a) to the individual case; and (b) genuinely to the age and condition of the dwelling in question. Thus, it was arguably incautious of a council to state simply that the reasonable practicability test was related to the 'public purse', without mention of the age and condition of the particular dwelling (*Harlow DC 2000*: although the local ombuds-man did not comment on this particular statement).

16.5.14 RECOVERY AND MAINTENANCE OF EQUIPMENT

The Housing Grants, Construction and Regeneration Act 1996, s.52, allows local authorities to impose additional conditions on grants – subject to consent from the Secretary of State.

One such consent allows local authorities to recover 'specialised' (removable equipment such as stairlifts), when it is no longer needed. They should consider carefully the condition of recovery to be imposed if the applicant has made a significant contribution to the equipment (i.e. pay the current value of the proportion of the equipment corresponding to the person's original contribution); and also make good damage to the property. It states that in practice social services are best placed to recover the equipment so that it can be reused by other people. However, where it is clear that the equipment will not be reused because of its age or condition, the local authority may waive its right to recovery (ODPM 2006, annex B, para 65: see specifically the *Housing Renewal Grants (Additional Conditions) (England) General Consent 1996*).

Some adaptations such as stairlifts or through-floor lifts require regular maintenance. Guidance states that it is good practice for such maintenance (and repair) arrangements to be put in place at time of installation. Thus the cost of an extended guarantee or service contract should be included in the calculation of the DFG payable (ODPM 2006, para 8.1).

16.5.15 SERVICES AND CHARGES

The cost of a range of various charges and services can be included within a DFG; for example, relating to design, advice, assistance in completing forms, surveys, supervision of works, application for building regulations approval – and the services of an occupational therapist (SI 1996/2889).

16.5.16 ELIGIBILITY ACROSS DIFFERENT HOUSING SECTORS

Eligibility for DFGs extends to all owner-occupiers, tenants or licensees who meet the criteria in ss.19–22 of the 1996 Act. This has been emphasised in guidance (ODPM 2006, para 3.21).

16.5.16.1 Council tenants

Notwithstanding the legislation, and the emphasis by guidance that it is 'not lawful for persons in any tenure to be obstructed in' applying for disabled facilities grants (ODPM 2006, para 3.26), some councils in practice deny this option to their tenants. Guidance makes clear that a local authority can carry out required adaptations to its own stock from its own resources, rather than through the DFG system (ODPM 2006, para 3.21). If it does so, it would presumably be acting under the Housing Act 1985 by considering housing conditions and needs with specific regard to disabled people (s.8 together with s.3 of the Chronically Sick and Disabled Persons Act 1970); and by altering, enlarging or improving its housing stock (s.9).

Nevertheless, guidance also states that the works should be carried out on terms as advantageous as if a DFG had been awarded (ODPM 2006, para 3.21). The following case clearly illustrates the local ombudsman's view of the disadvantages that might accrue if an individual council tenant is not offered a DFG or at least its equivalent – even though the alternative procedure offered by the council might have been more advantageous than a DFG for the generality of tenants:

DFGs and assessment for central heating. The case concerned the application for central heating by a council tenant who had been diagnosed in 1988 as HIV positive and was receiving income support. A complaint was made to the local ombudsman.

Original request. In August 1991, the Hackney Energy Audit Project wrote to the estate manager pointing out that the under-floor heating for the block in which the man lived had been defective since 1976, leaving tenants to heat their flats by using peak-rate electricity. The letter requested that affordable heating be installed for him and included supporting letters from the hospital and from an occupational therapist. The estate officer replied that there was no programme to fund central heating in individual cases, and that the man should apply for a transfer. However, the man did not wish to do this because of his network of friends and possible carers in the area.

Different procedure for council tenants. In June 1992, the man applied for both renovation and disabled facilities grants; he was sent information, but this did not explain that there was a special procedure for council tenants. By the end of 1992, the housing department had not agreed to fund the heating, so in December social services agreed to do so from its own budget. After some uncertainty about whether storage heaters should be installed rather than central heating (pending refurbishment of the whole estate), the heating was installed together with an electric shower in June 1993 at a cost of £3393.60 – though without thermostatic radiator valves. The man complained that radiators in two of the bedrooms were too small; the contractors confirmed that this was so and replaced them in February 1994.

Offering a choice of DFG or alternative. The local ombudsman congratulated the council on offering to its own tenants a procedure that was often better than the statutory procedure for disabled facilities grants. However, applicants should still have been given the choice between the two procedures; and if the council's own procedure was to be used, then it should 'be followed smoothly and without delay'. Neither of these things happened. Eventually, following confusion amongst council officers, the man had been told that he could not apply for a disabled facilities grant; his case was dealt with under the council's own procedure without his agreement being obtained. Furthermore, it took seven months for funding to be agreed and five months for the heating to be installed; this was 'too long' and was maladministration.

Disadvantage in time and nature of the adaptation. The injustice was that, had the council not made mistakes, the heating would have been installed by June 1992 rather than June 1993. In addition, the heating system installed was not what the man wanted (and which would have been specified if a disabled facilities grant had been awarded): there were no thermostatic valves, the water tank was wrongly positioned and the pipe-work not boxed in.

Important issue of public interest. The ombudsman recommended that the council check the heating against 'design temperatures', replace the valves, pay the man £700 compensation in respect of the delay, time and trouble – and review its procedures to enable council tenants to apply for disabled facilities grants, as is their statutory right. This last was an important issue of public interest: 'When a statutory entitlement exists and a Council considers that an alternative, non-statutory scheme would be preferable, the Council should publicise and explain both in an even-handed way and should leave the choice between the two schemes to the individual beneficiaries' (*Hackney LBC 1995*).

Thus, the local ombudsmen have in the past been highly critical of councils that have effectively prevented their own tenants applying for DFGs:

Not offering DFGs to council tenants. The local ombudsman has found maladministration when local councils fail to inform their own tenants of their right to apply for DFGs (e.g. *Hackney LBC 1995; Humberside CC 1996; Barnsley 1998, 1998a*) or are not even themselves sure what the position is (*Durham CC 1993; Bristol CC 1998*).

Likewise, when a council does offer adaptations to its own tenants, but simply manages the resulting demand by excessive waiting times, the local ombudsman will find maladministration:

Excessive demand in coal mining area. Three council tenants were kept waiting – for two years in two cases and over one and a half years in the other – for showers and stairlifts. The council explained that demand exceeded its budget; and that the demand was particularly high because it was an area formerly dominated by coal mining with the resultant problems of ill-health and disability. Nevertheless, the ombudsman refused to accept that lack of resources excused the excessive delays in helping people whose needs had been clearly assessed and accepted (*Bolsover DC 2003*).

16.5.16.2 Housing associations/registered social landlords

Housing associations, or registered social landlords, have the power to carry out home adaptations for their tenants. However, they are not under an obligation to carry out major adaptations for individual tenants; such individual obligations lie with housing and social services authorities.

Housing association tenants are eligible to apply for disabled facilities grants, a point stressed in guidance (ODPM 2006, para 3.26). It appears that in practice some local authorities adopt policies that preclude such applications; yet, as with council tenants, this would appear to be denying housing association tenants their statutory right (as the guidance states, it is 'not lawful': para 3.26).

Sometimes there are other options for housing association tenants; for works over £500 a grant might be available to the housing association, from the Housing Corporation under the Housing Act 1996, s.18, which gives a power to make grants. Alternatively, for minor or more major works, housing associations may pay for works out of their own revenue or reserves. In some areas, difficulties appear to arise when all concerned indulge in buck-passing and funding is not forthcoming from the Housing Corporation, the housing association, the local housing authority, or the local social services authority.

In some circumstances, when local authorities have transferred council housing to housing associations, part of the agreement has been that the housing association will carry out a certain level of adaptations for its disabled tenants. Such transfers are sometimes known as 'large-scale voluntary transfers'. In such circumstances, housing authorities may be tempted to refuse to approve DFGs for any of those tenants. This would seem to be a spurious ground for refusal, since any breach of an agreement concerning adaptations is a matter between local authority and housing association; the right of a disabled tenant to apply for a DFG is unaffected.

16.5.17 GIVING REASONS AND TIME LIMITS

Reasons must be given if applications for DFGs are refused, and applications must be approved or refused within six months from the date of application. If approved, payment must be made no longer than 12 months from the original date of application (ss.34–36). Guidance states that the 12-month limit should be used sparingly, especially where hardship or suffering would be caused (ODPM 2006, annex B, para 54).

Local authorities often run preliminary application schemes including long waiting lists. They sometimes do this when they are short of resources; the intention is to limit the annual expenditure on grants (as the local authority admitted in *Qazi v Waltham Forest LBC*). Such schemes tend to spin out the application process; and the statutory six months do not start to run until the application is finalised.

Previous guidance (now superseded) stated that local authorities 'should not use pre-application tests as a way of delaying applications or avoiding their statutory duty to process applications within 6 months' (DoE 17/96, annex I). Nevertheless, the local ombudsmen have in the past stated that they might not be 'critical of councils which have, in effect, introduced a rationing system for limiting the number of applications they approve provided that the system has been designed fairly and operates fairly, and provided that the council concerned has done what can reasonably be expected to secure the resources needed to meet its responsibilities in this area' (CLAE 1994, p.24). So, even if the process is going awry, the local ombudsman sometimes sympathises with those local authorities that are managing nevertheless still to act fairly:

Acting fairly despite breaching statutory time limits? Although the local ombudsmen have in the past been critical of delay in processing grants, they have also recognised the difficulties facing councils who have to operate a demand-led system of DFGs with insufficient resources. Thus, lack of resources leading to a failure to comply with housing grants legislation might not in itself necessarily be maladministration (*Cyngor Dosbarth Dwyfor 1994*).

Whilst breach of the timescale is maladministration (*Newham LBC 1993*), nevertheless the ombudsmen might accept that councils get into financial difficulty because of increased demand for grants; if complainants have not suffered injustice 'above and beyond' others in the same position, the ombudsmen might not recommend any remedy or compensation (*Middlesbrough BC 1996*) – other than that the council should get on and do all it can to eliminate delays (*Sheffield CC 1997a*).

Even so, the courts have, in passing, expressed doubt about the lawfulness of this sympathetic approach sometimes suggested by the local ombudsmen:

Preventing formal applications for grant. In a court case concerning waiting times for the processing of renovation and disabled facilities grants applications, the court held that restricting access to mandatory grant aid could be unlawful. The alleged approach of the local authority in that case included not indicating to applicants that they had not submitted a formal application, and not indicating the difference between an enquiry and an application. The court also expressed surprise that the local government ombudsman should have described as 'administratively unavoidable and proper' a queuing system that restricted access to mandatory grant (*Qazi v Waltham Forest LBC*).

The local ombudsmen have anyway condemned queuing on other occasions.

Preliminary enquiry system. Local authorities might operate preliminary enquiry systems; but preventing people from submitting formal applications or not telling that they have a right to do so is maladministration (e.g. *Walsall MBC 1996*).

More bluntly, the ombudsman found maladministration in a local authority's general approach of having disabled applicants at the enquiry stage queue for long periods, in order to avoid processing applications within the six-month statutory period. Lack of resources was not an acceptable reason for excessive delay in helping people whose needs had been clearly assessed and accepted (*Cardiff CC 2004*).

Withholding or failing to process application forms. When a council claimed that it could not process an application for a renovation grant because the woman had not submitted a certificate of owner occupation, the ombudsman found that technically this was correct. However, the situation had come about because the council had deliberately withheld the documents necessary for the woman to complete her application; this was maladministration (*Manchester CC 1998*).

Simply putting on hold a recommendation received from the social services department – so that the adaptations were not ready almost two years after referral – was maladministration (*North Yorkshire CC 1993*).

Where there are waiting lists and waiting times, the local ombudsman has stated that at the very least priorities should be made; date order is not be acceptable.

Priority systems and information. The local ombudsman has set out various steps necessary for applications for housing grants, including making known the details of priority systems to enquirers and applicants in a consistent and uniform way (e.g. by leaflet or information sheet), and treating requests for information with 'helpful and meaningful responses' (*Merthyr Tydvil 1994*).

It is maladministration if an authority fails to keep adequate records of information given to enquirers, and to explain clearly (a) the priorities; (b) the difference between initial enquiry and formal application; (c) the necessity of a council survey; (d) the importance of not starting works before grant approval (*Newham LBC 1997*). Failure to publish criteria about priority and to tell enquirers about them is maladministration, as is adopting a policy about priority without being able to produce a record of its formal adoption (*Dinefwr BC 1995*).

Whether or not delay itself is reasonable, failure to notify people about what is going on might be maladministration. For example, a borough council's 'failure to notify [the applicant] formally of the decision to delay the work and then its failure to notify him formally of its schedule for carrying out the work…was maladministration'. Similarly, in the same case, the failure to notify the applicant about the fluctuations in the authority's views of what the applicant's needs really were was maladministration (*North Yorkshire CC 1993*).

Methods of prioritisation: date order not acceptable. The local ombudsman has disapproved of systems in which applicants are treated solely in date order, because this prevents priority being given to those in greater need (*Liverpool CC 1996/1997*) – but has accepted that local authorities should adopt priorities and that this means people will have to queue (*Newham LBC 1997; Walsall MBC 1996*). Furthermore, giving priority for grants (renovation and disabled facilities) to certain groups such as disabled people or those with houses with dangerous structures is not a fettering of discretion when room is left to consider exceptional cases. However, if waiting lists are uneven in different areas of the authority and priority criteria are applied inconsistently, this is maladministration (*Newham LBC 1997*).

16.5.18 DWELLING (INCLUDING GARDEN)

Dwelling means a building or part of a building occupied or intended to be occupied as a separate dwelling, together with any yard, garden, outhouses and appurtenances belonging to it or usually enjoyed with it (s.101). Likewise, the definitions of houseboats and park homes (caravans: see 16.5.10.3) include yards, garden, outhouses and appurtenances (s.58). These definitions are sometimes overlooked.

Nevertheless, the definition of dwelling does mean that DFGs cannot be used for works outside the boundary of the dwelling; this can lead to complications and delay in organising and finding funding for such work (e.g. pavement vehicle crossover and dropped kerb: *Birmingham CC 2002*).

16.5.19 MAXIMUM MANDATORY GRANT

If all the relevant conditions are met, housing authorities are obliged to approve applications for DFGs up to a certain maximum, currently £30,000. Central government has advised that this maximum is to be applied before, rather than after, the assessed contribution of the applicant (see 16.5.20) has been deducted from the amount of grant payable (DTLR 3/2002). If this is the correct interpretation of both the 1996 Act and the relevant regulations (SI 2008/1189), it results in less generous provision of grant. For instance, if the works cost £35,000, and the applicant is assessed to contribute £5000, the grant awarded will be only £25,000 (i.e. £30,000 less £5000) rather than £30,000 (i.e. £35,000 less £5000).

Housing authorities have a discretion, but no obligation, to exceed this maximum amount of grant by exercising their general discretion under the *Regulatory Reform (Housing Assistance) (England and Wales) Order 2002* (see 16.8). Local authorities should beware of the importance of adhering to regulations rather than making up their own, unlawful, rules:

Making up the rules about grants. Before renovation grants were abolished (from July 2003), the legislation listed specific and exclusive factors that authorities had to take into account when deciding how much grant to give (just as there are for DFGs). Nevertheless, the authority had added its own rule that effectively limited the maximum grant payable to 20 per cent of the total cost of the works.

The judge found nothing in the Act which gave the council a discretion 'to impose some arbitrary limit on the amount payable or to take account of financial resources or their absence'. Express language in the legislation would have been required to sanction such a policy (*R v Sunderland CC, ex p Redezeus*).

16.5.20 TEST OF RESOURCES

Once an application has been approved, the applicant will be subject to a test of resources in order to determine his or her contribution to the cost of the works. The test is similar to that applied to housing benefit applications. It does not take account of outgoings. In the case of an adult, only that adult's resources, and those of his or her partner, will be taken into account (SI 1996/2890). In the case of children, the test of resources has been abolished; previously, the parents' resources were taken into account.

Where it can be shown that a couple no longer live as husband or wife, but are still living in the same dwelling, the resources of the applicant's spouse/partner would not be assessed (see, for example, the situation in *R(Fay) v Essex CC*). The sort of test to be applied is well known to social security law; it would involve matters such as independent financial arrangements, separate eating arrangements, independent arrangements for the storage and cooking of food, no evidence of family life, and separate commitment to housing costs.

Likewise, for instance, a person should be treated as a single person if his or her absence from other members of the family is likely to exceed 52 weeks:

Hospital stay and financial assessment of couple for DFG. When a man had been in hospital for nearly two and a half years, during period within which the assessment and application for a DFG had been made in order to make discharge possible, this rule should have applied. Instead the council conducted the means test on both himself and his wife. This was maladministration; it meant a year's delay in the husband's return home. Three years after the initial assessment had started, the council agreed that the assessment was a 'nil' assessment. Four later, he was on the point of returning home. He had suffered a severe stroke; his son was ten years old (*Stafford BC 2006*).

These cases illustrate a general point, namely, that councils should both understand and explain properly what the rules about DFGs are:

Failure of council to ensure woman with severely impaired mental capacity understood the grant conditions. A local authority failed to ensure that a woman understood the rule (which applied formerly to renovation grants) that if she moved within five years of the works being carried out, the grant would be repayable.

The woman did sell the house within this period and the local authority sought repayment of over £33,000. However, at the time that the woman agreed to the works, she had severely impaired mental capacity to the point of being detained in hospital under the Mental Health Act (where she agreed to the conditions and signed).

In these circumstances, the local ombudsman found that the council should have made particular efforts to ensure that she understood what she was agreeing to. Because she did not understand, she lost the chance of delaying the sale of her house for a further year (she had sold it after four years). The ombudsman recommended that the council waive repayment of the grant in full.

The council subsequently refused to accept this recommendation. The ombudsman published a further report, recording her dismay that the council had 'responded in what I can only describe as a cavalier manner to the prejudice of a very vulnerable citizen'. She asked the council to reconsider its decision, whilst recognising that it was under a legal obligation to agree to the remedy (*Trafford MBC 2006*).

Under s.51 of the HCGRA 1996, housing authorities may, with the consent of the Secretary of State, impose a condition requiring an applicant for DFG to pursue a legal claim for damages, or insurance claim relating to damage to the property. The Secretary of State has made a general consent in relation to s.51 claims (DoE 17/96: see specifically *Housing Renewal Main Grants (Recovery of Compensation) General Consent 1996*). Guidance states that authorities should consider imposing such a condition where such a legal claim is made and the cost of works to the property is part of the claim (or where the applicant has made or could make an insurance claim in respect of damage to the property). If the applicant receives the payment against the legal or insurance claim, he or she should use it to repay the authority, 'so far as is appropriate' (ODPM 2006, annex B, paras 59–62).

16.5.20.1 Successive applications and 'nil grant' applications

Guidance recognises that, for disabled people with degenerative conditions, more than one application might be required over time; the legislation imposes no express restriction on successive applications.

Any previously assessed contribution will be taken account of in a new application; this is why it is worthwhile for applicants to follow an application through to completion even when they receive 'nil grant' because their contribution equals or exceeds the cost of the works (ODPM 2006, annex B, para 11). The previously assessed contribution will then be taken account of in any future application within five or ten years (depending on whether the applicant is tenant or owner). Thus, the failure of a local authority to advise applicants of the advantages of pursuing such a nil grant application will constitute maladministration (*Cardiff CC 2004*).

16.5.20.2. Placing a legal charge on the dwelling

Since May 2008, a consent order has allowed local authorities to impose a legal charge on a person's dwelling by way of repayment for a disabled facilities grant awarded. Such a charge can be imposed only when the grant is for a sum exceeding £5000 and the applicant is the owner of the dwelling. The charge can be up to a maximum of £10,000 for such part of the grant exceeding £5000. Repayment of this charge can be demanded if the person disposes of the dwelling within 10 years. In addition, the local authority can only require repayment if it has first considered whether:

- the person would suffer financial hardship
- the disposal of the premises is connected to taking up or changing the location of employment
- the disposal is connected with the physical or mental health or well being of the recipient of the grant or of the disabled occupant, or
- the disposal is to enable the grant recipient to live with or near (a) any person who is either disabled or infirm and in need of care which the recipient is intending to provide, or (b) any person who is intending to provide care which the grant recipient needs because of disability or infirmity (Secretary of State for Communities and Local Government 2008).

16.6 REHOUSING INSTEAD OF HOME ADAPTATIONS

Increasingly in practice, local authorities encourage people to move dwelling rather than have adaptations carried out. This often occurs in the case of council tenants but sometimes also in the case of private tenants.

Sometimes authorities refuse to award a DFG and insist that people move. When local authorities make such a decision, they need in principle to be able to justify it against the terms of the 1996 Act. For instance, in the individual case, the works might be judged not to be necessary and appropriate or not to be reasonable and practicable. Guidance states that if a dwelling is unfit, to the extent that it is unreasonable and impractical to proceed with the proposed adaptations, the housing authority should, together with social services, consider alternatives. This might be renovation of the dwelling first, a reduced level of adaptations that would still meet the person's needs and considerations of practicality, or alternative accommodation (ODPM 2006, annex B, para 36).

More controversial, and sometimes legally suspect, is where the adaptation is judged to be necessary and appropriate, and reasonable and practicable, but the local authority simply refuses to countenance a DFG – instead offering rehousing only, because it judges this to be the cheaper option or better use of its own housing stock. First, the 1996 Act says nothing about people having to move house (in either public or private sector housing), simply because it would be cheaper than an adaptation or be a preferred strategic option in terms of management of its own housing stock. Second, even were this approach legally arguable, it would still need to be shown that the person's needs were being met by the rehousing to the extent that they would have been met by the DFG – and that the person was not in other ways being significantly disadvantaged by the move.

An offer of rehousing might seem reasonable on its face, but the following examples reveal that it is by no means plain sailing – quite apart from the major impact (psychological and physical) that moving house may have, particularly on older people. For instance, loss of a local support network might mean that a move would simply not meet a person's needs. The financial consequences of having to move might be high (including moving costs, cost of a higher mortgage, and the effect on benefits entitlements). In any case, rehousing might take a substantial length of time, before a suitable dwelling is identified – longer than a DFG would have taken. In which case, rehousing may be less advantageous and not be a suitable alternative to adaptations. The local ombudsman was in no doubt that it was maladministration in the following case to force the woman to move council house:

Trying to force a disabled woman to move: loss of support network. A couple had lived in a council house for 30 years. The woman was a permanent wheelchair user and depended on her husband for assistance. Three of their children lived in the same village and provided a support network. The woman was assessed as having no access to basic facilities such as toilet and bath; the occupational therapist considered the situation unacceptable and highly distressing to the woman. Adaptations were recommended. The council did not permit council tenants to apply for DFGs; it did carry out works to its own stock but allocated only £40,000 for these for the whole year. As the proposed works for the woman would have used up a quarter of this budget, the council declined approval. Instead it would offer to move them to a nearby village; provide new purpose-built accommodation in the same village in some three years' time; or fund a third of the cost of the works, and expect the couple to find charitable funding for the remaining two thirds.

The failure to approve the adaptations was maladministration. First, government guidance stated that council tenants should be eligible to receive home adaptations either through a DFG, or at least on the same terms as in the private sector. The ombudsman was in no doubt that, had the couple been owner-occupiers, they would have received a 100 per cent mandatory DFG. Second, the budgetary allocation was irrelevant to this mandatory duty. Third, the availability of alternative accommodation in another village was an irrelevant consideration given the couple's reliance on a local support network (North Warwickshire 2000).

The ombudsman also recommended a total of £4500 compensation. The council agreed to carry out the adaptations, but refused to pay the compensation because the couple had refused to move and because the money would have to come from the DFG budget and thus delay other applicants. The ombudsman found this to be irrational. There was no reason why their reasonable decision not to move should be used against the couple; likewise no reason why the compensation should not come out of another budget (*North Warwickshire BC 2000a*).

The following local ombudsman investigation reveals a situation that was anything but clear, and highlights the problems arising from imposing a highly restrictive policy in respect of DFG funding, in terms of a legally dubious financial ceiling (£15,000) well below the then statutory figure of £25,000 (up to which housing authorities had a duty to award DFG):

Restrictive policy on adaptations: rehousing offered instead. A local authority had a policy that for any adaptation costing over £15,000 there was an expectation that rehousing would be offered as the only alternative to meeting the need. Only exceptionally, where a suitable alternative adapted property owned by the council or housing association (that could be nominated by the council) was not available, would adaptations over £15,000 be considered. This policy was applied in the case of a family in private property with a disabled child. The family was prepared to move to another private property within the area; but would have to increase their mortgage, which they could not afford to do. They asked whether social services financial assistance to move might be available.

The family was also concerned about a move to council-owned property; the money realised would be taken into account in relation to their entitlement to benefits. In fact the council housing option that would have meant knocking two properties into one was anyway a remote possibility. Even so the local authority delayed in reaching the decision, and in producing a feasibility report (that was inadequate) for a through-floor lift. This led the council to approve a ground floor extension that was then judged not to be feasible. Further delay ensued while the council considered whether to financially assist the family with the purchase of another private property. In other words, the council was not considering all the relevant facts on each option. This was maladministration (*Kirklees MBC 2003*).

Likewise, the offering of alternative accommodation might not be straightforward, and result, after substantial delay, in reoffering a DFG:

Offering rehousing: confusion and delay. A complaint was made to the local ombudsman concerning a man who had early onset Alzheimer's disease, epileptic fits, and Parkinson's disease. He had had a heart attack, stroke, and transient ischaemic attacks. He was unable to feed himself, walk any distance or use the toilet unaided; he required care around the clock. His wife provided it, although she had back problems and had developed osteo-arthritis. Initially, an assessment concluded that certain adaptations would not meet his longer term needs. Other adaptations might have, but the district council miscalculated the couple's contribution, which put them off pursuing the application. The council then suggested council rehousing, but it took eight months for them to make clear that the couple would not be eligible; this was because the money from the sale of their existing house would exclude them from the council's allocation scheme. All this caused confusion and delay and was maladministration. The council subsequently reoffered a disabled facilities grant (*Maldon DC 2000*).

The local ombudsman in the next case uncovered a protracted rehousing process and a failure in the meantime to meet people's needs:

Failure to adapt and rehousing. When a couple applied to be rehoused, the local authority offered in early 1998 a two-storey property with a bathroom and toilet upstairs. This was maladministration since, on the medical evidence, the slightest exertion made the wife breathless, and there would be a problem with the stairs. A further offer of rehousing took until April 2002. Yet a downstairs toilet was assessed as required in June 1998; this was not provided, although a chemical toilet downstairs was supplied to mitigate the situation. By October 1999, the council stated that the downstairs toilet would not meet the longer term needs, therefore it had no obligation to adapt. Nevertheless the ombudsman criticised the fact that the council had previously stated that the toilet was required; it was maladministration not to have carried out the adaptation as required in 1998 – because of lack of funding (*Salford CC 2003*).

People sometimes find themselves caught within a vicious circle; having applied for rehousing, they are as a matter of policy then excluded from being on the adaptations list. Although defensible on a case-by-case basis, applied as a policy this can result in some cases in significant problems. Things are made even worse if there is then confusion amongst staff about whether or not there is such a policy (*Barking and Dagenham 2000*). Such policies can lead to patent absurdity, as became apparent in a Court of Appeal case:

Refusing to carry out adaptations. A local authority awarded 'nil points' to a mother who had applied for a council house transfer for herself and her two children, one of whom had been assessed as significantly disabled. This decision would have effectively ruled out a move in the foreseeable future; yet the council stated that while the mother remained on the housing transfer list, no adaptations could be carried out. The council in fact backed down, and the court suggested that the award of nil points could anyway have been susceptible to judicial review (*R v Ealing LBC, ex p C*).

It is worth noting that even in a case where the court suggested that an elderly disabled couple's needs could in principle be lawfully met either by means of a stairlift or by 'removing' them to another house, the judge referred to the potential complications of such a move – including the fact that it might be fatal:

Difficulty of moving house. The judge stated that the local authority was bound to take into account that the couple should remain in the area, to ensure continuity of service. Any new premises would have to be suitably adapted. Likewise there was a risk that, because of medical evidence as to the vulnerability of the couple, whatever was done would be fatal to the husband (both medical specialist and the GP said he was not fit to move house). Even so the judge (with some regret) was not prepared to state that a move to alternative accommodation was legally irrational – but did state that the local authority would have to reconsider the matter carefully about whether such a move should take place (*R v Kirklees MBC, ex p Daykin*).

(In the *Daykin* case, the court did not apparently consider the Housing Grants, Construction and Regeneration Act 1996; reference was made only to social services legislation (Chronically Sick and Disabled Persons Act 1970, etc.). Had the court been referred to the 1996 Act, with its specific duties in respect of adapting people's homes, its conclusions might have differed and come down in favour of adapting the home).

Local authorities now operate what are called 'choice-based letting schemes'. In one case a woman who was seriously ill and profoundly disabled sought to move house through the council's choice-based letting scheme. After several months, in the second highest category of priority, she was unsuccessful. She instead then applied for home adaptations, which application itself was then substantially delayed. In the end a suitable property was identified, after the local authority agreed to let it to her directly, on the basis of exceptional circumstances. The local ombudsman applauded the council for being prepared to directly let exceptionally; however, although it was insensitive to have expected somebody so ill and disabled to devote time and energy to bidding for properties, nonetheless it did not appear contrary to any law, regulation, guidance or council policy (*Leeds CC 2007*). The question of a possible breach of the Disability Discrimination Act 1995, by putting disabled applicants at a disadvantage, was not broached in the case.

However, in another case, involving housing allocation, the ombudsman found a highly restrictive approach which constituted maladministration and, in the ombudsman's view at least, a breach of human rights:

Prisoner in her own home: tragic and deplorable consequence of restrictive rehousing policy. An elderly woman could not cope with three flights of stairs up to her front door – and could only manage internal stairs with assistance. She applied to be rehoused in 2000, into a three-bedroomed property for herself, her daughter and grand-daughter, with whom she lived. She was an 86-year-old widow, partially sighted, deaf, arthritic, extremely frail and had bronchitic asthma. She used an oxygen concentrator and portable oxygen. By 2002, it was clear she needed to move as a priority. Instead, she was left to become more frail, with her health deteriorating, in 'completely unsuitable accommodation' – leaving her 'practically a prisoner in her own home' by the beginning of 2003.

This was a 'tragic, deplorable and wholly preventable circumstance'. In particular, the council had fettered its discretion, by adhering rigidly to its policy that three-bedroomed homes with gardens could only be allocated to families with young children only. This was maladministration, made worse by the fact that the Member for Parliament had been assured by the council that matters would be moved on – yet this reassurance seemed without substance. In addition, the ombudsman believed that the woman's human rights, under article 8 of the European Convention on Human Rights, had been breached (*Havering LBC 2007*).

16.7 LANDLORD CONSENT TO ADAPTATIONS

Landlord consent has been a significant obstacle to the carrying out of adaptations, since it will effectively prevent the work being carried out. However, legislation now restricts the freedom of landlords to refuse unreasonably.

16.7.1 HOUSING ACTS

First, the Housing Act 1980 (ss.81–85) and Housing Act 1985 (ss.97–99) write into the lease a term that the tenant will not make any improvement without the written consent of the landlord who, in turn, cannot unreasonably refuse. Improvement means any alteration in or addition to the dwelling, including (a) any addition to or alteration in the landlord's fittings and fixtures; (b) any addition or alteration connected with the provision of services to the premises; (c) erection of a wireless or television aerial; (d) carrying out of external decoration.

These Acts apply to protected tenancies, statutory tenancies and secure tenancies. The Acts also set out factors that are relevant to consideration of whether a landlord's refusal is unreasonable: safety issues, landlord expenditure arising, effect on sale or letting value of dwelling. They also make provision for the landlord to give consent, but with the attachment of reasonable conditions. If the landlord unreasonably refuses, consent is taken to have been given.

16.7.2 DISABILITY DISCRIMINATION ACT

Second, the Disability Discrimination Act 1995 applies to all leases of residential property other than protected, statutory and secure tenancies. It applies where the disabled person is the present or prospective lawful occupier of the premises, the premises are or are intended to be the only principal home, the tenant is entitled under the lease to make improvements, and the tenant applies to the landlord for consent to make a relevant improvement. If the landlord refuses unreasonably to give consent, then the consent is taken as given. If the landlord attaches unreasonable conditions, consent is taken to have been unreasonably withheld. Improvement to the dwelling is defined as in the Housing Acts 1980 and 1985 (DDA 1995, s.49G).

The DDA does not set out what might constitute unreasonable refusal and thus be discriminatory and unlawful. However, clearly, the factors set out in the Housing Acts are likely to be relevant. In addition, the relevant Code of Practice sets out, non-exhaustively, a number of other factors which should be taken into account, including impact upon the disabled person of any refusal of consent, ability of the tenant to pay for the improvement, scale of the proposed adaptation, feasibility of the works, length of the term remaining under the let, nature of the tenancy (type and length), nature of the premises (type, age, design, quality), extent of disruption, effect of, and compliance with, planning and building regulations requirements – and desirability or practicability of reinstatement of the premises at the end of the lease (DRC 2006, para 18.25). Certainly, separate guidance from central government states that in appropriate circumstances, 'every attempt should be made to secure the landlord's approval and in appropriate circumstances authorities should be prepared to assure the landlord that if requested by him they will "make good" when a tenant no longer requires the adaptation' (where it is arranging the adaptation) (ODPM 2006, para 6.3).

As to conditions which it might be reasonable for a landlord to attach to the consent, the Code of Practice suggests requirements that the tenant: obtain any necessary planning permission and other statutory consents, adhere to plans and specifications approved by the landlord, allow the landlord a reasonable opportunity to inspect, reimburse the landlord's reasonable costs in connection with giving consent, and be responsible for paying for and arranging ongoing maintenance (DRC 2006, para 18.29).

16.7.3 LANDLORD AND TENANT ACT 1927

Third, the Landlord and Tenant Act 1927 (s.19(2) applies to leases (not secure, protected, statutory or certain mining or agricultural leases) which contain a condition prohibiting the tenant from making improvements without consent. The Act makes any such condition subject to the landlord's consent not being unreasonably withheld. It allows for the landlord to demand payment of a reasonable sum from the tenant for a diminution in the value of the premises.

16.7.4 ABSOLUTE PROHIBITION OR SILENCE ABOUT IMPROVEMENTS OR ADAPTATIONS

Fourth, if the term in a lease prohibits absolutely the making of improvements, a duty may arise for that term to be changed under another part of the DDA – that is the duty to make reasonable adjustments by changing a term of the let of premises (DDA 1995, s.24D and SI 2006/887).

Fifth, if the lease says nothing about improvements, then the Code of Practice states that none of the above legislation is directly relevant and tenants can make alterations as long as they do not breach any other conditions (DRC 2006, para 18.39).

16.7.5 REFUSAL BY COUNCILS AS LANDLORDS TO PERMIT ADAPTATIONS TO THEIR OWN STOCK

Apart from potential refusal by private sector landlords, the question of landlord consent has in some areas assumed greater significance in respect of council tenants. It seems that, separate from any question of whether an adaptation is necessary and appropriate (and reasonable and practicable), some local authorities are in practice simply refusing consent as landlord as a matter of policy in respect of their own tenants. In other words, they are in principle allowing applications by their own tenants, but then refusing landlord consent wholesale. This is likely to be unlawful, since it would represent a systematic undermining of the DFG system by a local authority that simultaneously is legally responsible for DFGs and is landlord. In particular circumstances, it might potentially also breach the Disability Discrimination Act.

Other local authorities sometimes refuse landlord consent to their own tenants in individual cases (rather than wholesale) on grounds of overcrowding or under-occupation. Such grounds probably cannot be argued under the 'reasonable practicability' condition, since that relates to the age and condition of the dwelling: see 16.5.13). Sometimes local authorities attempt to connect overcrowding with the 'necessary and appropriate' condition; effectively stating that the need for extra space or an extra facility is not related to the need of the disabled occupant but to the whole family's situation. However, caution is again required:

Extra bedroom and overcrowding. When the parents of an autistic child applied for conversion of the attic into an extra bedroom, the local authority at one point suggested that this was simply an overcrowding issue. However, the parents rejected this, pointing out that if it were not for the child constantly attacking his brother with whom he shared a bedroom, the two boys could happily continue to share. Therefore the extra bedroom was disability, and not overcrowding, related. This point was not pursued by the local authority, nor taken up on the subsequent appeal (*R(B) v Calderdale MBC*, High Court).

The local government ombudsman has questioned undue application of the overcrowding argument:

Overcrowding. When adaptations were sought by the parents of a severely disabled girl, the council argued that the major problem was overcrowding. However, the ombudsman pointed out that although the daughter did not have her own bedroom, the family was not statutorily overcrowded; furthermore, the lack of a separate bedroom was only one reason why the home was not satisfactory. The ombudsman saw no evidence that the authority had adhered to its own policy on this matter; this was maladministration (*Sunderland CC 2002*).

The ground of under-occupancy is commonly used by local authorities to refuse consent to council tenants. It is doubtful, in the generality of cares, how lawful this is. The question might boil down to whether the courts would view strategic use of stock as a valid reason for refusing landlord consent; whatever the answer, it would almost certainly be complicated because of the local authority's dual role as landlord and DFG provider.

16.8 HOME ADAPTATIONS: REGULATORY REFORM ASSISTANCE

Under the Regulatory Reform (Housing Assistance) (England and Wales) Order 2002, housing authorities have a wide discretion to assist with housing in their locality. The assistance can include acquiring living accommodation but also adapting or improving it. This discretion could clearly cover the adaptation of people's homes.

The assistance may be provided in any form; it may be unconditional or subject to conditions, including repayment of, or contribution to, the assistance. The housing authority could take security, including a charge over the property.

Housing authorities must, under the Order, have a local, published policy, explaining what assistance it is able to give. Without it, the powers under the Order cannot be exercised. Central government guidance also points out that in order to avoid fettering their discretion (see 5.2.1), authorities should have a mechanism to consider individual requests, even if they fall outside the scope of the local policy (ODPM 5/2003, para 4.5). The following legal case was a reminder that, in even in the case of a discretion, the local authority must be prepared to consider exercising it:

Discretionary grants. The court held that a policy of never providing a particular type of discretionary grant (in this case a renovation grant) would amount to an unlawful fettering of discretion (R v Bristol CC, ex p Bailey).

Councils can get in a muddle about this, claiming to treat applications individually but nevertheless applying a concealed policy, as the local ombudsman found:

Muddled, shadowy policy on extensions. One local authority claimed to have no specific guidelines, because each application would be treated on its merits. However, it had also adopted a policy that, if an extension was required, consideration should be given to the reason the person needed to remain at the property. If it was more economic, a grant would be offered to the applicant to move. The applicant was, however, not told about this policy on extensions, nor did the council consider the need for an extension at an early stage. This was maladministration (Barnet LBC 2006).

An explanatory document issued by central government gave examples of how people with disabilities could be assisted under the Order. For instance, housing authorities could offer disabled applicants a choice of means-tested mandatory DFG or the option of a non-means-tested loan; the latter would avoid the need for the applicant to divulge their financial details. If the applicant was anyway not eligible for a DFG, the authority could offer assistance through a loan. Assistance could also be given toward relocation (rehousing) of a disabled occupant, where this would be a preferred option – for instance, if the existing dwelling was in a state of severe disrepair or adaptation would be unsuitable (DTLR 2001a, pp.11, 27–29). Otherwise, a consultative government paper suggested that the discretion could in principle be used, for instance:

- to assist a disabled person with small-scale adaptations to avoid the complexity of DFGs
- to top up mandatory DFGs (e.g. where the works are particularly expensive or an applicant cannot afford the assessed contribution, or where some of the works are not

mandatory – such as more satisfactory internal living arrangements for the disabled occupant)

- garden access if that is not already mandatory
- a safe play area for a child
- where a disabled occupant is receiving specialised care or medical treatment and where he or she is responsible for the works, or
- a 'complete solution' for the disabled person's needs (examples taken from DTLR 2001, para 9.7).

Finally, other guidance states that, since mandatory DFG is not adequate to deal with all likely requests for assistance, it would be 'very important' for the published policies of local authorities to include what additional assistance was available for adaptations for disabled people. It also reiterates that there is no restriction on the amount of discretionary assistance that can be given either as an addition or alternative to mandatory DFG. Assistance might be given for a person to acquire alternative accommodation, if the authority believes this will benefit the disabled occupant as much as improving or adapting his or her existing accommodation (ODPM 2006, paras 2.23–2.25).

The local ombudsman has stated that local authorities should give serious consideration to use of the discretion to go outside of mandatory disabled facilities grants, where the works required do not fall within DFG. This is especially in the light of the equality duty placed on local authorities by s.49A of the Disability Discrimination Act 1995 (*Kirklees MBC 2008*). The ombudsman has also found that local authorities should be clear with information about the mandatory maximum payable and the discretion (rather than duty) to go above this (*Walsall MBC 2008*) – and that they should not 'fetter' the exercise of the discretion:

Unacceptable fettering of discretion not to exceed the DFG maximum grant: was maladministration and not best use of council's resources. The consequence of a blanket policy of not exercising the discretion meant delay in funding the adaptations was a fettering of discretion. (At the time, the discretion to exceed the maximum was contained in 1996 regulations which have since been repealed in England). Absurdly, the consequence of the rigid policy and delay in eventually agreeing the adaptations was to cost the local authority £735 per week. This was to pay for residential care until the adaptations were completed and the man could return home; he had muscular dystrophy, a benign brain tumour and used a wheelchair. Yet no consideration had been given as to whether it would have been better use of resources to get on with the adaptations instead. All this was maladministration (*Walsall MBC 2008*).

16.9 HOME ADAPTATIONS AND LOCAL SOCIAL SERVICES AUTHORITIES

Central government guidance has always envisaged that local social services authorities have a significant part to play in the provision of home adaptations under s.2 of the Chronically Sick and Disabled Persons Act 1970. Views are sometimes expressed that the wording of s.2 does not place extensive obligations on social services to assist. However, it seems likely that in individual cases, where need cannot be met in any other fashion, a duty to provide substantial assistance will arise (see 11.2.5.6).

Guidance states that, even when an application has been made for a DFG, social services authorities might be asked to assist when (a) the assessed needs of the person exceed the scope of DFGs; (b) the person has difficulty meeting the assessed contribution for a DFG. In such circumstances, once social services have confirmed eligible need, it remains their duty to assist, even when the housing authority has either refused, or is unable to approve, the application (ODPM 2006, para 2.8).

Likewise, the courts appear to have accepted – admittedly without being pressed to the contrary – that social services authorities might have substantial responsibility for adaptations under the Chronically Sick and Disabled Persons Act 1970 (*R v Kirklees MBC, ex p Daykin; R v Kirklees MBC, ex p Good; CD(A Child) v Isle of Anglesey CC; R(Fay) v Essex CC; R(Spink) v Wandsworth LBC*).

Similarly, under the Northern Ireland version of the 1970 Act, the Chronically Sick and Disabled Persons (Northern Ireland) Act 1978, the courts have assumed that adaptations in the form of a heating system could come under s.2 of the 1978 Act (*Re: Teresa Judge*). And in another case brought in Northern Ireland concerning the provision of heating for a disabled person, the court held that it was quite acceptable for the health and social services trust to pass the matter on to the housing authority (the Northern Ireland Housing Executive). However, if the Executive could not satisfactorily deal with the problem, then the trust would retain 'overall statutory responsibility' for 'ensuring that the necessary requirements' of the person were met under the CSDPA (*Withnell v Down Lisburn Health and Social Services Trust*).

In other words, if a person's need for adaptations could be met through another channel, a duty would not arise for the trust to do so under the Chronically Sick and Disabled Persons Act. However, if the needs could not otherwise be met, then obligations would arise under that Act.

16.9.1 SOCIAL SERVICES: TEST OF ELIGIBILITY

The main ways in which social services could arguably be called on to assist are as follows. First, the adaptation required may simply not come under the purposes listed in the Housing, Grants, Construction and Regeneration Act 1996. Second, a person may, under the DFG test of resources, have to contribute an amount that he or she cannot reasonably afford. Third, the works required may exceed the £30,000 maximum that housing authorities are obliged to approve. In the latter two cases, social services might be asked to 'top up'; in the first, to assist with the whole of the cost.

When requested, social services authorities would be obliged to assess whether the person's needs come above their threshold of eligibility (see 6.10 and 6.12). They would also be entitled to take into account whether the person could reasonably afford any contribution he or she may have been asked for under the DFG test of resources. If social services authorities were not legally entitled to do so, every DFG applicant could as a matter of course demand that social services authorities make up the shortfall. This would in turn undermine, and indeed make redundant, the test of resources under the 1996 Act. Certainly the local ombudsman appears in the past to have accepted the reasonableness of this approach:

Inability to afford DFG contribution. It was maladministration when a council took two years to agree to provide an interest-free loan as part of its 'continuing duty', following the inability of a person to meet the contribution which had been assessed by the housing authority (*Wirral MBC 1994a*).

Again, the ombudsman has doubted a council's initial view (later reversed) that once it had assessed the need for a disabled facilities grant, it had done its duty under s.2 of the Chronically Sick and Disabled Persons Act. What it failed to do in this particular case was to establish whether the applicants could actually afford their contribution to the adaptations themselves, and if not, possibly offer an interest free loan (*Wirral MBC 1994*).

The courts anyway have held that, when the parents of two disabled children were assessed to pay a large contribution toward a DFG, the social services authority could take account of their (the parents') resources when deciding whether or not to assist with the adaptations under the CSDPA. In addition, if the authority did decide to assist, it would have the power to place a charge on the house under s.29 of the Children Act 1989. This was because functions exercised under s.2 of the CSDPA were under the umbrella of s.17 of the Children Act, to which the power to charge under s.29 of the 1989 Act applied. However the charge could only be placed on the house in respect of the younger (under 16 years old) of the two brothers. This was because under s.29 of the 1989 Act, the resources of the parents can only be taken account of in respect of a child under 16 years old (*R(Spink) v Wandsworth LBC*).

Placing such a charge on a house was challenged in one case on a number of grounds, but the courts confirmed that the charge was lawful:

Placing a legal charge on the parents' house for a period of 20 years. A three-year-old boy had severe mental and physical disabilities, including four-limb cerebral palsy, epilepsy, asthma and sleep problems. He needed assistance with all aspects of daily living and mobility. A disabled facilities grants under housing legislation had been approved up to the statutory maximum of £25,000. Social services had then agreed to make a further £10,000 non-repayable grant on top of this. In addition, in order to make the £65,000 total of the works, social services offered a further £30,000 to be secured against the house.

The court ruled that it was lawful (a) to exact the charge at all, despite the objections of the parents; (b) for repayment to be triggered even if the child died during the repayment period, or left the house to live elsewhere; (c) for interest to be payable once the liability to repay had been triggered; (d) for the loan period (within which the loan was repayable on occurrence of a triggering event) to last 20 years; (e) to apply a general policy of 20-year loans subject to the making of exceptions (so that the council did not fetter its discretion). In addition, the court found that the local authority had paid full regard to the parents' means. It also ruled that the facts of the case got nowhere near to establishing a breach of article 8 (*R(BG) v Medway Council*).

Whatever the precise extent of the duty to top up, the local ombudsman will in any case find maladministration if decisions are made arbitrarily because of the absence of a policy on such topping up (*Hertfordshire CC 1992; City and Council of Swansea 2005*). Furthermore, the ombudsman has been unimpressed by a council which seemed to believe that it could fulfil its duty under s.2 by advising people to fill in form for a disabled facilities grant – even though this route had already been unsuccessfully explored by the family (*City and Council of Swansea 2005*).

16.9.2 NATURE OF CONTINUING SOCIAL SERVICES DUTY

The local government ombudsmen have considered the question of social services responsibilities for home adaptations.

Continuing social services responsibility. Maladministration was found, when having identified a need for a downstairs extension, social services failed to act for 20 months – after the housing authority had offered a grant which the applicant family could not accept because it could not afford the contribution. The 'Council appear to have ignored the fact that their statutory responsibility to provide assistance did not come to an end with the offer of a grant [by the housing authority]' (*Salford CC 1993*).

Likewise, the local ombudsman has found that when a housing authority 'is not immediately able to provide the necessary funding, the Council must meet the costs of making provision under the terms of the Chronically Sick and Disabled Persons Act by other means in its capacity as Social Services Authority' (*Wirral MBC 1992*).

Interim provision by social services during wait for major adaptations. The duty on social services might in some circumstances be simply to make interim provision such as a commode (Barnsley MBC 1998a), until a grant is forthcoming (see e.g., *Liverpool CC 1996/1997*; also *Tower Hamlets LBC 1997*).

Drawing a veil over, and premature termination of, social services duty. Some social services departments appear to draw a veil over any continuing involvement, not even telling the person what its recommendation is and lacking a system of responding if the housing department does not act on that recommendation (*Durham CC 1993*). Closing files prematurely also attempts to avoid continuing duties, but is maladministration (*Durham CC 1993*; *Gravesham BC 1987*).

Disowning assessments. Alternatively, the social services department, when confronted with the continuing duty, might simply try to disown its original assessment of need (*Dyfed CC 1996*).

Expenditure moratorium and social services responsibilities. The ombudsman found that the housing authority had imposed a moratorium on expenditure, having discovered half way through the financial year that finance was 'tighter than anticipated'. The need for a stairlift identified by social services therefore remained unacted upon for a long period. Social services in turn did not act (as it might have, given the continuing duty potentially incurred). The ombudsman found maladministration which had caused a two-year wait (*Camden LBC 1993*).

In other investigations, the ombudsmen seem not to have been quite so certain of social services responsibilities, stating in one that 'the Chronically Sick and Disabled Persons Act 1970 does not place a statutory obligation on the council to make a financial contribution' (*Hertfordshire CC 1992*). In another, the ombudsman did not necessarily disagree with authorities who claim that advice and assistance might suffice in place of direct provision (*Wirral MBC 1992*); and in a third that, likewise, alternative accommodation would obviate the need for adaptations (*Manchester CC 1994*).

In a Northern Ireland legal case, there was a wait for the Northern Ireland Housing Executive to carry out an adaptation for a tenant in one of its properties. This was to replace an open fire with a non-manual heating system. During this period of delay, the court held that the health and social services trust's responsibility under s.2 of the Chronically Sick and Disabled Persons (Northern Ireland) Act 1978 – equivalent to s.2 of the CSDPA 1970 – had been discharged satisfactorily by means of interim provision. This consisted of the provision of a home help service to clean out, light and refuel the fire during the day, while the woman's sons would be expected to take responsibility on evenings and weekends (*Re Teresa Judge*).

The potential responsibility under s.2 of the 1970 Act is therefore not confined to assistance with the adaptations, when delay occurs. In addition to this, when an application for a disabled facilities grant had run into the sand, the local ombudsman found maladministration insofar as there was no direct social work contact with the family for 15 months (*Leeds CC 2007*).

16.9.3 DIVISION OF RESPONSIBILITIES FOR HOME ADAPTATIONS

The division of responsibility for adaptations between social services and housing authorities is by no means clear. Up to a point it is fluid. Central government guidance has in the past stated that social services authorities would normally provide equipment that could be easily installed and removed with little or no structural modification to the dwelling. Larger adaptations, involving structural modification, would be the responsibility of housing authorities and attract DFG. However, the guidance went on to state that ultimately it was for housing and social services authorities to decide how to meet people's needs, and that a disabled person's needs remained paramount (DoE 17/96, para 7.6).

Nevertheless, joint working has sometimes led precisely in the opposite direction and to a non-meeting of a person's need, as the local ombudsman has sometimes exposed:

Collusion in delay or non-provision. Sometimes, housing and social services departments apparently collude in strategies of delay – for instance, by the former asking the latter to suspend assessment visits, thereby creating waiting lists and taking the pressure off the housing grants budget. However, such an approach might in turn lead to the social services department's failing to assess within a reasonable time and to a finding of maladministration (e.g. *Bolton MBC 1992*).

In another ombudsman investigation, given the problems the housing department was having, the social services department suggested that baths at a day centre rather than a shower were the solution, in apparent misunderstanding of the law. This was maladministration (*Humberside CC 1996*).

16.9.3.1 Cost threshold to determine responsible authority

In practice, local housing and social services authorities often come to local agreement about divisions of responsibility for adaptions, on the basis of cost. Under a certain financial threshold, the social services authority normally takes responsibility, over that threshold the housing authority is expected to consider a DFG.

Since June 2003, the figure of £1000 is sometimes used to mark this threshold. This is because of the regulations effective since then, which state that if a social services authority provides an adaptation (as a community care service), costing £1000 or less, then it is to be regarded as 'minor' and cannot be charged for. Over that figure, social services authorities retain the power to charge (SI 2003/1196). Use of £1000 as a line of demarcation is convenient but is not explicitly demanded by the regulations; they are concerned with charges, not with divisions of responsibility.

Indeed, both housing and social services authorities should take care not to be rigidly bound by such a threshold. The reason for this is that not all adaptations costing over a certain threshold (whether £1000 or any other figure) will necessarily attract mandatory DFG. For example, an adaptation required to enable a person to work, but which did not otherwise come under the mandatory grant purposes (see 16.4.1), would not attract DFG. On the other hand, it could in principle attract a social services duty, since vital involvement in work is indicated in central government guidance as constituting a critical risk to independence (see 6.12).

Conversely, some adaptations falling under the financial threshold figure (whatever it may be) might not attract social services assistance because the person's needs are not sufficiently high to come over the local social services threshold of eligibility (see 6.12). However, in some cases, there could still be eligibility for a DFG. Indeed, although the bureaucracy of the DFG process should as a matter of practicality generally be avoided in the case of lower cost adaptations, there is no lower cost threshold beneath which DFGs are prohibited.

(Nevertheless blatant steering by local authorities of requests for adaptations that cost under £1000 – toward DFG rather than social services funding, in order simply to be able to charge people – might be legally questionable.)

Central government concludes that in practice it is likely that minor adaptations (under £1000) will be provided free of charge either through social services or through local housing authority discretionary powers (see 16.8) (ODPM 2006, para 6.21).

16.9.4 HOME ADAPTATIONS UNDER NHS LEGISLATION

The NHS is not normally associated with home adaptations, but in certain circumstances it may be potentially responsible. First, central government guidance issued in 1974 stated that home adaptations required for home renal dialysis should be funded by the NHS; it would be responsible for adaptation of people's homes to provide suitable accommodation for dialysis (HSC(IS)11). This guidance was reaffirmed in 1993 (HSG(93)48).

Second, the NHS has continuing health care responsibilities towards certain categories of patient (see 18.4.7), including some patients in their own home. It is arguable that, just as for renal dialysis, equipment and home adaptations required directly in relation to continuing health care treatment or services should likewise be the responsibility of the NHS.

16.10 HOME ADAPTATIONS: LANDLORD DUTIES UNDER THE DISABILITY DISCRIMINATION ACT 1995

Under the Disability Discrimination Act 1995, 'controllers' of let premises have a duty to make reasonable adjustments in relation to premises they have let, and in respect of an individual disabled person living lawfully under the letting in those premises (whether or not the person to whom the premises are let). For instance, it might be the disabled child or spouse of the tenant, or also a disabled person intending to take a let of the premises (DDA 1995, ss.24E, 24J).

The duty relies on a request by the disabled occupant (DDA 1995, ss.24A, 24C, 24D). It does not apply in the case of the so called 'small dwellings' exemption (landlord residing on premises, sharing accommodation on premises with people not part of his or her household, and normally only two households on the premises, s.23). Nor does it apply where the premises are or have been the principal or only home of the person letting them, and an estate agent is not being used to manage the premises (DDA 1995, ss.24B, 24H).

A controller of let premises is a landlord or manager of rented premises. This could include a management or residents' committee of a block of flats or anybody else who has control over how the premises are let or manage (DRC 2006, para 16.6).

16.10.1 REASONABLE ADJUSTMENTS

Discrimination occurs if the controller of the premises fails to comply with the duty to make reasonable adjustments and cannot show justification. The duty to make reasonable adjustments covers (a) provision of auxiliary aids and services; (b) changing practices, policies and procedures; (c) changing a term of the letting (DDA 1995, ss. 24A, 24C, 24D).

16.10.2 PHYSICAL FEATURES

In making reasonable adjustments, it would never be reasonable for the controller to have to remove or alter a physical feature (s.24E). A physical feature is (a) any feature arising from the design or construction of the premises; (b) any feature of any approach to, or exit from, access to the premises; (c) any fixtures in or on the premises; (d) any other physical element or quality of any land comprised in the premises (SI 2006/887). This clearly rules out major adaptations.

Nevertheless, furniture, furnishings, materials, equipment and other chattels are not to be treated as physical features. In addition, the following are not to be treated as changes to physical features: (a) replacement of or provision of any signs or notices; (b) replacement of any taps or door handles; (c) replacement, provision or adaptation of any door bell or door entry system; (d) changes to the colour of any surface, such as a wall or door. Thus these could come within the reasonable adjustments that may have to be made (SI 2006/887).

16.10.3 AUXILIARY AIDS AND SERVICES

The duty to provide an auxiliary aid or service, by way of making a reasonable adjustment, arises in two circumstances. First, where it would enable or make it easier for the disabled person to enjoy or take a let the premises – or make use of any benefit or facility which he or she is entitled to use – but which would be of little or no use if he or she were neither the tenant of the premises nor occupying them. Second, and in addition, if the auxiliary aid or service is not provided it would be impossible or unreasonably difficult for the person to enjoy or take a let of the premises or make use of the benefit or facility (DDA 1995, s.24C, 24J).

Auxiliary aids and services are defined to include: (a) removal, replacement or provision of any furniture, furnishings, materials, equipment or other chattels; (b) replacement of or provision of any signs or notices; (c) replacement of any taps or door handles; (d) replacement, provision or adaptation of any door bell or door entry system; (e) changes to the colour of any surface, such as a wall or door (SI 2006/887).

The Code of Practice suggests that attaching with a screw something to a physical feature, such as a wall, would be unlikely to amount to an alteration to a physical feature. But something more 'significant', such as a concrete ramp, would constitute alteration of a physical feature and so be excluded from the duty (DRC 2006, para 15.16). It goes on to discuss the nature of fixtures, which are generally excluded from the duty. It suggests that 'if an object cannot be removed without serious damage to, or destruction of, some part of the property, or if it is something which is done to effect a permanent improvement in the premises, then it is likely to be a fixture (for example, built-in cupboards). If something is fitted only to further the enjoyment of that thing, it is not likely to be a fixture but a chattel (for example, where a wall hanging is attached to the wall so that it can be properly displayed).' (DRC 2006, para 15.32)

The Code of Practice gives examples of a portable ramp which makes it possible for a disabled child in a wheelchair to negotiate the front step at the entrance to the block of flats; replacement of a chair, in a furnished let, which is too low for a person with arthritis to get out of; provision of telephone headphones, in a furnished let, to allow deaf tenant to watch the television without disturbing other tenants (DRC 2006, para 15.35).

16.10.4 PRACTICES, POLICIES AND PROCEDURES
There is also duty to change practices, policies and procedures, under the making of reasonable adjustments (DDA 1995, s.24D). For instance, a new policy for tenants prohibiting parking on the premises might be waived for a disabled occupant with mobility problems (DRC 2006, para 15.38).

16.10.4.1 Changing a term of the let and prohibition on making improvements
The duty to change terms of the let (s.24D) could involve a tenant with hearing impairment being permitted to have an assistance dog, despite the tenancy agreement generally prohibiting animals on the premises (DRC 2006, para 15.41). Regulations make it clear that this duty might oblige the controller of premises to change a term prohibiting alteration or improvements to the premises in the following circumstances when:
- the controller is subject to a duty to change a term of the let
- the duty arises because a term of the let prohibits alterations or improvements
- the term of the let allows no exception to this prohibition
- the tenant has requested permission to make an improvement to the premises
- if the improvement were allowed, the term would no longer have the effect of making it impossible or unreasonably difficult for the disabled person to enjoy the premises or make use of any benefit or facility
- it would be reasonable in all the circumstances for the tenant to make the improvement (SI 2006/887).

16.10.5 REASONABLENESS OF TAKING STEPS
Whether it is reasonable for a controller or premises to take steps and make reasonable adjustments depends on all the circumstances of the case. The Code of Practice lists non-exhaustively a number of factors, including nature of the letting, effect of the disability on the disabled person, effectiveness of any proposed step, practicability of steps, financial implications, disruption to other people, scale of controller's operation, extent of the controller's financial resources, amount of resources already spent on making adjustments, availability of financial assistance (DRC 2006, para 15.46).

16.10.6 JUSTIFICATION FOR NOT MAKING REASONABLE ADJUSTMENTS

Failure to comply with a duty to make reasonable adjustments can be justified if the controller holds a reasonable belief that the health and safety of any person would be endangered, or that the disabled person is incapable of entering into an enforceable agreement. However, this last justification does not apply if another person is acting for the disabled person by virtue of a power of attorney or deputy appointed by the Court of Protection (SI 2006/887).

16.11 HOME ADAPTATIONS: GENERAL

In practice, the system of home adaptations can be fraught with complications, and it would seem that it has often not worked well, in particular in relation to major, as opposed to minor, adaptations (Heywood 2001, p.38). Guidance was issued by central government in order to highlight good practice. It included reference to: proper application of the legislation, flexibility, equity, 'one-stop shops', provision of key information, self-assessment, interim help, use of agencies to facilitate adaptations, disability housing registers, involving service users, and time targets (ODPM 2006).

The same guidance emphasises that it is not acceptable for a disabled person to be left for weeks or months without interim help, if the process of adaptation is likely to be lengthy. Such interim help could include equipment, temporary works or practical and financial assistance to find 'decent' accommodation during the wait (ODPM 2006, paras 5.40–5.44). It also states that, for people with deteriorating conditions, consideration should be given to 'expedited procedures' (para 5.21).

Although the guidance is not of the legally stronger variety (see 5.1.6), the local ombudsman is prepared to make reference to it in findings of maladministration. In the following case a number of the issues related to the guidance:

Appalling response and breach of guidance. A man in his early twenties, quadriplegic with leukaemia, required adaptations to his parents' home. In dealing with his application the local authority was guilty of maladministration after its 'appalling' response, in relation to the following. It failed (a) to provide written information and written explanation at an early stage when it was most needed, (b) to provide a single point of contact which resulted in lack of continuity and inconsistency, (c) to respect the man's views and those of his family, (d) for 18 months to consider the needs of the foster child, whom the local authority itself had placed with the man's parents, (e) to pay any respect to the views of the family about the needs of the foster child to whom the local authority owed particular duties as a looked after child. The authority had also refused for over a year to fund adaptations to give him sufficient space to be able to meet and talk with his friends in private or to pursue the very limited leisure activities available to him. It had taken 18 months to agree a scheme that properly met the man's medical and social needs, as well as those of the foster child.

The ombudsman concluded that the man had battled against apparently impenetrable, insensitive and disrespectful decisions and processes. She recommend a payment of £7000 to the man, of £70 per week for the 20 weeks to the parents after he had left hospital to reflect their struggle to care for him, and of £1000 to the father in respect of the time and trouble in brining the complaint. She recommended also that the local authority apologise to the family through a personal visit from a director of head of service – and also review its current practices and procedures against the good practice guidance, report in six months to the authority's executive, and provide a copy of the report to the ombudsman (*Kirklees MBC 2008*).

In another case, the ombudsman likewise referred to the guidance, breach of which led to considerable distress and indignity:

Catalogue of delay and misinformation about equipment and adaptations: personal indignity distress resulting. The man was paralysed from the chest down following an accident. On discharge from hospital, the council took no action for ten weeks, with an NHS occupational therapist having to follow up the referral five times before the council did anything. He was wrongly told it would take 18 months to get a ramp for his three front door steps; so he arranged for friends to build him one. He spent 10-14 weeks at home with no access to washing facilities or a toilet, and with a shower chair which was too small for him to use as a commode. The only way he could defecate was to lie on an incontinence sheet and manually remove faeces.

The family asked the local authority to give greater priority to the adaptations required; it received no response. The man borrowed £10,000 and instructed a builder; the local authority failed to tell him that he could still have continued his DFG application which was only a few weeks away from approval. The occupational therapist delayed in ordering a new shower chair, and a replacement was only delivered six months after his hospital discharge.

All this was maladministration; furthermore the Council's practices did not reflect either its own published information or the government's good practice guide (from which it fell far short). The ombudsman recommended reimbursement of over £14,000 for the costs the man incurred of funding adaptations himself, and a further £2,000 in recognition of indignity, inconvenience and distress (*Sheffield CC 2008*).

Over the years, a relatively large number of investigations have been conducted by the local government ombudsmen involving home adaptations; some of these are illustrated in the following paragraphs.

16.11.1 DELAY IN HOME ADAPTATIONS

The system of home adaptations has generally been afflicted not just with the inevitable delay associated with major works to a dwelling, but with the potentially avoidable delay that comes with lack of resources or poor administration by local authorities. The courts have barely considered the issue of waiting times either in this context, although have commented on at least one occasion (*Qazi v Waltham Forest LBC*) (see 16.5.17).

In contrast, the local government ombudsmen have investigated such delay on many occasions. They have often been very critical; yet on some occasions they appear to have recognised the mismatch between demand and available resources and not found maladministration – even though the delay arguably breached the time limits set out in legislation. Sometimes the delay is simply cumulative, occurring at several stages:

Cumulative delay. The fact that a complex system requires considerable communication and cooperation between different departments and agencies does not mean that the local ombudsman will overlook administrative deficiencies. For instance, a 19-month period between application and final assessment was maladministration, including as it did insufficient record keeping, possible lost papers and the applicant's consequent uncertainty throughout the period about what was going on (*Wirral MBC 1994*). A four-year wait for home adaptations, made up of a series of delays, was 'entirely unacceptable' (*Gravesham BC 1987*).

A considerable lapse of time caused by obtaining medical opinion, drawing up plans and getting planning permission might be reasonable in the eyes of the ombudsman. However, once all this was done, a delay in approving and submitting plans was maladministration; as was inadequate monitoring by the council of a contractor whose defective work caused further delay (*Wirral MBC 1992a*).

Opportunities missed to progress works when finance was available and despite pressure from the hospital, the lack of finance when the application was submitted, a priority request not being progressed, availability of funding not checked, and misunderstanding between an occupational therapist and surveyors all constituted maladministration (*Tower Hamlets LBC 1992*).

Local authorities might have impressive policies but simply fail to follow them:

Not following own policy. The authority's policy was to raise an order (for a stairlift) within seven working days of an assessment visit; in practice, this did not happen for 22 months and was maladministration (*Camden LBC 1993*).

While there are many examples of effective arrangements between social services and housing departments, lapses also occur leading sometimes to findings of maladministration:

Housing and social services' lack of coordination. Things can go wrong in relation to different councils (*Durham CC 1993*), or even where social services and housing are different departments in the same council (*Camden LBC 1993*); and a breakdown in communication can result in nothing happening for months on end (*Leicester CC 1992*).

When attempts by senior officers to discuss delay with their opposite numbers in social services failed, 'officers in both departments should have taken responsibility to ensure such discussions took place'. Not to do so was maladministration (*Newham LBC 1993a*). Inadequate coordination between departments leading to delay in the meeting of assessed needs for equipment or adaptations was not acceptable; the council should 'exercise proper management to ensure that no unreasonable delays occur before those needs are met' (*Wirral MBC 1992*).

In yet another investigation, the 'process of establishing what needs were to be met, the drawing up of plans, the obtaining of grant aid, and the granting of planning permission involved three different departments of the Council (and two separate sections of one of those departments). If such a process is to work properly, then different parts of the Council must work together more effectively than happened in this case. The failure of officers to coordinate their activities led to the submission and processing of an unacceptable planning application and consequent delay. The Council's failure to coordinate their activities was maladministration' (*Salford CC 1993*).

The problems between housing and social services may come in the form of disagreement, unaccountable delays and problems of tracking correspondence:

Disagreements, delays, tracking correspondence. Allowing a disagreement, between the social services and housing departments about central heating for a man with AIDS to drag on for over a year, was maladministration – as was the concern about resources and about setting an unwanted precedent, which meant that genuine technical problems in installing the heating were identified only belatedly (*Tower Hamlets LBC 1997*). Delay caused by the seeking of medical advice will not be faulted; but subsequent failure to visit for three months, and a further three-month delay in approving a revised plan, would be (*Wirral MBC 1992a*).

Problems of correspondence in a large organisation did not make it 'right that a Council should rely on a service user to follow up delays caused by non-arrival of internal mail. It should not be beyond the capability of the Council to devise a system of keeping track of applications such as this' (*Liverpool CC 1992*). Thus, communication failure between a social worker and housing officer meant that a message was never received and led to a two-month delay; this was maladministration (*Rotherham MBC 1995*).

Again, a failure in coordination working between housing and social services can result in a catalogue of disasters and duplication:

Catalogue of disasters and duplication. The eight-month delay, between the approval and the placing of the order for an adaptation, was regarded as not unusual and with 'apparent equanimity' by the council. This was maladministration (*Wirral MBC 1993d*). Lack of 'effective liaison' between the social services and housing authority, resulting in delay for adaptations, was maladministration (*Camden LBC 1993*); the same fault might result in an occupational therapist's recommendations being omitted from a schedule of works drawn up by a technical officer – or in a 'catalogue of disasters and duplicated work' as well as the disappearance of an application in the architect's department (*Liverpool City CC 1996/1997*). A wait of seven and a half months between receipt of instructions from social services and the housing department's sending of a preliminary form to the applicants was also maladministration (*Wirral MBC 1994a*). When a grant had been awarded for a shower but the works carried out unsatisfactorily, remedial work was required. However, the council treated this as a new grant application, which entailed a 15-month wait. This was maladministration (*Wirral MBC 1993a*).

So, when there is disagreement between a social services occupational therapist and the grants section of the local authority, there needs to be a means of resolving the conflict. The absence of such means, with resulting delay, is maladministration:

Conflict between occupational therapist and grants section about sacrificing the family room. When a seriously ill woman left hospital, it should, reasonably, have taken no more than ten months to arrange the adaptations she required. As a result of delay in making a financial assessment for a DFG, of no means of resolving conflict between the occupational therapist and the grants section, and of the local authority not being prepared to reconsider the view that the family should sacrifice the only room useable as a family room, the time taken to arrange suitable accommodation was nearer three years. During this period she was confined to bed in the front living room, was unable to use a special NHS wheelchair which would have relieved pain and discomfort, was unable to use a toilet, bath or shower and was strip washed on her bed by carers adding to her pain and discomfort, unable to sit outside or with her family. This was maladministration (*Leeds CC 2007*).

Councils may themselves complicate matters through reorganisation; service users get caught in the crossfire and the local authority is found guilty of maladministration:

Forgetting people's needs: victim of council reorganisation. A council transferred management of its housing stock to six arms length management organisations (ALMOs), and also set up a new council department called the Adaptations Agency. Once an OT had assessed need, an adaptations application would be passed to the Agency to judge if it was reasonable and practicable, to draw up plans, tender the work and monitor it. The council, however, remained responsible overall for meeting people's adaptations needs.

The complainant suffered a stroke and required various minor adaptations. By March 2002, his condition had deteriorated, and he required either a through floor lift or an extension (he opposed the former because of space considerations in relation to his two children). Three and a half years later, the adaptations had not been carried out.

The ombudsman found that the man had been a victim of the reorganisation, made worse by a deterioration in the relationship between the Adaptations Agency and the relevant ALMO. His needs had been forgotten. Since April 2002, the man had been sleeping in the living room (first on the floor then on a camping bed), and using a commode there (which was unpleasant for the whole family). He believed that his children, with special educational needs, had been badly affected. He claimed he had suffered three further strokes as a result of having to sleep on the floor, and that his wife had attempted suicide five times.

The ombudsman recommended that the council find him a suitable property and pay the family £5000 for the delays and injustice. In addition, the council should recognise the strain on family life and pay for a two-week holiday (including travel) in the United Kingdom for the family (*Leeds CC 2006*).

Delay arising from lack of clarity or workload levels on staff might also constitute maladministration:

Workload and information. Failure to provide clear information to clarify the exact works involved and the amount of contribution required of an applicant is maladministration (*Nottinghamshire CC 1998a*). Workload might explain part of the delay in installing a shower, but the fact that an order marked urgent did not appear to have received the appropriate priority was maladministration (*Islington LBC 1988*).

Sometimes, the catalogue of failure leading to delay is extensive, suggesting – at least in hindsight – chaotic practices involving delay, deficient making of priorities, insufficient specification, lost document, uninformed change to the specification and so on:

Catalogue of failures in the adaptations process for disabled boy. Maladministration arose as a result of the following. There was a 13-month delay from the occupational therapist's recommendation to the installation of a heightened bath for a boy, to give carers safe access. The relevant policy document did not refer to the system of prioritising adaptations, nor was there any guidance as to how to implement it. There was no record of the acceptance of the recommendation, nor any written confirmation sent to the occupational therapy service. The agreed adaptation was not described in sufficient detail. There was no convincing explanation about why the height of bath was not sorted out on the first installation. The key document appeared to have been lost. The recommended height of the bath had been changed by another officer on health and safety grounds, without proper discussion with the occupational therapist and possible appeal. Contrary to its own policy, the council did not seek written confirmation from the parents of their satisfaction with the work. This was maladministration (*West Lancashire DC 2005*).

Of course not all delay will necessarily constitute maladministration. Sometimes, sheer complexity or unexpected problems might make it unavoidable:

No maladministration: design and construction issues. An 18-month wait for major adaptations following assessment, including design and construction taking a year, was deemed by the local ombudsman not to be 'unreasonable delay' (*Ealing LBC 1993*). The ombudsman did not criticise a council for failing to predict construction, foundation and drainage problems; nor the council's inability to get the work finished quicker by a contractor (*Cumbria CC 1992*).

Disagreement causing delay: no maladministration. Similarly, the council was not at fault when delay occurred because of disagreement between the person and council officers, the seeking of advice by the applicant from a doctor, and an indication by the applicant, without good cause, that she wished for no further help because of the delays. In addition, it was not the council's responsibility that the person had bought a home which was difficult to modify (*Wirral MBC 1993e*).

Swift correction of error: no maladministration. When an initial financial assessment was incorrect but was followed quickly by the formal assessment which correctly worked out the applicant's potential contribution, there was no evidence that the applicants were substantially misled (*Wirral MBC 1994a*).

Defective lift: no maladministration. The fact that a lift obtained through a disabled facilities grant broke down 16 times, the door was defective, it marked the wall when in use and turned out to be too small was not in the circumstances maladministration, though the ombudsman had some sympathy for the complainants. However, in the same case, the amending of the original recommendation for a shower to a smaller model (because of cost) meant that the shower was too small for the shower chair used by the disabled person; in addition the shower leaked and the water temperature varied too quickly. The failure to ensure provision of a satisfactory shower was maladministration (*Leeds CC 1995*).

Furthermore, the service user has certain responsibilities, as the local ombudsman has pointed out:

Responsibility of service users. It is the responsibility of grant applicants to obtain estimates, choose surveyors, choose contractors, etc., a point made by the local ombudsman when people complain after things have gone wrong (e.g. *Hounslow LBC 1994*). The council's role has been described by the local ombudsman as being about the monitoring of adaptations proceeding by way of grant to ensure that public money is spent wisely and building regulations adhered to; its inspections are therefore to protect the public revenue and not grant recipients. It is the latter's responsibility to ensure that works are carried out to a high standard (*Newham LBC 1995*). However, if a council is offering its own agency services to facilitate the adaptation, then it clearly takes on more responsibility (*Leicester CC 1992, Leicester CC 1995*); but in any case it should at least make clear to people the responsibilities they are taking on in relation to a grant (*Hounslow LBC 1994*).

CHAPTER 17

National Health Service provision

KEY POINTS

COMMUNITY CARE AND THE NHS

Law, policy and practice governing the NHS appears to be increasingly important in community care. The reason for this is twofold. First, central government is pursuing a policy of 'care closer to home', that is providing health care in, or nearer to, people's own homes. Underlying and preceding this policy has been significant closure of hospital beds, wards and day hospitals – for older people generally, people with mental health problems and people with learning disabilities. Second, there appears to be a continuing and sizeable shift of what were once perceived to be NHS responsibilities over to local authorities. This takes place either through a re-designation by NHS bodies, such as primary care trusts, of health care as social care. Alternatively, the means are cruder still. Local NHS bodies simply refuse to continue to fund certain services, and local social services authorities are left to pick up some, if not all, of the pieces.

NHS PROVISION OF SERVICES

The NHS has a general duty which includes the provision of medical and nursing services as well as the prevention of illness, care of people who are ill, and aftercare for people who have been ill. The duty is indeed a general one only (towards the local population, but not towards individuals) and extends only to providing services 'necessary to meet all reasonable requirements'. The effect is that the duty is far from absolute and is carried out within the resources which NHS bodies have available and according to priorities which they set.

The law courts have generally, although not always, denied a remedy to applicants complaining about the rationing or withholding of services, and have avoided the sort of close scrutiny they have brought to bear in some other welfare fields such as the provision of housing, education and social care provided by local authorities. The NHS has been left by the courts with very considerable discretion to ration services in the light of limited resources.

In the past, the discretion was regularly checked by the health service ombudsman. However, by and large, NHS bodies have had more to fear from public outcry than from serious legal challenge. In the last few years, public protests around the country at the closure of wards, beds, community hospitals and day hospitals have been perhaps unprecedented. In addition, central government has fuelled expectations about the wider availability of treatments for NHS patients – and individual patients are it seems readier to launch legal challenges about the refusal to provide particular treatment. These two factors seem to be responsible for the upturn of legal cases against the NHS in the last few years. One consequence seems to have been that the law courts have begun to explore a little more closely ways of holding NHS bodies to account, on grounds other than a simple lack of resources. For instance, legal fault is sometimes found if the NHS has not consulted properly on the closure of local services, or if it is implementing legally irrational, or insufficiently flexible, rationing policies.

Nonetheless, for patients, the situation remains one of considerable uncertainty. Service provision can vary greatly from place to place, which means that what services people get can depend on where they live. Even within the same area, provision could lawfully be uneven from week to week and from month to month, depending on the resources and facilities available. Thus, not only will there many be escape routes (see 3.1) for the NHS in terms of restricting expenditure, but many of them will be lawful, since concrete obligations are so hard to find.

REGISTERED NURSING CARE

People in nursing homes are eligible to have a certain element of their stay, namely the registered nursing care element, paid for by the NHS. This is paid at a flat rate of £101 per week. This is to be distinguished from the situation where people in nursing homes have NHS continuing health care status and have the whole cost of their stay – the accommodation, board, personal care and nursing care – funded by the NHS at no cost to the residents.

NHS SERVICES PROVIDED IN CARE HOMES AND IN PEOPLE'S OWN HOMES

In principle, the NHS is responsible for providing a range of community health care services, to people in care homes and to people in their own homes.

In practice, however, provision tends to be highly variable; this flows largely from a lack of both resources and lack of legal entitlement to such services. This situation takes on a more serious aspect, in the wake of central government policy of care closer to, and in, people's own homes, together with the closure of many hospital beds. In principle, NHS resources should have been diverted significantly into the community in order to implement this policy; in practice this appears not to have happened to the degree necessary. In other words, many acute and community hospital beds have closed, without adequate community services being in place. This was one of the reasons identified for the disastrous lapses of care identified in 2007 by the Healthcare Commission at acute hospitals in Kent, associated with excessive bed occupancy and a shortage of both beds and staff.

HOSPITAL DISCHARGE

Hospital discharge is now subject, in respect of acute beds, to time limits under the Community Care (Delayed Discharges) Act 2003. If these are not adhered to then, in some circumstances, local social service authorities have to make payments to the NHS by way of reimbursement for the 'blocked bed'. Hospital discharge continues to be a fraught issue. On the one hand, is the understandable consideration that people should not, and generally do not wish to, remain in hospital unnecessarily long. On the other hand are the acute NHS Trusts that continue to discharge people prematurely and sometimes highly inappropriately. Even when people in principle may not need to remain in hospital, there may be an absence of services in the community to support them in their own homes or elsewhere.

NATIONAL SERVICE FRAMEWORKS

The Department of Health has published a number of national service frameworks that amount to guidance (rather than legislation) and apply to both the NHS and local authorities. Three of particular relevance to community care concern older people, mental health and long-term conditions.

17.1 NHS BASIC DUTIES AND RESOURCES

The main duties in the NHS Act 2006 that ultimately underlie the provision of service for individual people are as follows:

- The Secretary of State must continue the promotion in England of a comprehensive health service designed to secure improvement (a) in the physical and mental health of the people of England; (b) in the prevention of, diagnosis and treatment of illness. For that purpose, the Secretary of State must provide or secure the effective provision of services (s.1).
- The Secretary of State has the power (a) to provide such services as he or she considers appropriate for the discharge of any duty in the NHS Act 2006; (b) to do any other thing to facilitate, or which is conducive or incidental to, the discharge of such a duty (s.2).
- The Secretary of State must, to such extent as he or she 'considers necessary to meet all reasonable requirements', to provide:
  - hospital accommodation or other accommodation for the purpose of any service provided under the Act
  - medical, dental, ophthalmic, nursing and ambulance services
  - other services for the care of pregnant women, women who are breastfeeding and young children as he or she considers appropriate as part of the health service
  - other services or facilities for the prevention of illness, the care of people suffering from illness and the aftercare of people who have suffered from illness – such as he or she considers are appropriate as part of the health service
  - such other services or facilities as are required for the diagnosis and treatment of illness (s.3).

The above functions are exercisable, on behalf of the Secretary of State, by strategic health authorities and NHS primary care trusts (NHS Act 2006, s.7; SI 2002/2375).

The Act is vague. It does not contain a detailed list of services, such as continence services, community nursing, stoma care, palliative care, respite care, physiotherapy, speech and language therapy, physiotherapy, chiropody. Even in respect of those services which are mentioned, such as medical or nursing, the duties in ss.1 and 3 of the Act are anyway aimed only at the population in general. They have been characterised by the courts as target or general duties, barely amenable to enforcement by individual patients (*R v Inner London Education Authority, ex p Ali*). Duties of this type are to be contrasted with specific duties towards individual people that are to be found in some of the community care legislation (see section 5.1 above).

Accordingly, the NHS has a very wide discretion to make priorities and allocate resources locally. Such is this discretion that the general duty to provide services under s.3 of the NHS Act 2006 is sometimes seen, in respect of any particular service, to be in effect a power only. It is flimsy. Thus, legal challenges to the provision, or more accurately non-provision, of NHS services have been relatively few. This contrasts with the comparatively large volume of negligence cases brought against the NHS by service users who claim to have suffered harm as a result of carelessness in the provision of NHS services. This illustrates the point that it is legally 'safer' for the NHS to refuse to accept patients and to provide services at all, rather than to provide services but to a negligent standard (Brazier 1992, p.23).

17.2 GENERAL PRACTITIONERS

Community care policy guidance states that, as a matter of good practice, general practitioners (GPs) will wish to make a full contribution to community care assessments. It also reminds local authorities that GPs are not always best placed to assess on behalf of a local authority, since GPs have a personal duty and relationship with their patients; in which case, local authorities might wish other practitioners to act in that capacity (DH 1990, paras 3.47–48).

Under their contractual terms, GPs have to provide a consultation at the request of a person at least 75 years old who has not had such a consultation in the previous 12 months. The inquiries and examinations to be undertaken are such as appears to the GP to be appropriate in all the circumstances (SI 2004/291, schedule 6). A GP may demand or accept a fee from any statutory body for services rendered for the purpose of that body's statutory functions (schedule 5). In addition, GPs must refer patients for other services provided under the NHS Act 2006 (r.15); this would include not just health services but also community care services provided by local authorities under s.254 and schedule 20.

17.3 NHS LEGAL CASES AND SCARCE RESOURCES

One of the legal consequences of the general duties contained in ss.1 and 3 of the NHS Act 2006 is that the NHS has been highly successful in legally defending the non-provision of services – at least when it has argued a lack of resources as the reason.

This has become clear in a series of legal decisions over a period of some two decades, involving orthopaedic patients who had been waiting some years for treatment (*R v Secretary of State for Social Services, ex p Hincks*), children with heart conditions requiring operations (*R v Central Birmingham HA, ex p Collier; R v Central Birmingham HA, ex p Walker*), a child with leukaemia (*R v Cambridge Health Authority, ex p B*) and women wishing for fertility treatment (*R v Sheffield HA, ex p Seale*).

Lack of resources for orthopaedic treatment: an illusion to think the courts could interfere. Some people in Staffordshire who had been on a waiting list for NHS orthopaedic treatment for some years sought a declaration that the Secretary of State was not providing a comprehensive health service. The applicants had waited for periods longer than 'medically advisable'; the delay occurred because of a shortage of treatment facilities that was due partly to a decision not to build a new block on the grounds of cost. They claimed that the Secretary of State, regional health authority and area health authority had all breached their statutory duties under both s.1 and s.3 of the NHS Act 1977 (since superseded by the 2006 Act).

One of the judges (Lord Denning) stated that s.3 of the NHS Act 1977 did not impose an absolute duty, since it was inevitably governed by resources. Indeed, the only way it could be read was to supply extra words which did not actually appear in the Act at all. These were as follows (italics added): 'duty to provide throughout England and Wales, to such extent as he considers necessary to meet all reasonable requirements such as *can be provided within the resources available*'. He went on to point out that it 'cannot be supposed that the Secretary of State has to provide all the latest equipment [or] to provide everything that is asked for… That includes the numerous pills that people take nowadays: it cannot be said that he has to provide all these free for everybody.'

Another of the judges, sounding a cautionary note, added that he felt 'extremely sorry for the particular applicants in this case who have to wait a long time, not being emergency cases, for necessary surgery. They share that misfortune with thousands up and down the country. I only hope that they have not been encouraged to think that these proceedings offered any real prospects that this court could enhance the standards of the National Health Service, because any such encouragement would be based upon manifest illusion' (*R v Secretary of State for Social Services, ex p Hincks*).

Another high profile case was decided in similar fashion:

Refusing potentially lifesaving treatment for a child. A health authority refused to provide possibly lifesaving treatment for a ten-year-old child suffering from leukaemia. One of the grounds for the refusal was that the proposed treatment would not be an effective use of resources. The Court of Appeal, on the same day, overturned the High Court's decision that the health authority should think again.

On the question of resources, it stated that it was not for the law courts to take decisions about the optimum – that is, utilitarian – allocation of resources. It was 'common knowledge that health authorities cannot make ends meet. They cannot pay their nurses as much as they would like; they cannot provide all the treatments they would like; they cannot purchase all the extremely expensive equipment they would like… Difficult and agonising judgements have to be made as to how a limited budget is best allocated to the maximum advantage of the maximum number of patients. That is not a judgement which the court can make.'

In addition, the court dismissed the argument that if the health authority had money in the bank which had not been spent, 'then they would be acting in plain breach of their statutory duty if they did not procure this treatment'. Indeed, 'it would be totally unrealistic to require the Authority to come to the court with its accounts and seek to demonstrate that if this treatment were provided for B then there would be a patient, C, who would have to go without treatment. No major Authority could run its financial affairs in a way which would permit such a demonstration' (*R v Cambridgeshire HA, ex p B*).

The chief reason for the failure of such cases is that the courts are generally (and understand-ably) not prepared to interfere with how the NHS allocates resources. This principle applies even to mental health and secure beds:

Bed required on secure unit: NHS under no obligation even to use best endeavours. A man had been given 'leave' under s.17 of the Mental Health Act 1983 by his responsible medical offi-cer (RMO), subject to conditions – namely a bed on a medium secure unit. The courts ruled that, since the funding fell to be provided by an NHS trust under s.3 of the NHS Act 1977 (now 2006), it still re-mained a question of the establishing priorities. The Secretary of State and the NHS trust had no obli-gation even to use their best endeavours to give effect to the decision of the RMO (*R(K) v West London Mental Health Trust*).

The courts may require in principle that reasons be given for decisions about the allocation of resources and services, but are unlikely to make that requirement onerous, certainly not in the case of the Secretary of State for Health:

Giving reasons for size of village community for people with learning disabilities. A dis-pute arose about the size of a village community that was to be created on the site of a long-stay hos-pital for people with severe learning disabilities, with additional physical disabilities. The Secretary of State ruled on the smaller size. She was challenged on the adequacy of her reasons. These seemed to boil down to the statement that she had concluded that the smaller size would take account of the needs of the residents and reflected government policy. The court found that this was sufficient (*R (Heimsath) v Secretary of State for the Home Department*).

The health service ombudsman, like the courts, will generally not tackle the matter of resources directly, but might nevertheless in some circumstances find fault in relation to resource-related matters. For instance, he has criticised a two-year wait for an assessment at a hearing clinic; and also the fact that the trust had not developed a coherent strategy for trying to remedy such long waits for this service (*Southampton University Hospitals NHS Trust 2003*).

The very general scope of s.3 of the 2006 Act not only allows extensive non-provision of services, but conversely allows extensive provision in both breadth and depth. For instance, in one case it was queried whether s.3, and in particular the word 'facilities' in it could cover pro-vision of an advice and assistance service about state benefits for people with mental health problems. The question was whether the word could cover not just accommodation, plant and other means but also human beings. The court held that it could (*R(Keating) v Cardiff Local Health Board*).

17.3.1 TREATMENT IN EUROPE AND REIMBURSEMENT

An alternative legal avenue has more recently been explored. This was to see whether, in case of undue delay in the provision of NHS services, patients who sought the required treatment in other European Community countries would then be entitled to reimbursement from the NHS. (Any such entitlement would not arise directly under the NHS Act 2006, but under article 22 of Council Regulation 1407/71 and a.49 of the European Community Treaty.) This was explored in the case of a woman who was waiting for a hip operation on the NHS in Bedford. Fed up, she instead made her own arrangements, went to France, had the operation carried out and then sought reimbursement from the NHS (*R(Watts) v Bedford Primary Care*

Trust). Given the significant implications of the case, the Court of Appeal referred the matter to the European Court of Justice.

The European Court stated that if a person waited for treatment on a waiting list unacceptably long (having regard to an objective medical assessment), then the NHS could not refuse authorisation of the treatment in another European Community country and reimbursement of the cost (*R(Watts) v Bedford Primary Care Trust*).

Of course this left open the all important question as to the circumstances in which an 'objective' medical assessment would conclude that the waiting time 'appeared to exceed an acceptable time'. In a subsequent case, the courts confirmed that it was the patient, and not the medical service provider, that would have to make the claim against the NHS. In addition, any liability would depend on whether the NHS commissioned the treatment, whether it would have commissioned it, whether there was undue delay, whether the treatment took place in the United Kingdom or elsewhere (*European Surgeries v Cambridgeshire PCT*).

The Department of Health has issued guidance to NHS commissioners, underlining that they should have systems for considering authorisation for patients to receive treatment abroad; that they can refuse to pay for health care abroad that they do not offer in their locality; that a patient is legally entitled to go elsewhere for treatment that the NHS should offer but for which there is undue delay; and that they are only obliged to fund up to the cost of the treatment in the United Kingdom (the patient having to pay the extra) (DH 2007g).

17.4 NHS LEGAL CHALLENGES ON GROUNDS OTHER THAN RESOURCES

The NHS has sometimes been legally challenged successfully, when the ground is not simply lack of resources.

For instance, central government guidance must be properly taken account of. A failure to do so in relation to drug treatment for multiple sclerosis meant that the health authority had acted unlawfully (*R v North Derbyshire Health Authority, ex p Fisher*).

In another court case, a health authority misinterpreted its responsibilities to provide continuing health care services under the NHS Act 1977 (now superseded by the NHS Act 2006). It expected the local authority to act unlawfully by providing a level of nursing service that was beyond the legal power of a local authority to provide (*R v North and East Devon HA, ex p Coughlan*). In the same case, the health authority acted unlawfully in respect of a breach of promise and the dashing of people's legitimate expectations:

Legitimate expectation. The breaking of an explicit promise to a disabled person constituted, without an overriding reason, a breach of legitimate expectations. The claimant, together with other patients, had received an explicit promise that when she moved into a specialist residential unit for disabled people, she could remain there for life. A few years later, the health authority tried to close the unit. The proposed closure was held to be unlawful (*R v North and East Devon HA, ex p Coughlan*).

Discrimination has sometimes been argued as a ground of challenge. For instance, the following case referred to human rights:

Human rights. In one case, about potential discrimination rather than lack of resources, the court did warn against the dangers of a breach of human rights. This was in the context of ensuring that a man with learning disabilities (and mentally incapable of giving or withholding consent) was not given less satisfactory treatment than a person who understood the risks, pain and discomfort of major surgery: 'To act in any other way would be contrary to the rights of a mentally incapacitated patient both under our domestic law and under the European Convention' (*An Hospital NHS Trust v S*).

Likewise, discrimination was the crux in a case about treatment for Alzheimer's disease:

Discrimination in drug treatment. The National Institute for Health and Clinical Evidence (NICE) issued guidance on the use of acetylcholinesterase inhibitors for treatment of people with Alzheimer's disease. The only successful ground of challenge related to discrimination. This was that the guidance had not sufficiently addressed the question of atypical groups. No proper consideration had been given to NICE's duties as a public authority to promote equal opportunities and to have due regard to the need to eliminate discrimination under s.49 of the Disability Discrimination Act 1995 (*Eisai Ltd v National Institute for Health and Clinical Excellence*).

The NHS is also regularly challenged, sometimes successfully, over defects in local consultations, when it is proposing to change or cut back services (see below).

17.4.1 BLANKET NHS POLICIES

One ground of challenge that has borne some fruit concerns the imposition of blanket, or rigid policies by the NHS. One of the common law principles applied by the law courts in judicial review cases is that public bodies should not 'fetter their discretion', that is, not blindly apply policies that are incapable of flexibility in at least exceptional cases:

Fettering discretion: blanket NHS policy about gender reassignment surgery. When a health authority applied a policy so rigidly such that it fettered its discretion, the Court of Appeal found that it had acted unlawfully. The health authority stated in one breath that exceptions could be made, but in another that the treatment in question, gender reassignment surgery, could never be clinically justified. Thus a policy would not be lawful unless it 'genuinely recognises the possibility of there being an overriding clinical need and requires each request for treatment to be considered on its individual merits'. This meant that there was therefore no genuine possibility of an exception; it was over-rigid application of a blanket policy (*R v North West Lancashire Health Authority, ex p G, A and D*).

The courts have started to explore such blanket policies with more frequency. Thus, if a policy sets out the types of exception to be made and for which funding should be made available, non-adherence to the exceptions policy might be unlawful:

Not following the policy on exceptions to the prohibition on treatment for cancer with particular drug. For instance, when a woman was denied treatment for cancer the decision was ruled unlawful on the following grounds: (a) the doctor concerned had raised an irrelevant question about use of the drug for this patient; (b) there were no other treatments available for the woman; (c) the funding Panel had not taken account of the slim but important chance that the treatment could significantly prolong the woman's life; (d) on any fair minded view of the 'exceptionality criteria' in the primary care trust's policy, her case was exceptional (*R(Otley) v Barking and Dagenham NHS Primary Care Trust*).

Thus, the NHS body must take into account relevant factors in the individual case, before deciding whether or not to make an exception. So when a primary care trust failed to consider whether a trial period for taking a cancer drug should be considered, the court gave permission for the patient to bring a judicial review case (*R(Gordon) v Bromley NHS PCT*). A policy that restricts or denies treatment, subject to exceptions, is rational, so long as it envisages the circumstances constituting a possible exception:

Irrational policy on drug treatment for cancer. An NHS primary care trust had a policy of not funding cancer with a particular non-licensed drug (Herceptin) unless there were exceptional clinical or personal circumstances. The policy was not based on the fact that the drug was unlicensed, nor was it based on resource constraints within the trust. The court found the policy to be irrational. This was essentially for two reasons.

First, there was no rational basis for making clinical distinctions within the potentially eligible group of patients, and – once it was clear that the PCT had decided that cost was irrelevant – the 'only reasonable approach was to focus on the patient's clinical needs and fund patients within the eligible group who were properly prescribed Herceptin by their physician.'

Second, had resource constraints been relevant, taking account of personal circumstances might have been rational – for instance, funding treatment for a woman with a disabled child, but not for a woman in different circumstances. However, remove the resources issue – as the PCT claimed to have done – and where clinical needs are equal, the court found that 'discrimination between patients in the same eligible group cannot be justified on the basis of personal characteristics not based on healthcare'.

The court would not order the treatment. Instead it was now for the PCT to reconsider and reformulate a lawful policy (*R(Rogers) v Swindon Primary Care Trust*).

The health service ombudsman also will consider if blanket polices have been imposed and whether there was a genuine mechanism to consider exceptions, as in the following cases concerning powered wheelchairs, breast reduction, homoeopathic treatment and growth hormone treatment.

Excessively rigid policies. The health service ombudsman has found maladministration when the NHS had no genuine mechanism for considering whether to make exceptions in terms of provision of electrically powered indoor and outdoor wheelchairs (*Epsom and St Helier NHS Trust 2001*).

Likewise when a health authority applied an over-restrictive – indeed arguably 'perverse and wholly unreasonable' – policy on breast reduction surgery. The woman had a spinal disorder and back pain, but had been refused surgery as a matter of policy, because the policy only allowed such surgery for psychiatric morbidity. This refusal was despite support for the surgery from her GP, consultant and surgeon (*North Essex HA 2001*).

A policy not to fund homoeopathic treatment was not objectionable; but the policy was adopted without sufficient thought as to whether there might be circumstances that could justify departure from it. The patient in question had a chronic skin disease that had previously responded to homoeopathic treatment, when other treatments had failed. Although the health authority's extra-contractual referral panel did review the case, it was not clear what considerations it took into account, and no clear indication as to what sort of circumstances might have led to an exception being made (*East Sussex, Brighton and Hove Health Authority 1999*). The health service ombudsman made similar objections in the case of non-provision of growth hormone treatment for a woman whose consultant had recommended it. The request was refused because there were no exceptional circumstances; but the health authority could shed no light on what might constitute exceptional circumstances (*North Essex HA 2003*).

17.5 CONSULTATION BY NHS BODIES ABOUT CHANGES AND CUTS TO SERVICES

In the light of changes, reconfigurations and closures of services, the NHS may well find itself challenged on the procedural ground that it has failed properly to consult. Apart from any common law obligation to consult, a legal framework for consultation is also in place. Inevitably, when NHS bodies attempt to push through changes and cuts to services too quickly, they go through the motions only of consultation, and rapidly attract local ire. Sometimes this results in legal cases.

In addition to the cases covered below, a number of others in both health and social care, have revolved around the duties to consult with, and to assess the needs of, residents of care homes or patients of hospitals before the closure of such homes or hospital beds (see 5.2.1.6).

17.5.1 HEALTH OVERVIEW AND SCRUTINY COMMITTEES

Local health overview and scrutiny committees have an important role in scrutinising and reviewing local health service provision. The committees are made up of local councillors, elected representatives. This is particularly important, given that the NHS trust and primary care trust boards are composed of members who are not elected and whose accountability is not to the local population but to the remote Secretary of State for Health.

These committees have the power to make referrals to the Secretary of State, who in turn has the power to appoint an Independent Reconfiguration Panel to investigate and review local NHS proposals. Up to July 2007, this power was little exercised by the Secretary of State, and the process had fallen into disrepute. A new Secretary of State began from that time to increase the involvement of the Panel.

17.5.1.1 Health overview and scrutiny committees: role

A local authority overview and scrutiny committee has the power to review and scrutinise any matter relating to the planning, provision and operation of health services within its area. It may make reports and recommendations to local NHS bodies.

In addition, when a local NHS body is considering any proposal – for a 'substantial development of the health service' in the area of a local authority, or for a 'substantial variation in the provision of such a service' – it must consult the overview and scrutiny committee. This duty does not apply if the NHS body is satisfied that a decision must be taken without consultation because of a risk to the safety or welfare of patients or staff. However, even then, the NHS body must notify the overview and scrutiny committee about the decision and why consultation has not taken place. If the committee is not satisfied that the consultation has been adequate or adequate reasons given for not consulting, then it may report this to the Secretary of State. The latter may, in turn, require the local NHS body to carry out such consultation or further consultation.

If, alternatively, the committee considers that the proposal will not be in the best interests of the health service in the local authority's area, it may report to the Secretary of State. The latter may make a final decision on the proposal, and require the local NHS body to take, or desist from such, action as the Secretary of State my direct (NHS Act 2006, s.244, and SI

2002/3048, and Local Government Act 2000, s.21 which gives local authorities a power for overview and scrutiny committee to scrutinise health services).

Guidance states that the following should be taken into account in considering whether the proposal is about 'substantial development': changes in accessibility of services (e.g. changes on a particular site or opening times for a particular clinic), the impact of proposals on the wider community (including economic, transport, regeneration), patients affected, methods of service delivery (eg. from hospital to community-based settings) (Department of Health 2003m, para 10.6.3).

Following referral by scrutiny committees to the Secretary of State, the latter will consider whether to refer the matter for review by the Independent Reconfiguration Panel (IRP), which is an advisory, non-departmental body. The IRP will take up cases only when all other options for local resolution have been explored.

17.6 PUBLIC AND PATIENT INVOLVEMENT

A further safeguard in the NHS decision-making process, beyond overview and scrutiny committees, is public involvement more generally. This includes a duty on NHS bodies to consult with the public.

Following the abolition of community health councils in 2003, public and patient and involvement forums (PPIFs) were created.

In addition, NHS bodies have a duty in respect of the planning of the provision of services, developing and considering proposals for the changes in the way services are provided, and decisions to be made by the NHS body affecting the operation of those services. The duty is to make arrangements to secure that people, to whom those services are being or may be provided, are involved (whether through being consulted or provided with information or in other ways) in such changes – either directly or through representatives (NHS Act 2006, s.242).

This duty was arguably watered down from its previous from, by legislative amendment through s.233 of the Local Government and Public Involvement in Health Act 2007. Previously, it stated that people had to be involved in and consulted on changes. Now the Act makes quite explicit that the duty could be discharged simply by the provision of information. In addition, the duty now only applies if the proposal under consideration would have an impact on the manner in which services are delivered to users of health services or on the range of health services available. Third, the reference to the delivery of services is to 'delivery at the point when they are received by users'. These provisos about the delivery of services appears to be in response to the case of *Smith v North Eastern Derbyshire PCT*, in which the courts held that the duty of consultation applied when it was proposed to run general practitioner services through a private company.

The House of Commons Health Committee referred to the concern that the Department of Health's real aim was to undermine the case law (under the previous version of the legislation), some of which had been successful. It pointed out that, that far from encouraging such cases to ensure such consultation takes place, the Department of Health had taken the lead in legally supporting local NHS bodies attempting to avoid consultation when reconfiguring services (HCHC 2007, chapter 5).

In this light, it is something of an irony that a Department of Health briefing issued in December 2007 about these legislative changes should refer to the importance of continuous and meaningful engagement with public and patients and to the consequences of not doing so. These include lack of understanding of local views, poor commissioning decisions, services that fail to meet local needs, a disillusioned and cynical local population with little trust in the NHS, weak and strained partnerships with local organisations (DH 2007l).

Regulations may also be made placing a duty on strategic health authorities to involve health service users in prescribed matters.

SHAs and PCTs must prepare a report on the consultation carried out before it makes commissioning decisions and on the influence that the results of the consultation had on its decisions (NHS Act 2006, ss.17A and 24A).

17.6.1 PATIENT INVOLVEMENT GROUPS

In 2008, legislation replaced PPIFs with Local Involvement Networks (LINKs). The House of Commons Health Committee advised against this change, fearing that it was more change for the sake of change, and yet one more tokenistic gesture on the part of the NHS (HCSC 2007, pp.3–5).

The legislation places a duty on the local authority to contract locally for the involvement of people in the commissioning, provision and scrutiny of local health and social care services (SI 2008/528). This will mean particular bodies undertaking this function and being referred to as a local involvement network (LINK), although the legislation does not use this name.

The legislation provides for regulations to be made placing a duty on service providers to respond to requests by a LINK for information, to deal with reports or recommendations from the LINK. Regulations have also been made making provision for service providers to allow access to premises owned by the service provider. Service providers are defined as: an NHS trust, an NHS foundation trust, a primary care trust, a local authority or any other pre-scribed body. The last category has been prescribed, in regulations, as people providing primary care, dental, ophthalmic and pharmaceutical services under the NHS Act 2006 (SI 2008/915). A major criticism of this is that increasingly health and social care provision is being made through independent providers, yet LINKS will not have the power to obtain information or to enter and inspect premises where health and social care services are provided.

If a LINK makes a referral to an overview and scrutiny committee about social care matters, the committee must acknowledge the referral, keep the referrer informed and decide whether to exercise any of its powers (Local Government and Public Involvement in Health Act 2007, ss.221–226, 230–231).

17.6.2 PUBLIC AND PATIENT INVOLVEMENT: POLICY AND PRACTICE

The general principle of public and patient involvement has been trumpeted to a considerable extent by government policy documents and guidance.

For instance, in 1999, it was important that 'public and patient partnership is genuine, not token, so that people at a local and national level, are fully involved in decisions both on their own care and the way in which services are provided' (DH 1999c, p.1).

In 2003, the government passed s.11 of the Health and Social Care Act (now superseded) to 'strengthen accountability to patients and the public and make that there is transparency and openness in decision-making procedures'. Discussion had to start 'before minds have been made up', and patients and the public had a 'central role as partners with the NHS' (DH 2003m, pp.2,7). One consequence would be that 'trust is built between communities and the health service' (DH 2003n, p.x).

Despite all this, the House of Commons Health Committee in 2007 identified that the policy was by no means being translated into practice. It referred to a weakening of s.11 by the Local Government and Public Involvement in Health Act 2007. It noted also that people 'feel that they are consulted after decisions have been made... Consultations in which a large proportion of the public reject plans which go ahead anyway must not continue to happen.' It noted that NHS bodies often sought to avoid consultation under s.11, and were supported in this by the Department of Health (HCHC 2007, p.5).

17.7 LEGAL CASES ON CONSULTATION

In the light of extensive cutbacks to health services from 2005 onwards, the duty to involve and consult with the public under s.242 of the NHS Act 2006 (formerly s.11 of the Health and Social Care Act 2001) has been subjected to judicial scrutiny. The duty has been held to be wide in scope, although the courts have also indicated a reluctance to hear too many such cases:

Independent Sector Treatment Centre: consultation. A primary care trust was seeking to set up an Independent Sector Treatment Centre contract to deliver certain local health services. It argued that a s.11 duty had not arisen because the arrangements were being made by the Department of Health at central government level, to whom the s.11 duty did not apply.

Mere involvement or consultation? First, use 'of different terms, involvement and consultation, only makes sense if something less than consultation may be appropriate in certain circumstances. The two concepts of involvement and consultation reflect the different stages at which the obligation may be triggered... Whether mere involvement or something more, namely [full] consultation...is required, will depend upon the circumstances...'. Thus, in some circumstances, no more than the giving of information will be required. This can be easily achieved by providing that to an Overview and Scrutiny Committee or a Public and Patient Involvement Forum (PPIF).

Full consultation: key principles. Second, full consultation should proceed upon well-established principles. The consultation must be undertaken at a time when the proposals are still at a formative stage. Sufficient reasons must be provided for particular proposals so as to permit those consulted to give intelligent consideration and response. Adequate time must be given. The product of consultation must be conscientiously taken into account.

Extensive obligation on primary care trust. Third, the s.11 duty could arise for the PCT, because although it was not responsible for making the decision, the decision nevertheless affected the services it (the PCT) was providing). Department of Health advice to the contrary was wrong.

Limited benefit of judicial review. Fourth, the court felt that in cases where the obligation under s.11 may be limited, little will be achieved in bringing proceedings for judicial review. Even though it had been established that the PCT should have shared information and that the Department of Health's advice was wrong, the court was not prepared to even to make a declaration. What had been done could not be undone.

The result in the case had been reached 'at the cost of a disproportionate amount of time and energy, exacerbated by the burden of files containing at least one thousand documents; the costs might have been better deployed in securing and maintaining health services within the region concerned. Public law falls into disrepute if it causes an unnecessary diversion of work and resources. It is dispiriting that we can discern little if any benefit to those in Avon, Gloucestershire and Wiltshire at having established that the Department erred in law in its views as to s.11' (*R(Fudge) v South West Strategic Health Authority*).

Nonetheless, the NHS sometimes goes to considerable lengths to avoid its obligations under what is now s.242 of the NHS Act 2006 (formerly s.11 of the Health and Social Care Act 2001), and it is certainly understandable that local people may feel obliged to turn to the courts. One argument used by the NHS not infrequently is to claim urgency and patient welfare as a reason not to consult. In the following case, such an argument was shown to be misguided and the court emphasised the importance of the duty of consultation. Yet, still, the court would not give the substantive remedy of ordering a reopening of the closed beds. Nor did it accept that the NHS body had acted in bad faith or taken the decision on financial grounds (notwithstanding a £12 million deficit):

Closing down rehabilitation beds on grounds of urgency and safety. An NHS trust closed down rehabilitation wards without first consulting.

History of planning closure. First, it transpired that the NHS trust had been considering closing the wards of Altrincham hospital, effectively a community hospital, for some time, but had taken no steps to conduct a public consultation.

Misinformation and defective premiss in PCT-commissioned report. Second, the PCT had commissioned a report from a professor. He had drawn attention to safety issues because of a lack of consultant cover. However, this deficiency affected patients with acute needs who were referred to the wards. In fact the wards were meant to be for non-acute rehabilitative care only. The professor had been misinformed by the PCT about the function of the wards. As the court pointed out, the position could have been stabilised whilst the trust consulted, by restricting the patients being referred from the district general hospital, to that category of patient for which the wards were intended.

High importance of consultation duty. The court further stated that the s.11 (Health and Social Care Act 2001) duty to consult was of 'high importance [now s.242 of the NHS Act 2006]. The public expect to be involved in decisions by healthcare bodies, particularly when the issues involved are contentious as they clearly were'.

Refusal of court to make substantial order to reopen beds; refusal to accept bad faith. However, the court refused to reorder the reopening of the wards, and the trust undertook to consult publicly. The court also did not accept that the trust had acted in bad faith; apart from anything else, the allegation had never been particularised as it should have been. Nor did the court accept that the closure decision had been made on financial, rather than clinical safety, grounds – notwithstanding the trust's deficit of some £12.5 million (*R(Morris) v Trafford Healthcare NHS Trust*).

This case was by no means the first in which the NHS body was tempted artificially to create an issue of urgency and then attempt to evade responsibilities of consultation. For instance, in an older case about closure of a community hospital at Lynton in Devon, such urgency was argued not on health and safety but on financial grounds:

Delaying announcements until it is too late to consult. The health authority argued that finances had suddenly become so pressing that it could not consult before temporarily closing the community hospital. Yet, the judge pointed out that health authority discussed closing the hospital at least three months – before the decision eventually was taken without consultation three months later. The authority suggested that because of the pressures, consultation would have been pointless or created anxiety. The court disagreed, stating that if this argument 'was correct, a belief that consultation was pointless or would merely provoke anxiety might lead a health authority to delay announcing a decision until it was too late to consult'. The judge found against the health authority, which was ordered to consult, despite the inconvenience this would cause and the obstruction to its making of urgent financial savings (*R v North and East Devon Health Authority, ex p Pow*).

The *Pow* case was also notable, because the proposed closure was only 'temporary', but the court was still clear that it represented a 'substantial variation' in service. This is an important point; years later, evidence to the House of Commons Health Committee was that NHS bodies sometimes attempt to avoid consultations by a series of temporary, small scale cuts to services over a period of time. Collectively they may result in the effective closure of a service, with no consultation or public or patient involvement – as pointed out in evidence to the House of Commons Health Committee:

Closure of services by stealth by NHS trusts wishing to avoid scrutiny. 'In many cases, where Trusts are short of money, they will run down the staffing levels so that the only safe step they can take is to close a ward or a service. Such steps are frequently taken without patients being involved in the decisions. Once such services have been closed, albeit on a supposedly temporary basis, they very rarely reopen and the decline takes place without any patient involvement as to the appropriateness of the change. This is seen by many NHS Trusts as a useful device for avoiding their responsibilities to involve patients and public' (HCHC 2007, p.75, evidence given by Richard Stein).

Second, in the *Pow* case, the health authority argued that, because the gist of local opposition to closure was already known, there would be no point in further consultation. Again, the court disagreed, noting that 'the mere fact that the grounds of opposition are already known or that it is well understood that the opposition is widespread and deeply felt does not mean that there is no room for a process of consultation whereby not just opposition but also the offer of alternative solutions is advanced'.

In a further case, the Court of Appeal again emphasised the importance of consultation, this time in relation to a proposal to contract out local general practitioner services:

General practitioner services: contracting out and consultation. A primary care trust attempted to avoid s.11 obligations to consult, when it controversially set about replacing local general practitioners with a large company, United Health Europe Ltd (UHE), to run local general practitioner services.

The parish council had written to the PCT, expressing its concern about the importance of a 'personal approach' in the area, which had high levels of social deprivation, and that the appointment of UHE was one more step toward privatisation of the NHS. The PCT had not responded to letters from the parish council.

Wide scope of s.11: 'reprovision' enough to trigger duty. The PCT argued that s.11 was not triggered because it was merely 'reprovision' of services. The judge was in no doubt that the duty did arise, since virtually any decision made by the PCT in connection with health services is capable of coming within s.11. The PCT then argued that it had, after all, complied with s.11 because (a) a member of the local Patients' Participation Group had sat on the interviewing panel, and (b) a meeting with this group had been held. However, those attending the meeting were subject to confidentiality; this could hardly qualify as public involvement or consultation. Furthermore, the letters from the parish council had not been answered.

Burden on PPIF to bring judicial review proceedings. However, the judge found that the claimant should have approached the local PPIF and persuaded it to intervene; it could then have brought a judicial review case if the PCT had not responded. In any case, he believed the PCT would not have reached a different decision even had the claimant's views been received – so he refused to give a relief (a remedy) to the claimant.

Latter day consultation insufficient. The Court of Appeal agreed that s.11 had been breached but held that the judge was wrong not to grant relief. It was the PCT's duty to consult with the PPIF, not the claimant's. It had failed to do so. The evidence was that the PCT had conducted the tender according to their understanding of local needs, but this understanding was not informed by proper statutory involvement and consultation with patients. The PCT was arguing that the court need not intervene because it would involve the PPIF in its negotiations with UHE, and that this would be an adequate cure for its breach of duty. The court was not impressed by this talk of 'latter day consultation'; it characterised the PCT's argument as 'trying to shut the stable door when the horse has bolted to the meadow'. It believed that had the s.11 duty been performed, the PCT might have negotiated with a different bidder.

Consultation: substance, not mere form. The court felt that the matter was one of substance, rather then mere form, but that in any case it was 'a field in which appearance is generally thought to matter' (*Smith v North Eastern Derbyshire PCT*).

When the National Institute for Clinical Excellence (NICE) consulted about the use by the NHS of drugs with which to treat Alzheimer's disease, it went wrong on two main grounds. First, the High Court held that, when reaching its decision, it had failed to take into account its obligations to promote equality of opportunity under the Disability Discrimination Act 1995 and the Race Relations Act 1976. This was in respect of people whose first language was not English or people with particular language problems. The NICE had relied on what is known as the 'mini mental state examination' (MMSE) as an indicator of severity, which in turn would determine when drugs should be prescribed. Second, the Court of Appeal went on to find a further flaw; procedural fairness was not achieved because the NICE provided a 'read-only' version of an economic model. For consultees to test out the NICE's claims, and so respond to the consultation by making informed representations, an 'executable' version was needed (*Eisai v National Institute for Clinical Excellence*).

17.8 NHS DIRECTIONS AND GUIDANCE

Directions issued to the NHS, though not legislation, will in effect impose a duty; this will be in contrast with guidance that would have merely to be taken account of but not necessarily followed (*R v North Derbyshire HA, ex p Fisher*). The courts have stated that directions should be clearly labelled as such, although it might still be possible to find a direction contained in guidance – if it was expressed in sufficiently forceful language (*R v Secretary of State for Health, ex p Manchester Local Committee*). For instance, two sets of directions have been issued in respect of NHS continuing health care (see 18.2 below).

Directions can be issued under ss.8, 15, 78, 272 and 273 of the NHS Act 2006.

17.9 REGISTERED NURSING CARE

People in nursing homes who are not eligible for NHS continuing health care (see Chapter 18) will be eligible to have some of their fee paid by the NHS (£101.00 flat rate) to cover the registered nursing care component (RNCC) of their stay. The basic rules are set out in directions (see below). The framework emphasises that this RNCC banding is not relevant to, and should not influence, the decision about a person's eligibility for NHS continuing health care (DH 2007a, annex D). A decision about NHS continuing health care should be made before, and separate from, a decision about eligibility for registered nursing care component.

Practice guidance clarifies. It makes a number of key points. First, the decision about such NHS-funded nursing care 'should be clearly distinct' from the NHS continuing health care decision. Second, some people's needs in a nursing home may require 'additional NHS services over and above the provision of registered nursing care. In such cases, the PCT needs to identify the necessary services and arrange the provision and funding of those services' (DH 2007f, paras 24, 37).

Guidance from the Association of Directors of Adult Social Services (ADASS) points out that some people will require more NHS funding than the flat rate in a nursing home and that sometimes this will relate just to additional registered nursing care, never mind other health services (ADASS 2007, pp.6–7). The ADASS document is envisaging registered nursing payments made by NHS primary care trusts beyond the flat rate.

A challenge to a decision about NHS-funded nursing care in a care home can be made by the same review process as for NHS continuing health care (DH 2007a, paras 90–91).

17.9.1 NHS (NURSING CARE IN RESIDENTIAL ACCOMMODATION) (ENGLAND) DIRECTIONS 2007

The directions on registered nursing care complement two other sets of directions about NHS continuing health care (see 18.2). They state:

- **(nursing needs in a care home)** where it appears to a PCT that a person in a care home providing nursing may require nursing care in a care home, then it shall carry out an assessment of his or need for nursing care (unless the person is receiving NHS continuing health care)
- **(continuing care assessment first)** before carrying out that assessment, the PCT shall consider whether its duty under the responsibilities directions (see above) is engaged and, if so, it must comply with that duty before carrying out an assessment of a person's need for nursing care
- **(then nursing care assessment)** if the person has been assessed as not eligible for NHS continuing health care, the PCT shall, where reasonably practicable, use that assessment to determine whether the person needs nursing care

- **(flat rate to care home)** if the PCT determines that the person does need nursing care, it shall pay the flat rate (£101.00) to the care home
- **(urgency)** in care of urgency, there is nothing to stop a PCT from temporarily providing nursing care to a person without having carried an assessment (DH 2007q).

The above sets of directions should mean that decision-making is in practice reasonably formal and transparent, something that the health service ombudsman has in the past found to be lacking – and contributing to the muddle between NHS continuing health care and registered nursing care:

Inadequate decision-making process. The health service ombudsman has found fault when a continuing care decision was taken without sufficient explanation being given (*West Kent HA 2001*); or when a district nurse simply decided that a woman, who had had a foot amputated as a result of diabetes, and then suffered a stroke, was not eligible for continuing care, without telling the family anything about continuing care – and the family was not given any information about the financial consequences of the nursing home placement (*Central Manchester PCT 2003*).

The ombudsman has also expressed concern about decision-making of the following type. A woman was assessed as being within the high band of registered nursing care, rather than continuing care. She was diagnosed with epilepsy, anaemia, contractures and fractures of her left arm and leg due to falls, and frequent urinary tract infections that made her confused and agitated. No evidence or rationale was presented to support the decision; only nine months later did the primary care trust give her husband a copy of the eligibility criteria against which his wife had been assessed. The trust undertook to 're-review' the case in June 2004, but did not do so until October 2004; the decision remained unchanged; the husband and daughter were told that they were not entitled to be present at the review panel meeting (HSO 2004b, para 20).

17.10 COMMUNITY HEALTH SERVICES IN CARE HOMES AND PEOPLE'S OWN HOMES

Department of Health guidance covers the provision of community services generally, as well as NHS continuing health care. For example, it states that residents of care homes, whether or not providing nursing, should have access to professional advice about incontinence, as well as incontinence products (DH 2007f, paras 42–43).

The guidance states that chiropody services and other therapies (such as physiotherapy, occupational therapy, speech and language therapy, podiatry) should be made available on a similar basis to their provision in other settings (such as for people in their own home). The guidance elucidates: 'Where such NHS services are not provided, or where individuals choose to pay a care home providing nursing care for these services that it is willing to provide, the NHS has no obligation to provide those services' (DH 2007f, para 44).

This is blunt; basically it is confirming that people do not have a right to receive these services from the NHS. Government health policy is to provide more care and treatment in the community and closer to people's homes, by way of diverting patients away from acute hospitals (Secretary of State for Health 2006). The guidance about the lack of obligation to provide community services is therefore unpromising for the policy. The sheer vagueness of this sort of guidance effectively means that the courts and the health service ombudsman can apparently do little, even in the face of clearly inadequate provision. For instance:

Lack of speech therapy for a child. The health service ombudsman investigated a complaint about delayed and intermittent speech therapy provided by a health authority for a two-and-a-half-year-old child with severe communication difficulties. The ombudsman accepted the health authority's position. This was that, although the speech therapy service was understaffed and under-funded by national and regional norms, the health authority was well aware of and concerned about the situation. The 'HA have to balance the needs of the STS against other services and I am aware, from other investigations, of the problems health authorities face in deciding between competing demands. The HA is vested with the discretion to decide how to allocate its resources…and the legislation which governs my work does not permit me to question such a decision unless I find evidence of maladministration in the way it was reached' (HSO W.783/85–86).

Nevertheless, even absent such absolute entitlements, the health service ombudsman might still find fault with the manner in which a decision not to provide a service is made, if not with the principle of non-provision itself:

Withdrawal of chiropody services. A woman received a regular home visiting chiropody service, involving dressing her feet and cutting her nails. At what she believed was a routine appointment, she was assessed that she was no longer eligible for home visits; she would no longer have her feet dressed, and the only service would be toenail cutting at four-monthly intervals. However, she was not told this; she only found out when she rang up the trust when the chiropodist failed to arrive on the next agreed date. The ombudsman also criticised generally the lack of system for informing patients of the planned review of chiropody services and possibility of withdrawal of service; and also that there were no agreed criteria for judging which patients would be eligible and which would not be (*Thames Gateway NHS Trust 2001*).

17.11 DISCHARGE OF PEOPLE FROM HOSPITAL

Two main issues seem to arise around hospital discharge. The first concerns the decision in principle about how, when and to where discharge should be made. The second concerns the adequacy of the arrangements made (see 17.12).

In terms of the first, the Community Care (Delayed Discharges) Act 2003 (CCDDA) was implemented in January 2004. In terms of the second, the health service ombudsman has investigated on many occasions, whilst the Department of Health continues to issue exhortative – but, it seems, largely ineffective, guidance from time to time about good practice.

17.11.1 DELAYED DISCHARGES

In the light of concerns about what had come to be known increasingly as 'blocked beds', the Community Care (Delayed Discharges) Act 2003 was passed essentially in order to expedite hospital discharges. It involves social services authorities having to reimburse the NHS for such blocked beds. Key points, deriving (unless otherwise stated) from the Act itself and regulations passed under it (SI 2003/2277), are set out below.

17.11.2 DELAYED DISCHARGES OVERALL POLICY

Generally, the pressure on the NHS and local authorities to effect speedy discharge of patients is greater than ever. Clearly such a policy has, in principle, an acceptable rationale. First, hospital beds are a scarce resource and it is poor use of public money to use them wastefully.

Second, prolonged hospital stays can be bad for people's health, whether in terms of loss of physical function and increased dependency, or of hospital-acquired infection. Equally, the danger of pressurised and premature discharge is that the policy and practice might lurch too far in the wrong direction and work to the active detriment of service users.

For example, local authorities and the NHS might in the past have tended to allow a person to remain in hospital some days or weeks while a care home placement of their choice became available. Indeed, within certain limits, service users have the right to choose residential accommodation (see section 9.5). Now, however, people are more likely to be placed in interim, or step-down, accommodation, so that reimbursement charges payable to the NHS by the local social services authority can be avoided.

For some people, such interim accommodation might be suitable and even more beneficial than remaining in hospital. However, for others it might be significantly detrimental to their physical and mental welfare. Even moving from ward to ward or hospital to hospital can be highly disruptive and upsetting for some patients; how much worse might be an inappropriate move to different interim accommodation altogether. In order to avoid such detriment, local authorities need to be aware that even an interim placement must legally meet a person's needs, as pointed out by Department of Health guidance. It states that interim arrangements must be based 'solely' on the person's assessed need, and sustain or improve independence. If this cannot be achieved by an interim placement, the person has to remain in hospital and social services will be liable for reimbursement (HSC 2003/9, para 97). It should also be recalled that need might, for example, be psychological and emotional as well as physical (see 6.8, 6.13).

A Commission for Social Care Inspection report issued in late 2004 identified both the positive effects of delayed discharge policies but also the more negative outcomes – for instance, where intermediate care and rehabilitation services are inadequate (CSCI 2004a, p.5).

17.11.3 DELAYED DISCHARGES FOR ACUTE CARE ONLY

At the time of writing, the rules under the Act apply in practice to acute care only. They do not cover paying patients, nor maternity care, mental health care, palliative care, intermediate care, recuperation or rehabilitation. However, there is a power in the Act to pass further regulations extending the applicability of the rules to other categories of patient.

Mental health care is defined as psychiatric services or other services for preventing, diagnosing or treating illness where a consultant psychiatrist is primarily responsible for those services (SI 2003/2276).

17.11.4 DELAYED DISCHARGE ASSESSMENT NOTICES

A 'section 2' notice must be given by the NHS to the social services authority, if it is unlikely to be safe to discharge the patient without community care services. The notice can be given up to eight days prior to a hospital admission. On the other hand, it can be given no more than two days before the date of proposed discharge. The patient and, if reasonably practicable, the carer must be consulted before the notice is given.

The notice must be withdrawn in certain circumstances if (a) the NHS considers that it would no longer be safe to discharge the person; (b) it considers that the person needs NHS continuing care; (c) if it considers safe discharge will not be achieved without further community care services provided than those already proposed by the local authority; (d) if the patient's proposed treatment has been cancelled or postponed. Alternatively it must withdraw it if it becomes aware that the person is ordinarily resident in a different local authority.

The assessment notice must be in written form and dated. It must also include various matters including likely date of discharge, a statement that the patient and carer have been consulted – and that the NHS has considered whether or not to provide NHS continuing health care and the result of that decision. It must refer to whether the patient has objected to the notice, and also to the name of the liaison person between hospital and social services. The minimum assessment period is set at two days; a notice issued after 2 pm is treated as having been issued on the following day. Sundays and public holidays do not count as part of the minimum interval; they are also excluded for the purpose of issuing an assessment notice (CCDDA 2003, ss.2 and 3 of the Act; SI 2003/2277).

17.11.5 CONTINUING CARE ASSESSMENT DIRECTIONS AND DISCHARGE
In order to emphasise the importance of taking a proper decision about possible NHS continuing health care status, directions have been issued in addition to the Act and Regulations. The Directions place a duty on the NHS to take certain steps before serving an assessment notice on the local authority (see 18.2).

17.11.6 DUTY OF SOCIAL SERVICES AUTHORITY ON RECEIPT OF ASSESSMENT NOTICE
On receipt of a s.2 assessment notice, the local authority must carry out an assessment of a person's needs for community care services to achieve a safe discharge. After consultation with the NHS, it must decide which of those services to make available.

The local authority must also assess an informal carer with a view to identifying services which may be provided under the Carers and Disabled Children Act 2000 – and, after consulting the NHS, decide which of those services to make available. However, the duty to assess the carer only arises if the carer requests the assessment or, if within the 12 months before the section 2 assessment notice was given, has previously requested an assessment under s.1 of the Carers and Disabled Children Act 2000.

The local authority must also keep under review both the patient's and the carer's needs in relation to the services required for safe discharge. The local authority can alter its decision in the light of changed circumstances following the assessment (CCDDA 2003, s.4).

17.11.7 DUTY OF NHS FOLLOWING ASSESSMENT NOTICE
The NHS must consult social services before deciding what services it will provide on discharge. It must give social services notice of the proposed day of discharge (the relevant day).

However, it cannot do this unless it has also issued an assessment notice. This notice may be withdrawn.

Discharge notices issued after 2 pm on Fridays or 5 pm on other days are treated as having been issued on the following day. The minimum interval between the giving of the notice and the discharge day is one day. Sundays and public holidays in England and Wales do not count as part of the minimum interval (CCDDA 2003, s.5; SI 2003/2277).

17.11.8 LIABILITY TO MAKE DELAYED DISCHARGE PAYMENTS

If the end of the relevant (discharge) day is reached and the patient has not been discharged because social services has failed (a) to carry out an assessment or to take a decision about what services are required; or (b) has not made available community care services it had decided to make available to the patient, or not made available carer's services it had decided to make available – then social services must make a payment for each day of the delayed discharge period.

The delayed discharge period begins with the day after (from 11 am) the relevant day and ends no later than the day of actual discharge (CCDDA 2003, s.6). Therefore, at the minimum a charge could not be made until three days after an assessment (and discharge) notice had been given – at the minimum 48 hours could be specified for assessment and arranging of services (DH 2004, paras 76–79).

If the reason for the delayed discharge is not solely due to the social services authority's failure, then the reimbursement duty does not arise (CCDDA 2003, s.6).

17.11.9 DELAYED DISCHARGE CRITERIA, DECISION-MAKING AND REVIEWS

A person can challenge a discharge decision by means of the review panels set up to deal with continuing care decisions (see 18.6).

17.11.10 DISPUTE BETWEEN PUBLIC AUTHORITIES ABOUT DISCHARGE

In case of dispute between public authorities, those authorities may apply to the strategic health authority for the appointment of a panel. Legal proceedings cannot be brought until such a panel has made a recommendation (CCDDA 2003, s.9 and SI 2003/2277).

17.11.11 REFUSAL OF PATIENT TO LEAVE HOSPITAL

If a person has been deemed suitable for discharge, then, subject to any review requested or complaint made, the question inevitably arises about what to do if he or she simply refuses to leave hospital. The guidance on hospital discharge states that patients do not have the right to stay in an acute hospital bed if they no longer need the care (HSC 2003/9, para 96); in fact that principle applies to any bed. However, the guidance is notably silent on what to do in difficult cases. In the following ombudsman case, the health authority seems to have backed down and continued to fund NHS inpatient care:

Refusal to enter a nursing home. In one health service ombudsman investigation, a woman had wanted the NHS to fund the nursing home care of her husband who had Alzheimer's disease. The health authority was prepared to provide the health care element of his care, but the local authority would arrange the accommodation and meet the level of costs for which it would be liable in the light of its statutory test of resources. However, the woman refused a financial assessment, without which the local authority would not arrange the care. The health authority acknowledged it could not force the husband into a nursing home, but at the same time clinical advice prevented his discharge to his own home. He was cared for in a community hospital and funded by the health authority; the ombudsman found that the health authority had acted reasonably (*Oxfordshire HA 1996*).

Nonetheless, in one case, the NHS primary care trust went to court, after a 72-year-old man had occupied a hospital bed he did not need for almost three years. He had been admitted in December 2002, and suffered from breathing problems, a left-sided foot drop and two bilateral hernias. Since May 2003, he had not required medical care. He refused to leave hospital. In March 2006, the High Court ordered that he leave the Finchley Memorial Hospital in London within 14 days and pay £10,000 to cover the cost of eviction attempts (*BBC News*, 6 March 2006).

17.12 HOSPITAL DISCHARGE PRACTICE

The Department of Health has issued guidance on the 'pathway, process and practice' of hospital discharge (DH 2003j). It is extensive and somewhat repetitive. Introducing itself as good practice guidance to assist the processes of discharge planning, it does not appear to be the type of guidance that carries legal weight or the 'badge of mandatory requirement' that a judge might search for (*R v North Derbyshire Health Authority, ex p Fisher*).

Further guidance was issued specifically about the discharge of people of homeless people and others living in insecure or temporary accommodation. All nine steps relate to management process, referring to identification of relevant organisations, setting up a steering group, reviewing existing systems, identifying training and resource requirements, developing a protocol, ensuring the protocol is fit for purpose, testing and monitoring the protocol, setting up audit arrangements, reviewing and refining the protocol (DCLG, DH 2006). Easy to parody, the guidance seems to be a triumph of process over substance.

That said, there are specific points made in the main 2003 guidance that might in any case be picked up on by the health service ombudsman or local government ombudsman, if not necessarily by the courts. Indeed one, concerning active engagement of the patient and carer, relates to the duty under directions to consult with the patient and carer (see 18.2).

The 'key messages' made in the Foreword include, for instance: (a) ensuring that service users and carers are actively engaged in planning and delivering care (including provision of information); (b) recognising the important role of carers; (c) effective communication between primary, secondary and social care services; (d) ensuring all patients are assessed for a period of rehabilitation before decisions are made on care options (DH 2003j). Indeed, the original community care policy guidance states that patients should not leave hospital until at least essential community care services have been agreed with them and their carers (DH 1990, para 3.44). Such points are typically picked up in health service ombudsman investigations; for instance, lack of involvement of carers in discharge decisions:

Discharge and suicide, inadequate consultation with relatives. A woman with a history of mental ill health was granted temporary home leave, having been detained under the Mental Health Act 1983. A day later she committed suicide. The health service ombudsman criticised the inadequate care plan, inadequate consultation with relatives, poor documentation and an inappropriate decision to discharge (*Nottinghamshire Healthcare NHS Trust 2003*).

In another mental health discharge case, also ending in suicide, the ombudsman criticised the failure to appoint a community psychiatric nurse for a person with complex mental health problems. The hospital consultant who was her key worker was also key worker for up to 30 patients, an arrangement that was 'not ideal' (*Newcastle, North Tyneside and Northumberland Mental Health NHS Trust 2001*).

The Healthcare Commission (which now deals with complaints at the stage prior to any ombudsman involvement) has, unsurprisingly, made similar findings:

Inadequate discharge arrangements for 91-year-old woman. A 91-year-old woman was admitted to hospital with pneumonia. She was the primary carer for her husband who was blind and arthritic. After a week she was discharged at short notice, at which point she was made to leave her bed, and sit around for hours waiting to be discharged. Her mobility was still limited. She had difficulties taking the medication required when she left hospital. Within four days she was readmitted. The hospital had not followed procedures. The discharge had not been discussed in advance with the family (at least 24 hours' notice should be given), and there was no consideration given to her circumstances as a care. Likewise neither recuperative care nor her social circumstances were considered. Furthermore, after the family complained, the NHS trust suggested a meeting but did not convene it for seven months. The complaint against the trust was upheld (HC 2007, p.22).

The health service ombudsman has repeatedly found shortcomings in terms of information provided. For instance:

Lack of information on discharge. The health service ombudsman has found fault when: an 89-year-old woman moved to a care home without being informed of alternatives (*East Norfolk HA 1996*); a woman who had suffered a stroke moved to a nursing home with no clear information (oral or written) provided for the family on the costs involved (*North Worcestershire HA 1996*); a woman with a broken leg was discharged to a care home and faced a bill of £900 for a month's stay without being told about the fees (HSO W.524/92–93); a brain damaged man was discharged to a nursing home without his wife being informed about the fees (*Leeds HA 1994*).

The ombudsman also found fault when the daughter of a woman who had suffered several strokes was not informed about the fees for a nursing home. The hospital staff relied on social services to provide this, but neglected to refer some patients to social services if they thought they would be ineligible for assistance (*East Kent HA 1996*).

Closely allied to lack of information is serious failure in communication that can result in clearly inappropriate discharges because the required arrangements are not in place:

Lack of communication resulting in inappropriate discharge arrangements. The health service ombudsman found fault when a woman with Huntington's chorea was discharged by the consultant, before he had ascertained whether the local authority and voluntary organisations could provide the assistance required (HSO W.40/84–85); similarly when a consultant had not found out whether the equipment and home adaptations required on discharge would be available (HSO W.113/84–85). It was clearly unacceptable when the carer first knew about the discharge through a telephone call telling her that her mother was already on her way home; when no hospital 'key worker' had been identified; and also that discharge policy and procedures were not fully operational and unknown to some staff (HSO W.254/88–89).

In another case, the ombudsman placed a considerable burden on the hospital staff; it was not enough that they had decided that clinically a person no longer needed to be in hospital; they had to ensure that the discharge would be to a satisfactory environment. It was insufficient for them to hope that the outcome would be satisfactory and otherwise offer readmission if necessary (HSO W.420/83–84).

In yet another case, the hospital clinicians overlooked vital information from the GP about the domestic circumstances of the man to be discharged, and about the fact that this wife could not cope with her husband's twice-daily bathing needs. There was considerable doubt about the registrar's communications, little evidence of a multi-disciplinary approach and no system of recording discharge arrangements on patients' notes (HSO SW.82/86–87).

In other cases, it appears that the arrangements are simply inadequate irrespective of communication issues, and will be criticised by the ombudsman. When an elderly man was admitted to hospital suffering from a head injury, multiple abrasions and confusion, he was discharged home later the same day – to his home where his dependent elderly wife lived – with no community nursing arrangements having been made. He was then readmitted to hospital because of subsequent community nursing concern, but discharged again without dressings for a pressure sore and again without arrangements for community nursing. He was then readmitted following an overdose; and died two days later, without his relatives being adequately informed about his deteriorating condition. This sequence of events had taken place over a period of about a month (*Southend Hospital NHS Trust 2001*).

The widespread closure of hospital beds in the last decade, amounting to some 16 per cent nationally, seems to have led to increasing pressures on beds in many areas. This is unsurprising given that the NHS Plan in 2000 had identified the need for 2000 more, rather than less, acute hospital beds, as well as some 5000 intermediate care beds (HSC 2001/03).

The resulting pressure on beds compromises patient care, and leads amongst other things to inappropriate discharge. For example, during 2007, Ipswich Hospital was reported as waking patients up in the middle of the night and discharging them (Bond 2007). Such continuing practices, which may in fact be worsening because of the high bed occupancy rates of many acute hospitals, put into perspective the essentially weak and tokenistic nature of Department of Health guidance. And it appears that although statistics seem to show a reduction in so called delayed discharges, or 'delayed transfers of care' as they are more euphemistically and sometimes optimistically described, readmission rates are increasing (Taylor 2007). This is unsurprising if people are being forced out of hospital prematurely.

17.12.1 TRANSFER OF FRAIL OLDER PATIENTS

The Department of Health has issued guidance on the transfer of frail older people from long-stay hospital settings. This followed a health service ombudsman investigation into one such, notorious, transfer:

Transfer against consultant's advice. In 1996, the health service ombudsman published an investigation in which an elderly man with dementia was transferred from a hospital, in which he had been a patient for four years, to a private nursing home. He died 17 days after the transfer which was (a) opposed by the man's consultant but approved, in her absence, by a colleague who was aware of the consultant's opposition but believed there was no alternative; (b) as a result of a planned closure of the ward which had been brought forward by 21 months – a change of plan approved at a health authority meeting which had not been open to the public.

The ombudsman doubted whether the second consultant's acquiescence in the discharge amounted to sufficient authority to sanction the discharge and was particularly concerned that, given the first consultant's opinion, the second consultant made no entry on the clinical records. The NHS trust did not comply with Department of Health discharge guidance (then HC(89)5) and drew the ombudsman's strong criticism, although he recognised that Winchester Health Authority's decision to speed up the closure gave the trust little time to consult and make practical arrangements.

The ombudsman found it 'totally undemocratic that a public body should have considered it justifiable to discuss a policy matter of such importance to patients and their families at a meeting closed to the general public', and criticised the authority's calling the meeting informal. He concluded by stating that the circumstances of the complaint 'should serve as a grim warning to any health authority or trust planning the discharge of patients from hospital or elsewhere' (*North and Mid-Hampshire HA 1996*).

Subsequent Department of Health guidance covered consultation, a project plan, the needs of the individual and their relatives or carers, the process of transfer and role to be played by staff in the new setting, and follow-up and monitoring. In particular, a care plan for each patient should be drawn up, be subject to regular review before the transfer, involve consultation with relatives and carers, and include the patient's preferences in terms of diet, eating habits, bathing arrangements and idiosyncrasies.

There should be a checklist of actions and tasks for each patient before and after the transfer. Information should be provided for patients, relatives and carers. Crucially, because a move can seriously threaten 'physical, psychological and social well-being', it is 'very important, therefore, to be aware of the risks, to handle the process sensitively and to be prepared to delay or halt a transfer if necessary' (HSC 1998/48, para 21).

The requirement in the guidance that a multi-disciplinary risk assessment be coordinated was found to have been breached by the High Court in *R v North and East Devon HA, ex p Coughlan*, although the Court of Appeal in the same case overturned this finding.

This NHS guidance has since been held not to apply to the closure of local authority care homes for reasons such as: (a) its being issued to the NHS and not to local authorities; (b) its being aimed at NHS (not local authority) long-stay patients; (c) uncertainty about whether the guidance is anyway still extant or is now obsolete; (d) the Department of Health's decision not to issue such guidance to local authorities about this issue; (e) the guidance is anyway not statutory or mandatory in nature (see: *R(Dudley) v East Sussex CC; R(Haggerty) v St Helens Council*).

17.12.2 HOSPITAL DISCHARGE: DOCUMENTATION, ROUTINES, PROCEDURES

The health service ombudsman has investigated hospital discharge situations on many occasions. The sort of issue consistently identified includes the following. Poor documentation may lead to problems:

Discharge after a stroke. A man who had suffered a stroke was discharged to his daughter's flat. She had health problems and used crutches to walk. A care package was not provided for three days, during which time he could not move unaided. However, the daughter had informed the hospital staff about her health problems, but this had not been properly recorded. Had it been so, a proper care package could have been in place before discharge; the ombudsman criticised the standard of nursing documentation (*St Mary's NHS Trust 2002*).

Slavishly following a discharge plan, but not varying this in the light of changes to the patient's needs and condition, might also result in poor discharge:

Not responding to changing needs prior to discharge. The health service ombudsman criticised a discharge when a man had suffered a fall the day before discharge at which time a chest infection was also identified – yet there had been no full physical examination prior to discharge (*West Sussex HA 2002*).

Similarly, a discharge took place on the basis of the nature of the person's previous admissions (for chemotherapy); whereas this time, the circumstances had been different but this had not been recorded in the nursing notes. This was faulted by the ombudsman (HSO W.286/86–87). The ombudsman criticised the progress of a planned discharge which was not adjusted to take account of the fact of changed circumstances – namely that the woman was now in severe abdominal pain, had been scalded and fallen on the morning of discharge (HSO W.24 and 56/84–85).

The local government ombudsman too sometimes explores hospital discharge from the local authority's point of view:

Failure to visit. A man was discharged from hospital following a major operation. He had been told in hospital that help would be provided when he got home. Normally a local authority officer would have visited the next day. Instead it took ten days, during which time the man survived mostly on tinned food and managed to get to the shops with considerable difficulty. This was maladministration for the local ombudsman, although the man had not been entirely alone or completely immobile – and he could have contacted the council during the ten days, which he chose not to do (*Sheffield CC 1996*).

Discharge to nursing home with pressure sore. When a local authority arranged for a woman to be discharged from hospital to a nursing home, it was unaware of the full extent of the pressure sores from which she was already suffering, and which would eventually lead to her death some weeks later. However, the local ombudsman found that the hospital told neither the council nor the nursing home the full facts of her medical condition (the pressure sores had been concealed beneath a bandage), and that therefore the council was not at fault in this particular respect (*Bexley LBC 2000*).

17.13 SPECIFIC COMMUNITY HEALTH SERVICES

A number of key community health services warrant mention, including wheelchair provision, continence (or incontinence) services, patient transport and mental health services under a process known as the Care Programme Approach.

17.13.1 WHEELCHAIRS

NHS wheelchair provision has long been the subject of reports which have suggested that it is inadequate in terms of the range of chair available, and the speed with which provision takes place. For instance, over 20 years ago, the McColl (1986) report identified serious shortcomings, many of which appear to remain (CSIP 2006a).

It is also clear that, depending on individual circumstances, wheelchairs are as much meeting social care, as health care, needs. Over the past 30 years or so, it appears that local authorities have in fact sometimes provided wheelchairs. This has occurred when the NHS has failed to provide the wheelchair, but the local authority has concluded that providing the wheelchair itself would be the most cost-effective way of meeting the person's community care needs. For instance, an outdoor powered wheelchair might meet a person's social, shopping and other related needs. Alternatively, a wheelchair provided by the local authority – with reclining backrest, elevating legrests removable armrests – might enable a disabled person to carry out more of his or her own personal care, than in the wheelchair provided by the NHS. In turn, this would give him or her more independence, privacy and dignity – whilst the local authority would save money on the personal care it no longer had to provide and pay for. Indeed, a report published by the Department of Health carries just such an example of a local authority providing a powered wheelchair (CSIP 2006a, p.15).

Nonetheless, local authorities will be very coy indeed about admitting that they might provide wheelchairs; given the inadequacy of NHS provision, they would be fearful of opening floodgates.

17.13.1.1 Guidance on powered wheelchairs and vouchers

The Department of Health has issued guidance on both the provision of electrically powered indoor/outdoor chairs, and on a voucher system for wheelchairs. The guidance on powered wheelchairs stated that the NHS should provide powered indoor/outdoor wheelchairs for severely disabled people, including children, who could benefit from them. Scooters were not to be included. Health authorities were told that they should formulate local eligibility criteria, which should be broadly based on the following three conditions:

- inability to propel a manual wheelchair outdoors
- ability to benefit, through increased mobility, from an improved quality of life
- ability to handle the chair safely.

It also states that if a person has such a powered wheelchair, but then moves to another area, where he or she would not be eligible, the wheelchair should not be withdrawn unless there is a good clinical reason for doing so (HSG(96)34).

Separate guidance set out the details of a wheelchair voucher scheme that should be offered by NHS wheelchair services. This involves the NHS giving a voucher equivalent to the cost to the NHS of providing a new wheelchair that, in the opinion of the assessing professional, would meet the clinical needs of the person. The person can then purchase a wheelchair with the voucher (the value of which the supplier can recover from the NHS), and 'top up' if he or she wishes.

Beyond this, there are two options. The 'independent option' involves the person becoming the owner of the wheelchair, being responsible for maintenance and repairs (and receiving those estimated costs for a specified period in the voucher). The 'partnership option' involves the NHS retaining ownership of the wheelchair, and also retaining responsibility for maintenance and repair.

The key principles of the voucher scheme are described as universal eligibility. It is open to anyone assessed as meeting the local eligibility criteria for a wheelchair. It follows assessment and review of needs leading to a wheelchair prescription, in consultation with the service user. Provision is made through agreed suppliers. There should be continued access in any event to NHS provision of special seating and pressure-relieving cushions where required (HSG(96)53). The legal power to operate the voucher scheme is contained in regulations (SI 1996/1503).

17.13.1.2 Application of eligibility criteria for wheelchairs

The health service ombudsman has considered the local application of wheelchair eligibility criteria provision on a few occasions.

Lightweight manual wheelchairs. An NHS primary care trust operated additional eligibility criteria for the provision of lightweight manual wheelchairs. A woman with cerebral palsy was assessed by a charity as needing one, so that she could perform certain activities that she could not manage in her standard wheelchair. Her request was refused; the ombudsman found nothing wrong with the application of such additional criteria for lightweight wheelchairs, which were more expensive than the standard chairs (*Plymouth NHS Primary Care Trust 2002*).

However, in another case, the ombudsman found that the NHS trust had applied its criteria too restrictively:

Applying guidance too restrictively. A complaint was made by the parents of their disabled son, respecting provision for him of an electrically powered indoor/outdoor wheelchair. The ombudsman found that the NHS trust had applied local and national guidance too restrictively and had not taken account of his previous experience of using such wheelchairs. It had also failed to consider whether he had exceptional needs not coming under the terms of the guidance (*Epsom and St. Helier NHS Trust 2001*).

17.13.2 CONTINENCE SERVICES AND EQUIPMENT

The Department of Health has repeatedly stressed, in relation to incontinence supplies, that the NHS has the power to make priorities locally. All too often, looking to exercise this power, it appears that the NHS continues, in many areas, to view incontinence services, pads and other supplies as an easy target when it wishes to save money. Yet incontinence remains a crucial issue. For older people in particular, single or double incontinence, seems often to be the trigger for admission to a care home, when the family feels unable to cope with it at home (over and above frailty, illness and various other physical and cognitive problems).

Providing for people's incontinence needs is sometimes vexed, not only because of the struggle over adequate funding for continence supplies, such as as pads. In addition, effects, both social and medical, are serious, and yet it – or the worst of its effects – is often avoidable. Indeed, with the right input, be it surgical, bladder retraining, adjustment of the environment or provision of the right mobility equipment (people are wrongly labelled incontinent if they cannot get to the lavatory in time because of mobility difficulties), it can be wholly remedied.

The importance of making such remedies available, and of professionals understanding incontinence, becomes all the greater if place of residence is at stake. The following dispute about what constituted 'incontinence' is informative:

Incontinence and care homes. A woman required a toileting regime (in order to get her to the toilet in time) in a care home (that did not provide nursing). Her daughter argued that this meant her mother was not incontinent. However, a medical doctor advising the local continuing care panel stated that, according to the local policy, a toileting regime meant that she was incontinent, and that therefore the mother required to be placed in a care home that provided nursing. The daughter maintained that her mother simply was not incontinent, since she passed urine on the toilet. The local authority for this, and other reasons, stated that the mother would have go to the nursing home. The court found this decision to be unlawful on various grounds, although it did not comment particularly on the incontinence point (*R(Goldsmith) v Wandsworth LBC*).

In addition, people may often be embarrassed to talk about incontinence, thus making the job of hard-pressed professionals that much more difficult.

17.13.2.1 Continence service provision: background

A little background will serve to highlight some of the issues concerning incontinence, and also illustrate the general point made earlier in this chapter about just how elusive are people's entitlements to NHS services, especially the distinctly unglamorous ones.

1977: aids and equipment. The Department of Health and Social Security wrote to nursing officers, having in mind 'positive action' even in the economic circumstances of the time. Although 'every effort should be directed towards maintaining continence, there are inevitably those whose control is so impaired as to make it necessary to meet as comprehensively as possible their need for the aids and equipment which will help to overcome this handicap' (CNO(SNC)(77)1).

1987: concerns about restrictions. Restriction of services in some areas had led to considerable concern about the situation and a request being made by the Department to health authorities for information about their practices (D(87)45).

1990: variability of provision. Central government conceded that health authorities' provision of incontinence aids to people in their own homes and in care homes was variable (*Hansard* 1990d).

1990: withdrawing continence aids. Example quoted in Parliament of a health authority's consultation document, proposing to withdraw 'free incontinence aids' from 400 to 500 people living in independent sector residential homes, though still continuing to advise home owners and sell supplies to them at cost price (*Hansard* 1990e).

1990: pressure sores and dealing with faeces and urine – none too pleasant. Baroness Masham reminded Members of the House of Lords about the realities of rationing of incontinence pads: 'The general public who are healthy and well have no idea that at such a basic level people who are incontinent are having many problems. They are having to buy pads or have them rationed or cut off. The mother of a spastic daughter who cannot speak and is doubly incontinent, living in a Cheshire Home, was told that she would have to pay for her daughter's incontinence pads as the Cheshire Home has nursing home status. The mother has to choose between supplying her daughter with pads or giving her a holiday. She cannot afford to do both. Other people have been told that they cannot have the pads which are the most suitable for them. If this goes on there will be an increase in pressure sores and all sorts of problems costing the health service millions of pounds. In addition to this, there are difficulties for carers who may find dealing with other people's urine and faeces none too pleasant. If people do not have adequate pads, life will become unbearable' (*Hansard* 1990c).

1990: failed legislative amendment to make incontinence services explicitly statutory. Baroness Masham of Ilton attempted, unsuccessfully, to remedy the vagueness of the NHS Act 1977, by an amendment to the NHS and Community Care Bill: 'In carrying out its primary functions a District Health Authority shall provide a district wide incontinence service and shall identify a continence advisor and a consultant to take a special interest in incontinence.'

The government's reply simply reaffirmed health authorities' discretion: 'In this as in other areas of health care provision district health authorities should be left free to determine the pattern and level of service in their districts in the light of local needs and circumstances' (*Hansard* 1990b).

1991: wide variations in provision. Government acknowledged 'wide variations in the level of services to people with incontinence' (*Hansard* 1991).

1991: withdrawal of pads. The Department of Health issued guidance stating that if local changes to the supply of incontinence pads were proposed, vulnerable patients or clients should not be exposed to anxiety; and there should be an assured alternative in place before withdrawal or reduction (EL(91)28).

1991: Department of Health report. Department of Health commissioned a report on an 'agenda for action on incontinence services' (Sanderson 1991).

1994: legal case illustrating rationing. A court case illustrated how a woman had to seek assistance with incontinence pads from the Social Fund. This was because she did not meet her local health authority's strict eligibility for NHS provision: double incontinence or terminal illness (*R v Social Fund Inspector, ex p Connick*).

2000: good practice guidance, but arbitrary rationing of pads irrespective of assessed need. The Department of Health published *Good Practice in Continence Services*. It told health authorities, primary care trusts and NHS trusts to work together to 'ensure that people with continence problems are identified, assessed and get the treatment they need' (DH 2000b). It pointed to geographical variations in people's eligibility for NHS continence services as well as in the range and quantity of treatment provided; it also noted with particular concern the 'gross difference' in NHS trust policies for supply of incontinence pads. Arbitrary rules and policies limited the supply of pads irrespective of the assessed needs of individual service users; there were also inflexible rules concerning the provision of either washable or disposable pads (p.8).

2001: reusing paper sheets, and getting infections and pressure sores. Parliament was reminded about how important continence supplies are: 'We know about the problems which arose when there was a hiccup or a cut-back in the community in relation to the incontinence service. People were reusing paper sheets, drying them on radiators. You end up with infections; your skin condition breaks down; and you may get pressure sores. If that happens, you then have to go into hospital because you cannot be looked after in a care home. Pressure sores cost the NHS millions of pounds per year' (*Hansard* 2001a).

2001: issuing a direction about continence supplies in nursing homes. A government minister undertook in Parliament to issue a direction to the NHS about free continence supplies in nursing homes (*Hansard* 2001b). In the event, no such formal direction (which would have been stronger than guidance) is ever issued.

2001 and 2003: guidance on continence supplies in nursing homes. Department of Health guidance stated that incontinence aids should be free of charge to meet the assessed needs of residents in care homes providing nursing (HSC 2001/17, HSC 2003/6: guidance since superseded).

2005: national audit of continence care. Funded by the Healthcare Commission, and undertaken by the Royal College of Physicians – with a running footnote to 'St Elsewhere's Hospital' – this audit concluded that management of incontinence in the United Kingdom was inadequate. Findings included the fact that pads were often provided, rather than treatment to manage the underlying problem. Pads were anyway rationed; despite 80 per cent of services stating that pads were to be provided on the basis of clinical need, nonetheless 81 per cent of primary care services, and 76 per cent of care home services, limited the maximum number of daily pads per patient. In addition, the audit found lack of adequate assessment, lack of policies of continence, poor documentation, limited staff training, high use of indwelling catheters in hospital settings (RCP 2005).

In 2008, it would seem that continence supplies, at least in some areas, continue to be rationed arbitrarily (i.e. not according to assessed need) for people in their own homes, in care homes (not providing nursing) and, despite, Parliamentary undertakings and guidance issued to the NHS to the contrary, in nursing homes as well.

17.13.2.2 Continence services in care homes providing nursing

Entitlement to continence services and equipment is generally vague and weak because of the flimsiness of the underpinning NHS Act 2006.

However, in the case of residents of nursing homes, Department of Health guidance states that 'continence products should be made available by the NHS to residents of care homes who are also receiving NHS-funded Nursing Care, if required' (DH 2007f, paras 42–43). This seems to bear the inescapable implication that the guidance is telling the NHS that it must meet, free of charge, all the assessed continence-related needs of a resident in a care home that provides nursing. In other words, the rationing of incontinence products, including pads, in nursing homes is inconsistent with the guidance. This would be in contrast with such provision for people in other types of care home or in their own homes, where rationing is in principle possible. Nevertheless, it seems that in many areas the NHS continues in practice to ration incontinence supplies not just to people in their own homes and care homes that do not provide nursing, but also to people in care homes that do (i.e. nursing homes). In the light of the Department of Health guidance, this sort of systematic rationing in nursing homes is legally questionable – especially given the Parliamentary undertaking in 2001 that a 'direction' (which is more than guidance and creates a duty) would be issued (*Hansard* 2001b). It never has been issued.

17.13.3 PATIENT TRANSPORT

Department of Health guidance outlines the rules for NHS 'patient transport services' (PTS). It states that patients should reach, and travel home from, health care locations in both secondary and primary care settings in 'reasonable time' and 'reasonable comfort', and without detriment to their medical condition. The travel distance should be taken into account because the need for patient transport may be a function of the effect of the distance on the person's medical condition. It states also that what is a 'reasonable' journey time needs to be defined locally, since circumstances vary. It states that eligible people are those:

- whose medical condition is such that they require the skills or support of PTS staff on or after the journey – and/or where it would be detrimental to the patients' condition or recovery to use other means of transport
- whose medical condition affects their mobility to such an extent that they would be unable to access the health care, and/or it would be detrimental to their condition or recovery if they travelled by other means
- who are the recognised parent or guardian of a child who is being conveyed.

It goes on to state that PTS could also be provided for the escort or carer of a patient, where their particular skills and/or support are needed – in the case of, for example, those accompanying a person with a physical or mental incapacity, vulnerable adults, or interpreters. It states that only one escort should travel with the patient.

Eligible patients should receive transport free of charge. However, the guidance points out that the NHS has the discretion to use its income generation powers to provide transport for 'social', rather than 'medical' needs. This would be under s.7 of the Health and Medicines Act 1988.

The guidance also points out that the Hospital Travel Costs Scheme provides financial assistance to those patients who do not have a medical need for ambulance transport, but who require assistance in meeting the cost of travel to and from their health care. Reimbursement of travel fares is available for services related to the care of a consultant (but not a GP), a traditional hospital diagnostic or treatment (i.e. non-primary care) at whatever location, and paid for by the NHS whether carried it out by an NHS or independent professional (DH 2007i). This is under s.183 of the NHS Act 2006. Reimbursement is also available for a companion, where the patient is a child or because of the adult's medical condition (SI 2003/2382).

17.13.4 CARE PROGRAMME APPROACH: MENTAL HEALTH

It is beyond the scope of this book to cover the Mental Health Act 1983 generally. Nevertheless, the book does refer to it in various places, in particular in respect of s.117 of the Act (aftercare services: see 11.5), and of interventions potentially relevant to adult protection (see 21.9).

The Care Programme Approach (CPA) applies to the NHS and stems from guidance issued in 1990 concerning the management of people with mental health problems (HC(90)23). The four key elements identified were systematic assessment, a care plan, a key worker and regular review (para 10). Despite the emphasis placed by central government on CPA, it is not to be found not in legislation but in Department of Health guidance. Launched in 1990, it was updated in 1999, and then again in 2008, with the latest changes being effective from October 2008 (DH 2008b). It abandons the two-pronged approach of 'standard CPA' and 'enhanced CPA'; effectively, 'new CPA' will apply only to those who previously would have been regarded as enhanced CPA . The courts have confirmed that the CPA framework constitutes good practice guidance but is not the source of duties and powers which an NHS trust exercises in relation to people with a mental disorder (*K v Central v North West London Mental Health NHS Trust*).

17.13.4.1 Standard and enhanced CPA to October 2008

Updated guidance was issued in 1999, the gist of which was as follows (DH 1999b). It stated that even though the CPA was aimed at those most in need, nevertheless it should be applied to all service users in contact with the secondary mental health system (para 18). The four key elements remained the same as in the 1990 guidance (para 4). It referred to two levels of CPA: standard and enhanced. It also stated that people receiving aftercare services under s.117 of the Mental Health Act 1983 would be subject to the same principles as CPA, and the guidance recommended that the s.117 register should be a subset of the overall CPA register (para 71). Standard CPA was referred to as applying to people with some of the following characteristics:

- requiring support or intervention of one agency or discipline or only low key support from more than one agency/discipline
- being more able to manage their mental health problems themselves
- having active informal support network
- posing little danger to themselves or others
- being more likely to maintain appropriate contact with services (DH 1999b, para 57).

Enhanced CPA was referred to as applying to people with some of the following characteristics:

- having multiple care needs, including housing, employment, etc., requiring inter-agency coordination
- only being willing to cooperate with one professional or agency despite having multiple care needs
- being in contact with a number of agencies (including the criminal justice system)
- being likely to require more frequent and intensive interventions, perhaps with medication management
- being more likely to have mental health problems co-existing with other problems such as substance misuse
- being more likely to be at risk of self-harm or of harming others
- being more likely to disengage with services (DH 1999b, para 58).

17.13.4.2 Single approach to CPA from October 2008

New guidance issued in 2008, calling itself confusingly policy, positive practice and best practice guidance all at once, revises the approach to CPA from October 2008. The status of the guidance in terms of its strength is therefore unclear. Certainly it is not labelled as constituting 'directions'. The courts prefer guidance to be clearly labelled, although may pay some heed to the word 'must' (*R v North Derbyshire HA, ex p Fisher*); there are a few 'musts' scattered, albeit sporadically, in the guidance.

In summary, it states that individuals with a wide range of needs relating to a number of services, or those who are most at risk, should receive a higher level of coordination support. And it is to this group only that CPA will apply. This will typically cover people needing multi-agency support, active engagement, intense intervention, support with dual diagnoses – and who are at higher risk. Thus, people with more straightforward needs, with contact with one agency only, will not be within CPA.

The characteristics to be considered as indicative of the 'new' CPA are:

- severe mental disorder (including personality disorder) with a high degree of clinical complexity
- current or potential risks including suicide, self-harm, harm to others, relapse history, self-neglect, non-compliance with treatment plan, vulnerability (e.g. exploitation, financial difficulties, disinhibition, physical/emotional abuse, cognitive impairment, child protection issues)
- current or past severe distress/instability or disengagement
- non-physical co-morbidity (e.g. substance/alcohol/prescription drugs misuse, learning disability)
- multiple service provision from different agencies
- current or recent detention under the Mental Health Act 1983, or referral to crisis/home treatment team
- significant reliance by person on carers or has significant caring responsibilities
- experiencing disadvantage or difficulty because of parenting responsibilities, physical health problems or disability, unsettled accommodation issues, employment issues related to mental illness, significant impairment of function due to mental illness, ethnicity issues (immigration, race/culture, language, religion), sexuality or gender issues.

All service users subject to supervised community treatment (under the amended Mental Health Act 1983) or subject to guardianship under the 1983 Act should be supported by the CPA. CPA should not be withdrawn prematurely just because a service user is stable when a high level of support is being given. Key components of CPA include care coordination by a care coordinator (with specific care coordination responsibilities); comprehensive, multi-disciplinary, multi-agency assessment (including regular review, likely to be more frequent than annual); comprehensive, formal written care plan (DH 2008b, pp.11–17)

17.13.4.3 Shortcuts in joint working in mental health

Ultimate responsibility for implementing the CPA lies with the NHS. However, the Department of Health has long since repeatedly stressed the importance of an integrated approach covering both CPA and social services assessment and care management under community care legislation. This is to minimise confusion and distress for service users and duplication (DH 1999b, paras 35, 38).

Nevertheless, the most recent guidance has finally recognised that CPA is a 'process' and should not be simply equated as a 'gateway' to social services or as a badge of entitlement to any other service. Thus, 'services that currently equate CPA levels with Fair Access to Care Services (FACS) eligibility levels should review their policies accordingly' (DH 2008b, p.13).

Clearly then, care must be taken that, if health and social care assessment processes are integrated, it is on the basis of a proper legal understanding of the respective duties lying on social services and the NHS. Such integration approached in the wrong way can result not in helpful 'streamlining' of assessment and services, but in depriving service users of these. In 2004, the courts effectively sounded a warning that joint working was not to be regarded as synonymous with legal shortcuts (*R(HP) v Islington LBC*).

17.14 NATIONAL SERVICE FRAMEWORKS

In addition to the general mass of guidance that it otherwise publishes, central government has also drawn up what it has called national service frameworks (NSFs), in order to target and improve specific types of service. Three of the frameworks drawn up are particularly relevant to this book and concern older people, long-term conditions and mental health. Although the frameworks have received a significant amount of publicity, they are no more than mostly rather vague guidance. It is also arguable that as far as social services authorities are concerned, these two frameworks are of the weaker variety of guidance (see 5.1.6), since no reference to s.7 of the Local Authority Social Services Act 1970 is to be found. In sum, the frameworks contain laudable aspiration but lack legal bite. For instance, standard 1 of the NSF for older people states that age discrimination should not be part of health and social care. Yet such discrimination continues unabated in both obvious and less obvious ways (Forder 2008; Steel *et al.* 2008).

17.14.1 NATIONAL SERVICE FRAMEWORK FOR OLDER PEOPLE

The National Service Framework (NSF) for Older People applies across both health and social care and contains a number of standards (DH 2001c).

- **Age discrimination**. NHS services will be provided, regardless of age, on the basis of clinical need alone. Social care services will not use age in their eligibility criteria or policies, to restrict access to available services (standard 1).
- **Person-centred care**. NHS and social care services treat older people as individuals and enable them to make choices about their own care. This is achieved through the single assessment process, integrated commissioning arrangements and integrated provision of services, including community equipment and continence services (standard 2).
- **Intermediate care**. Older people will have access to a new range of intermediate care services at home or in designated care settings, to promote their independence by providing enhanced services from the NHS and councils to prevent unnecessary hospital admission and effective rehabilitation services to enable early discharge from hospital and to prevent premature or unnecessary admission to long-term residential care (standard 3).
- **General hospital care**. Older people's care in hospital is delivered through appropriate specialist care and by hospital staff who have the right set of skills to meet their needs (standard 4).
- **Strokes**. The NHS will take action to prevent strokes, working in partnership with other agencies where appropriate. People who are thought to have had a stroke have access to diagnostic services, are treated appropriately by a specialist stroke service, and subsequently, with their carers, participate in a multidisciplinary programme of secondary prevention and rehabilitation (standard 5).
- **Falls**. The NHS, working in partnership with councils, takes action to prevent falls and reduce resultant fractures or other injuries in their populations of older people. Older people who have fallen receive effective treatment and rehabilitation and, with their carers, receive advice on prevention through a specialised falls service (standard 6).
- **Mental health in older people**. Older people who have mental health problems have access to integrated mental health services, provided by the NHS and councils to ensure effective diagnosis, treatment and support, for them and their carers (standard 7).
- **Promotion of health and active life in older age**. The health and well-being of older people is promoted through a coordinated programme of action led by the NHS with support from councils (standard 8).

17.14.2 NATIONAL SERVICE FRAMEWORK FOR MENTAL HEALTH

The NSF for Mental Health (DH 1999a) applies across both health and social care and contains a number of standards. Standard 6 in particular is for social services authorities to take a lead on because it relates to the carers' legislation (see 13.5). In summary, the standards are as follows:

- Health promotion (standard 1).
- Identification and assessment of mental health needs, offering of effective treatments (standard 2).
- Round-the-clock contact with local services. Ability to use NHS Direct (standard 3).
- All service users on Care Programme Approach should:
  - receive care optimising engagement, preventing or anticipating crises and reducing risk
  - have a copy of a written care plan including action required in a crisis, advice to GP – and the care plan should be regularly reviewed
  - be able to access services 24 hours a day, seven days a week (standard 4).

- Each service user assessed as requiring a period of care away from home should have:
  - timely access to appropriate (hospital) bed, which is in the least restrictive environment consistent with self- and public protection, and is as close to home as possible
  - have a copy of a written care plan agreed on discharge setting out care and rehabilitation to be provided, identifying care coordinator and specifying action in a crisis (standard 5).
- All individuals providing regular and substantial care for a person on CPA should have:
  - an annually repeated assessment of caring, physical and mental health needs
  - have their own written care plan, given to them and implemented in discussion with them (standard 6).
- Health and social care communities to prevent suicides (standard 7) by:
  - promoting mental health for all (standard 1)
  - delivering high quality primary mental health care (standard 2)
  - ensuring people with mental health problems can contact local services (standard 3)
  - ensuring that people with severe and enduring mental illness have a care plan (standard 4)
  - providing safe hospital accommodation where needed (standard 5)
  - enable, by support, carers to continue caring (standard 6)
  - support local prison staff
  - ensure that staff are competent to assess the risk of suicide
  - develop local systems to audit suicide, to learn lessons and to take any necessary action.

17.14.3 NATIONAL SERVICE FRAMEWORK FOR LONG-TERM CONDITIONS

A further national framework concerns long-term conditions (DH 2005b). It consists of a list of quality requirements:

1. **Person-centred service**. There should be integrated assessment and planning of health and social care needs. Information should be provided to enable informed decisions about care and treatment and to support people with long-term neurological conditions them to manage their conditions themselves.
2. **Early recognition, prompt diagnosis and treatment**. People suspected of having neurological condition should have prompt access to specialist neurological expertise for accurate diagnosis and treatment.
3. **Emergency and acute management**. People needing hospital admission for neurosurgical or neurological emergency should be assessed and treated in timely manner by teams with appropriate neurological and resuscitation skills.
4. **Early and specialist rehabilitation**. There should be timely, ongoing, high quality rehabilitation services in hospital or other specialist setting – also community rehabilitation and support.
5. **Community rehabilitation and support**. People at home should have ongoing access to a comprehensive range of rehabilitation, advice and support to meet needs, increase independence and autonomy and help them to live as they wish.
6. **Vocational rehabilitation**. There should be access to assessment, rehabilitation and ongoing support for finding, regaining, remaining in work, and to access other occupational and educational opportunities.

7. **Providing equipment and accommodation**. People with long-term neurological conditions are to receive timely, appropriate assistive technology/equipment and adaptations to accommodation to support them to live independently; help them with their care; maintain their health and improve their quality of life.

8. **Providing personal care and support**. Health and social care services work together to provide care and support to enable people with long-term neurology conditions to achieve maximum choice about living independently at home.

9. **Palliative care**. There should be a comprehensive range of palliative care services to control symptoms, offer pain relief and to meet needs for personal, social, psychological and spiritual support.

10. **Supporting family and carers**. Carers of people with long-term neurological conditions should have access to appropriate support and services that recognise their needs as carers and in their own right.

11. **Care in health or social care setting**. People with long-term neurological conditions should have their specific neurological needs met when receiving health or social care for other reasons.

17.15 NHS AND CHARGES FOR SERVICES

Health services and equipment provided by the NHS, unless otherwise specified, are by default free of charge to patients (NHS Act 2006, s.1). Despite this relatively clear position, misunderstandings and illegal charges do sometimes occur; hence the Department of Health issues guidance from time to time, in order to remind NHS bodies of the legal position (e.g. EL(91)129; EL(92)20).

Generally speaking, the charges that are specified cover equipment and drugs prescribed by general practitioners; dental services and appliances; spectacles and contact lenses; and elastic hosiery, wigs, abdominal or spinal supports and surgical brassieres (SI 2000/620). There are further distinctions to be made depending on the status of a patient, since not even these charges apply to NHS inpatients (NHS Act 2006, s.173). There are anyway also exemptions from, or reductions in, payment depending on factors such as the age, condition and financial status of patients (NHS Act 2006, s.182 and SI 2000/620). The system of medical exemptions from prescription charges has been heavily criticised. Unchanged since 1968, it is riddled with anomalies, not taking account of conditions such as cystic fibrosis and HIV/AIDS, and making confusing distinctions by exempting diabetes in some circumstances but not others (HCHC 2006, p.33)

In addition, separate rules govern charges for private patients (NHS Act 2006, schedule 2, para 15) and overseas visitors (see 14.3).

Patients cannot be charged if there is a defect in the appliance as supplied (NHS Act 2006, s.173), but can be charged if the need for repair or replacement is required due to an 'act or omission' of the patient (NHS Act 2006, s.186; SI 1974/284).

Improper charging policy for shoe repairs. A man had severe lower limb problems (caused by thalidomide) that caused excess wear and tear on the several pairs of NHS supplied orthopaedic shoes that he required. The NHS trust had a policy of making patients pay for the first two repairs per year per pair of shoes – on the basis that anyone using ordinary shoes might have to repair their shoes twice a year. The health service ombudsman stated that this policy was inconsistent with the 1974 regulations, that only gave a power to charge for a repair caused by a specific act or omission of the patient (*North Bristol NHS Trust 2000*).

If a person has received a compensation payment for an injury, and was treated by the NHS at a hospital, or provided with ambulance services, the person making the payment is liable to reimburse the NHS (Health and Social Care (Community Health and Standards) Act 2003, s.150).

17.15.1 NOT PROVIDING SERVICES AT ALL

The NHS does not have the same wide powers to charge as social services authorities. It does, ironically, have a wide discretion not to provide services at all. Sometimes confusion arises as to whether NHS patients have had to pay for NHS services or equipment (which would be unlawful) or been asked to purchase them privately (which would be lawful):

People buying their own equipment. The health service ombudsman investigated a case where the complainant had bought a transcutaneous nerve stimulator (TNS) for the relief of pain and wanted reimbursement from the hospital. The ombudsman accepted the hospital's explanation that normally it could not loan its own stock of TNS machines on a semi-permanent basis because of demand and a finite budget. One of the hospital staff explained that there was a point at which people 'had to look after themselves', since if they attended the hospital indefinitely, the system would grind to a halt. It transpired however that a long-term loan might have been possible from elsewhere, but that the hospital had not given a proper explanation of the possibilities; the ombudsman therefore found fault with the lack of information given to the complainant (HSO W.263/83–84).

Non-provision of chiropody services. Some 25 years ago, the health service ombudsman considered the use of a means test in relation to chiropody services. He found the authority's policy vindicated and quoted a DHSS letter to the authority: 'We know that many [authorities] do not have the manpower or other resources to provide a satisfactory service for even the elderly and have therefore decided to introduce their own criteria for determining priority amongst this and other groups…decisions as to level of provision rest with individual [authorities] and if your [authority] considers that a "means" type test is the best way of determining priority amongst those seeking treatment that is entirely a matter for the authority' (HSO W.68/77–78). One suspects that, given the sensitive nature of NHS rationing, such a policy would, if publicised, nowadays generate lively debate – if not in terms of the rationing itself, then of the criterion used to determine eligibility.

In one case, the health service ombudsman found it unobjectionable that a hospital occupational therapy department had made a charge for a reaching stick; perhaps on the basis that responsibility lay with the local authority social services department, but the person (understandably) did not want to wait (HSO W.340/80–81). Though a probably helpful practice, its lawfulness might have been open to question. Indeed, a decade later, the health service ombudsman investigated unlawful charging for chiropody appliances:

Charging for chiropody appliances. A health service ombudsman investigation found that a health authority had improperly tried to make charges for chiropody appliances supplied to a 13-year-old girl. The attempted justification by the authority referred to local financial constraints; but such constraints could not permit either a health authority or NHS trust to breach their statutory duties. Furthermore, Circular guidance had made clear that services, new or existing, should be planned within resources. Thus, the health authority could at its discretion decide to continue or discontinue altogether the bio-mechanics service; what they could not do was make unlawful charges for it. There were possibly 20 patients involved in such charging: the health authority was urged to investigate all 20 (HSO W.226/91–92).

It has been reported that some NHS trusts request deposits from £5 to £40 for the loan of equipment. In one case the NHS trust said that this was 'voluntary' but the notices to this effect were apparently unclear and in very small print (Clark *et al.* 1998, p.29). Such deposits are typically taken for items such as walking aids and wheelchairs. The Association of Community Health Councils expressed the view that such deposits amount to charges and are therefore unlawful (Ford, McLeish and Chester 2002, p.13).

Where the NHS has failed to accept responsibility for NHS continuing health care, then people have had either to fund their own nursing home care, or pay local authorities to arrange for it them – by using up their savings and selling their homes. The extent to which a charge has been in effect imposed by the NHS – via its refusal to provide the free services it was in principle obliged to – became evident in 2008. The Department of Health admitted that the NHS had had to repay at least £180 million to people who paid for their own continuing health care – on average £90,000 was owing to each person (Womack 2008).

17.15.2 INCOME GENERATION: HEALTH AND MEDICINES ACT 1988

Under the Health and Medicines Act 1988, the NHS is permitted to make charges for some services, as long as this does not interfere with the performance of duties under the 2006 Act or be to the disadvantage of NHS patients (s.7).

Under the 1988 Act, the NHS can operate income-generation schemes so long as they are profitable, the profit is used for improving health services, the goods or services must be marketed outside the NHS, they do not interfere with the provision of NHS services to patients, they must not be used to deliver core functions, they do not become so large so as to move from trading on the margins to becoming significant businesses which are relied in order to carry out core functions etc. (DH 2006a, pp.4–5). Income generation could include, for example, amenity beds for NHS patients involving extra facilities, items or services that are not an integral part of a patient's treatment, hearing aids (as long as the NHS ensures there is a clear demarcation between NHS and commercial provision), transport needed for social rather than medical needs, and car parking (DH 2006a, pp.7–8).

The Department of Health has issued extensive guidance on car parking income generation schemes. In chapter 5 of the guidance, it reminds NHS bodies to be 'sensitive' to the position of patients or visitors who use their car parks regularly. They are strongly recommended to have some sort of 'season ticket' arrangements for regular users, as well as a weekly cap on charges for people attending on a daily basis (DH 2006b, p.14).

The extensive use of these income generation powers has been called into question on matters such as hospital car parking charges and bedside telephones. For instance, cancer patients may be making frequent visits to hospital and have to pay very considerable parking charges. Rates in England vary from £0.30 per hour to £4.00. Likewise, patients have ended up paying very high costs for use of bedside telephones, ten pence per minute for outgoing calls, but £0.49 per minute for incoming calls (HCHC 2006, pp.35,39). In Wales, the Welsh Assembly took the decision in 2008 to abolish hospital car parking charges in Wales, thus removing an income stream to NHS trusts of some £5.4 million a year (HSJ 2008).

CHAPTER 18

NHS continuing health care

KEY POINTS

People with a continuing primary health need should in principle qualify for what is called 'NHS continuing health care'. This enables them to receive NHS services in hospital, a care home, a hospice or in their own home. Apart from benefiting from the services themselves, there can be very substantial financial advantages for service users. For example, if the person is in a care home providing nursing, the NHS is responsible for funding, free of charge, the accommodation, board, personal care and nursing care. This would compare to a nursing home resident who was deemed not to be in need of NHS continuing health care; he or she would receive only a certain amount of nursing care free of charge. The rest would be subject to a local authority means test that could result in the resident paying and having to sell his or her house. Similarly if a person is at home, then the NHS is responsible for funding not just the health care, but the personal care required as well, in which case the person would not be paying the local authority for the letter.

This situation has led to a great sense of injustice and unfairness amongst many older people and their families who understood that, having worked all their lives and paid tax and national insurance, that the National Health Service would look after them in their hour, literally, of greatest need and vulnerability.

Department of Health guidance about NHS continuing health care has been unclear and difficult to understand for some two decades. The health service ombudsman repeatedly, as well as the courts on occasion, has pointed this out forcibly. Equally persistently, the Department of Health has failed properly to sort the problem out. It has arguably fostered and encouraged not only uncertainty but evasion of legal obligations.

In 2007, the Department issued further procedural directions about continuing care assessments, a national framework, a 'decision support tool', and a 'needs checklist'. Notwithstanding this glut, early indicators are that legal questions and doubts remain – given, for example that some NHS primary care trusts are continuing to query whether a person has health care needs even if they are a mere few days from death.

18.1 NHS CONTINUING HEALTH CARE: BACKGROUND

In order to understand the present position, the background needs first to be outlined. The whole issue is also symptomatic of just how difficult it is to establish what the NHS is or isn't obliged to do, and how evasive and ambivalent central government has been when it comes to clear commitment to care for needy, older people with complex and expensive needs.

By the beginning of the 1990s, unease had been growing about the degree to which the NHS had surreptitiously been shedding long-stay beds. In 1994, it came as little surprise that the health service ombudsman should publish a hard-hitting report on the non-provision of NHS continuing health care by Leeds Health Authority:

Failure to provide NHS care for people with neurological conditions. A health authority had decided not to provide directly, or pay for elsewhere (e.g. a nursing home), continuing care for people with neurological conditions: the health authority neuro-surgical contract did not refer to institutional care at all. The person discharged was doubly incontinent, could not eat or drink without assistance, could not communicate, had a kidney tumour, cataracts in both eyes and occasional epileptic fits. There was no dispute that when he was discharged he did not need active medical treatment but did need 'substantial nursing care'. The health authority defended its position with reference to resources, priorities and national policy (which was being followed by other health authorities).

The health service ombudsman found a failure in service. He cited s.3 of the NHS Act 1977 at the beginning of the report, including s.3(1)(e) which refers to 'aftercare'. His findings read: 'This patient was a highly dependent patient in hospital under a contract made with the Infirmary by Leeds Health Authority; and yet, when he no longer needed care in an acute ward but manifestly still needed what the National Health Service is there to provide, they regarded themselves as having no scope for continuing to discharge their responsibilities to him because their policy was to make no provision for continuing care. The policy also had the effect of excluding an option whereby he might have the cost of his continuing care met by the NHS. In my opinion the failure to make available long-term care within the NHS for this patient was unreasonable and constitutes a failure in the service provided by the Health Authority. I uphold the complaint.'

The ombudsman recommended that the health authority reimburse nursing home costs already incurred by the man's wife and meet future costs; and also that it should review its 'provision of services for the likes of this man in view of the apparent gap in service available for this particular group of patients' (Leeds HA 1994).

In the wake of the Leeds case the following sequence has unfolded:

- **1995: Department of Health guidance**. In 1995, largely in response to the Leeds investigation, the Department of Health published specific guidance on continuing care in 1995 (HSG(95)8).
- **1995–6: more ombudsman investigations**. By 1995 and 1996 the health service ombudsman was publishing further reports of highly restrictive policies being operated by health authorities – such as not contracting for continuing care nursing home beds, even though the authority's hospital beds were inadequate to meet continuing care needs (*North Worcestershire HA 1995*), simply not funding continuing care beds either in hospitals or nursing homes (*Avon HA 1996*), not informing patients and their families about continuing care (*East Kent HA 1996*), quite improperly making even partial continuing care funding dependent on whether the patient received income support (*North Cheshire HA 1996*), or prejudging people's continuing care status and simply not telling them about it (*Buckinghamshire HA 1996*).
- **1999: Coughlan judgment**. In 1999, the Court of Appeal criticised the Department of Health's 1995 guidance, finding aspects of it both elusive and unclear. The court stated that the local authority should be responsible for nursing services in a care home, only if they were incidental or ancillary to the provision of the accommodation, or of a nature 'which it can be expected that an authority whose primary responsibility is to provide social services can be expected to provide'. Any other nursing care the NHS would be responsible for; in turn this would mean that a resident requiring such nursing care would be deemed to have NHS continuing health care status (*R v North and East Devon Health Authority, ex p Coughlan*).
- **1999: interim guidance and inaction**. In response to the *Coughlan* judgment, the Department of Health issued interim guidance in August 1999 (HSC 1999/180), stating that it would issue final guidance later in 1999; as a consequence the NHS and local authorities appeared to do little pending the imminent guidance. Unfortunately, it was almost a two-year wait before the guidance was issued. The health service ombudsman has since found evidence that during this time the Department of Health did little to encourage the NHS to review its practices; one letter sent out by a regional office of the Department could justifiably have been interpreted as a 'mandate to do the bare minimum' (HSO 2003c, para 21). At one meeting with such a regional office, a health authority was told to 'duck and dive' for a while (*Suffolk HA 2003*).
- **2001: guidance**. In 2001, in belated response to the *Coughlan* case, the Department of Health finally issued revised continuing care guidance (HSC 2001/15). Also in 2001, the Department of Health introduced what it termed 'free nursing care' and, in so doing, added an additional variable to the continuing care equation (not present at the time of the *Coughlan* case).
- **2001: NHS plan**. The government published, under the umbrella of its NHS Plan, its response to its own Royal Commission on Long Term Care. The response was totally silent about the issue of NHS continuing health care status (Secretary of State for Health 2000a).

- **2003: highly critical ombudsman report**. In 2003, the health service ombudsman published a special report on continuing care matters, this time severely criticising the 2001 guidance and the Department of Health's policy on continuing care. She found that the 2001 guidance was not only as unclear as the 1995 guidance (itself criticised by the Court of Appeal), but in fact was 'weaker'. This meant it would be even harder to judge under the 2001 guidance whether local NHS criteria were in line with the national guidance. She stated that any system should be 'fair and logical and should be transparent in respect of the entitlement of individuals'. Yet from what she had seen, 'the national policy and guidance that has been in place over recent years does not pass that test' (HSO 2003c, paras 28, 31). The ombudsman also recommended reimbursement of nursing home fees to all those service users who had as far back as 1996 themselves paid – when the NHS should have (HSO 2003c, para 39). The Department of Health instructed the NHS to comply with this recommendation by conducting retrospective reviews.
- **2004: ombudsman report on person with Alzheimer's disease in own home**. In 2004, the health service ombudsman published a further special report on continuing care, this time concerning a man with advanced Alzheimer's disease in his own home (*Cambridgeshire HA 2004*).
- **2004: directions**. In 2004, the Department of Health passed two sets of directions in respect of continuing care concerning assessment, the application of eligibility criteria and reviews (see immediately below).
- **2004: further ombudsman report**. In December 2004, the health service ombudsman issued yet another report (HSO 2004b), pointing to the continuing difficulties, casting doubt on the process of retrospective reviews and reimbursement (see 2003 report above), and making the following recommendations for action to be taken by the Department of Health in respect of:
    - ° (a) the establishment of clear, national minimum eligibility criteria which are understandable by health professionals, patients and carers
    - ° (b) the development of a set of accredited assessment tools and good practice guidance to support the criteria
    - ° (c) supporting training and development to expand local capacity and thus ensure that continuing care cases are assessed and decided properly and promptly
    - ° (d) clarification of standards for record keeping and documentation
    - ° (e) seeking assurance that the retrospective reviews have covered all those who might be affected
    - ° (f) monitoring the progress of retrospective reviews.
- **2004: Department of Health report**. A report commissioned by the Department of Health was published in December 2004, making a number of findings similar to that of the health service ombudsman's report of December 2004 (Henwood 2004).
- **2004: Department of Health undertaking to publish further guidance**. In December 2004, a government minister (Stephen Ladyman) announced that he would commission a 'new national framework' on continuing care, although he still maintained (despite the health service ombudsman's withering criticisms) that the existing criteria were 'fair and legal' (DH 2004g).
- **2005:** The House of Commons Health Committee reported that the system was 'beset with complexity', had been contentious for over a decade, was a postcode lottery, and

that the system should have built in incentives to promote rehabilitation and independence (HCHC 2005, p.3).

- **2006: Grogan judgment**. The High Court found that the NHS in the Bexley area was applying Department of Health guidance in such a way that was unlawful, because it was not asking the right legal questions as set out in the *Coughlan* judgment back in 1999. Furthermore, although the case was not brought against the Department of Health, the judge subjected the latter's guidance to serious criticism (*R(Grogan) v Bexley NHS Care Trust*).

- **2006: BBC Panorama programmes**. The BBC broadcast two *Panorama* programmes, entitled *The National Homes Scandal*. The reason for running two programmes within months of each other was because of the unprecedented level of public response to the first (BBC 2006).

- **2007: Health Service Ombudsman** criticises the Department of Health guidance on restitution (HSO 2007).

- **2007:** Department of Health reissues guidance on restitution (DH 2007m).

- **2007: Department of Health's new guidance comes into force in October 2007**. Nearly three years after the commitment to new guidance given in December 2004, a new 'national framework' was implemented in October 2007, together with a 'decision support tool', a 'checklist' (for screening purposes), and a 'fast-track pathway tool'. It was underpinned by three sets of directions, imposing various obligations on the NHS (see below).

- **2008: tens of millions of pounds repaid**. Department of Health confirms that over £180 million was repaid to thousands of elderly people who had wrongly been charged for what should have been free, NHS continuing health care. The final amount was reported as possibly exceeding £200 million, with the average restitution amounting to some £90,000 per person (Womack 2008).

In sum, right up to the bringing into force of new guidance and directions in October 2007, the Department of Health had, for well over a decade, maintained that there was nothing wrong with its guidance, despite the criticism that rained in from all quarters. Nonetheless, it did concede that it expected the new rules to mean that some 5000–10,000 people, previously deemed ineligible, to be eligible (CSCI 2008, p.13). Yet reports in early 2008 showed that numbers began to drop in a significant number of NHS primary care trust (PCT) areas, especially in the case of people with a terminal illness (Gainsbury 2008). It is also possible that some of the guidance produced by the Department of Health, particularly its 'decision support tool' (see below) was inconsistent with the legal position and would provoke a rash of new challenges to NHS decisions on continuing care. Such uncertainties are unsurprising in the light of the highly restrictive and wildly varying policies applied by PCTs. If Department of Health statistics for 2005/6 are to be believed, a person might at an extreme have been 1000 times more likely to have been given continuing health care status in one PCT rather than another. Even allowing for such statistical outliers to be suspect, the statistics still showed huge discrepancies across some 300 PCTs (DH 2007n).

18.1.1 REIMBURSEMENT OF MONEY TO PEOPLE WRONGLY CHARGED FOR CARE

Following the health service ombudsman's report of 2003 (HSO 2003c), the Department of Health had instructed strategic health authorities to conduct reviews of people who might have wrongly been charged for care, which should have been free as NHS continuing health care. Such reviews should have been directed not just at past nursing home placements, but also at situations where people at home might have been paying for services that should have been free from the NHS (see e.g. *Cambridgeshire HA 2004*).

The outcome of these reviews was that a great deal of money was repaid; although the health service ombudsman has since criticised the speed of the efforts being made (HSO 2004, p.13). Further criticism by the health service ombudsman at the end of 2004 pointed out that:

- The Department of Health had assured the ombudsman that retrospective reviews of cases would be finished by December 2003, but it was now clear that the backlog might not be dealt with even by the end of 2004.
- The Department of Health had not collected central statistics relating to retrospective reviews since July 2004 and had no plans to do so.
- In more than 50 per cent of review cases examined by the ombudsman, the assessments had not been carried out properly due to a lack of consistency of approach, variable quality of assessments, confused and inconsistent panel procedures (e.g. some lacked clinical or professional input), failure to record reasons for decisions, and poor communication with patients and relatives. There had also been delays in the payment of restitution following retrospective reviews.
- In the absence of support and leadership from the Department of Health and some strategic health authorities, the ombudsman's office was regularly receiving requests for advice, interpretation of the guidance and even training. However, it was for the Department of Health to clarify procedures, which it had itself initiated, rather than for the ombudsman to do so (HSO 2004b, Summary and paras 5, 29, 32).

The scale of the problem of retrospective review and reimbursement was indicated by the number of reviews involved (nearly 12,000), the number of complaints made to the health service ombudsman (reported in December 2004 as numbering 4000 since February 2003), and the amount of money allocated by the Department of Health for restitution (£180 million). The ombudsman pointed out that she could not say with certainty whether all strategic health authorities had made extensive and comprehensive efforts to locate patients (and their relatives) eligible for retrospective review (HSO 2004b, paras 5, 40, 12). Finally, in July 2007, ahead of the implementation of the new national framework on continuing care in October 2007, the Department of Health signalled an end to the review process – subject to exceptional cases – on 30 November 2007 (Nicholson 2007).

In the meantime the Parliamentary and health service ombudsman (that is the same person exercising both roles) had found fault with the guidance issued by the Department of Health on how primary care trusts should decide on recompense to be paid. The guidance had stated that such restitution would only apply to monies paid out in care home fees, but not to other circumstances such as premature sale of a property, or inconvenience or distress that individuals had suffered in making unnecessarily difficult decisions about how to fund care. The guidance had resulted in a PCT refusing to make financial recompense for the sale of a person's property to fund care. This maladministration had resulted in inconsistency of payments (HSO 2007).

18.2 NHS CONTINUING HEALTH CARE DIRECTIONS ON PROCEDURAL ASPECTS

In 2007, the Department of Health passed two sets of directions in respect of continuing care, which impose specific duties on the NHS. Although procedural only, they nevertheless could be the basis for challenging decisions made by PCTs. An additional set of directions was made in relation to 'free nursing care', that is, the registered nursing care component payable for people in nursing homes – in contrast to NHS continuing health care (see 17.9).

18.2.1 DELAYED DISCHARGES (CONTINUING CARE) DIRECTIONS 2007

One set, in respect of delayed patient discharges from hospital, stipulates that before the NHS gives notice to a social services authority to assess a person in relation to hospital discharge (under the Community Care (Delayed Discharges) Act 2003), it must take reasonable steps to ensure that an NHS continuing care assessment is carried out. This is where it appears to the NHS body – in consultation, where it considers this appropriate, with the local social services authority – that the patient may have a need for such care. The NHS body:

- **(consultation with patient)** must consult with the patient and, where it considers it appropriate, the patient's carer
- **(screening)** must use the 'needs checklist' for screening purposes (if it wishes to use an initial screening process), in order to decide whether to undertake an assessment for NHS continuing health care, inform the person about the decision as to whether to carry out an assessment of his or her NHS continuing health care needs, and make a record of the decision in the patient's notes
- **(multi-disciplinary assessment)** must ensure that a multi-disciplinary assessment is used to inform the decision about eligibility for NHS continuing health care
- **(decision support tool)** must ensure that the 'decision support tool' is completed and used to inform the decision as to whether a person has a primary health need
- **(primary health need)** must, in deciding about a primary health need, consider whether – if the person is going into a care home – his or her needs are more than incidental or ancillary to the provision of the accommodation, or are of a nature beyond that which a social services authority, whose primary responsibility is to provide social services, could be expected to provide. If either of these conditions is satisfied, then the NHS body must determine that the person has a primary health need
- **(notification to patient)** must, where an NHS continuing health care assessment has been carried, notify in writing the person assessed and make a record of the decision in the person's notes
- **(review of decision)** must, where the decision is that the person is ineligible, inform the person (or somebody acting on his or her behalf) that he or she can apply for a review in connection with either the procedure followed by the NHS body in reaching the decision about eligibility, or the application of the criterion (i.e. primary health need) of eligibility (DH 2007o).

18.2.2 NHS CONTINUING HEALTHCARE (RESPONSIBILITIES) DIRECTIONS 2007

The second set of directions sets out the responsibilities of NHS primary care trusts (PCTs), strategic health authorities (SHAs) and local social services authorities. They state that:

- **(PCT to ensure assessment)** a PCT must take reasonable steps to ensure that an NHS continuing care assessment is carried out. This is where it appears to the NHS body (in consultation, where it considers this appropriate, with social services) that the patient may have a need for such care or for a variation in the provision of such care. This must be before an assessment is carried about a person's need for nursing care in residential accommodation under the NHS

- **(screening)** the PCT must use the 'needs checklist' for screening purposes (if it wishes to use an initial screening process), in order to decide whether to undertake an assessment for NHS continuing health care, inform the person about the decision as to whether to carry out an assessment of his or her NHS continuing health care needs, and make a record of the decision in the patient's notes

- **(multi-disciplinary assessment)** the PCT must ensure that a multi-disciplinary assessment is used to inform the decision about eligibility for NHS continuing health care

- **(decision support tool)** the PCT must ensure that the 'decision support tool' is completed and used to inform the decision as to whether a person has a primary health need

- **(primary health need)** the PCT must, in deciding about a primary health need, consider whether – if the person is going into a care home – his or her needs are more than incidental or ancillary to the provision of the accommodation, or are of a nature beyond that which a social services authority, whose primary responsibility is to provide social services, could be expected to provide. If either of these conditions is satisfied, then the PCT must decide that the person has a primary health need

- **(notify the patient)** the PCT must, where an NHS continuing health care assessment has been carried, notify in writing the person assessed and make a record of the decision in the person's notes

- **(review of decision)** the PCT must, where the decision is that the person is ineligible, inform the person (or somebody acting on his or her behalf) that he or she can apply for a review in connection with either the procedure followed by the PCT in reaching the decision about eligibility, or the application of the criterion (ie primary health need) of eligibility

- **(social services involvement)** the PCT shall, as far as is reasonably practicable, consult with the social services authority, before making a decision about a person's eligibility for NHS continuing health care. The authority shall, as far as is reasonably practicable, provide advice and assistance to the PCT

- **(community care assessment)** nothing in this direction affects the duty of a social services authority to carry out an assessment under s.47 of the NHS and Community Care Act 1990

- **(disputes between NHS and social services)** any dispute between the PCT and social services authority about eligibility for NHS continuing health care, or about the contribution of either to a jointly funded package of care, should be resolved in accordance with an agreed local dispute resolution procedure

- **(strategic health authority panels)** each SHA must establish a panel, including an independent chairman, to consider reviews of decision concerning either the procedure followed by a PCT or by an NHS trust (under the delayed discharge directions: see above) in reaching a decision about eligibility, or the application of the criterion (primary health need) of eligibility

- on application by the person, or a person on his or her behalf, expressing dissatisfaction about an NHS continuing health care decision, the SHA may refer the decision to the review panel (DH 2007p).

18.3 NHS CONTINUING HEALTH CARE: GUIDANCE

In addition to the directions set out above, which provide a procedural framework, further Department of Health guidance sets out the substance of how NHS continuing health care decisions should be made:

- a national framework (DH 2007a)
- core values and principles (DH 2007b)
- a decision support tool (DH 2007c)
- a checklist for screening purposes (DH 2007d)
- a fast-track pathway tool (DH 2007e)
- guidance on NHS-funded nursing care (DH 2007f).

In addition, the Association of Directors of Adult Social Services and the Local Government Association have issued guidance of their own (ADASS 2007).

18.4 DECIDING ABOUT CONTINUING CARE ELIGIBILITY

Department of Health guidance states that NHS continuing health care means 'care provided over an extended period of time to a person aged 18 or over to meet physical or mental health needs which have arisen as the result of disability accident or illness. NHS continuing health care means a package of continuing care arranged and funded solely by the NHS' (DH 2007a, para 7).

Continuing care needs can result also in jointly funded packages of care. But the key legal test for NHS continuing health care is whether the person has a 'primary health need' (DH 2007a, para 23). This is because the courts have held this to be so in *R v North and East Devon Health Authority, ex p Coughlan* and in *R(Grogan) v Bexley NHS Care Trust.*

Thus, the primary health need test should be applied so that a person is only ineligible for NHS continuing health care if the nursing or other health services are (a) no more than incidental or ancillary to the provision of residential accommodation which the local authority is under a duty to provide, and (b) are not of a nature beyond which a local authority, whose primary responsibility is to provide social services, could be expected to provide (DH 2007a, para 24). Again this derives from the *Coughlan* and *Grogan* cases, and is enshrined in the continuing care directions (see 18.2 above).

The ADASS guidance is blunter. It points out that for local authorities to fund more than what is incidental or ancillary – that is, to fund a person with nursing needs that are a major, rather than a lesser, part of what is being provided – is simply unlawful (ADASS, 2007, p.11).

The Department of Health guidance states that there should not be a gap between what the NHS and social services provide (DH 2007a, para 24). However, it is unclear quite what it means by this. This is because it is established that even if the NHS incurs a duty in principle under s.3 of the NHS Act 2006, nonetheless it is a target duty only – and lack of resources is nearly always a defence for non-provision of a service. For instance, in the following case, there clearly was a gap between what the NHS would provide and what the local authority was legally able to provide:

No help with tracheostomy care. A woman was caring for her child at home, who had a tracheostomy. The woman also had another, older, disabled daughter, who visited home fortnightly. The woman was struggling to cope. She was receiving a certain amount of assistance from the NHS primary care trust, but felt she needed more, especially in light of her exhaustion resulting from sleep deprivation. The case centred mainly on the provision of ten extra hours of help a night. The PCT did not accept that this was required. But, in any case, the s.3 target duty could not be enforced. Although human rights considerations could 'crystallise' this target duty into a specific, enforceable duty, none-theless this case did not raise human rights issues under articles 2, 3 or 8.

The mother had turned to social services for the extra assistance. But the court found that the particular nursing care required, including tube replacement and unblocking, was nursing care of a type beyond that which social services legally could provide. To hold that social services might be obliged to provide such care under s.17 of the Children Act 1989 or s.2 of the Chronically Sick and Disabled Person Act 1970 would mean turning a social services authority into a substitute or addi-tional NHS for children.

Thus, the PCT was not obliged to provide the extra care, and the local authority was not empow-ered to (R(T) v London Borough of Haringey).

And, some years ago, the health service ombudsman elicited from the Department of Health, in respect of continuing care investigations, a response as follows suggesting just such a gap. The Department stated that there were three options legally open to the NHS: (a) to provide a hospital bed; (b) to purchase a bed in a private hospital or nursing home; (c) to advise that 'their resources did not extend' to providing full NHS continuing health care (HSO W.194/89–90).

In 2008, the Court of Appeal reiterated that 'there can be no gap' and that 'if a person's care needs are not primarily health care needs, they will be social services needs'. Thus the PCT will 'take account of the social services authority's statutory competence so that the resulting decision will define the services which the social services authority is obliged to provide' (St Helens BC v Manchester PCT). This is a clear statement that in principle there should be no gap; but such a statement of principle does not necessarily translate into the real world for every patient – since it would seem clear that the NHS can, at least in individual cases, still decline to meet some or even all of a person's primary health care needs, needs which the local authority would lack the statutory power to meet.

18.4.1 PRIMARY HEALTH NEED

The Department of Health guidance states that certain characteristics of need may help deter-mine whether the quantity or quality of care required goes beyond what local authorities can legally provide under the rules established in the *Coughlan* case:

- **nature**: type of needs and overall effect, including type (quality) of interventions required
- **intensity**: extent (quality) and severity (degree) of the needs including the need for sustained care (continuity)

- **complexity**: how the needs arise and interact to increase the skill needed to monitor and manage the care, or
- **unpredictability**: degree to which needs fluctuate, creating difficulty in managing needs, and level of risk to person's health.

The guidance states that 'each of these characteristics may, in combination or alone, demonstrate a primary health need, because of the quality and/or quantity of care required to meet the individual's needs.' It also states that one or more these characteristics may well apply to those people approaching the end of their lives (DH 2007a, paras 26–27). This means that any one characteristic could be sufficient and that it would not be necessary for a person's condition, for example, to be unstable or unpredictable – something that PCTs have often wrongly argued to be a pre-requisite for full NHS continuing health care. However, the courts have pointed out that none of this means that 'care needs are [by definition] health care needs if they are by nature complex, intense or unpredictable, since they have to be health care needs in the first place' (*St Helens BC v Manchester PCT*). In other words, the court seemed to be saying that a social care need could be complex, intense or unpredictable.

To minimise variation in how these principles are interpreted, the Department of Health has published a decision support tool (see below) which covers the following 'domains' of a person's needs: behaviour, cognition, communication, psychological/emotional needs, mobility, nutrition (food/drink), continence, skin, breathing, drug therapies and medication (symptom control), altered states of consciousness (DH 2007c).

The term 'primary health need' is a legal one, identified as the key test in the case of *Coughlan* and followed in a later, 2006, case (*R(Grogan) v Bexley NHS Care Trust*).

18.4.1.1 NHS is the decision-maker about a primary health need

Ultimately, a legal challenge by a local authority (or by anybody else) to an NHS decision – for example, that a person's needs were not of the primary health variety – is not without difficulty. Indeed, in terms of local authorities challenging the NHS, with a legal case resulting, the Court of Appeal was distinctly unenthusiastic. This is perhaps an unfortunate outcome, given the poor standards of decision-making to be found in some primary care trusts, and the intransigence of those trusts in the face of anything less drastic than a legal challenge. It is also not clear, from the comments of the court about the money 'all coming out of the same purse', whether it had in mind how drastic the financial consequences may be for service users if continuing care decisions go wrong:

NHS is primary decision maker, NHS legislation is dominant, the courts will interfere with caution – and the courts deplore two publicly funded bodies engaging in expensive litigation. The case involved a woman with dissociative identity disorder. The local authority argued that (a) the views of the multi-disciplinary team had been inaccurately recorded and communicated to the panel, (b) the team had not applied the right criteria, (c) the decision-making panel had not taken account of all the relevant material, (d) the panel had misapplied the criteria, (e) the patient's condition was unique, complex and fluctuating and the panel's decision was irrational. Indeed, the local authority argued that the woman's condition could not be more serious and that if her needs were not health care needs, then nobody with a mental disability would ever have a primary health need. She required support with daily living, with medication and with her aggressive and self-harming behaviour; this required three carers during the day and two at night. The cost of her care package was £675,000 per annum.

The Court of Appeal held (a) that the primary decision-maker was the NHS, (b) that the NHS Act 2006 was dominant (over social services legislation), (c) that the local authority did not have an equivalent decision-making process that could hold its own against the NHS in respect of continuing care needs, (d) that the court would not get involved in 'substantive' issue about the merits of the conflicting decisions reached by the primary care trust and local authority, and (e) that the decision would be challengeable only on traditional public law grounds (e.g. rationality). The court also found it unsatisfactory that two publicly funded public authorities should engage in expensive litigation, especially when 'the money for the care and the money for the litigation is all coming out of the same purse' (*St Helens BC v Manchester PCT*).

However, if this case appears heavily to stack the cards in favour of the NHS in continuing care disputes, there were three provisos. First, even if the NHS is the primary decision maker, and it is for the local authority to pick up the remaining pieces, the court reiterated that the local authority cannot lawfully provide services and care beyond its statutory competence. (And this decision, about the limits of its statutory functions, must be for the local authority to take). Second, the primary status of the NHS decision was not in the sense that it would 'trump' that of the local authority, but that it was to the NHS legislation (and NHS body) that the court would look for the decision about health care. Third, the case concerned guidance in force prior to October 2007; the Court of Appeal expressly noted that it would refrain from stating what the position would be under the national framework guidance (DH 2007a) in force since that date (*St Helens BC v Manchester PCT*).

18.4.2 AVOIDING PITFALLS IN THE DECISION-MAKING PROCESS

Department of Health guidance sets out some further core principles which, on their face, at least, are to remedy some of the serious defects in NHS decision-making over the past decade and longer.

It states that NHS continuing health care may be provided by PCTs in any setting (including, but not only, a care home, hospice, person's own home). Thus, eligibility decisions should not be based on setting of care (DH 2007a, para 37). The issue of setting or location has sometimes surfaced in health service ombudsman investigations:

Equating hospital with continuing care. The local eligibility criteria for NHS continuing health care were being applied such that if a person could be cared for in a nursing home rather than an NHS facility, an assumption was made that the person would not be of continuing health care status. The ombudsman criticised this, notwithstanding that the criteria did in principle allow for exceptions; but in practice, this aspect of the criteria was 'likely to be missed by those interpreting the policy' (*Dorset HA 2003*).

Undue emphasis on hospital care. A health authority stated that people in specialist nursing home care could be eligible for continuing care funding. However, the criteria went on to state that this would only be where there was a constant availability of on-site specialist medical expertise 24 hours a day, or of highly complex or specialist medical equipment to maintain life. In reality, this was only possible in hospital; thus the issue of whether a person needed hospital medical provision was overly significant in the decision about eligibility for continuing care (*Berkshire HA 2003*).

Likewise, criteria that left no scope for the NHS to fund the full cost of care in a nursing home were defective and over-restrictive, since such an approach might raise questions about quality of life (a person might be better off elsewhere than in a hospital) and, in any case, many authorities would have insufficient hospital beds available to sustain such a policy but still properly fund NHS continuing health care (*Shropshire Health Authority 2003a*).

Respite care only as NHS inpatient. In another case, the ombudsman criticised the fact that continuing care funding would only be available for respite care if the person concerned became an NHS inpatient, but would not be available in his own home, so as to give his main carer, his wife, a break (*Cambridgeshire HA 2004*).

No continuing care other than in hospital. The health authority had decided, as a matter of policy, not to contract for private nursing home places for continuing care needs. Yet the 24 long-stay hospital beds for continuing care were insufficient for that purpose. Therefore, in order to manage this shortfall, the authority's policy simply excluded NHS funding for the continuing care of younger, highly dependent patients not in need of hospital inpatient treatment. The health service ombudsman found this to be a failure to provide a service that it was a function of the health authority to provide (*North Worcestershire HA 1995*).

The guidance maintains that the decision should not be based on whether or not the person's needs are currently being successfully managed, on use or not of NHS employed staff to provide care, on need for/presence of 'specialist staff' in care delivery, on existence of other NHS-funded care, or on any other input-related (rather than needs-related) rationale (DH 2007a, para 42). This point about specialist staff not necessarily being required answers the health service ombudsman's criticism in the past that the requirement of 'specialist' intervention was unduly restrictive (HSO 2004, para 19). Similarly, the question of current successful management, or use or not of NHS staff, not being decisive was dealt with by the ombudsman in the following case (the *Pointon* case which received considerable publicity at the time):

Eligibility for continuing care without input by a registered nurse. One health service ombudsman case involved the care at home by a woman (and personal assistants) of her husband, who had Alzheimer's disease. One of the grounds on which the NHS had held that he was not continuing health care status was that he was not receiving regular care from registered nurses. Two of the senior staff involved in continuing care decisions (the manager and director, both nurses) stated that the wife was not providing nursing care, since nursing qualifications and skills could not be self-taught and took many years to acquire. Therefore the care being given by the wife could not be highly professional. Yet both an independent medical consultant and the consultant psychiatrist involved disagreed with this view; they said that the severity of the man's condition meant he had health care needs 'well beyond' anything that the average care worker was competent to deal with.

The consultant psychiatrist also gave the view that the care was being provided in a professional manner, and was equal to, if not superior to, the care the husband would have received on an NHS dementia ward. Indeed, the 'atmosphere was not one that could be replicated in a continuing care ward' (*Cambridgeshire HA 2004*).

The guidance states that the decision-making process should be 'accurately and fully recorded' (DH 2007a, para 39). This point is well made:

Inconsistency and lack of clarity. A woman had suffered a stroke, was admitted to hospital and then discharged to a nursing home. She had insulin dependent diabetes, and had been left by the stroke immobile and unable to speak. Prior to her discharge, a feeding tube was removed. She was assessed as ineligible for continuing care.

The health service ombudsman criticised the decision, on the grounds that the assessment documentation was incomplete, and that the family had been neither given information about the eligibility criteria, nor involved properly in the discharge process. The health authority's criteria had been reviewed in the light of the *Coughlan* judgment, but the support documentation for assessment had not been. This led to inconsistency and a lack of clarity (*Gloucestershire HA 2003*).

The health service ombudsman further expressed disquiet that some NHS bodies simply view continuing care funding as a 'top band' above the high band of registered nursing care funding. This might mean that they fail to consider the 'totality' of a person's health care needs, instead carrying out only nursing, rather than multi-disciplinary continuing care, assessments. The ombudsman found evidence of this occurring, and suggested that one causative factor might be the confusing similarity of wording in the registered nursing care guidance with the wording in the continuing care guidance (HSO 2004, para 22). The judge in the *Grogan* case made the same point (*R(Grogan) v Bexley NHS Care Trust*).

Likewise in a case investigated by the Scottish Public Services Ombudsman, the health board had failed, contrary to the clinical evidence, to consider a patient eligible for even an assessment as to whether he would qualify for NHS continuing health care (*Ayrshire and Arran Health Board 2007*).

The guidance also makes clear that financial issues should not be considered as part of the eligibility decision; that PCT panels should not play a financial monitoring role; that multi-disciplinary team recommendations should be overturned only rarely by the panel; and that eligibility decisions should not delay treatment or appropriate care. In addition it states that an assessment should always consider further potential for rehabilitation, and that the risks and benefits of change of location should be considered before move or change takes place (DH 2007a, paras 39–40).

Such points are also well made. The sheer arbitrariness of PCT decisions, largely driven by concern about finances, would seem to be borne out by statistics issued by the Department of Health (DH 2007n). In addition, the reference to rehabilitation is important, although the significant reduction in specialist rehabilitation units and services around the country may make this point all too often academic – especially since decisions may increasingly be made by health care professionals without adequate specialist knowledge and experience in rehabilitation.

18.4.3 END OF LIFE ELIGIBILITY

The guidance states that there should be a fast-tracking process for people rapidly deteriorating. Also, that one or more of the characteristics of need (nature, intensity, complexity or unpredictability) may well apply to a person nearing the end of his or her life (DH 2007a, para 27).

Other guidance states: 'Individuals with a rapidly deteriorating condition and short-term life expectancy will immediately qualify for NHS continuing health care. For the purposes of determining eligibility to NHS funding, 'short-term' should not be defined prescriptively or restrictively, but should be based on an assessment of the person's care needs and considered as a period of time which can be expressed in days and weeks. Strict time limits are not relevant for end of life cases and should not be imposed – it is the responsibility of the assessor to make a decision based on the relevant facts of the case' (DH 2007b, para 36).

The ADASS guidance is more specific, suggesting that people with a prognosis of 12 weeks to live or less, should receive NHS funding (p.13). The Department of Health has published a fast-track assessment tool, to help clinicians make decisions 'where an individual not previously awarded NHS continuing health care on the basis of need has a rapidly deteriorating condition, which may be entering a terminal phase. They may need NHS continuing health care funding to enable their needs to be urgently met (e.g. to allow them to go home to die or to allow appropriate end-of-life support to be put in place)' (DH 2007e, para 2). Anecdotal reports received since October 2007, when the new guidance and directions came into force, suggest that some PCTs have made even stricter their approach to terminal illness. Prior to that date, a period of four, eight or ten weeks of remaining life was adopted in some PCTs as a local guideline for intervention. Since October, it appears some PCTs have reduced this to as little as two days; in practice, by this time, the person is dead before the PCT intervenes and accepts responsibility.

18.4.4 LEGAL AND OMBUDSMAN CASES INDICATIVE OF CONTINUING CARE

The guidance states that PCTs should be aware of cases which have indicated circumstances where a finding of NHS continuing care eligibility should have been made (e.g. the *Coughlan* case and some health service ombudsman cases). It is clearly suggesting that such cases may be indicative of eligibility, if the patient currently being considered has similar needs.

However, the guidance dilutes this somewhat when it warns also that PCTs should be 'wary of trying to extrapolate generalisations about eligibility' and that there is 'no substitute for a careful and detailed assessment of the needs of the individual whose eligibility is in question' (DH 2007a, para 61). Nonetheless, it seems clear that PCTs should give very serious consideration to awarding NHS continuing health care to patients who are similar to those at the heart of these indicative legal and ombudsman cases. The following are examples of ombudsman cases, together with the *Coughlan* legal case, in which continuing care status was established or was a strong possibility:

Substantial nursing care. A man was doubly incontinent, could not eat or drink without assistance, could not communicate, had a kidney tumour, cataracts in both eyes and occasional epileptic fits. There was no dispute that when he was discharged he did not need active medical treatment but did need 'substantial nursing care'. Failure to provide continuing care was unreasonable and a failure in the duty to provide a service for a highly dependent person (*Leeds HA 1994*).

More than incidental and ancillary. A woman, who had been badly injured in a road traffic accident, was described as tetraplegic, doubly incontinent, requiring regular catheterisation, partially paralysed in respiratory function, subject to problems attendant on immobility and also to recurrent headaches caused by an associated neurological condition. She required regular nursing input but not active medical treatment. Her nursing needs were held to be more than just 'incidental or ancillary' to the provision of accommodation, and were not of a nature that social services could be expected to provide (*R v North and East Devon HA, ex p Coughlan*).

More than incidental and ancillary. A woman had suffered several strokes, had no speech or comprehension, was unable to swallow and required feeding by a PEG tube into the stomach, and was doubly incontinent. Her needs were more than just incidental or ancillary to the provision of nursing home accommodation or of a nature that social services could be expected to provide; they were on a par with those in the *Coughlan* case, and should have attracted continuing health care funding (*Wigan and Bolton HA 2003*).

Intensive and complex care package. A woman had vascular dementia, confusion and challenging behaviour; she had been assessed as having multiple and complex nursing and medical problems. These required an 'intensive and complex' personal care package, well beyond the customary level of care offered by a nursing home. The ombudsman could not see how the nursing care required could be only 'incidental or ancillary' to the provision of accommodation, or of a nature that social services could be expected to provide (*Berkshire HA 2003*).

Constant supervision. A man with Alzheimer's disease was now living at home, being cared for by his wife and other personal assistants. He was totally reliant on others for his needs to be met. He was subject to epileptic seizures, muscular spasms, panic attacks and episodes of choking, visual spatial difficulties and hallucinatory experiences. He required constant supervision (*Cambridgeshire HA 2004*).

Significant nursing care beyond incidental or ancillary. A woman in a nursing home was assessed as requiring full assistance with all personal care tasks including washing, dressing, feeding and toileting. She was doubly incontinent, dependent on others for her safety and could mobilise only with assistance. The health authority refused a request for an independent review. The ombudsman was advised by her independent clinical assessor that it was debatable whether the significant nursing care required could properly be regarded as incidental or ancillary. The ombudsman recommended that a reassessment take place to determine the status of the woman (*Shropshire HA 2003*).

Primary health need? A woman was discharged to a nursing home without continuing care funding. The assessment included the fact that she was unable to manage any aspect of personal care independently, had an in-dwelling urinary catheter, suffered from occasional faecal incontinence, required a soft puréed diet, had a PEG (percutaneous endoscopic gastrostomy) feed, needed a hoist for all transfers because of hemi-paresis and contracture, required re-positioning every two hours in order to manage pressure risks, communicated by eye contact and head movement, could not speak, and was totally reliant on others for safety. The ombudsman's assessor concluded that the health authority's decision to deny continuing care status was debatable. The ombudsman recommended that the health authority re-determine whether the woman should have continuing health care status (*Shropshire HA 2003a*).

Head injured woman requiring sustained nursing care, mental stimulation and physiotherapy. A woman sustained severe head injuries in a road traffic accident. She was admitted to the neuro-surgical unit of a hospital. After she was over the acute stage, some six months later, she was discharged to a private nursing home charging £200 per week. The district health authority (DHA) denied it was responsible for funding her placement. Basically, the health authority considered that it lacked the resources to fund non-acute health needs for such a patient. The relevant hospital consultant told the ombudsman that although she no longer needed to be in the unit, she still required nursing care, mental stimulation and physiotherapy. She would remain severely incapacitated and would 'sustained nursing care for the rest of her life'. The ombudsman found it 'incontrovertible, therefore, in the light of the level of continuing care [she] will require...that the DHA had a duty to continue to provide the care...at no cost to her or her family'. This meant the DHA should meet the cost of provision and should reimburse the complainant (the woman's son) who had receivership from the Court of Protection (HSO W.478/89–90).

Man with serious medical needs: if he did not qualify who would? A 55-year-old man had a stroke and was admitted to hospital. Six months later, his wife was told that nothing more could be done for him and a nursing home would be required. He was discharged; the health authority refused to pay for the nursing home placement or even the transport to the home. His general practitioner was enlisted to help and he wrote to the family's MP to the effect that the man was in the nursing home because 'he continues to have several serious medical problems for which he is under consultant medical care. Because of his stroke he cannot walk and because he is a relatively young man his severe stroke condition causes him to be chronically depressed. He is incontinent of urine and has difficulty feeding himself although he does so. His diabetes is controlled by insulin. His care is coordinated by a consultant physician at the Alexandra Hospital, Redditch, but the specialist nature of his blood condition requires that he is also under the care of a consultant haemotologist at the same hospital. He likely to remain under the consultant for the rest of his life because of the serious state of his Crohn's disease [inflammatory disease of the bowel], his diabetes and his idiopathic thrombocytopenia [a blood disorder]. In addition he has hypertension and is on treatment for that as well'.

The chairman of the regional health authority had stated to the district health authority that the man appeared to have very complex needs and 'that begs the question, if people like [the patient] do not qualify for continuing care by reason of ill-health, then who does?'

The health service ombudsman found that 'the continuing care of a highly dependent patient like the complainant's husband is a service which the NHS should provide'. The policy adopted by the district health authority represented a 'failure to provide a service which it is the authority's function to provide'. The ombudsman recommended that the authority pick up the cost of the nursing home placement and make an *ex gratia* payment to the wife to cover the cost of the care already incurred (*North Worcestershire HA 1995*).

Another type of case, heard by a social services tribunal, shed further light on the chaotic nature of NHS continuing health care saga, revealing clearly how the issue is so often financial, patient need relegated to a virtual sideshow. The financial dispute was played out between a government department, the Department of Work and Pensions, and a health authority (now an NHS primary care trust). The tribunal criticised heavily the NHS for spending its time devising flawed schemes for saving money, which in the end simply wasted public resources:

Dispute between the NHS and the Department of Work and Pensions over people with severe learning disabilities. The NHS had placed a number of people with severe learning disabilities in a care home. They had substantial nursing care needs, and the Social Security Commissioners ruled that it clearly counted as 'hospital accommodation', and that these residents should have been given NHS continuing health care status. They were not. Instead, they claimed benefits and were charged for their accommodation. Those receiving the care component of disability living allowance handed this over to the home by way of payment.

The Tribunal found that the residents clearly were a continuing NHS responsibility. 'The legislation is clear and so are the principles behind it. Whilst the benefit system may be properly required to bear part of the costs of local authority provision of accommodation…it is not obliged or empowered to pay any of the legitimate costs of the National Health Service. To determine whether needs fall to be catered for by the National Health Service or by the local authority or by the benefits system, there must be a proper assessment of those needs…[but] no assessment was formally made.' Nonetheless the NHS had 'regarded it as legitimate to make every effort to minimise its proper liabilities under the 1977 Act by seeking to transfer them to the budget of another limb of Government through a wholly artificial scheme. Even if the scheme had been successful, there would have been no apparent advantage to the tax payer and no sensible advantage to the patients. On the contrary, devising schemes and forcing the DWP to respond to them merely results in a waste of public resources... Those responsible for National Health Service funds could perhaps consider whether devising and defending such schemes is the most effective use of public money' (CDLA/3161/2003).

18.4.5 HEALTH SERVICES

Apart from registered nursing, Department of Health guidance states that the NHS is expected to arrange and fund the following (as well as other) services, as part of a person's care plan: primary health care, assessment involving doctors and registered nurses, rehabilitation and recovery, respite health care, community health services, specialist health care support, palliative care (DH 2007a, para 79).

18.4.6 MENTAL HEALTH AFTERCARE SERVICES

Guidance states that it does not apply to services provided under s.117 of the Mental Health Act 1983. However, it might apply if, in addition to s.117 services, a person required services relating to their physical health (rather than a mental disorder) (DH 2007a, paras 65–67).

18.4.7 NHS CONTINUING HEALTH CARE FOR PEOPLE IN THEIR OWN HOMES

Guidance is slightly unclear about the position of people in their own homes. It states that local authorities might still provide some services, even if a person qualifies for NHS continuing health care. But it also maintains that a jointly funded package would only arise if a person was not eligible for NHS continuing health care (DH 2007a, paras 76–78).

The answer is more clearly provided by the ADASS guidance, which states that – in the case of a person having NHS continuing health care status – the NHS would be responsible for all health and personal care services, as well as associated social care services essential to daily living, such as equipment provision, routine and incontinence laundry, daily domestic tasks such as food preparation, shopping, washing up, bed making etc. Whereas local authorities might still assist in terms of adapting the property, essential parenting activities, access to leisure or other community facilities, carer services including additional general domestic support (ADASS 2007, p.7).

It may be arguable that home adaptations, closely and directly linked to a person's continuing health care needs or treatment, should be funded by the NHS as well. Certainly, there is a precedent for this; longstanding Department of Health guidance made clear that adaptations needed directly for renal dialysis in a person's home, should be an NHS responsibility – including, if necessary, a separate room and direct water supply (HSC(IS)11 and HSG(93)48: both Circulars, although the first was issued in 1974, remain on the Department of Health website).

Nonetheless, the NHS is likely to be reluctant to fund adaptations more generally; for example, the local government ombudsman investigated the case of a woman living at home with NHS continuing health care needs. The NHS trust funded her personal care from 8 am to 5 pm, Monday to Friday; the family wished to provide care the rest of the time. She was seriously ill and profoundly disabled; she required adaptations to enable her to use the bath or shower and toilet – her inability to use these caused much additional pain and discomfort.

The adaptations she required, and the failure to provide them, came under the responsibility of the local authority – both its housing and social services functions in the Housing Grants, Construction and Regeneration Act 1996 and the Chronically Sick and Disabled Person Act 1970 (*Leeds CC 2007*).

The National Assistance Act 1948, s.29 – of which the 1970 Act has been held to be an extension – states that local authorities are not permitted to provide what is required to be provided under the NHS Act 2006. Thus, local social services authorities would legally be unable to provide NHS continuing health care services – because the latter are required, under guidance and directions, to be provided by the NHS. However, any service, equipment or adaptation which was not directly linked to the continuing care, could arguably be provided by the NHS – or the local authority (because although the NHS might have the power to provide it, it would not be required to).

18.4.8 LOCAL AUTHORITY PROVISION OF HEALTH SERVICES

Confusingly, the Department of Health guidance also states that in accordance with the *Coughlan* judgment, local authorities can provide some health services (DH 2007a, para 81).

On this issue, the ADASS guidance reminds local authorities that they can lawfully provide only a 'low level of general nursing services (and since 2001 cannot provide any registered nursing at all)' (ADASS 2007, p.11).

The Department of Health guidance states that continuing care decisions should be reviewed no later than three months following initial assessment. Neither NHS nor local authority should withdraw unilaterally from an existing funding arrangement without a joint reassessment of the individual (DH 2007a, paras 82, 87).

The ADASS guidance emphasises that it is unlawful for local authorities to provide, purchase or charge for care that should legally be the responsibility of the NHS. It urges local authorities not simply to accept PCT decisions and fund placements by default (ADASS 2007, p.8).

Thus, there is clearly an onus on local authorities not to fall into the trap of unlawfully providing NHS continuing health care. By the same token they should make reasonable efforts on behalf of their clients, efforts the local ombudsman found to be lacking in the following case:

Social worker failing to act in respect of continuing care: maladministration. A social worker failed to set in motion an application for continuing care funding for a man with Alzheimer's disease. Despite the fact that the NHS officer who was head of continuing care stated retrospectively that the man would have qualified, the social worker involved seemed to doubt this at the time. No application was made. The local ombudsman found maladministration. In response to his draft recommendations, the local authority and health authority agreed to reimburse the nursing home costs in full which his wife had paid – over £26,000 (*Hertfordshire CC 2003a*).

Nonetheless, local authorities have a track record of not challenging the NHS, for a number of highly unsatisfactory but potent reasons including lack of expertise, lack of political will and the imperative of joint working between local authorities and PCTs (Score and McCabe 2007).

18.5 SCREENING BY CHECKLIST, ASSESSMENT BY DECISION SUPPORT TOOL

18.5.1 SCREENING BY CHECKLIST

The Department of Health has published a checklist (DH 2007d) for screening people's needs, in order to encourage 'proportionate' assessments. If the checklist indicates that a person might be eligible for NHS continuing health care, then a full assessment using the decision support tool (see below) should be carried out. The threshold at the checklist stage 'has been set deliberately low, to ensure that all those who require a full consideration of their needs do get this opportunity' (DH 2007a, para 46).

Use of the checklist is not discretionary, if the NHS body is using an initial screening process. The ADASS guidance suggests that anybody who crosses the checklist threshold, but is subsequently deemed not to need NHS continuing health care, is likely to qualify for joint PCT and local authority funding (ADASS 2007, p.5).

18.5.2 ASSESSMENT BY DECISION SUPPORT TOOL

The Department of Health's decision support tool is to support practitioners reach a decision about whether a person has a primary health need in terms of the complexity, nature, intensity or unpredictability of their health care needs. It sets out a number of 'domains'. Use of the tool is not discretionary; it is referred to explicitly in the directions issued in October 2007 (see 18.2 above). However, guidance also emphasises that the guidelines in the tool are indicative only and should not be viewed prescriptively (DH 2007a, para 59).

The assessment for NHS continuing health care should be comprehensive and multi-disciplinary, as stated in the directions (above) and in the guidance (DH 2007a, para 53).

Within each domain are different levels of need, ranging from priority to low, with severe, high, and moderate in between. However, not all domains contain the priority or severe categories. The domains are as follows with P indicating a top category of priority, S a top category of severe; the others going up to high only: behaviour (P), cognition (S), psychological and emotional needs (H), communication (H), mobility (S), nutrition (S), continence (H), skin (S), breathing (P), drug therapies and medication (P), altered states of consciousness (P) (DH 2007c, para 9).

The inclusion of behaviour in this list of domains, for example, relates to the ombudsman's concern that in the past local eligibility criteria focused inadequately on aspects of dementia such as mood changes, delusions, hallucinatory experiences and visual spatial difficulties – causing staff to produce inappropriate assessments based only on physical need (*Cambridgeshire HA 2004*).

The guidance states that NHS continuing health care would be indicated by:
- a priority need in any one of the four domains
- severe needs in at least two domains
- one domain recorded as severe, together a needs in a number of other domains
- a number of domains with high and/or moderate needs (DH 2007c, para 16).

On the last point, the ADASS guidance suggests that if a person has two or more high needs and also three or more moderate needs, they should normally be beyond the scope of local authority provision (ADASS 2007, p.5).

The Department of Health guidance also states that some people's needs may not fit easily into the specified care domains, in which case an additional domain should be recorded. When in doubt about the level at which to place needs in a particular domain, the guidance states that the practitioner should choose the higher level of need under consideration and explain the problem (DH 2007c, para 10).

The tool contains examples of patients against each of the levels within each domain. It is clear from these examples that it is not necessarily easy to achieve continuing care status by using the tool. The concern is that if applied to the patient in *R v North and East Devon Health Authority, ex p Coughlan*, she would not be deemed to have continuing care status. Yet, in law, she does; this raises the possibility that the decision support tool is not consistent with the law.

For instance, even to score 'high', the top level for the domain of communication, the person must be unable reliably to communicate their needs at any time and in any way, even when all practicable steps to do so have been taken. To score 'severe', the top level for mobility, the person must be completely immobile and/or have a clinical condition such that on movement or transfer there is a high risk of serious physical harm, and where positioning is critical. For severe in respect of nutrition, the person must be unable to take food and drink by mouth. All nutritional requirements must be taken by artificial means requiring ongoing skilled professional intervention or monitoring over a 24-hour period to ensure nutrition/hydration – or inability to take food and drink by mouth, with intervention inappropriate or impossible. To score the most on incontinence, which anyway only goes up to 'high', the continence care must be problematic requiring timely and skilled intervention. Severity in relation to skin means open wounds, pressure ulcers with full thickness skin loss with extensive destruction and tissue necrosis extending to underlying bone, tendon or joint capsule – or multiple wounds which are not responding to treatment (DH 2007c).

18.6 REVIEWS/APPEALS OF CONTINUING CARE AND NURSING CARE DECISIONS

Under the continuing responsibilities directions (see 18.2 above), PCTs are responsible for telling people about how to apply for a review of a decision about NHS continuing health care or about NHS-funded nursing care (in a care home). PCTs should deal promptly with review requests, usually in the form of a local review panel.

Normally, the time between referral for a full consideration of need and communication of the funding decision to the patient, should not exceed two weeks. However, if the referral has taken place and NHS funding is still ongoing, the process may take longer. Where a longer period is required for valid and unavoidable reasons, time scales should be clearly communicated to the person and their carers (DH 2007a, paras 62–63).

If the person remains dissatisfied, the case should be referred to the Strategic Health Authority's Independent Review Panel (IRP) to assess whether the PCT has correctly applied the Framework. The convening of a review panel is a power, not a duty; the directions state that a strategic health authority may refer an appeal to a panel. The panel reports back to the

SHA, which must then give notice to the applicant and the PCT or NHS trust. But the health service ombudsman has in the past stated that such a discretion should be exercised properly:

Improperly not convening a review panel. In respect of the discretion to convene a panel not being exercised, the health service ombudsman referred to the guidance (HSC 2001/15) that stated that the decision not to convene should be confined to those cases where the patient falls outside the criteria or is otherwise clearly not appropriate for the panel to consider. In the particular circumstances, the ombudsman criticised the failure to convene a panel, although the woman involved could not be seen 'as anything other than borderline', given the 'scoring' she had received when assessed (*Herefordshire HA 1999*).

Department of Health guidance states that the IRP must gather and scrutinise all available and appropriate evidence, compile/identify needs, involve the individual and carer as far as possible, fully record panel deliberations, reach clear and evidenced decisions with the rationale set out. There should be consistency between the panel deliberations, the recommendations and the decision letter. The IRP function is advisory but the PCT should accept its recommendations in all but exceptional circumstances (DH 2007a, paras 93–94).

The directions state that the review can be requested in relation to the procedure adopted by the PCT, or to the way in which the primary health criterion has been applied. Guidance makes clear, however, that the IRP procedure does not apply in the case of challenges to the content of eligibility criteria, the type and location of NHS funded continuing care services on offer, the content of any alternative care package which has been offered, or treatment or any other aspect of services being received. Complaints about these issues should be made through the ordinary NHS complaints procedure (DH 2007a, annex E).

Beyond the IRP, the case can then be referred to the Healthcare Commission and, ultimately, to the Health Service Ombudsman. Guidance states that where the dispute arises between different NHS bodies or between the local authority and the PCT, there should be an agreed local dispute resolution process. The dispute should not delay the provision of the care package (DH 2007a, para 98).

The ADASS document states that, during a dispute between local authority and PCT, any charges collected by the local authority from the client pending resolution, should be set aside in an interesting bearing account, in order to facilitate full restitution if the NHS is ultimately deemed to be responsible for meeting the person's needs (ADASS 2007, p.8). The NHS may, at least in some circumstances, be expected to continue funding until the review procedure is complete:

Discharged improperly from NHS care despite request for review. A woman with Alzheimer's disease was admitted to hospital in April. On 4 October her husband handed hospital staff a letter, dated 2 October, disagreeing with the proposal that she be discharged to a care home. He thought his wife was entitled to NHS care. On 10 October she was moved to a care home on a trial basis. The hospital wrote to him on 18 October telling him he could appeal, but not explaining how to do that. On 1 November, his letter of 2 October was accepted as a request for a review. On 9 January, the chair of the panel refused to convene a panel. The woman was held liable for charges for her stay in the care home from 10 October.

The health service ombudsman stated that the letter of 2 October should have been sufficient to trigger a review; and that NHS funding should have continued until the review procedure was complete on 9 January (*Barnet Healthcare NHS Trust 2000*).

Department of Health guidance states that during a dispute between NHS bodies or between an NHS body and a local authority, 'the bodies should put in place a local dispute resolution process, which proceeds in a robust and timely manner. Disputes should not delay the provision of the care package and the protocol should make clear how funding will be handled during the dispute' (DH 2007a, para 98).

CHAPTER 19

Joint working between local authorities and the NHS

KEY POINTS

JOINT WORKING

Department of Health policy has long been to encourage joint working between the NHS and local authorities, and a number of legislative provisions allow for this. For instance, the NHS Act 2006 permits pooled budgets, lead commissioning of services and transfer of functions (e.g. where an NHS primary care trust discharges community care duties on behalf of the local authority). In principle, joint working would appear to have much to recommend it, insofar as it circumvents the rigidity, inflexibility, artificial demarcation, and duplication of assessment that can afflict health and social care.

Nonetheless, far from working jointly, local authorities and NHS bodies all too often continue to find themselves at loggerheads, as they attempt to pass the financial buck, in order to avoid unwanted responsibilities. Because of the political imperative to be seen to be working jointly, transparency is sometimes a casualty; sometimes even, this imperative has militated against local authorities challenging NHS bodies over matters such as NHS continuing health care (see Chapter 18); even if this has meant local authorities ending up unlawfully providing services, charging for them, and effectively forcing people to use up their savings and sell their homes to pay for care that should have been free.

An additional trend has been for local authorities and the NHS sometimes to assume that the usual legal obligations to assess and provide services no longer apply in the context of joint working. If thinking of this type takes hold, joint working becomes a byword for excising certain legal duties from everyday practice.

INTERMEDIATE CARE AND REHABILITATION

Under guidance issued by the Department of Health, the NHS and local authorities provide intermediate care services, which are designed either to prevent admission to hospital or other institution, or alternatively to enable people to return home by means of (usually up to six weeks) provision of rehabilitation or other services. The policy of intermediate care, which was intended to enhance and add to existing rehabilitation services, has in some areas arguably been misused and exploited by NHS bodies as an excuse to run down other rehabilitation beds, services and units. Although difficult to challenge legally (but it has been done), this has had an unfortunate effect. This is because, whilst intermediate care may be suitable for a significant number of people, it is usually insufficient to deal with more complex needs for rehabilitation and recuperation. Intermediate care is generally intended to represent a short, sharp response for people with simpler needs.

COMMUNITY EQUIPMENT SERVICES

Community equipment services have long been an enigma, perceived to be important in principle, but in practice badly neglected. Department of Health policy has stated that community equipment services should be integrated between health and social care. It would appear that after several years this policy has not resulted in significant improvements for service users. With some exasperation, central government has proposed a radical change to the way in which equipment is provided, taking provision largely away from local authorities and NHS bodies and replacing it with a 'retail market model' of provision. However, to date no legislation or definitive guidance has been issued.

SINGLE ASSESSMENT PROCESS

Guidance on a single assessment process for older people provides for the NHS and local authorities to streamline and integrate health and social care assessments, and to organise it in terms of four levels: contact, overview, specialist and comprehensive assessment. However, arguably the guidance and policy has been superficial both in practice and law and is of limited significance. In practice, this is because older people and disabled people can still find themselves subject to a range of different assessments from varying professionals – partly of course because they need such multiple assessments. For example, general practitioner, consultant, district nurse, occupational therapist, physiotherapists all have expertise to contribute. In law, it is because the guidance represents a veneer only; disparate social and health legislation remains beneath, thus hindering a true merging of local policy, assessment and provision of services.

19.1 JOINT WORKING BETWEEN NHS AND LOCAL AUTHORITIES

There has long been legislation allowing, and sometimes demanding, joint working between the NHS and local authorities. However, more recent legislative provisions passed by central government are designed to facilitate such working and make it more prevalent.

The reasons for joint working would appear to be compelling, namely, to simplify assessment and provision of services for service users, to reduce duplication of function – and to reduce the unseemly wrangling and cost shunting between local authorities and the NHS that sometimes results in delay in the provision, or even non-provision, of services. Thus, original community care policy guidance stated that the objective was to provide a service in which the boundaries between primary health care, secondary health care and social care did not form barriers from the perspective of the service user (DH 1990, para 1.9). Examples of legislation (as amended) allowing or demanding joint working include the following:

- **Cooperation**. NHS bodies and local authorities must cooperate in order to advance the health and welfare of the people of England and Wales (NHS Act 2006, s.82).
- **Joint strategic needs assessments**. A local authority and local NHS primary care trust(s) must prepare an assessment of relevant local needs – which either the local authority or PCT could meet to a significant extent, and which the other could meet, or affect, to a significant extent (Local Government and Public Involvement in Health Act 2007, s.116).
- **Local authorities**. A local authority must make services available to each NHS body acting in its area, as far as is reasonably necessary and practicable, to enable the NHS to discharge its functions (NHS Act 2006, s.74).
- **Arrangements with other organisations**. The NHS can arrange with any person or body, including a voluntary organisation for that person or body to provide, or assist in providing, any service under the NHS Act 2006; also the NHS may make available to such a person or body goods, materials, premises, etc. (NHS Act 2006, s.12).
- **Arrangement with local authorities**. The NHS must make available to local authorities services, facilities, etc., so far as is reasonably practicable to enable local authorities to discharge their functions relating to social services, education and public health (NHS Act 2006, s.80).
- **NHS payments to local authorities**. A primary care trust may make payments to various bodies including a social services authority, a housing authority, education authority, voluntary organisation or registered social landlord, in connection with the functions of those bodies. Payments may also be made, if such an NHS body thinks fit, to a local authority in connection with any of that authority's functions if the NHS body believes that those functions have an effect on the health of any individuals, have an effect on or are affected by any NHS functions, or are connected with any NHS functions (NHS Act 2006. s.256).
- **Local authority payments to NHS**. A local authority may make payments to a primary care trust, strategic health authority or local health board (Wales) (NHS Act 2006, s.76).

- **Agreements involving staff**. Local authorities and the NHS may enter into agreements involving the making of each other's staff available to each other (Local Government Act 1972, s.113).

19.2 JOINT WORKING AND THE NHS ACT 2006

Section 75 of the NHS Act 2006 (formerly s.31 of the Health Act 1999) refers specifically to the pooling of budgets and to the delegation of functions. It does not impose a duty, but instead places a power on the NHS and local authorities to work jointly in this way. Section 75 empowers the Secretary of State to make regulations enabling prescribed NHS bodies and prescribed local authorities to enter into particular arrangements in relation to their respective functions. This is on condition that any such arrangements are likely to improve the way in which those functions are exercised. The section goes on to state that the prescribed arrangements may include (a) the establishment and maintenance of joint funds; (b) the exercise by an NHS body of prescribed health-related functions of a local authority and vice versa; (c) the provision of staff, goods, services or accommodation in connection with (a) or (b).

19.2.1 NHS ACT 2006: SERVICES INVOLVED IN JOINT WORKING

Regulations spell out the detail of which bodies and services the joint working arrangements apply to. Relevant NHS functions are those under s.2 and s.3(1) of the NHS Act 2006, including rehabilitation services and those services intended to avoid admission to hospital. Also included is aftercare under s.117 of the Mental Health Act 1983. Excluded are surgery, radiotherapy, termination of pregnancies, endoscopy, Class 4 laser treatment, other invasive treatment and emergency ambulance services, medical and dental inspections of school age children – and advice, examination and treatment on contraception, substances and appliances (SI 2000/617).

Relevant local authority functions are many (with a few specific exclusions). The regulations were amended in 2003 to allow charging functions, for both residential and non-residential accommodation, to be included. Other local authority functions covered, in addition to social services functions, include education authority functions, and housing authority functions under both Part 1 of the Housing Grants, Construction and Regeneration Act 1996 (containing disabled facilities grants), and under Parts VI and VII of the Housing Act 1996 (housing allocation and homelessness).

The Regulations state that partners may establish and maintain a pooled fund, and that NHS bodies may exercise health-related local authority functions, and that local authorities may exercise NHS functions (SI 2000/617).

19.3 CARE TRUSTS

Joint working can take the form of a care trust, comprising an NHS trust or primary care trust that may exercise health-related functions of a local authority (NHS Act 2006, s.77).

19.4 JOINT WORKING: LEGAL FUNCTIONS AND AVOIDANCE OF PITFALLS

The NHS Act 2006 makes quite clear that any arrangements made under it affect neither the liability of NHS bodies or local authorities for the exercise of their functions, nor the powers or duties of local authorities to recover charges for services (s.75). Likewise, in respect of care trusts, it states that existing functions of both NHS and local authority are not affected (s.77).

This is a cautionary reminder to those local authorities and NHS bodies who enter joint working agreements without an appreciation of the legal implications. When joint working takes place, it is sometimes forgotten that existing duties on each partner (local authority or NHS) remain unaltered. This can lead to unlawfulness where either partner improperly gives up its decision-making responsibilities. Single health and social care assessments are one thing, unduly restrictive assessment quite another. This was illustrated in a court case where the local authority improperly determined the outcome of its community care assessment with reference to NHS matters. It had therefore in effect lost its own legal identity:

Fundamental error of local authority in giving up its decision-making responsibility. An assessment was carried out as to whether a man was eligible for assistance through the Care Programme Approach (CPA), which is primarily an NHS responsibility. The final decision was that he was not eligible, because he did not have a severe and enduring mental illness. It was then concluded, on the basis of the CPA decision, that he was not eligible for community care services either. This was legally impermissible; before a decision was taken about community care, an assessment was required to investigate the risk, self-neglect and vulnerability to deterioration that had already been identified. There had never been a proper and comprehensive community care assessment; this was a demonstrable, fundamental and serious error (*R(HP) v Islington LBC*).

Likewise in another court case, reliance on health reports was not enough for the local authority to discharge its decision-making obligations:

Local authority failing to take community care decision. A medical doctor made recommendations to a local continuing care panel about whether a woman should be placed in a nursing home. They were based on the reports of health professionals during the woman's hospital stay. They took no account of the social work team manager's detailed assessment and report. However, the local authority simply followed the panel's recommendations, even though the latter's function was advisory only, and it had made those recommendations on the basis of limited or flawed information.

In deciding whether to place the woman in a nursing home, the final decision lay with the local authority; but it had to take account of all relevant factors, including an up-to-date community care assessment. This it had not done. The Court of Appeal held that the local authority's decision was manifestly flawed (*R(Goldsmith) v Wandsworth LBC*).

If joint working is to be effective it needs somehow to grapple with the cost-shunting exercises that typically take place, as described by the local ombudsman when making a finding of maladministration:

Joint working and cost shunting. A woman had severe physical and learning disabilities and challenging behaviour. Following a local authority's assessment of need, two years passed until she actually received the day care she needed. Over a year after assessing the need, the local authority attempted to persuade the NHS to fund it. However, there was no record that the woman's needs had changed from the previous year when the local authority had accepted that it had responsibility. Thus, it was clear that financial reasons lay behind the council's reluctance to secure a service.

The ombudsman found it was inappropriate for the council to attempt to shift the burden, given the additional delay this would cause; the failure to 'grasp the nettle' was maladministration. Furthermore, no strategy was developed to further joint working and to ensure that gaps in care were filled and that a 'seamless service' existed. Instead the authority chose to place the woman in the 'grey area' of responsibility, rather than accepting the financial burden that the five-day care package would have entailed. The ombudsman recommended £15,000 compensation for this (*Calderdale MBC 1998*).

Further caution must be exercised when joint health and social care packages are delivered. This is because the NHS for the most part is unable legally to charge for services. Thus, however 'seamless' or joined up a care package is, a seam nevertheless needs to be identified and unpicked in order to pinpoint the social care elements that can be charged for, and the health care that cannot be.

19.5 JOINT WORKING WITHIN ORGANISATIONS

Although local authorities and the NHS are urged to work jointly across agency boundaries, nevertheless coordinated working may also be lacking within a single agency. At times such fragmented working can bear consequences that will attract censure from both the courts and the ombudsmen:

Lack of coordinated working within a local authority. In one local authority, the social services and housing departments failed to meet the needs of a severely disabled woman over a period of two years. As a consequence she was left in a situation in the family home, such that her human rights (article 8 of the Convention) were breached. The judge found that one cause of this had been what he referred to as 'corporate failure' (*R(Bernard) v Enfield LBC*).

In another case, the lack of coordinated working between departments resulted in an 'outrageous' breach of an undertaking given to the court by the local authority:

Lamentable and outrageous breach of undertaking to the court. A local authority gave an undertaking to the High Court to carry out a community care assessment and not to enforce any warrant for possession of the premises. Six days later, in breach of the undertaking, the woman was evicted. The judge referred to this as lamentable and outrageous. The local authority explained this as an administrative oversight and lack of communication between departments. The undertaking had been given on behalf of social services, whereas the eviction had been arranged by the housing department. This division of responsibility was mirrored in the legal department of the council. For the court, this was a systematic inadequacy with the potential for disaster. Required were procedures that were adequate, understood by relevant staff and rigorously enforced. The local authority appeared to 'fall down on every count' (*R(Bempoa) v Southwark LBC*).

Such occurrences seem not necessarily to be isolated. The local ombudsman investigated similarly:

Corporate failure of local authority. The local ombudsman identified corporate failure when the housing department served a possession order in respect of a person with mental health problems, vulnerable and unwell, but failed to inform social services, in particular the mental health division. Had this happened, the council's social workers would have been able to offer help to the man in managing his money and avert the eviction (*Barnet LBC 2000*).

Similarly, in the following case, the ombudsman found a failure in communication between several local authority departments, including those responsible for letting, repairs, rent collection and social services:

Failure of four council departments in respect of disabled occupant requiring adaptations to property. A disabled applicant was offered a council house on the understanding that it would be adapted to her needs. However, it was not in suitable condition and she was unable to move in for eight months until a broken stairlift was removed, the property cleaned and various necessary adaptations removed. As a result she and her daughter could not claim the full housing benefit to which they were entitled, and so could not pay their rent. The council then took possession action to recover the property; this resulted in a suspended court order and a four-figure sum of arrears to repay. Furthermore, the council had failed to make the tenancy in joint names, despite it being a joint application and the tenancy being awarded on the basis of their joint medical circumstances. This resulted in further loss of right to housing benefit, because although the tenancy was made joint, it was not backdated. Two years after the property had been made suitable to live in, the tenants were still struggling to pay the rent arrears and court costs. They had also lost their right to buy because of legislative changes during the relevant period.

The ombudsman found maladministration because the property was not suitable and it should have been; there was a failure in communication between the several council departments responsible for letting, repairs, rent collection and social services; failure to identify why the tenants had not moved in and why court action was not necessary since the tenants were entitled to full housing benefit, and failure to keep proper records. She recommended that rent arrears or outstanding council tax as a result of the maladministration be removed, as well as £3000 compensation for inconvenience, distress and expense suffered (*Kirklees MC 2007*).

In another case that resulted in the severe housing and social care needs of a disabled boy and his family not being met, the local ombudsman identified poor communication between housing and social services officers of the same council. This in turn meant that even those local authority officers who were attempting to help were rendered helpless by other officers responding to their own priorities (*Bristol CC 1998*). Likewise, following a failure to provide a stairlift that would have made the last two years of her life easier for her, the ombudsman found a 'sorry tale of confusion' within and between the two councils involved (*Durham CC 1993*).

Sometimes the failings are apparently trivial, but can have serious results, such as an application for assistance being delayed for a year; for example, when an internal memorandum between the social services and housing department of the same council never arrived and there was no system for checking the safe arrival of internal mail (*Liverpool CC 1992*). Unawareness of funding sources even within the same department of the same council may mean a person's needs are not met promptly, and exacerbate a fragmented approach to assessing and meeting people's needs. The local ombudsman found maladministration:

Special fund for HIV/AIDS. A social worker, involved in the assessment of a man with HIV/AIDS, was unaware of the special fund which the social services department had for people with AIDS. This caused delay. An occupational therapist subsequently visited; she recorded his serious condition and recommended various items including walking sticks, height adjusters and a sheepskin. These were delivered within days; a shower was later installed, paid for by the special AIDS fund, since the housing department said it had no resources. Between March and April, the man was assessed on three separate occasions by three different parts of the social services department – a fragmented approach which, the carer claimed, added to the stress the man was under in trying to obtain appropriate services. This was maladministration; the consequent delay meant that at a time when he was dying, appropriate and essential services had been denied him (*Salford 1996*).

Sometimes, unusual needs or uncertainty as to what the need is result in people 'falling between stools'. For instance, team or specialism boundaries may effectively exclude people from assistance, as the following local ombudsman investigation found:

Team boundaries failing service users. A man was born with physical problems (mild cerebral palsy) that remained undiagnosed until adulthood (1995, when a voluntary body carried out an assessment). He suffered throughout life from difficulty in defecating and micturition. He was caused great unhappiness, embarrassment and loss of confidence because of difficulty in keeping himself clean. He became socially withdrawn. His mother had in 1994 requested (when he was 17 years old) social services involvement; amongst other things a Clos-o-mat was requested – i.e. an automatic washing/drying toilet.

Over an extended period, he was referred between the social services learning disability and physical disability teams, a consultant neurosurgeon, consultant psychiatrist and gastro-enterologist in an attempt to diagnose the problem. He seemed not to 'fit' into any team or any specialism. Social services had stated that it would not provide the Clos-o-mat until the cause of the problem had been identified. However, by 1999 definite medical advice had still not been provided; social services finally decided to provide the Clos-o-mat. The ombudsman accepted that the council had now agreed to review its procedures; this would include ensuring that boundaries between teams did not prevent people's needs from being met (*Northumberland CC 2000*).

Reflecting a similar type of issue, a report published by the Joseph Rowntree Foundation in 2004 highlighted the difficulties faced by people with both a physical disability and mental health problems; people's needs were treated unhelpfully and in fragmented fashion between physical disability and mental health teams (Morris 2004).

19.6 INTERMEDIATE CARE

Guidance was issued by the Department of Health in 2001 on what it called intermediate care (HSC 2001/01). Overall, the guidance stemmed from central government's concern about 'blocked' hospital beds; as such it was a forerunner of the legislation relating to delayed hospital discharges. However, it also serves to a degree to support the concept of rehabilitation, although the six-week general limit will of course be relevant to short-term rehabilitation only. The guidance states that intermediate care should be:

- for people who would otherwise face unnecessarily prolonged hospital stays or inappropriate admission to acute inpatient care, long-term residential care or NHS continuing inpatient care
- provided on basis of comprehensive assessment, resulting in a structured individual care plan involving active therapy, treatment or opportunity for recovery
- planned with an outcome of maximising independence and typically enabling people to live at home
- time limited, normally no longer than six weeks and frequently as little as one to two weeks

• inclusive of cross-professional working, with a single assessment framework, single professional records and shared protocols.

The guidance lists the following as constituting intermediate care services: rapid response, hospital at home, residential rehabilitation, supported discharge, day rehabilitation (HSC 2001/1). It states that intermediate care should normally last no more than six weeks, but may sometimes be slightly longer (e.g. for stroke patients). In any event, it states that all individual care plans should have a review date specified within a six-week period; exceptional extensions should be based on full reassessment and authorisation of a senior clinician. It also stipulates that individual care plans should specify what care, therapy or support may be needed on discharge from intermediate care (HSC 2001/001).

The guidance recognises what was at the time the legal discretion of local authorities to charge for the social care element of non-residential intermediate care (and a legal duty to charge for residential elements) but stated that the Department of Health considered that intermediate care in either residential or non-residential form should be free of charge (HSC 2001/001).

However, since June 2003, the social care element of intermediate care must under regulations anyway be provided free of charge. For the purpose of these regulations, intermediate care is defined as a 'structured programme of care provided for a limited period of time to assist a person to maintain or regain the ability to live in his home'. The prohibition on charging applies to both residential and non-residential care and is limited to a maximum of six weeks (SI 2003/1196).

19.6.1 INTERMEDIATE CARE AND REHABILITATION

Intermediate care is meant to be one form of rehabilitation service, whether in a person's own home, a community hospital or a specialist care home (HSC 2001/001). It was always meant to be an addition to other, specialist rehabilitation services – not to replace them (Audit Commission (2000b, p.21). One size does not fit all patients; different types and settings of rehabilitation are required for different patients (O'Connor *et al.* 2006). Yet it appears that NHS primary care trusts, responsible for commissioning health services, have both taken far too a narrow view of intermediate care (by failing to see the clinical and financial value of community hospital beds), as well as forcing NHS trusts to run down other rehabilitation services.

For example, many community hospital beds have been lost, 3000 since 1999 (*Hansard* 2007). This is despite evidence showing their cost-effectiveness (Green *et al.* 2005; O'Reilly *et al.* 2006) and how important they may be for people to step down to, from acute hospital beds, before returning to their own homes (CSCI 2004, p.5). More generally, the British Geriatric Society reports the loss, between 2003 and 2007, of 35 per cent of acute medical emergency beds, 59 per cent decrease in rehabilitation beds in an acute setting, 62 per cent decrease in community hospital rehabilitation beds and 71 per cent decrease in NHS continuing care beds. It found an apparently small increase only, in intermediate care (4.6%) and transitional care (11%) beds (BGS 2007).

It is recognised widely, including at the Department of Health, that placing people in care homes, other than those with a specialist rehabilitation function, is likely to result in institutionalisation and dependency (CSCI 2005a, p.6; DH 2002c, p.11, Appendix 3). Yet this is the policy followed by some PCTs, even in spite of continuing Department of Health guidance emphasising the need for community hospitals to take the pressure off acute hospitals and provide friendly, supportive care – particularly 'step-down' facilities from the acute hospital (Philp 2007). This was referred to in a White Paper which indicated the desirability of replacing acute beds with less intensive beds, so that people could 'recover faster in a more appropriate setting' (Secretary of State for Health 2006, p.136).

The apparent loss of rehabilitation facilities and beds seems also contrary to the government's national framework for long-term conditions, which stresses the importance of specialist inpatient rehabilitation services (DH 2005b, p.32). Likewise the *National Service Framework for Older People* speaks of a 'new range of acute and rehabilitation services' being needed – in acute hospital beds, step-down beds in acute hospitals, community hospitals and people's own homes (DH 2001c, pp.41–48).

The NHS Plan in 2000 envisaged an increase of some 7000 NHS beds, 2100 in acute and medical wards, 5000 intermediate care beds – as well as more services in people's own homes (HSC 2001/003, para 7). Yet the net loss of beds between 1997 and 2007 nationally has been some 16 per cent, with some areas losing up to 20 per cent of NHS beds (*Ipswich Evening Star* 2007). It seems that these cuts have heavily involved rehabilitation beds.

19.7 COMMUNITY EQUIPMENT SERVICES

The provision of community equipment services – by both local authorities and the NHS – has long been recognised as inadequate. Reports stretching back over three decades have repeatedly exposed a chaotic and inefficient system; these culminated in a highly critical Audit Commission (2000) report.

19.7.1 COMMUNITY EQUIPMENT SERVICES GUIDANCE

The Department of Health finally issued guidance in 2001, setting out 'action that should be taken' to improve provision of community equipment services. In particular, the guidance stated that local authorities should increase the number of people benefiting from community equipment services by 50 per cent and integrate local authority and NHS community equipment services by March 2004. In order to achieve this, central government stated that it was making extra funding available. For the NHS, this extra funding was quantified, but not ring fenced; for social services authorities there was no quantification (HSC 2001/008). The result has apparently been that in a significant number of areas, the extra funding has been merely theoretical, and has instead been spent on other things. Community equipment cannot be charged for either by local authorities (see section 12.2) or by the NHS (see 17.15).

19.7.2 RANGE OF COMMUNITY EQUIPMENT SERVICES

Further guidance (DH 2001) attached to HSC 2001/008 gives a non-exhaustive definition of community equipment. Although the list is useful, local authorities should bear in mind that it is non-exhaustive, and that obligations may arise to provide all sorts of equipment – depending on the assessed needs of a service user.

The guidance refers to home nursing equipment such as pressure relief mattresses, commodes and daily living equipment such as shower chairs and raised toilet seats. It also lists minor adaptations (e.g. grab rails, lever taps, improved lighting), sensory impairment equipment (e.g. liquid level indicators, hearing loops, assistive listening devices, flashing doorbells), communication aids, wheelchairs for short-term loan and telecare equipment (e.g. fall alarms, gas escape alarms, health state monitoring devices). Wheelchairs (see 17.13.1) were excluded from the ambit of the guidance and the 'reforms' being promulgated by the Department of Health.

In addition is a new development referred to as 'telecare'. This signifies preventative technology to enable people to remain in their own homes with assistance from a range of new technologies, including alarms, sensors and monitors, backed up by control centres. Department of Health guidance does warn that telecare should be a part of care planning and that the risks of social isolation need to be taken into account (LAC(2006)5. See also generally: DH 2005c).

19.7.3 COMMUNITY EQUIPMENT IN CARE HOMES

Regulations made under the Care Standards Act 2000 are vague concerning equipment provision in care homes. Likewise even the care standards made under the Act give little away. For example, the national minimum standards on care homes for older people refer only to the home providing grab rails, other aids, hoists, assisted toilets and baths, communication aids such as loop systems and storage areas for equipment (DH 2003a).

One of the consequences of this vagueness is uncertainty and sometimes dispute as to who should be providing particular items of equipment in a care home; the care home as part of its basic provision within its basic fee level, or the NHS or local authority.

Department of Health guidance states that: 'care homes providing nursing care are expected to be fit for purpose, which, in the main, means they will have in place basic handling, mobility, and lifting equipment and adaptations. There may be some situations where they will need to draw on the resources of the local community equipment service.'

It goes on to differentiate between equipment that the care home should be providing for the generality of residents, and equipment needed for a particular individual resident: 'Where the NHS has determined that an individual requires a particular piece of equipment, it should ensure either that the care home provides it; or provide it on a temporary basis until the care home is able to provide it; or provide it to the individual for as long as they need it. It would be unreasonable to expect care homes to provide items of equipment that, by the nature of the design, size, and weight requirements, need to be specifically tailored to meet the individual's needs and would not be capable of being utilised by other care home residents. Further information on community equipment is available' (DH 2007f, paras 40–41).

19.7.4 TRANSFORMING EQUIPMENT SERVICES

The Commission for Services Improvement Partnership (some sort of a Department of Health backed quango) has proposed changes to the way in which community equipment is provided by local authorities and the NHS, although it is attempting to do so without making any legislative change.

The precise details are not wholly clear. Roughly, however, the following is being suggested. First, people will receive assessment of needs as normal. Second, for people with complex needs, local authorities and the NHS will remain responsible for directly providing the equipment. Third, those with less complex needs, but nonetheless eligible for statutory services by local authorities or the NHS, will be given vouchers. These vouchers may cover both further specialist, detailed assessment in the independent sector, and provision of the equipment deemed to be required. In principle, before this happens, people should be offered rehabilitation where appropriate – which may make equipment unnecessary. Fourth, those with less complex needs who are assessed to be ineligible for local authority or NHS services will be advised that they should seek detailed assessment of their equipment needs, and provision of that equipment, through the independent sector. However, they will have to pay for both the assessment and the equipment (CSIP 2007).

This new policy has been called the 'retail market model'. In part, it represents a laudable attempt to shake up a system of equipment provision which has long been criticised for serious failings. However, in part, it also represents an admission that the statutory services cannot cope with the increasing numbers of older people who require assistance and equipment.

19.7.5 COMMUNITY EQUIPMENT CASES

A number of the local ombudsman cases referred to elsewhere in this book, particularly concerning assessments and waiting times for services, concern community equipment. However, the health service ombudsman too has considered equipment on a few occasions:

Four-month delay in equipment for man with dementia. An elderly man suffered from multi-infarct dementia. At a care programme approach (CPA) meeting involving the senior consultant psychiatrist and GP, a number of recommendations were made for the provision of occupational therapy equipment. This took four months; the day after it was received, he fell and had to be admitted to a nursing home for rehabilitation. The health service ombudsman criticised the delay in implementing the recommendations; the ordering arrangements for equipment had been complex and unwieldy (*Wiltshire and Swindon Health Care NHS Trust 2002*).

Delay in commode and toilet seat provision. A complaint was upheld by the health service ombudsman when, despite the need for a commode and toilet seat extension having been assessed at least a week before discharge from hospital, they were not provided in time (HSO W.24 and 56/84–85).

Rationing is generally assumed to take place on the basis of clinical priority:

Rationing of crutches. When the health service ombudsman investigated the non-provision of crutches for a patient leaving hospital, he found maladministration because the decision not to provide was not clinical but administrative, made as it was by a technician and founded on a shortage of crutches (HSO WW.3/79–80).

19.7.6 CHARGING FOR EQUIPMENT

Local authorities are prevented by legislation from charging from equipment provided under community care legislation (SI 2003/1196). The same legislation, however, allows authorities to charge for adaptations costing £1000 or more. In accordance with these rules, Department of Health policy guidance states that the telecare equipment itself provided by a local authority to an individual at home – for assisting with nursing or aiding daily living – should be provided free of charge, but that a charge could be made for the service elements. If, however, it is being used as a preventative service it can be charged for (DH 2005c, p.16). This has led some local authorities to consider charging for the maintenance, but not the for the hardware itself, of a much wider range of equipment – such as hoists, for example. Whether or not this is lawful is unclear.

The NHS is unable to charge for equipment provided to NHS patients unless prescribed under the Drug Tariff, or in the case of certain outpatient appliances including wigs, elastic hosiery, spinal supports and surgical brassieres. There are exemptions and reduction depending on medical and financial status.

19.8 SINGLE ASSESSMENT PROCESS

In 2002, the Department of Health issued guidance on what it named the single assessment process for older people (HSC 2002/001). The main thrust of the guidance is twofold. First, it urges that local authorities and the NHS should work jointly when older people are assessed. Second, it sets out what it considers to be an effective approach to assessment in terms of different levels of assessment, and what it calls contact, overview, specialist and comprehensive assessments.

Somewhat confusingly however, this guidance does not formally replace the plentiful guidance issued to local authorities (but not the NHS) on community care assessment over a decade before, and which itself had plenty to say about levels of assessment (DH 1990; SSI/SWSG 1991). Some of the salient points are as follows (HSC 2002/001):

- **Place of the older person in the assessment**. 'During assessment, care planning and other processes, the older person's account of their needs and their views and wishes must be kept at the centre of all decisions that are made… Agencies should remember that the person who is most expert in the care of an individual older person is that older person.'
- **Four levels of assessment**. Four levels of assessment are envisaged: contact, overview, specialist and comprehensive.
- **Contact assessment**. Basic personal information can be collected or verified by trained, but not necessarily professionally qualified, staff. The exploration of potential needs should be undertaken by a trained and competent single professional (health or social care), whether qualified or not (HSC 2001/1).
- **Overview assessment**. An overview assessment is a more rounded assessment, in which some or all of the domains (see below) of assessment are explored. The overview assessment could be carried out by a single health or social care professional, who need not necessarily be a qualified professional. However, it states that local agencies should nevertheless be clear as to just who is competent to carry out such an assessment.
- **Specialist assessment**. Specialist assessments are to explore specific needs. Professionals should confirm the presence, extent, cause, likely development of a health condition or

problem or social care need – and establish links to other conditions, problems, needs. Such assessments should rely on the involvement and judgement of appropriately qualified and competent professionals. The assessment should be administered and interpreted by the most appropriate professionals – with access to other professionals to contribute.

- **Comprehensive assessment**. Comprehensive assessments should involve all or most of the domains of assessment, and a range of different professionals or specialist teams.
- **Domains of assessment**. 'Domains' of assessment comprise: the perspective of the service user, clinical background, disease prevention, personal care and physical well-being, senses, mental health, relationships, safety, immediate environment and resources.

Nevertheless, the guidance does not really add a great deal to what had gone before. Furthermore, it was not accompanied by changes to underpinning NHS and social services legislation – which is so divergent – so that any 'single' assessment will from a legal point of view constitute a veneer only.

PART IV

Decision-making capacity, safeguarding adults

CHAPTER 20

Mental capacity

KEY POINTS

The law about a person's capacity to make decisions is of at least threefold importance in relation to this book. First, when local social services authorities and NHS bodies are assessing, providing services for and treating people who do or may lack capacity, it is essential that they understand the law about capacity. Otherwise, their interventions run the risk of being unlawful and of not being in a person's best interests. Second, more specifically, the law about capacity relates closely to adult protection and safeguarding adults, since an adult lacking capacity to take important decisions is by definition more vulnerable (see Chapter 21). Third, the numbers of people who may lack capacity are increasing, for example, with the increase in prevalence of dementia.

During 2007, the Mental Capacity Act 2005 came into force in England and Wales. First, it consolidated the 'common law' legal rules about mental capacity that the law courts had developed over some 20 years. That is, in the absence of adequate legislation, the courts had increasingly been forced to decide about health and welfare interventions, in the case of people lacking capacity to decide for themselves. Second, the Act also introduced new legal rules.

In summary, the 2007 Act sets out a number of key principles that run throughout the Act and which should govern decisions and interventions in relation to people lacking capacity. It defines lack of capacity, and states that interventions have to be in people's 'best interests'. It provides legal protection for people who provide care and treatment for a person lacking capacity, so long as they have done so reasonably and in good faith. At the same time the Act prohibits excessive restraint of a person. It contains separate rules about going beyond restraint and instead depriving a person, lacking capacity, of his or her liberty.

A major change introduced by the Act is to replace enduring powers of attorney with lasting powers of attorney. This means that a donor, with capacity, can create such a power authorising the attorney in the future to take not only financial decisions but also health and welfare decisions for the donor, when the latter loses capacity to take those decisions. Parallel with this change in the law, the Act creates a new Court of Protection which can intervene not only in financial, but also in health and welfare, matters. This contrasts with the previous position, in which the Court of Protection (under the Mental Health Act 1983) was limited to interventions relating to finance, business and property.

The Act clarifies the law about advance decisions or 'living wills' as they are sometimes called. They involve a person with capacity, stipulating in advance their refusal of specified medical treatment, in case at the relevant time he or she lacks the capacity to do so directly.

The Act also underpins a statutory independent mental capacity advocacy (IMCA) service, which means that in certain circumstances local authorities and NHS bodies have an obligation to instruct an advocate before a decision is made.

A new offence of wilful neglect or ill-treatment of a person lacking capacity, with a maximum sentence of five years in prison, is contained in the Act.

Overall, the Act is intended to empower people by, for example, making sure that they are not too readily deemed to lack capacity to make decisions; at the same time it serves a protective function also. It thus serves a dual purpose.

A helpful way of understanding the 'substituted decision-making' set out by the Act, in relation to the care and treatment of a person lacking capacity, is to consider it in terms of a hierarchy. First, and outweighing the others when it comes to a refusal of medical treatment, are advance decisions (sometimes known as living wills). Second, come the powers exercised by the donee of a lasting power of attorney (given to the donee when the donor still had capacity). Third, the Court of Protection may make orders in relation to care and treatment. Fourth, the Court may appoint a deputy to make ongoing decisions. Lastly, s.5 of the 2005 Act provides protection for those providing care or treatment less formally – but this does not extend to overriding an advance decision, or a decision made by a person with lasting power of attorney or by a deputy (Bowen 2007, p.172).

20.1 BACKGROUND

Most of the Mental Capacity Act 2005 came into force in October 2007. Prior to the passing of this Act, the position as regards decision-making capacity was as follows.

As far as finance-type matters were concerned, a person as donor could make an enduring power of attorney, authorising the attorney (typically a family member) to take finance, business and property decisions on behalf of the donor, in case of the donor losing capacity to manage such affairs. This was under the Enduring Powers of Attorney Act 1985. In the absence of such a power of attorney, the Court of Protection could intervene in such matters under the Mental Health Act 1983, making orders or appointing a receiver for ongoing management of a person's affairs. If the only finance to be dealt with was in the form of social security benefits, then an appointee could be appointed by the Benefits Agency. The law remains the same in this latter respect.

If health or welfare decisions had to be made, the law did not allow anybody directly to consent or make decisions on behalf of the person lacking capacity. However, it did allow 'best interests' and 'necessity' (making lawful what would otherwise be unlawful) interventions. These could range from deciding about what somebody should eat, what clothes they should wear and when they should get washed – to major medical interventions or decisions about where somebody should live. Where significant issues were in question, resort had to be made to the Family Division of the High Court in case of uncertainty, of dispute or of some very serious interventions. The court would exercise its 'inherent jurisdiction' by making a declaration or order as to what should happen. Sometimes the court was called on to decide whether a person himself or herself had capacity to decide the issue in question. Through this legal case law, the court developed a set of rules about decision-making capacity. Many of these rules have found their way into the Mental Capacity Act 2005, and so past case law remains highly relevant to the new Act.

Central government had proceeded slowly and cautiously toward the new Act. During the 1990s, the Law Commission carried out a great deal of work on the topic and produced a number of reports, culminating in a final report entitled *Mental incapacity law* (Law Commission 1995). This was then followed by a government consultation paper, *Who decides?* (Lord Chancellor's Department 1997), and a report, *Making decisions* (Lord Chancellor 1999). In 2003 the government published a draft Mental Incapacity Bill, and followed it up with a Mental Capacity Bill in 2004. The Act was passed in 2005 and brought into force mainly toward the end of 2007, together with a substantial and helpful statutory Code of Practice.

Some years previously, the Scottish Parliament had enacted and implemented its own legislation, the Adults with Incapacity (Scotland) Act 2000.

20.2 PRINCIPLES RUNNING THROUGH THE MENTAL CAPACITY ACT 2005

Section 1 of the Act sets out five core principles which apply to the whole Act.

20.2.1 ASSUMPTION OF CAPACITY

First, a person is assumed to have capacity to take a decision unless it is established otherwise (Mental Capacity Act 2005, s.1). The effect of this principle is that whoever is seeking to show lack of capacity has to work all the harder in doing so. In case of doubt, one would therefore lean to capacity rather than incapacity. Prior to the Act, this approach was anyway to be found in the common law and the exercise of the High Court's inherent jurisdiction.

The principle in common law has also been that, once capacity has been shown to have been lost, there is a presumption of continuance of that loss. However, the Court of Appeal rejected this approach in the case, for example, of head injury, from which there might be recovery. One reason for taking this approach is because of the drastic consequences of being judged to lack capacity: a person is deprived of important civil rights (*Masterman-Lister v Brutton*). In another case, in which a man with learning disabilities clearly lacked the capacity to consent to marriage, the court noted that the possibility of future improvement in his capacity had to be borne in mind (*X City Council v MB*).

20.2.2 TAKING PRACTICABLE STEPS TO HELP A PERSON DECIDE

All practicable steps should be taken to help a person take the decision (s.1).

Such practicable steps could be various. The Code of Practice refers to the importance of relevant information, including all relevant information, avoidance of excessive detail, outlining risks and benefits, explanation of the effects of the decision, balanced presentation and consideration of obtaining specialist advice. In terms of communication, 'all possible and appropriate means of communication should be tried'. This may include finding out the best means of communication, using simple language, pictures, objects, illustrations, picture boards, hearing interpreter, mechanical or electronic communication aids, interpreting behaviour which is indicative of feelings, speaking at the right volume and speed with appropriate sentence structure and vocabulary, breaking down information into smaller bits, allowing the person time to understand each bit of information, repeating information, getting help from people the person trusts, awareness of cultural, ethical or religious factors, using a professional language interpreter, using an advocate.

Location might be decisive, for instance, a quiet one free of background noise or other distractions, and one where privacy and dignity is respected; taking a person to the relevant location (such as a hospital) may assist the person to understand what is in issue and make the decision. Likewise timing may be decisive; a person may be more alert in the morning, less alert immediately after taking drowsiness-inducing medication, become tired or confused if asked to decide too much in one go – or simply delaying the decision may be helpful so that more steps can be taken to assist the person take the decision. Support from other people may of benefit; the presence of a relative or a friend may (or may not be) reassuring and reduce anxiety (Lord Chancellor 2007, paras 3.9–3.15).

20.2.3 UNWISE DECISIONS DO NOT NECESSARILY MEAN INCAPACITY

The fact that a person with a disorder or disability of mind takes what is considered to be an unwise decision does not necessarily mean that he or she lacks capacity (s.1).

This is a key principle. It recognises the fact that everybody makes unwise decisions. As the courts have put it: 'It is not the task of the courts to prevent those who have the mental capacity to make rational decisions from making decisions which others may regard as rash or irresponsible' (*Masterman-Lister v Brutton*). After all, many people 'make rash and irresponsible decisions, but are of full capacity'. However, this does not mean that vulnerability to exploitation is not relevant to the question of capacity. The question is not whether the person is making a rational decision but whether he or she has the capacity to make a rational decision (*Lindsay v Wood*). Nonetheless, the courts have stated that outcomes can often 'cast a flood of light on capacity', and are likely to be important, though not conclusive, indicators (*Masterman-Lister v Brutton*).

So, when a woman person with learning disabilities wished to marry a 37-year-old man with a substantial history of sexually violent crimes, the court was called on to consider whether or not she had capacity to marry. It did not simply assume that she lacked capacity, nor was it minded to set too high a threshold of capacity to marry:

Marriage. The question of whether E has capacity to marry is quite distinct from the question of whether E is wise to marry; either wise to marry at all, or wise to marry X rather than Y, or wise to marry S. In relation to her marriage the only question for the court is whether E has capacity to marry. The court has no jurisdiction to consider whether it is in E's best interests to marry or to marry S. It is not concerned with the wisdom of her marriage in general or her marriage to S in particular (*Sheffield CC v E*).

Legal cases involving the question of unwise decisions are discussed further below (see 20.4.2).

20.2.4 INTERVENTIONS MUST BE IN A PERSON'S BEST INTERESTS

Acts done or decisions made for people lacking capacity must be in their best interests (s.1). Best interests are defined in section 4 of the Act (see below).

20.2.5 LEAST RESTRICTIVE INTERVENTION

Before an act is done for a person lacking capacity, regard must be had to whether the purpose of the act can be as effectively achieved in a way that is less restrictive of the person's rights and freedom of action (s.1).

Intervention in the case of a person lacking capacity is a major intrusion because, by definition, it is without the person's consent. Therefore the Act makes clear that it should be no more restrictive than necessary. This principle could apply to a range of situations, including restraint, restriction of liberty, restrictive daily routines (e.g. how washing, dressing, mealtimes, getting up and going to bed are handled and organised).

Nor is it necessarily about minimising risk at all costs. As the court put it in one case involving a highly vulnerable woman, 'what good is it making someone safer if it merely makes them miserable?' This was where allowing the continuation of a sexual relationship (to which she could consent) with her longstanding boyfriend, would be a clear benefit to her – but also carry a number of risks in relation to her mental health and to other matters on which she lacked the capacity to decide (*Local Authority X v MM*).

20.3 LACK OF CAPACITY

Section 2 deals with lack of capacity:

- a person lacks capacity if, at the material time, he or she is unable to take a decision in relation to a particular matter, because of impairment of, or disturbance in the functioning of, the mind or brain
- it doesn't matter whether the lack of capacity is permanent or temporary
- lack of capacity cannot be established merely be reference to age, appearance, condition or aspect of behaviour
- capacity is to be decided on the balance of probabilities
- the Act does not apply in the case of somebody under 16, but the Court of Protection may make decisions or appoint a deputy in relation to the property and affairs of a person under 16 (s.2).

The test for capacity is essentially twofold. First, whether there is an impairment or disturbance in the functioning of the mind or brain; and, second, whether is there an inability to take a particular decision at a particular time.

The Code of Practice states that examples of impairment or disturbance in the functioning of the mind or brain might include:

- conditions associated with some types of mental illness
- dementia
- significant learning disabilities
- brain damage
- physical or mental conditions causing confusion, drowsiness or loss of consciousness
- delirium

- concussion following head injury
- symptoms of alcohol or drug abuse (Lord Chancellor 2007, para 4.12).

20.3.1 CAPACITY: ISSUE AND TIME SPECIFIC

Section 2 makes clear that capacity is both issue and time specific, a principle emphasised by the courts in the past. Capacity is not all or nothing. It generally relates to the taking of a particular (type of) decision (*Masterman-Lister v Brutton*).

For instance, a person might have the capacity to decide what to eat for breakfast, but not where he or she should live. Likewise, a person may lack capacity to take a decision one week, only to regain it the next, once a chest infection or urinary infection has cleared up. Nonetheless, in case of marriage, the question is not whether the person has the capacity to marry one person rather than another, but rather whether he or she has the capacity to marry at all (*Sheffield CC v E*). The same principle applies to capacity to consent to sexual relations; it cannot depend on the particular partner. Thus it is issue, not person or partner, specific (*Local Authority X v MM*).

Things may become complicated. In one case, in which a local authority was attempting to protect a woman with learning disabilities, she was judged to lack the capacity to decide where to live, with whom (generally) to have contact, to marry or to litigate. However, she was deemed to have the capacity to consent to sexual relations. The local authority was faced with the task of working out a care plan which balanced these factors (*Local Authority X v MM*).

20.4 INABILITY TO TAKE A DECISION

The second part of the test for incapacity is elaborated upon in section 3 of the 2005 Act which states that:

- a person is unable to take a decision if he or she is unable to understand the relevant information, or to retain it, or to use or weigh it as part of the decision-making process, or to communicate it
- however, the person is not to be regarded as unable to take the decisions if he or she can understand an explanation in a way appropriate to his or her circumstances (e.g. using simple language, visual aids or any other means)
- if the person can retain the information relevant to the decision for a short time only, this does not necessarily mean the person cannot make decision
- information relevant to a decision includes information about the reasonably foreseeable consequences of deciding one way or another, or of failing to make the decision (s.3).

The test of capacity embodied in s.3 of the Mental Capacity Act 2007 equates with what has been called the functional approach, as opposed to a status or outcome approach, to capacity (Law Commission 1995, para 3.3). Its inclusion in the Act derives from past judge-made law, in the exercise of the inherent jurisdiction of the High Court in the absence of applicable legislation. It contrasts with what may be called a status or outcome approach. The following example was a landmark case, illustrating the courts' rejection of the status and outcome, in favour of the functional, approach. The outcome of the person's decision was that he might well die; the status issue was that he was a mental health patient in a special hospital. However, neither fact meant that he necessarily lacked the requisite decision-making capacity:

Amputation of gangrenous leg. A patient detained in a special secure hospital suffered from chronic paranoid schizophrenia. He was found to be suffering from an ulcerated, gangrenous foot and transferred to a general hospital, where the surgeon recommended amputation. The patient refused but agreed to conservative treatment; and sought an injunction to stop amputation unless he consented in writing. The court held that his schizophrenia did not mean that he could not understand the nature, purpose and effects of the treatment. He understood the relevant information, believed it and arrived at a clear choice. The court granted the injunction (*Re C (Adult: refusal of treatment)*).

20.4.1. EXISTING COMMON LAW TESTS OF CAPACITY

Tests of capacity for some particular decisions have been formulated in the common law by the courts – including for medical treatment, residence, contact, litigation, gifts, wills, marriage, sexual relations.

It is expected that the courts will consider these rules in the light of the general test of capacity in the 2005 Act. However, these particular rules remain applicable. The Code of Practice states that the judges will adopt the 2005 Act test 'if they think it is appropriate' (para 4.33). The courts have stated that this does not mean judges can simply disregard the 2005 Act test but that in cases, other than in the Court of Protection – for example, cases about capacity to make wills, gifts, to litigate, to marry – the court can 'adopt the new definition if it is appropriate – appropriate, that is, having regard to the existing principles of the common law' (*Local Authority X v MM*).

In the case of capacity to litigate, however, the relevant civil procedure rules have adopted the definition of capacity contained in the 2005 Act – thus, the latter does directly apply, outside of the Court of Protection, to the question of capacity to litigate (*Saulle v Novet*).

20.4.2 ASCERTAINING INABILITY TO TAKE A DECISION

Ultimately the question of capacity is a legal, not a medical, one. Indeed, the Act and Code of Practice envisage that all manner of person may be taking this decision, because the onus lies on the person – who may be a professional, but who may alternatively be a family member, for example – proposing to make a decision in somebody else's best interests.

The Code of Practice states that the person who assesses capacity will usually be the person directly concerned with the decision that has to be made. This means, for 'most day-to-day' decisions, the immediate carer. For acts of care or treatment, the assessor must, under s.5 of the Act, have a reasonable belief that the person lacks capacity. More complex decisions are likely to need more formal assessments, but the final decision is to be made by the person intending to make the intervention in terms of care or treatment. Of course professionals such as doctors or solicitors will have to assess capacity in relation to proposed medical treatment or legal transactions respectively.

The Code goes on to state that carers, including family carers, do not have to be expert assessors, but must be able to explain the reasonable steps they have taken to ascertain the lack of capacity. Thus reasonable steps will depend on individual circumstances and the urgency of the decision; professionals would normally be expected to undertake a fuller assessment than family members without formal qualifications. However, a professional opinion may be required when a complex or major decision has to be made. This might be from a general practitioner or, for example and depending on the condition or disorder, consultant psychiatrist, psychologist or speech and language therapist (Lord Chancellor 2007, paras 4.38–4.51).

Yet medical evidence is by no means all. For instance, a family member or professional (such as a social worker) with close knowledge of and contact with a person may be better positioned to make a judgement about capacity, than a medical doctor coming to the situation 'cold'. In the same vein, in coming to the conclusion in one case that a person did not lack capacity to manage his affairs, the court took particular account of the person's diary entries made over a period of many years. The medical experts giving evidence in the case had failed to reach a consensus, and so the judge had to look particularly hard at non-medical evidence, including the man's diaries (*Masterman-Lister v Brutton*). In another case, the evidence to the court was from many quarters:

Evidence about a woman's capacity. In a case concerning exploitation by carers of an elderly woman (now dead), and whether the transfer of her home to the carers should be set aside in civil law, the court heard evidence from a whole range of people including three general practitioners, a hospital senior house officer, a pathologist and another hospital consultant who had examined histological slides of the woman's brain, a chiropodist, friends, neighbours, a social worker, a retired Methodist minister, a solicitors' clerk, and a borough council emergency contact service supervisor (*Special Trustees for Great Ormond Street Hospital v Rushin*).

In practice, factors to be considered in a capacity assessment (by a medical doctor) might include appearance, speech, mood, thinking processes, perceptual disorders, delusional ideas, cognitive functions, orientation, memory, insight and pre-morbid personality. Apparent incapacity may simply be very temporary owing to a chest infection or urinary infection that can rapidly be cleared up. It might well be better to visit a person in his or her own home, choosing the time carefully so that the person is not too tired or otherwise distracted; a couple of visits may be necessary. Even then, the doctor may be unable to decide and refer the matter to the courts (Singh 2002).

20.4.2.1 Refusal of assessment of capacity

Some people might refuse or object to an assessment of mental capacity. The Code of Practice states that nobody 'can be forced to undergo an assessment of capacity. If someone refuses to open the door to their home, it cannot be forced'. It points out that that if there were serious concerns about a person's mental health, it may be possible to obtain a warrant and force entry under s.135 of the Mental Health Act 1983. However, the Code underlines that 'simply refusing an assessment of capacity is in no way sufficient grounds for an assessment' under the 1983 Act (Lord Chancellor 2007, para 4.59).

20.5 BEST INTERESTS

If an act is done or decision taken for a person lacking capacity, it must be in that person's bests interests (s.4):

* **(best interests)** any act done or decision taken, for or on behalf of a person lacking capacity, must be in that person's best interests

- **(avoiding unjustified assumptions)** in determining best interests, the person making the determination must not make it merely on the basis of the person's age or appearance or a condition or aspect of behaviour, which might lead others to make unjustified assumptions about what might be in his best interests
- **(considerations)** best interests involve the decision-maker:
  - **(regaining of capacity)** considering whether it is likely that the person will at some time have capacity and, if so, when that is likely to be
  - **(participation of person)** permitting and encouraging the person to participate as fully as possible in the decision and any decision affecting him
  - **(not desiring to bring about death)** where life sustaining treatment is in issue, the decision-maker must not be motivated by a desire to bring about the person's death
  - **(past and present wishes etc.)** considering, if reasonably ascertainable, the person's past and present wishes and feelings (and, in particular, any relevant written statement made by the person when he or she still had capacity), beliefs and values, other factors
  - **(consulting others)** taking into account, where consultation is appropriate and practicable, the views of anyone named person by the person, any person caring for the person or interested in the person's welfare, any donee of a lasting power of attorney, any Court of Protection appointed deputy.
- **(reasonable belief)** this section of the Act is complied with if the person doing the act or making the decision reasonably believes that the act or decision is in the best of the interests of the person concerned (s.4).

There is no indication in the Act as to which, if any, of these factors should take precedence in the reaching of a decision about best interests. The Code of Practice states that, for example, that a person's wishes and feelings, values and beliefs 'will not necessarily be the deciding factor in working out their best interests'. Yet the Code notes the legal requirement to pay special attention to any written statements the person may have made before losing capacity (Lord Chancellor 2007, para 5.38–5.42). The courts have stated in this respect, that the 'further capacity is reduced, the lighter autonomy weighs' (*Re C (Adult: refusal of treatment)*). So, conversely:

The nearer to capacity, so greater weight on wishes in determining best interests. 'The nearer to the borderline the particular adult, even if she falls on the wrong side of the line, the more weight must in principle be attached to her wishes and feelings, because the greater distress, the humiliation and indeed it may even be the anger she is likely to feel the better she is able to appreciate that others are taking on her behalf decisions which vitally affect her – matters, it may be, as here [a personal, sexual relationship], of an intensely private and personal nature' (*Local Authority X v MM*).

The person making the decision ultimately has to decide about the best interests, after applying the above test. It may not be plain sailing. For instance, consulting with relatives may bring about anything but a consensus:

Family pressure. A complaint to the local ombudsman concerned a woman with dementia and a family dispute amongst her three children. Unhappy with the care their mother was receiving at a home within the Doncaster area, the brother and one sister suggested their mother move down to a residential home in the south-west of England. The second sister objected, but the council agreed to fund the placement.

The following year, the second sister contacted the council and alleged that the first sister was not visiting frequently and that her mother was unhappy. The council agreed to arrange for the mother's return to a council-owned home in Doncaster. It was maladministration to take this decision without the reassessment which was 'clearly desirable and mandated by the Council's own policy' – and without at least some attempt at verifying the sister's claims. The second sister collected her mother from the home in the south-west without explaining her intention of removing her permanently, but the council did not inform the brother and first sister. This was maladministration also (*Doncaster MBC 1997*).

Although it is the decision-maker who has to decide about best interests, nonetheless those best interests are not confined to issues within the expertise of that decision-maker. For instance, a decision about a medical intervention would encompass not just medical but also emotional and all other welfare issues. Furthermore, deciding about a person's best interests is not just about identifying a range of acceptable options, but instead is about identifying the 'best', a superlative term. This does not therefore equate with the common law duty of care owed by professionals, which is at least to adopt a reasonable course of action, but not necessarily the best (*SL v SL*). The courts have also made clear that the best interests in issue are those of the person lacking capacity – even if, for example, the decision in question affects the life or death of a close family member (*Re Y (Adult Patient) (Transplant: Bone Marrow)*).

Over a number of years, the courts have been increasingly called on to make important welfare decisions about best interests – for example, about whether a person should receive medical intervention (e.g. sterilisation of a woman with learning disabilities for non-therapeutic reasons), where people with learning disabilities should live (*Newham LBC v BS*), whether they had capacity to marry or have sexual relations (*Sheffield CC v E*), or whether elderly people with dementia should remain at home cared for by a spouse or be admitted to hospital or care home (*B Borough Council v Mrs S*). The decisions are not always easy, as the court attempts to draw up a balance sheet, weighing up the pros and cons of a particular course of action.

The courts will wish to ensure that, as section 4 of the Act states, assumptions about a person's best interests are not made on the basis of a person's condition:

Hospital treatment of person with severe learning disability. An 18-year-old had the capacity of a five- to six-year-old child – with severe learning disability, autism and epilepsy. He was admitted to hospital for acute renal failure; haemodialysis was required. A dispute arose between the hospital and mother as to whether or in what circumstances a kidney transplant would ever be suitable for him and whether there was a possibility of a different form of haemodialysis by use of AV fistula.

The court found that the medical and nursing team's approach had been coloured by past experience with the man and the difficulties of verbal communication. However, other evidence in the case showed that steps could be taken to enable him to cope with certain treatment and that the possibility of an AV fistula should not be ruled out and kidney transplantation should not be ruled on non-medical grounds.

The court made the point that it was crucial that he was not given less satisfactory treatment than a person who understood the risks, pain and discomfort of major surgery. 'To act in any other way would be contrary to the rights of a mentally incapacitated patient both under our domestic law and under the European Convention' (*An Hospital NHS Trust v S*).

20.5.1 MOTIVATION TO BRING ABOUT DEATH

The Code of Practice explains that in case of deciding about best interests and life-sustaining treatment, the decision-maker must not be motivated to bring about the death of the person. However, if treatment is futile, overly burdensome or there is no prospect of recovery, a decision may sometimes be made that further life-sustaining treatment is not in the person's best interests. This however is not same as being motivated to bring about the person's death, even if this stems only from a sense of compassion. By the same token, this rule cannot be interpreted to mean that doctors are obliged to provide life-sustaining treatment where this is not in the person's best interests (Lord Chancellor 2007, paras 5.31–5.33).

20.6 DEPRIVATION OF LIBERTY

Some years ago, the English courts held that in the case of a mentally incapable, but compliant, person being detained by reason of mental disorder, it is not necessary that he or she be formally sectioned under the Mental Health Act 1983. The common law of best interests and necessity sufficed. However, the case exposed the lack of safeguards available to such informal patients:

Removal to hospital. A 48-year-old man had been autistic since birth. He was unable to speak and required 24-hour care, and unable to go outside alone. He had no ability to communicate consent or dissent to treatment or to express preferences as to where he should live. He was frequently agitated, had no sense of danger and had a history of self-harm. From the age of 13, for over 30 years, he was resident at a hospital. He was then discharged on a trial basis into the community, going to live with paid carers.

One day he was attending a day centre and became agitated and was banging his head against a wall, and hitting his head with his fists. The day centre got in touch with a local doctor who came and administered a sedative; the social worker with overall responsibility for him was contacted and recommended that he be taken by ambulance to accident and emergency. There, after further agitation, a psychiatrist assessed that he needed inpatient treatment. However, it was decided that he could be admitted informally, rather than making use of s.2 or s.3 of the 1983 Act, because he appeared to be fully compliant and did not resist admission. He subsequently remained in hospital for several months on this informal basis, before being belatedly sectioned under the Mental Health Act. Shortly afterwards this formal detention, he was in fact discharged.

The House of Lords, overruling the Court of Appeal, held that it was permissible to admit informally to hospital (s.131 of the Mental Health Act 1983) patients who lacked the capacity to consent but who did not positively object. The court stated that the removal, care and treatment of the person had been in his best interests and was justified by the common law doctrine of necessity, which was not excluded by the provisions of the 1983 Act. Nevertheless, one of the law lords pointed out that this conclusion was not wholly satisfactory, since it meant that the formal safeguards contained in the Mental Health Act did not apply to this particular class of vulnerable informal patient (*R v Bournewood Community and Mental Health NHS Trust, ex p L*).

The case was then taken to the European Court of Human Rights, which found that both article 5.1 and article 5.4 had been breached. The former (article 5.1, concerning lawful deprivation of liberty) was breached because of the arbitrary nature, without fixed procedural rules, of his detention for a period of over three months (at which point he was actually formally detained). The latter (article 5.4, concerning entitlement to a speedy decision as to the lawfulness of detention) was also breached (*HL v United Kingdom*).

The health service ombudsman had also, between the House of Lords and European Court decisions, separately criticised the prolonged 'detention' in this case, finding that the man should have been discharged back to the family the same, or following, day (*Bournewood Community and Mental Health NHS Trust 2002*).

In the light of the judgment of the European Court, the Department of Health issued guidance in December 2004 stating that it would bring forward proposals for appropriate procedural safeguards. However, until these were in place, the guidance made clear that to provide care or treatment (whether in hospital or other residential settings) for a mentally incapacitated patient, amounting to a deprivation of liberty, was unlawful unless the person was detained under the Mental Health Act 1983. It suggested, amongst other things, that:

- the NHS and local authorities should ensure they have systems in place to assess whether a person is being deprived of his or her liberty
- wherever possible to avoid situations in which professionals take 'full and effective control' of a person's care and liberty
- decisions should be taken in a structured way
- there should be effective, documented care planning
- there should be consideration of alternatives to hospital admission or residential care, and that any restrictions placed on the person are kept to the minimum necessary in all the circumstances
- both assessment of capacity and care plan should be kept under review, and an independent element to this may well be helpful
- if it is concluded that there is no way of providing appropriate care without a deprivation of liberty occurring, then consideration should be given to use of the formal powers of detention under the 1983 Act.

However, the guidance also included a note of caution, pointing out that not all patients, subject to restrictions amounting to deprivation of liberty, can be detained lawfully under the 1983 Act. For instance, their mental disorder might not warrant detention in hospital. In addition, there were dangers in using the Act simply to be on the 'safe side'; formal detention might be perceived as a stigma. Further, significant increased use of the 1983 Act would place considerable pressure on local authority approved social workers, second opinion appointed doctors (SOADs) and on the operation of Mental Health Review Tribunals (DH 2004e).

Between the European Court ruling in *HL v UK* and the coming into force of legal rules about the authorising of deprivation of liberty (see below), the courts made clear that – in this interim period – a court order represented the necessary safeguard to prevent human rights being breached (*City of Sunderland v PS*; and *JE v DE and Surrey County Council*).

20.6.1 DEPRIVATION OF LIBERTY: PERMITTED UNDER THE MENTAL CAPACITY ACT 2005

The Mental Capacity Act 2005 does not authorise any person to deprive any other person of his or her liberty – subject to certain exceptions, in which case the Act applies specific safeguards for allowing the authorisation of a deprivation of liberty. These are expected to come into force in April 2009.

Deprivation of liberty will be defined in the MCA 2005 with reference to article 5 of the European Convention on Human Rights (s.64, expected in force in late 2008). The European Court itself has struggled with the concept, and has outlined it as follows. The difference between deprivation of, and restriction of, liberty is one of degree or intensity, not one of nature or substance. Relevant issues include type, duration, effects and manner of implementation (*Ashingdane v UK*). Compliance by a person in giving up himself or herself for detention is not determinative (i.e. there could still be a deprivation of liberty: *HL v UK*). Indicators of deprivation of liberty might include, as the European Court found in *HL v UK*:

- professionals having complete, effective, continuous and strict control and supervision over a person's care, movements, assessment, residence, treatment, contacts
- attempts to leave informal detention would have resulted in compulsory detention (under the Mental Health Act)
- whether a ward is locked or lockable is relevant but not determinative of the issue (*HL v UK*).

In a subsequent case, the High Court identified three relevant propositions to whether deprivation of liberty has occurred:

- an objective element of a person's confinement in a restricted space for a not negligible length of time
- a subjective element, in that the person has not validly consented
- the deprivation must be imputable to the State (*JE v DE and Surrey CC*).

With such factors in mind, the English court found a deprivation of liberty in the following case.

Refusal to let a person go home: deprivation of liberty? A man had a major stroke aged 76 years old. This left him blind with significant memory impairment. He suffered from dementia, although could express wishes and feelings with some force. The evidence suggested strongly that he lacked capacity. On a particular day, his wife, who had intermittent mental health problems of her own, felt she could no longer cope and placed in him a chair on the pavement. He was dressed in pyjama bottoms, shirt and slippers. His wife informed the police who informed the local authority.

The local authority subsequently placed him in a nursing home. While there, significant restrictions were put in place. He was not allowed to visit his wife at home, not even at Christmas. His wife was not to remove him. The local authority said on a number of occasions that it would call the police if his wife tried to take him home. During this period of over a year, the man repeatedly asked to go home; repeatedly he was told he could not.

In its evidence to the court, the local authority stated that had he tried to go home, it would not have prevented him – but the court pointed out that this had never been communicated to the man or his wife. The court also dismissed the authority's claim that, first, his wishes largely flowed from his wife's urgings. Second, that it had no objection to him living elsewhere – just not with his wife. Third, that the police would not in fact have had any power to prevent him leaving. This last, the judge dismissed as 'legal sophistry', pointing out that a person can be deprived of his or her liberty 'by the misuse or misrepresentation of even non-existent authority as by locked doors and physical barriers' (*JE v DE and Surrey CC*).

However, in another case, the judge concluded that a man who had been placed in a care home may have had his liberty restricted but he had not been deprived of it. Some of the relevant factors he took into account were (a) that the care home was an 'ordinary care home where only ordinary restrictions of liberty applied; (b) the family was able to visit on a largely unrestricted basis and could take him on outings; (c) the man was personally compliant and expressed himself happy; and (d) there was no occasion on which he was objectively deprived of his liberty (*LLBC v TG*). Prior to the amended Mental Capacity Act coming into force, the courts identified in the following case that the safeguard needed in case of deprivation of liberty was for the local authority to seek a court order – as it was doing:

Preventing daughter discharging mother from hospital: court order. The daughter of a woman lacking capacity and in physical ill health, wished to discharge her mother from hospital into her own care – rather than back to the residential unit her mother had been living in previously. The local authority was greatly concerned about the welfare of the mother, but was concerned about depriving the mother of her liberty if it took steps to prevent her leaving or from being removed from the unit. The court made an order stating that it was 'lawful being in the [mother's] best interests for the local authority by its employees or agents to use reasonable and proportionate measures to prevent [the mother] from leaving the unit'. This could involve 'perimeter security' and in an extreme situation, the use of reasonable force to prevent removal, the force being applied to the daughter rather than the mother (*City of Sunderland v PS*).

20.6.2 AUTHORISATION OF DEPRIVATION OF LIBERTY: RULES

The amended Mental Capacity Act 2005 (MCA) sets out a complex system of safeguards, to ensure that a person is not arbitrarily deprived of his or her liberty. These are due to come into force in April 2009. It is beyond the scope of this book to set out the detail.

In summary only, deprivation of liberty is lawful under the Mental Capacity Act 2005 (a) when the Court of Protection has ordered it, or a court's decision is impending and life is at stake or serious deterioration at stake, or (b) if it is otherwise authorised under the Act in terms of a 'standard' or 'urgent' authorisation, by a 'supervisory body' (local authority of NHS primary care trust) or 'managing authority' (hospital or care home) respectively.

The Act states that its deprivation of liberty provisions – that is safeguards – apply if a person lacking capacity to decide is 'detained in circumstances which amount to a deprivation of liberty' in a hospital or care home (schedule A1, paras 1(2) and 15).

For deprivation to be lawful, the person must meet a number of qualifying requirements which have to be assessed by the supervisory body before it grants what is called a standard authorisation. These requirements relate to age, mental health, mental capacity, best interests, eligibility (that is the person is not excluded because of overlap with the Mental Health Act 1983) and 'refusals' (any valid advance decision). Regulations govern who can carry out these assessments as well as other procedural aspects.

Urgent authorisation can be given for up to seven days by managing authorities, if there is not time for the supervisory body to undertake these assessments and grant a standard authorisation.

The length of time of a standard authorisation must be specified, with a maximum of 12 months. Provisions are made for review which must, in certain circumstances, be carried out.

There are also provisions for a personal representative to be appointed and, in certain circumstances, an independent mental capacity advocate (Mental Capacity Act 2005, schedule A1 and 1A).

20.7 ACTS IN CONNECTION WITH CARE OR TREATMENT

Section 5 of the Act provides a general defence for people providing care or treatment for a person lacking capacity. It states that:

- a person is protected from liability if he or she does an act in connection with care or treatment, and
- he or she took reasonable steps to establish that the person lacked capacity in respect of the matter in question, and reasonably believed that the person lacked that capacity and that it was in his or own best interests that the act be done
- however, this does not exclude civil liability for loss or damage, or criminal liability, arising from negligence in doing the act. And nothing in this section affects the rules about advance decisions or overrides the decision of a person with lasting power of attorney.

The Code of Practice points out that simply because somebody has come to an incorrect conclusion about a person's capacity or best interests does not mean that he or she will not be protected from liability. But they must 'be able to show that it was reasonable for them to think that the person lacked capacity and that they were acting in the person's best interests at the time they made their decision or took action' (Lord Chancellor 2007, para 5.59). As a consultant psychiatrist has put it, decisions regarding mental capacity and best interests should be carefully documented, not least because there may be in many cases no 'right answer' – and good documentation will go a long way in protecting both patient and doctor (Hotopf 2005). Nonetheless, the Department of Health reported eight months after implementation of the Mental Capacity Act that many staff and managers were 'not taking and recording all best interests decisions' (LAC(DH)(2008)4).

The protection from liability is in respect of both civil and criminal liability that could otherwise arise from doing things for or to a person without their consent. For instance, as the Code of Practice points out, a carer dressing a person without the latter's consent could theoretically be prosecuted for assault. A neighbour entering and cleaning the house of a person lacking capacity to give permission could be trespassing on the person's property (Lord Chancellor 2007, para 6.2).

The Code gives a non-exhaustive list of the sort of actions that are covered by way of care under s.5. These include help with washing, dressing, personal hygiene, eating, drinking, communication, mobility – and with a person's taking part in education, social or leisure activities. Also, going to a person's house to see if they are alright, doing the shopping with the person's money, arranging household services, providing home help services, undertaking actions related to community care services (e.g. day care, care home accommodation, nursing care), helping a person move home.

Health care and treatment might include diagnostic examinations and tests, medical or dental treatment, medication, taking a person to hospital for assessment or treatment, nursing care, other procedures or therapies (e.g. physiotherapy or chiropody), emergency care (Lord Chancellor 2007, para 6.5).

20.8 LIMITATIONS ON RESTRAINT AND ON SECTION 5

Section 6 of the Act states that:

- to restrain a person and be protected under s.5, the person (the restrainer) must reasonably believe it is necessary to prevent harm to the person lacking capacity
- the response must be proportionate in relation to the likelihood of the person suffering harm and the seriousness of that harm
- however, this section does not apply if the intervention is more than just restraint and the person is being deprived of their liberty (due to be repealed in April 2009)
- restraint involves use or threats to use force to secure the doing of an act which the person resists – or restriction of liberty of the person's movement whether or not the person resists
- section 5 does not authorise a person to do an act which conflicts with a decision made, within the scope of the authority of a donee of a lasting power of attorney or a court-appointed deputy. But this does not stop a person providing life-sustaining treatment, or doing any act which he or she believes necessary to prevent a serious deterioration in the person's condition – while a decision about any relevant issue is sought from the court.

The Code of Practice points out that the common law also imposes a duty of care on healthcare and social care staff to take appropriate and necessary action to restrain or remove a person – with challenging behaviour or who is in the acute stages of illness – who may cause harm to themselves or other people (Lord Chancellor 2007, para 6.43).

20.9 PAYMENT FOR NECESSARY GOODS AND SERVICES

Section 7 deals with the question of a person entering into a contract for goods or services, even though he or she lacks the capacity to do so. It states that:

- if necessary goods or services are supplied to a person lacking capacity to contract for them, the person must nevertheless pay a reasonable price for them
- necessary means suitable to a person's condition in life and to his or her actual requirements at the time when goods or services are supplied.

The Code of Practice explains that in general, a contract entered into by a person lacking capacity cannot be enforced if the other person knows, or should have known, about the lack of capacity. The Act modifies this rule by stating that such a contract is enforceable if the goods or services contracted for are 'necessary' (Lord Chancellor 2007, para 6.57).

20.10 EXPENDITURE: PLEDGE OF PERSON'S EXPENDITURE

In relation to section 5 (care or treatment), it is lawful for the carer to pledge the person's (who lacks capacity) credit for the purpose of expenditure or to use money in the person's possession. The carer can reimburse himself or herself from money in the person's possession or be otherwise indemnified by the second person (MCA 2005, s.8). The Code of Practice explains that the carer could use cash that the person lacking capacity may have, or use his or her own money with a view to being paid back by the person lacking capacity (Lord Chancellor 2007, para 6.61).

20.11 LASTING POWER OF ATTORNEY

Sections 9–14 deal with lasting power of attorney, which enables a donee of such a power to take a range of finance and welfare decisions on behalf the donor of the power, when the latter has lost capacity to take them:

- **(capacity and age of donor)** a person, the donor, is able to create a 'lasting power of attorney', whilst he or she retains the capacity to do so, and must be at least 18 years old
- **(scope of power)** such a lasting power can give the attorney authorisation to deal with property and financial affairs, as well as personal welfare matters (including health care decisions) – when the donor no longer has capacity
- **(prescribed form)** the power must be contained in an instrument of a certain form and must be registered with the the Public Guardian, otherwise it is not effective
- **(principles of Act apply)** a lasting power of attorney is subject to the provisions of the Act, in particular the principles in s.1 of the Act, as well as any conditions or restrictions specified in the instrument (s.9)
- **(age of donee)** a donee must be at least 18 years old
- **(attorneys acting jointly or severally)** may be appointed to act jointly, jointly and severally – or jointly in respect of matters, and jointly and severally in respect of others (s.10)
- **(restraint)** the use of the power to restrain the donor is restricted to where it is necessary and proportionate (to the likelihood of the person suffering harm), and the person lacks capacity or the attorney reasonably believe that the person lacks capacity in relation to the matter
- **(welfare powers useable only on loss of capacity)** the personal welfare powers cannot be used unless the donor lacks capacity or the attorney reasonably believes that the donor lacks capacity
- **(relation to advance decisions)** the personal welfare power would be subject to any advance decisions on treatment made by the donor – and would not cover decisions about life-sustaining treatment, unless this had been expressly included by the donor in the lasting power of attorney
- **(health care treatment)** the personal welfare power can be specified so as to include consent, or refusal of consent, to health care treatment (s.11)
- **(restrictions on gifts)** there are restrictions on gifts, other than on customary gifts or charities to whom the donor might have made gifts, insofar as the value of any such gift is reasonable in respect of the donor's estate
- **(prescribed information)** the document must include prescribed information
- **(donor signature)** the donor must sign a statement that they have read the information and want the power to apply when they have lost capacity
- **(named people to be informed)** the document must name people who should be informed when an application is made to register the power
- **(attorneys' signature)** the attorneys must sign to say they have read the information and understand their duties, including the duty to act in the person's best interests

- **(certification by third party of donor's understanding)** the document must include a certificate completed by an independent third party to the effect that that in their view, the donor understands the power being created, no undue pressure of fraud has been used, and there is nothing to stop the power being created (schedule 1)
- **(identity of certifying third party)** the independent third party (not a family member) can be someone who has known the donor personally for two years, or a person chosen by the donor on account of their professional skills and expertise, and whom the donor reasonably considers to be competent to certify the relevant matters (SI 2007/1253)
- **(Public Guardian and registration)** the Public Guardian charges registration fees (SI 20072051)
- **(separate forms and fees for welfare and finance)** There are separate forms for a welfare power and a finance power (SI 2007/1253, and the fee of £150 payable for each (SI 2007/2051).

In summary, a person aged 18 years or over, with capacity to do so, can make what is called a lasting power of attorney. This authorises the attorney to deal with property and financial affairs and (or) welfare matters when the donor loses capacity to take such decisions. Welfare decisions can include matters such as health care, place of residence, contact etc. More than one attorney can be appointed. There is a choice of appointing the attorneys to act jointly, or jointly or severally. Acting jointly is clearly a safeguard but could be more cumbersome. There are restrictions on gifts that can be made; otherwise, application must be made to the Court of Protection.

The Code of Practice spells out that attorneys must follow the principles of the Act, make decisions in the donor's best interests, have regard to the Code and remain within the authority contained in the power of attorney. In addition, as agent of the person lacking capacity, the attorney has a common law duty of care to apply reasonable standards of care and skill, a fiduciary duty (including principles such a trust, good faith, honesty, not taking advantage of the position and acting so as to benefit the donor, not themselves), should not delegate their authority, has a duty of confidentiality, a duty to comply with Court of Protection directions, a duty not to give up the role without notifying the donor and the Office of the Public Guardian, a duty to keep accounts, a duty to keep the donor's money and property separate from their own (Lord Chancellor 2007, paras 7.52–7.68).

20.11.1 LASTING POWER OF ATTORNEY: FINANCE, HEALTH AND WELFARE

The Act allows a donor of a lasting power of attorney to specify not just finance, business and property issues, but also health or welfare matters. However, the power does not have to cover all these things. The donor can specify. It is not all or nothing. Equally, the donor might appoint one attorney to deal with finance, and another to deal with welfare. Joint attorneys must always act together; joint and several attorneys can act either together or independently. The donor could specify that some matters could be dealt with severally, but others jointly.

The distinction between finance and welfare issues will usually be clear enough. There will nevertheless be a grey area, in which a decision concerning property or finance will overlap with welfare matters. For instance, a decision about whether to enter a care home is strictly speaking a welfare decision; but deciding how much to spend on the care placement is financial.

Lasting powers of attorney can be registered with the Office of the Public Guardian at any time and cannot be used until registered. A property and affairs power can be used by the attorney before the donor loses capacity; but a welfare power can be used only when the donor lacks the capacity to take a relevant welfare decision.

20.11.2 REVOCATION OF LASTING POWER OF ATTORNEY

Lasting powers of attorney may be subject to revocation in a number of situations. One of these is where the donor, at any time he or she has capacity, decides on revocation (s.13).

Section 22 of the Act sets out the power of the Court of Protection to intervene and determine whether the requirements for creation of a lasting power of attorney have been met, whether the power has been revoked, whether fraud or undue pressure was exercised, whether the donee is behaving inconsistently with the authority given by the power or not behaving in the donor's best interests. The court has the power to prevent registration of the power (s.22)

20.11.3 EXISTING ENDURING POWERS OF ATTORNEY

From October 2007, no new enduring powers of attorney could be made. Any made before that date remain valid, whether or not the donor has yet lost capacity and the power has been registered with the Court of Protection (Mental Capacity Act 2005, schedule 4).

Unlike lasting powers of attorney, enduring powers can only cover finance, business and property – and not health or welfare matters. This limitation sometimes leads to misunderstanding on the part of the attorney, who believes he or she is authorised under the power to make health or welfare decisions. In the past, professionals too have likewise been unclear. For example, in one case, the local ombudsman found social workers failing to involve attorneys in relevant matters, such as the management of personal finances, because the former were 'very woolly' about what such the enduring power entailed (*Nottinghamshire CC 2002*).

20.12 COURT OF PROTECTION

Sections 15 to 20 outline the function of the new Court of Protection. Some of the key points are as follows:

- **(declarations about capacity and interventions)** it has the power to make declarations about whether or not a person has capacity, lawfulness of any act done or proposed to be done in relation to the person (s.15)
- **(making orders, appointing deputies)** it can make a decision (by making an order) or alternatively, appoint a deputy, whose powers may extend to personal welfare, as well as to property and affairs
- **(orders preferred to deputies)** a decision of the court is to be preferred to the appointment of a deputy. The powers conferred on a deputy should be as limited in scope and duration as is reasonably practicable

- **(court subject to principles of Act)** the powers of the court are subject to the provisions of the Act, in particular the principles in s.1 and the test of best interests in s.4 (s.16)
- **(scope of welfare decisions)** personal welfare decisions could include in particular where the incapacitated person is to live, with whom he or she should have contact, consent or refusal to health care treatment (s.17)
- **(age of deputy, joint or several)** a deputy must be at least 18 years old. Two more deputies may be appointed to act jointly or severally (s.19)
- **(restraint)** if a deputy restrains the person, such intervention must be within the scope of the deputy's authority, necessary and proportionate, and the person lack capacity or the deputy reasonably believe that the person lacks capacity in relation to the matter)
- **(property, wills)** a deputy cannot be given power to settle any of the person's property, to execute the person's will or to exercise any power vested in the person (e.g. trusteeship)
- **(life sustaining treatment)** a deputy cannot refuse consent to life-sustaining treatment
- **(limit to authority)** a deputy cannot make a decision inconsistent with the scope of his or her authority or with a decision made by the donee of a lasting power of attorney
- **(contact and health care)** a deputy cannot be given powers to prohibit a named person from having contact with the person lacking capacity, nor to direct a person responsible for the person's health care to allow somebody else to take over the responsibility (s.20)
- **(fees)** where deputies are appointed, there are both appointment fees and supervision fees (specified at three levels) charged by the Public Guardian. There are exemptions in relation to receipt of benefits and also reduction and remission and fees in exceptional circumstances involving undue hardship (SI 2007/2051)
- **(deprivation of liberty)** in relation to standard authorisations concerning deprivation of liberty, the court can determine questions about whether the person meets the qualifying requirements, the period the authorisation is to be in force, the purpose of the authorisation, the conditions attached to the authorisation. It can vary or terminate the authorisation or direct that the supervisory body do so (s.21A).

Receiverships (dealing only with property, business, finance) - previously put in place before October 2007 by the former Court of Protection under Part 7 of the Mental Health Act 1983 - remain valid to the extent that they are converted to deputyship with the same functions as had been attached to the receivership (schedule 5).

20.12.1 APPLICATIONS TO THE COURT OF PROTECTION

Court of Protection involvement is intended to be a last resort. For instance, the Code of Practice states that in a dispute about best interests, a decision-maker could be challenged through use of an advocate, getting a second opinion, holding a case conference, mediation, or use of a complaints procedure. Only then, the Code states, should application be made to the Court (Lord Chancellor 2007, para 5.68).

The Code states that application to the Court about personal welfare, including health, interventions, may be necessary in case of particularly difficult decisions, disagreements that cannot otherwise be resolved, or situations where ongoing decisions may need to be made. The courts have in the past stated that certain serous medical interventions should always go to court, including decisions about artificial nutrition and hydration for patients in a persistent vegetative state (*Airedale NHS Trust v Bland*), bone marrow donation (*Re Y (Mental incapacity: bone marrow transplant)*), non-therapeutic sterilisation (*SL v SL*). Sometimes uncertainty as to whether the court needs to be resorted to for a decision (even in the absence of disagreement about intervention), in which case it is applied to for clarification:

Lawfulness of cessation of artificial ventilation. A man with motor neurone disease had slight eyelash movement as his only means of communication to express his wishes. He indicated that when he lost this last means of communication, he wished the artificial ventilation to cease. The doctors wanted the legal position clarified; in fact the court stated that the law was so clear (since the man had capacity to take this decision) that the doctors need not have applied to the courts and instead simply proceeded in accordance with the man's wishes. In fact, because one of the doctors had received conflicting legal advice, the court held that the court application was a proper one, although would not be necessary in every case (*Re AK (medical treatment: consent)*).

However, for finance and property, a court order will usually be necessary unless the only income involved consists of state benefits, or an enduring or lasting power of attorney exists. The Code of Practice states that the court may make a particular finance decision, for example, to terminate a tenancy or to make or amend a will. However, it may appoint a deputy for ongoing management of such affairs (a) for dealing with cash assets over a specified amount; (b) for selling a person's property; or (c) where the person has a level of income or capital that the court thinks a deputy needs to manage (Lord Chancellor 2007, paras 8.27–8.35).

20.12.1.1 Procedure

Permission is not needed to make an application to the Court by a person lacking, or alleged to lack capacity, by a person with a parental responsibility for a person under 18 years old, by a donor or donee of a lasting power of attorney, by a court-appointed deputy, or by a person named in an existing court order (with which the application is concerned). Otherwise permission is required (s.50). Applications to the Court are governed by detailed rules (SI 2007/1744).

Fees are charged, but there are exemptions in relation to receipt of benefits and also reduction and remission of fees in exceptional circumstances involving undue hardship (SI 2007/1745).

20.12.2 ORDERS MADE BY COURT

Prior to October 2007, the High Court (Family Division), was accustomed to giving declarations or orders in relation to a person's best interests. These cases form a good guide to function of the Court of Protection since October 2007.

The Court of Protection may be called on to confirm a lack of capacity and make an order – as in one case about preventing a woman's parents (motivated by strong cultural and religious influences) from entering into a contract of marriage for her, and forbidding them to take her abroad (to Pakistan) without permission from the court (*M v B*). Alternatively, it may decide not to make an order. In a case concerning a possible marriage in Pakistan for a man with learning disabilities who clearly lacked capacity to marry, the court refrained from such an order on the grounds that his parents were honourable people and the court would accept their undertakings not to contract a marriage or take him to Pakistan without application to the court (*X City Council v MB*).

In another case, the local authority sought an order to prevent the wife of a person with dementia from interfering with his transfer from a nursing home to hospital. It also sought to prevent her visiting hospital without the prior written agreement of the local authority and even then, only in the presence of a local authority employee. The court granted the order sought. She had previously been caring for him at home; he was 90 years old, lacked capacity, had difficult and challenging behaviour, together with extensive care needs including incontinence and lack of mobility (*B Borough Council v Mrs S*).

In that case, the court stressed that 'without notice' applications should not be the norm – since they did not allow the other side to be heard before an order was granted. It noted with regret how, frequently, without notice applications were made on the basis of 'largely unparticularised assertions', without any third party to material to support them. The court appreciated that in 'many instances there is a very real urgency and there will not be third party evidence of allegations of abusive behaviour that are readily available but in others there will be'.

The points made in this case were endorsed subsequently. This involved another without notice application, seeking an order to transfer a 78-year-old man with dementia out of the care of his daughter and grand-daughter into a care home. He lacked capacity to decide for himself. A first court hearing had granted a without notice order to have him removed. A second court hearing challenged the making of that without notice application, in the first hearing, by the local authority. Virtually all the local authority's assertions, on which it had relied to obtain the without notice order, were shown to be false (*LLBC v TG*).

20.12.3 OBLIGATIONS OF DEPUTY

The Code of Practice states that deputies must follow the statutory principles of the Act, make decisions in a person's best interests, have regard to the Code of Practice, and remain within the authority given them by the Court. In addition, as agent of the person lacking capacity, the deputy has a common law duty of care to apply reasonable standards of care and skill, a fiduciary duty (including principles such a trust, good faith, honesty, not taking advantage of the position and acting so as to benefit the donor, not themselves), a duty to indemnify the person against liability arising from the deputy's negligence, should not delegate their authority, has a duty of confidentiality, a duty to comply with Court of Protection directions, a duty to keep accounts, a duty to keep the donor's money and property separate from their own (Lord Chancellor 2007, paras 7.52–7.68).

20.13 ADVANCE DECISIONS

Sections 24–26 set out the rules about advance decisions or 'living wills' as they have commonly been known. They concern advance refusals of medical treatment, applicable when the person no longer has capacity to take the decision at the relevant time that treatment is in issue:

- **(age and capacity to specify refusal of medical treatment)** a person aged 18 or over, with the capacity to do so, may specify the circumstances in which at a future date, if he or she lacks capacity, specified treatment is *not* to be given
- **(withdrawal)** the person may withdraw or alter an advance decision; a withdrawal need not be in writing
- **(alteration)** an alteration need not be in writing, unless it relates to life-sustaining treatment s.24)
- **(treatment)** treatment is defined to include a 'diagnostic or other procedure' (s.64)
- **(invalidity)** the advance decision is not valid if the person has withdrawn it, subsequently conferred authority for the making of such a decision through a lasting power of attorney, or done anything inconsistent with the advance decision
- **(non-applicability)** the advance decision is not applicable to the particular treatment in issue if at the time the person has capacity to refuse or to consent to the treatment, or if the treatment in question is not specified in the advance decision, or if the circumstances specified in the advance statement have not arisen, or if there are reasonable grounds for believing that circumstances now exist that the person did not anticipate at the time of the advance decisions, but which would have affected that decision had they been anticipated
- **(life sustaining treatment: must be in writing)** the advance decision is not applicable to life-sustaining treatment unless the decision is verified by the person that it is to apply to that treatment even if life is at risk – and is in writing, signed by the person or by somebody else in the presence of, and by the direction, of the person, the signature is made or acknowledged by the person in the presence of a witness, and the witness signs it or acknowledges his/her signature in the person's presence (s.25)
- **(effect of valid and applicable decision)** otherwise an advance decision that is both valid and applicable to the treatment in question has effect as if the person had made it (and had the capacity to do so) at the time when the question arises about whether to carry out the treatment
- **(liability)** a person does not incur liability for providing treatment unless he or she know there was a valid and applicable advance decision
- **(Court of Protection)** the Court of Protection can make a declaration about the existence, validity or applicability of an advance decision
- **(interim treatment)** nothing in an apparent advance decision prevents the provision of life-sustaining treatment of prevention of serious deterioration in the person's condition, while a decision is sought from the Court (s.26).

Under the Act, an advance decision about life-sustaining treatment must be in writing, but not necessarily written by the person making the decision. For instance, somebody else can sign at the direction of the person making the decision, and in the presence of a witness. For instance, in the following case the person making the decision could not have written and signed anything, but somebody else could have signed in the presence of a witness:

Advance statement by means of slight eyelash movement. A man with motor neurone disease had slight eyelash movement as his only means of communication to express his wishes. By this means, he stated that when he lost this last means of communication, he wished the artificial ventilation to cease. The court stated that such a valid advance indication would be effective and that doctors would not be entitled to act inconsistently with it – so long as he did not subsequently indicate that his wishes had changed (*Re AK (medical treatment: consent)*).

The person must have the requisite capacity at the time of making the statement. For instance, a person with borderline personality disorder, who self-harmed by cutting herself and by blood-letting, made such a statement by which refusing blood transfusions. She believed her blood was evil and contaminated the blood that was being transfused. The evidence showed that she lacked capacity at the time of making the statement; it was therefore not legally effective (*An NHS Trust v Ms T*).

Advance decisions concern refusal of medical treatment only. Any other advance statement – for example, about medical treatment desired, or about location of care – would have to be taken account of in the best interests test applied under s.4 of the Act, but would not be binding. The following case, heard before the Mental Capacity Act 2005 was in force, well illustrates the questions of whether an advance decision is both valid and applicable:

Religious beliefs and validity. A 24-year-old woman had been born to Muslim parents. Her parents separated. Her mother became a Jehovah's Witness, as did her daughter. When she was 22 years old she made an advance decision, which expressly stated an absolute refusal to have a blood transfusion. She suffered from aortic valve disease. Two years later she was taken seriously ill and was rushed to hospital. She was unconscious. Her mother and other relatives were adamant that the advance directive should be observed. The situation became critical over the next couple of weeks.

The matter was referred to the High Court. The father made a statement including the following points. First, for the past few months, his daughter had been betrothed to a Turkish Muslim man on condition she would revert back to being a Muslim. Second, following a promise to her fiancé, she had during this time not attended any Jehovah's Witness meetings, which she used to attend twice weekly. Third, prior to her collapse, she had admitted herself to hospital for two days, did not mention the advance directive and had said to her aunt and brother that she did not want to die. Fourth, she had announced to the family two months previously that she would not allow anything to get in the way of marrying her fiancé, and that she would follow his Muslim faith.

The judge set out certain principles. First, the burden of proof lies on those seek to establish the existence, validity and applicability of an advance directive, because if there is doubt, that doubt should be resolved in favour of life. The proof needs to be clear and convincing, no more than the civil standard (balance of probability), but nonetheless stronger and more cogent in relation to the gravity of the issue.

He went on to point out that it is 'fundamental that an advance directive is, of its very essence and nature, inherently revocable'. Furthermore, such revocation need not be in writing because, clearly, a 'patient who has changed his mind is not to be condemned to death because pen and ink are not readily to hand'.

Ultimately, in this case, the judge found compelling the evidence of the father that his daughter had rejected her faith in the Jehovah's Witness religion, on which the advance directive was entirely founded. The directive was no longer valid. Even if he was wrong about this, the father's evidence – at the very lowest – threw 'considerable doubt' on the validity and of the directive. And such doubt had to be resolved in favour of preservation of his daughter's life (*HE v A Hospital NHS Trust*).

Nothing in the Act changes the law relating to murder, manslaughter or assisted suicide (s.62). Thus, assisted suicide remains unlawful, even in the light of human rights legislation (*Pretty v United Kingdom*). The courts have also stated that a doctor who deliberately interrupts 'life-prolonging treatment in the face of a competent patient's expressed wish to be kept alive, with the intention of thereby terminating the patient's life, would leave the doctor with no answer to a charge of murder' (*R(Burke) v General Medical Council*).

An advance decision could refuse the artificial nutrition and hydration but not basic care: 'An advance decision cannot refuse actions that are needed to keep a person comfortable (sometimes called basic or essential care). Examples include warmth, shelter, actions to keep a person clean and the offer of food and water by mouth. Section 5 of the Act allows health care professionals to carry out these actions in the best interests of a person who lacks capacity to consent... An advance decision can refuse artificial nutrition and hydration' (Lord Chancellor 2007, para 9.28).

Artificial nutrition and hydration (ANH) will be clinically indicated, unless a clinical decision has been taken that the life in question should come to an end. However, such a decision could not lawfully be taken if a competent patient expresses a wish to remain alive. Nonetheless, a competent patient could refuse to receive life-prolonging treatment, including ANH. Where a person lacks capacity, and a best interests decision needs to be taken about ANH, the decision will depend 'on the particular circumstances' (*R(Burke) v General Medical Council*).

20.13.1 OLDER ADVANCE DECISIONS

If an advance decision, refusing life-sustaining treatment, was made before the coming into force of the MCA (1 October 2007), it may still be valid and applicable in certain circumstances. These are that:

- a person providing health care to the individual reasonably believes that such an advance decision had been made before 1 October 2007 and that since 1 October the individual has lacked the capacity (a) to verify by a statement that the advance decision is to apply to the treatment in question even if life is at risk, and (b) to carry out the requirement that the advance decision be signed and witnessed
- the advance decision is in writing
- the person did not withdraw the decision when he or she still had capacity to do so, and has not done anything else clearly inconsistent with the advance decision
- the person lacks the capacity to decide about the treatment in question at the material time
- the treatment in question is specified in the advance decision
- the circumstances specified in the advance decision are present
- there are no reasonable grounds for believing circumstances exist which the individual did not anticipate at the time of the advance decision and which would have affected that decision (SI 2007/1898).

The requirements that then do not have to be met are (a) the verifying statement that the decision is to apply to treatment even if life is at risk, and (b) the signing and witnessing of the decision.

20.14 EXCLUSIONS

Sections 27 and 29 sets out a range of decisions that are not permitted under the Act, where the person themselves lacks capacity to take the decision. These exclusions include consent to marriage or civil partnership, consent to sexual relations, consent to divorce based on two years' separation, consent to a dissolution order in relation to civil partnership based on two years' separation, consent to child being placed for adoption, consent to making of an adoption order, discharging parental responsibilities in matters unrelated to child's property, giving consent under Human Fertilisation and Embryology Act 1990 (s.27). Voting is also excluded (s.29).

The courts have pointed out that, in relation to such questions and capacity, best interests are simply irrelevant. If the person has capacity to take such a decision, then best interests have no part to play because the person can do as he or she likes. If there is lack of capacity, then likewise best interests are irrelevant, because the person cannot take the decision anyway. In a case about whether a young woman had the capacity to marry, the court noted that there was significant confusion underlying an important part of the case. The local authority was asking the court to decide whether it was in the woman's best interests to marry. But, the court had 'no business – in fact…no jurisdiction – to embark upon a determination of that question' (*Sheffield CC v E*).

20.15 MENTAL HEALTH ACT 1983

Under s.28 of the 2005 Act, the Mental Capacity Act 2005 (MCA) does not authorise the giving of treatment for mental disorder if it is treatment regulated by part 4 of the Mental Health Act 1983. This rule is not without some complexity.

The MCA Code of Practice states that the MHA may have to be used if a person cannot be given care or treatment without a deprivation of liberty, treatment cannot be given under the MCA because of an advance decision, restraint may be required that is not allowed under the MCA, compulsory treatment is required (and the person may regain capacity to consent or to refuse consent), the person has the capacity to refuse a vital part of the treatment, or there is some other reason why the person might not get the treatment and they or somebody else will suffer harm.

However, the MHA cannot be used unless the patient's mental disorder justifies detention in hospital. It also cannot be used if the treatment required is only for physical illness or disability.

The MCA will apply to people subject to the MHA as it applies to anybody else with four exceptions: (a) if a person is detained under the MHA, decision-makers cannot normally rely on the MCA to give treatment for mental disorder; (b) if a person can be treated for mental disorder without their consent under the MHA, then health care staff can override an advance decision refusing that treatment; (c) if a person is subject to guardianship under the MHA, the guardian has an exclusive right to take certain decisions including where the person is to reside; (d) health care staff cannot (under the MHA or MCA), in any circumstances, give psychosurgery or surgical implantation of hormones to reduce sex drive to a person who lacks the capacity to consent to such treatment (Lord Chancellor 2007, pp.225–6).

This guidance has to be read in the light of the changes to the Mental Capacity Act, due in April 2009, which will enable the authorisation of deprivation of liberty in some circumstances (see 20.6 above). Also the position will be affected by other changes under the 2005

Act and the Mental Health Act 1983, as amended by the Mental Health Act 2007, which will probably be in force by April 2009.

As amended, s.28 of the Mental Capacity Act will be as follows. The general prohibition will remain, to the effect that nothing in the 2005 Act authorises anyone to give, or consent to, a patient's medical treatment for mental disorder – if the treatment is regulated by Part 4 of the Mental Health Act 1983. Section 5 of the Act (legal defence for care or treatment given under the Mental Capacity Act: see above) does not apply to treatment of supervised community treatment patients (under Part 4A of the 1983 Act) who have not been recalled to hospital. However, there is authority to give the treatment to such a patient if the person has capacity to consent to it and does so, or a donee or deputy or the Court of Protection authorises it. In addition a number of other conditions have to be met (other than in the case of immediately necessary treatment) (Mental Capacity Act 2005, s.28; Mental Health Act 1983, as amended, ss.64A-64G). It is beyond the scope of this book to set out the detail.

20.16 INDEPENDENT MENTAL CAPACITY ADVOCATES (IMCAS)

The Act provides for independent mental capacity advocates (IMCA) to be appointed. There is both a duty and a power for NHS bodies or local authorities to appoint such an advocate.

20.16.1 ROLE OF IMCA

Generally, section 35 places a duty on the Department of Health to make arrangements for independent mental capacity advocates. Local authorities are responsible for contracting with appropriate organisations. Such an advocate has the power to:

- interview the person whom he or she has been instructed to represent
- at all reasonable times examine and take copies of a health record, a local authority social services record, or a record of registered care provider – which holder of the record considers may be relevant to the advocate's investigation.

The advocate's core functions are to provide support, obtain and evaluate relevant information, ascertain what the person's wishes, feelings, beliefs and values might be (if the person had capacity), ascertain alternative courses of action, and obtain a further medical opinion where treatment is proposed (if the advocate thinks this should be obtained) (s.36). The advocate must prepare a report for the authorised person who instructed him or her. The advocate subsequently has the same rights to challenge the decision as if he or she were any other person engaged in caring for the person or interested in his or her welfare (s.36 and SI 2006/1832).

20.16.2 DUTY TO APPOINT IMCA: ACCOMMODATION OR SERIOUS MEDICAL TREATMENT

Appointment of an IMCA may be a duty or power. A duty arises (a) if the person lacking capacity is unbefriended – that is, if the local authority or NHS body is satisfied that there is no other person (other than one providing care or treatment in a professional capacity or for remuneration) whom it would be appropriate to consult about the person's best interests; and (b) if serious medical treatment or placement in a hospital or care home is in question. In the case of a hospital the placement must be likely to last longer than four weeks, in a care home longer than eight weeks.

The Code of Practice makes clear that just because a 'family disagrees with the decision-maker's proposed action, this is not grounds for concluding that there is nobody whose views are relevant to the decision' (Lord Chancellor 2007, para 10.79). There is also no duty to appoint an advocate if there is another person, nominated by the person lacking capacity, to be consulted on matters to which the duty relates; if there is a donee of a lasting power of attorney authorised to make decisions on those welfare matters; or if there is a court-appointed deputy with the power to make decisions in relation to those welfare matters (s.40).

Serious medical treatment involves providing, withdrawing or withholding treatment in the following circumstances:

- in the case of a single treatment, there is a fine balance between benefit, and burden and risk, to the patient
- where there is a choice of treatments, a decision as to which one to use is finely balanced or
- what is proposed would be likely to involve serious consequences for the patient (SI 2006/1832).

The duty to appoint an IMCA falls either on the NHS in the case of serious medical treatment, or hospital or care home placement – or on the local authority in case of a care home placement.

There are in addition special IMCA provisions relating to authorisations to deprive a person of his or her liberty under schedule A1 of the MCA 2005. Basically, if a person does not have a personal representative but is subject to the deprivation of liberty principles, or the supervisory body believes that the person and the representative are not exercising relevant rights, then it must appoint an IMCA (ss.39A–39E: due in force in October 2008).

In case of urgency, the rules about appointing the IMCA are relaxed, although in the case of provision of accommodation, the IMCA should be appointed subsequently (ss.37–39).

20.16.3 POWER TO INSTRUCT ADVOCATE IN CASE OF ABUSE OR NEGLECT

A power (rather than a duty) arises to appoint an IMCA in two circumstances. First, if adult protection measures are being or are going to be taken – whether or not there are family or friends appropriate to consult (see immediately below). Second, if the hospital or care home accommodation is being reviewed, where the person has been in the accommodation for at least 12 weeks continuously (ss.36–39 and SI 2006/2883).

The power in relation to adult protection arises if the NHS body or local authority proposes to take, or has taken protective measures, for a person lacking capacity (a) following receipt of allegation of abuse or neglect (by another person), or (b) in accordance with arrangements made under adult protection guidance issued under s.7 Local Authority Social Services Act 1970. This is referring to the *No secrets* guidance issued in 2000 (DH 2000). Protective measures are defined to include measures to minimise risk of abuse or neglect.

Unlike the rules concerning IMCAs and accommodation or serious medical treatment, the power is not dependent on the absence of another person, other than one providing care or treatment in a professional capacity or for remuneration, whom it would be appropriate to consult about the person's best interests (SI 2006/2883).

20.17 CODES OF PRACTICE

Section 42 places a duty on the Lord Chancellor to prepare and issue one or more codes of practice. Failure to comply with a code must be taken into account in legal proceedings.

20.18 OFFENCE OF ILL-TREATMENT OR WILFUL NEGLECT

Section 44 creates an offence of ill-treatment or wilful neglect by any person who has the care of another person who lacks or who the first person reasonably believed to lack capacity – or by any deputy or person with lasting power of attorney (see 21.17).

20.19 PUBLIC GUARDIAN

A new Public Guardian is created, supported by the Office of the Public Guardian (MCA 2005. s.57). The functions of the Public Guardian are to protect people lacking capacity include: (a) setting up and managing separate registers of lasting powers of attorney, of enduring powers of attorney, of court order appointing deputies; (b) supervising deputies; (c) sending Court of Protection visitors to visit people who may lack capacity and also those who formal powers to act on their behalf; (d) receiving reports from attorneys acting under lasting powers of attorney and from deputies; (e) providing reports to the Court of Protection; (f) dealing with complaints about the way in which attorneys or deputies carry out their duties (Lord Chancellor 2007, para 14.8).

20.20 APPOINTEES

The law relating to appointeeship remains outside of the Mental Capacity Act 2005. Where a person is receiving social security benefits, but is 'for the time being unable to act', then an appointee may be appointed to manage the benefits, assuming that no deputy with the relevant power has been appointed by the Court of Protection (SI 1987/1968).

20.21 INHERENT JURISDICTION OF THE HIGH COURT

The MCA means that many decisions previously taken by the Family Division of the High Court under common law, in the form of the inherent jurisdiction, will now be made by the Court of Protection. However, some issues may arise that fall still outside of the 2005 act and will call still for the exercise of the inherent jurisdiction (*KC v Westminster Social and Community Services Department*).

For instance, the High Court has held that it can exercise the jurisdiction in respect of a competent adult whose capacity to consent to marriage is overborne by fear, duress or threat, such that she is deprived of the capacity to make relevant decisions (*Re SK*).

In addition, it could extend to a vulnerable adult who 'even if not incapacitated by mental disorder or mental illness, is, or is reasonably believed to be, either (i) under constraint, or (ii) subject to coercion or undue influence, or (iii) for some other reason deprived of the capacity to make the relevant decision, or disabled from making a free choice, or incapacitated or disabled from giving or expressing real or genuine consent'. In the case in question, the woman in question had profound sensory disabilities, but did have the capacity to understand marriage. However, the danger lay in her being unable to understand what was going on and genuinely to consent to marriage, if she found herself in a situation in Pakistan where she was unable to communicate with anybody – since her main form of communication was use of British Sign Language (*Re SA*).

However, the courts have made clear that this does not mean that they can exercise the jurisdiction in order to protect a vulnerable adult from harm when the person has the capacity to take the decision in question, even though the decision would lead to harm (*Ealing LBC v KS*).

20.22 EFFECT OF THE MENTAL CAPACITY ACT ON COMMUNITY CARE DUTIES

The MCA is, amongst other things, about establishing the best interests of a person. On the other hand, local authorities and NHS bodies provide care, treatment and other services under separate statute, such as the NHS and Community Care Act 1990 and the NHS Act 2006. A possible tension could, in principle, arise – and could be relevant to actions or decisions being taken in the context of protection and safeguarding of vulnerable adults. The issue could boil down to a local authority or NHS body stating that it is not obliged to make statutory provision to achieve those best interests. This could be a logical decision in some circumstances because local authorities and NHS trusts are not obliged to provide the 'best' for anybody, with or without capacity. To provide the best for a person lacking capacity would in fact put the latter at an advantage over a person with capacity.

The courts have considered the issue in terms of the orders they might make. Thus, orders about a person's best interests may now be made by the Court of Protection under the MCA 2005. On the other hand, it is still the Administrative Division of the High Court which considers judicial review applications about the lawfulness of local authority or NHS decision-making under the NHS and Community Care Act 1990 and NHS Act 2006 respectively.

The courts have pointed out that different principles are involved. Court of Protection involvement is in the sphere of private law, involving judicial identification of the best course of action for the person concerned. Judicial review on the other hand is a public law, supervisory jurisdiction concerned basically with whether a public body has made a decision within a reasonable band of possible decisions that lay open to it within the relevant legislative context (e.g. community care legislation). Judicial review is essentially not about whether the 'best' decision has been taken.

In the past, the question arose as to how a decision about best interests might impact on a local authority's or NHS body's duty to provide services:

Where a person should live: best interests and community care duties. A man with learning disabilities, deaf and with no verbal communication lived for many years at a long-stay hospital. He was then resettled in a small care home, funded by the health authority. Following a hip fracture, he was admitted to hospital; he was subsequently removed by his father and taken to the latter's home, where he had since been living. A dispute then arose about where he should live and about contact with his parents (long since divorced). One of the issues considered was the extent to which a declaration by the court as to best interests could bind the local authority or NHS to make particular provision in public law (*A v A health authority*).

The answer in the above case was that a best interests declaration could not in principle bind the local authority or NHS to take a particular decision concerning the service user in the exercise of their statutory functions (i.e. under community care and NHS legislation). Although such a declaration would be persuasive, the court seemed not to accept that it would be 'coercive', unless a mandatory order were made. The court was at pains to point out the different principles underlying the exercise of (what was then still) the inherent jurisdiction by the Family Division of the High Court, and the exercise of its public law jurisdiction by the Administrative Division of the High Court. The court was careful to distinguish these in the following case:

Best interests decision. In one case, the court pointed out that the issue in dispute was not in fact a public law issue, concerning the propriety of a public body's decision to close certain premises – but was one relating to the taking of a decision in the best interests of a person lacking capacity to decide for herself. The court declined to rule on the lawfulness or otherwise of a proposed closure, and instead held that a case should be taken to the Family Division of the High Court to seek a best interests declaration (*R(Payne) v Surrey Oakland NHS Trust*).

The courts have continued to treat this distinction cautiously. In another case heard prior to the Mental Capacity Act coming into force, they expressed hesitation about making a declaration that it was 'lawful' to act in a certain way to achieve the best interests of a person – because a public body might construe that as meaning that all other courses of action were unlawful. This would give the court's declaration a coercive effect which, as against a public body, might be inappropriate. Thus, a 'bare statement' of best interests was a legitimate and appropriate exercise of the court's jurisdiction (*St Helens BC v PE*).

Nonetheless, maintaining the dividing line between the two jurisdictions may not be easy – and in some instances, human rights may make the bridge between the two. In a case heard in the Family Division of the High Court, the court was clear that a local authority's care plan was inadequate. It ordered the local authority to amend it and provide facilities, so as to allow a woman with mental health problems and learning disabilities (whose life the authority was otherwise largely controlling) to continue a sexual relationship. Otherwise her human rights would be breached. On the basis of this potential breach, the court stated that the local authority could not 'toll the bell of scarce resources…the additional financial burden…is comparatively modest… And the right in play here is, to repeat, too important, too precious in human terms, to be swept aside by such purely fiscal considerations' (*Local Authority X v MM*).

20.23 MCA'S APPLICATION TO CHILDREN AND YOUNG PEOPLE

The Mental Capacity Act 2005 does not apply to people under 16 years old, unless the Court of Protection is making a decision about a child's (without capacity) property and if the child is likely still to lack capacity at age 18 (Mental Capacity Act 2005, s.18). In addition, the offence of ill-treatment or wilful neglect of a person who lacks capacity can also apply to people under 16.

The Act does apply generally to people aged 16 or 17 years old but a) only people aged 18 or over can make a lasting power of attorney (s.9), b) only people aged 18 or over can make advance decisions (s.24), and c) the Court of Protection can only make a statutory will for a person aged 18 or over (s.18). Legal proceedings in respect of 16 or 17 year olds who lack capacity to make the relevant decisions may be heard either by the Court of Protection or the family courts. Proceedings can be transferred between the two (s.21 and SI 2007/1899).

The deprivation of liberty safeguards in relation to standard or urgent authorisations, due to come into force in April 2009 (see 20.6.1), do not apply to people under 18 years old. The rules concerning the detention and treatment of children, particularly 16 and 17 year olds, are somewhat complex.

CHAPTER 21

Protecting and safeguarding vulnerable adults

KEY POINTS

During the 1990s concern grew about the phenomenon of what has been termed adult abuse – and a corresponding need to protect and to safeguard vulnerable adults.

In 2000, the Department of Health published guidance about this. The guidance gave local social services authorities the lead in the development of local policies and practices, involving cooperative working with other local agencies, including the police, housing organisations, NHS bodies etc. Adult protection, or safeguarding adults, as it is increasingly called in England, is growing rapidly as an area of work for local social services authorities.

However, substantially no new social services legislation was passed concerning adult protection, equivalent for example to child protection provisions contained in the Children Act 1989. Indeed, central government in England has so far failed to adopt proposals made by the Law Commission (1995) that local authorities should given be explicit protective powers. This is in contrast to Scotland, where the Scottish Parliament has passed just such legislation in the form of the Adult Support and Protection (Scotland) Act 2007. There is concern that the lack of clear statutory obligation on statutory bodies, such as local authorities and NHS organisations, undermines efforts to achieve effective protection and safeguarding.

Therefore, in order to understand the legal framework, a twofold approach is required. First, from the social services point of view, adult protection issues have to be set in the context of existing community care legislation and related guidance. Second, in order to understand how other agencies are able to act, an appreciation of other, non-social services legislation is needed – in order to identify possible legal remedies to prevent or to respond to certain types of abuse.

This chapter outlines a range of legal issues, in addition to community care legislation. This includes the protection of vulnerable adults list (POVA) and future 'barring' scheme, criminal record certificates, removing people from their homes under the National Assistance Act 1948, mental health law interventions, environmental health powers, civil wrongs (e.g. assault, battery, false imprisonment), criminal justice legislation (including offences against the person, sexual offences and theft), and the principle of undue influence in relation to financial abuse. In addition, use of the Mental Capacity Act 2005, to protect people lacking capacity and to act in their best interests, is a major legal route to consider in safeguarding adults. This is covered in Chapter 20 of this book.

Particularly notable, and an additional complication, is the degree to which local authorities and the NHS, two key types of statutory agency in the protection of vulnerable people, are themselves so heavily implicated – both directly and indirectly – in some of the physical and financial harm to which vulnerable people come.

The legal and practical scope of adult protection and safeguarding is ill-defined but is potentially very wide. For that reason, this chapter provides a bird's eye view only. This is expanded upon in a companion volume to this book, *Safeguarding vulnerable adults and the law.*

21.1 DEPARTMENT OF HEALTH GUIDANCE: *NO SECRETS*

In 2000, the Department of Health published policy guidance under s.7 of the Local Authority Social Services Act 1970. Entitled *No secrets*, it stated that local authority social services departments should take the lead in 'inter-agency' working to combat such abuse. It set out a framework only, on which local authorities could base more detailed local policies and procedures (DH 2000).

21.1.1 DEFINITION OF VULNERABLE AND ADULT AND OF ABUSE

The guidance states that it is concerned with the protection from abuse of vulnerable adults. A vulnerable adult is defined as a person 'who is or may be in need of community care services by reason of mental or other disability, age or illness; and who is or may be unable to take care of him or herself, or unable to protect him or herself against significant harm or exploitation'.

Abuse can be physical, sexual, psychological, financial or material, neglect and acts of omission, discriminatory, institutional. Some forms of abuse are criminal offences, for example physical assault, sexual assault and rape, fraud, etc. (DH 2000).

21.1.2 INTER-AGENCY WORKING

The guidance stresses the importance of inter-agency working including the NHS and social services, sheltered and supported housing providers, regulators of services, polices and Crown Prosecution Service, voluntary and private sector agencies, local authority housing and education departments, probation service, DSS benefit agencies, carer support groups, user groups and user-led services, advocacy and advisory services, community safety partnerships, legal advice and representation services, and so on (DH 2000). It suggests the setting up of local adult protection committees.

21.1.3 INFORMATION SHARING

The Department of Health guidance points out that, as part of inter-agency working, agreement on the sharing of information will be required, in order to balance on the one hand confidentiality, and on the other the importance of sharing information (even in the absence of consent). The guidance summarises the principles of sharing confidential information as follows (DH 2000, para 5.6):

- information must be shared on a 'need to know' basis only
- confidentiality should not be confused with secrecy
- informed consent should be obtained but, if this is not possible and other vulnerable adults are at risk, it might be necessary to override this requirement
- assurances of absolute confidentiality should not be given where there are concerns about abuse.

It also goes on to state that principles of confidentiality designed to safeguard and promote the interests of service users should not be confused with those 'designed to protect the management interests of an organisation' (DH 2000, para 5.8).

21.2 SOCIAL SERVICES LEGISLATION

Since no specific new legislation was passed to accompany central government policy as set out in the *No secrets* guidance, local social services authority safeguarding work primarily rests on the existing community care legislation as set out previously in this book. Hence the guidance refers to a vulnerable adult as being a person who may be in need of community care services. This is a direct reference to the condition in s.47 of the NHS and Community Care Act 1990, which is the legal trigger for community care assessment of a person's needs and possible intervention.

The absence of any specific adult protection legislation has been recognised by the courts. In one case, concerning an assisted suicide, whilst acknowledging the *No secrets* guidance, the judge held that a local authority's duties were limited to addressing the community care needs of the particular person as assessed by the authority. Any common law duties that it might owe 'did not extend the scope of the statutory duties' under the relevant community care legislation. Furthermore, such duties were not 'all-embracing' in the ways provided for children under s.33 and Part 3 of the Children Act 1989 (*Re Z*).

Community care legislation contains a wide variety of services that local authorities can potentially arrange for people (see Chapters 9 and 11) – and which may be relevant in the context of preventing or reacting to abuse and harm. These include, for example, placing a person in a care home, as well as providing practical assistance in a person's own home, advice, support, visiting services, and so on. Such non-residential services referred to are available for both disabled people under the National Assistance Act 1948 (s.29) and the Chronically Sick and Disabled Persons Act 1970 (s.2). They are also available for older people generally, who are not disabled, under the Health Service and Public Health Act 1968 (s.45).

The carers' legislation, too, may be useful (see section 13.5 above). For instance, sometimes the physical and mental stress of continual caring might start to lead to possible or actual abuse or neglect. An assessment and provision of a short break for the carer – either as a carer's service under the Carers and Disabled Children Act 2000, or as community care service under the National Assistance Act 1948 or Chronically Sick and Disabled Persons Act 1970 – might defuse the threat of abuse.

21.2.1 SOCIAL SERVICES IMPLICATED IN HARM TO VULNERABLE PEOPLE

Local authorities are charged with safeguarding adults under the *No secrets* guidance. Typically they are increasingly aware of abuse or neglect being perpetrated in care homes or in people's own homes by carers or family.

However, sometimes, unwittingly, local authorities themselves appear to be the root cause of abuse or neglect. Alternatively, while not being the root cause, they may display a blind spot; typically this seems to be the case in relation to the NHS, when social services often appears powerless or unwilling to protect, or even to attempt to protect, vulnerable adults from sometimes highly neglectful practices.

21.2.1.1 Local authorities' failure to monitor and review contracted out services

First, local authorities sometimes continue to contract out services to independent care providers even when they are well aware that those care providers are not delivering care to a suitable standard, and are putting vulnerable service users at significant risk – but have not acted to remedy the problem. The consequences may literally be fatal, as the local government ombudsmen have found. In such circumstances, the ombudsmen have little hesitation in finding maladministration on the part of local authorities (see section 8.2.3).

21.2.1.2 Failure to meet people's needs

Second, the failure sometimes on the part of local authorities to discharge their clear duties to fund the care that people clearly need may result in severe detriment, including abuse, for vulnerable people. For instance, the local government ombudsman has investigated several cases involving younger adults with severe learning disabilities and autism whom the local authority refused adequate funding for. The consequences were serious, including people being shut up (inappropriately) in a secure psychiatric unit and heavily sedated for up to a year, and being forgotten about in hospital for ten years and suffering abuse there. The ombudsmen were duly scathing in these cases (see 6.11).

21.2.1.3 Breach of the rules about topping up of care home fees

Third, it would appear that many local authorities knowingly breach the rules about when families can, and can't be asked, to top up care home fees (see 9.5.1). This can result in older people's families having to part with considerable sums of money which the local authority should in fact be paying.

21.2.1.4 Persistent charging for NHS continuing health care

Fourth, for at least 14 years, significant numbers of people – almost certainly numbering tens of thousands – have wrongly been denied NHS continuing health care (see Chapter 18). This has meant many having to use up savings and sell their houses. However, in such cases it is not just that the NHS has unlawfully denied responsibility for there care, but that local authorities have unlawfully provided services and charged people for them. Local authorities would protest that they have merely been stepping in to help people wrongly denied by the NHS, but this would be less than candid. For the most part, local authorities have stood back at senior level and accepted this pattern without serious challenge. However, given that they have been given the lead to protect vulnerable adults from abuse, including financial abuse, it is astonishing that they should have displayed such passivity. Front line practitioners have often been left to fight lonely battles on behalf of individual clients.

This is especially so since (a) to fund the services at all in such circumstances is unlawful; (b) it is the local authority not the NHS which charges and forces people to use up savings and sell their homes; and (c) if people cannot afford to pay the charges or run out of assets, the local authority steps in and uses public money to fund, unlawfully, the services itself. The measure of local authorities' ineffectual approach over a long period of time has been revealed by the fact that even central government has admitted to having to repay to people and their families some £180 million in unlawfully taken fees for health services.

21.2.1.5 Charging for aftercare services under the Mental Health Act 1983

Fifth, local authorities for many years made unlawful charges for people receiving mental health aftercare services under s.117 of the Mental Health Act 1983. Some of these charges, before the courts had dispelled doubts about the true position, could perhaps be excused. But even after the position was clear, some local authorities have continued to act in such a way as to suggest serious impropriety. For example, one local authority, short of funds, even tried to get a woman to sign away her legal rights to such free aftercare – threatening the alternative that she might have to stay unnecessarily in hospital for up to a year if she did not do so (*York CC 2006*). As with NHS continuing health care, significant sums of money have had to be repaid by local authorities to users of services.

21.2.1.6 Strict eligibility criteria as to who will be assisted

Lastly, the ever increasing strictness of eligibility rules means that vulnerable people are no longer being assisted by local authorities. The Commission for Social Care Inspection has identified that this trend is removing quality, dignity and self-worth from significant numbers of older people (CSCI 2008).

Younger adults, too, may be affected. In Cornwall, it appeared that a man with learning disabilities whose life was taken over by people who were exploiting him, before he was tortured and murdered, would probably not have been eligible for social services assistance in the final year of his life under the 'fair access to care' policy (Cornwall Adult Protection Committee 2007, p.9).

21.3 NHS IMPLICATED IN ABUSE OR NEGLECT

A significant number of reports and investigations over the last few years have indicated that the NHS is implicated in significant and widespread neglectful and arguably abusive practices.

The examples that have come to light are many, including tying people on commodes for extended periods of time (HC, CSCI 2006), tying people up in wheelchairs likewise (HC 2007b), placing abusive and restrictive care regimes on people with learning disabilities (HC 2007c), not helping people eat and drink in hospital even when they cannot do so themselves (HC 2007d), deliberately taking short cuts with infection control measures in order not to jeopardise performance targets and thus directly contributing to scores of deaths from *Clostridium difficile* (HC 2006), maintaining hospital wards and equipment in filthy condition

(HC 2007a), telling patients to evacuate their bowels and bladder in the bed (HC 2007a), running hospitals at excessive bed occupancy causing not only infection problems but under-mining the clinical welfare and dignity of patients (HC 2006a), premature discharge of patients – including waking up and discharging patients in the middle of the night, unplanned (Bond 2007). In addition, the improper denial of NHS continuing health care to people, thus forcing them to use up their savings and sell their houses, has caused huge finan-cial harm to vulnerable older people and their families.

21.4 PROTECTION OF VULNERABLE ADULTS LIST

Under the Care Standards Act 2000, there has been a duty on the Secretary of State to keep a list of care workers who are considered unsuitable to work with vulnerable adults because they have, through misconduct, harmed or placed at risk of harm vulnerable adults – and the employer has, or would have, dismissed the person, or transferred him or her to a non-care position (s.81). The protection of vulnerable adults (POVA) list was started in July 2004. In October 2009, a new system of barring is due to be in place and will have replaced the POVA list scheme.

Care providers have a duty to check the POVA list, and not offer employment if the pro-spective employee is included on the list (whether or not provisionally). This duty covers existing employees moving or being transferred from a non-care to a care position. If the employer discovers that an existing employee is on the list, the employer must cease to employ the person in that care position (Care Standards Act 2000, s.89; DH 2004c, para 29).

It is an offence for a person on the POVA list (unless the inclusion is provisional only) to apply for, offer to do, accept or do any work in a care position (Care Standards Act 2000, s.89).

21.5 BARRING PEOPLE FROM WORKING WITH VULNERABLE ADULTS

From October 2009, a new scheme of regulating the social and health care work force replaced the previous scheme that had regulated personal care and independent health care. *In summary only*, the new scheme is as follows.

First, an independent barring board (IBB), to be known as the Independent Safeguarding Authority (ISA) has a duty to establish an 'adults barred list' (and a children's also). If a person is included in the list he or she is barred from engaging in a 'regulated activity' with vulnera-ble adults (ss.2–3).

The ISA will place an individual on the barred list in four main ways. First, if certain pre-scribed criteria apply to the individual, relating to sexual offences involving a mentally disor-dered victim, inclusion is automatic. Second, if certain other prescribed criteria apply, relating to a wide range of offences, inclusion is also automatic, but the individual must be allowed to make representations as to why he or she should be removed from the list. If the ISA considers that it is not appropriate to include the individual on the list, then it must remove him or her.

Third, if it appears to the ISA that the person has engaged in relevant conduct and it proposes to include the individual on the list, it must give the person the opportunity to make representations as to why he or she should not be included. If the ISA is satisfied that the person has engaged in the relevant conduct of endangering a vulnerable adult, and that it appears to the IBB that it is appropriate to include him or her on the list, then it must do so (schedule 3). Relevant conduct is conduct:

- endangering, or likely to endanger, a vulnerable adult
- which if repeated would endanger, or be likely to endanger, a vulnerable adult
- involving sexual material relating to children
- (inappropriate) conduct involving sexually explicit images depicting violence against human beings, or
- (inappropriate) conduct of a sexual nature involving a vulnerable adult (schedule 3).

Endangering a vulnerable adult occurs where the individual harms, causes to be harmed, puts at risk of harm, attempts to harm, or incites somebody else to harm – a vulnerable adult (SVGA 2006, schedule 3).

Fourth and last, is the 'risk of harm' test. If it appears to the ISA that a person may harm a vulnerable adult, cause a vulnerable adult to be harmed, put a vulnerable adult at risk of harm, attempt to harm a vulnerable adult, or incite another person to harm a vulnerable adult – then the ISA must give the person an opportunity to make representations as to why he or she should not be barred. If it appears appropriate to include the person on the barred list, the ISA must do so (SVGA 2006, schedule 3).

Appeals can be made against barring to a Care Standards Tribunal (s.4).

The Act creates various offences in relation to the employment of a person who is barred (ss.7–11). In order to work with vulnerable adults, a person must be subject to monitoring under the Act. If a person is barred, he or she ceases to be subject to monitoring. Workers have to apply to be subject to monitoring and pay a fee.

The Act does not apply to activity carried out in the course of family or personal relationships (s.58).

21.6 PROFESSIONAL BODIES

The General Social Care Council (GSCC) is responsible for maintaining a register of qualified social workers, as well as social care workers more generally (Care Standards Act 2000, Part 4). Currently, however, it covers only the former. Applicants must provide evidence of their good character (including fitness to practice), good conduct, physical and mental fitness, competence, relevant qualifications. It is an offence for a social worker to use the title of 'social worker' if he or she is not on the register. The Council may remove or suspend people from the register on grounds of misconduct (Care Standards Act 2000, Part 4; also the *General Social Care Council (Registration) Rules 2003; General Social Care Council (Conduct) Rules 2003*, published by the General Social Care Council).

21.6.1 OTHER PROFESSIONAL BODIES

Other professional bodies deal with cases of abuse in disciplinary hearings, which may result in the professional being suspended or struck off from the profession.

The Nursing and Midwifery Council has reported that abuse of older people accounts for increasingly more of its misconduct hearings (*Nursing Times* 2005). Thus, for instance, when a nurse put a patient's glass eye in a ward sister's drink, painted a smiley face on a patient's fist-sized hernia, and falsified patient records with a magic pen – she was struck off by the Council (Ward 2006).

21.7 CRIMINAL RECORD CERTIFICATES

Under the Care Standards Act 2000 and associated regulations, care providers have a duty to obtain criminal record certificates from the Criminal Records Bureau (CRB) in respect of certain types of worker under the Police Act 1997. For example, such certificates have to be obtained by care providers under the Domiciliary Care Agencies Regulations 2002 (SI 2002/3214, schedule 2) under the Care Home Regulations 2001 (SI 2001/3965, schedule 2) and under the Adult Placement Schemes (England) Regulations 2004 (SI 2004/2070, schedule 3).

An application for a standard or enhanced disclosure must be countersigned by a person registered with the CRB. However, it is possible for persons or bodies not so registered to find out such details, if they ask another registered body to countersign an application on their behalf. Another body acting in this way is known as an 'umbrella body' (CRB 2001, para 4).

21.7.1 LEVELS OF DISCLOSURE

The Police Act 1997 provides for three different levels of disclosure. The first is basic disclosure, which contains details of convictions held in central police records that are not 'spent' under the Rehabilitation of Offenders Act 1974 (s.112). However, the CRB does not, at time of writing, issue such disclosures.

The second is standard disclosure, containing details of spent and unspent convictions, but also cautions, reprimands, warnings, recorded centrally by the police. The disclosure will also indicate whether the person is on the POVA list (see 21.4) and thus unsuitable to work with vulnerable adults (s.113).

The third level is enhanced disclosure, which contains the same information as a standard disclosure, but it can also include additional 'soft', non-conviction information held in local police records, which a chief police officer considers may be relevant. The legislation states that the Secretary of State must request the chief police officer to provide any information relevant as to the person's suitability that the chief police officer thinks (a) ought to be included in the certificate; or (b) ought to be provided but not included in the certificate in the interests of the prevention or detection of crime (s.115).

21.7.2 ENHANCED DISCLOSURE: VULNERABLE ADULTS

In respect of community care services for adults, enhanced disclosure applies to workers who occupy a position involving regular care for, training, supervising or being in sole charge of people aged 18 or over – and enables the person to have regular contact in the course of his or her duties with a vulnerable adult (Police Act 1997, s.115; SI 2002/446).

21.8 REMOVAL OF PEOPLE FROM HOME: NATIONAL ASSISTANCE ACT 1948, S.47

Under s.47 of the National Assistance Act 1948, local authorities (district councils or borough councils) can by magistrate's order remove to institutional care people who

- are suffering from grave chronic disease or, being aged, infirm or physically incapacitated, are living in insanitary conditions, and
- are unable to devote to themselves, and are not receiving from other persons, proper care and attention.

A medical officer of health (i.e. community physician) must certify to the authority that removal is necessary either in the person's best interests, or to prevent injury to the health of, or serious nuisance to, other people.

The authority can apply to a magistrates' court for an order that may authorise the person's detention for up to three months; although this may be extended by court order. Seven days' notice is required to be given to the person before a court can consider the application. The period of notice can be dispensed with under powers in the National Assistance (Amendment) Act 1951, if it is certified both by the medical officer of health and another registered medical practitioner that in their opinion it is necessary in the interests of the person that he or she be removed without delay.

However, the person does not have to be mentally incapacitated or mentally disordered for s.47 to operate. Thus, there exists a view that s.47 of the 1948 Act is potentially contrary to the Human Rights Act 1998 – at least in some circumstances. This would be on the basis that self-neglect, without more, is not a ground on which people may be deprived of their liberty under s.5 of the European Convention on Human Rights. The article refers to people of unsound mind, alcoholics, drug addicts or vagrants – but not to people who neglect themselves or are neglected, who have the mental capacity to decide where and how they want to live (and so are not of unsound mind), and who are not otherwise diagnosed as mentally disordered.

It appears that s.47 has fallen largely into desuetude, although some councils still report occasional usage.

21.8.1 PROTECTION OF PROPERTY: NATIONAL ASSISTANCE ACT 1948, S.48

A duty to protect property arises if:

- a person is admitted to hospital, admitted to residential accommodation under s.21 of the 1948 Act, or removed under s.47 of the 1948 Act
- it appears to the local social services authority that there is danger of loss of, or damage to, any of the person's movable property by reason of his or her temporary or permanent inability to protect or deal with the property
- no other suitable arrangements have been or are being made.

If these conditions are satisfied, then the local authority must take reasonable steps to prevent or mitigate the loss or damage. The authority has the power, at all reasonable times, to enter the person's place of residence and to deal with any movable property in a reasonable way to prevent or mitigate loss or damage. The local authority can recover reasonable expenses either from the person concerned or anybody else liable to maintain him or her (National Assistance

Act 1948, s.48). Examples of reasonable steps might include, for example, securing the premises, informing the police about an empty property, taking an inventory, turning off utilities, disposing of perishable food, and arranging for pets to be cared for (Jones 2004, para D1–088).

21.9 MENTAL HEALTH ACT INTERVENTIONS

Where mental disorder is in issue, adult protection may be served by certain interventions under the Mental Health Act 1983. For instance, such interventions may serve to break or prevent a cycle of abuse or neglect. However, these grounds of intervention must be used properly and in this respect it will be noted that the threshold for intervention varies. Nevertheless, such drastic interventions can only be exercised if the relevant statutory grounds are made out.

The amending Mental Health Act 2007 creates a new duty on the Department of Health to make such arrangements as are considered reasonable for independent mental health advocates for people detained under the Act (other than for those under ss.4,5(2)or (4), 135, 136), or subject to guardianship or a community patient (community treatment order) (MHA 1983, s.130A–D).

Interventions include detention under s. 2 (assessment for limited period and treatment), s.3 (detention for longer period for treatment), s.7 and 8 (guardianship), s.115 (entry and inspection by approved social worker), s. 135 (warrant for removal from premises to place of safety by constable), s.136 (removal from public place to place of safety by constable).

21.9.1 GUARDIANSHIP UNDER THE MENTAL HEALTH ACT 1983

Under s.7 of the Mental Health Act 1983, a guardianship order can be made for a patient aged 16 years or over on the following grounds:

- that he or she is suffering from mental disorder in terms of mental illness, severe mental impairment, mental impairment or psychopathic disorder (under the amending Mental Health Act 2007, this changes just to mental disorder, the specific diagnoses are deleted)
- that the mental disorder is of a nature of degree that warrants his or her reception into guardianship
- that this is necessary in the interests of the welfare of the patient – or for the protection of other persons that the patient be so received.

Under s.8 of the Act, the guardian (either the local social services authority or other person) has the power:

- to require the patient to reside at a place specified by the authority or person named as guardian
- to require the patient to attend at specified places and times for medical treatment, occupation, education or training
- to require access to the patient to be given, at any place where the patient is residing, to any registered medical practitioner, approved social worker or other specified person.

Guardianship is a potentially useful tool in adult protection. The Mental Health Act 2007 (schedule 3, para 3) amends s.18 of the 1983 Act, so that not only can a person subject to guardianship be fetched back but also taken and conveyed to the required place of residence in the first place. Prior to this amendment, there was no explicit power in the Act to convey the person to the place of residence, there is a power to return him or her, if he or she has absconded (Mental Health Act 1983, s.18). However, in practice, persistent non-cooperation generally might render guardianship ineffective.

The courts have previously held that there is an implied duty under s.7 of the 1983 Act to act generally for the person's welfare in ways not explicitly referred to in s.8 (*R v Kent CC, ex p Marston*). However, more recently, the courts have set boundaries. For instance, if the issue of contact arises in addition to place of residence (which is explicitly covered by s.8 of the Act), then s.8 would not confer sufficient authority. There would be a statutory lacuna, and a declaration from the courts would be required (*Lewis v Gibson*). Since October 2007, the avenue would be the Mental Capacity Act 2005 and the Court of Protection.

For some people with learning disabilities, guardianship might be desirable but is simply not available. This is because the definitions in the Act of impairment and severe mental impairment, which would apply to people with learning disabilities, include the requirement that the impairment be associated with abnormally aggressive or seriously irresponsible conduct. This proviso will remain in the Mental Health Act 1983 as amended by the Mental Health Act 2007. In future, grounds of guardianship will simply refer to mental disorder (rather than the more specific diagnoses). But in the case of learning disability, it will still be necessary that it be associated with abnormally aggressive or seriously irresponsible conduct.

This requirement is likely to exclude many people with learning disabilities, since the courts have taken a restrictive approach to the term, serious irresponsibility (*Re F (Adult Patient)*). Thus neither a young person's wish to go home against a background of possible sexual exploitation (*Re F (A Child)*), nor a person's lack of road sense (*Newham LBC v BS*), constituted seriously irresponsible conduct. On the other hand, historical conduct and the potential for aggressive or irresponsible behaviour to recur will be relevant and may provide ground for guardianship even if there has been amelioration in a person's condition (*Lewis v Gibson*).

This accounts for the courts' being increasingly asked instead to intervene in order to declare or order where the best interests of people with learning disabilities lie, when guardianship is unavailable – for example to protect an 18-year-old woman with learning disabilities from chronic neglect, lack of minimum standards of hygiene and cleanliness in the home, serious lack of parenting, and exposure to people engaged in sexual exploitation (*Re F (Adult Patient)*).

21.9.2 INFORMAL MENTAL HEALTH PATIENTS

There is nothing in the 1983 Act to prevent a person who needs treatment for mental disorder from being admitted to hospital without formal detention, nor from remaining in hospital informally following any formal detention (Mental Health Act 1983, s.131). However, legal problems arise if the person (a) is effectively detained to the extent that a deprivation of liberty occurs; and (b) lacks the capacity to consent to this. The Mental Capacity Act 2005 accordingly has been amended so as to apply legal safeguards (see 20.6).

21.10 ENVIRONMENTAL HEALTH INTERVENTIONS

Gaining entry into domestic premises (via an appropriate legal channel) in cases of neglect is not necessarily easy. However, local authority environmental health departments do have statutory powers to enter premises under the Environmental Protection Act 1990 and the Public Health Act 1936, to deal with statutory nuisance – and with filthy, unwholesome, verminous premises and verminous people.

21.11 POLICE POWERS OF ENTRY

A constable may enter premises in order, amongst other things, to recapture any person whatever who is unlawfully at large and whom he is pursuing – or to save life or limb or prevent serious damage to property (Police and Criminal Evidence Act 1984, s.17).

21.12 INTERVENTIONS ON GROUNDS OF LACK OF MENTAL CAPACITY

In the adult protection context, recourse may be had to the Mental Capacity Act 2005 to protect vulnerable adults who lack capacity.

In the past, the courts exercised their 'inherent jurisdiction' to make orders and declarations about people's capacity, and about their best interests if they were deemed to lack capacity. Now the 2005 Act provides the legal underpinning (Chapter 20).

21.13 GAS AND ELECTRICITY OPERATORS

There are some powers of entry associated with utility companies: for instance, gas operators have such powers under the Gas Act 1986 (schedule 2B, paras 20–28) and Rights of Entry (Gas and Electricity Boards) Act 1954.

21.14 CARE STANDARDS AND REGULATION

The Commission for Social Care Inspection (CSCI) regulates and inspects care services, and has a power of entry and can investigate by inspecting and copying documents and interviewing employees (Health and Social Care (Community Health and Standards) Act 2003, ss.88–89). Such regulation and inspection under the Care Standards Act 2000 is intended to be a safeguard against abuse taking place.

Under the 2000 Act, CSCI takes account of national minimum standards when registering and inspecting providers. For care homes, standard 18 relates to abuse, from which the registered person must protect residents. Various aspects are referred to, including policy and practice concerning residents' money and financial affairs (DH 2003a). Under the standards for domiciliary care agencies, there is likewise a standard (14) on abuse and a separate one (13) on the safe handling of service users' money and property. This includes reference to matters such as bills, shopping, pension collection, acceptance of gifts, making use of the service user's telephone, borrowing money, etc (DH 2003b).

These standards in turn derive from the regulations made under the Act for care homes (SI 2001/3965, rr.13, 16) and domiciliary care agencies (SI 2002/3214, r.14), which make explicit reference to the prevention of harm or abuse and to the handling of money.

Under the Health and Social Care Act 2008, the CSCI is due to be replaced, and its functions subsumed in a new Care Quality Commission from April 2009. The Act provides for new regulations and standards.

21.15 CRIME AND DISORDER STRATEGIES

Under the Crime and Disorder Act 1998 (ss.5–7), 'responsible authorities' have certain obligations. The authorities comprise the local authority (county or unitary) and the following (any part of whose area comes within that of the local authority: chief officer of police, police authority, NHS primary care trust, and fire authority). These authorities must formulate and implement a strategy for the reduction of crime and disorder and for combating the misuse of drugs in the area.

21.16 OFFENCES AGAINST THE PERSON

A range of offences against the person exist in criminal law. The following are but a few examples.

When a care assistant bent back the thumbs of residents as part of the way she handled them, she was found guilty of six offences of assault under s.39 of the Criminal Justice Act 1988 (which makes common assault or battery summary offences, allowing for a fine or up to six months' imprisonment). She was sentenced to six weeks' custody (*Mwaura v Secretary of State for Health*).

Manslaughter through gross negligence may be charged:

Pressure sores and manslaughter. Pressure sores accounted for the conviction for manslaughter of a nursing services manager of a care home and her deputy. Septicaemia had resulted from pressure sorest the size of a fist, which had penetrated to the bone and gave off an overpowering smell of rotting flesh. The resident died in July 1999, having been in the home since March. The home had passed an inspection in May of that same year. The jury rejected the defendant's claim that it was the system that was to blame (*BBC News 2003*).

When violence was deliberate, but death was not intended, manslaughter through an unlawful act may also be charged. For instance, a man with learning disabilities was subjected to a campaign of physical abuse in his home, by a group of teenagers, which resulted in his death – and convictions for manslaughter (Carter 2007). Manslaughter through diminished responsibility may be charged instead of murder. This happened when a mother killed her 36-year-old son who had Down's syndrome, having suffered unbearable pressure for some 30 years (Laville 2005). It may instead be murder:

Social services unable to protect vulnerable adult from murder. A man with severe learning disabilities was befriended by a 'gang'. He thought they were his best friends. For a year, they exploited and cheated him, taking control of his money, his flat and his life, dragging him around his bedsit on a dog's lead. They then tortured him into confessing falsely that he was a paedophile, sentenced him to death, forced him to swallow 70 painkilling tablets, marched him to the top of a viaduct and forced him over, stamping on his hands as he hung on. He fell 30 metres and died. Three of the gang were convicted of murder, another of manslaughter. During the period in question, social services had been visiting him but stopped some time before his death, apparently in response to his wishes (Morris 2007).

The Corporate Manslaughter and Corporate Homicide Act 2007 contains rules about charging an organisation with corporate manslaughter. There has been speculation about whether it might in future apply to circumstances such as pertained in Buckinghamshire and Kent, where seemingly deliberate shortcuts in infection control and standards of care contributed to the deaths of scores of older people from the bacterium *Clostridium difficile* (Carvel 2006; Rose 2007).

Under the Suicide Act 1961, it remains against the law to assist a person to commit suicide. It has been established that this law is not contrary to human rights. When a woman suffering with motor neurone disease wanted an assurance that her husband would not be prosecuted if he assisted her to commit suicide, she brought a human-rights based legal challenge. The challenge failed first in the English courts and then in the European Court of Human Rights (*Pretty v United Kingdom*). Nonetheless, the courts are sometimes minded to impose light sentences:

Husband assists suicide of wife suffering from multiple sclerosis. For instance, a husband was found guilty of aiding and abetting his wife's suicide, but was sentenced to nine months in prison, suspended for a year – and to unpaid work of 50 hours. His wife, suffering from multiple sclerosis, had already attempted suicide twice. When he came home from work, he found a note stating that she had taken 175 valium tablets. She had a plastic bag over her head. He chose to tighten the string around the bag, rather than see his wife fail in her suicide attempt. She blamed him for the failure of her previous attempts. The judge noted that he was entirely of good character and no risk to the community (Cumming 2006).

21.17 ILL-TREATMENT OR NEGLECT

It is an offence for employees or managers of a hospital, independent hospital or care home to ill-treat or wilfully neglect a person receiving treatment for mental disorder as an inpatient in that hospital or home; likewise, ill-treatment or wilful neglect, on the premises of which the hospital or home forms a part, of a patient receiving such treatment as an outpatient. It is an offence for any individual to ill-treat or to wilfully neglect a mentally disordered patient who is subject to his or her guardianship under the 1983 Act or otherwise in his or her custody or care. It is an offence for any individual to ill-treat or wilfully to neglect a mentally disordered patient who is subject to aftercare under supervision (Mental Health Act 1983, s.127). The section was amended in October 2007 and the maximum prison sentence increased from two years to five years.

Under the Mental Capacity Act 2005, an offence of ill-treatment or neglect is created in respect of people lacking capacity, who have been so treated by a person in whose care they are (s.44).

Care home manager locking vulnerable people in car. A care home manager and an employee went to a betting shop and amusement arcade. For three hours during the visit, they locked three vulnerable people in a car on a hot and muggy day. The three had severe learning disabilities, autism and epilepsy. They were rescued when passers-by spotted them in distress and trying to get out. The police freed them and found them dehydrated and very hot. The judge in the Crown Court sentenced, on the basis of wilful neglect, the manager and employee to 300 hours and 250 hours of community service respectively. They were in serious breach of their responsibilities, and the three men must have suffered very considerable stress and discomfort in the unventilated vehicle. They had been on the 'cusp' of going to prison, but were previously model citizens. Both were sacked by their employer (*Daily Mail* 2007).

21.18 OFFENCE OF CAUSING DEATH OF VULNERABLE ADULT

The Domestic Violence, Crime and Victims Act 2004 contains an offence of causing or allowing the death of a vulnerable adult. In outline, it will apply when:

- the vulnerable adult dies as a result of an unlawful act
- the person who committed the act was a member of the same household and had frequent contact with the victim
- the victim must have been at significant risk of serious physical harm by an unlawful act by such a member of the household
- the person either caused the victim's death, or was or ought to have been aware of the risk, failed to take reasonable steps to protect the victim, and the act occurred in circumstances that the person foresaw or should have foreseen.

For the offence to be made out, the prosecution does not have to prove whether the person actually did the act or instead failed to protect the victim. The purpose of the offence is to overcome the problem of showing which of two perpetrators committed the act when, for example, each is blaming the other and the evidence is otherwise inconclusive.

A person could be classed as a member of the same household even if he or she does not live there but visits so often and for such periods of time that it would be reasonable to regard him or her as such a member. A vulnerable adult means a person aged 16 or over whose ability to protect himself or herself from violence, abuse or neglect is significantly impaired through physical or mental disability or illness, through old age or otherwise (s.5).

For instance, in 2001, a 78-year-old woman went to live with relatives. Five weeks and 49 injuries later, she died. All the relatives denied responsibility for the injuries, the cause of her death could not be established, and so no charges were laid. It is thought that cases such as this could be caught by the offence under the 2004 Act (Hamilton 2005). So, when a 19-year old woman was killed, not only was her brother convicted of murder after systematically beating and abusing her for three months, but other relatives living in the house were convicted under the 2004 Act for doing nothing to stop it (Jenkins 2008).

21.19 SEXUAL OFFENCES

The Sexual Offences Act 2003 reformed the law on sexual offences. In relation to adult protection, there are, in addition to the basic offences (rape, sexual assault, etc.), a number of offences specifically related to mental disorder, which bears the same meaning as in s.1 of the Mental Health Act 1983 (see 21.9).

These specific offences related to mental disorder fall into three categories; those involving sexual activity where the allege victim lacked the capacity to refuse or the ability to communicate the refusal (ss.30–33); those involving inducement, threat or deception but not requiring a lack of capacity to refuse (ss.34–37); and those involving care workers and not requiring and ability to refuse (ss.38–41). An example of the first type of these offences, requiring inability to refuse or to communicate that refusal was as follows:

Inability to communicate choice. The victim lived in a public house with her parents. She was 27 years old (but had a much lower developmental age) and had cerebral palsy. A 73-year-old man, of previous good character, allegedly touched her over her clothing in the area of her vagina, whilst exposing himself and placing her hand on his soft penis. The defence accepted that the woman suffered from a mental disorder, but argued that she did not lack the capacity to agree to the touching. The magistrates' court had accepted that she understood the nature of sexual relations but did not have the capacity to understand that she could refuse. The High Court took this reasoning to mean that, whilst she might have understood about sexual activity, she was unable to communicate her choice (*Hulme v Director of Public Prosecutions*).

An example of the third type, involving a care worker, involved a senior social worker:

Senior social worker having consensual sexual intercourse with client suffering from depression. A senior social care practitioner, who was an approved social worker, had sexual intercourse on three occasions with a service user; he was convicted under s.38 of the Act. At the time, the woman concerned was suffering a mental disorder in the form of depression. Following the last occasion, she confessed to her husband and they subsequently informed the social worker's manager. The police were then involved. She had consented to the sexual activity. He was sentenced to 17 months' imprisonment (*Bradford v General Social Care Council*).

21.20 VULNERABLE WITNESSES AND SUSPECTS

The detention, treatment and questioning of vulnerable persons by police officers is governed by special provisions, in particular the provision of an appropriate adult under Code of Practice C, made under the Police and Criminal Evidence Act 1984 (see s.6) (Home Office 2008).

In addition, both legislation and guidance now seek to provide assistance for vulnerable witnesses as well. The Youth Justice and Criminal Evidence Act 1999 provides for special measures to be taken in the case of both vulnerable and intimidated witnesses. Eligibility includes the fact that the witness suffers from a mental disorder under the Mental Health Act 1983, or otherwise has a significant impairment of intelligence and social functioning (s.16). The special measures listed include screening the witness from the accused, evidence by live link, evidence given in private, removal of wigs and gowns, video recorded evidence in chief, video recorded cross-examination or re-examination, examination of witness through intermediary, and aids to communication (ss.23–30; see also the rules on special measures directions in respect of magistrates' courts and crown courts: SI 2002/1687 and SI 2002/1688).

Live link evidence given from elderly persons' homes. Two elderly women aged 72 and 91, whose carer had stolen cash from their homes, were able to give evidence by live link under s.24. Real time sound and images were relayed to the courtroom using a mobile video conferencing kit set up in their living room. The jury convicted the carer for theft; she was sentenced to 18 months in prison (*R v Atkins*).

In addition, the Home Office has published a set of guidance as part of its 'achieving best evidence' policy covering vulnerable or intimidated witnesses, including children. In particular, in respect of vulnerable adults, various aspects are covered. These include a definition and identification of vulnerable witnesses, and support for the witness in terms of planning for an interview, at interview, during the investigation, pre-court hearing, during the court hearing and after the hearing. In addition, court-based intermediaries are referred to, and issues around capacity (and oath taking) discussed (Home Office 2002).

Separate guidance has been issued on the use of therapy in relation to the welfare of the witness, and on precautions to be taken so that the therapy does not unnecessarily 'contaminate' the evidence to be given by the vulnerable witness. The guidance does emphasise, though, that 'priority must be given to the best interests of the vulnerable or intimidated witness' (Home Office 2002a, p.19).

21.21 CIVIL TORTS

Trespass to the person, false imprisonment and negligence are all civil torts which may give rise to civil legal actions for damages.

Trespass to the person is the civil law equivalent of assault and battery in criminal law (see 21.16). In a case concerning an NHS trust's failure to withdraw a medical intervention on the request of the patient, the court concluded that the trust had acted unlawfully in terms of the tort of trespass to the person (*Re B (Adult: refusal of treatment)*). Likewise a caesarean section, carried out against a woman's will, constituted unlawful trespass to the person (*R v Collins, ex p S*). Following the neglect and death of a man in hospital, a negligence case was settled out of court for some £15,000:

Neglect in hospital leading to death. A former metal worker, he had been admitted for a broken leg, but within a few days became ill. He became dehydrated ill-nourished, eventually dying of renal failure, septicaemia and a chest infection. Fluids and nutrition had not been administered and his poor state of health was only identified when he had been discharged to a rehabilitation unit. He was immediately readmitted to hospital intensive care but died (BBC News 2004). Despite instructions from doctors to do so, staff had failed to provide a saline drip for 12 days. The hospital stated that it could have done things better, but was under-funded (Wright and Carson 2002).

21.22 PHYSICAL RESTRAINT

The physical restraint of adults, as well as of children, remains of considerable concern. On the one hand, total prohibition on restraint might result in harm to both the service user and other people. Equally, improper restraint runs the risk of resulting in, for example, injury to the restrained or the restrainer, breach of human rights, the criminal offence of assault and battery, and the civil tort of trespass to the person.

In response to such concerns, the Department of Health issued guidance in 2002 on physically restrictive interventions for people with learning disabilities or autism in health, education and social care settings (DH 2002). In summary, the guidance emphasises that interventions are legally permissible in certain circumstances (e.g. self-harm or injury to others) – and that any interventions should be the least restrictive necessary. They should be planned as far as possible, result from multi-disciplinary assessment and be part of a wider therapeutic strategy detailed in individual care plans. Prevention should be the primary aim, in order to avoid the use of restraint if possible. There should be clear organisational policies and adequate training (DH 2002).

Although aimed at people with learning disabilities or autism, the principles set out in the guidance would arguably apply to some other groups of people with a mental disorder where restraint is sometimes necessary. The Mental Health Act 1983 Code of Practice also contains guidance on restraint (DH 2008c, Chapter 15). The Mental Capacity Act 2005 confirms the lawfulness of restraint of a person lacking capacity, but only if it is for the purpose of preventing harm to the person and is proportionate (s.6).

In 2007, the Commission for Social Care Inspection published a report on the use of restraint in the care of older people. It found a range of examples of the use of restraint which were unacceptable and constituted a breach of human rights. These included people fastened into wheelchairs, people kept in chairs by means of trays, the use of low chairs to stop people getting up, wrapping up people in bed to the point of immobility so they could not remove their incontinence pads, excessive use of bed rails, dragging a person by her hair and tying her to a chair, excessive drug-based sedation, not taking people to the toilet when they want to go, punishing people by leaving them sitting in soiled pads – and so on (CSCI 2007).

21.23 FINANCIAL ABUSE

When financial abuse has occurred, transactions such as gifts or wills can sometimes be set aside in civil law. Alternatively or additionally, the criminal law can sometimes be invoked and a charge such as theft be brought. The organisation Action on Elder Abuse believes that family financial abuse is a serious issue, and observes that 'middle-aged sons and daughters are the people most likely to rob older people of their cash, valuables and even their homes' (Action on Elder Abuse 2007).

21.23.1 LACK OF CAPACITY: SETTING ASIDE A FINANCIAL TRANSACTION

If it can be shown that a transaction has taken place at a time when a person lacked capacity to take the relevant decision, the transaction will, as a matter of civil law, be void (unless it involved the provision of 'necessaries': see 20.9) and be set aside by a court – as happened when a woman transferred her house to carers. She had left her house to Great Ormond Street Hospital in her will; the hospital brought a civil case and succeeded on the ground that the woman lacked capacity when she made the transfer (*Special Trustees for Great Ormond Street Hospital v Rushin*).

Decision-making capacity is issue and time specific, and the courts will look carefully at both the nature of the transaction and when it was performed (see 20.3.1). Thus a person may have the capacity to make a power of attorney, but at the same time lack the capacity to manage their affairs (*Re K*). And, the validity of a will may depend on whether the executor had enjoyed a period of lucidity on a particular afternoon, in between confusion both in the morning and later the same afternoon. In the circumstances, the court thought not – and the will was declared invalid (*Richards v Allan*).

Similarly, in criminal law, lack of capacity to make a gift may make prosecution of a theft case more straightforward (see below).

21.23.2 UNDUE INFLUENCE

Apart from lack of capacity, there is sometimes an alternative ground on which a transaction may be set aside in civil law. This is on the basis of a legal, equitable concept known as undue influence. Generally speaking, undue influence can be summarised as follows. First, the exploited person has capacity, otherwise it is arguable that he or she cannot be unduly influenced (e.g. *Tchilingirian v Ouzounian*). Second, he or she is influenced to enter into a transaction not of his or her own free, informed will. Third, the undue influence can be either 'express' (in the case of gifts of wills) or 'presumed' (in the case of gifts only).

If undue influence is argued to be express, then evidence is required of how exactly the influence was exercised in terms of overt, improper pressure or coercion (*Royal Bank of Scotland v Etridge (no.2)*). For instance, a woman changed her will and left everything to her heavily drinking son, with whom she lived and of whom she was afraid, whilst disinheriting her other son. The court found sufficient evidence of express undue influence and set aside the new will (*Edwards v Edwards*).

Alternatively, presumed undue influence relies on a relationship of trust and confidence, and on a disadvantageous transaction, or at least a transaction that 'calls for an explanation'. Once these two elements are established, then the evidential burden shifts to the other party to give an innocent explanation for the transaction. If this explanation is not forthcoming, undue influence will be made out. Importantly it is not necessary to prove that the other party did anything 'wrong'. Relationships of trust and confidence are recognised by the law courts in well-known categories (such as doctor–patient) but also in other relationships (such as carer and cared for person).

Under the proverbial wing of a neighbour. In one case, an elderly man was taken under the proverbial wing of a neighbour. He made a gift of nearly £300,000, 91 per cent of his liquid assets. The court emphasised the significance of the presumption of undue influence and of the carer having to provide an innocent explanation for what had occurred. In the absence of such an explanation, 'public policy' demanded a finding of undue influence, even were there no direct evidence of a wrongful act (*Hammond v Osborne*).

21.23.3 THEFT AND FRAUD

Under s.1 of the Theft Act 1968, a person is guilty of theft if he or she dishonestly appropriates property belonging to somebody else. This must be with the intention of permanently depriving the other person of it.

Such an appropriation is not dishonest if the person believes he or she had a right in law to deprive the other person of it. Alternatively it is not dishonest if he or she believed that the other person would consent, and if the other person knew of the appropriation and the circumstances.

In the context of adult protection, the question of theft might arise where, for instance, carers financially exploit vulnerable adults. The significance of one particular legal case was that theft could be made out on the basis of the jury's overall view of whether there had been dishonesty; and that this would not necessarily depend on the man being shown to have lacked the requisite capacity to make a gift of the money involved:

Giving money away amounting to theft. A man of 'limited intelligence' had gone to the building society every day with a privately arranged carer. He transferred £300 to her every day for six months, until he had transferred £60,000. The question of whether he lacked capacity to make these daily gifts was unclear; but the House of Lords on appeal refused to overturn the carer's conviction. Whether or not he had capacity, it was for the jury to decide whether, in all the circumstances, it was dishonest (*R v Hinks*).

21.23.3.1 Fraud

The offence of fraud is to be found in the Fraud Act 2006 (not Scotland). The three main offences are fraud by false representation, by failure to disclose information or by abuse of position (ss. 1–4).

The last is perhaps particularly relevant to adult protection concerns. The ingredients are that a person (a) occupies a position in which he is expected to safeguard, or not to act against, the financial interests of another person; (b) dishonestly abuses that position; and (c) intends, by means of the abuse of that position to make a gain for himself or another – or to cause loss to another or to expose another to a risk of loss. Abuse can be made out even if the conduct consists of an omission rather than an act (s.4).

21.24 SAFEGUARDING PROCEDURES AND INVESTIGATIONS

Clearly, effective investigations will be a crucial part of a local authority's adult protection activity. The following local ombudsman cases illustrate failures in policies, procedures and such investigations. One concerned a gift to a carer and the question of whether undue influence had been exercised:

Bequest to council carer. In 1984, guidance on the receipt of gifts was issued to its staff by a local authority; in 1990 a further instruction was issued. However, in the case of one particular carer (against whom the complaint of undue influence had been made), it could not be shown that she had received either the guidance or further instruction. She was not asked to sign a record that she had done so. This in itself was maladministration.

The carer was left a significant amount of money in the will of one of the service users for whom she provided care, and had also received £1000 as a lifetime gift. When the service user died, her granddaughter complained to the council that the bequest and gift had been procured by undue influence.

The local ombudsman found maladministration on a number of grounds; one was that the local authority did not investigate the complaint for three years; when it did so, its response was inadequate since it sought no evidence from third parties who might have contributed the relevant evidence (*Suffolk CC 2001*).

Local authorities may fail to investigate physical injuries suffered by a severely brain injured woman at a local authority day centre (*Bedfordshire CC 2003*), or to inform either the police or the father of a woman with severe learning disabilities about the catalogue of injuries she had suffered (*Southwark LBC 2001a*).

Equally, where councils do act decisively in relation to safeguarding, they need to be careful to ensure that they keep in focus the overall welfare of the service user. For instance, in one local ombudsman investigation, adult protection concerns were responded to swiftly by arranging an emergency residential placement for her the same day. However, the woman was extremely physically vulnerable and had complex postural needs; she died a few days later of a chest infection. Although the ombudsman did not directly blame the council for her death, he concluded that it could have managed the placement better and should have considered the case on a 'deeper level' (*Kent CC 1999*).

Adult protection work is described in Department of Health guidance as being essentially multi-agency in nature. Thus, the health service ombudsman has criticised an NHS Trust for not having a complaints procedure that was sensitive to adult protection, following a complaint about rough handling which effectively was an allegation about assault (*Warrington Hospital NHS Trust 2001*).

21.24.1 EVIDENCE PUT FORWARD BY LOCAL AUTHORITIES TO THE COURTS

The courts have sometimes been less than impressed with the evidence of abuse put forward by local authorities. Such cases are a reminder that councils must take safeguarding adults seriously but at the same time have reasonable grounds for actions they propose to take.

For instance, in one case, it appeared that the local authority gave the impression that it had dredged up old and largely unsubstantiated allegations concerning abuse by a father against his daughter with learning disabilities. The court largely discounted this evidence, finding most of it not made out, although granted on other grants the order sought by the local authority (*Newham LBC v BS*).

Non-specific and unbalanced evidence will be criticised and discounted by the court (*B Borough Council v Mrs S*). And, in one case, when a local authority sought a 'without notice' order (giving the other side no chance to oppose it in the first instance), the court found that virtually all the allegations made by the local authority were factually incorrect – a defect that could have been remedied had the order not been sought without notice (*LLBC v TG*). It is nonetheless of interest that in all three of these cases the local authority obtained the order it sought, largely on general welfare grounds rather than on the grounds of abuse put forward.

21.25 PUBLIC INTEREST DISCLOSURE ACT 1998: 'WHISTLE-BLOWING'

If employees have serious concerns about matters at work, they are protected if in certain circumstances, they 'whistle-blow' – that is, raise their concerns outside of the organisation (Employment Rights Act 1996, as amended by the Public Interest Disclosure Act 1998). The protection may of course only be retrospective insofar as the employees who raise their concerns may have to resort to an Employment Tribunal in order to gain compensation for losing their jobs.

21.26 HEALTH AND SAFETY AT WORK LEGISLATION

In some circumstances, health and safety at work legislation may be employed to prosecute in relation to adult protection. For instance, people with physical and learning disabilities living in a care home in Hull had been subject to a regime of sustained abuse for three years. Seven carers were sent to prison under s.127 of the Mental Health Act 1983, for ill-treatment and wilful neglect. However, in addition, under the Health and Safety at Work Act 1974, the company was prosecuted and fined £100,000 together with £25,000 costs. It pleaded guilty to failing to take appropriate action to investigate and prevent the ill-treatment of vulnerable adults. Also, five senior managers were prosecuted individually for failing to protect residents from this ill-treatment; they had failed to act on reports of abuse. They were fined sums ranging from £4000 down to £360 (Mark 2005).

References

LEGAL CASES

A v A health authority [2001] EWHC Fam/Admin 18.

A Child 'A' (By his mother and litigation friend 'B') v Ministry of Defence and Guy's and St Thomas Hospital NHS Trust [2004] EWCA Civ 641.

Ahsan v University Hospitals Leicester NHS Trust [2006] EWHC 2624 QB.

Airedale NHS Trust v Bland [1993] AC 789.

Alternative Futures Ltd v Sefton Metropolitan Borough Council and National Care Standards Commission [2002] EWHC 3032 (Admin).

An Hospital NHS Trust v S [2003] EWHC Admin 365.

An NHS Trust v Ms T [2004] EWHC Fam 1279.

Ashingdane v UK (1985) 7 EHRR 528, European Court of Human Rights.

Associated Provincial Picture Houses v Wednesbury Corporation [1947] 2 All ER 680, Court of Appeal.

Avon County Council v Hooper [1997] 1 All ER 532, Court of Appeal.

B Borough Council v Mrs S [2006] EWHC Fam 2584.

Baker v Baker [1993] 2 FLR 247, Court of Appeal.

Barber v Somerset County Council [2004] UKHL 13, House of Lords.

Barrett v Enfield London Borough Council [1999] 3 WLR 79, House of Lords.

Beasley v Buckinghamshire County Council [1997] PIQR P473, High Court (QBD).

Bell v Todd [2002] LR Med 12, High Court.

BetterCare Group v Director General of Fair Trading [2002] CAT 7, Competition Commission Appeal Tribunal.

BetterCare Group v North and West Belfast Health and Social Services Trust (2003) Case no. CA98/09/2003, Office of Fair Trading, 2003.

Bluett v Suffolk County Council and Others [2004] EWCA Civ 1707.

Botta v Italy (1998) Case no. 21439/93, European Court of Human Rights.

Brent LBC v SK [2007] EWHC 1250, Fam.

British Oxygen v Board of Trade [1971] AC 610, House of Lords.

Brooklyn House Ltd v Commission for Social Care Inspection [2006] EWHC 1165 Admin.

Buck v Nottinghamshire Healthcare NHS Trust [2006] EWCA Civ 1576.

Bull v Devon Area Health Authority (1983) 4 Med LR 177.

Burke v General Medical Council [2004] EWHC Admin 1879.

Campbell v Griffin [2001] EWCA Civ 990.

Casewell v Secretary of State for Work and Pensions (2008) Court of Appeal.

CD (A Child) v Anglesey County Council [2004] EWHC Admin 1635.

Cheese v Thomas [1994] 1 All ER 35, Court of Appeal.

Chief Adjudication Officer v Palfrey [1995] SJLB 65, Court of Appeal.

Chief Adjudication Officer v Quinn [1996] 1 WLR 1184, House of Lords.

Chief Constable of Hertfordshire v Van Colle; Smith v Chief Constable of Sussex [2008] UKHL 50.

City of Sunderland v PS [2007] EWHC Fam 623.

Clunis v Camden and Islington Health Authority [1998] 3 All ER 180, Court of Appeal.

Cocks v Thanet District Council [1983] 2 AC, House of Lords.

Colclough v Staffordshire County Council [1994] CL 94/2283, County Court.

Cole v Davis Gilbert [2007] EWCA Civ 396.

Collins v United Kingdom (2002) Application 11909/02, European Court of Human Rights.

Commons v Queen's Medical Centre Nottingham University Hospital NHS Trust (2001) unreported, County Court.

Cook v Bradford Community NHS Trust [2002] EWCA Civ 1616.

Council of Civil Service Unions v Minister of State for the Civil Service [1985] AC 374, House of Lords.

Crofton v NHS Litigation Authority [2007] EWCA Civ 71.

Croydon London Borough Council v Moody (1999) 2 CCLR 93, Court of Appeal.

Dennis Rye Pension Fund v Sheffield City Council (1998) 1 WLR 840, Court of Appeal.

Derbyshire County Council v Akrill [2005] EWCA Civ 308.

Dodov v Bulgaria (2008) European Court of Human Rights, case no. 59548/00.

Donoghue v Poplar Housing Association [2001] EWCA Civ 595.

Douce v Staffordshire County Council [2002] EWCA Civ 506.

E (By her litigation friend PW) v X London Borough Council [2005] EWHC 2811 Fam.

Ealing London Borough Council v KS [2008] EWHC 636 (Fam).

Edwards v Edwards [2007] EWHC Chancery 119.

Edwards v National Coal Board [1949] 1 All ER 743, Court of Appeal.

Eisai Ltd v National Institute for Health and Clinical Excellence [2007] Admin EWHC 1941, High Court; [2008] EWCA Civ 438, Court of Appeal.

European Surgeries v Cambridgeshire Primary Care Trust [2007] EWHC Admin 2758n.

Faulkner v Talbot [1981] 3 All ER 468, Court of Appeal.

Firth v Ackroyd and Bradford Metropolitan District Council (2000), High Court (QBD).

Freeman v Lockett [2006] EWHC 102.

Gaskin v UK (1989) 12 EHRR 36 (Series A, no.160), European Court of Human Rights.

Gichura v Home Office [2008] EWCA Civ 697.

Godbold v Mahmood [2005] EWHC 1002.

Gwilliam v West Hertfordshire Hospital NHS Trust [2002] EWCA Civ 1041.

Hall v Monmouthshire County Council, Gwent Healthcare NHS Trust and others [2004] EWHC QB 2748.

Hammond v Osborne [2002] EWCA Civ 885.

Hampson v Department of Education and Science [1990] IRLR 302, House of Lords.

Hampstead Health Winter Swimming Club v Corporation of London [2005] EWHC 713 Admin.

Harris v Perry [2008] EWHC 990 QB; [2008] EWCA 907, Court of Appeal.

Harrison v Cornwall County Council (1991) 156 Lg Rev R 703, Court of Appeal.

Hawkes v Southwark London Borough Council (1998) unreported, Court of Appeal.

HE v A Hospital NHS Trust [2003] EWHC Fam 1017.

Health and Safety Executive v BUPA Care Homes Ltd (2006) Southwark Crown Court, 7 September 2006. HSE Press Release, 7 September 2006.

Health and Safety Executive v Dukeries Health Care (2004) 24 August 2004, Magistrates Court (unreported).

Health and Safety Executive v London Borough of Barnet (1997) unreported, Crown Court.

Health and Safety Executive v Norfolk and Norwich Healthcare NHS Trust (1999) Crown Court.

Health and Safety Executive v Prime Life Ltd (2007) Leicester Crown Court, 8 October 2007. *Health and Safety Bulletin* December 2007, p.5.

Health and Safety Executive v South Church Care Ltd (2005) 24 August 2005, Magistrates Court.

Health and Safety Executive v Southern Cross Care Homes (2007) 30 November 2007, Crown Court.

HL v United Kingdom (2004) 40 EHRR 761, European Court of Human Rights.

Hulme v Director of Public Prosecutions [2006] EWHC Admin 1347.

Islington London Borough Council v University College London Hospital NHS Trust [2004] EWHC 1754 (QBD); [2005] EWCA Civ 596 (Court of Appeal).

Jain v Trent Strategic Health Authority [2007] EWCA Civ 1186.

JE v DE and Surrey County Council [2006] EWHC Fam 3459.

Jones v National Care Standards Commission [2004] EWHC Admin 918; [2004] EWCA Civ 1713, Court of Appeal.

JT v United Kingdom [2000] 1 FLR 909, European Court of Human Rights.

K v Central and North West London Mental Health NHS Trust, and Kensington and Chelsea Royal London Borough Council [2008] EWHC 1217 QB.

K v X Grammar School Governors [2007] EWCA Civ 165.

KC v City of Westminster Social and Community Services Department [2008] EWCA Civ 198.

Kent v Griffiths (2000) 3 CCLR 98, Court of Appeal.

King v Sussex Ambulance Service [2002] EWCA Civ 953.

Koonjul v Thameslink NHS Health Care Trust (2000) PIQR 123, Court of Appeal.

Knott v Newham Healthcare NHS Trust [2003] EWCA Civ 771.

Lambeth London Borough Council v A [2002] EWCA Civ 1084.

Law Society v Southall [2001] EWCA Civ 2001.

Lewis v Gibson [2005] EWCA Civ 587.

Lindsay v Wood [2006] EWHC QB 2895.

LLBC v TG [2007] EWHC Fam 2640, High Court.

Local Authority X v MM [2007] EWHC Fam 2003.

M v B [2005] EWHC Fam 1681.

McCarthy v Richmond London Borough Council [1991] 4 All ER 897, House of Lords.

McGlinchey v United Kingdom (2003) Application 50390/99, European Court of Human Rights.

MacGregor v South Lanarkshire Council (2001) 4 CCLR 188, Court of Session (Outer House).

McKellar v Hounslow London Borough Council [2003] EWHC 3145, Queens Bench.

Malcolm v Lewisham London Borough Council [2007] EWCA 763; [2008] UKHL 43.

Manchester City Council v Romano; Manchester City Council v Samari [2004] EWCA Civ 384.

Masterman-Lister v Brutton [2002] EWHC 417, High Court (QBD); [2002] EWCA Civ 1889, Court of Appeal.

MG v United Kingdom (2002) Application 39393/98, European Court of Human Rights.

Miao v Secretary of State for the Home Department [2006] EWCA Civ 75.

Moore v Care Standards Tribunal [2005] EWCA Civ 627.

N v Secretary of State for the Home Department [2005] UKHL 31, House of Lords.

N v United Kingdom (2008), European Court of Human Rights (Application 26565/05, 27 May 2008).

Newham London Borough Council v BS [2003] EWHC Fam 1909.

NHS Trust A v M (2001) 2 WLR 942.

NHS Trust v MB [2006] EWHC Fam 507.

NHS Trust v Ms D [2005] EWHC Fam 2439.

North Devon Homes v Brazier [2003] EWHC 574 (QBD).

O'Rourke v Camden London Borough Council [1997] 3 All ER 23, House of Lords.

Patchett v Leathem (1949) TLR 4 February 1949, High Court, Kings Bench Division.

Peters v East Midlands Strategic Health Authority [2008] EWHC 778 QB.

Pfizer Corporation v Ministry of Health [1965] AC 512, House of Lords.

Phelps v Hillingdon London Borough Council (2000) 3 WLR 776, House of Lords.

Pratley v Surrey County Council [2003] EWCA Civ 1067.

Pretty v United Kingdom [2002] 2 FCR 97, European Court of Human Rights.

Price v United Kingdom (2001) Application 33394/96, European Court of Human Rights.

Purves v Joydisc Ltd (2003) SC694/01, Sheriff Court (Scotland), appeal to the Sheriff Principal.

Purves v Southampton University Hospitals NHS Trust (2004) Employment Tribunal case no. 3103968/2002.

Qazi v Waltham Forest London Borough Council (1999) unreported, High Court (QBD).

R v A local authority in the Midlands, ex p LM (2000) 1 FLR 612, High Court.

R v Ali Sed [2004] EWCA Crim 1295.

R v Ashworth Special Hospital Authority, ex p E [2001] EWHC Admin 1089.

R v Ashworth Special Hospital Authority, ex p N [2001] EWHC Admin 339.

R v Atkins, reported in: Humberside Crown Prosecution Services (2004) *Humberside Annual Report 2003–04*, p.5.

R v Avon County Council, ex p M [1994] 2 FCR 259, High Court.

R v Barnet London Borough Council, ex p Shah (1983) 2 AC 309, House of Lords.

R v Berkshire County Council, ex p Parker [1996] 95 LGR 449, High Court.

R v Bexley London Borough Council, ex p B [1995] CL 3225, High Court.

R v Birmingham City Council, ex p A [1997] 2 FCR 357, High Court.

R v Birmingham City Council, ex p Birmingham Care Consortium [2002] EWHC Admin 2118.

R v Birmingham City Council, ex p Killigrew (2000) 3 CCLR 109, High Court.

R v Birmingham City Council, ex p Mohammed [2002] EWHC Admin 1511.

R v Birmingham City Council, ex p Taj Mohammed [1998] 1 CCLR 441, High Court.

R v Bournewood Community and Mental Health NHS Trust, ex p L [1998] 1 CCLR 390, House of Lords.

R v Brent, Kensington and Chelsea and Westminster NHS Trust, ex p C [2002] EWHC 181.

R v Brent London Borough Council, ex p D [1998] 1 CCLR 235, High Court.

R v Bristol City Council, ex p Bailey [1995] 27 HLR 307, High Court.

R v Bristol City Council, ex p Penfold [1998] 1 CCLR 315, High Court.

R v Cambridge Health Authority, ex p B [1995] 6 MLR 250, Court of Appeal.

R v Central Birmingham Health Authority, ex p Collier (1998) unreported, Court of Appeal.

R v Central Birmingham Health Authority, ex p Walker [1987] 3 BMLR 32, Court of Appeal.

R v Chief Constable of North Wales, ex p AB [1998] 3 WLR 57, Court of Appeal.

R v Cleveland County Council, ex p Cleveland Care Homes Association [1993] 158 LGRevR 641, High Court.

R v Cleveland County Council, ex p Ward [1994] COD 222, High Court.

R v Collins, Pathfinder Mental Health Services NHS Trust and St George's Healthcare NHS Trust, ex p S (1998) 1 CCLR 578, Court of Appeal.

R v Collins, Pathfinder Mental Health Services NHS Trust and St George's Healthcare NHS Trust, ex p S (no.2) (1998) 3 WLR 936, Court of Appeal.

R v Commissioner for Local Administration, ex p Liverpool City Council [2001] 1 All ER 462, Court of Appeal.

R v Commissioner for Local Administration, ex p PH (1999) COD 382, High Court; [1999] ELR 314, Court of Appeal.

R v Cornwall County Council, ex p Goldsack (1996) unreported, High Court.

R v Coventry City Council, ex p Coventry Heads of Independent Care Establishments (CHOICE) and Peggs [1998] 1 CCLR 379, High Court.

R v Department of Health and Social Security, ex p Bruce [1986] TLR 8 February 1986, High Court.

R v Devon County Council, ex p Baker and Johns; R v Durham County Council, ex p Curtis and Brown [1992] 158 LGRevR 241, Court of Appeal.

R v Ealing District Health Authority, ex p Fox [1993] WLR 373, High Court.

R v Ealing London Borough Council, ex p C (2000) 3 CCLR 122, Court of Appeal.

R v Ealing London Borough Council, ex p Leaman [1984] TLR, 10 February 1984, High Court.

R v East Kent Hospital NHS Trust, ex p Smith [2002] EWHC Admin 2640.

R v East Sussex County Council, ex p Tandy [1997] 3 FCR 525, Court of Appeal; [1998] 2 All ER 769, House of Lords.

R v East Sussex County Council, ex p Tandy [1997] 3 FCR 525, Court of Appeal; (1998) 1 CCLR 352, House of Lords.

R v Essex County Council, ex p Bucke [1997] COD 66, High Court.

R v Further Education Funding Council and Bradford Metropolitan District Council, ex p Parkinson [1997] 2 FCR 67, High Court.

R v Gloucestershire County Council, ex p Barry [1995] 160 LGRevR 321, High Court; [1996] 4 All ER 422, Court of Appeal; [1997] 2 All ER 1, House of Lords.

R v Gloucestershire County Council, ex p Mahfood [1995] 160 LGRevR 321, High Court.

R v Gloucestershire County Council, ex p RADAR [1996] COD 253, High Court.

R v Hackney London Borough Council, ex p J (1999) unreported, High Court.

R v Hammersmith Hospitals NHS Trust, ex p Reffell (2000) Lloyd's Rep Med 350, Court of Appeal.

R v Haringey London Borough Council, ex p Norton [1998] 1 CCLR 168, High Court.

R v Hereford and Worcester County Council, ex p Chandler (1992) unreported, noted in Legal Action 15, September 2002.

R v Hillingdon Area Health Authority, ex p Wyatt (1977) unreported, Court of Appeal.

R v Hinks (2001) 2 AC 241, House of Lords.

R v Inhabitants of Eastbourne (1803) 4 East 103.

R v Inner London Education Authority (ILEA), ex p Ali [1990] 2 ALR 822, High Court.

R v Islington London Borough Council, ex p McMillan [1995] 160 LGRevR 321, High Court.

R v Islington London Borough Council, ex p Rixon [1997] 1 ELR 477, High Court.

R v Kensington and Chelsea RB, ex p Kujtim (1999) 2 CCLR 340, Court of Appeal.

R v Kent County Council, ex p Marston (1997) unreported, High Court.

R v Kent County Council, ex p Salisbury (2000) 3 CCLR 38, High Court.

R v Kingston upon Thames Royal Borough, ex p T [1994] 1 FLR 799, High Court.

R v Kirklees Metropolitan Borough Council, ex p Daykin [1996] 3 CL 565, High Court.

R v Kirklees Metropolitan Borough Council, ex p Good [1996] 11 CL 288, High Court.

R v Lambeth London Borough Council, ex p A [1997] 10 ALR 209, Court of Appeal.

R v Lambeth London Borough Council, ex p Sarhangi (1999) 2 CCLR 145, High Court.

R v Lancashire County Council, ex p RADAR [1996] 4 All ER 422, Court of Appeal.

R v Lewisham London Borough Council, ex p Pinzon and Patino (1999) 2 CCLR 152, High Court.

R v Lynsey (1995) 3 All ER 654.

R v Manchester City Council, ex p Stennett (1999) 2 CCLR 402, High Court; [2002] UKHL 34, House of Lords.

R v Mental Health Review Tribunal, Torfaen County Borough Council and Gwent Health Authority, ex p Hall (1999) 2 CCLR 361, High Court, Administrative Division.

R v Merton, Sutton and Wandsworth Health Authority, ex p Andrew (2001) Lloyd's Rep Med 73, High Court.

R v Newcastle upon Tyne Council, ex p Dixon [1993] 158 LGRevR 441, High Court.

R v Newham London Borough Council, ex p Gorenkin [1997] 30 HLR 278, High Court.

R v Newham London Borough Council, ex p Medical Foundation for the Care of Victims of Torture [1998] 1 CCLR 227, High Court.

R v Newham London Borough Council, ex p Plastin [1997] 30 HLR 261, High Court.

R v North Cornwall District Council, ex p Singer (1994) *The Times* 12 January 1994, High Court.

R v North Derbyshire Health Authority, ex p Fisher [1998] 8 MLR 327, High Court.

R v North and East Devon Health Authority, ex p Coughlan (1999) 2 CCLR 285, Court of Appeal.

R v North and East Devon Health Authority, ex p Pow (1998) 39 BMLR 77.

R v North West Lancashire Health Authority, ex p G,A,D (1999) 2 CCLR 419, Court of Appeal.

R v North Yorkshire County Council, ex p Hargreaves [1994] 26 BMLR 121, High Court.

R v North Yorkshire County Council, ex p Hargreaves (no.2) [1997] 96 LGR 39 High Court.

R v Northavon District Council, ex p Smith [1994] 2 FCR 859, House of Lords.

R v Partnerships in Care Ltd, ex p A [2002] EWHC Admin 529.

R v Plymouth City Council, ex p Stevens [2002] EWCA Civ 388.

R v Powys County Council, ex p Hambidge [1998] 1 CCLR 458, Court of Appeal.

R v Powys County Council, ex p Hambidge (no.2) [1999] 2 CCLR 460, High Court; (2000) LGR 564, Court of Appeal.

R v Redbridge London Borough Council ex p East Sussex County Council [1993] COD 256, High Court.

R v Responsible Medical Officer Broadmoor Hospital, ex p Wilkinson [2001] EWCA Civ 1545.

R v Richmond London Borough Council, ex p H (2000) unreported, High Court.

R v St Edmundsbury Housing Benefit Review Board, ex p Sandys (1999) 48 BMLR 24, Court of Appeal.

R v Secretary of State for the Environment, ex p Nottinghamshire County Council [1986] AC 240, House of Lords.

R v Secretary of State for Health, ex p Hammersmith and Fulham London Borough Council (1998) LGR 277, Court of Appeal.

R v Secretary of State for Health, ex p Manchester Local Committee [1995] 2 CL 3621, High Court.

R v Secretary of State for Social Services, ex p Hincks [1980] 1 BMLR 93, Court of Appeal.

R v Secretary of State for the Home Department, ex p Adam, Limbuela, Tesema [2005] UKHL 66, House of Lords.

R v Secretary of State for the Home Department, ex p Doody [1994] 1 AC 531, House of Lords.

R v Secretary of State for the Home Department, ex p Joint Council for the Welfare of Immigrants [1996] 4 All ER 385, Court of Appeal.

R v Secretary of State for the Home Department, ex p Zakrocki (1998) 1 CCLR 374, High Court.

R v Sefton Metropolitan Borough Council, ex p Help the Aged [1997] 3 FCR 392, High Court; [1997] 3 FCR 573, Court of Appeal.

R v Servite Houses, ex p Goldsmith (2000) 3 CCLR 325, High Court.

R v Sheffield City Council, ex p Low (2000) unreported, Court of Appeal (renewed application for permission to bring judicial review case).

R v Sheffield Health Authority, ex p Seale [1994] 25 BMLR 1, High Court.

R v Social Fund Inspector, ex p Connick [1994] COD 75, High Court.

R v Somerset County Council, ex p Harcombe [1997] 96 LGR 444, High Court.

R v Southampton University Hospitals NHS Trust [2006] EWCA Crim 2971.

R v Staffordshire County Council, ex p Farley [1997] 7 CL 572, High Court.

R v Sunderland City Council, ex p Redezeus [1994] 27 HLR 477, High Court.

R v Sutton London Borough Council, ex p Tucker [1998] CCLR 251, High Court.

R v Swindon Borough Council, ex p Stoddard (1998) unreported, High Court.

R v Waltham Forest London Borough Council, ex p Vale [1985] TLR, 25 February 1985, High Court.

R v Wandsworth London Borough Council, ex p Beckwith [1996] 1 FCR 504, House of Lords.

R v Wandsworth London Borough Council, ex p Beckwith (no.2) [1995] 159 LGRevR 929, High Court.

R v Wandsworth London Borough Council, ex p M [1998] ELR 424, High Court.

R v Wandsworth London Borough Council, ex p O (2000) 3 CCLR 237, Court of Appeal.

R v Westminster City Council, ex p A [1997] 1 CCLR 69, High Court; [1997] 30 HLR 10 (reported as R v Hammersmith and Fulham London Borough Council, ex p M), Court of Appeal.

R v Westminster City Council, ex p P [1998] (1998) 1 CCLR 486, Court of Appeal.

R v Wigan Metropolitan Borough Council, ex p Tammadge [1998] 1 CCLR 581, High Court.

R(A) v Liverpool City Council [2007] EWHC 1477 Admin.

R(A) v National Asylum Support Service [2003] EWCA Civ 1473.

R(A) v National Probation Service [2003] EWHC Admin 2910.

R(A) West Middlesex University Hospital NHS Trust [2008] EWHC 855.

R(AA) v Lambeth London Borough Council [2001] EWHC Admin 741.

R(Gunter) v South Western Staffordshire Primary Care Trust [2005] EWHC 1894 Admin.

R(H) v Mental Health Review Tribunal, North and East London Region and the Secretary of State for Health [2001] EWCA Civ 415.

R(H) v Wandsworth London Borough Council [2007] EWHC 1082 Admin.

R(Haggerty) v St Helens Metropolitan Borough Council [2003] EWHC Admin 803.

R(Hands) v Birmingham City Council [2001] EWHC Admin.

R(Heather) v Leonard Cheshire Foundation [2002] EWCA Civ 366.

R(Heffernan) v Sheffield City Council [2004] EWCH Admin 1377.

R(Heimsath) v Secretary of State for the Home Department [2003] EWHC 3478.

R(Hide) v Staffordshire County Council [2007] EWCA Civ 860.

R(Hillingdon London Borough Council) v Secretary of State for Education and Skills [2007] EWHC 514 Admin.

R(HP) v Islington London Borough Council [2004] EWHC Admin 07.

R(Hughes) v Liverpool City Council [2005] EWHC 428 Admin.

R(IH) v Secretary of State [2003] UKHL 59, House of Lords.

R (Ireneschild) v Lambeth LBC [2007] EWCA Civ 234.

R(J) v Caerphilly County Borough Council [2005] EWHC 586 Admin.

R(J) v Enfield London Borough Council [2002] EWHC Admin 432.

R(J) v Newham London Borough Council [2001] EWHC Admin 992.

R(J) v Southend Borough Council [2005] EWHC 3457 Admin.

R(Johnson) v Havering London Borough Council [2007] EWCA Civ 26.

R(K) v Camden and Islington Health Authority [2001] EWCA Civ 240.

R(K) v Lambeth London Borough Council [2003] EWCA Civ 1150.

R(K) v West London Mental Health Trust [2006] EWCA Civ 118.

R(Keating) v Cardiff Local Health Board [2005] EWCA Civ 847.

R(KB,MK,FR,GM,PD,TB,B) v Mental Health Review Tribunal and Secretary of State for Health [2003] EWHC 193.

R(Kelly) v Hammersmith and Fulham London Borough Council [2004] EWHC Admin 435.

R(Khan) v Oxfordshire County Council [2004] EWCA Civ 309.

R(Khana) v Southwark London Borough Council (2000) unreported, High Court; [2001] EWCA Civ 999, Court of Appeal.

R(L) v Commissioner of Police for the Metropolis [2007] EWCA Civ 168.

R(LH) v Lambeth London Borough Council [2006] EWHC 1190 Admin.

R(Limbuela) v Secretary of State for the Home Department [2004] EWHC 219, High Court; [2004] EWCA Civ 540, Court of Appeal.

R(Lindley) v Tameside Metropolitan Borough Council [2006] EWHC 2296 Admin.

R(Lloyd) v Barking and Dagenham London Borough Council (2001) 4 CCLR 196, Court of Appeal.

R(Longstaff) v Newcastle Primary Care Trust [2003] EWHC Admin 3252.

R(M) v Hammersmith and Fulham LBC [2008] UKHL 14.

R(M) v Islington London Borough Council [2004] EWCA Civ 235.

R(M) v Secretary of State for Health [2003] EWHC Admin 1094.

R(M) v Slough Borough Council [2008] UKHL 52.

R(M) v Suffolk County Council [2006] EWHC 2366 Admin.

R(Madden) v Bury Metropolitan Borough Council [2002] EWHC Admin 1882.

R(Mani) v Lambeth London Borough Council [2003] EWCA Civ 836.

R(Mooney) v Southwark London Borough Council [2006] EWHC 1912 Admin.

R(Morris) Trafford Healthcare NHS [2006] EWHC Admin 2334.

R(N) v Lambeth London Borough Council [2007] EWHC Admin 3427.

R(O) v Haringey London Borough Council [2004] EWCA Civ 535.

R(Otley) v Barking and Dagenham Primary Care Trust [2007] EWHC Admin 1927.

R(P) v Camden London Borough Council [2004] EWHC 55.

R(P) v Hackney London Borough Council [2007] EWHC 1365 Admin.

R(P) v Newham London Borough Council [2004] EWHC 2210 Admin.

R(Pajaziti) v Lewisham London Borough Council [2007] EWHC 1874 Admin, High Court; [2007] EWCA Civ 1351, Court of Appeal.

R(Panic) v Secretary of State for the Home Department [2004] EWCA Civ 494.

R(Patnaik) v Sunderland Teaching Primary Care Trust (2007). Digested in: Ashton K, Gould J (2008). Community care law update. Legal Action, May 2008. Also reported: Booler T (2008). Victory for family in home-care case. Sunderland Echo, 2 February 2008.

R(Patrick) v Newham London Borough Council (2001) 4 CCLR 48.

R(Payne) v Surrey Oakland NHS Trust [2001] EWHC Admin 461.

R(PB) v Haringey London Borough Council [2006] EWHC Admin 2255.

R(Rodriguez-Bannister) v Somerset Partnership NHS and Social Care Trust [2003] EWHC Admin 2184.

R(Rogers) v Swindon NHS Primary Care Trust [2006] EWCA Civ 392.

R(Rowe) v Walsall Metropolitan Borough Council (2001) unreported (leave to apply for judicial review).

R(S) v Leicester City Council [2004] EWHC Fam 533.

R(S) v Lewisham LBC, Lambeth LBC, Hackney LBC [2008] EWHC 1290 Admin.

R(SH) v Camden London Borough Council and Camden Primary Care NHS Trust [2007] EWHC 1697 Admin.

R(SSG) v Liverpool City Council (2002) 5 CCLR 639, High Court.

R(Selmour and 42 Others) v West Sussex County Council [2004] EWHC 2414 (Admin).

R(Spink) v Wandsworth LBC [2004] EWHC 2314 Admin, High Court; [2005] EWCA Civ 302, Court of Appeal.

R(Stephenson) v Stockton-on-Tees Borough Council [2004] EWHC 2228 (Admin), High Court; [2005] EWCA Civ 960, Court of Appeal.

R(T) v Enfield London Borough Council [2004] EWHC Admin 2297.

R(T) v Haringey LBC [2005] EWHC 2235 Admin.

R(W) v Doncaster Metropolitan Borough Council [2004] EWCA Civ 378.

R(Wahid) v Tower Hamlets London Borough Council [2002] EWCA Civ 287.

R(Watts) v Bedford Primary Care Trust [2004] EWCA Civ 166, Court of Appeal; European Court of Justice, Case C-372/04, 16 May 2006.

R(Whapples) v Birmingham East Primary Care Trust [2008] EWCA Civ 465.

R(Wooder) v Feggetter [2002] EWCA Civ 554.

R(Wright) v Secretary of State for Health [2007] EWCA Civ 999.v.

Re AK (Medical treatment: consent) (2001) 1 FLR 129, High Court.

Re B (Adult: refusal of treatment) [2002] EWHC 429.

Re C (Adult: refusal of treatment) [1994] 1 WLR 290, High Court.

Re F (A child) (1999) 2 CCLR 445, Court of Appeal.

Re F (Adult Patient) (2000) 3 CCLR 210, Court of Appeal.

Re K [1988] 2 FLR 15, High Court.

Re O (A child) [2001] EWCA Civ 16.

Re SA [2005] EWHC Fam 2942.

Re SK [2004] EWHC Fam 3202.

Re Teresa Judge [2001] NIQB 14, High Court (Northern Ireland).

Re Y (Mental incapacity: bone marrow transplant) [1996] 2 FLR 787.

Re Z [2004] EWHC Fam 2817.

Richards v Allan (2000) unreported, High Court (Chancery).

Roads v Central Trains [2004] EWCA Civ 1541.

Robertson v Fife Council (2001) 4 CCLR 355, Court of Session (Inner House); [2002] UKHL 35, House of Lords.

Rose v Bouchet (1999) IRLR 463, Sheriff's Court, Lothian (appeal to the Sheriff Principal).

Ross v Ryanair (2004) Claim CL 209468, Central London County Court; [2004] EWCA Civ 1751, Court of Appeal.

Rowley v Director of Public Prosecutions [2003] EWHC Admin 693.

Royal Bank of Scotland v Etridge (no.2) [2001] UKHL 44, House of Lords.

Ryan and Liverpool City Council v Liverpool Health Authority (2001) High Court (QBD).

S V Floyd [2008] EWCA CIV 201.

Sandford v Waltham Forest LBC [2008] EWHC 1106 (QB).

Saulle v Nouvet [2007] EWHC QB 2902.

Secretary of State for Social Security v Fairey [1995] 26 BMLR 63, Court of Appeal.

Sentges v Netherlands (2003) Application 27677/02, European Court of Human Rights.

Sheffield CC v E [2004] EWHC Fam 2808.

Siddorn v Patel [2007] EWHC 1248 Queen's Bench.

SL v SL (2000) 3 WLR 1288, Court of Appeal.

Slater v Buckinghamshire County Council [2004] EWHC 77, High Court (QBD); [2004] EWCA 1478, Court of Appeal.

Smith v North Eastern Derbyshire Primary Care Trust and Secretary of State [2006] EWHC Admin 1338, High Court; and
     [2006] EWCA Civ 1291, Court of Appeal.
Smith v South Lanarkshire Council (2000) Employment Appeal Tribunal (Edinburgh).
Sowden v Lodge [2004] EWCA Civ 1370, Court of Appeal.
Special Trustees of Great Ormond Street Hospital v Rushin (1997) unreported, High Court (Chancery).
Springette v Defoe (1992) 24 HLR 552, Court of Appeal.
St Helens BC v PE [2006] EWHC Fam 3460.
Stainton v Chorley and South Ribble NHS Trust (1998) unreported, High Court.
Steane v Chief Adjudication Officer [1996] 1 WLR 1195, House of Lords.
Strickland v Woodfield Lodge [2003] EWHC 287 (QBD).
T (A minor) v Surrey County Council [1994] 4 All ER 577.
Tchilingirian v Ouzounian [2003] EWHC 1220 (Chancery).
Tidman v Reading Borough Council [1994] 3 PLR 72, High Court.
Tinsley v Sarkar [2005] EWHC 192 (QBD).
Tomlinson v Congleton Borough Council [2003] UKHL 47, House of Lords.
Trustees of the Portsmouth Youth Activities Committee (A charity) v Poppleton [2008] EWCA Civ 646.
Urquhart v Fife Primary Care Trust [2007] CSOH 02, Court of Session, Scotland.
Vandyk v Oliver (Valuation Officer) [1976] AC 659, House of Lords.
Vicar of Writtle v Essex County Council [1979] 77 LGR 656, High Court.
W v Edgell [1990] 1 All ER 835, Court of Appeal.
Walker v Northumberland County Council (1995) 1 All ER 737.
Walton v Calderdale Healthcare NHS Trust [2005] EWHC 1053.
Welton v North Cornwall District Council [1997] 1 WLR 570, Court of Appeal.
Westminster v NASS (National Asylum Support Service) [2002] UKHL 38, House of Lords.
White v Clitheroe Royal Grammar School (2002) Claim BB 002640, Preston County Court.
Wilkinson v Chief Adjudication Officer [2000] 2 FCR 82, Court of Appeal.
Williams v Williams [2008] EWHC QB 299.
Withnell v Down Lisburn Health and Social Services Trust (2004) High Court (Northern Ireland).
Woolgar v Chief Constable of Sussex Police (2000) 1 WLR 25, Court of Appeal.
Wyatt v Hillingdon London Borough Council [1978] 76 LGR 727, Court of Appeal.
X v Bedfordshire County Council [1995] 3 All ER 353, House of Lords.
X City Council v MB & Ors [2006] EWHC 168 (Fam).
X,Y v Hounslow London Borough Council [2008] EWHC 1168.
Yorkshire Care Developments v North Yorkshire County Council (2004) unreported, Case no. NE 307141, Newcastle upon
     Tyne County Court.
YL v Birmingham City Council [2007] UKHL 27, House of Lords.
Yule v South Lanarkshire Council (1998) 1 CCLR 571, Court of Session, Outer House.
Yule v South Lanarkshire Council (no.2) (2001) 4 CCLR 383, Court of Session (Inner House).
Z v United Kingdom [2001] 2 FCR 246, European Court of Human Rights.

CARE STANDARDS TRIBUNAL CASES

Alternative Futures Ltd v National Care Standards Commission [2002] 101–111 NC, Care Standards Tribunal.
Bhatnagar v Commission v Social Care Inspection [2002] 0360 EA.
Bradford v General Social Care Council [2006] 792 SW-SUS.
DG v Secretary of State [2006] 824 PVA.
Dixon v Secretary of State for Health [2005] 621 PVA.
EK v Secretary of State [2006] 0716 PVA/0717 PC.
Hillier v Commission for Social Care Inspection [2003] 0187 NC.
Joyce v National Care Standards Commission [2003] 0190 NC.
Mrs P v Secretary of State for Education and Skills [2005]562 PVA/563 PC.
Mwaura v Secretary of State for Health [2006] 687 PVA/688 PC.
Pain v Secretary of State [2006] 636 PVA.
Simpson v National Care Standards Commission [2004] 255 EA.
Wilkinson v National Care Standards Commission [2003] 231 EA.

SOCIAL SECURITY COMMISSIONERS CASES

CDLA/3161/2003, 27 JULY 2005.
CH/1326/2004, 26 APRIL 2005.
CIS/1068/2006, 14 MARCH 2007.
CIS/2208/2003, 25 SEPTEMBER 2003.
CIS/3197/2003, 21 APRIL 2004.

LOCAL GOVERNMENT OMBUDSMAN (AND PUBLIC SERVICES OMBUDSMAN FOR WALES) CASES

Avon County Council 1997 (95/B/5144).
Barking and Dagenham London Borough Council 1997 (94/A/4229).
Barking and Dagenham London Borough Council 1998 (97/A/0337).
Barking and Dagenham 2000 (98/A/0322).
Barnet London Borough Council 2000 (98/A/0280).
Barnet London Borough Council 2006 (03/A/08718).
Barnsley Metropolitan Borough Council 1998 (97/C/0433).
Barnsley Metropolitan Borough Council 1998a (97/C/1096).
Bath and North East Somerset Council 2007 (06/B/16774).
Bedfordshire County Council 2003 (02/B/16654).
Bexley London Borough Council 2000 (97/A/4002).
Birmingham City Council 1993 (91/B/1262).
Birmingham City Council 2002 (00/C/19154).
Birmingham City Council 2006 (04/C/16195).
Birmingham City Council 2008 (05/C/18474).
Blackpool Borough Council 2006 (03/C/17141).
Bolton Metropolitan Borough Council 1992 (92/C/0670).
Bolton Metropolitan Borough Council 2004 (03/C/02451).
Bolton Metropolitan Borough Council 2004a (02/C/17068).
Bolsover District Council 2003 (02/C/08679, 02/C/08681, 02/C/10389).
Brent London Borough Council 1994 (93/A/0523).
Bridgend County Borough Council 2004 (2003/0386/BR/250).
Bristol City Council 1998 (96/B/4035 and 96/B/4143).
Buckinghamshire County Council 1992 (90/B/1340).
Buckinghamshire County Council 1998 (97/B/0876).
Buckinghamshire County Council and Oxfordshire & Buckinghamshire Mental Health Partnership Trust 2008 (03/1/04618
   local ombudsman, and HS-2608 health service ombudsman).
Bury Metropolitan Borough Council 2004 (02/C/14188).
Calderdale Metropolitan Borough Council 1998 (96/C/3868).
Cambridgeshire County Council 2001 (99/B/04621).
Cambridgeshire County Council 2002 (01/B/00305).
Cambridgeshire County Council 2004 (02/B/10226).
Camden London Borough Council 1993 (91/A/1481).
Cardiff City Council 2004 (2003/0671/CF/490).
Carmarthenshire County Council 1999 (99/0117/CM/210).
Castle Morpeth Borough Council and Northumberland County Council 2003 (02/C/04897, 02/C/13783).
City and Council of Swansea 2005 (2003/0948).
City and County of Swansea 2007 (B2004/0707/S/370).
Cleveland County Council 1993 (92/C/1042).
Clwyd County Council 1997 (97/0177, 97/0755).
Cornwall County Council 1996 (95/B/0166).
Croydon London Borough Council 2000 (98/A/2154).
Croydon London Borough Council 2006 (05/B/00246).
Cumbria County Council 1992 (90/C/2438).
Cumbria County Council 2000 (99/C/0619).
Cumbria County Council 2001 (98/C/4738).

Cyngor Dosbarth Dwyfor 1994 (93/465).

Derbyshire County Council 2001 (00/C/19118).

Derbyshire County Council 2004 (02/C/14235 and others).

Devon County Council 1996 (94/B/2128).

Dinefwr Borough Council 1995 (94/0772).

Doncaster Metropolitan Borough Council 1997 (95/C/4390).

Durham City Council and Durham County Council 1993 (92/C/2753, 92/C/2754).

Durham County Council 1998 (96/C/4083).

Durham County Council 2000 (99/C/1983).

Dyfed County Council 1996 (95/0227).

Ealing London Borough Council 1993 (91/A/3466).

Ealing London Borough Council 1999 (97/A/4069).

Ealing London Borough Council 2008 (06/A/08746).

East Sussex County Council 1995 (93/A/3738).

East Sussex County Council 1995a (92/A/2085).

East Sussex County Council 2003 (00/B/18600).

Essex County Council 1991 (90/A/2675).

Essex County Council 2001 (99/B/00799).

Essex County Council 2006 (05/A/00880).

Gateshead Metropolitan Borough Council 2001 (99/C/02509, 99/C/02624).

Gravesham Borough Council 1987 and Kent County Council (194/A/86).

Greenwich London Borough Council 1993 (91/A/3782).

Hackney London Borough Council 1992 (91/A/0482).

Hackney London Borough Council 1992a (90/A/3447).

Hackney London Borough Council 1995 (93/A3690).

Hackney London Borough Council 1997 (96/A/3762).

Hackney London Borough Council 1997a (96/A/3072).

Hackney London Borough Council 1997b (96/A/0743).

Hackney London Borough Council 1998 (97/A/2959).

Hackney London Borough Council 1998a (97/A/1649).

Halton Borough Council 2002 (01/C/09625).

Hampshire County Council 2001 (99/B/03979).

Haringey London Borough Council 1993 (92/A/3725).

Haringey London Borough Council 2000 (99/C/2060).

Harlow District Council 2000 (97/B/4324)

Harrow London Borough Council 2004 (02/B/03622).

Havering London Borough Council 2007 (06/A/10428).

Hertfordshire County Council 1992 (90/B/1676).

Hertfordshire County Council 2002 (00/B/09315).

Hertfordshire County Council 2003 (01/B/09360).

Hertfordshire County Council 2003a (00/B/16833).

Hounslow London Borough Council 1994 (92/A/2493).

Hounslow London Borough Council 1995 (93/A/3007).

Hounslow London Borough Council 1999 (96/A/2313).

Humberside County Council 1992 (91/C/0774).

Humberside County Council 1996 (and East Yorkshire Borough Council) (94/C/2151).

Isle of Anglesey County Council 1999 (98/0374/AN/082).

Isle of Anglesey County Council 1999a (98/0092/AN/067).

Islington London Borough Council 1988 (88/A/303).

Islington London Borough Council 1994 (92/A/4104).

Islington London Borough Council 1995 (94/A/2369).

Kensington and Chelsea Royal Borough 1992 (90/A/2232).

Kent County Council 1998 (97/A/1305).

Kent County Council 1999 (98/A/1612).

Kent County Council 2001 (99/B/3078).

Kent County Council 2001a (00/B/00721).

Kingston upon Hull C 2000 (99/C/1757).
Kirklees Metropolitan Borough Council 1993 (90/C/1911).
Kirklees Metropolitan Borough Council 1997 (94/C/3349).
Kirklees Metropolitan Borough Council 2002 (01/C/02370).
Kirklees Metropolitan Borough Council 2003 (01/C/00627).
Kirklees Metropolitan Borough Council 2007 (05/C/04684).
Kirklees Metropolitan Borough Council 2008 (07/C/05809).
Knowsley Metropolitan Borough Council 1997 (95/C/4681).
Leeds City Council 1995 (93/C/2475).
Leeds City Council 2001 (00/C/14156).
Leeds City Council 2006 (04/C/16622).
Leeds City Council 2007 (05/C/13157).
Leicester City Council 1992 and Leicestershire County Council (91/B/2154 and 91/B/2155).
Leicester City Council 1992a and Leicestershire County Council (91/B/0254 and 91/B/0380).
Leicester City Council 1995 (94/B/2813).
Leicester City Council 1998 (97/C/3498).
Leicestershire County Council 2001 (00/B/08307).
Lewisham London Borough Council 1993 (92/A/1693).
Lincolnshire County Council 2004 (03/C/09384).
Liverpool City Council 1992 (91/C/0121).
Liverpool City Council 1996/1997 (common points included within the reports involving Liverpool City Council:
    95/C/0867, 93/C/1485, 92/C/2848, 94/C/0805, 92/C/1165, 93/C/1173, 93/C/4112, 94/C/ 1902,
    95/C/0859).
Liverpool City Council 1997 (96/C/0581).
Liverpool City Council 1997a (97/C/1256).
Liverpool City Council 1998 (96/C/4284).
Liverpool City Council 1998a (96/C/4315).
Liverpool City Council 1999 (98/C/2564).
Liverpool City Council 2007 (05/C/08592).
Maldon District Council 2000 and Essex County Council (98/B/1691, 98/B/1791).
Manchester City Council 1993 (90/C/2147).
Manchester City Council 1994 (92/C/2376).
Manchester City Council 1996 (93/C/2330).
Manchester City Council 1996a (94/C/1571).
Manchester City Council 1998 (97/C/1814).
Manchester City Council 2005 (04/C/04804).
Merthyr Tydfil 1994 (93/218).
Merthyr Tydfil County Borough Council 2005 (2003/0648/MT/147: Public Services Ombudsman for Wales).
Merton London Borough Council 1999 (97/A/3218).
Middlesbrough Borough Council 1996 and Cleveland County Council (94/C/0964 and 94/C/0965).
Middlesbrough Council and Tees, Esk and Wear Valleys NHS Trust 2008 (O6/C/10526 and JW-11585). Joint local
    government ombudsman and health service ombudsman investigation.
Neath Port Talbot County Borough Council 1999 (99/0149/N/142).
Neath Port Talbot County Borough Council 2000 (99/0824/N/173).
Newham London Borough Council 1993 (91/A/3602).
Newham London Borough Council 1993a (91/A/3911).
Newham London Borough Council 1995 (92/A/4120).
Newham London Borough Council 1996 (94/A/3185).
Newham London Borough Council 1997 (94/A/0503).
North Somerset County Council 1999 (98/C/4033).
North Tyneside Metropolitan Borough Council 2004 (03/C/04610).
North Warwickshire District Council 2000 (99/B/0012).
North Warwickshire District Council 2000a (99/B/0012: further report).
North Yorkshire County Council 1993 and Harrogate Borough Council (91/C/0565 and 92/C/1400).
North Yorkshire County Council 2002 (01/C/03521).
North Yorkshire County Council 2005 (04/C/06322).

North Yorkshire County Council 2007 (05/C/13158).
Northumberland County Council 2000 (99/C/1276).
Northumberland County Council 2006 (05/C/07195).
Nottinghamshire County Council 1998 (97/C/3705).
Nottinghamshire County Council 1998a (97/C/2126).
Nottinghamshire County Council 1999 (98/C/2295).
Nottinghamshire City Council 2000 (99/C/3355).
Nottinghamshire County Council 2002 and Nottingham City Council (00/C/03176, 00/C/05525).
Oldham Metropolitan Borough Council 2006 (04/C/12489).
Oldham Metropolitan Borough Council 2007 (05/C/08648).
Oxfordshire County Council 1999 (97/B/3440).
Poole Borough Council 2007 (06/B/07542).
Redbridge London Borough Council 1993 (92/A/4108).
Redbridge London Borough Council 1993a (92/A/1173).
Redbridge London Borough Council 1998 (95/C/1472, 95/C/2543).
Redcar and Cleveland Borough Council 1999 (98/C/2796).
Rochdale Metropolitan Borough Council 1995 (93/C/3660).
Rotherham Metropolitan Borough Council 1995 (94/C/2287).
Salford City Council 1993 (91/C/1972).
Salford City Council 1996 (94/C/0399).
Salford City Council 2003 (01/C/17519).
Sandwell Metropolitan Borough Council 1995 (93/B/3956).
Sheffield City Council 1989 (88/C/1048).
Sheffield City Council 1994 (93/C/0005).
Sheffield City Council 1995 (93/C/1609).
Sheffield City Council 1996 (95/C/2483).
Sheffield City Council 1997 (95/C/3741).
Sheffield City Council 1997a (95/C/4413).
Sheffield City Council 2002 (00/C/07439).
Sheffield City Council 2004 (02/C/08690).
Sheffield City Council 2007 (05/C/06420).
Sheffield City Council 2008 (06/C/16349).
South Tyneside Metropolitan Borough Council 1999 (98/C/1055, 98/C/1802).
Southend-on-Sea Borough Council 2005 (04/A/10159)
Southwark London Borough Council 2001 (99/A/00988).
Southwark London Borough Council 2001a (99/A/4226).
St Helens Metropolitan Borough Council 1998 (97/C/2492).
Stafford Borough Council 2006 (05/B/06334).
Staffordshire County Council 2000 (99/C/4295).
Stockport Metropolitan Borough Council 2003 (02/C/03831).
Stockton-on-Tees Borough Council 1997 and the former Stockton-on-Tees Borough Council and the former Cleveland County Council (96/C/1523 and others).
Stockton-on-Tees Borough Council 2005 (03/C/16371).
Suffolk County Council 2001 (99/B/1651).
Sunderland City Council 2002 (00/C/12118, 00/C/12621).
Tower Hamlets London Borough Council 1992 (91/A/0726).
Tower Hamlets London Borough Council 1993 (92/A/1374).
Tower Hamlets London Borough Council 1997 (96/A/1219).
Tower Hamlets London Borough Council 2004 (03/C/02410).
Trafford Metropolitan Borough Council 1996 (94/C/3690).
Trafford Metropolitan Borough Council 2006 (04/C/17057 and 2007, 04/C/17057).
Trafford Metropolitan Borough Council 2007 (05/C/11921).
Trafford Metropolitan Borough Council 2008 (05/C/11921).
Wakefield Metropolitan District Council 1992 (90/C/2203).
Wakefield Metropolitan District Council 1993 (91/C/1246).
Wakefield Metropolitan District Council 2000 (98/C/4884).

Wakefield Metropolitan District Council 2003 (01/C/15652).
Wakefield Metropolitan District Council 2004 (02/C/14023).
Walsall Metropolitan Borough Council 1996 (94/B/3584).
Walsall Metropolitan Borough Council 2008 (07/B/07346).
Waltham Forest London Borough Council 1993 (92/A/0543).
Waltham Forest London Borough Council 1994 (93/A/2536).
Wandsworth London Borough Council 2006 (05/B/02414)
Warwickshire County Council 1997 (96/B/2562).
West Lancashire District Council 2005 (04/C/12312).
Westminster County Council 1996 (93/A/4250).
Wigan Metropolitan Borough Council 2001 (99/C/05493).
Wigan Metropolitan Borough Council (and Medway Council) 2008 (06B/12247 and 12248).
Wiltshire County Council 1999 (98/B/0341).
Wiltshire County Council 2007 (05/B/12629).
Wirral Metropolitan Borough Council 1992 (89/C/1114).
Wirral Metropolitan Borough Council 1992a (90/C/2413).
Wirral Metropolitan Borough Council 1992b (91/C/2038).
Wirral Metropolitan Borough Council 1992c (91/C/0729).
Wirral Metropolitan Borough Council 1993 (91/C/0381).
Wirral Metropolitan Borough Council 1993a (91/C/1258).
Wirral Metropolitan Borough Council 1993b (91/C/1852).
Wirral Metropolitan Borough Council 1993c (91/C/3108).
Wirral Metropolitan Borough Council 1993d (91/C/3811).
Wirral Metropolitan Borough Council 1993e (92/C/1254).
Wirral Metropolitan Borough Council 1994 (91/C/2376).
Wirral Metropolitan Borough Council 1994a (92/C/0298).
Wirral Metropolitan Borough Council 1994b (92/C/1403).
York City Council 2006 (04/B/01280).

HEALTH SERVICE OMBUDSMAN (AND SCOTTISH PUBLIC SERVICES OMBUDSMAN) CASES

Avon Health Authority 1996 (E.615/94–95 in HSC 1996).
Ayrshire and Arran Health Board 2007 (Case 200500976, Scottish Public Services Ombudsman).
Barnet Healthcare NHS Trust 2000 (E.33/99–00 in HSO 2000).
Berkshire Health Authority 2003 (E.814/00–01 in HSO 2003c).
Bexley and Greenwich Health Authority 1999 (E.1610/97–98 in HSO 1999a).
Bournewood Community and Mental Health NHS Trust 2002 (E.2280/98–99 in HSO 2002a).
Buckinghamshire Health Authority 1996 (E.118/94–95 in HSC 1996).
Cambridgeshire Health Authority 2004 (E.22/02–03 in HSO 2004a).
Central Manchester Primary Care Trust 2003 (E.629/01–02 in HSO 2003).
Dorset Health Authority 2003 (E.208/99–00 in HSO 2003c).
East Kent Health Authority 1996 (E.685/94–95 in HSC 1996).
East Norfolk Health Authority 1996 (E.213/94–95 in HSC 1996a).
East Sussex, Brighton and Hove Health Authority 1999 (E.1316/98–99 in HSO 1999).
Epsom and St Helier NHS Trust 2001 (E.559/99–00 in HSO 2001b).
Gloucestershire Health Authority 2003 (E.112/02–03 in HSO 2003).
Herefordshire Health Authority 1999 (E.1321/98–99 in HSO 1999).
HSC (1978) Health Service Commissioner. HC 343. *2nd report 1977–1978.* London: HMSO.
HSC (1981) Health Service Commissioner. HC 9. *1st report 1981–1982.* London: HMSO.
HSC (1982) Health Service Commissioner. HC 372. *2nd report 1981–1982.* London: HMSO.
HSC (1984) Health Service Commissioner. HC 418. *2nd report 1984–1985.* London: HSC.
HSC (1985) Health Service Commissioner. HC 33. *1st report 1984–1985.* London: HMSO.
HSC (1985a) Health Service Commissioner. HC 418. *2nd report 1984–1985.* London: HMSO.
HSC (1988) Health Service Commissioner. HC 232. *3rd report 1987–1988.* London: HMSO.
HSC (1988a) Health Service Commissioner. HC 511. *4th report 1987–1988.* London: HMSO.

HSC (1990) Health Service Commissioner. HC 199. *1st report 1989–1990*. London: HMSO.

HSC (1991) Health Service Commissioner. HC 482. *2nd report 1990–1991*. London: HMSO.

HSC (1992) Health Service Commissioner. HC 32. *1st report 1991–1992*. London: HMSO.

HSC (1994) Health Service Commissioner. *Failure to provide long term NHS care for brain damaged patient*. London: HMSO.

HSC (1994a) Health Service Commissioner. HC 498. *Selected investigations completed October 1993 to March 1994*. London: HMSO.

HSC (1995) Health Service Commissioner. HC 11. *Selected investigations completed April to September 1995*. London: HMSO.

HSC (1996) Health Service Commissioner. *Investigations of complaints about long term NHS care*. London: HMSO.

HSC (1996a) Health Service Commissioner. HC 464. *Selected investigations completed October 1995 to March 1996*. London: HMSO.

HSC (1996b) Health Service Commissioner. HC 87. *Selected investigations completed April to September 1996*. London: HMSO.

HSC (1996c) Health Service Commissioner. *Guide to the work of the health service ombudsman*. London: HSC.

HSO W.68/77–78 (in HSC 1978).

HSO WW.3/79–80 (in HSC 1981).

HSO W.340/80–81 (in HSC 1982).

HSO W. 420/83–84 (1983: HSC publication unknown).

HSO W.40/84–85 (in HSC 1984).

HSO W.113/84–85 (in HSC 1984).

HSO W.263/83–84 (in HSC 1985).

HSO W.24 and W.56/84–85 (in HSC 1985a).

HSO W.783/85–86 (in HSC 1988).

HSO W.286/86–87 (in HSC 1988a).

HSO SW.82/86–87 (in HSC 1988a).

HSO W.254/88–89 (in HSC 1990).

HSO W.194/89–90 (in HSC 1991).

HSO W.478/89–90 (in HSC 1991).

HSO W.226/91–92 (in HSC 1992).

HSO W.524/92–93 (in HSC 1994a).

HSO (1999) Health Service Ombudsman. HC 19. *Investigations completed April–September 1999*. London: TSO.

HSO (1999a) Health Service Ombudsman. HC 497. *Investigations completed October 1998–March 1999*. London: TSO.

HSO (2000) Health Service Ombudsman. HC 541–I. *Summaries of investigations completed October 1999–March 2000*. London: TSO.

HSO (2001) Health Service Ombudsman. HC 287–I. *Selected investigations completed April–July 2001*. London: TSO.

HSO (2001a) Health Service Ombudsman. HC 4–I. *Selected investigations completed December 2000–March 2001*. London: TSO.

HSO (2001b) Health Service Ombudsman. HC 278–I. *Selected investigations completed August–November 2000*. London: TSO.

HSO (2002) Health Service Ombudsman. HC 924–I. *Selected investigations completed December 2001–March 2002*. London: TSO.

HSO (2002a) Health Service Ombudsman. HC 679–I. *Selected investigations completed August–November 2001*. London: TSO.

HSO (2003) Health Service Ombudsman. HC 119. *Selected investigations completed April–September 2003*. London: TSO.

HSO (2003a) Health Service Ombudsman. HC 787. *Selected investigations completed December 2002–March 2003*. London: TSO.

HSO (2003b) Health Service Ombudsman. HC 532. *Selected investigations completed August–November 2002*. London: TSO.

HSO (2003c) Health Service Ombudsman. *NHS funding for long term care*. London: TSO.

HSO (2004) Health Service Ombudsman. *Annual report 2003–4*. London: TSO.

HSO (2004a) Health Service Ombudsman. HC 704. *Selected investigations completed October 2003–March 2004*. London: TSO.

HSO (2004b) Health Service Ombudsman. HC 144. *NHS funding for long term care: follow up report*. London: HSO.

HSO (2007) Health Service Ombudsman. *Retrospective continuing care funding and redress*. HC 386. London: TSO.

Leeds Health Authority 1994 (E.62/93–94 in HSC 1994).
Newcastle, North Tyneside and Northumberland Mental Health NHS Trust 2001 (E.2495/99–00 in HSO 2001).
North and Mid-Hampshire Health Authority 1996 (E.639/94–95 in HSC 1996a).
North Bristol NHS Trust 2000 (E.2041/98–99 in HSO 2000).
North Cheshire Health Authority 1996 (E.672/94–95 in HSC 1996).
North Essex Health Authority 2001 (E.1099/00–01 in HSO 2001b).
North Essex Health Authority 2003 (E.1033/01–02 in HSO 2003a).
North Worcestershire Health Authority 1995 (E.264/94–95 in HSC 1995).
North Worcestershire Health Authority 1996 (E.985/94–95 in HSC 1996b).
Nottinghamshire Healthcare NHS Trust 2003 (E.410/00–01 in HSO 2003b).
Oxfordshire Health Authority 1996 (E.787/94–95 in HSC 1996).
PCA (1982) Parliamentary Commissioner for Local Administration. *5th report for session 1981–1982*. London: HMSO.
PCA (1988) Parliamentary Commissioner for Local Administration. HC 672. *6th report for session 1987–1988*.
    London: HMSO.
PCA C.799/81 (in PCA 1982).
PCA C.656/87 (in PCA 1988).
Plymouth NHS Primary Care Trust 2002.
Shrophire Health Authority 2003 (E.5/02–03 in HSO 2003a).
Shropshire Health Authority 2003a (E.2119/01–02 in HSO 2003a).
St Mary's NHS Trust 2002 (E.231/01–02 in HSO 2002).
Southampton University Hospitals NHS Trust 2003 (E.2333/01–02 in HSO 2003).
Southend Hospital NHS Trust 2001 (E.2087/99–00 in HSO 2001b).
Suffolk Health Authority 2003 (E.2339/01–02 in HSO 2003a).
Surrey Oaklands NHS Trust 2002 (E.1742/00–01 in HSO 2002).
Thames Gateway NHS Trust 2001 (E.2380/99–00 in HSO 2001a).
Warrington Hospital NHS Trust 2001 (E.1846/99–00 in HSO 2001a).
West Kent Health Authority 2001 (E.1079/99–00 in HSO 2001b).
West Sussex Health Authority 2002 (E.2080/00–01 in HSO 2002).
Wigan and Bolton Health Authority 2003 (E.420/00–01 in HSO 2003c).
Wiltshire and Swindon Health Care NHS Trust 2002 (E.1982/00–01 in HSO 2002).

SECRETARY OF STATE DETERMINATIONS: ORDINARY RESIDENCE

Determinations can be found at: www.dh.gov.uk

STATUTORY INSTRUMENTS

SI 1974/284. *NHS (Charges for Appliances) Regulations 1974.*
SI 1987/1968. *Social Security (Claims and Payments) Regulations 1987.*
SI 1989/306. *National Health Service (Charges to Overseas Visitors) Regulations 1989.*
SI 1992/2793. *Manual Handling Operations Regulations 1992.*
SI 1992/2977. *National Assistance (Assessment of Resources) Regulations 1992.*
SI 1996/1455. *Disability Discrimination (Meaning of Disability) Regulations 1996.*
SI 1996/1503. *National Health Service (Wheelchair Charges) Regulations 1996.*
SI 1996/2889. *Housing Renewal Grants (Services and Charges) Order 1996.*
SI 1996/2890. *Housing Renewal Grants Regulations 1996.*
SI 1998/3132. *Civil Procedure Rules 1998.*
SI 1999/3242. *Management of Health and Safety at Work Regulations 1999.*
SI 2000/413. *Data Protection (Subject Access Modification) (Health) Order 2000.*
SI 2000/415. *Data Protection (Subject Access Modification) (Social Work) Order 2000.*
SI 2000/417. *Data Protection (Processing of Sensitive Personal Data) Order 2000.*
SI 2000/617. *NHS Bodies and Local Authorities Partnership Arrangements (Amendment) Regulations 2000.*
SI 2000/620. *NHS (Charges for Drugs and Appliances) Regulations 2000.*
SI 2001/441. *Carers (Services) and Direct Payments (Amendment) (England) Regulations 2001.*
SI 2001/3067. *National Assistance (Residential Accommodation) (Disregarding of Resources) (England) Regulations 2001.*
SI 2001/3069. *National Assistance (Residential Accommodation) (Relevant Contributions) (England) Regulations 2001.*

SI 2001/3441. *National Assistance (Residential Accommodation) (Additional Payments and Assessment of Resources) (Amendment) (England) Regulations 2001.*

SI 2001/3712. *Mental Health Act 1983 (Remedial Order) 2001.*

SI 2001/3965. *Care Homes Regulations 2001.*

SI 2002/446. *Police Act 1997 (Enhanced Criminal Record Certificates) (Protection of Vulnerable Adults) Regulations 2002.*

SI 2002/1687. *Magistrates' Courts (Special Measures Directions) Rules 2002.*

SI 2002/1688. *Crown Court (Special Measures Directions and Directions Prohibiting Cross-examination) Rules 2002.*

SI 2002/2375. *NHS (Functions of Strategic Health Authorities and Primary Care Trusts and Administration Arrangements) (England) Regulations 2002.*

SI 2002/3048. *Local Authority (Overview and Scrutiny Committees Health Scrutiny Functions) Regulations 2002.*

SI 2002/3078. *Withholding and Withdrawal of Support (Travel Assistance and Temporary Accommodation) Regulations 2002.*

SI 2002/3214. *Domiciliary Care Agencies Regulations 2002.*

SI 2003/628. *National Assistance (Sums for Personal Requirements) (England) Regulations 2003.*

SI 2003/712. *Disability Discrimination (Blind and Partially Sighted Persons) Regulations 2003.*

SI 2003/762. *Community Care, Services for Carers and Children's Services (Direct Payments) (England) Regulations 2003.*

SI 2003/907. *Local Authorities (Charges for Specified Welfare Services) Regulations 2003.*

SI 2003/1196. *Community Care (Delayed Discharges) (Qualifying Services) (England) Regulations 2003.*

SI 2003/1216. *Carers and Disabled Children (Vouchers) (England) Regulations 2003.*

SI 2003/2276. *Delayed Discharges (Mental Health Care) (England) Order 2003.*

SI 2003/2277. *Delayed Discharges (England) Regulations 2003.*

SI 2003/2382. *National Health Service (Travel Expenses and Remission of Charges) Regulations 2003.*

SI 2004/291. *NHS (General Medical Services Contracts) Regulations 2004.*

SI 2004/1768. *NHS (Complaints) Regulations 2004.*

SI 2004/2070. *Adult Placement Schemes (England) Regulations 2004.*

SI 2005/930. *The Immigration and Asylum (Provision of Accommodation to Failed Asylum-Seekers) Regulations 2005.*

SI 2006/1003. *Social Security (Persons from Abroad) Amendment Regulations 2006.*

SI 2006/1681. *Local Authority Social Services (Complaints) Regulations 2006.*

SI 2006/887. *Disability Discrimination (Premises) Regulations 2006.*

SI 2006/1681. *The Local Authority Social Services Complaints (England) Regulations 2006.*

SI 2006/1832. *The Mental Capacity Act 2005 (Independent Mental Capacity Advocates) (General) Regulations 2006.*

SI 2006/2883. *The Mental Capacity Act 2005 (Independent Mental Capacity Advocates) (Expansion of Role) Regulations 2006.*

SI 2007/76. *The Smoke-free (Exemptions and Vehicles) Regulations 2007.*

SI 2007/1744. *Court of Protection Rules.*

SI 2007/1745. *Court of Protection Fees Order.*

SI 2007/1898. *Mental Capacity Act 2005 (Transitional and Consequential Provisions) Order 2007.*

SI 2007/1889. *Regulatory Reform (Collaboration etc. between Ombudsmen) Order 2007.*

SI 2007/1899. *The Mental Capacity Act 2005 (Transfer of Proceedings) Order 2007.*

SI 2007/2051. *The Public Guardian (Fees, etc.) Regulations 2007*

SI 2008/528. *Local Involvement Networks Regulations 2008.*

SI 2008/593. *The National Assistance (Sums for Personal Requirements and Assessment of Resources) Amendment (England) Regulations 2008.*

SI 2008/915. *Local Involvement Networks (Duty of Services Providers to Allow Entry) Regulations 2008.*

SI 2008/1189. *Disabled Facilities Grants (Maximum Amounts and Additional Purposes) (England) Order 2006.*

CENTRAL GOVERNMENT GUIDANCE AND DIRECTIONS

ADASS, LGA (2007) Association of Directors of Adult Social Services; Local Government Association. *Commentary and advice for local authorities on the national framework for NHS continuing healthcare and NHS-funded nursing care.* London: ADASS, LGA.

Barnes, J. (2006) *Making referrals to the Protection of Vulnerable Adults (POVA) list.* London: SCIE.

Cabinet Office (Regulatory Impact Unit) (2004) *Code of practice on consultation.* London: Cabinet Office.

CNO(SNC)(77)1. Department of Health and Social Security. *Standards of nursing care: promotion of continence and management of incontinence.* London: DHSS.

CRAG (2008) Department of Health. *Charging for residential accommodation guidance.* London: DH.

CRB (2001) Criminal Records Bureau. *Code of practice and explanatory guide for registered persons and other recipients of disclosure information.* London: CRB.

CSIP (2007) Care Services Improvement Partnership. *Transforming community equipment and wheelchair services programme.* London: CSIP.

D(87)45. Department of Health and Social Security. *Provision of incontinence pads.* London: DHSS.

DCLG, DH (2006) Department of Communities and Local Government, Department of Health. *Hospital admission and discharge: people who are homeless or living in temporary or insecure accommodation.* London: DCLG, DH.

DCLG (2007) Department of Communities and Local Government. *Disabled facilities grant programme: the government's proposals to improve programme delivery.* London: DCLG.

DCLG (2008) Department of Communities and Local Government. *Disabled facilities grant: the package of changes to modernise the programme.* London: DCLG.

DH (1990) Department of Health. *Community care in the next decade and beyond: policy guidance.* London: DH.

DH (1999) Department of Health; Welsh Office. *Code of practice: Mental Health Act 1983.* London: DH.

DH (1999a) Department of Health. *National Service Framework for Mental Health.* London: DH.

DH (1999b) Department of Health. *Effective care coordination in mental health services: modernising the care programme approach.* London: DH.

DH (1999c) Department of Health. *Patient and public involvement in the new NHS.* London: DH.

DH (2000) Department of Health. *No secrets.* London: DH.

DH (2000a) Department of Health. *Framework for the assessment of children in need and their families.* London: DH.

DH (2000b) Department of Health. *Good practice in continence services.* London: DH.

DH (2001) Department of Health. *Guide to integrating equipment services.* London: DH.

DH (2001a) Department of Health. *Carers and people with parental responsibility for disabled children: policy guidance.* London: DH.

DH (2001b) Department of Health. *Carers and people with parental responsibility for disabled children: practice guidance.* London: DH.

DH (2001c) Department of Health. *National service framework for older people.* London: DH.

DH (2001d) Department of Health. *Valuing people: a new strategy for learning disability for the 21st century.* London: Stationery Office.

DH (2002) Department of Health. *Guidance on physically restrictive interventions for people with learning disability and austistic spectrum disorder in health, education and social care settings.* London: DH.

DH (2002a) Department of Health. *Fairer charging policies for home care and other non-residential services: practice guidance.* London: DH.

DH (2002b) Department of Health. *Supported housing and care homes: guidance on regulation.* London: DH.

DH (2002c) Department of Health. *Intermediate care: moving forward.* London: DH.

DH (2003) Department of Health. *Establishing the responsible commissioner.* London: DH.

DH (2003a) Department of Health. *Care homes for older people: national minimum standards.* London: DH.

DH (2003b) Department of Health. *Domiciliary care: national minimum standards.* London: DH.

DH (2003c) Department of Health. *Direct payments guidance: community care, services for carers and children's services (direct payments).* London: DH.

DH (2003d) Department of Health. *Carers and Disabled Children Act 2000: vouchers for short term breaks.* London: DH.

DH (2003e) Department of Health. *Section 54 of the Nationality, Immigration and Asylum Act 2002 and community care and other social services for adults from the European Economic Area living in the UK.* London: DH.

DH (2003f) Department of Health. *Identification, referral and registration of sight loss: action for social services department and optometrists, and explanatory notes.* London: DH.

DH (2003g) Department of Health. *Fair access to care services: practice guidance.* London: DH.

DH (2003h) Department of Health. *Code of practice on openness in the NHS.* London: DH.

DH (2003i) Department of Health. *Fairer charging policies for home and other non-residential social services: guidance for councils with social services responsibilities.* London: DH.

DH (2003j) Department of Health. *Discharge from hospital: pathway, process and practice.* London: DH.

DH (2003k) Department of Health. *Protocol on cross-border issues for NHS-funded nursing care in care homes in England and Wales.* London: DH.

DH (2003l) Department of Health. *Overview and scrutiny: guidance.* London: DH.

DH (2003m) Department of Health. *Strengthening accountability, involving patients and the public: policy guidance, section 11 of the Health and Social Care Act 2001.* London: DH.

DH (2003n) Department of Health. *Strengthening accountability, involving patients and the public: practice guidance, section 11 of the Health and Social Care Act 2001.* London: DH.

DH (2003o) Department of Health. *Keeping the NHS local: a new direction of travel.* London: DH.

DH (2004) Department of Health. *Delayed Discharges (Continuing Care) Directions 2004.* London: DH.

DH (2004a) Department of Health. *Implementing the overseas visitors hospital charging regulations: guidance for NHS Trust Hospitals in England.* Revised January 2007. London: DH.

DH (2004b) Department of Health. *Proposals to exclude overseas visitors from eligibility to free NHS primary medical services: consultation.* London: DH.

DH (2004c) Department of Health. *Protection of vulnerable adults scheme in England and Wales for care home and domiciliary care agencies: a practical guide.* London: DH.

DH (2004d) Department of Health. *Community care assessment directions.* London: DH.

DH (2004e) Department of Health. *Advice on the decision of the European Court of Human Rights in the case of HL v UK (the 'Bournewood' case).* London: DH.

DH (2004f) Department of Health. *Direct choices: what councils need to make direct payments happen for people with learning disabilities.* London: DH.

DH (2004g) Department of Health. *New national framework on continuing care.* Department of Health press release (Stephen Ladyman). London: DH.

DH (2005) Department of Health. *Carers and Disabled Children Act 2000 and Carers (Equal Opportunities) Act 2004 combined policy guidance.* London: DH.

DH (2005a) Department of Health. *Creating a patient–led NHS.* London: DH.

DH (2005b) Department of Health. *National Service Framework for Long-term conditions.* London: DH.

DH (2005c) Department of Health. *Building telecare in England.* London: DH.

DH (2006) Department of Health. *Future regulation of health and adult social care in England.* London: DH.

DH (2006a) Department of Health. *Revised guidance on income generation in the NHS.* London: DH.

DH (2006b) Department of Health. *Income generation: car parking charges, best practice for implementation.* London: DH.

DH (2006c) Department of Health. *Learning from complaints: social services complaints procedure for adults.* London: DH.

DH (2007) Department of Health. *Making experiences count: the proposed new arrangements for handling health and social care complaints: detailed policy background.* London: DH.

DH (2007a) Department of Health. *National framework for NHS continuing health care and NHS-funded nursing care.* London: DH.

DH (2007b) Department of Health. *National framework for NHS continuing health care and NHS-funded nursing care in England: core principles.* London: DH.

DH (2007c) Department of Health. *Decision-support tool for NHS continuing healthcare.* London: DH.

DH (2007d) Department of Health. *NHS continuing healthcare checklist.* London: DH.

DH (2007e) Department of Health. *Fast-track pathway tool for NHS continuing healthcare.* London: DH.

DH (2007f) Department of Health. *NHS-funded nursing care: practice guide 2007.* London: DH.

DH (2007g) Department of Health. *Patient mobility: advice to local healthcare commissioners on handling requests for hospital care in other European countries following the ECJ's judgment in the Watts case.* London: DH.

DH (2007h) Department of Health. *National Health Service (Charges to Overseas) Regulations 1989. Notification of changes: amended 30 April 2007.* London: DH.

DH (2007i) Department of Health. *Eligibility criteria for Patient Transport Services (PTS).* London: DH.

DH (2007j) Department of Health. *Guidance to local authorities on the use of funding for emergency respite care which was a new component of the carers grant payable from 1 October 2007.* London: DH.

DH (2007k) Department of Health. *Determining ordinary residence disputes between English and Welsh authorities.* London: DH.

DH (2007l) Department of Health. *Duty to involve patients strengthened: briefing on section 242 of NHS Act 2006.* London: DH.

DH (2007m) Department of Health. *NHS continuing healthcare: continuing care redress.* London: DH.

DH (2007n) Department of Health. *Number of people receiving continuing care in England 2005–6.* PQ01216. London: DH.

DH (2007o) Department of Health. *Delayed Discharges (Continuing Care) Directions 2007).* London: DH.

DH (2007p) Department of Health. *NHS Continuing Healthcare (Responsibilities) Directions 2007.* London: DH.

DH (2007q) Department of Health. *NHS (Nursing Care in Residential Accommodation) (England) Directions 2007.* London: DH.

DH (2007r) Department of Health. *Duty to involve patients strengthened: briefing on section 242 of NHS Act 2006.* London: DH.

DH (2007s) Department of Health. *Valuing people now: from progress to transformation.* London: DH.

DH (2007t). Department of Health. *Who pays? Establishing the responsible commissioner.* London: DH.

DH (2007u). Department of Health. *Independence, choice and risk: a guide to best practice in supported decision making*. London: DH.

DH (2008) Department of Health. *Code of practice for the promotion of NHS funded services*. London: DH.

DH (2008a) Department of Health. *Making experiences count*. London: DH.

DH (2008b) Department of Health. *Refocusing the Care Programme Approach: policy and positive practice guidance*. London: DH.

DH (2008c). Department of Health. *Code of Practice: Mental Health Act 1983*. London: DH.

DH (2008d). Department of Health. *Failed asylum seekers and ordinary residence: advice to overseas visitors managers*. Chief Executive Letter, 1st May 2008. London: DH.

DH (2008e). Department of Health. (Draft regulations). *Community Care, Services for Carers and Children's Services (Direct Payments) (England) Regulations 2009*. London: DH.

DHSS 12/70. Department of Health and Social Security. *Chronically Sick and Disabled Persons Act 1970*. London: DHSS.

DHSS 19/71. Department of Health and Social Security. *Welfare of the elderly: implementation of section 45 of the Health Services and Public Health Act 1945*. London: DHSS.

DoE 17/96. Department of Environment. *Private sector renewal: a strategic approach*. London: HMSO.

DRC (2006) Disability Rights Commission. *Code of practice: rights of access: services to the public, public authority functions, private clubs and premises*. London: DRC.

DTLR (2001) Department of Transport, Local Government and the Regions. *Private sector housing renewal: a consultation paper*. London: DTLR.

DTLR (2001a) Department of Transport, Local Government and the Regions. *Regulatory Reform (Housing Assistance) (England and Wales) Order 2002: explanatory document*. London: DTLR.

DTLR (2002). Department of Transport, Local Government and the Regions. *Housing Grants, Construction and Regeneration Act 1996, Part 1: amendments to the renovation grant system*. London: DTLR.

EL(91)28. NHS Management Executive. *Continence services and the supply of incontinence aids*. London: Department of Health.

EL(91)129. NHS Management Executive. *Charging NHS patients*. London: DH.

EL(92)20. NHS Management Executive. *Provision of equipment by the NHS*. London: DH.

HC(89)5. Department of Health. *Discharge of patients from hospital*. London: DH.

HC(90)23. Department of Health. *Care programme approach for people with a mental illness referred to the specialist psychiatric services*. London: DH.

HMG (2007) Her Majesty's Government. *Putting people first: a shared vision and commitment to the transformation of adult social care*. London: HMG.

Home Office (2001) *Immigration directorates' instructions*. Chapter 17, section 2. Available at www.ind.homeoffice.gov.uk/documents/idischapter17, accessed 10 October 2007.

Home Office (2008) *Police and Criminal Evidence Act 1984 (PACE) Code C: Code of Practice for the detention, treatment and questioning of persons by police officers*. London: HO.

HSC(IS)11. (1974) Department of Health and Social Security. *Services for chronic renal failure*. London: DHSS.

HSC 1998/48. *Transfer of frail older NHS patients to other long stay settings*. London: DH.

HSC 1999/180; LAC(99)30. Department of Health. *Ex parte Coughlan: follow up action*. London: DH.

HSC 2000/3; LAC(2000)3. Department of Health. *After-care under the Mental Health Act 1983*. London: DH.

HSC 2001/001; LAC(2001)11. Department of Health. *Intermediate care*. London: DH.

HSC 2001/003. Department of Health. *Implementing the NHS Plan: developing services following the National Beds Inquiry*. London: DH.

HSC 2001/008; LAC(2001)13. Department of Health. *Community equipment services*. London: DH.

HSC 2001/15; LAC(2001)18. Department of Health. *Continuing care: NHS and local council's responsibilities*. London: DH.

HSC 2001/17; LAC(2001)26. Department of Health. *Guidance on free nursing care in nursing homes*. London: DH.

HSC 2002/001; LAC(2002)1. Department of Health. *Guidance on the single assessment process for older people*. London: DH.

HSC 2003/006; LAC(2003)7. Department of Health. *Guidance on NHS funded nursing care*. London: DH.

HSC 2003/9; LAC(2003)21. Department of Health. *Community Care (Delayed Discharges) Act 2003*.

HSE (1998) Health and Safety Executive. *Manual handling: Manual Handling Operations Regulations 1992, guidance on regulations*. Sudbury: HSE.

HSE SIM 7/2000/8. Health and Safety Executive. *Social services: social inclusion and elective risk*. Sudbury: HSE.

HSG(92)42. Department of Health. *Health services for people with learning disabilities (mental handicap)*. London: DH.

HSG(93)48. Department of Health. *Home dialysis patients: costs of metered water for home dialysis.* London: DH.

HSG(95)8; LAC(95)5. Department of Health. *NHS responsibilities for meeting continuing health care needs.* London: DH.

HSG(96)34. Department of Health. *Powered indoor/outdoor wheelchairs for severely disabled people.* London: DH.

HSG(96)53. Department of Health. *Wheelchair voucher scheme.* London: DH.

HSS(OS5A)4/76. Department of Health and Social Services. *British Wireless for the Blind Fund: batteries supplied by health and social services boards.* Belfast: DHSS.

HSS(OS5A)5/78. Department of Health and Social Services. *Telephones for the handicapped and the elderly.* Belfast: DHSS.

HSS(PH)5/79. Department of Health and Social Services. *Help with television.* Belfast: DHSS.

Home Office (2002) *Achieving best evidence in criminal proceedings: guidance for vulnerable or intimidated witnesses, including children.* London: Home Office.

Home Office (2002a) *Provision of therapy for vulnerable adults or intimidated witnesses prior to a criminal trial: practice guidance.* London: Home Office.

HSC 1999/018. Department of Health. *Overseas visitors' eligibility to receive free primary care: a clarification of existing policy together with a description of the changes brought in by the new EC health care form E128.* London: DH.

ILF (2007) Independent Living Fund. Letter, 17 December 2007. Nottingham: ILF.

Joint Committee (2004) *Joint Committee on the Draft Disability Discrimination Bill: volume 1, report.* London: Stationery Office.

LAC(92)13. Department of Health. *Further and Higher Education Act 1992: implications of sections 5 and 6 of the Disabled Persons (Services, Consultation and Representation) Act 1986.* London: DH.

LAC(92)15. Department of Health. *Social care for adults with learning disabilities (mental handicap).* London: DH.

LAC(92)27. Department of Health. *National Assistance Act 1948 (Choice of Accommodation) Directions 1992.* London: DH.

LAC(93)2. Department of Health. *Alcohol and drug services within community care.* London: DH.

LAC(93)7. Department of Health. *Ordinary residence.* London: DH.

LAC(93)10. Department of Health. *Approvals and directions for arrangements from 1st April 2003 made under schedule 8 to the NHS Act 1977 and sections 21 and 29 of the National Assistance Act 1948.* London: DH.

LAC(93)12. Department of Health. *Further and Higher Education Act 1992: implications for sections 5 and 6 of the Disabled Persons (Services, Consultation and Representation) Act 1986.* London: DH.

LAC(93)18. *National Assistance Act 1948 (Choice of Accommodation) (Amendment) Directions 1993.* London: DH.

LAC(98)19. Department of Health. *Community Care (Residential Accommodation) Act 1998.* London: DH.

LAC(2001)8. Department of Health. *Social care for deaf-blind children and adults.* London: DH.

LAC(2001)10. Department of Health. *Charges for residential accommodation.* London: DH.

LAC(2001)23; HSC 2001/16. Department of Health. *Valuing people: a new strategy for learning disability for the 21st century: implementation.* London: DH.

LAC(2001)25. Department of Health. *Charges for residential accommodation: CRAG amendment no. 15.* London: DH.

LAC(2001)32. Department of Health. *Fairer charging policies for home and other non-residential social services: guidance for councils with social services responsibilities.* London: DH.

LAC(2002)001. Department of Health. *Guidance on the single assessment process for older people.* London: DH.

LAC(2002)2. Department of Health. *Implementing the Caldicott standard in social care: appointment of 'Caldicott Guardians'.* London: DH.

LAC(2002)13. Department of Health. *Fair access to care services: guidance on eligibility criteria for adult social care.* London: DH.

LAC(2003)13. Department of Health. *Guidance on accommodating children in need and their families.* London: DH.

LAC(2003)14. Department of Health. *Changes to local authorities' charging regime for community equipment and intermediate care services.* London: DH.

LAC(2004)20. Department of Health. *Guidance on National Assistance Act 1948 (Choice of Accommodation) Directions 1992.* London: DH.

LAC(2004)24. *Community care assessment directions 2004.* London: DH.

LAC(2006)5. Department of Health. *Preventative technology grant 2006/07–2007/08.* London: DH.

LAC(DH)(2007)4. Department of Health. *Charges for residential accommodation: CRAG amendment no. 26.* London: DH, annex.

LAC(DH)(2008)1. Department of Health. *Transforming social care.* London: DH.

LAC (DH) (2008)3. Department of Health. *AIDS support grant for social care for people HIV/AIDS: financial year 2008/2009.* London: DH.

LAC(DH)(2008)4. Department of Health. *Mental Capacity Act.* London: DH.

LASSL(2004)20. Department of Health. *National protocol – inter-authority arrangements negotiating support for care leavers resident outside of their responsible authority.* London: DH.

Lord Chancellor (1999) *Making decisions: the government's proposals for making decisions on behalf of incapacitated adults.* London: Stationery Office.

Lord Chancellor (2007) *Mental Capacity Act 2005: code of practice.* London: TSO.

Lord Chancellor's Department (1997) *Who decides? Making decisions on behalf of mentally incapacitated adults.* London: Stationery Office.

Lord Privy Seal, Leader of the House of Commons, Minister for Women and Equality (2008). *Framework for a fairer future: the Equality Bill. Cm 7431.* London: Government Equalities Office.

LSC (2006) Learning and Skills Council. *Funding guidance: placement for learners with learning difficulties and/or disabilities at specialist providers 2007/08.* Coventry: LSC.

ODPM (2003) Office of the Deputy Prime Minister. *General power for best value authorities to charge for discretionary services: guidance on the power in the Local Government Act 2003.* London: ODPM.

ODPM 5/2003. Office of the Deputy Prime Minister. *Housing renewal.* London: ODPM. London: ODPM.

ODPM (2005) Office of The Deputy Prime Minister. *Guidance on Contracting for Services in the light of the Human Rights Act 1990.* London: ODPM.

ODPM (2005a) Office of the Deputy Prime Minister. *Reviewing the disabled facilities grant programme.* London ODPM.

ODPM (2006) Office of the Deputy Prime Minister; Department for Education and Skills; Department of Health. *Delivering housing adaptations for disabled people: a good practice guide (June 2006 edition).* London: ODPM.

Philp, I. (2007) *A recipe for care: not a single ingredient.* London: DH.

Scottish Executive (2001) *Community Care and Health (Scotland) Bill: policy memorandum.* Edinburgh: Scottish Executive.

Secretaries of State (1989) Secretaries of State for Health, Social Security, Wales and Scotland. *Caring for people: community care in the next decade and beyond.* London: HMSO.

Secretary of State (1996) *Guidance on matters to be taken into account in determining questions relating to the definition of disability.* London: HMSO.

Secretary of State for Communities and Local Government (2008). *Housing Grants, Construction and Regeneration Act 1996: Disabled Facilities Grant (Conditions Relating to Approval or Payment of Grant) General Consent 2008.* London: DCLG.

Secretary of State for Health (1998) *Modernising social services: promoting independence, improving protection, raising standards.* London: TSO.

Secretary of State for Health (2000) *The NHS Plan.* London: TSO.

Secretary of State for Health (2000a) *The NHS Plan: the government's response to the Royal Commission on Long Term Care. Cm 4818–II.* London: TSO.

Secretary of State for Health (2004) *NHS improvement plan: putting people at the heart of public services.* London: TSO.

Secretary of State for Health (2005) *Independence, well-being and choice. Cm 6499. Green Paper.* London: TSO.

Secretary of State for Health (2006) *Our health, our care, our say. Cm 6737.* London: TSO.

SSI/SWSG (1991) Social Services Inspectorate; Social Work Services Group. *Care management and assessment: practitioners' guide.* London/Edinburgh: Department of Health, Scottish Office.

SW7/1972. Social Work Services Group. *Telephones for severely disabled persons living alone.* Edinburgh: Scottish Office.

SWSG 6/1994. Social Work Services Group. *Choice of accommodation: cross border placements.* Edinburgh: Scottish Office.

OTHER REFERENCES

ACC, AMA (1971) Association of County Councils, Association of Metropolitan Authorities. *Chronically Sick and Disabled Persons Act 1970: provision of telephones as amended by ACC/AMA letter 20/4/72.* London: Association of County Councils, Association of Metropolitan Authorities.

Action on Elder Abuse (2007) '£Millions stolen, defrauded or conned from older people by their own sons and daughters each year.' News release, 30 January 2007.

Age Concern England (2008) *Out of sight, out of mind: social exclusion behind closed doors.* London: Age Concern England.

al Yafai, F. (2005) 'NHS trust is fined £28,000 for incompetent safety procedures that cost a nurse his life.' *Guardian,* 6 May.

All Party Parliamentary Groups: Primary Care and Public Health and Social Care (2006) *Report of joint inquiry on:White Paper: Our health, our care our say: a new direction for community services.* London: TSO.

Amnesty International (2006) *Down and out in London.* London: Amnesty International.

Audit Commission (2000) *Charging with care: how councils charge for home care.* London: Audit Commission.

Audit Commission (2000a) *Fully equipped: the provision of equipment to older or disabled people by the NHS and social services in England and Wales.* London: Audit Commission.

Audit Commission (2000b). *The way to go home: rehabilitation and remedial services for older people.* London: Audit Commission.

Audit Commission (2003) *Waiting list accuracy.* London: Audit Commission.

Baldwin, R. (1995) *Rules and government.* Oxford: Clarendon Press.

BBA (undated). British Bankers' Association. *Banking for mentally incapacitated and learning disabled customers.* London: British Bankers' Association.

Bewley, C. (2002) *Pointers to control: consent and control by people with learning difficulties using direct payments.* London: Values into Action.

Bichard, M. (2004) Sir Michael Bichard. *Bichard enquiry report.* London: Stationery Office.

Bilson, A. (2004) 'Time to buck the system.' *Community Care,* 9–15 September 2004, pp.38–39.

Binmore, K. (2007) 'Rules of the game.' *Prospect Magazine,* November 2007. Available at www.prospect-magazine.co.uk/printarticle.php?id=9880, accessed 7 October 2008.

Black, D. (1980) *Inequalities in health: the Black report.* London: Department of Health and Social Security.

Bond, A. (2007) 'Hospital hit by bed crisis.' *East Anglian Daily Times,* 22 December.

Booler, T. (2008) 'Victory for family in home-care case.' *Sunderland Echo,* 2 February.

Bowen P (2007). *Blackstone's guide to the Mental Health Act 2007.* Oxford: Oxford University Press.

Bowen, P., Markus, K. and Suterwalla, A. (2008) 'Discharged prisoners' rights to health care, housing and community care: part 1.' *Legal Action,* January 2008, p.18.

Bradley, G. and Manthorpe, J. (1997) *Dilemmas of financial assessment: a practitioner's guide.* Birmingham: Venture Press.

Brazier, M. (1992) *Medicines, patients and the law,* 2nd edn. London: Penguin.

British Geriatric Society (2007) *Rehabilitation beds report on the second England council survey.* London: British Geriatric Society.

Bulstrode, M. (2006) 'Surgeon says morale is down at hospital.' *East Anglian Daily Times,* 12 August.

'Care homes under closure threat', BBC News, 18 July 2007. Available at http://www.news.bbc.co.uk/1/hi/england/devon/6904593.stm, accessed 7 October 2008.

Caring Choices (2008) *Future of care funding: time for a change.* London: Caring Choices.

Carter, H. (2007) 'He couldn't say "no".' *Guardian,* 15 August.

Carvel, J. (2006) 'Hospital's focus on waiting time targets led to 41 super-bug deaths.' *Guardian,* 25 July.

CCC (2007) Continuing Care Conference. *Paying for care: third party top-ups and cross-subsidies.* London: CCC.

CIPFA (2004) Chartered Institute of Public Finance and Accountancy. *Community care direct payments: accounting and financial management guidelines,* 2nd edn. London: CIPFA.

CIPFA (2007) Chartered Institute of Public Finance and Accountancy. *Direct payment and individual budgets: managing the finances.* London: CIPFA.

CLAE (1992) Commission for Local Administration in England. *Devising a complaints system.* London: CLAE.

CLAE (1993) Commission for Local Administration in England. *Good administrative practice.* London: CLAE.

CLAE (1994) Commission for Local Administration in England. *The Local Government Ombudsmen 1993/1994.* London: CLAE.

CLAE (2000) Commission for Local Administration in England. *The Local Government Ombudsmen as an alternative to judicial review.* London: CLAE.

CLAE (2003) Commmission for Local Administration. *Special report: advice and guidance on the funding of aftercare under section 117 of the Mental Health Act 1983.* London: CLAE.

CLAE (2004) Commission for Local Administration in England. *Local Government Ombudsman: annual report 2003/4.* London: CLAE.

CLAE (2007) Commission for Local Administration in England. *Special report: local partnerships and citizen redress.* London: CLAE.

Clark, H., Dyer, S. and Horwood, J. (1998) *That bit of help: the high value of low level preventative services for older people.* Bristol: Policy Press.

Clark, H., Gough, H. and Macfarlane, A. (2004) *It pays dividends: direct payments and older people.* Bristol: Policy Press.

Clements, L. and Thompson, P. (2007) *Community care law,* 4th edn. London: Legal Action Group.

Clout, L. (2008) 'War hero refused treatment by NHS.' *Daily Telegraph,* 26 February.

CO, DH (2005) Cabinet Office, Department of Health. *Making a difference: direct payments.* London: CO, DH.

Coalition on Charging (2008) *Charging into poverty?* London: Coalition on Charging.

Community Care (2005) News. *Community Care,* 29 September–5 October 2005, p.9.